CIVILISING
SUBJECTS

*Metropole and Colony in the
English Imagination, 1830–1867*

Catherine Hall

Polity

First published in 2002 by Polity Press in association with Blackwell Publishers Ltd.

Editorial office:
Polity Press
65 Bridge Street
Cambridge CB2 1UR, UK

Marketing and production:
Blackwell Publishers Ltd
108 Cowley Road
Oxford OX4 1JF, UK

ISBN 0-7456-1820-0
ISBN 0-7456-1821-9 (pbk)

A catalogue record for this book is available from the British Library.

Typeset in 10 on 12 pt by SNP Best-set Typesetter Ltd., Hong Kong
Printed in Great Britain by PG Books Ltd., Bodmin, Cornwall

This book is printed on acid-free paper.

For Stuart and Gail

Contents

༼༽

Illustrations

Acknowledgements

I am deeply grateful to the Economic and Social Research Council, for their grant (ref. no. R000232169) from 1990 to 1992 to do some of the work for this book. At that stage I had no idea that it would be such a long project. The fellowship from the Nuffield Foundation for 1995–6 was also invaluable, and enabled me to extend the original scale of the research. I have worked in three institutions since 1988 (when I conceived the idea of working on England and Jamaica in the mid-nineteenth century): the University of East London, the University of Essex and University College London. Each institution has made it possible for me, even in these times, to research and write.

This piece of work has taken over ten years to complete, and I have received much help and support along the way. I have given papers based on the research in innumerable institutions: each occasion has helped me to formulate my own ideas and to debate with audiences. I have been especially fortunate in being able to present the work across some parts of that erstwhile empire with which I have engaged. Papers presented to the Conference on 'Engendering the History of the Caribbean' at the University of the West Indies at Mona, Jamaica; to the Association of Australian Historians in Perth; to the Association of New Zealand Historians in Wellington; and to the Association of Canadian Historians in St Johns, Newfoundland, have been particularly significant moments. In addition, I have given papers in many US and British universities, in Ireland, South Africa and Brazil over the years, and have always learned from these occasions. The group of scholars in history and anthropology at the University of Michigan at Ann Arbor have been particularly supportive. I thank all those who have invited me.

I owe an especial debt to the Sisters at Immaculate Conception Convent in Kingston – in particular, my dear cousin Sister Maureen

Clare Hall – who have given me a home in Kingston for all my research trips. They have been most tolerant of the years of work involved in this project, while they have been preoccupied with more immediate needs on the island. Joan Tucker, Audrey Cooper, Annie Paul and David Scott have all helped me to think about Jamaica. Margaret Allen, Vicki Crowley, Ann Curthoys, Marilyn Lake and Kay Schaffer helped me to focus on Australia. In New Zealand Charlotte Macdonald and Raewyn Dalziel were my main interlocutors. In every instance it has been a wonderful experience to visit and explore the places on which I am working.

The librarians at the Birmingham Central Library have been most helpful. Thanks to Sue Mills at the Angus Library, Regent's Park College, and Elizabeth Douall, who had special responsibility for the Baptist Missionary Society archive when I was working there. More recently Jennifer Thorp, the current archivist, has been most helpful. Thanks also to the archivists at the National Library of Jamaica and to the staff at the Jamaica Baptist Union. Between 1990 and 1992 I spent many happy hours in the reading room of the British Library, then housed in the British Museum, and I have also found the London Library a wonderful resource. Megan Doolittle's research assistance at the University of Essex was invaluable. Ruth Percy and Ralph Kingston at University College both helped me to get the manuscript together at critical points. Richard Smith's assistance with the illustrations has been much appreciated, as has Bill Storey's photography and Keith McClelland's help with the bibliography.

Many friends have supported me. My talks with Sally Alexander about history over nearly thirty years have been, and continue to be, a joy and a pleasure. Michèle Barrett, Avtar Brah, Leonore Davidoff, Miriam Glucksmann, Alison Light, Jokhim Meikle, Judy Walkowitz and Sophie Watson have all listened to me, argued with me and sustained me. David Albury thought of the title *Civilising Subjects* many years ago. Gad Heuman and Mary Chamberlain welcomed me to the field of Caribbean history in Britain. Tom Holt and Brian Stanley both kindly allowed me to see material before it was published. Clyde Binfield has shared his unrivalled knowledge of nineteenth-century nonconformity with me. I have found intellectual sustenance in the growing community of feminist historians engaged in rethinking empire both in Britain and the USA. Particular thanks to Antoinette Burton, Joanna de Groot, Clare Midgley, Sonya Rose, Mrinalini Sinha, Carroll Smith-Rosenberg and Ann Laura Stoler. The seminar on 'Reconfiguring the British', which Linda Colley and I have organised at the Institute of Historical Research since 1999, has provided an important intellectual space. The untimely death of Rachel Fruchter in July 1998 was a great blow. Her expeditions

x   Acknowledgements

with me in Jamaica were a tremendous pleasure, and I like to think she would have liked this book.

My friends Peter Hulme, Cora Kaplan, Gail Lewis, Keith McClelland, Jane Rendall and Bill Schwarz have all read and given me invaluable comments on the entire manuscript, for which I am very grateful. In addition, the comments from readers at Polity and the University of Chicago Press have been very helpful. David Held and the editorial team at Polity have been most supportive.

Since this book has been a long time in the making, versions of some of the material have already been published. Part of the prologue appeared as 'Imperial Man: Edward Eyre in Australasia and the West Indies, 1833–66', in Bill Schwarz (ed.), *The Expansion of England: Race, Ethnicity and Cultural History* (Routledge, London, 1996), pp. 130–70. An early version of the account of the missionaries in chapter 1 appeared as 'Missionary Stories: Gender and Ethnicity in England in the 1830s and 1840s', in Lawrence Grossberg, Cary Nelson and Paula A. Treichler (eds), *Cultural Studies* (Routledge, London and New York, 1992), pp. 240–70. This was published subsequently in my own collection of essays, *White, Male and Middle Class: Explorations in Feminism and History* (Polity, Cambridge, 1992), pp. 205–54. The account of the free villages in chapter 1 draws on my article 'White Visions, Black Lives: The Free Villages of Jamaica', *History Workshop*, 36 (Autumn 1993), pp. 100–32. The material on Knibb in chapter 1 draws on 'William Knibb and the Constitution of the New Black Subject', in Martin Daunton and Rick Halpern (eds), *Empire and Others: British Encounters with Indigenous Peoples 1600–1850* (UCL Press, London, 1998), pp. 303–24. Some of the material in chapter 3 appeared as 'A Jamaica of the Mind: Gender, Colonialism and the Missionary Venture', in Robert Swanson (ed.), *Gender and Christian Religion*, Studies in Church History 34, published for the Ecclesiastical History Society by the Boydell Press, 1998, pp. 362–90. Some of the material in chapter 4 draws on 'Going a-Trolloping: Imperial Man Travels the Empire', in Clare Midgley (ed.), *Gender and Imperialism* (Manchester University Press, Manchester, 1998), pp. 180–99. An early account of the differences between George Dawson and R. W. Dale which are explored in chapters 6 and 7 appeared as 'From Greenland's Icy Mountains . . . to Afric's Golden Sand: Ethnicity, Race and Nation in Mid-Nineteenth Century England', *Gender and History*, 5, 2 (Summer 1993), pp. 212–30. I am grateful to all these publishers for allowing me to reprint material.

Much of the book was written in Wivenhoe, where the Colne estuary has provided both solace and inspiration. My immediate and my extended family have lived with this book for years, some of them very difficult ones. My father and mother are both threaded through the work. I am only sorry that my father did not live to know that I was doing it. My sister, Margaret Rustin, is an unfailing source of love and support. My daughter, Becky, and son, Jess, both know what it means to be black and British. The book is dedicated to Stuart, who first took me to, and helped me to think about, Jamaica and the relation between metropole and colony, and to Gail, who helped me to know England differently.

Catherine Hall
Wivenhoe, June 2001

Abbreviations

ASR	*Anti-Slavery Reporter*
BDP	*Birmingham Daily Post*
BFASS	British and Foreign Anti-Slavery Society
BH	*Baptist Herald and Friend of Africa*
BJ	*Birmingham Journal*
BM	*Baptist Magazine*
BMS	Baptist Missionary Society
BRL	Birmingham Reference Library
CND	Campaign for Nuclear Disarmament
DNB	*Dictionary of National Biography*
JBU	Jamaica Baptist Union
JRC	Jamaica Royal Commission
LMS	London Missionary Society
LNFS	Ladies' Negro's Friend Society
MH	*Missionary Herald*
NAPSS	National Association for the Promotion of Social Science
NLJ	National Library of Jamaica
PP	Parliamentary Papers
YCND	Youth Campaign for Nuclear Disarmament

Cast of Characters

John Bright (1811–1889)
John Bright was educated as a Quaker, and first worked in the family business. A leading campaigner for the Anti-Corn Law League, he became MP for Durham in 1843, and for Manchester between 1847 and 1857. In the 1850s he was a leading advocate of parliamentary and financial reform, an opponent of the Crimean War, and a critic of the British response to the 'Indian Mutiny'. Defeated at Manchester in 1857, he became MP for Birmingham. He was an active supporter of the North in the American Civil War, and one of the most important campaigners and orators on parliamentary reform outside the House of Commons in 1866–7.

Thomas Burchell (1799–1846)
Son of a Tetbury wool-stapler, he was converted while an apprentice, and accepted as a trainee missionary by the BMS in 1819. He went to Jamaica with his wife, Hester, in 1823, and they settled in Montego Bay, where black Baptists were already established. In the 1820s, despite many difficulties with the planters, his congregations grew. In 1831 he was one of the Baptist missionaries seen as responsible for the rebellion. He was arrested and forced to leave the island: the Montego Bay chapel was destroyed. In Britain, he became an active supporter of emancipation, and after his return to Jamaica in 1834, emerged as a powerful figure, running numerous mission stations and establishing free villages.

Thomas Carlyle (1795–1881)
Son of a Dumfriesshire mason, educated at the parish school and Edinburgh University, he abandoned his first plan to become a Presbyterian minister, and made a career by reviewing and translating Goethe

from the German. He moved to Chelsea in 1834, and in his historical writing focused especially on the careers of great men. He warned of the dangers of revolution, democracy and *laissez-faire* in *The French Revolution* (1837), *Chartism* (1839) and *Past and Present* (1843). In 1849 he published anonymously his 'Occasional Discourse on the Negro Question'. After the events at Morant Bay in 1865, Carlyle led the support for Governor Eyre and celebrated him as a hero. In his *Shooting Niagara: And After?* (1867), Carlyle's fear of democracy was linked with his contempt for black people and their white supporters.

John Clark (1809–1880)

He worked as a printer in London, and became fascinated by the missionary venture in Jamaica. In 1836 he established a new chapel in Brown's Town, where he stayed for the rest of his life. The same year he began a correspondence with Joseph Sturge, who visited him in 1837. In 1839, with the help of his wife, he established the new village of Sturge Town, and in 1840 the new mission station of Clarksonville. By the mid-1840s times were much more difficult, and his regular visits to England always involved seeking financial aid from Birmingham and elsewhere. In 1866 he was visited by William Morgan. In 1870 his church split, a source of much distress to him.

John Clarke (1802–1879)

Cousin of John Clark (above), he was inspired by hearing a missionary preach, and became a teacher and trainee missionary. He sailed to Jamaica in 1829 with his new wife, the daughter of his minister. They settled in Jericho, and Clarke was amongst the first to work with native agents. He was selected to lead the mission to West Africa, where he stayed until 1847, despite difficult relations with some of his co-workers. Between 1848 and 1852 he was in England, where he published on African languages. He then returned to Jamaica.

Robert William Dale (1829–1895)

Son of a dealer in hat trimmings, his mother longed for him to be a minister, and at fifteen he preached his first sermon. He initially worked as a teacher, but then went to Spring Hill College in 1847 to train as a minister. As a student, he regularly attended George Dawson's church. Invited by John Angell James to become his assistant at Carrs Lane in 1853, he became co-pastor in 1854. At James's death in 1859 he became sole pastor. A champion of nonconformity and liberalism in Birmingham, he established a national reputation from the 1860s as a leading theologian and public man. One of the great pulpit preachers of his generation, he believed in the responsibilities of Christian citizenship.

George Dawson (1821–1877)

The son of a Baptist schoolmaster, he started out teaching, but wanted to be a minister. He was at Glasgow University 1839–41, and started to preach soon after. In 1844 he became minister of Mount Zion chapel in Birmingham. A powerful preacher and lecturer, he soon established a reputation in Birmingham and beyond. In 1846 his followers built a new church for him, the Church of the Saviour, dedicated to a spirit of free inquiry. He enthusiastically supported the struggles for Italian, Polish and Hungarian freedom. By the late 1850s he had become increasingly convinced of the importance of the town as a site of social improvement and reform, and was an architect of Birmingham's 'civic gospel'.

Walter Dendy (?–1881)

A Wiltshire Baptist, he married a cousin of William Knibb, and sailed for Jamaica as a missionary (with the Burchells) in 1831. He and his wife worked initially in Annotto Bay, where they experienced persecution in the wake of the 1831 rebellion. They then settled in Salter's Hill, near Montego Bay, where a church had originally been formed by the black Baptist, Moses Baker. A new chapel was opened in 1836, along with a schoolroom and a house. In 1841 he travelled to England with two of his deacons. He remained in Salter's Hill through the anxious years from the late 1840s. In 1865 he attended one of the Underhill meetings, and was a critic of Eyre.

David Jonathan East (1816–1904)

A student at Stepney College, which became Regent's Park, he wrote *Western Africa: Its Condition and Christianity the Means of its Recovery* in 1843. In 1851 he agreed to become the principal of Calabar, the training college which had been established in Jamaica in 1841. He was a great friend of Edward Underhill's, and they corresponded for many years. He retired in 1892, and returned to England.

Edward John Eyre (1815–1901)

Third son of a Yorkshire vicar, and originally intended for the army, he went to seek his fortune in Australia in 1833, where he became well known as an explorer. Sympathetic to Aboriginal peoples, he became associated with Governor Grey's policy of assimilation in South Australia. His first Colonial Office appointment was in New Zealand (1847), followed by St Vincent, then Antigua, and in 1862, Jamaica. When rebellion broke out in Morant Bay in 1865, he imposed martial law with brutality. He was removed from his post by the Liberal government, and retired to Devon.

John Edward Henderson (1816–1885)

Trained as a missionary at Stepney College, he sailed to Jamaica with his wife, Ann, in 1840. He initially worked in Falmouth with Knibb, and then established a new church nearby at Waldensia. His initial enthusiasm for the island and its future was displaced by increasing gloom from the late 1840s, as he was beset by financial and other troubles. In 1853 they moved to Montego Bay. In 1865 he was named by Eyre as one of the most troublesome of the Baptist missionaries. He came to regard Jamaica as his home, and despite many difficulties remained on the island, where he died in 1885.

John Angell James (1785–1859)

Son of a draper, he was converted and decided to become a minister. In 1805 he became pastor at Carrs Lane in Birmingham, and stayed there until his death. The chapel rapidly became a centre of town life, and James himself a celebrated figure. A prolific writer, well-known evangelical preacher and powerful protagonist of separate spheres, his most influential book was *The Anxious Enquirer after Salvation* (1834). An enthusiastic supporter of missionary and abolitionist ventures, he played a significant role in the development of the Congregational Union. In 1840 he represented Birmingham and Jamaica at the Anti-Slavery Convention.

William Knibb (1803–1845)

Born in Kettering, he was apprenticed in Bristol, where he became a Sunday school teacher. Inspired by the example of his brother, Thomas, who died while teaching in Kingston, he decided to go to Jamaica. He sailed with his wife, Mary, in 1825. Initially working in Savanna-la-Mar, they moved to Falmouth in 1830. In 1831 he became the spokesman for the Jamaican missionaries at a time when they faced serious persecution. He came out publicly against slavery, and lectured throughout Britain to rally support. A regular visitor to Birmingham, he was well known to Sturge, Morgan and James. In the aftermath of emancipation, he became the best-known protagonist of the rights of freed men and women and the acknowledged leader of the missionaries in Jamaica.

John Stuart Mill (1806–1873)

The young Mill's education, at home with his Utilitarian father, and his reaction against it were famously recorded in his *Autobiography* (1873). He first met Harriet Taylor in 1830, and their relationship increased his interest in the position of women. He supported the Philosophic Radicals in the 1830s, and from 1840 concentrated on writing on philosophical and political subjects. His major works were *A System of Logic*

(1843), *Principles of Political Economy* (1848), *On Liberty* (1859), *Considerations on Representative Government* (1861), and *The Subjection of Women* (1869). In the 1860s Mill was an active supporter of the North in the American Civil War and the central public figure in the Jamaica Committee, set up in 1866 to campaign for justice in the wake of Morant Bay. From 1865 to 1868 he was MP for Westminster, and spoke on parliamentary reform, women's suffrage, Jamaica and Ireland.

Thomas Morgan (1776–1857)
The son of a Welsh Anglican farmer, he trained as a Baptist minister at Bristol College with Dr Ryland, and succeeded Samuel Pearce at Birmingham's Cannon Street chapel in 1802. He was forced to resign because of illness in 1811, and his wife Ann ran a school to support the family. In 1815 he began preaching again, and became pastor at Bond Street in 1820. An enthusiast for missionary and abolitionist ventures, he was a founder member of the town's Anti-Slavery Society and a lifelong friend of John Angell James and Joseph Sturge. William Knibb stayed with the family in 1833.

William Morgan (1815–?)
Third son of the above, he trained as a solicitor, and practised in Birmingham. From an early age he was engaged with missionary and abolitionist ventures, and was active in liberal and philanthropic causes. Co-founder of the Birmingham Baptist Union, he was also secretary of the Birmingham Anti-Slavery Society in the 1830s. In 1840 he served as one of the honorary secretaries of the Anti-Slavery Convention. In the 1840s and 1850s he worked closely with Sturge. In 1866 he went to Jamaica for the BFASS.

Samuel Oughton (?)
Born in London, and in business with his father, he married the niece of Hester Burchell, and became a missionary. His first work was with Thomas Burchell, and then he settled in Kingston, where he became the minister of the important church on East Queen's Street. Difficulties within the church embittered him, and he became increasingly sceptical of the potential of Africans to become fully civilised. In 1866 he expressed support for Eyre, and left Jamaica to settle in England. He appears to have had no further connections with the Baptists.

James Mursell Phillippo (1798–1879)
The son of a master builder, he was converted as a young man, and determined to become a missionary. He was accepted as a trainee in 1819, and sailed to Jamaica with his new wife, Hannah, in 1823. (In 1822 he

stayed with Thomas Morgan in Birmingham, and established a long-term friendship with the family.) They settled in Spanish Town, and lived there for the rest of their lives. They faced many difficulties with the plantocracy in the 1820s, and he spoke out against slavery in the wake of 1831. A great defender of the free peasantry, he established numerous free villages in the period after 1838. His church in Spanish Town split, and there were years of dispute as to the property and the pastor's power. Phillippo came to terms with this, and remained a patriarchal champion of freed men and women to the end of his life.

Joseph Sturge (1793–1859)
Born into a Quaker family near Bristol, his father died when he was twenty-four, and he became responsible for his mother and seven younger brothers and sisters. A corn merchant, he moved to Birmingham in 1822, living initially with his sister Sophia. He became involved in a wide range of philanthropic and political activities. An enthusiast for missionary and abolitionist ventures, he was central to the struggle for the abolition of apprenticeship. In 1837 he travelled to the West Indies to investigate conditions for himself. Founder of the BFASS in 1840, he was a key figure in the Anti-Slavery Convention. Increasingly radicalised by his experience both at home and in the colonies, he was a lifelong believer in the universal family of man and a supporter of freed men and women.

Edward Bean Underhill (1813–1901)
The son of a Baptist, he was himself converted at sixteen. Initially he went into business, but his fascination with Baptist history and missionary work took him into the BMS in 1849. In 1854 he went on a deputation to India for two and a half years, and in 1859 to Jamaica. His letter to the Secretary of State for the Colonies in 1865, about conditions in Jamaica, was seen by Eyre as a provocation. Between 1865 and 1867 he was very heavily involved with Jamaican affairs. Effectively he directed the BMS for twenty-seven years.

Introduction

People are trapped in history and history is trapped in them.
James Baldwin, 'Stranger in the village'

The origins of this book lie in my own history. I was born in Kettering, Northamptonshire, in 1946. My father, John Barrett, was a Baptist minister, my mother a budding historian who had become a clergyman's wife. My father was at that time the minister of Fuller Baptist Chapel, named after the nonconformist divine and first secretary of the Baptist Missionary Society, Andrew Fuller. The church, first established in 1696, now stands in the centre of the town, and is a handsome building, resonant of a proud dissenting culture. My parents lived in Kettering throughout the Second World War, a time when churches and chapels were particularly important in providing a focus for communities struggling with the experience of war and major conflict. Fuller, as it was known by everybody, had always played a significant part in the life of the town. Dissent had had a powerful presence in the county since the seventeenth century, and it was in Kettering that the Baptist Missionary Society was formed in 1792, the first of the great missionary ventures of the late eighteenth century. William Knibb, a Baptist missionary to Jamaica who was closely associated with the end of British colonial slavery, was intimately connected with Fuller. So proud was the town of its place in the making of abolition that the arms of the borough depict the figure of a freed man.[1] In September 1945 my father held a service of memorial and celebration at Fuller, 100 years after Knibb's death. The mayor and town dignitaries attended, a recognition of the significance of the legacy of radical abolitionism to the town's sense of itself. Fuller now boasts a Heritage Room where this history is told.

Kettering was built on the boot and shoe trade, and still has the character of a small provincial town. With a population of c.76,000, it is predominantly white, and has a very different feel from those cities where the peoples of the erstwhile empire, African-Caribbeans, Africans, and South and East Asians and others, have settled, had children, and changed these 'contact zones' of the second half of the twentieth century into something new. In the late 1940s the community around Fuller was close-knit, including a few well-to-do families but dominated by small manufacturers and traders, many still working in leather. As young children my brother, my sister and I were surrounded by kindly pretend aunts and uncles, all members of the congregation, binding us into a narrow, restricted world where propriety and respectability were highly valued, and membership of Fuller was a critical part of a good life. Belonging to this community brought great benefits: warmth, friendship, companionship, a sense of purpose and a place of belonging, where the ritual moments of life and death were collectively celebrated and mourned. Yet it had its costs: a privileging of respectability, the requirement to live in certain prescribed ways, a disapproval of anything perceived as delinquent, social conformity, assumptions about the truth of the faith, a fear of critical thinking, a limited intellectual vision. The narrowness of this world was offset, however, by the wider communities to which the congregation was attached, not only throughout Britain, but across the empire and the globe. The radical Baptist tradition with which Fuller was associated was committed to a notion of a universal family of man and, more specifically, to a Baptist family which stretched across the oceans, linking West Indians, Africans, Chinese and Indians in the embrace of its mission. There were friends in Baptist chapels everywhere. This was, in its own way, a transnational world.

In 1949, when I was three, we left Kettering. My father had been appointed superintendent of the north-eastern area of the Baptist Union, and we went to live in Leeds. We returned to Kettering to visit on a very regular basis, and Fuller continued to be a place of belonging, of warmth and acceptance, where our family was loved and my parents revered. Leeds was a very different experience. My father now had no church of 'his own', and travelled across the north-east preaching in different chapels every Sunday, but the rest of the family attended the local Baptist church, South Parade. My father's version of the Baptist faith, with its focus on the potential of all men and women to become Christians, connected to the founding fathers of the seventeenth century in its emphasis on social and political justice, was only one strand within the denomination. A more rigid, dogmatic and excluding version, with conservative rather than radical instincts, was always present. In Leeds, no longer protected by my father's inclusive style of preaching and teaching, I experienced the Baptist congregation as much less like a kindly extended family. The disapproving, narrow-minded and self-righteous aspects of this nonconformist culture became ever more apparent as my sister and I moved into adolescence, hated having to go to church and Sunday school, and resisted the pressure to become believers. Since the key doctrine which distinguishes the Baptists from other nonconformists is their belief in adult baptism on the basis of individual conversion, a high premium is placed on personal conviction. Without the experience of faith, there can be no full membership of the church. Each individual, male or female, black or white, Jew or Greek, as St Paul said, must make their own choice. On that choice depended their entry into the community and into salvation. Individual autonomy on matters of faith was sacrosanct, and this gave a certain freedom, albeit a negative one, to children of the manse.

At home the sense of a Baptist family stretching across the globe was always part of domestic life: missionaries from 'the field', 'on furlough', bringing me stamps for my collection; African students studying at the university who were invited for Christmas or Sunday tea; the small concerts we held to raise money for 'good causes' both near and far. My mother's involvement in the United Nations Association meant that some of the specifically Christian dimensions of a connection with other parts of the world could be displaced by a focus on internationalism. But there were uncomfortable moments as to quite what the nature of these connections were. A visiting West African student was upset with me when I exclaimed about the 'funny' feel of her hair and kept wanting to touch it. A great United Nations enthusiast, an acquaintance of my mother's, was deeply disapproving of my sister's friendship with some Trinidadian students. What was the nature of this supposedly universal family? And how were black people and white people placed within it?

Living in a city made it much easier to find other forms of identity, other kinds of belonging, beyond that of the church. There was school and the political activities to which I became attached: YCND (the Youth Campaign for Nuclear Disarmament) in particular, an extension of my parents' radical sentiments. It was the political aspects of my parents' thinking that I took up, while the religious dimensions were cast off. At one of the CND Easter marches to demonstrate against the nuclear base at Aldermaston, I met my partner-to-be, Stuart Hall, a Jamaican who had come to England in 1951 to study. He had never gone home but settled, one of the first post-war generation of West Indians to 'come home' to the mother country.

In 1964, now married, I arrived in Birmingham as a student in the Department of History. Birmingham was not a city that appealed to me. Leeds in the 1950s was proud of its radical traditions and its labour movement. Birmingham, represented by Liberals from its inception as a parliamentary borough, had followed Joseph Chamberlain and turned conservative and imperialist at the end of the nineteenth century. In the early 1960s the city fathers were busy destroying much of what was left of the Victorian town and building the Bull Ring and the motorway which circled the heart of the city, ugly monuments to the car and consumption. The city was conservative in its culture, celebratory of the 'small man' and his struggles, profoundly unwelcoming to the migrants from the Caribbean and South Asia whose labour was needed in the car industry, the metal trades and the public sectors which serviced the population of the West Midlands. In the election of 1964 race and immigration had surfaced explicitly in Wolverhampton when Patrick Gordon Walker, the Labour MP, was defeated by the Conservative candidate Peter Griffiths, who made direct use of what came to be called 'the race card'. This was a foretaste of things to come, and the ripples were all too apparent in Birmingham. Travelling on the bus as a mixed-race couple, or looking for a flat to rent, was a difficult venture, to say the least.

In the late 1960s and 1970s, however, it was student politics and then being a mother to my daughter and son, feminist politics and feminist history, which absorbed my energies. My 'Englishness' and my 'whiteness', as I have written elsewhere, seemed irrelevant to my political project.[2] Of course I knew about Enoch Powell's 'Rivers of Blood' speech in Birmingham in April 1968. I watched the burgeoning of far-right groups demanding an end to immigration and the repatriation of the black and Asian migrants already here. I followed the development of the many organisations based in the West Indian, Indian, Pakistani and Bangladeshi communities across Birmingham, from Sparkbrook, Sparkhill and Balsall Heath to Handsworth. There were groups based in churches, dealing with housing, welfare, youth, police harassment, employment. What is more, they became preoccupied in different ways with the question of what it means to be a migrant, how to create some new kind of place for themselves in postcolonial Britain. For some the issue became how to construct a new way of being, that of the black Briton, and here black was an inclusive political identity.[3] But the division of labour in our household was that Stuart worked on race, which meant black men, and I worked on gender, which meant white women: a variation on that common phenomenon on the Left, where men dealt with class and women with gender. At moments of crisis, it was taken for granted that 'we' – anti-racists, women's groups, trade-unionists, Labour movement activists, socialists – would all be out for the demonstrations against the National Front. Anti-racism was assumed as part of the socialist feminism with which I was engaged: what might be characterised as a humanist universalism, an assumption that all human beings are equal, was integral to the shared vocabulary of the Left. 'Black and White together, we shall not be moved,' we sang, just as once I had sung those missionary hymns which celebrated the Christian family across the empire. But the unspoken racial hierarchy which was the underlying assumption of that humanist universalism had not been confronted in my psyche, any more than I had worked through just what was meant by the Baptist family of man.

I first visited Jamaica in 1964, soon after independence, but thereafter went only irregularly until the late 1980s. I found it a difficult place because it meant encountering my whiteness, meeting hostility simply because I was white, being identified with the culture of colonialism in a way which stereotyped me and left no space for me as an English woman to define a different relation to Jamaica. A new experience for a white woman, albeit one of the defining experiences of being black, as Frantz Fanon has so eloquently explored.[4] But it was also an exciting place, so different from England, so profoundly connected: yet that connection was colonialism and slavery. Africa was being rediscovered in Jamaica, in part through Rastafarianism and the music of Bob Marley. But in white England, amnesia about empire, which was so characteristic of the period of decolonisation, was prevalent. The empire was best forgotten, a source of embarrassment and guilt, or alternatively a site of nostalgia.[5]

In the summer of 1988, having finished the joint project with Leonore Davidoff on the intersections of gender and class which appeared as *Family Fortunes. Men and Women of the English Middle Class 1780–1850*, and with time to wonder about what I was going to work on next, we went as a family to Jamaica. Our daughter, Becky, was going to stay for a year, in between school and university, intrigued to discover what her Jamaican heritage meant to her. It was a difficult summer: family life was about to change drastically; our children were angry adolescents and had little patience with the foibles of their parents. Stuart was deeply troubled by his relation to 'home'. Jamaica was not 'home' any more; indeed, it had not been home for a long time: yet part of him wanted to be seen as Jamaican and was fighting with the difficulty of accepting that this was no longer the case, that his clothes and his ways of walking and talking and being identified him as one of those migrants who had lived in England for longer than in the land of their birth, who, in the language of Jamaicans, 'came from foreign'. Perhaps his unease with who he was, Jamaican and/or black Briton, made it more possible for me to reflect on my Englishness, my whiteness.

'It is a very charged and difficult moment', argues James Baldwin, when the white man confronts his own whiteness and loses 'the jewel of his naiveté'. Whiteness carries with it authority and power, the legacy of having 'made the modern world', of never being 'strangers anywhere in the world'.[6] White women carry this legacy in different ways from men, but they carry it none the less. The white construction of 'the African', the black man or the black woman, depends on the production of stereo-types which refuse full human complexity. When the black man insists, wrote Baldwin, 'that the white man cease to regard him as an exotic rarity and recognise him as a human being', then that difficult moment erupts, and the naiveté of not knowing that relation of power is broken. 'The white man prefers', he argued, 'to keep the black man at a certain human remove because it is easier for him thus to preserve his simplic-ity and avoid being called to account for crimes committed by his fore-fathers, or his neighbours.' The Christian version of the family of man and the Left's universal humanism had both acted as screens for me, allowing me to avoid the full recognition of the relations of power between white and black, the hierarchies that were encoded in those two paradigms. But the dismantling of those screens was not simply a matter of personal will-power (though that is necessarily a part of the process): rather, it was something which became possible in a particular conjunc-ture, the postcolonial moment, a moment of crisis for the whole culture. As Salman Rushdie wrote in 1982:

> I want to suggest that racism is not a side-issue in contemporary Britain; that it's not a peripheral minority affair. I believe that Britain is undergo-ing a critical phase of its postcolonial period, and this crisis is not simply economic or political. It's a crisis of the whole culture, of the society's whole sense of itself.[7]

The postcolonial moment, argues Simon Gikandi, can be understood as a moment of transition and cultural instability. It is the time when it becomes clear that decolonisation has not resulted in total freedom.[8] It was the time when the new nations which had become independent began to recognise the limits of nationalism, and in the old centres of empire the chickens came home to roost: in the case of Britain, in the guise of those once imperial subjects who 'came home'. While first-generation migrants felt compelled for the most part to make the best they could of the inhospitable mother country, their children, born here, made very different claims.[9] At this point of transition, Gikandi suggests, the foundational histories of both metropolitan and decolonised nations began to unravel: a disjunctive moment when 'imperial legacies' came 'to haunt English and postcolonial identities'.[10] This was also the time when questions of culture, of language and of representation began to be understood as central to the work of colonialism. While anti-

gos

colonialism had focused on the expulsion of colonising powers and the creation of new political nations, the postcolonial project is about dismantling the deep assumption that only white people are fully human and their claim to be 'the lords of human kind'.[11] In the metropole this was the moment when second-generation black Britons asked what it meant to be black and British, when black feminists asked who belonged, and in what ways, to the collective 'we' of a feminist sisterhood. That question was posed very sharply in the editorial meetings of *Feminist Review*, a journal which I had worked on for some years and which was forced to rethink its practice at every level by the group of black feminists who had agreed to join the collective. How inclusive were those humanist visions that white feminists took for granted? The idea of the unity of black and white could not simply be taken for granted: its founding assumptions needed radical re-examination. Whiteness was problematised for me in a way that it had never been before. My assumption that my black husband and mixed-race children somehow made me different, that I need not think about the privilege and power associated with my white skin and white self, was challenged and undermined, particularly in my encounters with Gail Lewis, Avtar Brah and Ann Phoenix.[12] At the same time, in the wider society, Powellite formulations regarding the threat to 'our island race' had passed into the common sense of Thatcherism and conservatism, provoking more explicit racial antagonisms. Race was an issue for British society in new ways by the late 1980s: racial thinking had been around for a very long time, but the bringing of it to consciousness, the making explicit of the ways in which the society is 'raced', to use Toni Morrison's term, is another matter.

Driving along the north coast of Jamaica that summer of 1988, on the main road from Falmouth, once the prosperous port at the centre of a trade in enslaved peoples and the market for a complex of sugar plantations, to Ocho Rios, with its modern economy tied to tourism, we came to the small village of Kettering. I was immediately struck by its name, and by the large Baptist chapel with the name of William Knibb, the Emancipator, blazoned upon it. Why was this village called Kettering? What was its relation to the Northamptonshire town in which I was born? And why did the Baptist chapel occupy pride of place in the village? Who was William Knibb, and why was he remembered? What part did nonconformists play in the making of empire? This was the beginning of an unravelling of a set of connected histories linking Jamaica with England, colonised with colonisers, enslaved men and women with Baptist missionaries, freed people with a wider public of abolitionists in the metropole. How did the 'embedded assumptions of racial language' work in the universalist speech of the missionaries and their supporters?[13] The links between Jamaica and England were not neutral, not simply a chain of connection. The relations between colony and metropole were relations of power. More significantly, they were relations which were mutually constitutive, in which both coloniser and colonised were made. That mutual constitution was hierarchical: each was party to the making of the other, but the coloniser always exercised authority over the colonised. My project, as I elaborated it, was to try to understand the making of this particular group of colonisers: that was my task, from where I stood, the politics of my particular location, driven by my 'trans-generational haunting'.[14]

If Kettering, in both its manifestations, provided one point of departure, Birmingham provided another. The city which had seemed so alien to me in 1964 was my home for seventeen years, the place where my children were born, and I continued to grow up. Powerfully identified with Powellism, it was in the heartlands of the new forms of racial thinking of the 1970s and 1980s: a reworking of the legacy of Joseph Chamberlain with his passionate belief in empire as essential to the well-being of Britain. Race, it was clear, was deeply rooted in English culture. Not always in forms which were explicitly racist, but as a space in which the English configured their relation to themselves and to others. Racial thinking was a part of the everyday, part of instinctive English common sense: and there was no better base from which to try and unpick this than Birmingham. The work which I had done in the 1980s on the nineteenth-century Birmingham middle class had focused on the centrality of gender to middle-class culture.[15] It had not reflected on the national culture, in the sense of how racial thinking inscribes or is inscribed in the national, or what was peculiarly English, or the imperial aspects of this culture. These now became much more pressing concerns for me, not invalidating the previous preoccupations, but recognising the partial nature of the picture I had produced. There was so much I had not seen because I had not been looking for it. Class and gender were indeed crucial axes of power, differentiating men and women and bisecting this divide in cross-cutting and complicated ways. But questions of race and ethnicity were also always present in the nineteenth century, foundational to English forms of classification and relations of power. The vocabulary of the men and women of Birmingham, whether they knew it or not, was a racialised vocabulary, for supposed racial characteristics were always an implicit part of their categorisations. This was nothing new, this was part of being English. This was what I wanted to understand.

In his classic account of the revolution in San-Domingue, *The Black Jacobins*, C. L. R. James demonstrated the complex dialectic running across and between colony and metropole. He challenged the assumption that causality always ran from the centre to the colony, and that metropolitan politics were unrelated to those of the periphery. James knew the extent to which he was himself a product of both Trinidad and Britain, his ways of thinking and being constituted through the Caribbean and the 'mother country', in, but not fully part of, Europe.[16] The idea that colonies and their peoples were made by the colonisers was of course nothing new: what was new was the argument that this relation went both ways, even if in unequal relations of power. In the context of the French and Haitian revolutions, James was interested in the political, economic and intellectual aspects of this cross-over: how events in both locations affected each other, shaped what happened and defined what was possible.

The imperative of placing colony and metropole in one analytic frame, as Frederick Cooper and Ann Stoler have succinctly phrased it, has been one of the starting points for this study.[17] I was a historian of Britain who assumed that Britain could be understood in itself, without reference to other histories: a legacy of the assumption that Britain provided the model for the modern world, the touchstone whereby all other national histories could be judged. World history had been constructed as European histories, and the division of labour that academics made in the nineteenth century has left deep legacies. As a result, historians took on the ancient Mediterranean and Europe; orientalists dealt with Mesopotamia, Egypt, Persia, India and China; and the 'peoples without history' in Africa, South-East Asia, tropical America and Oceania fell to anthropologists.[18] I have become a historian of Britain who is convinced that, in order to understand the specificity of the national formation, we have to look outside it. A focus on national histories as constructed, rather than given, on the imagined community of the nation as created, rather than simply there, on national identities as brought into being through particular discursive work, requires transnational thinking. We can understand the nation only by defining what is not part of it, for identity depends on the outside, on the marking both of its positive presence and content and of its negative and excluded parts. Being English means being some things, and definitely not others – not like the French, the Irish or the Jamaicans. 'I cannot assert a differential identity', as Ernesto Laclau argues, 'without distinguishing it from a context and in the process of making the distinction, I am asserting the context at the same time.'[19] Identities are constructed within power relations, and that which is external to an identity, the 'outside', marks the absence or lack which is constitutive of its presence.[20] We need, then, to consider how modernity begins, in Paul Gilroy's phrase, 'in the constitutive relationships with outsiders that both found and temper a self-conscious sense of western civilisation'.[21]

In this study it is Jamaica which constitutes one kind of inside/outside to England, though other colonial locations figure to a lesser extent. In the nineteenth century Jamaica was understood both as a kind of extension to Britain, a useful source of that necessity, sugar, and as somewhere completely separate and different. The right to colonial rule was built on the gap between metropole and colony: civilisation here, barbarism/savagery there. But that gap was a slippery one, which was constantly being reworked. In one sense Jamaica was a colony. Colonies were thought of as offshoots of the mother country, new places where the English (or Irish or Scots) settled: colonies were children, with all the meanings of connection and separation carried by that familial trope. Dependencies, on the other hand, conquered territories or wartime acquisitions, with majority non-white populations, were a different matter. The West Indies were awkwardly placed between these two categories. Jamaica had a long-established white settler population and a form of representative government. Yet the vast majority of the population were black or 'coloured' – that is, of mixed race – and were not indigenous peoples who, according to nineteenth-century thinking, could be confidently expected to die out. Jamaica therefore sat uneasily between colony and dependency, an in-between place whose position was constantly being re-negotiated between the 1830s and 1867.

Metropolitan power, as Partha Chatterjee observes, was structured through 'a rule of colonial difference' and 'the preservation of the alienness of the ruling group'.[22] But in a world in which sexuality was locked into racial and class thinking, with their complex logics of desire, the boundaries between rulers and ruled were necessarily unstable. Mixed-race children were particularly problematic, for how was the in between to be categorised? The impossibility of fixing lines, keeping people in separate places, stopping slippage, was constantly at issue in Jamaica. And this was mirrored in England: Jamaican commodities, Jamaican family connections, Jamaican property in enslaved people, did not stay conveniently over there; they were part of the fabric of England, inside not outside, raising the question as to what was here and what was there, threatening dissolution of the gap on which the distinction between colony and metropole was constructed. Europe was only Europe because of that other world: Jamaica was one domain of the constitutive outside of England.

My reasons for choosing to work on Jamaica are perhaps self-evident by now: it was the site of empire to which I had some access. It was the largest island in the British Caribbean and the one producing the most wealth for Britain in the eighteenth century. 'Discursively the Caribbean is a special place,' as Peter Hulme notes, 'partly because of its primacy in the encounter between Europe and America, civilization

and savagery.'[23] It was through the lens of the Caribbean, and particularly Jamaica, that the English first debated 'the African', slavery and
anti-slavery, emancipation and the meanings of freedom; and Jamaica
occupied a special place in the English imagination between the 1780s
and 1860s on these grounds. Jamaicans were to re-emerge as privileged objects of concern in Britain in the post-war period, but in a
very different context. Now the Jamaicans were those who had left
their island to come to Britain between 1948 and the 1960s, who had
settled, had children and claimed full national belonging. In so doing
they once again put Jamaica at the heart of the metropolitan frame: questions of identity and national belonging were again crucially in play, and
Jamaica and England were part of the same story. But this was a repetition with a difference. England was no longer at the heart of a great
empire, and its domestic population was visibly diverse. One historical
power configuration, the colonial, had been displaced by another, the
postcolonial:

Problems of dependency, under-development and marginalization, typical
of the 'high' colonial period persist into the post-colonial. However, these
relations are *resumed* in a new configuration. Once they were articulated
as unequal relations of power and exploitation between colonized and col-
onizing societies. Now they are re-staged and displaced as struggles
between indigenous social forces, as internal contradictions and sources of
destabilization *within* the decolonized society, or between them and the
wider global system.[24] *shows how power relations between oppressor
a) oppressed persist even after decolonization*

It was this new configuration with its repetition, the same but different,
which made possible both the return to the past and a rewriting of connected histories.

My focus is England, not Britain, and my detailed case study is
Birmingham, particularly its nonconformists. Evangelical Christians
were always central to the anti-slavery movement, but the Baptists had
a particular significance in Jamaica. Baptist missionaries were seen
by the plantocracy as responsible for the rebellions of both 1831 and
1865: their teaching had stirred up sedition. In the wake of emancipation in 1834, freed men and women themselves believed that Baptist
support had been essential to the ending of slavery, and joined the church
in large numbers. The Baptists remain a powerful presence in contemporary Jamaica. Baptists, and more generally nonconformists, were
also a significant grouping in Birmingham. In focusing on a particular
provincial town, Birmingham, known by its nineteenth-century inhabitants as 'the midland metropolis', my aim has been to find out what
provincial men and women knew of the empire, and how they knew it.

What representations of empire circulated in a mid-nineteenth-century town, and in what ways, if any, did the associated knowledge shape political and other discourses? Did the empire make any difference 'at home'? The case study has been central to my method.[25] Birmingham's nonconformist and abolitionist population had very close connections with the Baptist missionaries in Jamaica. The island, its peoples, its geography and its politics were familiar to the Birmingham public in the early to mid-nineteenth century. Birmingham, I argue, was imbricated with the culture of empire.[26]

My hypothesis, that colony and metropole are terms which can be understood only in relation to each other, and that the identity of coloniser is a constitutive part of Englishness could have been explored on many different sites. I have chosen to take the Baptist mission to Jamaica and the town of Birmingham as ways into my investigation of how race was lived at the local level. I have been careful to set these case studies in their wider context, asking, for example, whether a text such as Thomas Carlyle's 'Occasional Discourse on the Negro Question' had an impact locally as well as nationally.

The period with which I am concerned, 1830–1867, is framed both by emancipation and the rebellion at Morant Bay in Jamaica and by the Reform Acts of 1832 and 1867 in England. The historical significance of these events, I argue, can be understood only in a transnational frame: hardly a novel idea when the impact of the metropole on the colony is at issue, but much less accepted when the impact is seen as travelling both ways.[27] This is a period commonly seen as critical to Jamaican history, the formative years of post-emancipation society, but somewhat in between in relation to imperial history. This was the time after the expansion of empire which followed the recovery from the loss of the United States and before the expansion of the late nineteenth century. It was the time of free trade and of the development of responsible government in the white settler colonies. But it was also a time when racial thinking in the metropole hardened, in response, it is usually argued, to the 'Indian Mutiny'/Sepoy Rebellion of 1857, the American Civil War and the events at Morant Bay in 1865. There is already a considerable literature both on the Baptists in Jamaica and on the shift in racial thinking in the metropole which has been invaluable to me.[28] But my focus is different.

My questions concern the ways in which a particular group of English men and women, mainly Baptists and other varieties of nonconformists, constituted themselves as colonisers both in Jamaica and at home. Did nonconformists, in their own particular ways, conceive of themselves as 'lords of human kind', superior to others? I take the development of the missionary movement, one formative moment in the emergence of modern racial thinking, as my point of departure. What difference did the missionary enterprise, the anti-slavery movement and emancipation make to thinking about race? What vision of metropole and colony did these men and women have? What did people in England know about Jamaica in the heady days of abolitionism? And what happened when those days were over? What other sites of empire were significant for them, and why? And how did they know what they knew? Which forms of representation mattered?

More precisely, my questions concern the missionaries, their wives and children, their supporters and friends, their enemies and critics. Who were the men who decided to be missionaries? Where did they come from? What did they think they were doing? How was their vision different from that of other colonisers, such as planters? How did their dream relate to the world of plantation owners and colonial officials? How did the family figure in their 'new world'? They went to Jamaica to convert 'the heathen', but became agents in the winning of emancipation and the construction of a new society. But what was the nature of the transformation they sought? And what happened to their dream? Who were their supporters at home? What picture of the empire did Birmingham Baptists have? What forms of belonging to town, nation and empire did nonconformists in the middle decades of the nineteenth century share? Was it the same or different for men and women? How did it change over the period from the 1830s to the end of the 1860s? What was the relation between missionary and abolitionist thinking about race and that in the wider society? What did Birmingham men and women know about Thomas Carlyle or Robert Knox? What were the connections between the abolitionists' paternalistic forms of racial discourse, with their notions of black sisters and brothers, and those of the 'scientific racists', with their emphasis on fixed, immutable racial differences?[29] How did race work in nonconformist thinking about Englishness?[29] It is everyday racial thinking that is at the heart of my investigation, its 'stubborn persistence' in English culture, and the ways in which it structures English ways of life and being.[30] Through a focus on the Baptist missionaries who went to Jamaica and the men and women of Birmingham, I explore the making of colonising subjects, of racialised and gendered selves, both in the empire and at home.[31]

In thinking about the mutual constitution of coloniser and colonised, Fanon has been an important influence. A child of the French Caribbean, Fanon left his native Martinique to train as a psychiatrist in Paris. There he encountered the meanings of blackness in a new way. Best known for his thinking about the black male subject, Fanon is less often cited for his recognition of the double inscription of black and white. Deeply troubled by the psychic dimensions of colonialism, he explored his own fractured sense of himself as a black man. 'The black is not a man', he believed, until he was liberated from himself. 'What I want to do is to help the black man to free himself of the arsenal of complexes that has been developed by the colonial environment.' Colonisers assumed that black men had no culture, no civilisation, no long historical past. In learning their masters' language, black men took on a world and a culture – a culture which fixed them as essentially inferior. Drawing on his clinical experience as a psychiatrist and his self-knowledge, he explored the 'epidermalization' of inferiority, how the meanings of blackness were taken inside the self by the colonised, both inscribed on the skin and internalised in the psyche. Lack of self-esteem, deep inner insecurity, obsessive feelings of exclusion, no sense of place, 'I am the other' characterised what it was to be black.

But Fanon did not dissect only the psyche of the colonised. If blackness was constituted as a lack, what was whiteness? In his work as a psychiatrist in Algeria and Tunisia, treating victims from both sides of the conflict over decolonisation, he studied the torturers as well as the tortured. Those torturers were formed by a culture of settlement. Settlers had to become colonisers, had to learn how to define and manage the new world they were encountering. Whether as missionaries, colonial officials, bounty hunters, planters, doctors or military men, they were in the business of creating new societies, wrenching what they had found into something different. As Sartre noted in his introduction to *The Wretched of the Earth*, 'the European has become a man only through creating slaves and monsters'. Europeans made history and made themselves through becoming colonisers. For Fanon, decolonisation was inevitably a violent phenomenon, for it meant 'the replacing of a certain "species" of men by another species of men'. This involved the 'veritable creation of new men ... the "thing" which has been colonised becomes man', and the coloniser in his or her turn had to be made anew. In Fanon's mind the world which the settlers created was a Manichean world. 'The settler paints the native as a sort of quintessence of evil.' 'Natives' could become fully human again only by violently expelling their colonisers, both from their land and from their own psyche. The settlers meanwhile were the heroes of their stories, the champions of a modern world, expunging savagery and barbarism, as they construed it, in the name of civilisation and freedom.

The settler makes history; his life is an epoch, an Odyssey. He is the absolute beginning: 'This land was created by us'. 'If we leave all is lost and we go back to the Middle Ages.' Over against him torpid creatures, wasted by fevers, obsessed by ancestral customs, form an almost inorganic background for the innovating dynamism of colonial mercantilism. The

[Margin annotations:]

The coloniser indoctrinates the colonised

To be white was to be "Civilised" ↔ to be black was to always be inferior

The colonised are not even human before being colonized

Not enough to cast them off the physical shackles

[handwritten: The settler makes history - constantly referring to the history of his mother country. History of his own nation]

settler makes history and is conscious of making it. And because he constantly refers to the history of his mother country he clearly indicates that he himself is the extension of that mother country. Thus the history which he writes is not the history of the country which he plunders but the history of his own nation in relation to all that she skims off, all that she violates and starves.

[handwritten: "Old" history. Europe as an idea, not just continent]

'Europe', he insisted in a critical formulation, 'is literally the creation of the Third World.' Europeans made themselves and made history through becoming colonisers, becoming new subjects. Without colonialism, there would have been no Europe.[32]

[handwritten: NEW FIELD of STUDY]

Fanon's Manichean binary, coloniser/colonised, was in part a product of anti-colonial wars. From his own position in one such war, the struggle for Palestine, Edward Said also emphasised the hegemonic identities of 'the West' and 'the Orient'. Said's utilisation of Foucault's theory of the relation between knowledge and power was critical to the development of a new field of study. His insistence on the cultural dimensions of imperialism and the impetus he gave to the analysis of colonial discourse ('an ensemble of linguistically-based practices unified by their common deployment in the management of colonial relationships') have contributed to the breakdown of the idea of a common vision and a single colonial project, of Manichean binaries and hegemonic blocs.[33]

[handwritten: hegemonic identity of the West. Knowledge + power]

An important shift in understanding has taken place as anthropologists, cultural critics, geographers, art historians and historians have struggled to describe, analyse and define the complex formations of the colonial world. There were the colonialisms associated with the different European empires and the different forms of colonialism which operated within the British empire. On each of those sites different groups of colonisers engaged in different colonial projects. Travellers, merchants, traders, soldiers and sailors, prostitutes, teachers, officials and missionaries – all were engaged in colonial relations with their own particular dynamics.

Different colonial projects give access to different meanings of empire. The empire changed across time: there was the First Empire, the Second Empire, the 'informal empire', 'the empire of free trade', the 'scramble for Africa', the moment of high imperialism and the struggles over decolonisation, each with the different preoccupations of those specific temporalities, places and spaces. And there were contestations over meaning: who had the power to define the empire at any one time? The early nineteenth-century Baptist missionaries, for example, who believed that empire could be articulated to particular notions of freedom and liberty associated with the free-born Englishman? Or planters whose freedom, they were convinced, entailed the right to own enslaved men and women?[34] And who had the power to define the relation of colony to metropole? Whose meanings won in any particular struggle?[35] The discourses of imperialism, as Kathleen Wilson argues in the context of her study of eighteenth-century English national culture, produced contradiction and complexity.[36]

And then there is gender. Feminist scholars have been in the forefront of the effort to write new imperial histories, cognisant of the centrality of masculinity, femininity and sexuality to the making of nations and empires. Both men and women were colonisers, both in the empire and at home. Their spheres of action were delineated, their gendered and racialised selves always in play.[37] In the postcolonial moment we are perhaps more aware of the multiplicity of positionalities located across the binary of coloniser/colonised: the distinctions of gender, of class, of ethnicity. The distinctions between one kind of coloniser and another, one colonised subject and another, were indeed significant. Colonial officials, planters and missionaries had very different aims and preoccupations. An enslaved man acting as gang leader on a plantation exercised forms of power over others which an enslaved woman serving as maid-of-all-work in an urban household could not hope to emulate. The black lover of a white plantation owner was entirely subject to his power in some respects, although their sexual relationship meant that power might not flow only one way.[38] The times when the collective identity of coloniser or colonised overrode all other distinctions were rare, and were the effect of particular political articulations: the rebellion of 1831 in Jamaica or the aftermath of Morant Bay, for example. But even then there were those who refused to be positioned in that way. The framework of them/us, or what is absolutely the same versus what is absolutely other, will not do. It is not possible to make sense of empire either theoretically or empirically through a binary lens: we need the dislocation of that binary and more elaborate, cross-cutting ways of thinking.[39] Part of the task of the historian is to trace the complexity of these metropolitan and colonial formations across time, to look at the multiple axes of power through which they operated, and to chart the moments in which binaries were fixed, even if only to be destabilised.

The time of empire was the time when anatomies of difference were being elaborated, across the axes of class, race and gender. These elaborations were the work of culture, for the categories were discursive, and their meanings historically contingent. The language of class emerged as a way of making sense of the new industrial society in Britain of the late eighteenth and early nineteenth centuries.[40] The language of 'separate spheres' became a common way of talking about and categorising sexual difference in this same period of transition.[41] It was colonial encounters which produced a new category, race, the meanings of which, like those of class and gender, have always shifted and been contested and challenged. The Enlightenment inaugurated a debate about racial types, and natural scientists began to make human races an object of study, labouring to produce a schema out of the immense varieties of human life, within a context of relatively few physical variations. On the one hand, there were those who operated within a Christian universalism which assumed that all peoples were the descendants of Adam and Eve, and that the differences between peoples could be explained by differences in culture and climate. But this did not mean that all were equal: white people, it was widely thought, were more advanced, more civilised, than others. Given the right conditions, those who lived in less developed cultures would be able to advance. Many indigenous peoples, however, were seen as destined for extinction. On the other hand, there were those who focused on the notion of permanent physical differences which were inherited and which distinguished groups of people one from another. In the context of evolutionary thinking, classificatory racial schemes which involved hierarchies from 'savagery' to 'civilisation', with white Anglo-Saxons at the apex, became common.[42] But these two discourses, that of cultural differentialism and that of biological racism, were, as Stuart Hall has argued, not two different systems, but 'racism's two registers', and in many situations discourses of both were in play, the cultural slipping into the biological, and vice versa.[43]

Nineteenth-century discourses of sexual identity and difference, as Joanna de Groot has argued, drew upon, and contributed to, discourses of ethnic and racial identity and difference; these analagous languages drew on understandings of both domination and subordination.[44] The scientific theorising which was so strategic to understanding human variation, Nancy Stepan notes, depended heavily on an analogy linking race to gender: women became a racialised category, and non-white peoples were feminised.[45] Similarly, class divisions were racialised, the poor constructed as 'a race apart'.[46] In the colonial order of things, as Ann Stoler argues, the Dutch, the British and the French all made new bourgeois selves, across colony and metropole. Each defined 'their unique civilities through a language of difference that drew on images of racial purity and sexual virtue'.[47] Marking differences was a way of classifying, of categorising, of making hierarchies, of constructing boundaries for the body politic and the body social. Processes of differentiation, positioning men and women, colonisers and colonised, as if these divisions were natural, were constantly in the making, in conflicts of power. The most basic tension of empire was that 'the otherness of colonised persons was neither inherent nor stable: his or her difference had to be defined and maintained'. This meant that 'a grammar of difference was continuously and vigilantly crafted as people in colonies refashioned and contested European claims to superiority'.[48] The construction of this 'grammar of difference' was the cultural work of both colonisers and colonised.

Fanon's settlers were men. But women were colonisers too. The mental world of a Birmingham middle-class female abolitionist was peopled with numerous others: imagined 'sisters' suffering under slavery, her male relatives – husband, father and brothers – and the female servants working in her household, to name a few. Gayatri Chakravorty Spivak has drawn attention to the gendered constitution of imperial subjects and the making of the white feminist woman. This is a woman constituted and interpellated not only as bourgeois individual but as 'individualist'. 'This stake is represented', she continues, 'on two registers: child bearing and soul making. The first is domestic-society-through-sexual-reproduction cathected as "companionate love"; the second is the imperialist project cathected as civil-society-through-social mission.'[49] The imperialist project, Spivak insists, was at the heart of this white woman's subjecthood. It is family and empire which are proposed here as the constitutive agents in the construction of the female bourgeois subject, and it is the discourses of race which form the Western female as an agent of history, while the 'native' woman is excluded. The social mission is as important at home as in the empire: the civilising of others had to take place on multiple fronts, from the civilising work which women did on men in the drawing-room or parlour, to their work with servants in the back kitchen, fallen women in the city, or the enslaved women of their imaginations. No binary, whether of class, race, or gender, is adequate to these multiple constructions of difference.

Spivak is working with Jacques Derrida's notion of *différance*. Derrida argues that, rather than meaning being produced through binary oppositions, it is produced through endless proliferation and constant deferral: the 'logic of the supplement'. As Deborah Cherry puts it: 'Alluding to the double meaning in French of *supplement* as addition and replacement, Derrida writes in *La dissemination* that the supplement is dangerous precisely because its textual movement is unstable and slippery, disrupting binary oppositions and securities of meaning.'[50] *Différance* is 'a playing movement' across a continuum of similarities and differences which refuses to separate into fixed binary oppositions. *Différance* characterises a system in which 'every concept [or meaning] is inscribed in a chain or in a system within which it refers to the other, to other concepts [meanings], by means of the systematic play of differences'.[51] Meanings, then, cannot be fixed, but are always in process. Cherry utilises these insights in her analysis of egalitarian feminism in the 1850s. The term 'sister', she argues, widely adopted by feminists, was doubly inscribed.

It slipped between registers of meaning, marking both kinship and a gap, between philanthropic ladies at home and those they supported and helped. 'As it conjured a communality', she writes, 'it denied differences and disavowed the violence of colonial conquest.' The term hinted at proximity, but established a distance between 'the native female', 'not quite/not white', and the Western feminist, 'not quite/not male'. Far from fixing 'native women' in a close sibling relationship to white feminists, 'sister' destabilised and unsettled, leaving meanings ambiguous and unresolved.[52]

Working with these same issues, John Barrell utilises a notion of 'this/that/the other' in his analysis of de Quincy's psychopathology of imperialism. He draws on the distinction which Spivak makes between 'self-consolidating other' and 'absolute other'. The difference between self and other in de Quincy's writing, he suggests,

> though in its own way important, is as nothing compared with the difference between the two of them considered together, and that third thing, way over there, which is truly *other* to them both . . . what at first seems other can be made over to the side of the self – to a subordinate position on that side – only so long as a new, and a newly absolute 'other' is constituted to fill the discursive space that has thus been evacuated.

These are the mechanisms, he argues, through which an imperial power produces a sense of national solidarity; 'for it enables the differences between one class and another to be fully acknowledged', only then to be recognised as trivial in comparison with the civilisation which they share and which is not shared by 'whatever oriental other, the sepoys or the dervishes, is in season at the time'. De Quincy was constantly terrorised by his fear of infection from the East, argues Barrell, and inoculated himself by splitting, taking in something of the East, projecting whatever he could not acknowledge on to the East beyond the East, the absolute other. But there was always something of the East inside himself, precluding any possibility of a metropolitan identity safe from colonial invasions.[53] Splitting is central, then, to thinking 'otherness', splitting between good and bad, taking in or identifying with those aspects which are seen as good, projecting the bad on to absolute others.

These insights have helped me to think about the nineteenth-century men and women whose mental worlds and structures of feeling I have tried to make sense of. In tracing some of the shifts and turns in racial thinking over three decades, the historical specificity of the distinctions made between such pairs of terms as good/bad, docile/hostile, industrious/lazy, civilisation/barbarism, are very apparent. The 'good negro' of the abolitionists became the 'nigger' of the mid-Victorian imagination, the 'docile' sepoy became the terrifying mutineer. The mapping of difference, I suggest, the constant discursive work of creating, bringing into being, or reworking these hieratic categories, was always a matter of historical contingency. The map constantly shifted, the categories faltered, as different colonial sites came into the metropolitan focus, as conflicts of power produced new configurations in one place or another.[54] Generation mattered too. Those who came to adulthood in the early 1830s tended to share an optimism about the possibilities for reform and change. It was a different moment for those growing up in the 1850s: a different political culture, a more defensive relationship to the world outside, a bleaker view of racial others. Both coloniser and colonised were terms the meanings of which could never be fixed. Yet this did not mean that these terms did not have political effectivity: far from it. This mapping of difference across nation and empire had many dimensions: subjects were constituted across multiple axes of power, from class, race, and ethnicity, to gender and sexuality.[55] The map provided the basis for drawing lines as to who was inside and who was outside the nation or colony, who were subjects and who were citizens, what forms of cultural or political belonging were possible at any given time.

The making of an imperial man, Edward John Eyre, provides the prologue to this book. Eyre's narrative, spanning the decades from the 1830s to the late 1860s, linking metropole and empire, making connections between the Antipodes and the Caribbean, offers a starting point to a history concerned with the making of selves through the making of others. Eyre's life in the empire spanned the chronological frame of the book, and I have used it as a way into the shifts in racial thinking between 1830 and 1867. The two case studies of Jamaica and Birmingham, both within this same chronology, then follow. The two places and two sets of people are intimately connected and constantly cross over: ideally the narrative would have been written as a seamless web, but this would have been difficult to follow. The colony comes first, in part to emphasise Jamaica's historical agency in this story.

Part 1, 'Colony and Metropole' is about the Baptist missionaries in Jamaica. It tells the story of the formation of the Baptist Missionary Society, the beginnings of the mission to Jamaica, and the decision of three young men – William Knibb, Thomas Burchell and James Mursell Phillippo – to go there in the 1820s. It documents their establishment of the 'mission family', the hostility they met from the plantocracy, their recognition that slavery and Christianity could not coexist, and their engagement with the struggles for emancipation, both in Jamaica and 'at home'. Both planters and missionaries attempted to win public support for their cause, and a struggle over the representations of slavery ensued

Missionary views of a new society.

in the metropole. This part of the book tells the tale of the missionary vision of a new society, peopled with black Christian subjects, guided and led by patriarchal pastors. But this was a dream, a dream which fragmented as the missionaries came to realise, to a greater or lesser extent, that they could not control the destinies of others, or indeed of themselves. Meanwhile, in England opinion was shifting too, and attempts by the missionaries and their supporters to maintain faith in the 'great experiment' of emancipation was undercut by travellers such as Anthony Trollope, who told different stories. By 1865 the mission family was divided, and the events at Morant Bay brought these divisions into the public domain. Those missionaries who remained in Jamaica were a less optimistic group, their utopian visions of an empire of new Christian subjects sadly diminished.

Part 2, 'Metropolis, Colony and Empire' focuses on Birmingham, the 'midland metropolis', and its relation to both Jamaica and the empire. Birmingham was not an imperial city in any conventional sense, yet the town was imbricated with empire. A stronghold of missionary and abolitionist activity in the 1830s, to be a 'friend of the negro' was an energising identity for both men and women. The Baptists of Birmingham, *Self-centred activism* alongside their nonconformist brothers and sisters, and with the inspiring leadership of the Quaker, Joseph Sturge, a great friend to the missionaries, enthused the town with a vision of a universal family, to be led by the inhabitants of 'the midland metropolis'. By the 1850s, however, thinking about race was shifting away from ideas of black men and women as brothers and sisters, to a racial vocabulary of biological difference. The popular lecturer and preacher George Dawson, disciple of Thomas Carlyle, was a critical figure in harnessing the energies of Birmingham men to a new cause, that of European nationalisms. In the 1830s emancipation and reform had been linked in the minds of the men of 'the midland metropolis', but by the mid-1860s and the debates in the aftermath of Morant Bay, the rights of white male citizens had been very clearly delineated from those of black male subjects. While both men and women could be 'friends of the negro', manly citizenship, as it was defined in the Reform Act of 1867, was an exclusively white male prerogative.

My title, *Civilising Subjects*, has a double meaning. The non- *The 'Civilising Subjects' became new subjects* conformist men on whom I have focused – and there are more men than women because of the sources available and the period on which I have concentrated – believed that they could make themselves anew *New Self = more civilised* and become new subjects. That was their most important task. An aspect of that new self would be a more civilised self, for Christianity and civilisation were intimately linked in their minds. But they also carried the responsibility to civilise others, to win 'heathens' for Christ, whether at home or abroad. The 'heathen' subjects of the empire were a particular responsibility for those in the metropole, since they had a special relation to other British subjects. But 'heathen', 'subject' and 'civilisation' were all terms with complex meanings: each apparently named one category while masking ambivalent understandings. Colonial subjects were, and were not, the same as those of the metropole, 'not quite/not white': colonial heathens were, and were not, more in need of civilisation than heathens at home. And there was no certainty that England was civilised: even Dickens, in his moments of harshest racial thinking, could turn the categories around, terrified of the savage within.[56] In constructing imagined worlds across colony and metropole, the men and women who are the subject of this book were struggling with questions of difference and power. As Baldwin so eloquently puts it, they were trapped in history, and history was trapped in them.[57]

A note on terminology

Since I regard the categories of 'race', 'gender', 'class' and 'civilisation' as discursive categories, with no essential referents, there is an argument for the use of inverted commas throughout. I have decided against it, however, since the text would then be littered with them, making it difficult to read. Nevertheless, the book should be read with the historically located and discursively specific meanings of these terms always in mind.

Similarly, I work for the most part with the terminology of the mid-nineteenth century, and have decided against signalling the constructed nature of these terms with inverted commas, since the book is about those changing representations. Thus 'negro' is the word used by the abolitionists and commonly adopted by those who wished to adopt a respectful term for black people. 'Coloured' is the word used to denote those of mixed-race parentage. 'Mother country' was in common use to refer to the metropole. I use 'English', not 'British', in part because it is England and the English which form the object of my study, in part because English was constituted as a hegemonic cultural identity in this period. Even Scots such as Thomas Carlyle thought of themselves as English. 'British', however, was often used in relation to the empire: a recognition that it was connected to the wider political unit of the four nations.

In constructing imagined worlds across
colony + metropole (GB empire)
difference + power.

So. she from her own experience has imagined a
'new subject' - the missionaries.

Prologue: The Making of an Imperial Man

In October 1865 a riot occurred outside the court house in the small
town of Morant Bay on the south-eastern coast of Jamaica. Months of
tensions between black people and white over land, labour and law
erupted after an unpopular verdict from magistrates led to a demonstration and attempted arrests. The police had been resisted, and an
angry crowd had gathered and marched on the court house. The Volunteers had been called up in anticipation of trouble, and were marshalled as the crowd came into the square. The local official had already
asked the British governor, Edward John Eyre, for troops, and they were
on their way by sea. Stones were thrown, sticks brandished, the Riot Act
read. The Volunteers fired, and several people in the crowd were killed.
In the subsequent violence, more killings occurred, including eighteen
officials and members of the militia, and thirty-one were wounded.
The next day Governor Eyre received a message, 'the blacks have risen'.[1]
The 13,000 Europeans on the island had long feared a rising from the
350,000 black people. More troops were immediately despatched, and
martial law declared. In the month that followed, horrific reprisals took
place. Despite the absence of organised resistance, troops under British
command executed 439 people, flogged more than 600 men and women,
and burnt more than 1,000 homes. A mixed-race member of the
Jamaican House of Assembly, George William Gordon, was hanged.[2]
    The initial response of the British government was cautiously to
endorse Eyre's actions. Jamaica, conquered almost by chance by the
troops of Oliver Cromwell in 1655, had become the jewel in the British
crown during the halcyon days of Caribbean sugar production in the
eighteenth century. By the 1780s, however, the anti-slavery movement
was challenging the permanence of the plantation economy built on
enslaved labour, and the island increasingly became the source of trouble

and strife for the colonial authorities. The abolition of the slave trade in 1807, and of slavery and apprenticeship in 1833 and 1838 respectively, put Jamaica, as the largest of the British Caribbean islands, at the heart of 'the great experiment' of the abolitionists – the attempt to construct a successful free-labour economy with black labour. By mid-century this experiment looked, from the British line of vision, less than successful, and Jamaica increasingly appeared in the British imagination as a place of disappointment and decay, its black population lazy, its planter class decadent and archaic. The riot at Morant Bay, following in the wake of the 'Indian Mutiny'/Sepoy Rebellion of 1857 and the Maori wars of 1861–5, was further evidence for the Colonial Office and the Liberal government of the day of the rebellious nature of 'native' populations and the need for strong government.

The government's initial support for Eyre soon came under attack, however, from abolitionist and dissenting groups. Delegations were organised to petition the Colonial Office; public meetings were held following lurid newspaper reports of the actions of the British troops; questions were asked in Parliament. The government was forced to establish a Royal Commission to inquire into the events in Jamaica. Meanwhile, a Jamaica Committee had been set up, chaired by Charles Buxton, the son of that veteran anti-slavery leader, Sir Thomas Fowell Buxton, in order to monitor the official inquiry and keep the British public informed of the issues.[3]

The Royal Commission report, based on evidence collected from witnesses in Jamaica, was published in April 1866. It claimed that the initial violence had presented a genuine danger, and that Eyre had been right to react vigorously in order to prevent the spread of the disturbance. However, the report also concluded that martial law had continued for too long, that deaths had been unnecessarily frequent, that the floggings had been excessive and in some instances 'barbarous', and that the burning of so many homes was 'wanton and cruel'.[4] Faced with this critical report, the new Tory government decided that since Eyre had already been suspended on account of the criticisms, a resolution in the House of Commons deploring the excessive punishments would be an adequate response. The official leniency provoked the Jamaica Committee to consider prosecuting Eyre privately, a move which alarmed Buxton and led to his resignation. He was replaced by that most prominent liberal intellectual, John Stuart Mill. The threatened prosecution of Eyre itself caused a backlash and led to a reaction in his defence, culminating in the formation of an Eyre Defence Committee, pledged to raise money for any necessary legal action.[5]

For months the debate over the Eyre case raged in Britain. On either side were leading intellectuals and public men. Behind John Stuart Mill were the doyens of the liberal intelligentsia – Charles Darwin, Charles Lyell, Herbert Spencer, Thomas Huxley, John Bright and Frederick Harrison. They believed that martial law had been misused: British subjects had been denied their right to the rule of law.[6] Jamaica was part of the British empire, its peoples were British subjects. This was not a problem without, it was a problem within. The behaviour of the British governor and the British army had constituted an attack on English notions of the freedom of the subject. The move from British to English was crucial: the Empire was a British project, but it was the English, who defined its codes of belonging, and Englishness which were under attack when codes of conduct were forgotten.[7]

Spearheading the defence of Eyre was Thomas Carlyle, the prophetic voice of mid-nineteenth-century England, backed by Charles Dickens, John Ruskin, Charles Kingsley and Alfred Lord Tennyson. Carlyle argued that Eyre's actions had been heroic, that he had saved the white people from massacre, and that black people were born to be mastered.[8] Between the summers of 1866 and 1867 public opinion swung away from the Jamaica Committee to the supporters of Eyre. By June 1868, when the third, last and still unsuccessful attempt was made to prosecute Eyre, it was clear that the defence of black Jamaican rights was no longer a popular cause. Only a small core of middle-class radicals was left, led by a disillusioned and disheartened Mill, and relying for support on working-class radicals. A considerable body of opinion had concluded that black people were, essentially, different from whites, and thus could not expect the same rights. British subjects across the empire were not all the same.

At stake in this debate were issues about the relations between the mother country and her colonies, the place of martial law and the rule of law, and the nature of black people. But also at issue were questions about Englishness itself. The debate over Eyre marked a moment when two different conceptions of 'us', constructed through two different notions of 'them', were publicly contested. Mill's imagined community was one of potential equality, in which 'us', white Anglo-Saxon men and women, believed in the potential of black Jamaican men and women to become like 'us' through a process of civilisation. Carlyle's imagined community was a hierarchically ordered one in which 'we' must always master 'them'.

These questions about the representation of 'us' and 'them', about colonisers and colonised, about colony and metropole, about the civilising process, about hierarchy and differentiated forms of power, are some of the preoccupations which thread through this book. But first let us see who Edward John Eyre was, and what light his story might shed on the making of a coloniser. How and why did he come to occupy such a

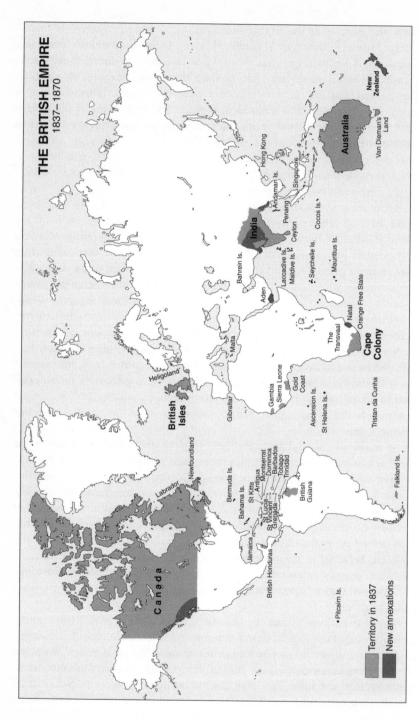

The British Empire 1837–1870.

Adapted from Paul Knapland, *The British Empire 1815–1939* (Hamish

significant position in relation to debates on race, nation and empire in the mid-1860s? Eyre's story takes us from England to Australia, New Zealand and the Caribbean. It documents the new openings for 'imperial men' from the 1830s and the complex sets of relations across different sites of empire between explorers, colonial officials, missionaries and those they attempted to colonise. It illustrates how racial thinking was made and re-made across the span of colony and metropole.

Australia

In the 1830s, respectable English middle-class men supported the anti-slavery movement and emancipation. To be a supporter of the weak and dependent – women, children, enslaved people and animals – constituted a part of the 'independence' of middle-class masculinity. True manliness was derived not from property and inheritance, but from 'real religion' – the faith born from religious conversion and a determination to make life anew.[9] True manliness also encompassed a belief in individual integrity and freedom from subjection to the will of another. Furthermore, it encompassed the capacity to establish a home, protect it, provide for it and control it: all these were a part of a man's good standing. Indeed, domesticity was integral to masculinity.[10] Such beliefs were in part rooted in a refusal of aristocratic patronage, a conviction that client relationships were demeaning and that 'a man must act'.[11] True manhood was defined by the capacity to work for oneself in the world, to trust in the dignity of labour, and to make money, rather than to live off an existing fortune. Such a definition rested on fragile foundations in a society in which economic crises were frequent – when banks collapsed and bankruptcy constantly threatened – and when, for many men, the activities of the marketplace brought not sturdy independence but fearful anxieties. The vulnerability of manhood was repressed in the fictions of integrity and independence – whether in the marketplace, the political arena or the home – but arguably it was this unspoken vulnerability which gave discourses of masculinity in this period their dynamic intensity.[12]

In the troubled decade of the 1830s, when opportunities for young men with only modest capital were limited, the empire beckoned as a source of riches, opportunities and adventure. The American and French revolutions, together with industrialisation, were changing attitudes to the colonies. In economic terms the colonies already offered much to Britain. As Peter Marshall argues, the political loss of the North American colonies did not mean that Britain had lost its economic hold on the new USA. But British governments wanted both trade and dominion. By 1818, as a result of grants and conquests, the East India Company ruled 40 million people, had an army of 180,000 men, and offered tremendous opportunities of employment. At the same time the West Indies still appeared to offer considerable rewards, and the Pacific was increasingly looking like a place of possibility. The empire was an exciting place, and old and new empires, that of the Atlantic and that of the East, coexisted alongside the trading ventures of the non-imperial world.[13] Eighteenth-century mercantilists, as Bernard Semmel argues, had hoped to fit colonial possessions, particularly those to which emigrants from the homelands went, into a system that would benefit both colony and mother country, though the latter might be expected to benefit more. The colonies would supply raw materials in exchange for manufactured goods, and each party would have a monopoly position in the market of the other, protected by tariffs. Mercantilist nations expected to use violence to retain or expand their possessions, and believed that one nation's gain was only possible from the losses of another. Adam Smith attacked this orthodoxy, arguing that the world's wealth was not fixed but could increase. He proposed the novel idea of an international division of labour and a competitive marketplace within and between nations that would determine the terms of this division. 'In such a world, formal colonies would provide no particular advantages while imposing the expense of governing.'[14] Late eighteenth-century political economists emphasised the burden of the colonies.

Issues of emigration and settlement were also being widely debated. Vocal critics of emigration such as Cobbett were arguing that emigrant paupers were being deprived of their British rights, while Rowland Hill and other advocates of 'home colonies' argued that emigration was needless and costly when thousands of acres in Great Britain were awaiting development. By the mid-1820s, however, such arguments were under attack, and the establishment of the London Emigration Committee was one sign of the unravelling of the consensus on the colonies.[15] Of strategic importance in challenging the old consensus was a group which called itself the Colonial Reformers, which advocated empire building as a necessary – indeed, vital – response to the serious internal problems faced by Britain. Systematic colonisation and the development of responsible government in the white settler colonies were seen as essential to the prosperity of Britain and Empire.

The chief theorist of this group was Edward Gibbon Wakefield, who had no independent income and had to find ways of making a living. In 1827 he was confined to Newgate for three years as a result of one of his less respectable ventures: the abduction of an heiress to Gretna Green. In prison he became fascinated by the colonies and their potential. In his unfettered imagination, Australia became a new and better England, a construct of desire.[16] In *A Letter from Sydney*, he transported himself from his prison cell to Australia, a land he had never seen and which he assumed to be empty, with no indigenous population, and imagined himself as a farmer with a large tract of land which could not be worked because of the dearth of labour. He addressed himself to 'young men of rank and connections' and those 'in the intermediate ranks of life', arguing that the colonies provided 'the most certain means of obtaining a comfortable settlement'. Industrialising Britain had more capital than it could usefully employ: this surplus needed new fields of investment. Australia offered a solution to over-population of England, and Wakefield eloquently developed the case for an organised system of emigration for both the middle and the working classes. Wakefield rejected both slavery and the convict system, a 'system full of evil', as solutions to the labour problem. He maintained that planned emigration was possible if colonial lands were sold at a reasonable price and the proceeds of the land sales were used to pay for working-class emigration. The effect of this would be to transform 'a waste country' into a profitable and civilised extension of Britain, with its class hierarchy firmly in place.[17]

In 1833 Wakefield published *England and America*, which developed the case he had made in the earlier volume, but emphasised that improving the conditions of the working classes was crucial if social revolution was to be avoided at home. The increase of population meant that new outlets were essential if prosperity was to be maintained: empire building provided a key. Properly planned colonisation, which meant supporting the emigration of young couples so that each colony would become 'one immense nursery', would furthermore contribute to the ending of slavery in America, which arose because of the need for labour.[18] Family and class were both central to Wakefield's scheme. 'A new colony is a bad place for a young single man,' he argued, for 'to be single is contrary to the nature of a new colony, where the laws of society are labour, peace, domestic life, increase and multiply.' It was the woman's moral influence, he believed, which would ensure both that money was saved and that her husband's energy and prudence would be encouraged.[19]

Wakefield, a brilliant publicist, was successful in making systematic colonisation a public issue. His insistence on mixed-class emigration was central to finally breaking the link between Australia and convicts, making it a respectable place for the middle classes. From the arrival of the First Fleet in 1788, New South Wales had been associated with transportation. It seemed to offer a wondrous solution to fears about crime, for the evil could be taken to another world. Botany Bay could take up what American Independence had made impossible. A population of 7,500 in 1807 had grown to 36,598 by 1828, but the 'convict stain' became an increasing issue in the 'New World'.[20] Australia needed new, and clean, blood. The development of pastoralism in New South Wales and Van Dieman's Land meant that Australia became an area of growing interest to men who wanted to make their fortunes.[21] It might be an alternative to America, a place where a man could return to the land. Wakefield succeeded in converting both Bentham and John Stuart Mill to his views, the latter insisting that, 'There needs to be no hesitation in affirming that Colonization, in the present state of the world, is the best affair of business, in which the capital of an old and wealthy country can engage'.[22] James Mill, Ricardo and other earlier political economists had emphasised the crucial importance of free trade to the ways in which Britain could wield informal dominion. Wakefield, as Semmel argues, was crucial to the development of another strand of colonial thinking amongst the political economists, one which stressed the importance of emigration and colonisation. His scheme became the radical alternative to the old colonial system.[23]

From a very different starting point Thomas Carlyle also came to be convinced of the virtues of systematic colonisation. He saw emigration as a solution to the problem of 'over-population' and as a way to deal with the economic ills of the time. With characteristic hyperbole he conceptualised the non-European world as a 'vacant earth', calling to be tilled, and white European man as miraculously benevolent:

> If this small western rim of Europe is overpeopled, does not everywhere else a whole vacant Earth, as it were, call to us, Come and till me, come and reap me! Can it be an evil that in an Earth such as ours there should be new Men? Considered as mercantile commodities, as working machines, is there in Birmingham or out of it a machine of such value? 'Good Heavens!, a white European Man, standing on his two legs, with his two five-fingered hands at his shackle-bones, and miraculous Head on his shoulders, is worth something considerable, one would say!'

Malthusians, he argued, those dismal scientists who felt helpless in the face of inexorable economic laws, should stop being so gloomy and encourage emigration, which promised such riches both for Anglo-Saxons and for the rest of the world. It was time to revive the heroic actions of a Clive, to send the 'iron missionaries' – the wonders of Britain's Industrial Revolution – into the wilder vineyards of the Lord. The time was ripe for another major expansion, and white European man, the powerful, phallic 'fire-pillar' would burst forth from 'swelling, simmering, never-resting Europe' and plant his seed.

Is it not as if this swelling, simmering, never-resting Europe of ours stood, once more, on the verge of an expansion without parallel; struggling, struggling like a mighty tree again about to burst in the embrace of summer, and shoot forth broad fondant boughs which would fill the whole earth? A disease; but the noblest of all – of her who is in pain and sore travail, but travails that she may be a mother, and say, Behold, there is a new Man born! . . . Alas, where now are the Hengsts and Alarics of our still-glowing, still-expanding Europe; who, when their home is grown too narrow, will enlist and, like fire-pillars, guide onwards those superfluous masses of indomitable living Valour; equipped, not now with the battle-axe and war-chariot, but with the steam-engine and ploughshare.[24]

Both Mill and Carlyle were convinced, on very different grounds, that colonisation could provide a key to a better world.

The proselytising of Wakefield, the support he mobilised and the organised activities of the Colonial Reformers were to bear fruit. Radical and Utilitarian pressure groups had plenty of experience to offer. They knew which influential men to approach, how to organise public meetings, and how to raise issues in Parliament. South Australia, a supposedly 'vacant' land, became the locus of activity, and the South Australia Association was formed to orchestrate the campaign to introduce systematic colonisation. Active amongst its supporters was the Hill family, a family which took the business of reform, in its widest definition, most seriously. The energetic sons of the educational innovator Thomas Wright Hill had been devoting themselves to liberal and reforming causes from their adolescence. Matthew Davenport and Rowland were both founding members of the Society for the Diffusion of Useful Knowledge when it was established in 1826. In 1832 Matthew stood successfully for Parliament (arguing for women's suffrage on his platform), representing Hull. In the House of Commons he spoke on municipal reform, discrimination against Jews, anti-slavery and systematic colonisation. While his brother Rowland, by now a thorough convert to colonisation beyond the homeland, acted as secretary of the South Australia Association, Matthew Davenport took on responsibility for raising the issue in Parliament. Their sister Caroline, who had married into the Clark family, old family friends, was amongst the early white settlers in South Australia. Their house in Adelaide was named after the famous family school, Hazelwood.[25]

The efforts of the Hill brothers and their friends bore fruit. By 1834 long negotiations with the Colonial Office resulted in an Act of Parliament which opened South Australia to British colonisation with a system of land sales and free passages, as Wakefield had proposed. South Australia, a land conceived of as empty, its Aboriginal population forgotten, was to be a land for free men, enjoying civil liberties, social and economic opportunities, and religious toleration. There were to be no convicts there. Great efforts were made to encourage the right kind of people to emigrate, 'proper men' who would establish an appropriate, serious, hard-working ethic for the colony.[26] Authority would be divided between the Colonial Office and a Board of Colonisation Commissioners, drawn from the association. Rationalists and Utilitarians were not the only protagonists of a South Australian dream. Enthusiastic dissenters were also active participants in this scheme for a new Jerusalem in the Antipodes. George Fife Angas, for example, a successful Baptist shipowner with interests in the West Indies and South America as well as Britain, and a staunch supporter of missionary ventures, linked his philanthropic interests closely with commercial enterprise. He was involved with plans for South Australia from early on, and in 1836 started the South Australia Company. In the early days of the colony he was the largest individual landowner.[27] His first 'great object' was

> to provide a place of refuge for pious Dissenters of Great Britain, who in their new home could discharge their consciences before God in civil and religious duties without any disabilities. Then in the second place, to provide a place where the children of pious farmers might have farms on which to settle and provide bread for their families; and lastly, that I might be the humble instrument of laying the foundation of a good system of education and religious instruction for the poorer settlers.

A place for dissenters, a place for families, a place for 'proper men', as he put it in a letter to Wakefield, even, in Angas's view, a place where Aboriginal people could be protected.[28] Thought was given as to how to reconcile indigenous people to the new settlers. As an official seal for the new colony, the planners suggested 'a draped figure of Britannia accompanied by a sheep and an unclothed Aboriginal receiving in exchange for the land the gift of British "civilization"'.[29] This view regarding the protection of native peoples was not shared by many of the new enthusiasts for colonial settlement, but it had the support of the evangelical Lord Glenelg, then at the Colonial Office. Meanwhile, for Colonel Torrens, another supporter of Wakefield and propagandist for South Australia, who had assumed much of the responsibility for attracting capital and emigrants to the new colony, this settlement marked only the beginning of what could become a vast Anglo-Saxon empire, for it was the mission of the race to increase and multiply across the earth.[30]

The settlement of South Australia began in 1836, and in four years there was a population of 15,000, Adelaide had been laid out, the Torrens River named.[31] Over-speculation in land, however, brought a crisis and the financial collapse of the colony in 1840. George Grey, a young explorer, was brought in as governor in 1841, and encouraged a move from land speculation to agricultural pursuits. A new South Australia Act in 1842 abolished the existing governing body, and gave authority to the governor and a legislative council, as in other crown colonies. These difficult early years are powerfully evoked in Catherine Spence's domestic novel *Clara Morrison*, the first South Australian novel.[32] Spence, born into a Scottish middle-class family, had emigrated in 1839 after the decline of the family fortunes. She initially worked as a governess and teacher, and later became a well-known writer and social reformer. She was a friend of Caroline Clark, the Hill daughter who had settled in Adelaide.[33]

While plans for South Australia were developing, new schemes for New South Wales were also in train. In 1837 the Select Committee on Transportation provided a public platform for a critique of that form of punishment and the effects it was having on the colony. New South Wales was presented as a colony crippled by its criminal origins. Transportation to New South Wales was abolished in 1840. New schemes of free emigration meant that between 1830 and 1850, 125,000 new emigrants settled in the old convict colonies, while 60,000 went to Western Australia and South Australia. As a result of this process the white population exceeded the black for the first time.[34] Australia had become a place for white settlers in the English imagination. Samuel Sidney's popular writing on Australia in the early 1840s encouraged Arcadian visions, and constructed Australia as a place for men with large families and small capital, for the Irish, even for Chartists. Australia could turn from a prison into a land of promise for the adventurous, a home for the Peggottys or the Micawbers from Dickens's *David Copperfield*, a place in which poverty need never arise.[35] The discovery of the Australian gold-fields in the 1850s set the seal on this transformation from convict settlement to land where fortunes could be made.

Edward Eyre was destined to be one of these new migrants. Born into a clerical family in Yorkshire in 1816, he was the third son of a rector without land, but with claims to a long lineage. He soon learnt, as he reflected in his autobiography, that 'There was no landed property for me to inherit and my attention was in consequence early directed to the necessity of engaging in some employment as a means of providing for myself'.[36] That autobiography, written in the Caribbean in 1859, describes his early years in Australia. Through his writing, he retrospectively constructed himself for himself as a man whose masculinity was expressed through action, independence and work. Writing in his early forties, he narrated his young manhood as a success story, and one which he feared he could not sustain. Through hard work, duty and determination, he had made his way in the world with only superior character and Christian gentility to support him.

Eyre had originally been intended for the army but his father was seized with the notion that his son could go to Australia, which 'was then just beginning to be known . . . [as] a desirable field for a young man commencing life'. In 1833, aged only seventeen, Eyre set out, armed with modest capital and some letters of introduction. He cherished the idea that soon he would be his 'own master, free from all contracts and taking an independent position in life'. In his later account of these years, he conveys the certainty that he would do well, his motto 'Si je puis', blessed as he was by Providence with the virtues of duty, diligence, abstemiousness, pride in physical hardship, all of which would enable him to prove his manhood and return with a fortune. While the disappearance of the 'white cliffs' of Dover brought many tears to his eyes, he recorded later that 'I never once regretted that I had not chosen an easier and less solitary path; whilst the very impossibility of my now turning back or my receiving aid from others made me feel more reliance on myself and determined me to spare no efforts to make my own way in the world'.[37]

On the lengthy voyage Eyre enjoyed the company of his fellow first-class travellers, especially the pretty Mrs Abell who sang 'Home Sweet Home' to the assembled group on Christmas Day. He read Madame de Stael on the commencement of a career alone, and quoted Byron to the sea on the beauties of the rainbow, and the Bible on the wonders of the deep. He also learnt all he could 'from books relative to the new regions which were soon to become at once our home and the theatre of our struggles to advance ourselves in life'.[38]

On arrival in Sydney, New South Wales, he found no lucrative government post open to him, despite his letters of introduction. Taking advice from a colonist who befriended him, he decided to become a sheep farmer. He entered into an agreement with a Mr Bell, a gentleman settler, for a year to learn the trade. Pastoral farming had rapidly expanded in New South Wales since 1815, resulting in huge seizures of land and conflict with Aboriginal people.[39] During that year he bought sheep and land, and was assigned convict labour under the government scheme. Setting up his own farm (which he named 'Woodlands'), together with his work with Mr Bell, required continuous, intensive labour, and Eyre soon discovered that 'With the possession of property came an increase of care and anxiety'.[40] Brought up amidst the comforts of a Yorkshire vicarage, accustomed to having his food prepared, his washing done, his fires laid, Eyre learnt not only how to care for stock, build and do carpentry, and grow food crops, but also how to sew on buttons and care for his clothes, cook, often after catching the fish or fowl first, render down fat, make candles, salt beef and bake bread, twist up tobacco and make his own wool bags for the wool from his first shearing. In what spare time he had, he liked to follow the pursuits favoured by middle-class men in an age when the spirit of scientific enquiry was widespread: reading, writing, stuffing birds, and catching and classifying insects and butterflies.

Eyre's later narration of these years is structured through a powerful sense of the qualities of English middle-class gentility, which for him included both a commitment to hard work and a recognition of the need for the deferral of gratification. Conversion of a small capital into income required industry and diligence. A colonist must look to his farm first, and the comforts of his home second; but he must also struggle to maintain the civilities of English life, to hold on to notions of respectability which served to distinguish him from the convicts and 'natives' who were his daily companions. Remembering Christmas Day 1834, a bright, hot day just after the first shearing, Eyre bemoaned the lost comforts of home, and evoked the delights of English paternalism in comparison with the harsh life of master and men in the colony:

> Christmas Day at last arrived . . . but how unlike Christmas at home. There was no solemn chants to awake you from your rest at the approach of the sacred day, no greetings in the morning, no affectionate wishes, no presents, no peel of merry bells, no cheerful voices of village children loud and clamorous in their greetings of the season as in their solicitations for the customary remembrance of it . . . there was no anticipation of pleasure, no prospect of meeting kind friends, no expected enjoyment of any innocent recreation or amusement. All that the men wished for or cared for was that they might have grog and get tipsy. If they could accomplish this they were satisfied to remain dirty and comfortless and miserable in all other respects.[41]

Thus Eyre demarcated himself from those men who shared his daily life, underpinning his own fragile self-esteem by denigrating the lack of self-control, the base impulses, of those around him.

Eyre was convinced that the system of convict labour was valuable, and that transportation provided a solution to the problem of punishment, both freeing Britain of criminals and reforming them. 'For the most part', he argued, 'the convicts, or Government men as they liked to be called, were well and kindly treated from the natural feelings and kind disposition inherent in Englishmen.' 'It was also', he noted, in 'the masters' interests to make them comfortable and contented.' He was impressed by the care, industry and trustworthiness of many of the convicts, and believed that the combination of a healthy rural life and the prospect of freedom brought out the best in most Englishmen. There were, unfortunately, instances of tyranny on the part of the masters: he was shocked by the sight of men being flogged, a punishment which the colonists insisted was an absolute necessity. Writing in 1859, Eyre recalled that 'It was a sickening sight to see the scarred and bleeding backs of human beings, convicts tho' they were. Could I ever divest myself', he asked himself rhetorically (little knowing what his answer would be in 1865), 'of the impression that the punishment of flogging was not only revolting and degrading but hardening also?'[42] As auto-biographer, Eyre reconstructed his young manhood in terms of the enlightened, serious Christianity of the evangelicals, with their emphasis on the sensitive, responsible man, caring for, encouraging and correcting dependents, all of whom had the potential to become new men and women. Physical brutality should be something of the past, a form of punishment no longer necessary in a rational and enlightened age. Another voice in Eyre, a harsher voice, less convinced of the capacities of all people to be reformed, was, by the 1860s, to be more insistent.

After a year, Eyre left Mr Bell and set up on his own. His experiment with sheep farming went well until he entered an unwise partnership, impelled primarily by his desire for companionship, tired of a life in which his everyday contacts were only with convicts and 'natives'. This proved financially disastrous, and he decided to try his hand as an over-lander, taking sheep and cattle across the country to the new settlements in South Australia. Despite the hardships of the life, he was able to make a considerable amount of money; for, as George Grey, explorer and colo-nial administrator to be, remarked, 'The first entrance of an Overlander into a district, may be compared to the rising of the Nile upon a thirsty land of Egypt; then does the country bear fruit and the land give forth her increase.' Overlanding required some capital and plenty of confi-dence; it was an exciting, romantic and dangerous life, a frontier life, with the constant possibility of conflict with Aboriginal people.[43]

Grey, the son of a lieutenant-colonel, had entered Sandhurst in 1826, been sent to Ireland on his first assignment, been horrified by the misery there, and become interested in liberal ideas about colonisation. He decided to go into the colonial service. From 1834, concern about land and colonisation – as, for example, the public regret over excesses against the natives in Van Dieman's land – had inspired a series of House of Commons inquiries into 'wastelands' and the fate of native peoples. This was in part associated with efforts to redirect humanitarian efforts towards people untouched by the African slave trade, but suffering from largely uncontrolled British expansion. There were hopes that it would be possible to define the principles of a system which would make it possible to enforce the observance of some indigenous rights.[44] The main report on Aboriginal people was submitted by Buxton and revised by George Grey; it reflected what might be called a humanitarian wisdom on these questions. The evidence collected vindicated a system whereby the government would negotiate with people for the 'purchase' of their land and then resell it to settlers. The report stressed the importance of obtaining consent from local peoples for settlement. When barbarous customs had been removed, and conversion effected, all native peoples should receive full civil rights and come under British law.[45] Now was the moment, the report declared,

> for the nation to declare, that with all its desire to give encouragement to emigration, and to find a soil to which our surplus population may retreat, it will tolerate no scheme which implies violence or fraud in taking possession of such a territory; that it will no longer subject itself to the guilt of conniving at oppression, and that it will take upon itself the task of defending those who are too weak and too ignorant to defend themselves.[46]

In 1836 George Grey led an exploration north from Perth which was designed to investigate the possibilities of further colonisation in Western Australia. His journals of the expeditions included an account of Aboriginal peoples, and were read with interest in the Colonial Office. He was subsequently appointed resident magistrate in Albany, and there formulated his principles of native policy which focused on the civilisation and assimilation of Aboriginal peoples. In 1841, as we have seen, he arrived in South Australia, newly appointed from London.[47]

Eyre thrived on this travelling life, and became increasingly interested in the land, its potential for wealth and its mysteries. While overlanding, he took on two 'Aborigine' boys (the generic term used by the British for the many different indigenous peoples they encountered), intending to educate and civilise them. From his first contacts with Aboriginal people, Eyre had been fascinated by their differences from Europeans, both physically and culturally. Eyre had left England in the year of the great Reform Act, just before the new Parliament, elected by its wider franchise, emancipated enslaved people in the colonies, a statement of faith from the anti-slavery and humanitarian public in the potential of black people to be brothers. A true child of the era of emancipation, Eyre carried that faith to Australia, and while never doubting the European right to possess the land, he firmly believed in British responsibility towards those they had dispossessed, denouncing those settlers who 'think as little of firing at a black, as at a bird'.[48]

By 1839 Eyre had made a considerable amount of money from overlanding, and he decided to devote his energies to an exploration of parts of the north and west of South Australia, impelled by 'an innate feeling of ambition and a desire to distinguish myself in a more honourable and disinterested way than the mere acquisition of wealth'.[49] Australia was still a vast unexplored continent, a field of adventure for the ambitious. Both overlanding and exploration were quintessentially male activities, and exploration allowed a powerful expression of frontier masculinity, the extension in the European mind of man's conquest over 'virgin' territory. In an article in the *South Australian Register* of 1840, Eyre's metaphorical language of conquest, like that of Carlyle, evokes the psychic links between power over other men, over women and over nature. Thus the web of connections established in the first encounters between the European and the 'new world', and later richly elaborated in the popular fictions of African conquest, were spun for Australia too.[50] Making use of the trope of conquest as sexualised narrative, Eyre noted:

> In a geographical point of view it will be exceedingly interesting to know the character of the intervening country between this colony and theirs, and to unfold the secrets hidden by those lofty and singular cliffs at the head of the Great Bight. . . . it is possible that a light party might, in a favourable season, force their way across . . . it is possible the veil may be lifted from the still unknown and mysterious interior of this vast continent.[51]

When Eyre's second expedition set out from Adelaide, following the writing of this article, his friend and fellow explorer Charles Sturt presented him with a Union Jack, worked by the ladies of the town as their contribution to exploration – a manifestation of their particular relation to the public world of men – which he was to plant in the centre of the mighty continent 'as a sign to the savage that the footstep of civilised man has penetrated so far'; an evocative moment in the complex of relations between English men and their 'others', whether black men or women or white females.[52]

Overlanders would occasionally have a woman with them, explorers never. The men had to survive on their own, and the skills that Eyre had learnt as a bachelor-farmer – cooking, washing and mending his clothes, dealing with sickness – were quite as essential as those associated with the driving of stock, the keeping of journals and charts, the daily observation of the barometer, the thermometer, the winds and the weather. When times were hard, Eyre, trained in the ways of cleanliness and godliness, retreated to nursery lore and found there was nothing better than 'a good wash' to recover himself.[53]

The entire land of Australia had been claimed by the British crown in 1788, but only relatively small areas had been settled by the 1830s, providing, in the words of Charles Sturt, a 'girdle of civilisation'.[54] Since Aborigines did not share the Western concept of property and had no fixed settlements, no arable farming, no stock raising, they were utterly strange to the settlers, as were the settlers to them.[55] The British saw the land as theirs to take, to improve and, in their terms, to make valuable. The introduction of sheep farming, profitable for the colonists, was a disaster for Aboriginal people, resulting in the destruction of the traditional hunting environment. Aboriginal resistance to the invasion, once they understood that this was what it was, was considerable, but the combination of guns, the ravages of new diseases, and the destruction of the traditional means of survival resulted in the deaths of tens of thousands. For many of the settlers it became a self-fulfilling orthodoxy that the Aborigines were doomed to extinction.

As a farmer, Eyre had been glad to employ casual Aboriginal labour, making use, for example, of traditional skills in stripping bark which could then be used for building sheep pens.[56] As an overlander, he again had need of Aboriginal skills, and was dependent on Aboriginal knowledge of the countryside. As an explorer, this knowledge was even more essential, and on his expeditions into the heartlands of South Australia, Eyre would not have survived without Aboriginal help. His journals, as Julie Evans has argued, expressed an immediacy and uncertainty: these were new experiences in new kinds of spaces and places, and it was possible for him to experience difference without hierarchy.[57] Nothing was as he expected it to be, and it was Aboriginal knowledge which saved him. At numerous points on his ill-fated exploration of the Great Bight in 1840–1, it was Aboriginal knowledge of the waterholes which saved at least some of the party. 'In how strong a light does such a simple kindness of the inhabitants of the wilds to Europeans travelling through his country (when his fears are not excited or his prejudices violated) stand contrasted', he noted, 'with the treatment he experiences from them when they occupy his country, and dispossess him of his all.'[58]

Eyre's expeditions were unsuccessful as regards the discovery of new lands which could be settled and farmed. But his terrifying experiences on the Great Bight provided the makings of an adventure narrative which Eyre himself wrote and which Henry Kingsley, Charles Kingsley's brother, was later to take up.[59] On Eyre's return from his year-long expedition to the Great Bight, he was enthusiastically welcomed by the residents of Adelaide. His bleak 'discoveries', marked by names such as Mt Hopeless and Mt Deception discouraged further exploration, however, and he invested his remaining savings in some land at Moorundie on the Murray River. A month later a massacre of Aboriginals by overlanders in this area prompted Grey to invite Eyre to take on a new post as resident magistrate. In 1840 Grey had submitted a memorandum to the Secretary of State arguing for a different approach to the 'native problem'. He argued that the Aborigines 'are as apt and intelligent as any other race of men I am acquainted with', and that the future must lie in their incorporation into settler society. Drawing on his observation of their 'particular code of laws', he insisted that until these 'barbarous' laws were dispensed with, there was no hope for civilisation. A programme of regular employment and improvement should be combined with subjection to British laws. South Australia was to be the testing ground for this new policy.[60] Eyre was to establish friendly relations, adjust grievances, and shepherd overlanding parties through the area. To make amends for the driving away of game and the interference with their lands, Eyre distributed food periodically, and attempted to instruct Aboriginal people in 'good behaviour'. His initial optimism as to his success gradually diminished, however, and he decided to return to England and seek another appointment.[61]

In 1845 Eyre returned to England, and on the voyage followed the example of Grey and wrote up his journals of his expeditions. His English audience was able to follow the thrilling narrative of his adventures. By now, however, his construction of his Aboriginal subjects had been codified into a more clearly paternalistic story. But his paternalism had its limits. As Kay Schaffer argues, like many of the early explorers, Eyre collapsed in his mind the punishing landscape with the natives who inhabited this terrain. The landscape is bare, barren and inhospitable, a young female native 'miserably thin and squalid, fit emblem of the sterility of the country'.[62] In addition, he wrote an ethnographic portrait separate from the narrative proper – 'The Manners and Customs of the Aborigines of Australia' – drawing heavily on his experiences in South Australia, classifying and ordering the practices of another society for both the English reader and himself.[63] Eyre's account of the Aborigines was a powerful plea 'on behalf of a people, who are fast fading away before the progress of a civilisation, which ought only to have added to their improvement and prosperity . . . it is most lamentable to think that the progress and prosperity of one race should conduce on the downfal [sic] and decay of another'. Eyre was convinced that 'the Australian is fully equal in natural powers and intelligence, to the generality of mankind', and he believed that the interests of settlers and Aborigines could coexist.[64] He insisted that in his experience the Aborigines were 'generally of a very inoffensive and tractable character', and could be 'rendered peaceable and well disposed by kind and consistent treatment'. 'We must remember', he reminded his readers, 'That our being in their country at all is, so far as their ideas of right and wrong are concerned, altogether an act of intrusion and aggression.'

Settlement meant dispossession. The Aborigines had become 'strangers in their own land', subject to summary violence from settlers, while the law, 'which merely lays down rules for the protection of the privileged robber', offered no protection.[65] But Eyre had now constituted himself as the one with knowledge, able to codify and classify Aboriginal culture, and able to see that it was doomed to extinction. Sovereignty belonged only to the elders: once they had gone, dependence was inevitable. As Evans argues, his ethnographic portrait had a quite different tone from his earlier writing. He had now become the colonial administrator.[66]

While acting as resident magistrate on the Murray River, Eyre developed a system which he strongly recommended was worthy of general notice. The area had been one in which considerable violence had taken place between Aborigines and overlanders. Under Eyre's control it had become peaceful. Through his account of events, he hoped to convince readers of the failure of the white settlers to raise these 'children of the wilds', these 'poor untutored children of impulse', higher in the scale of civilisation. Eyre did not doubt that the Aboriginal people were 'savages', in that, for example, they treated their wives as slaves (always a key index for the Victorian Englishman as to the scale of a civilisation). He was also quite ready to denounce them as 'silent and cunning in all they do', needing to be watched all the time. He doubted, however, that they were cannibals. They had, he was sure, no thought for the morrow, a natural taste for a rambling, indolent life, and no idea of temperance and prudence. They lacked those characteristics which the middle-class Englishman valued: a commitment to the values of labour and discipline and a willingness to put off immediate pleasures in the interests of pleasures to come. Eyre described with amazement and disapproval the capacity of his Aboriginal companions, having caught a kangaroo, to eat vast quantities of meat, just like his white, male, working-class companions who drank gallons of water after having been deprived of it, while he, ever prudent, ate only a modest amount of his share, keeping the rest for another day, content with his usual pot of tea.[67] Nevertheless, he recognized that, contrary to many European assumptions, Aboriginal peoples had their own relationship to the land, their own feelings, their own value system, their own legal code, their own marriage customs, their own religious ideas, their own language. In Eyre's view their culture was different from, and inferior to, that of the English; the proper response to this was to make it genuinely possible for 'them' to become 'like us'.

'Englishmen have ever been ready to come forward to protect the weak or the oppressed,' he believed. English men must make the Aborigines into dependants. But the 'native' was constructed as victim only as long as he or she was docile and compliant. 'Natives' were also intemperate, unreliable, untrustworthy, always in danger of acting on impulse. Eyre, at the time of writing his tract in 1844, crossed philanthropic humanitarianism with the sterner tone of the colonial official, but he still exuded a degree of optimism. Typically, he argued that having deprived the Aborigines of their subsistence, 'we' must provide for them and give them blankets and food, must separate the children from the parents and the boys from the girls, teach them entirely in English, educate them for work, find jobs for them so that they would not be tempted back to the wandering life, take them to church on Sundays, and give presents to those parents who were willing to abandon 'savage or barbarous ceremonies' for their children. Eyre argued that 'we', the collective white English 'we', 'must adopt a system which may at once administer to their wants, and at the same time give us a controlling influence over them'.[68] English men must act to protect the 'savages' from their own savagery and make them anew as men and women in their own – English – image. Coexistence meant existence in their brothers' image. Humanitarian ideas about Aboriginal peoples were closely linked to ideas about 'the African' and slavery. And, as Philip Curtin argues, humanitarian ideas about 'the African' had little space for notions of African culture. Most humanitarians, he suggests, 'believed in the spiritual equality of all men before God. Perhaps a majority believed that Africans might achieve equality with the Europeans on this earth as well, but only a very few saw much value in African culture as it was.' Equality was seen as for the future. In the 1830s both science and religion pointed to the possibility of improvements. Africans were not condemned to a permanent condition of barbarism, and the mood was optimistic.[69] But the assumption of European superiority was always in danger, and the construction of native peoples as childlike younger brothers and sisters could always slip. Once Aboriginal or African peoples were seen as not in their brothers' image, the seeds of other ways of perceiving these 'natives' were already contained in the interstices of the philanthropic mind.

New Zealand

Eyre left Australia in 1845, hoping to find employment in the colonial service. He returned to England, taking with him the two Aboriginal boys who he was educating and 'civilising', his personal experiment in the construction of the 'new man'.[70] While in England, he met Ada Ormond, daughter of a captain in the Royal Navy, a meeting 'that eventually became the turning point of my whole destiny and led to the most important occurrence of my whole life'. Miss Ormond was not only highly suitable socially, she was also 'a fair and beautiful girl, then in her teens, with all the attractive charms of incipient womanhood, the freshness, grace and loveliness of the rosebud ere it expands into the opening flower'.[71] Like many middle-class men, Eyre preferred to marry a younger woman, whose adulthood would be formed in relation to him. In November 1846, after a year spent visiting friends and family, he was appointed lieutenant-governor of the South Island of New Zealand, under the governorship of Grey, who had been transferred from South Australia. He set out for New Zealand at the beginning of 1847.

New Zealand had become an object of public concern in Britain in the late 1830s, when the Aborigine Protection Society was founded and the House of Commons Select Committee Report on Aborigines in British settlements was published. The report, articulating the concerns of the anti-slavery lobby, as we have seen, argued that the expansion of the empire must involve the trusteeship of 'native races', protecting them from the worst effects of uncontrolled European contact. New Zealand, still only in the early stages of settlement, and with a modest European population of about 2,000 in 1840, seemed to offer the possibility for a happier outcome than Australia. The amalgamation of Maori society into the settler community might be feasible there.[72] This was the hope of the Aborigine Protection Society and the New Zealand missionaries who were closely connected with it.

In the 1830s, however, Wakefield and the Colonial Reformers also sought the ear of the Colonial Office with a very different agenda. Disappointed with their unfulfilled desires in Australia, they turned their attention to New Zealand, seeing it as a land rich in opportunities. Increasing French interest in New Zealand lent force to Wakefield's proposals that the territory be seized for Britain. Wakefield was active in promoting the cause of systematic colonisation through his evidence to the Parliamentary Inquiry on Colonial Lands in 1836, for which he was the chief witness, and the Select Committee of the House of Lords on New Zealand, in 1838.[73] In 1837 the New Zealand Association was formed, soon to be transformed into a joint-stock company, the New Zealand Land Company, which acquired land and sent ships and settlers out to New Zealand, with Wakefield's son and brother on the first ship. The company was anxious to force the government to declare sovereignty, concerned to protect settler interests and dismissive of any conception of a Maori culture in need of protection. In this vision, as in that of Carlyle, the islands were of no value until the settlers got there. 'Wilderness land', the company argued in its prospectus, is worth nothing to its native owners, or worth nothing more than the trifle they can obtain for it. We are not therefore to take much account of the inadequacy of the purchase money according to English notions of the value of the land. This land is really of no value, and can become valuable only by means of a great outlay of capital on emigration and settlement.[74]

As Charles Buller, an energetic spokesman for the Colonial Reformers and Colonial Secretary in 1842 imagined it, New Zealand could become 'the Britain of the southern hemisphere; there you might concentrate the trade of the Pacific; and from that new seat of your dominion you might give laws and manners to a new world, upholding subject races, and imposing your will on the strong'.[75]

The missionaries, who provided vital information on events in the islands, were extremely hostile to the naked commercial greed, as they saw it, of the company, and they had the support of Lord Glenelg at the Colonial Office, who had been vice-president of the Church Missionary Society. The Anti-Slavery Society and the Aborigine Protection Society were both active in warning the British government of the dangers to native peoples associated with colonial expansion. They wanted to ensure that colonisation went hand in hand with the protection of native rights. By 1838, the Colonial Office had become convinced that more intervention was essential in order to protect Maori interests from the settlers and ensure that colonisation proceeded in an orderly, civilising fashion. Furthermore, there was an issue of European rivalry: the French already had a significant presence in New Zealand, and threatened to expand their control over the whole of the South Island. New Zealand Protestant missionaries were especially anxious to keep out the Catholic French.[76] The official view had moved from the idea of 'a Maori New Zealand in which a place had to be found for British intruders' to 'a settler New Zealand in which a place had to be found for the Maori'.[77]

The Treaty of Waitangi of 1840 was the government's attempt to resolve the competing claims of the New Zealand Land Company, on the one hand, and the missionaries, on the other. The context was that the British government had come to believe in its own myth of empire: New Zealand was already, in effect, a colony.[78] Maori tribes lived in relatively permanent settlements, with chiefs and recognised hierarchies. Such social and political organisation facilitated negotiations between settlers and Maoris. The official account was that the government persuaded a substantial number of Maori chiefs to cede their sovereignty to the Queen and give the crown exclusive rights to the pre-emption of such lands as Maori people wished to sell. In exchange, Maori people were granted full rights of ownership of their lands, forests and fisheries. They were also granted 'the rights and privileges of British subjects' and royal protection.[79] The government relied on substantial help from the missionaries – many of whom had built up a relation of trust with Maori chiefs – to conclude this treaty. 'There was considerable excitement amongst the people', one missionary recalled,

> greatly increased by the irritating language of ill-disposed Europeans, stating to the chiefs, in most insulting language, that their country was gone, and they now were only taurekareka [slaves]. Many came to us to speak upon this new state of affairs. We gave them but one version, explaining clause by clause, showing the advantage to them of being taken under the fostering care of the British Government, by which act they would become one people with the English, in the suppression of wars, and of every lawless act; under one sovereign, and one Law, human and divine.

As each Maori chief signed the treaty, the British representative shook hands and said in Maori, 'We are now one people.'[80] Both 'we' and 'one people' were highly contentious. The official version was only official for the British and the Pakeha (the Maori name for white settlers).

The Treaty of Waitangi broke new ground in British colonial history, in that the 'native' population was officially recognised as owning the land. In this sense it was a triumph for the humanitarian lobby and an experiment akin to emancipation, demonstrating a faith in the future of non-white peoples. The detailed interpretation of the clauses of the different versions of the treaty were subjects of dispute from the very beginning, however, and have remained so ever since. As Belich argues, Aotearoa, independent Maoridom, persisted alongside the old New Zealand, with its interface between Maori and incomers of many kinds, from whalers and traders to missionaries, and the new New Zealand, of mass European settlement. But Maori were willing to allow the machinery of British law and state in, and were willing to sell land to settlers. 'The likely Maori view was that neither state nor settlers were to have control over them', while 'the Pakeha expected control over Maori.' The treaty did not achieve real sovereignty over New Zealand: that was to take a further twenty-five years.[81] Rights over land were at the heart of conflicts between Maori and Pakeha, and these conflicts erupted into open violence at several points in the early 1840s, most dramatically in 1845. Grey, fresh from his success in saving South Australia from financial ruin and racial conflict, was appointed to rescue the new colony, and arrived with a significant increase in military strength. New Zealand was to provide a more ambitious site for his policy of racial assimilation.

It was Grey who had appointed Eyre as a resident magistrate in South Australia, part of his planned programme of 'native civilisation', teaching so-called savages the ways of civilised life and showing them the benefits which could accrue to them. In his report on 'The Aborigine' Grey had argued that they were both like and unlike other men. The dissimilarities arose from their system of law, which not only made it impossible 'that any nation subject to them could ever emerge from a savage state', but also meant that 'no race, however highly endowed, however civilised, could in other respects remain long in a state of civilisation, if they were submitted to the operation of such barbarous customs'.[82] Grey believed that British laws, British missionaries, British education, British patterns of work, British culture, would transform Australian Aborigines and New Zealand Maoris and allow their underlying intelligence to flower. It was this belief which underpinned the policies which Grey and Eyre followed in South Australia and New Zealand. They were the protectors and guides who would bring their charges to full manhood or womanhood.

Eyre was active in attempting to foster amicable relations between black and white, and to raise the level of Maori 'civilisation', in accordance with the framework which Grey had set out. On one of his trips, for example, he took with him a Maori chief and his wife, 'to show the feelings and intentions of the White people towards the native race'. He was quite prepared to be seen kneeling at services with natives, rather than pompously displaying his power. Most strikingly, his own marriage was a double ceremony in which the second couple was Maori, and the lunch and the singing were shared, a symbolic expression of the brotherhood of man.[83] This policy of friendship and assimilation was combined with an energetic programme of land buying by the crown from Maori, in order significantly to reduce the latter's overall holdings. Between 1846 and 1853, 32.6 million acres were bought by the crown at very low prices: just under half the whole country.[84] Grey envisaged that in time Maori would be 'trained to become useful labourers for the colonists'.[85] He believed that military possession of part of the land was not enough: a new society had to be created, and police and resident magistrates were utilised to open lines of communication throughout the country, a plan based on the Irish constabulary system.[86]

A young Englishwoman, Mary Swainson, who arrived in New Zealand in 1840 as a girl of fourteen, was not quite so convinced of Maori potential, though she believed that 'for savages they are universally allowed to be the most intelligent'. She vividly described her life to her grandparents in Birmingham in her letters home. Her father, John Swainson, had lost most of his money in Mexican speculations, and in the late 1830s had decided to emigrate. He started farming in the

Wellington area. In this tiny white society the family knew everyone – the Greys, Eyre, the Molesworths and the Wakefields, the colonial officials, the missionaries and the settlers. She described Eyre as 'a very nice person . . . he appears to have every wish to be sociable, and agreeable and counteract the effect of his being a bachelor'. His marriage, when it took place, produced a 'great deal of gaiety' in Wellington with balls, dinners and evening parties. Ada Eyre was pronounced by Mary to be 'a very pleasing ladylike person', but this was after the difficulties of their courtship had become the topic of much settler gossip. For Mary, Maori were intelligent and cunning, dirty and irrational, capable of being caring of their children yet coolly killing others, cannibals and victims of European rapacity. This was one young English settler's personal view, as distinct from the public discourse of a Grey or an Eyre. 'I must say,' she wrote to her friend Isabel, 'I believe in the extinction of races . . . It seems to me in the order of God's providence that it should be so.' She was also convinced that Grey 'makes every endeavour to hide everything that is bad on the native side'.[87]

The policies of Grey and Eyre were vigorously opposed by many Pakeha, who were alienated by their autocratic style of government, and also by many Maori, who recognised the threat associated with European claims. Grey's private and public relationship with Eyre became very strained. It broke down completely, despite their common approach to the 'native question', when Eyre opposed Grey in a matter of policy.[88] Grey deprived Eyre of any authority, and Eyre returned to England in 1853, now with a wife and two children and looking for a new post.[89]

The 1850s saw a hardening of attitudes on all sides. Maori were increasingly resolved to resist the imposition of British supremacy. The settlers were intolerant of what they saw as soft attitudes to 'the natives' and anxious to extend their landholdings in the north, which meant a further challenge to the Treaty of Waitangi. The Colonial Office and public opinion in Britain were moving away from the influence of the humanitarian lobby, with its emphasis on native welfare, and were increasingly preoccupied with settler development and self-government.[90] The dream of 'one people' was beginning to look outdated, the 'we' collapsing into 'them' and 'us'.

St Vincent and Antigua

Eyre spent some time in England before being appointed lieutenant-governor for the Caribbean island of St Vincent. The England he encountered in the early to mid-1850s was changing. The respectable abolitionist orthodoxy about black people as brothers and sisters was breaking up, and ideas about racial inferiority were more openly discussed. The great experiment of emancipation in the West Indies had not been entirely successful from the British point of view. Anxieties focused on the collapse, as it was seen in Britain, of the plantation economy. While the planters' lobby loudly bemoaned their ruin at the indolent hands of lazy 'blacks', abolitionists were increasingly defensive in their accounts of the West Indies. Reflecting the signs of the times and articulating new thoughts on the relations between black and white, Carlyle published his 'Occasional Discourse on the Negro Question' in 1849; this was republished as a pamphlet and retitled in 1853 'Occasional Discourse on the Nigger Question'. This piece, instantly repudiated by the abolitionist press, marked the moment when it became legitimate for public men to profess a belief in the essential inferiority of black people, and to claim that they were born to be mastered and could never attain the level of European civilisation.[91] Carlyle came to stand for a particular view of racial difference whereby it became the fashion amongst some who saw themselves as racial scientists to aver that distinct and fixed racial types provide the key to human history. This represented a shift from the orthodoxy most influentially expressed by J. C. Prichard, who minimised the small number of phenotypical and other physical variations between racial groups and argued for negro potential. In his view, language was the only valid criterion for classifying peoples into distinct categories.[92]

As Nancy Stepan has argued, the battle against slavery might have been won, but the war against racism was lost. Indeed, it was emancipation which provoked the rise of new ways of categorising racial difference, for it raised the spectre of black peoples as free and equal.[93] It was in this context that race became more, rather than less, important, in the metropole. By the 1850s, '"Race" increasingly became a primary form of self and group identification.'[94] In 1845 Robert Knox, soon to be celebrated as the author of *The Races of Men*, travelled the country visiting major provincial cities and lecturing on race. He noted that while the provincial press reported him, the national press did not. By 1850, when his lectures were published as a book, he reflected retrospectively that the situation was now very different. The world had moved on, and the climate had changed. Race had indeed become an issue. Knox had served as an army surgeon in South Africa between 1817 and 1820 and become interested in the place of race in history. Following a too close association with the Burk and Hare scandal in Edinburgh over illegal methods of obtaining bodies for anatomical purposes, he was barred from professional work and forced to make a living by his pen. Knox was convinced that climate was a crucial factor in racial difference. Here he was elaborating the work of eighteenth-century social theorists who argued for a connection between tropical vegetation and particular social forms. As early as 1770 James Steuart had codified his law of tropical society:

> If the soil be vastly rich, situated in a warm climate, and naturally watered, the productions of the earth will be almost spontaneous: this will make the inhabitants lazy. Laziness is the greatest of all obstacles to labour and industry . . . Manufactures will never flourish here . . . It is in climates less favoured by nature, and where the soil produces to those only who labour, and in proportion to the industry of every one, where we may expect to find great multitudes.[95]

This notion, that it was labour which gave rise to civilisation, was widely adopted, by evangelicals as well as moral philosophers. Knox took a rather different view of climate. Europeans, in his thinking, could only flourish in Europe. And their natural enemy was the negro, who could survive in a tropical climate: here, as Curtin points out, was a new note of fear. Knox's imagined negro did not 'walk like us, think like us, or act like us'. He had energy and, aided by the sun, could repel the white invader. He had driven the Celt from San-Domingue and would drive the Saxon from Jamaica. According to Knox's thinking the war of races was inevitable.[96] As he argued from his own distinctive radical and anti-imperialist position in 1850, 'That race is in human affairs everything is simply a fact, the most remarkable, the most comprehensive, which philosophy has ever announced. Race is everything: literature, science, art – in a word – civilisation depends on it.' Knox believed that races were organically distinct and 'not convertible into each other by any contrivance whatever'; races could not amalgamate, and hybridity could result only in withering and death.[97] Civilisation depended, in other words, on racial purity, on the separation of races, not on their harmonious integration.

It was in this climate that Eyre began to write his autobiography, working from his old journals. His understanding of race and empire came from both colony and metropole. Humanitarian discourse, white settler wisdom, Colonial Office speak – all played a part in the story he told. While Knox, holding to the radical tradition of the Norman yoke, believed that the Norman conquest of England had been a disaster and emphasised Saxon virtues, Eyre was anxious to demonstrate his Norman origins as the root of his gentility. 'The family of Eyre or le Eyre', he wrote, 'is an ancient and honourable one, said to have come to England with William the Conquerer.'[98] This good stock from which he claimed descent had by the eighteenth and early nineteenth centuries turned from land to the professions, and Eyre combined his aspirations to nobility (entirely rejected, it should be noted, by the Jamaican whites who were to be outraged in the years to come that a 'nobody' should be made their governor[99]) with a conviction that it was his personal characteristics of hard work, duty and temperance which made it possible for him to succeed to fame and fortune. 'Although beginning life under great disadvantages, I have ever maintained the character and standing of a gentleman,' he told himself and others, even in the strange conditions of the colonies, which offered a career to 'the steady, the energetic and the persevering'.[100] It was providential in his eyes that his superior characteristics allowed him to succeed, while improvident 'blacks' and convicts wasted themselves.

The optimistic tone of his narrative may well have been regretted not long after, as he languished in a public silence unbroken between 1868 and his death in 1901. But his account of his daring exploration, his determined disciplining of his 'men', his social conquests, sit ill at ease with the description of him in his thirties as having a badly proportioned head, narrow chest, a speech impediment and a tiptoeing awkward gait, and with the stories of his difficult courtship of Ada and his troubled times socially in Jamaica.[101] The retrospective tales of his years in Australia, in other words, have to be seen as part of the person he desperately wanted to present to himself and others in 1859, as he sat in the heat of St Vincent and hoped against hope that the Colonial Office would see fit to send him back to Australia. In Knox's view, that land was one of the few in which Europeans might hope to thrive, since the climate was temperate, and black people would soon have disappeared, for 'by shooting the natives as freely as we do crows in other countries, the population must become thin and scarce in time'.[102] Climate and natives were the twin challenges to the equilibrium of the white 'fire-pillar' of Carlyle's imagination. For Eyre the parts of Australia he liked best were those which were well watered, like England. His notions of beauty were entirely conventional, the landscape valued according to its potential for wealth. He was determined to remain an Englishman, to maintain 'the good old traditions of the English race' – never, in other words, to be a stranger in his own land.[103] Black people might conceivably be able to become like 'us' – 'we' were certainly not going to become like 'them'. Australia offered more hope of such a scenario in the 1830s and 1840s than did the Caribbean twenty years later, to an older, less confident man.

Eyre arrived at the end of 1854 in St Vincent, one of the tiny islands of the Caribbean, with his wife, his two children, a private secretary, a manservant and three women servants – a thoroughly English party.[104] St Vincent was a late colonial conquest, and the British had only finally secured it in 1796 when a Carib revolt, supported by the French, was defeated. Despite its mountainous topography, it was an important plantation island and had had a large number of enslaved people. Eyre was shocked by the contrast between the white settler colonies of Australia and New Zealand and the tropical world of the plantation economy with its long-established white population, its coloured inhabitants and its black freed peoples. He found the financial state of the colony 'deplorable', with its large debt and its annual expenditure exceeding its revenue. Public services were 'most unsound and unsatisfactory', with the hospital closed, the gaol dilapidated, no aid being given to schools, no refuges for the destitute or orphans, no mental institution – indeed, the island lacked 'the most essential laws and the most necessary institutions'. His own residence was 'deficient in many of the essential and commonest conveniences of an ordinary English dwelling'. This was more than disappointing to a man much concerned with status who wanted his official position to give him authority, dignity and respect. A child of the Reform Act, who had strongly supported the establishment of an elective legislative council in New Zealand, he saw himself as a strong advocate for representative institutions in the colonies. But white settler colonies might be suited to forms of representative government; sugar colonies with substantial black majorities in the population were not. The institutions of representative government, he soon came to think, were not workable in St Vincent. With a population of over 30,000, only 293 electors were registered, and in the previous election only 130 had voted for the nineteen members. At various times, he discovered, 'four members have been returned by ten votes, three members by four votes, three members by three votes, one member by one voter and in one instance a single voter actually returned two out of the nineteen members'. Furthermore, those members who were returned were not up to their duties, for there were, in his view, 'few persons of intelligence, education and respectability' willing to take up public service. The Speaker of the House at the time Eyre was there wrote:

> During the time I have been Speaker, it has scarcely been possible to find a member who could, as chairman, conduct the business of a Committee of the House – Very many cannot read a manuscript at all – some cannot read a manuscript law bill at all – and on one occasion a gentleman in the chair could neither read nor write.[105]

Eyre pressed for intervention by the British government, believing the island incapable of effecting reform for itself. Henry Taylor, who had long been responsible for the West Indies at the Colonial Office and had been arguing for direct crown rule for Jamaica since 1839, in the belief that it was the only appropriate form of government for the sugar colonies, commented that 'there is nothing that the Home Government can do to bring about a more prosperous state of things'. His colleague Herman Merivale, after reading one of Eyre's depressed despatches, thought that despondency 'strikes him the more forcibly as coming so recently from a new and rising colony'.[106] The comparison between the virgin lands of Australia and New Zealand and the white man's vision of a declining plantation economy was indeed striking. The young enterprising middle-class English settlers, whose presence was seen as so vital by Wakefield, were certainly not to be found in St Vincent. Indeed, as a visiting American noted a few years later, 'the island was utterly destitute of the spirit of enterprise'.[107] The absence of white people and the dependence on 'coloured' shopkeepers and tradesmen for public office were responsible, in Eyre's view, for the prevailing decadence. These were men lacking in talent and 'greatly deficient even in ordinary education and information'.[108] Whereas in Australia and New Zealand, natives were children to raise up, the 'uppity coloureds' of St Vincent, whether in the House of Assembly or acting as magistrates, special constables or volunteers, occupied an uncomfortable space in Eyre's mental map of empire. Long-established patterns of racial intermixing and the existence of a coloured middle class brought what to Eyre was a serious problem, and one he had not previously encountered: the presence of non-white men in positions of power and responsibility.

'Public opinion', he complained, 'has no influence and can scarcely be said to exist amidst the proverbial apathy and indolence of West Indian colonists.'[109] It was public opinion alongside the spirit of co-operation and a responsible press which had, in the eyes of liberal reformers, created the conditions in which democratic institutions could flourish in England.[110] Whereas the Colonial Office had long been dismissive of the capacity of white planters to supersede self-interest, Eyre bemoaned the absence of them on the island, an absence which resulted in the prominence of urban coloureds. He compared the island unfavourably with Barbados, where there were more resident white people 'interspersed amongst the coloured population and above all there is the moral influence of a large body of disciplined European troops'.[111]

The missionaries and their allies in England had, since emancipation, been preoccupied with encouraging independent black proprietors who would be capable, in their eyes, of conducting responsible government in the future.[112] Given Eyre's history of attachment to the protection of native races, it might have been expected that he would align himself to just such a policy; but this was not to be. Just as the presence of coloured merchants, tradesmen and newspaper editors troubled him, so the black people whom he encountered in St Vincent were disturbingly different from the indigenous natives he was used to, those 'children of the wilds', 'strangers in their own lands', who were to be pitied as victims and made into dependants, or those Maori who, in the New Zealand he had encountered, seemed to have found a way to coexist with the settlers. The black peoples of the British Caribbean were freed slaves, still riven with the memory of slavery and ever watchful of any attempt to reimpose that hated institution, whether in the guise of new penal codes or the importation of indentured labourers from Asia. They had been brought forcibly from Africa, but had become independent peoples: their property, skills and aspirations now had to be recognised. On French and Spanish territory, all too close, slavery still flourished. Their own children had never experienced slavery, but had been raised in its shadow. Numerically, black people outnumbered white on St Vincent by twenty to one and had the potential, if they won the vote, to provide the electoral majority. Thousands of acres were being cultivated by small independent black proprietors, enjoying unparalleled prosperity.[113]

Eyre's first encounters with black St Vincentians left him disappointed with the extent to which, in his view, they were 'so little improved a race'.[114] The promise of emancipation had not been realised; and, far from considering any extension in the franchise to raise the degree of representation, he was convinced that the executive should increase its powers at the expense of the elected bodies, a conviction which he was able to translate into new constitutional legislation. Eyre's fears about public order, in an island on which no white troops were stationed and boasting 'so excitable a population', were stirred by riots over the case of a coloured woman accused of stealing canes in 1855. On attempting to swear in special constables, Eyre found that few coloured men would volunteer, his first recognition of the bond between people of colour against white men. In describing this event to his superior, Eyre complained that the coloureds 'were resolutely banded together for the purpose of preventing the awards of law being carried out in cases where they disapproved of the decisions'. He needed white soldiers, to exert a 'moral influence' and 'to keep within proper bounds that innate conviction of their own power which is so often apt to mislead a population such as that of St Vincent in cases where they imagine . . . their interest as a class to be concerned'. His fears were seen as exaggerated by his chief-of-staff in Barbados, however, who firmly told him that 'there is no reason to mistrust the black population when properly appealed to'.[115] But Eyre became increasingly nervous as to the 'mine' upon 'which all the West Indian colonies rested'; the 'mine' being the 'very excitable and easily misled' people, the non-European population.[116] This fear and anxiety, this sense of white insecurity, made him ever more prone to turn to more authoritarian solutions.

Eyre sailed to England on six months leave in 1857, the year of the 'Indian Mutiny', when even the abolitionist public had difficulty in refusing the construction of Indian events as a racial and religious war in which white people were the victims. 'How little we know of the heart of the native!' was the cry on every lip.[117] Abolitionists were still ready to defend Christian black peoples, but had little to say about the persecution of Hindus and Moslems.

Eyre returned reluctantly to the Caribbean on his own, his wife's health having suffered severely from living in the tropics. He hoped for an appointment in Australia, so that he could be reunited with his family, for they would travel with him there. Having a limited private income, he also desperately wanted a better-paid post as his frequent correspondence with the Colonial Office makes clear. The impact of the Mutiny spread to St Vincent after a suggestion that 'mutineers' of a less dangerous kind could be transported to provide labour for the desperate West Indian planters who were convinced that a plentiful supply of cheap labour was the one thing needful to transform their enterprise. Eyre was in favour of this, provided a small garrison of white troops was available. Furthermore, he wanted wives and children to come too, in order to establish a proper family life –

> always supposing that they are of a class from which a reasonable amount of labour may be obtained: for I am not sufficiently acquainted with the character of the high caste Mutineers of India to be able to judge how far it would be practicable to get them to apply themselves cheerfully to manual labour in the fields.[118]

India was a far cry from the Caribbean in the imperial imagination. It was a place with an ancient civilisation and its own established hierarchies, a very different world from that of the uneducated, 'excitable' negroes.

At Christmas and New Year there were riots in the capital of St Vincent again. With the experience of the 'Indian Mutiny' behind him, and an increasing sense of the island as a 'small and isolated colony', Eyre did not hesitate to interpret the dangers in racial terms. The riots had begun with drunken British sailors rampaging in the town, offending local inhabitants. An angry crowd collected, 'nearly the whole population of Kingstown'. Eyre's only available peace-keeping force consisted of volunteers drawn from this very same crowd and 'just as much excited as the rest of the people'. He envisaged an ugly confrontation between 'resolute English sailors' and the 'excited crowd'. 'It was evident', he reported to his superior, 'that in the event of any collision taking place it would become one of race – the coloured against the white man.' He concluded that without white troops there could be no security.[119]

It was in the midst of all this that Eyre was writing his autobiography, sending bundles of it back to his wife, who was in Plymouth with the children. Alone in the heat of the tropics, cut off from ordinary social intercourse by his position as lieutenant-governor, and from England by the absence of white settlers and the irregularity of the post, surrounded by – as he increasingly interpreted them – hostile 'coloureds' and 'blacks', it is hardly surprising that memories of his young manhood seemed deeply enticing. At the same time, he was penning regular letters to the Secretary of State for the Colonies, asserting his qualifications for any posts which he heard about, in the hope of escaping his predicament. These letters focused on his long-term experience with the different native peoples of the empire, and also served, alongside his autobiographical writing, to heighten his sense of his own identity as 'a white Englishman'. His persistence demonstrated that he was, as Taylor noted, 'certainly a very urgent and indefatigable suitor'. The Colonial Office, however, was not entirely convinced by his credentials, but in April 1859 a reasonably satisfactory solution was found when he was offered a slightly better temporary post in Antigua.[120]

This promotion, together with his pleasure at leaving St Vincent in a more orderly state than he had found it, may account for a more optimistic note in his first comments on Antigua, first colonised by the British in 1632. A tiny island, it was nevertheless sugar producing and the site of one of Britain's most important military bases in the Caribbean. His first task was to attempt to form a local militia. He discovered that Europeans were afraid to arm black people even against a common enemy, but reported that, 'I do not in the least share this feeling; for however excitable or disposed to occasional excesses whilst under excitement . . . the labouring classes of the West Indies are, I believe, as a Body both truly loyal and fully alive to the advantages of living under British rule'.[121] Such a positive note was soon dissipated, however, in more gloomy comments on the fall in population which was occurring on the island. Eyre explained this odd phenomenon in 'a people naturally so prolific as the Negro race' in terms of their lack of proper family life, their neglect of their children, and their desperate need for 'respectable and influential residents in their neighbourhood', who could improve by their moral example. While 'excitable' almost always signified black, 'respectable' meant white, civilised and European.[122]

In 1860 Eyre returned once more to England, where he had to wait eighteen months before being appointed deputy governor of Jamaica. The New Zealand wars were replacing the 'Indian Mutiny' as the new source of colonial disillusionment. Eyre's old superior, Grey, sent back

to New Zealand from South Africa in 1861, in order to regain ground
lost in the first months of the war, was increasingly determined to make
British sovereignty real and more sympathetic to Pakeha aspirations.[123]
The Pakeha bemoaned the fact that

> We have dealt with the natives of this country upon a principle radically
> wrong. We have conceded them rights and privileges which nature has
> refused to ratify . . . [In reality the Maori is] a man ignorant and savage,
> loving darkness and anarchy, hating light and order; a man of fierce,
> ungoverned passions, bloodthirsty, cruel, ungrateful, treacherous.[124]

Such voices were not the only ones heard in Britain. John Eldon Gorst's
passionate plea in his widely read *The Maori King*, that 'the Maori view
of this colonial question is worthy of attention', reworked humanitarian
discourse for the 1860s, providing a critique of British colonisation and
attitudes and settler greed.[125]

As discourses of racial difference multiplied, the conflation of 'native'
with 'irredeemable savage' became more common. In New Zealand,
Grey's erstwhile assimilationist policy toward the Maoris was abandoned
in favour of military conquest. In Jamaica, where a similar dynamic was
being played out, the common sense of the planter class – that negroes
no longer held in check by violence would revert to savagery – began to
touch more closely the 'official mind' of the empire.[126] In the parliamentary debates on emancipation and apprenticeship, those who were
fearful of sudden freedom had argued that it might result in the adop-
tion of 'primitive habits of savage life', habits which had been contained
only by the regime of the whip.[127] The language of brotherhood was
increasingly under threat. The fear now articulated was that black people
would sink back into the barbarism from which they had been briefly
lifted, by their enforced enslavement and encounter with Europe. The
confidence and enthusiasm which had permeated Eyre's account of his
young manhood and his successful engagement with Aboriginal improvement was gone. Public and private disappointments, the responsibility
of supporting a growing family of five, his wife's ill health, and his separation from her and his children all combined with the new racial
discourses of the 1850s and 1860s to construct a more threatened,
defensive, disturbed identity, one which depended on an assertion of
established white authority and power.

Mill, reflecting on debates in England about the American Civil War,
and observing the absence of a strong tide of anti-slavery feeling, pointed
to the generational change which had taken place: those who fought for
abolition and believed slavery to be an issue which went right to the
heart were no longer active in public debate.[128] Eyre was only too

ready to ponder a different generational change which had occurred in Jamaica. Europeans on the island widely agreed that the most respectful black men and women were those who had been born into slavery; it was their children who had become idle and profligate. And it was they who had not felt the whip who were the future.[129]

Furthermore, whereas Eyre's early ideas about Aboriginal peoples had been formed through daily contact and dependence, as sheep farmer, overlander and explorer, his life as a colonial dignatory was very different. His personal intimates were white: his household included a white manservant, two women servants and a tutor for his children, though of course his food was prepared, the establishment maintained and the horses stabled by brown and black men and women. On his tour of the island in 1864, Eyre did come face to face with black people: he could still recognise warmth and hospitality before recodifying those encounters through a language of fear and of racial difference. Jamaican 'blacks', as he constructed them in his imagination, through the troubles in St Vincent and Antigua, Maori wars, 'Indian Mutinies' and the newly popular discourses of racial difference, were much more fearful and dangerous than those Aborigines whose help he had once relied upon for his survival.

Jamaica

Eyre was sent to Jamaica as deputy governor in 1862, after an anxious year and a half without employment. His first months there convinced him of the centrality of race to an understanding of the society; it was a place where every opportunity was taken 'to make the question one of colour'. With a population of thirty-two blacks and coloureds to every one European, this could appear very threatening, especially when the vast majority were, in Eyre's terms, 'always liable to be easily imposed upon by designing persons'. The declining white population was a source of serious concern to him, as it had been in St Vincent, for colonists with 'ability and intelligence' were leaving or dying off, with the consequence that the executive had to rely on a 'very different class of persons'.[130]

That 'very different class of persons' was predominantly coloured and was fairly well represented in the House of Assembly. When coloureds united with Jews (there was a significant Jewish mercantile presence in Kingston) in the House, they could form a majority. Eyre found many of the middle-class coloured men exceedingly difficult to deal with, especially George William Gordon, the son of a planter and an enslaved woman who had become a planter himself and was a prominent member of the House of Assembly and a severe critic of the governor on many counts.[131] But nor could he count on the support of the Europeans, whom he would have expected to be his natural allies. He was convinced that 1863, for example, was a good year economically for the colony, since – though planters had not done well – the small settlers, the black independent peasantry, had, and in 1863 he was still willing to celebrate their success. The planters, however, 'will not recognize and do not like to be told of a prosperity in which they are not sharing'. The *Jamaica Guardian* admiringly quoted Eyre as providing evidence which would tell against the prejudices of Carlyle:

> Mr Eyre is the first Governor we have had who has recognised the small settler of the country, as forming an important element in the industrial activity and enterprise of Jamaica . . . We rejoice to have such convincing evidence afforded us, and to be able to put forth such proof to the world, that they are making creditable progress in those pursuits which become a people worthy of freedom. Carlyle and his disciples will see that the pumpkin-eaters of this island – the men 'up to the eyes in pumpkin' as he has described them – are not such lazy and worthless fellows after all.[132]

Eyre's clashes with the House led him speedily to the same conclusion he had reached in the other Caribbean islands: that representative institutions could not work in the sugar colonies. In a recent election forty-seven members had been returned by 1,457 voters, out of a population of 441,264, so that the vast majority of the population 'had no voice in returning their so called Representatives'. He was not in favour of increasing the franchise, however, since he regarded the 'general population' as 'quite unfitted for the exercise of political privileges'. Representative institutions were the 'great bulwark of British liberty and British greatness' – but Jamaica was not Britain, and the Jamaican population were not black Anglo-Saxons.[133]

In May 1864 Eyre was finally made governor, against the wishes of many prominent white Jamaicans, after a long period of uncertainty which he felt deeply undermined his authority in 'this most troubled colony'. Under attack from many sides, with his own position 'anomalous and doubtful', suffering again from the absence of his wife and children, who could not stand the climate and had returned to England, with no proper 'establishment' or 'Lady' to dispense the hospitality which might have eased his isolation, he claimed that only his sense of duty sustained him.[134] In his new, more prestigious capacity, however, he decided on a tour of the island. His response to the addresses of the peasantry detailing their distress, reported to the Colonial Secretary, was, as Thomas Holt puts it, 'laced with classic mid-Victorian platitudes and irrelevancies'.[135] He instructed the small settlers that the Queen was 'most anxious you should progress in civilisation, in education, in morality and in material prosperity', and that such improvements depended on their own efforts, particularly in relation to their children. It was their lack of proper family life, as he defined it, which ensured that there was no base from which 'civilisation' – meaning English society with its particular economic and gender order – could develop. 'All Ages and all Sexes promiscuously occupy the same apartment,' he noted disapprovingly. 'The natural and necessary result is that all sense of propriety or decency, all morality and all cleanliness are utterly wanting.' While he was impressed by the relative prosperity of the small settlers with their lands, carts, horses and Sunday clothes, his final judgement of them as 'a people' was that in 'their own homes, and in their social habits and relations', they were 'little better than absolute savages'.[136]

Having in his own mind constructed the population of the island as 'absolute savages', the shift to a highly coercive regime appeared quite logical. Theft, for example, had become a serious problem. The culprits, it appeared, were not the old and the needy, but the young and able-bodied of both sexes, 'those who are well able to work'. 'I fear', argued Eyre, moving towards the logic of Carlyle and the planters, 'it is rather an indisposition to labour than an inability to procure work' which led them to steal. Far from feeling shamed by imprisonment, Eyre believed, such offenders returned home to 'their people' with no stigma attached. From June 1864 Eyre began to inquire of the Colonial Office whether the treadmill had ever been officially banned; and after his tour of the country he pressed for the reintroduction of the whip, together with a system of enforced apprenticeship. The proposed number of stripes was well in excess of what was allowed in the British army or under the old apprenticeship system. Given 'the peculiar state of things' in the West Indies, Eyre maintained, flogging had become a necessary remedy, though not one that he had expected to have to resort to in his younger days. He insisted that propertied black people – indeed, all classes of the community – were in favour of such action, a view from which Gordon, for one, dissented.[137]

In March 1865 Eyre received a letter forwarded to him by Cardwell, Secretary of State at the Colonial Office, from the secretary of the Baptist Missionary Society, Edward Bean Underhill. The Baptists had long been active in Jamaica, and had been powerfully identified as 'the friend of the negro'.[138] Underhill's letter expressed great concern at the level of want and starvation on the island, and asked for action. Eyre, a committed Anglican, had previously maintained reasonable, if not warm, relations with the Baptists on the island; but the letter outraged him. Allying himself with the white establishment, he collected reports on the state of the population, emphatically denied Underhill's claims, and placed responsibility for all ills squarely on the shoulders of 'excitable blacks' and dangerous agitators. At the heart of the problem, he was now convinced, was race – the character of the creole labourer, born in Jamaica, and the 'difficulty of elevating him'. 'It must . . . be borne in mind', he argued, reproducing the rhetoric of the slave-owners of the 1830s and Carlyle in the 1840s,

> that even when he does work, the Creole labourer requires an amount of direction, supervision and watching unknown in other Countries, and detracting greatly from the value of his services; and this remark is equally applicable to the best and most intelligent tradesman and mechanic as to the mere field labourer . . . If he can obtain a bare subsistence by little effort or exertion, he will not extend his labours to secure comfort and independence.

'The people' suffered from 'an utter want of principle or moral sense', a 'total absence of parental control or proper training of children', 'incorrigible indolence, apathy and improvidence', and a 'degraded and immoral existence'. They were 'easily misled' by 'political agitators or designing Men'. At the core of their degradation lay immorality, most sharply signified by promiscuity, parental irresponsibility, and the neglect of the old and the sick by familial networks. These were all indices of sin; only the Christian household with its proper division of labour between the sexes and a proper sense of responsibility for the awesome duties entailed by parenthood could provide the fundamentals for a good society. 'Deterioration, Decadence and Decay' were everywhere apparent, with white people leaving and no 'fresh influx of European energy, intelligence, enlightened views and moral principles' replacing them, 'qualities which are so essential as examples to stimulate and influence races, only just emerging from, and without such influences likely to fall back rapidly into a state of barbarism'.[139]

For Eyre, convinced as he was and always had been of the superiority of European civilisation, the recognition of Aboriginal culture, albeit as a dying culture, which had been possible in the early 1840s, was no longer possible. West Indian negroes were 'savages' and 'barbarians', without culture, unable to adapt to the requirements of civilisation. Mastery and control were the only remedies. Given this construction of 'them' as essentially, utterly different from 'us', of the Caribbean islands as minefields, and Europeans as beleaguered and in great jeopardy, it became inevitable that Eyre would see the rising at Morant Bay only as the preordained fulfilment of his worst fantasies, in which the white people of Jamaica faced extinction and all manner of torment. His first despatch recounted horrific brutalities committed by black rioters – later proved by the Royal Commission never to have occurred – which 'could only be paralleled by the atrocities of the Indian mutiny'. The women, he asserted, 'as usual on such occasions, were even more brutal and barbarous than the men', a sign for the English that the veil of illusion had been torn away. Only white troops (with the help of loyal black Maroons who had co-operated with the colonisers for many years in return for relative freedoms) could save the white population from the 'evil passions' of black savagery, wickedly stirred up by 'wolves in sheep's clothing' (as Eyre perceived the Baptist missionaries), who found it easy to sway the rioters, but 'impossible to guide, direct or control them when once excited'. 'It is scarcely necessary to point out', Eyre insisted to the Colonial Office when he heard intimations of criticism from England, 'that the negro is a creature of impulse and imitation, easily misled, very excitable, and a perfect fiend when under the influence of an excitement which stirs up all the evil passions of a race little removed in many respects from absolute savagery'. By such logic, justice could be meted out only by the imposition of the most severe retribution.[140]

Eyre's wife Ada, known in the family as Fanny, was in Jamaica at the time of the rebellion. Her letter to her mother describing the 'very terrible' events she had experienced exudes an upper middle-class English femininity. She was a weak, dependent woman who assumed both the loyalty of her white servants, who 'would have fought to the death for me and the children', and the barbarism of unknown black people. 'No one can tell what I have endured for my precious husband,' she wrote; he had been 'an entire slave to duty', had worked ceaselessly 'to uproot and utterly destroy this fearful rising amongst the Blacks'. They had been in their house in the mountains when the uprising had begun. Her husband had had to leave, though very worried for 'his delicate little wife and children'. Fortunately there were officers in the house, so, despite the 'shouts and yells' which she heard all night and the fact that she could not sleep a wink for days, she was safe. 'Proof is hourly being evinced', she told her mother, 'that this was a widely planned insurrection and that the massacre of the white and coloured races was determined.' This was the fate from which her 'brave and noble' husband had saved the island.[141]

Morant Bay finally convinced Eyre that he had been right in his political assessment: Jamaica was not capable of self-government, the people were 'incompetent to judge for themselves'. Direct rule from Britain was the only solution. The terrified white population concurred. Despite the objections of some of the 'coloured' members, the House of Assembly

and the Legislative Council abolished themselves.[142] Jamaica became a
crown colony in 1866. By the time Eyre left Jamaica earlier that year,
having been suspended from duty, he was immensely popular with the
white inhabitants of the island. His departure provided an opportunity
for grateful addresses, thanking him for saving the colony from anarchy.
The shared common sense of the white population was articulated by
Eyre in his despatches to the Colonial Office and in his subsequent evidence to the Royal Commission. Negroes, in his view, were not black
Anglo-Saxons; indeed, 'there are feelings of race within the black man's
breast impenetrable to those without', preventing many in England from
understanding the true 'character and tone of thinking of the negro population'.[143] There were powerful echoes here of the arguments of the
planters in the 1830s, the insistence that only people who knew 'blacks'
could 'know', and that 'Nigger-Philanthropists', to use Carlyle's term (a
term which placed the enemy firmly within), were deluded in their fantasies of black equality.[144] 'I know of no general grievance under which
the negroes of the colony labour,' insisted Eyre.[145] Their pursuit of a
rebellious plot against 'buckra', as black people named the colonisers,
could, therefore, be blamed on designing others. The enemy, it turned
out, was within as well as without. Uncivilised, ignorant black people
had been misled and encouraged by 'pseudo-philanthropists' from
England, who could not be aware of what terrible harm they were
causing, by 'political demagogues' and 'evil minded men' who excited
them to 'rebellion, arson, murder'. There was an unresolved tension in
the thinking here, as there had been in the 'Indian Mutiny': black people
were both incapable of acting for themselves, puppets on strings, and a
source of conspiracy and evil, awaiting only the lifting of white surveil-
lance to explode. They were at one and the same time objects of contempt – effeminate and dependent – and objects of terror and fear,
rapists, torturers and murderers.

For Eyre's supporters in England, shocked at the unrelenting persecution of him, as they saw it, by the Jamaica Committee, it was vital to
make the British public understand the true character of their hero.
Henry Kingsley's celebration of Eyre the adventurous explorer and friend
of the Aborigine in *Macmillan's Magazine*, published right at the time of
Morant Bay, was a godsend, for Kingsley constructed Eyre as a man
whose 'life work had been, and was to be, the protection of these savages
against the whites'.

> He knew more about the aboriginal tribes, their habits, language and so
> on, than any man before or since. He was appointed Black Protector for
> the Lower Murray and did his work well. He seems to have been . . . a
> man eminently kind, generous, and just . . . he pleaded for the black and

tried to stop the war of extermination which was, is, and I suppose will be, carried on by the colonists against the natives in the unsettled districts beyond reach of the public eye. His task was hopeless. It was easier for him to find water in the desert than to find mercy for the savages.[146]

It was essential to the Eyre Defence Committee, set up in 1866, that the true character of the negro as it had been revealed all too clearly by the events at Morant Bay, in their view, should be exposed. Thus a key protagonist of Eyre's, Commander Bedford Pim, presented a paper to the Anthropological Society of London (a new society of which Eyre was a founder member, that combined 'science' with politics) in February 1866, in which he stated that the rebellion meant that 'my country-men, whether they like it or not, were brought face to face with the negro'. Pim gave himself the task of laying out the 'negro's peculiarities' to his respectable, enthusiastic audience. Reminding the crowded room that 'We do not admit equality even amongst our own race, as is provided by the state of the franchise at this hour in England', Pim asserted that 'to suppose two alien races can compose a political unity is simply ridiculous. One section must govern the other.' 'The principles', he continued,

> on which alien and dissimilar races ought to be governed, is not yet under-stood by our rulers. Jamaica is not the only proof of this: the state of St Vincent, Antigua, New Zealand, the Cape of Good Hope, to say nothing of India, attests that 'how to govern alien races' has yet to be learnt. Let us take the negro as we find him, as God designed him, not a white man, nor the equal of a white man.[147]

Similarly, Hamilton Hume, Australian explorer and contemporary biographer of Eyre, who was closely involved in establishing the Eyre Defence Fund, sought to vindicate his hero and show the nature of the dangers he had faced. His descriptions of the events at Morant Bay, heavily laced with fantasy, dwelt on 'those fearful and bloody acts', 'the cries for mercy, the savage yells of the women hounding on the men as each new victim was discovered', and 'the bodies of the butchered', dia-bolically hacked to death. The negroes were 'drunk with blood' and 'mad with excitement', all of which justified the view that 'Nothing can be more absurd than to compare a negro insurrection with a rebel-lion in England'.[148] The supporters of Eyre felt compelled to defend their own race, to counter the tendency of those who 'in their desire to white-wash the black man, too often blacken the white man'.[149] William Finlason, in his concern to provide an accessible, edited version of the hundreds of official papers dealing with events, published several books, all attempting to exonerate Eyre. He was narrated as a hero: 'one of the very finest types of English manhood', who had 'preserved the lives of 7,000 British men, and the honour of 7,000 British women, from the murder and the lust of black savages'. In his defence of Eyre, Carlyle poured scorn on the humanitarians, painting them as effeminate just as he had done in his 'Occasional Discourse'. He celebrated Eyre as the manly hero, the silent doer, who had responded to threat and acted with strength, saving Europeans from 'black unutterabilities'.[150]

Eyre himself must have been profoundly shocked by his recall to England and the discovery of the bitter controversy attached to his name. His only public statements after his return aimed to portray him as a faithful public servant, a man who had done his Christian duty as he had seen fit. Having spent most of his adult life in the colonies, dreaming of an England that was more attractive in memory than in reality, it must have been a bitter experience to return to life in retirement, his pension secured only after long negotiation, his reputation high with many, but his figure burnt in effigy by working-class radicals.[151]

His response to the personal prosecution by the Jamaica Committee, Finlason claims, 'echoed throughout England'.

> I have only this to say, that not upon me, but upon those who brought me here, lies the foul disgrace that a public servant who has faithfully discharged his duty for upwards of twenty years, has been now, after two years and a half of persecution, brought to a criminal court and committed for trial for having performed his duty at a trying moment, and thereby saved, indubitably, a great British colony from destruction, and its well-disposed inhabitants, white and black, from massacre or worse...I am satisfied that the large majority of my fellow-countrymen do not sanction these proceedings against me, and to their sense of justice, and to their common sense, I may say, I confidently entrust my honour as a gentleman and my character as a public officer.[152]

He was correct in his judgement. Successive prosecutions were thrown out by juries of 'twelve good men and true' who determined that an Englishman's rights and liberties were more important than those of black Jamaicans. His own career, however, was at an end. The support for crown colony status for Jamaica and the conviction that black people were not white Anglo-Saxons did not necessarily go hand in hand with respect for Eyre. He was something of an embarrassment, something of a liability, once the heat of the moment had passed. He was himself a bitterly disappointed man. ''Tho I have signally defeated and triumphed over my Persecutors in every instance,' he wrote to one correspondent, 'I am ruined in prospects and in fortune and the result of a lifetime's career in the Public Service is taken from me.'[153] In 1872 his pension was awarded to him, though without enthusiasm. As the *Daily News* commented, no speaker of any influence in the House of Commons spoke on his behalf.[154] Instead of having the pleasure of a little patronage at his disposal, as an ex-governor of a colony might have hoped, he was left anxious about the situation of his dependants after his death and feared that his daughter Mary, who had not married, would have to work for a living.[155] He lived quietly in the country until his death in 1901.

Eyre spent most of his working life as a colonial administrator, ruling 'subject peoples', attempting to manage white settlers, negotiating his relation with metropolitan society through family and friends and the Colonial Office. As farmer and overlander, as explorer, as colonial official, he was always one of the colonisers, albeit in a complex web of relations to other colonisers and to the colonised. England was always 'home', yet he spent most of his time between the ages of seventeen and fifty-nine in Australia, New Zealand and the Caribbean. His identity, his sense of self and his notions about the world were formed as much by his experiences abroad as by his time in England. His 'imperial identity', his individual history, can be mapped across these different sites of empire. The theatres of empire constructed different possibilities. Metropolitan society, white settler societies, sugar colonies, each provided a site for the articulation of different relations of power, different subject positions, different cultural identities. White Englishmen were able to use the power of the colonial stage to disrupt the traditional class relations of their own country and enjoy new forms of direct power over 'subject peoples'. At the same time, as 'imperial men' who moved across those societies, their own identities were ruptured, changed and differently articulated by place. Public metropolitan time was cross-cut with public colonial time; both were cross-cut again by familial time, private time, the time of birth, emigration, marriage, new homes and death. It was these cross-cutting patterns which constituted 'imperial men', and out of which they made, and told, their stories. Eyre's story, set in the time scale of this book, linking metropole and empire, the Antipodes and the Caribbean, through individual voyages and racialised histories, mapping the shift from black peoples as brothers to black peoples as a new kind of 'other', provides a point of departure for a history concerned with connection and complexity.

PART I

COLONY AND METROPOLE

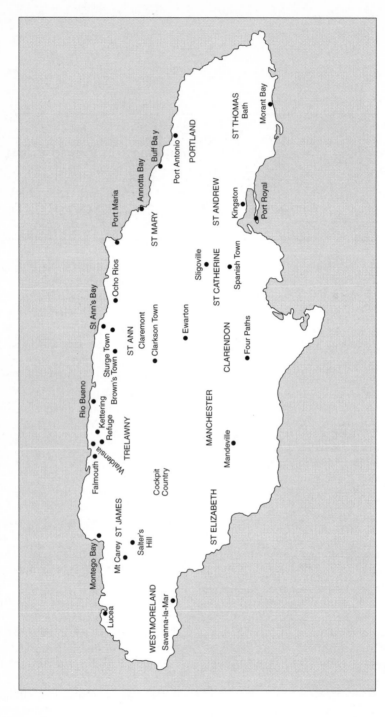

Map of Jamaica showing the main places mentioned in the text.

Mapping Jamaica: The Pre-emancipation World in the Metropolitan Mind

Ada Eyre found Jamaica a very uncongenial place. Knowing her duty as the wife of a colonial official, she accompanied her husband on his tours of duty, spending time in St Vincent, Antigua and Jamaica. But the tropics did not suit her or their children, and for much of the time that Eyre was in the Caribbean he suffered the loneliness of being separated from his family. While it was accepted that imperial men had to travel the empire, there were questions in the metropolitan mind as to which sites of empire were appropriate for white women. The image of Jamaica in the 'metropolitan mind' was not, of course, a fixed phenomenon: rather, it was constantly made and re-made by varying individuals and groups, carrying sediments across generations, but absorbing new possibilities in new conditions of existence. In the nineteenth century the Caribbean was widely seen as peculiarly devoid of the forms of civilisation which would make it appropriate for 'ladies'. But how else was it characterised, and what did the English know of it? What kind of place was it in the early nineteenth century?

Jamaica was situated ninety miles south of Cuba. From its first days as a colonial settlement it had been seen as a place to acquire a fortune which could then be spent at home. And 'home' was England, or Scotland, or possibly Ireland. Jamaica was a place of riches and danger, intimately linked with the metropolis, yet fortunately at a distance. A place of gamblers, Jamaica was Britain's 'Wild West' of the seventeenth century, a frontier society. Outside the limits of European treaties, it was a site of unlimited greed and atrocity.[1] In the early seventeenth century the association with sugar began. Between the 1640s and the 1660s Barbadian planters had started to grow sugar and had hugely increased their riches, supplying the growing demand in Europe for the sweetener which by 1800 had become a necessity, and by 1900 was supplying

nearly one-fifth of the calories in the English diet. After 1655 and
the seizure of Jamaica by Cromwell's troops, 'the sugar supply of the
English people', as Sidney Mintz argues, 'would be provided substantially within the skein of the empire'. Sugar consumption became a
national habit, 'like tea, sugar came to define English "character"'.[2] The
English became famous for puddings, and sugar became a part of the
English self.[3] The first place from which it came on a significant scale,
the British West Indies, was understood as a kind of outpost of the
metropolis, an extension, or perhaps excrescence, of the self, rather than
somewhere entirely separate: inside rather than outside, a place that
could be milked for all its worth with no returns, a breast on which to
feed. John Stuart Mill characterised the trade with the West Indies as not
really an external trade, more like the trade between town and country.
'Our West Indian colonies', he wrote, 'cannot be regarded as countries
with a productive capital of their own ... [but are rather] the place
where England finds it convenient to carry on the production of sugar,
coffee and a few other tropical commodities.'[4] The British West Indies
provided an essential item for the home consumer and a source of wealth
for planters and merchants.

To the early English colonists Jamaica was the most fascinating, but
also the most disturbing, of the Caribbean islands. There was no peace
with the humming and biting of the insects, the heat, the humidity, the
torrential tropical rains, the summer hurricanes, the dramatic earthquakes. In the early seventeenth century it became the chief buccaneer-
ing base for ventures against the Spanish Main. Port Royal, the main
port just outside Kingston, was depicted as a place of drunkenness, prostitution and crime. Its terrible destruction in the earthquake of 1692 was
understood by many as a punishment from God.[5] By the end of the
seventeenth century, the buccaneers had been displaced by planters, and
the land had been consolidated into estates, worked by enslaved men
and women, and often run by managers and attorneys, since their owners
were in Britain. Jamaica became identified as the place of sugar and
slavery, the sugar plantations the distinctive icon of a different and disturbing culture.

Sugar planters generally were different kinds of capitalists from those
at home who were busy enclosing and reorganising the land. They were
manufacturers as well as farmers, merchants as well as landlords. Unless
ripe canes were cut and crushed within forty-eight hours and the cane
juice boiled, the crop was spoilt. Farms had to be factories too. Planters
supervised the growing of canes, the manufacture of sugar, molasses and
rum, and arranged the business side of the plantation.[6] They needed
heavy capital investment to bring their labour force from Africa, to buy
their machinery to extract the sugar from the cane, and to sustain their

ventures in the long period between planting and the sale of the crop. The plantation was the prototype of the modern capitalist venture. Its combination of agriculture and processing, the time/work discipline required by the scale of the work-force on the large estates and the cycle of production, the organisation of a skilled and unskilled enslaved labour force, the coercion required to extract the labour, the separation of production from consumption, the need for careful accounting and the organisation of credit – all this made it a peculiarly modern form.[7] London merchants and finance capitalists were intimately connected with West Indian planters. Immense fortunes could be made, 'created by the labor of millions of slaves stolen from Africa, on millions of acres of the New World stolen from the Indians, wealth in the form of commodities like sugar, molasses and rum to be sold to Africans, Indians, colonials, and the British working class alike'.[8] Plantations could vary hugely in size, from 80 to 2,000 or more acres, the latter requiring the labour of 500 or more slaves. The British Caribbean islands were very different. Jamaica, with a range of high mountains running down the spine, had large areas of land which could not be used for sugar. Barbados, on the other hand, could be cultivated for sugar throughout. These different spatial patterns made for significant variations in the social relations of the two islands: in Jamaica the mountains provided places of refuge, in Barbados the plantocracy ruled throughout.[9]

The mid-eighteenth century saw the high point of this system. The number of plantations, as well as of the enslaved who worked them, more than doubled: this was the golden period of prosperity for the planters, before the American War of Independence disrupted the triangular trades – between Britain, Africa and the New World, and New England, Africa and the West Indies – and initiated the long-term decline of sugar production in the West Indies. The war meant that supplies of food and capital goods needed on the plantations were either not available or more expensive, so the cost of sugar production went up. At the same time increasing competition – from Brazil, Cuba, the French Caribbean islands and the East India Company – confronted the planters with new concerns.

Meanwhile the growth of the anti-slavery movement in the metropolis in the 1770s and 1780s was a seriously destabilising factor, raising questions as to the long-term viability of the system. Nevertheless, the 1790s was a period of expansion in Jamaica, because of the revolution in San-Domingue which disrupted French sugar supplies. But the prosperity was short-lived. There were attempts by the planters to improve productivity, raise efficiency, and 'ameliorate', in response to the anti-slavery critique, but innovation was limited by absenteeism and delegated management.[10] The abolition of the slave trade in 1807 meant that it was necessary to ensure that enslaved people would live longer and reproduce themselves, since constant new supplies of labour could no longer be relied upon. But the enslaved population continued to fail to reproduce itself, a failure associated primarily with the poor health of enslaved mothers. Amelioration – the improvements insisted upon by the imperial government in the 1820s under pressure from the abolitionists – did not deliver what it was meant to deliver.[11] Jamaica's plantation economy was in crisis in the 1820s: sugar exports fell by 40 per cent between 1805 and 1835, the number of the enslaved fell by one-tenth, and a quarter of the estates ceased production.[12] It was this crisis which provided the backdrop to the major rebellion of 1831 and the abolition of British colonial slavery by the imperial parliament in 1833.

Jamaica was organised for sugar production; that was its purpose and place in the British empire. One of fourteen British sugar colonies in tropical America, its trade was protected by the mercantilist system, its ships, its harbours and its wealth being defended by the British army and navy. In return, it sent home substantial rewards in commodities and cash. In the eyes of the British, it was a place in which to make a fortune, not to make a life, and its white population comprised at least two men to every woman.[13]

In this situation, England was for families, Jamaica was for sex. Illicit forms of sexuality which transgressed racial and social lines characterised the gender order which developed as an integral part of the system of slavery. The aim of the planters was to acquire fortunes to enjoy at home. A family was an incumbrance: a mistress more convenient.[14] Many of those planters were absentee, approximately one-sixth in 1774, but that one-sixth owned most of the property and most of those enslaved on the island.[15] They were like Sir Thomas Bertram, the patriarch of *Mansfield Park*, whose troublesome estates in Antigua required a long absence from the family property financed by West Indian spoils, an absence which resulted in near breakdown of the patriarchal order at home.[16] Absenteeism was dangerous both at home and in the colonies. By 1830 it is estimated that probably two-thirds of the planters were absentees.[17] Deficiency laws had been passed in an attempt to fix a ratio of white to black on each estate and to ensure that enough able-bodied white men were available to serve in the militia and discourage insurrection amongst the enslaved. But absenteeism in Jamaica meant that, far from the 'higher orders' providing a model for a proper bourgeois life, they offered instead a model of disorder, licentious sexuality, illegitimacy, irregularity, with coloured mistresses kept openly, and concubinage a completely accepted form. For the anti-slavery movement, formed in the crucible of the evangelical revival, deeply committed to the notion of the ordered

Christian household as prototype of the family in heaven, this was profanity indeed.[18]

Few white women went to Jamaica in the nineteenth century except as companions to men – as wives and daughters of colonial officials, high-ranking army and naval officers, clergymen and missionaries. It was her peculiar, isolated status as a white woman, the wife of the most powerful man on the island, which particularly struck Maria, Lady Nugent, in her five years as the governor's wife between 1801 and 1805. Lady Nugent was born in the USA, of Irish descent. Her husband was the illegitimate son of an Irish peer who became a soldier and an MP before being appointed to the governorship of Jamaica in 1801. Jamaica ranked highly as an appointment, second only to India and Canada, worth something in the region of £10,000 per annum, since it was still a wealthy island, albeit with increasing problems. Nugent's term of office coincided with the Napoleonic wars, dramatic events in Haiti, and the employment of black troops in Jamaica. As commander-in-chief of the armed forces, his time was much occupied with military matters. Questions about slavery continued to reverberate in the metropolis despite the relative quiescence induced by wartime fever, however, and Lady Nugent read Wilberforce and Cowper, one of the poets of anti-slavery, and reflected on what she saw as the relatively good conditions enjoyed by the slaves in comparison with the Irish.[19]

General Nugent had been the commander in Ireland charged with quelling the rebellion there in 1798, and Lady Nugent had been only too pleased to leave 'all the horrors of a civil war'. A short period of recovery in Hampstead was most enjoyable, and she would have preferred to remain there rather than 'playing the Governor's lady to the *blackies*', but 'we are soldiers, and must have no will of our own'. They arrived in Spanish Town, the capital of the island, and were 'much amused' at their first encounter with the black population and 'the odd appearance of everything'.[20] The governor's residence, the King's House, was a superb palace reflecting the wealth of eighteenth-century Jamaica.[21] The square in which it stood, with the House of Assembly, the Court House and the impressive statue of Admiral Rodney, victor over the combined French and Spanish fleets in 1782, who had made the island safe from invasion, was worthy of any colonial capital. Close to the square was the great military barracks, built in 1791 to house both soldiers and officers of the British army. Nearby was the Anglican church of St James, which was to become a cathedral in 1843. This, however, was the extent of Spanish Town's grandeur. Built on the banks of the Rio Cobre, about six miles from the sea, the town was on the southern coastal plain of the island, one of the most fertile areas for sugar. Its population was about

5,000, and in November and December when the House of Assembly was sitting, it became a hive of activity.[22] In February 1816, however, when Monk Lewis visited it, he found it a most melancholy place, with 'no recommendations whatever'. The houses were mostly built of wood, the streets narrow and irregular, many buildings were in a ruinous state, and the whole place deeply gloomy.[23]

Spanish Town was the administrative centre of Jamaica. The governor, the 'king' of Jamaica, had considerable powers, though not as many as that description would imply.[24] He was the military commander-in-chief, could proclaim martial law, summon and dissolve the House of Assembly, and veto its measures. He established courts, appointed justices, pardoned and reprieved. He was the dispenser of offices and privileges, in control of the church and the militia. Together with a council of twelve, nominated by the government at his recommendation, he carried executive authority on the island. But the administration depended on the taxes granted yearly by the assembly, and this provided a rich source of tension. A proclamation of 1661 had granted that all settlers should have 'the same privileges to all intents and purposes as our free-born subjects of England'.[25] The House of Assembly had engaged in a long struggle with the crown, claiming rights equivalent to those of the House of Commons, and had succeeded in 1728 in getting confirmation of all the laws and privileges of the island in exchange for an annual revenue bill. Their claim was that Jamaica was a colony, an offshoot of the mother country, loyal to the crown, with the same laws as those 'at home'.[26] The distance from London, however, meant that, subject to the king's prerogative, they should tax and govern themselves. American independence posed a strong challenge to Jamaica, but there was no equivalent basis for full autonomy, and the island necessarily became more dependent on Britain in the aftermath of the war.[27] Fear of interference from the Imperial Parliament, therefore, was a constant anxiety, given the fragility of any separate identity for Jamaica, that sugar-laden extension of the metropolis. That fear was to come to a head over the abolition of slavery.

Edwards estimated that at the end of the eighteenth century the population of the island comprised about 30,000 white people, 10,000 freed black and coloured people, 1,400 Maroons (freed men and women from the Spanish period of colonisation who had settled in the mountains and fought the British to secure rights for themselves) and 250,000 of the enslaved.[28] The European population fell by half between 1820 and 1834, from 30,000 to 15,000, while the enslaved population rose to 311,000, and the free coloured and black population to 45,000.[29] Resistance to slavery was endemic, with major rebellions in 1760 and 1831. The militia, therefore, which included both free black and white, but in

which all the officers were white, was vital if inefficient, and had military training and plenty of arms.[30] In the Napoleonic wars, the Caribbean
was a key theatre of conflict, as it had been throughout the European
struggles of the eighteenth century, and both army and navy were quar-
tered on the island, accentuating the masculinity of the colonial culture
which Lady Nugent encountered.

The white population was divided between the creoles, those born on
the island, and those English, Scottish and Irish soldiers, sailors, overseers, doctors and attorneys who were there to make money and take it
home. Brathwaite estimates that approximately 6,000 of these men and
women belonged to the upper classes.[31] The great majority of the white
population were dependent on the plantation system, whether owners
themselves, on a greater or lesser scale, or as the managers, attorneys
and doctors who serviced those plantations. In addition, there were the
overseers and craftsmen, the men who ran the cattle pens which supplied
the estates, the coffee and cotton proprietors, and the shopkeepers, merchants and urban craftsmen who lived in Spanish Town, the rapidly
expanding city of Kingston, and the ports and market centres ringing the
island – from Falmouth and Montego Bay on the north coast, to Morant
Bay on the east and Savanna-la-Mar on the west. The majority of that
white population thought of England, or Scotland, as home, but they
were no longer English. The culture to which they belonged was a creole
culture, a colonial culture. 'It would be difficult to find a white man in
the island of Jamaica who does not regard England as his home and the
colony as his place of exile,' wrote James Stephen; but when they went
home, they were labelled West Indian and ridiculed and envied for their
ways.[32] West Indians were not like the English: it was whiteness which
distinguished them from those they held as slaves, and it was slavery
which characterised their society. There was a pervasive assumption of
a hierarchical racial order: three ranks of men, white, brown and black,
each with their proper place. As Edward Long put it in his enormously
influential *History of Jamaica*,

> The general *order*, since the whole began,
> Is kept in *nature*, and is kept in *man*.
> *Order* is heaven's first law; and, this confest,
> *Some are* and *must be*, *greater* than the rest.[33]

White men living in the West Indies, argued Edwards, were characterised
by 'an impatience of subordination ... a consciousness of self-
importance', while creolised whites were too indolent, but full of courage, warmth, imagination and high spirits.[34] James Stewart, who visited
the island in 1823, deplored the 'arbitrary habits', the 'irritation and

violent passions' of the white inhabitants, and the way in which 'feelings are gradually blunted by the constant exercise of a too unrestrained power, and the scenes to which it is continually giving birth'. Girls grew up with harsh ideas about the treatment of the enslaved, and this resulted in a troubling juxtaposition of the cruel mistress with the 'tender mother and agreeable companion'.[35] Civil society in Jamaica might be relatively weak, with little educational or cultural provision: sons, especially, were educated 'at home', and daughters too if it were possible financially. But there were newspapers (about fifteen of them, mostly weeklies, strongly pro the plantocracy, owned by individual entrepreneurs and carrying little local news), periodicals, even agricultural improvement societies. White Jamaicans had their own colonial culture: a culture of exile, but nevertheless one which produced its own architecture, its own cuisine, its own elaborate forms of hospitality.

One white discourse on Jamaica focused on it as a 'horrid country' characterised by cruelty and fear, licentious in its habits, where making money was the chief occupation, and the three main topics of conversation were death, disease and debt.[36] Another discourse focused on the beauty of the island: planters, medical men, travellers, historians, missionaries, all those white men who wrote about Jamaica and represented it to the British waxed lyrical about its natural wonders, though sometimes linking unrestrained nature to an unrestrained society. From Columbus onwards, its majestic scenery, luxurious rivers, waterfalls and streams, wondrous fertility, sublime mountains and forests, its exotic vegetation such that a Scotsman could comment that 'the weeds of your public roads are the ornamental plants of our green-houses and hothouses', its beautiful birds, particularly the humming-birds, 'the brilliance of whose plumage no combination of words, nor tints of the pencil, can convey an adequate idea', all combined to test the poetic powers of writers.[37] The beaches and the sea rated scarcely a mention. There were no poisonous snakes or animals of prey, the mountains were covered with trees worthy of kings, sugar cane flourished along with coffee, cotton, pimento, ginger and dozens of varieties of fruit and vegetable which the palate could savour. The year was divided into two seasons, the wet and the dry, but the plenteous rain kept the land green. The island, 150 miles long and roughly forty miles wide, probably only one-quarter of which was cultivated at the end of the eighteenth century, was divided into three counties, Middlesex, Surrey and Cornwall, each of which was divided into parishes, the basic administrative unit. Each parish had its rector and its custos, or chief magistrate, who was appointed by the governor. Vestries, annually elected by freeholders and dominated by middle-ranking planters, attorneys and traders, ensured that local administration remained in the hands of the white population.

Crucial also to the maintenance of that power were the JPs, whose juris-
diction was extensive.

The Church of England was the established church, but its hold on
hearts and minds was tenuous indeed. It was not a mission church, and
it was unsympathetic to missionaries. An attempt at revitalisation in the
early nineteenth century, inspired by metropolitan evangelicalism,
resulted in an attempt to reduce clerical abuses and provide more spiritual sustenance. The first bishop was appointed in 1825. But the majority of Anglican clergy were involved in slave management until
emancipation, and the planters were their friends and their patrons, part
of the same social world. Few missionaries arrived on the island until
the 1820s. The planters were deeply suspicious of missionary teaching,
despite the missionary societies' insistence that their task was the salvation of souls, a matter which was above and beyond politics. The
planters' need for the support of the imperial government after 1815,
however, given fears of French competition and the anti-slavery movement, meant that they had to acquiesce in the demand for religious toleration and the right of the enslaved to receive religious instruction.[38]

The enslaved men and women addressed by the missionaries constituted the vast majority of Jamaica's population, outnumbering Europeans by ten to one, providing 'the sinews of West Indian property', as
Long put it.[39] Of diverse origins, though the largest number came from
West Africa, they had created a shared language and a culture, a culture
which had emerged out of the encounter between Africa and Europe,
between the enslaved men and women and their owners. Subject to a
slave code, and to a personal regime of coercion, the most powerful
icon of which was the whip, locked with their masters and mistresses in
intimate interdependence, most memorably evoked in Thomas Thistlewood's diary, they were at one and the same time persons and non-
persons in the eyes of their owners.[40] Across the British West Indies in
1815, 60 per cent of the enslaved were attached to sugar plantations, 20
per cent were engaged in the production of coffee, cotton and livestock,
10 per cent were involved in other rural activities, and 10 per cent were
in towns.[41] On the eve of emancipation, almost half of Jamaica's enslaved
were held on estates having more than 150 male and female labourers,
with a quarter of them living on estates with labour forces of over 250.[42]
Their conditions of life and work were likely to be better than those of
their brothers and sisters in small settlements or in urban households.
But the work regime on coffee and cotton plantations, usually relatively
small scale, was less severe than that associated with sugar.

By the early nineteenth century, three-quarters of the men and women
on the plantations were living in family groupings, most often made up
of a single woman with her children. Some 10 per cent of the enslaved

were coloured: the children of white masters and their black mistresses. Some 15 per cent of the adult enslaved were given tasks that involved special skills: men learned the crafts associated with sugar production or stock rearing and maintenance, women were the cooks, nursemaids and domestics.[43] In Jamaica about 37 per cent of enslaved people were 'new blood' from Africa, the rest were creole and, according to Patterson, held the Africans in contempt.[44] Hierarchies existed amongst the enslaved: gang drivers and skilled men often held positions of relative power, and age carried respect. By the mid-eighteenth century, the practice of the enslaved growing food for themselves on provision grounds had resulted in a well-developed marketing system which they dominated, and many owned poultry or pigs, perhaps even a cow. Coming as they did from many different regions and peoples, there was no common religion, but the religious practices which developed on the plantations derived chiefly from elements of cosmologies and spiritual systems common to ethnic groups of West Africa. Obeah was used to make charms, discover secrets, punish crimes, administer revenge and interpret the spirit world. Obeah men were feared and respected in the community, as were the myal men who were seen to be in direct communion with the spirit world. Funeral rites were vitally important in the community, and it was widely believed that death meant a return to Africa. Ancestor worship survived.[45] Three days' holiday was usually granted at Christmas, which gave opportunities for music and dancing linked to religious forms. Resistance to slavery took many forms for both men and women: from the passive refusal to work and the spoiling of crops or food to the violent acts associated with running away or armed resistance.[46]

Between black and white were the free men and women of colour: a growing population, particularly in urban areas. The descendants of white masters and black women, some were freed, and those who stayed enslaved tended to be given higher-status tasks, the men gaining skills, the women working in the household. Free men and women of colour could not vote, could not be jurors or give evidence in criminal cases against white people. Burial laws excluded them from white burial grounds, and seats were reserved for them at the back of Anglican churches. Restrictions on their economic rights meant that they tended to gravitate to the towns, where more job opportunities existed. They were excluded socially from white society, and were widely characterised as despising black people and behaving more tyrannically towards those they held as slaves than did the Europeans. Men of colour were thought of as timid and effeminate, lacking the manly vigour and courage of white men.[47] Amongst white people the ambition of coloured women was seen as to be the mistress of a white man, with no expectation of marriage or acceptance in society, for that was not the 'custom of the country'. James Stewart noted that while an unusual brown man might occasionally be admitted to white society, a woman would never be: 'if she has one drop of African blood in her veins, however remotely derived, it operates as effectually to shut her out from the society of the white ladies, as a moral stain in her character would do in European society'.[48] By the early nineteenth century, some free men of colour were claiming admittance to the 'high privileges of Englishmen'.[49] Between 1813 and 1830 a campaign was waged for full political and civil rights, and British government support was sought in the face of sustained resistance from the plantocracy. It was the crisis over abolition, however, which forced the House of Assembly to grant the same 'rights, privileges, immunities, and advantages' to 'all free blacks and browns' as those enjoyed by white men, in the hope that they would enjoy coloured support against the enslaved, a hope that was disappointed.[50]

In theory, Jamaican society was divided neatly into men and women, white, brown and black. In practice, despite the absence of legal rights for married women, many single women and widows operated on the fringes of the urban economy, as in the mother country. There were poor whites and well-to-do brown merchants, men and women who did not fit into the 'epidermal schema'.[51] This was especially likely to be the case in the towns, where white women owned a significant amount of small property and ran taverns, brothels and lodging houses, rented out their enslaved labour and kept shops.[52] Spanish Town was officially the capital, but it was fast being superseded by Kingston, and it was there that urban life was most developed. Settled by refugees from the earthquake at Port Royal at the end of the seventeenth century, and boasting a superb natural harbour, commerce and trade flourished during the eighteenth century, and it had a population of close to 30,000 by the beginning of the nineteenth century. For some, it was a 'place of great trade and opulence' with fine brick houses. Others were less impressed.[53] It was indeed beautiful from a distance, but in the eyes of some visitors it proved to be terrible close up. Situated as it was with the sea providing the main point of access and the Blue Mountains a spectacular backdrop, it was a trading city, dominated by its port, with the crowded wharves and vessels, the men and women plying their wares, and the sailors and merchants congregating down at the docks. Originally the city had been laid out in a compact square, enclosed by North Street, West Street, East Street and the sea, but it grew rapidly, in higgledy-piggledy fashion, and all too often the main roads were ploughed up, the place looking dirty, desolate and decayed. Still, it was a city. It boasted a mayor and aldermen, a town guard and police force, a public hospital, some schools and charitable institutions, and a number of churches and chapels. Most of the English, Irish and Scots residents lived at

Falmouth taken from the church tower (*c*. 1840).

A daguerotype by Adolphus Duperly, reproduced by permission of the British Library, BL Maps 19b12. This makes clear the scale of building in the town by 1840 and the significance of the harbour.

a distance from the city, in which creoles, French residents, Spanish settlers and a significant number of Jews lived alongside free men and women of colour, sailors, street sellers, prostitutes, apprentices and slaves.

On the other side of the island, on the north coast, was Falmouth, originally planned by Edward Barrett in the 1770s. The first Barrett had come to Jamaica as an officer in the conquering army of Penn and Venables. A Samuel Barrett settled on the north coast in the early eighteenth century, and left a prosperous property on his death in 1760. His son Edward introduced many improvements on the plantation, and built Cinammon Hill, the estate's Great House for generations.[54] He needed wharves to unload the enslaved who worked on his plantations and to load the sugar, rum and molasses which he produced. By the 1790s, Falmouth, a busy slaving port, was laid out on a grid plan, with a church, for which Barrett had given the land, sporting a tall tower and marble monuments to planters and army officers. In 1815 the imposing stone court house was built, overlooking the harbour and the town house of the great planting and mercantile family of Tharpe, whose beautiful Great House was at Good Hope, about five miles from the town. By the late 1820s, Falmouth was a fashionable seaport town with two to three thousand inhabitants, broad streets and brick and timber houses. Now that 'new blood' was no longer arriving from Africa, its wharves were dominated in the early part of the year by imported goods from Britain and North America, on which the colony lived – from pork, butter and salt fish to saucepans and stationery, needles and pins – and then by the sugar and rum, brought from the nexus of plantations which surrounded the town. A busy market, selling the provisions grown by the enslaved as well as other goods, served the area, and the town boasted shop-keepers and professionals as well as its own paper, the *Cornwall Courier*, soon to be rivalled by the *Falmouth Post*.[55]

Those newspapers were often taken up with news from London: news of the debates over slavery which had finally culminated in 1807 in the abolition of the slave trade and which had gathered strength again by the 1820s, as it became clear that slavery as an institution had survived the abolition of the trade. The news from London focused on the activities of the colonial agents, men employed from the islands to represent West Indian interests in the metropole, the questions and debates in the House of Commons and the House of Lords, and the doings of the Colonial Office. From 1794 government business concerning the colonies had been conducted through a new office which dealt with war and colonial affairs. This office gradually moved towards systematising its business: collecting information, building up reports from the colonies, and getting regular returns from them. In 1801 a new position was created of Secretary for War and the Colonies, in 1812 the colonies got their own parliamentary under-secretary, and in 1825 a permanent under-secretary. The work of the Colonial Office was to deal with the government of con-quered colonies, to supervise convict settlements, to regulate emigration, to respond to pressure groups, particularly the anti-slavery movement, to liaise with the agents in London who represented the colonial assem-blies, and to deal with governors' letters and reports. The accession of new Caribbean colonies at the end of the revolutionary and Napoleonic wars meant that West Indian matters occupied a very considerable amount of attention, particularly since the debate over slavery was of such public significance. By 1816 the Office had nine clerks, a librarian, a translator servicing the Secretary of State, his under-secretary and private secretary. In the early 1820s the Office was reorganised, and the empire divided into geographical areas, with one senior clerk responsi-ble for each register of incoming correspondence.[56] Amongst the perma-nent officials were James Stephen and Henry Taylor, both of whom were to play a significant role in formulating policy on the West Indies. James Stephen spent his first five years in the West Indies. His father was a successful lawyer there, but returned to England, where, an ardent activist for evangelical and anti-slavery causes, he became an MP. James Junior entered the Bar after Cambridge, and was appointed as a legal adviser to the Colonial Office in 1813. In 1825 he became a salaried legal counsellor, and stayed at the Colonial Office until 1847, becoming a permanent under-secretary in 1836.[57] Henry Taylor served briefly in Barbados in 1820, and then joined the Colonial Office as a clerk in 1824, staying until his retirement in 1872.[58]

The American Revolution meant that in the late eighteenth century the emphasis was on the rights of colonists as Englishmen, and a premium was placed on non-interference in the internal affairs of those colonists. No repetition of the American débâcle was desired. Parliament played no regular part in colonial affairs, though the king and his ministers were concerned with supervising the activities of the governors, looking at the laws which had been passed and considering petitions which were presented. The anti-slavery movement, however, was increasingly demanding that the British government do more to regulate and control colonial governments. James Stephen and Henry Taylor both assumed that colonial executives should be subject to the direction of the British government. As D. J. Murray argues, their initiatives were important, stemming from administrative imperatives rather than legislative ones. From the mid-1820s they were emphasising the positive policy-making role of the senior permanent staff. Stephen went into the Colonial Office with the abolition of slavery as his priority; he worked initially on the establishment of a Slave Register and issues of amelioration, particularly how these could be enforced. He then turned to the drafting of legislation on emancipation.[59] Since colonial secretaries seldom lasted long, the permanent officials were able to wield considerable influence. As Taylor was to write about Stephen many years later:

> For more than twenty-five years, during short tenures of strong Secretaries of State, and entire tenures, whether short or not, of some who were not strong, he, more than any other man, virtually governed the Colonial Empire. Not that he was otherwise than profoundly subordinate; but he found the way to bring men to his own conclusions.[60]

There may be some delusions of grandeur here. As William Green emphasises, there were great difficulties in exercising colonial government in a systematic way. 'Wary of a capricious Parliament and constrained by the treasury', he argues, 'the Colonial Office was in no position to afford dynamic leadership to the Empire.'[61]

In 1831 the new Whig Under-Secretary for the Colonies was Lord Howick, and he facilitated further change and control from London, leading up to the passing of emancipation by the British Parliament. The Jamaican House of Assembly saw abolition as unwarranted interference with their rights as colonists to manage their own internal affairs, but were compelled to accept it. In the aftermath of emancipation, the assumption at the Colonial Office was that there was no longer any reason to interfere, but a close watch was kept, the appointment of governors was more carefully considered, and their activities vetted. By the late 1830s Henry Taylor had come to the conclusion that the only proper method of government for Jamaica was government from London, crown colony government, a system which had already been established in Trinidad, St Lucia and British Guiana.[62]

In the metropolitan mind, Jamaica was associated with sugar and with slavery. As a colony, it existed because of sugar, which it produced for the mother country. Its population, black, white and brown, was there because of sugar, its economy was centred on sugar, its social relations were defined by the sugar plantation, its politics structured through the tensions and antagonisms between the plantocracy and the enslaved. Successive imperial governments and their colonial officials saw the island through a sugared lens, reflecting on forms of government in terms of their commitment to maintaining a sugar monoculture. What part were the Baptist missionaries to play in this society? What kind of colonisers were they? And how did they imagine their imperial project and their African flock?

1
The Missionary Dream 1820–1842

In the Knibb Baptist Chapel in Falmouth, Jamaica, an impressive marble monument hangs on the wall behind the communion table. As the *Baptist Herald* reported in February 1841:

> The emancipated Sons of Africa, in connexion with the church under the pastoral care of the Rev. W. Knibb, have recently erected in this place of worship a splendid marble monument, designed to perpetuate the remembrance of the glorious period when they came into the possession of that liberty which was their right, and of which they have proved themselves to be so pre-eminently worthy. It is surmounted with the figure of Justice, holding in her left hand the balances of equity, whilst her right hand rests upon the sword which is placed at her side. Beneath this figure the likenesses of Granville Sharp, Sturge, and Wilberforce are arrayed in bas-relief, and that of the Rev. W. Knibb appears at the base. The inscription reads:

DEO GLORIA

ERECTED

BY EMANCIPATED SONS OF AFRICA

TO COMMEMORATE

THE BIRTH-DAY OF THEIR FREEDOM

AUGUST THE FIRST 1838

HOPE

HAILS THE ABOLITION OF SLAVERY

THROUGHOUT THE BRITISH COLONIES

AS THE DAY-SPRING OF

UNIVERSAL LIBERTY

TO ALL NATIONS OF MEN, WHOM

GOD "HATH MADE OF ONE BLOOD"

"ETHIOPIA SHALL SOON STRETCH OUT HER
HANDS UNTO GOD" LXVIII PSALM 31 VERSE

Immediately under this inscription two Africans are represented in the act
of burying the broken chain, and useless whip – another is rejoicing in the
undisturbed possession of the book of God, whilst associated with these,
a fond mother is joyously caressing the infant which for the first time she
can dare to regard as *her own*. The monument, as a whole, is one of the
best executed pieces of workmanship, and is certainly well worthy of the
people by whom it has been created.[1]

What can this monument, made in Birmingham, tell us of the meanings
of emancipation and of the complex relation between Jamaica and
Britain? What entwined histories are revealed in this celebration of
Granville Sharp, Joseph Sturge and William Wilberforce in a large Baptist
chapel in a small Jamaican town? Who was William Knibb, and why
was this chapel named after him?

The first day of August 1838 marked the moment of full emancipation when 'apprenticeship' was abolished. (Apprenticeship was the
system introduced alongside compensation for the planters by the Imperial Government, to soften the blow of emancipation for those who had
lost their 'property'.) Those once enslaved were now fully free. That
moment marked the end of a prolonged struggle in both Britain and the
Caribbean to secure the abolition of slavery, a struggle which always had
both its British and its Caribbean forms. In Britain efforts to abolish the
slave trade and question the whole system of slavery were launched by
Granville Sharp amongst others in the 1770s, sustained under the leadership of William Wilberforce in the late eighteenth century and early
nineteenth century, and culminated in the abolition of the slave trade by
the Imperial Parliament in 1807. Popular pressure was central to the
passing of that legislation. In the 1820s the recognition that the demise
of the British slave trade had not been effective in transforming the
system of slavery resulted in a revival of anti-slavery activity in the
country.

In the Caribbean the resistance of those enslaved peaked in Demerara (British Guiana) in 1823 and in Jamaica in 1831. Both rebellions
were widely reported in Britain, partly because of the central involvement of missionaries in the events and the way in which they were held
responsible by planters and colonists for the eruptions which took place.
In 1832 the Baptist missionaries in Jamaica decided to send one of their
brethren, William Knibb, pastor of the mission in Falmouth, to Britain.
He was to answer the charges which had been made against them and
raise funds for the rebuilding of the churches which had been destroyed
as part of the backlash. Once in Britain, Knibb defied the authority of
the Baptist Missionary Society, which, like all missionary societies, cau-
tioned its agents against any form of political involvement, and came out
publicly against slavery. His subsequent public speaking tour mobilised

large numbers for the campaign against slavery, a campaign which was finally successful in 1833, when slavery was abolished from 1 August 1834. A subsequent campaign against apprenticeship, in which Joseph Sturge, the Birmingham Quaker and corn merchant, played a vital part, resulted in the abolition of that system from 1 August 1838, as the monument records.[2] Sharp, Wilberforce, Sturge and Knibb were key figures in the anti-slavery movement. Neither Sharp nor Wilberforce ever went to Jamaica, but Sturge visited the West Indies in 1837, and William Knibb lived there from 1825 to his death in 1845.

The Baptist Missionary Society and the missionary project

The name Knibb is still well known in Jamaica. But why did missionaries become so crucial to the anti-slavery struggle? Jamaica had been nominally a Christian country from the time of its British settlement, but it was only with the arrival of missionaries that substantial efforts were made to Christianise the enslaved people. The Baptist Missionary Society (BMS) had been sending missionaries to Jamaica from 1814. Initially they had been invited by the black Baptists who had arrived on the island in the wake of American Independence, having supported the British, and had established a network of chapels and congregations amongst both the enslaved and free black men and women. Both enslaved men and women and free black people had flocked to the British army during the American Revolution, and 'were then dispersed around the Atlantic after 1783'. Some of them went to Jamaica, and Lord Balcarres, governor of the island, deeply regretted the 'Pandora's Box' that had been opened up in the West Indies. George Liele, for example, enslaved in Virginia, had founded the first Baptist church in Georgia. He was evacuated by the British, and established a following in Jamaica.[3]

The BMS had its roots in the evangelical revival of the late eighteenth century, that re-emergence of vital, serious or real Christianity, as compared with the nominal forms which had come to dominate Christian worship. Both nonconformists and Anglicans were inspired by the revival, and shared a common insistence on the centrality of individual sin and the conversion experience; on the individual's capacity to be born anew and to construct a new Christian identity, whether as man or as woman, built around their particular relation to the Christian household; and on a close monitoring both by the individual and by his or her pastor and his or her congregation of each soul and its progress towards salvation.[4]

Formed in the crucible of radical Protestantism in the seventeenth century, and surviving as a small dissenting sect in the eighteenth century, the Baptists enjoyed a great revival from the 1780s, associated with evangelicalism and bringing in significant numbers of new recruits to the faith.[5] In 1838 Gilbert estimates that there were about 100,000 members of Baptist churches, and by 1851 this had grown to 140,000 in a population of 20 million in England and Wales.[6] Women dominated that world in numbers, but not in status: as with all denominations, women constituted the majority of the congregation, but men occupied the positions of power.[7] The social base of New Dissent was predominantly artisanal, as Gilbert has shown, but with a small yet significant number of merchants, manufacturers, professional men, shopkeepers and farmers. As Clyde Binfield argues, 'the undenominational religious outpourings of the later eighteenth century caught the aspirations of the mobile classes of a new society. Its natural tendency was towards Dissent, since its values could not be established values as traditionally interpreted.' But renewed denominationalism, he suggests, was an inevitable outcome of this growth, as 'Dissent turned into Nonconformity and *movements* became *Churches*'.[8] The formation of the BMS in 1792, and of the General Union of Particular Baptists in 1812, was part of this process of definition.

For evangelicals, the key struggle of the late eighteenth century, in the wake of the French Revolution and English radicalism, was for hearts and minds. The nation had become warm in politics, but 'cold in religion'.[9] Heathens at home and abroad must be won for Christ, and an army of God must be mobilised for this work. William Carey, a Baptist minister in Northamptonshire, inspired others with his belief that Christians must not confine their mission to home but should take it to other parts of the world. 'Our own countrymen have the means of grace, and may attend on the word preached if they chuse it,' he wrote, but those 'who have no Bible, no written language . . . no ministers, no good civil government, nor any of those advantages which we have', call out for sustenance.[10] Inspired by this appeal, a small group of Baptist ministers met in Kettering, and decided to 'act together in society for the purpose of propagating the gospel among the heathen'.[11] The Baptists were the first to organise a society, but were soon followed by the London Missionary Society, initially interdenominational but soon to become Congregationalist, and the Church Missionary Society, an Anglican venture.[12]

The first field of activity for the BMS was in India, and Carey, together with William Ward and Joshua Marshman, established the station at Serampore which was to dominate the early years of the Baptist missionary endeavour.[13] In 1814, after pleas for support from the black Baptists who had well-established networks in Jamaica, and correspondence between Dr Ryland, the Baptist divine, and William Wilberforce, the BMS sent John Rowe as their first emissary to the West Indies. His instructions from the committee impressed on him that he must not despise the enslaved on account of 'their ignorance, their colour, their country or their enslaved condition'.[14] The first years in Jamaica were dogged by ill health, death and political problems, for the planters were for the most part extremely hostile to missionary activities; but in the early 1820s the general revival of British interest in anti-slavery affected the Baptists too, and they committed more resources to Jamaica. Three of the men who were to be most influential both in Jamaica, where each of them has a chapel named after him, and in Britain, went to the island at this time – William Knibb, Thomas Burchell and James Mursell Phillippo. Missionaries had the distinction of being the first white men on the island not primarily interested in making a fortune.

The BMS venture in Jamaica grew steadily. By 1827 there were eight Baptist chapels with approximately 5,000 members; by 1831 there were twenty-four chapels with 10,000 members and 24,000 inquirers (that is, people seeking membership and being observed by the missionary and his auxiliaries); by 1835 this had increased to fifty-two stations with 13,795 members; and for some years these figures went up as the missionaries benefitted from the conviction amongst the freed black peoples that the missionaries had been crucial to the ending of slavery and apprenticeship.[15]

Most Baptist missionaries came from artisan families, some from the borders of the middle classes. From the beginning, missionaries had to deal with planter contempt, derision and harassment, but they were used to being laughed at for their faith, used to a society in which they were discriminated against and in which they had to fight to make their voices heard, used to being part of the army of God, outfacing sin, in whatever manifestations it appeared. Their struggle both at home and abroad, as they conceptualised it, was with the forces of evil, reaction, 'dark savagery', heathenism and superstition, all of which could as easily be met in the back streets of Birmingham as in the markets of Calcutta or the plantations of Jamaica. Slavery, however, offered a particular challenge, for in the anti-slavery imagination the 'poor negro' was scorned by all. As the most favoured of the abolitionist poets, Montgomery, wrote:

> And thou, poor Negro! scorned of all mankind;
> Thou dumb and impotent, and deaf and blind;
> Thou dead in spirit! toil degraded slave,
> Crush'd by the curse on Adam to the grave;
> The messengers of peace, o'er land and sea,
> That sought the sons of sorrow, stoop'd to thee.[16]

Thomas Burchell, who came from a solidly middle-class mercantile background and was used to being treated with respect, was shocked, despite
all preparation, at the way in which he was treated by planters and officials in Jamaica. 'No Englishman, except a missionary, would be treated
with so much contempt,' he wrote home.[17] Similarly, James Mursell
Phillippo noted that even an invitation from the governor to meet him
did not save him from the disdain of Jamaican whites. 'I was treated with
superciliousness and contempt,' he noted.[18] The Baptist missionaries
occupied a liminal space in Jamaica: white, yet allied with the enslaved
and free black and coloured peoples, coming from a very different class
background to that of the planters and the Anglican clergy.

The contempt they faced, however, could be offset by the influence
which they established with the black population. Missionaries loved to
tell their brethren in England of the 'hunger' for Christianity which they
found amongst the enslaved, a sharp contrast with the situation at home.
Thomas Burchell was moved by the comparison between the 'frozen congregations' which he had known in England and the voracious demand
for missionary preaching in Jamaica, which threatened exhaustion, but
was deeply enlivening.[19] The missionaries delighted in sending home
computations of the numbers they had baptised, of their members and
inquirers, all demonstrations of the power of the Word amongst the
heathen.

The first necessity for a missionary life was the experience of conversion. For Thomas Burchell, son of a wool-stapler, conversion meant
freedom from sin, the only true freedom there was; 'his captivity was
exchanged for freedom, and his mourning turned into joy'.[20] Conversion
brought with it the need for action, for in his mind Christian manliness
was defined through the work he would do in the world. For evangelical Christians the action of combating sin, of enlisting in the army of
God, provided a worthy arena. For aspirant artisans or lower middle-
class men, missionary work abroad offered an exciting opportunity;
indeed, in the early days of the Jamaica mission it proved to be a great
deal more exciting than working as a minister in England, where congregations were often pitifully small. In Jamaica, converts came in their
thousands up to the early 1840s, and the influence of the missionaries
appeared to be profound. Not unusually, Philip Cornford found himself
at age twenty-four the minister of a congregation of 2,800.[21] The
encounter with both planters and the enslaved gave an intensity to the
work which was hard to maintain in the mean streets of Manchester.[22]

Some of the missionaries recorded that they had been preoccupied
since childhood with stories of 'the heathen', witness Thomas Burchell,
who as a young man had loved to read conversion stories in the missionary press. These provided tales of triumph against all odds, promises

of crowns of glory.[23] Boys dreamt of a missionary martyrdom, rather than the adventures of Crusoe; the imperial project and the imaginations it engendered took many forms. Such dreams inspired Bernard Barton, the Quaker evangelical poet, when he was invited to write some introductory verses for the Rev. F. A. Cox's official *History of the Baptist Missionary Society*. Barton celebrated the men who went to the colonies not for the more traditional prizes of wealth or land, not for excitement or to chart the wonders of nature. Rather, their noble task was to save sinners, for they were the tools of the living God:

> For they went forth as followers of the Lamb,
> To spread his gospel-message far and wide,
> In the dread power of Him, the great I AM,
> In the meek spirit of the Crucified, –
> With unction from the Holy Ghost supplied,
> To war with error, ignorance and sin,
> To exalt humility, to humble pride,
> To still the passions' stormy strife within,
> Through wisdom from above immortal souls to win.[24]

Burchell's reading of the missionary press made him long 'to tread their shores, to mingle with their swarthy people, and to unfurl in their midst the banners of salvation'. As he became 'more acquainted with their barbarous atrocities and superstitious rites', he was increasingly convinced that he could find the strength to give up home. As he declared at his ordination, 'All my thoughts were occupied on missionary themes, and my chief happiness was associated with solicitude for the heathen.' His dreams were of India, for this was where Baptist missionaries were then active. 'India,' he wrote in a letter in 1820, 'I long to place my foot on thy polluted shores. I long to enter the field of action as an ensign in the army of the Saviour, bearing the banner of his cross. I long to exert myself in the glorious revolution now taking place.'[25]

Entry into missionary work meant applying to the BMS committee as a suitable candidate. Once accepted, the young men would undergo some training, either at one of the dissenting academies or in the home of a Baptist minister deemed suitable to take in a small group for preparation. Most of the trainees had a very limited educational background, having left school to go into trade at the age of twelve or thirteen. This lack of a 'proper' education was another source of derision from their class superiors both at home and abroad. Ordination followed their training, and the ritual of 'setting apart' the missionaries for their work, usually performed by a group of established ministers, some of whom would have personal connections with the ordinand. The training was designed to foster and entrench the forms of Christian manliness which missionaries were to possess. Many of the Baptist missionaries in Jamaica were trained together and 'set apart' together, often with senior missionaries officiating, thus affirming the existence of a 'mission family', which it was a primary objective to sustain. The BMS committee decided where missionaries were to go, and each missionary was responsible to the committee for his actions. In the hostile situations into which so many missionaries went, support from home was a necessary part of survival, and there was a constant flow of letters between Jamaica and England. Missionaries were always at least partially dependent on money from home to finance their activities, and also needed the committee to intervene with the Colonial Office at times of acute tension.

The final 'necessary preparation' before sailing was marriage, for it was assumed that a married missionary would be of more use than a single one.[26] Not only would his masculinity be tamed by domesticity, and fears as to his going 'astray' much reduced, but missionary wives were a crucial part of a mission partnership. In the 1820s all the missionaries who were sent out by the BMS were married. When unmarried ones did arrive, there was general joy and relief when they made appropriate marriages. 'We were much pleased with Mrs. Taylor', reported a senior missionary to the BMS after he and his wife had visited a newly married missionary in Old Harbour, 'and think she is likely to assist our good brother well in his important work.'[27] The debauchery, as evangelicals saw it, of planter society, with its practice of concubinage, made Jamaica a dangerous place for a man on his own. For Baptist women who were seized with the missionary spirit, this meant a window of opportunity. They could not themselves become missionaries, but were needed to accompany men, it was argued, for it would be impossible to have access to many of 'the heathen' without workers of their own sex. It was widely believed in early nineteenth-century England that Western women owed their superior position to Christianity, for it was Christianity which had raised society from its superstitions and freed women from the degradations associated in the English mind with heathenism – in particular, the practice of 'sati' in India. It was proper, argued the protagonists of a special missionary sphere for women, that the daughters of Eve, first in transgression, be the first in restoration.[28] There was no question, however, of accepting women as trainees or granting them equal access with men. Marriage, therefore, offered the only route into the work for those women who wanted to do it. Mary Ann Chambers was able to take this route to satisfy her missionary ambitions, marrying the Rev. James Coultart and going with him to Jamaica.[29] Similarly, Mary Ann Middleditch, living in Northamptonshire and fired with dreams of assisting in the great anti-slavery struggle in the early 1830s, married a missionary and got to Jamaica.[30] Accompanying an unmarried brother was also sometimes possible, and by the 1830s a small number of unmarried women were going out to the Caribbean as teachers. A Miss J. Clack, for example, went out from England to teach the young, for which she was well qualified on account of her 'affectionate disposition', which made her the admiration of the mission circle. A fever seized her, however, and her untimely death is commemorated in the graveyard of St Ann's Bay Baptist church.[31]

Outfits had to be purchased before missionaries could leave England, for anything not bought at home would be imported and consequently more expensive. It would help if a list of necessary items could be compiled, suggested the *Missionary Herald*, the official organ of the BMS. It should include stockings, neckerchiefs, handkerchiefs, collars, hats both of straw and of gossamer, linen and cotton shirts, towels, blankets, sheets and pillow-cases, flannel and calico articles, and materials 'for the usual articles of dress'. 'The outfit of a missionary's wife', it continued, 'is composed of the articles of dress used in this country, and light-coloured prints and muslins, and flannel articles are of great value.'[32] Knibb noted in the diary that he kept of his voyage how surprised his friends in Bristol and Kettering would have been to see him in 'light trousers and waistcoat and a short jacket', rather than the usual dark suit of the dissenting minister.[33] That dark suit functioned as an outward symbol of the inner transformation through which he had gone. Furthermore, for middle-class men, dark clothes which cloaked masculinity rather than drawing attention to it in the style of their fathers and grandfathers, were among the signs of a new focus on morality.[34] Some small concessions, however, were made for the tropics.

Faith was at the heart of the missionary endeavour: a belief in the depravity of mankind and the absolute necessity of a change of heart with Christ as the only route to salvation. The rebirth of the Christian man and woman, embedded in the Christian household, the finding of a new sense of self in Christ, was central to the evangelical project. The abandonment of self, the belief that men and women were but 'worms' in God's eyes, the most abject creatures at his command, coexisted with the powerful sense of self which both sexes derived from their convictions. Thomas Burchell, described by many visitors as a patriarch and a gentleman, dispensing hospitality in ample style from his very comfortable country residence in beautiful Mount Carey, one of the free villages set up after emancipation in the hills behind Montego Bay, reported to the secretary of the BMS a series of new mission stations he had established. 'I do not wish to mention anything boastingly,' he wrote; 'I feel my own nothingness, and my anxious desire is to be found at the foot of the cross.'[35] Part of this abjection was associated with the constant struggle for self-improvement, for missionaries sought to evangelise in part through their own spiritual example. A careful watch over the self was central to any evangelical Christian's faith, but this took on an extra dimension when ministering to others.

The strength of the missionaries lay in their sense of righteousness, their necessary dependence on their flocks because of their exclusion from white society, their capacity to face persecution linked to their oft-invoked spirit of Protestant martyrdom, their commitment to the voluntary principle and, therefore, their conviction that it was only through the agency of men and women such as themselves that the new moral world would be created. The narrowness of their set of beliefs held them in a relatively secure framework, and enabled them to withstand multiple difficulties. The savagery and barbarism, as they constructed it, of the societies they went to justified their intervention. In bringing Christianity, they were bringing civilisation, for the two were linked in their discourse. The contest over slavery was a contest with Christianity; freedom meant the light of the Word of God, the chains of bondage being infidelity and ignorance. In the 'contest for empire' between Christianity and slavery, the light had triumphed, and Satan was defeated.[36] The missionaries were the 'messengers of mercy'.[37]

Inevitably they struggled not to acknowledge doubts as to the absolutism of their faith, for in their isolation it was hard to keep their fears at bay. Their certainties were rooted in what they saw as their superior faith. Whatever the inadequacies of their own education, as perceived in England, for Baptist missionaries were denounced as low mechanics and tradesmen, they did not hesitate to scoff at their opponents in Jamaica. They were possessed of the truth, *the* reading of the Gospel. Those first missionaries who had to establish themselves on the basis of the work done by black Baptists found much to contend with. They were shocked by the bad teaching, as they saw it, of the 'pretend preachers' on the island who claimed to teach the Gospel. Missionary disapproval of their popular preaching was compounded by their difficulties in understanding patois, and with making themselves understood. 'Their understandings are very limited,' wrote Thomas Knibb to an English friend, 'exceedingly so with field negroes, so that we find the greatest difficulty in understanding what they mean.'[38]

Any hopes for the construction of a New Jerusalem depended on the ceaseless industry and activity of the little band of missionaries, who had set themselves the task of converting the heathen. Their project was rooted in the 'mission family' which they worked hard to create and sustain. The Baptist missionaries came from a society in which family enterprises were at the heart of economic, social and cultural life.[39] They were used to a world which was physically organised around the family, to which men, women and children each contributed in their particular ways: men as the public and legal front, women as the informal partners, children by running errands or undertaking tasks. In the world of tradesmen, small proprietors and merchants, artisans and ministers, from which they came, women played a vital part. Men might provide the driving force and the public face, but women were often the source of capital, labour and contacts; they were the ones who bore children to carry on the family business and reproduce it in its daily life. Missionary wives, it was assumed, needed no training for any of this; it was their vocation.

But the family enterprise was only the starting point for the mission family. Family was crucial to the missionaries themselves, for they were isolated figures, white men with black congregations, facing the hostility of much of the white community on the island, and often living in places where there were very few white people. Furthermore, as one of the missionaries noted, if any minister became too involved with white people, black people would lose their confidence in him.[40] Mission stations thus became the site of an extended family, stretching across the island, linking one isolated mission family to another. The family, moreover, was defined not by blood but by religious kinship: 'friend', 'brother' and 'sister' were all terms whose meanings crossed blood relations and ties of friendship. Stations might begin with only one couple, but would hope to bring in others as their work expanded and the numbers of chapels, schools and Sunday schools under their care grew. When new stations were established, they kept in close touch with their 'parent' stations, and relied on them for succour and support. A Jamaica Baptist Association was formed in 1824 to link the missions across the island. Family was indeed a many-layered concept in this context: there was the family of origin, the family of marriage, the family of the chapel, the mission family, the family of Baptists at home and the family-to-be in the sky – this last providing the key to the overarching spiritual nature of the Christian family. Without a religious family, individuals would be hard pressed to maintain their faith. The family was a bulwark, a defence against the immorality of 'the world', a haven in which Christian morality was practised.

The overlapping family networks provided a series of settings in which people could live their daily lives and enjoy a promise for the future to come. The initial pain of leaving home was lessened by the dream of a shared heavenly future, 'a family anew, unbroken in the skies'.[41] New missionaries were welcomed to the island by those already established, and the mission family was literally tied by a web of cross-cutting relationships. Many of the missionaries came from Baptist families and carried their fathers' and grandfathers' activities into pastures new. They married into Baptist families, named their children after Baptist luminaries and friends, saw their children marry missionaries or become missionaries themselves. Thomas Burchell's grandfather was a Baptist minister, his wife's sister married another Jamaican Baptist missionary, Samuel Oughton, his daughter married a missionary, Edward Hewett.[42] William Knibb's brother was a schoolteacher in Jamaica; his nephew, left orphaned, was cared for by him and returned to Jamaica also to work as a teacher; one of his daughters married one of the newly trained 'native' pastors in the early 1840s, and their son became a minister; his other daughter Catherine married Captain Milbourne, the commander of a schooner specially designed for BMS work in West Africa. Two sisters, the Misses Drayton, who came to Jamaica in the 1840s as teachers, both married missionaries. Missionaries who were widowed married relatives of their extended mission families; widows often remarried other missionaries or ministers.

Naming patterns confirmed these connections and friendships. Two of William Knibb's sons were named after missionary friends, James Coultart and Thomas Burchell. Knibb's second son was originally to have been named Augustus Africanus, but the missionary connection triumphed. Knibb's first son was named after Andrew Fuller, one of his mentors and a celebrated Baptist divine. James Phillippo sealed a friendship for life with a Baptist brother when they were both undergoing their missionary training. They exchanged names and each took the other's surname as a middle name. He became James Mursell Phillippo.

Like all families, the mission family was subject to acute tensions and conflicts. Its structure was patriarchal. It was the missionary who was appointed by the BMS and had all formal responsibilities. Direct correspondence between missionary wives and the BMS was usually when the wives were acting for their husbands, in cases of illness or death, for example. The missionary's role in the family enterprise was closely linked to his fatherhood – head of household, father of the family, father of the congregation, father of the children in 'his' schools. The range of his activities was immense, his working hours prolonged. Hours for prayer and reflection, family worship, superintendence of schools, chapel, class meetings, singing classes, training leaders, adult evening schools, sessions with individual church members, these were part of the pattern of each week. On Sundays there were the services and the Sunday schools. In addition there were monthly meetings with members and inquirers, visits to the sick, chapel meetings, the settlement of disputes, marriages, burials, baptisms, meetings with other missionaries, encounters with officials and all the other myriad responsibilities of the pastor. They acted as mediators of the public world to the enslaved and those who were freed, they were 'everything religiously, politically, civilly' as Knibb put it.[43]

He and his brothers relied heavily on their wives to support them in whatever ways were appropriate. Hannah Phillippo lived above the school in which she worked alongside her husband. She taught the girls, while he taught the boys, a division of labour firmly established in evangelical schools, whether Sunday or day schools, from the late eighteenth century. In addition, she ran the household, bore nine children, five of whom died, and suffered extreme ill health. As a missionary's wife, her home was one in which hospitality was always available, and callers and visitors could be received. She would also visit sick and poor women and children, and question female applicants for church membership. Mrs Coultart, one of the earliest missionary wives on the island, described to a friend how she had 'thirty-five little ragged black children' whom she taught for two hours every evening. At that time there was only one member of the church who could read, and young children, having learned themselves, would then teach their aged grandparents.[44]

Missionary wives received none of the public praise which was heaped on their successful husbands in the heady years of the 1830s and 1840s. The grand funerals, the public meetings, the obituaries, memorials and biographies were not for them. They had to be satisfied with a quieter form of praise; they were buried beside their husbands, as their helpmeets and supporters. When husbands were ill, wives did as much of the work as they could for them, even to the point of occasionally reading a sermon. When wives were ill, husbands found their labours greatly increased. 'The affliction of a wife, accustomed to take every domestic care is peculiarly trying to a missionary,' wrote James Coultart to the BMS committee.[45] The death of a spouse was a common affliction, for in the 1820s and 1830s the average duration of service of a missionary in Jamaica was three years, as a result of illness and death.[46] Philip Cornford mourned the loss of his wife, which left him 'a poor lonely widower in a foreign land'. His wife had comforted him, worked alongside him, taken care of the Sunday school and of the teaching of the young women. The house felt large and desolate without her, and he did not want to go back to it.[47] 'To be alone in Jamaica is solitary indeed,' wrote Edward Hewett after the death of his wife.[48] When wives died before husbands, daughters often took on the task of providing help and support, running the establishment for the mission family under God the father and the father/head of household. The pressure to do this was immense. Sons or daughters who did not move in a clear line towards adult baptism and a life of service were pressured, prayed for, publicly urged to identify themselves with Christ.

Since, during slavery, the plantation provided the major community to which the slaves belonged, one of the essential tasks of the missionaries, both before and after emancipation, was to build an alternative community around the chapel. The chapel could potentially provide a place of belonging, a source of identity, a social life. Much of the strength of dissenting congregations in England derived from this sense of community, the cohesion of the chapel world, with its voluntary principles and clear rules of conduct. The missionaries worked to develop equivalent structures in Jamaica. In order to extend their supervision and build up a band of helpers outside the immediate family but within the family of the church, missionaries took up the pattern already established by black Baptists and used by Wesleyans: that of appointing class leaders. Teachers, deacons, leaders – all were appointed by the missionary and delegated by him. He sat at the centre of this web, aiming to manage and organise. 'The characteristics of this organization', wrote Phillippo, 'are union, division of labour, and classification, combined with the most vigilant pastoral direction and supervision.'[49]

Each congregation was divided into classes, each class superintended and fuelled with the 'holy ambition' to surpass their brothers in duty. Each individual was encouraged to see himself as part of the whole, and there were frequent social meetings to foster a sense of union and mutual effort. The leaders 'instructed inquirers, visited the sick, sought after backsliders, superintended funerals, and reported cases of poverty and distress throughout their respective districts'. Each member of the church was encouraged to think of himself as his brother's keeper; together they were one family. 'Bound closely to each other by mutual knowledge, intercourse and love, "there is neither Jew nor Greek, there is neither male nor female, there is neither bond nor free, but all are one in Christ Jesus",' wrote Phillippo, quoting St Paul. But at the centre, 'planning, improving, and directing all its movements', was the pastor himself, the white patriarch.[50]

If gender hierarchy was inscribed at the heart of the missionary enterprise, so was that of race. Missionaries arrived on the island with their heads full of images of 'poor Africans', 'savages' and 'heathens'. Dr Ryland's charge to Knibb reiterated contemporary wisdom: 'the Negro and coloured population are generally very ignorant, and are like children of a larger growth, who will need the simplest and plainest instruction to be given them line upon line.'[51] But there was also a long tradition of thinking of Africans as natural Christians, open to salvation.[52] The missionary task was to bring these 'poor creatures' to salvation, manhood and freedom. Missionaries were the angels of mercy with the news of the Gospel. 'From isle to isle the welcome tidings ran,' wrote Montgomery,

> The slave that heard them started into man:
> Like Peter, sleeping in his chains, he lay, –
> The angel came, his night was turn'd to day:
> 'Arise!' his fetters fall, his slumbers flee;
> He wakes to life, he springs to liberty.[53]

Their encounter with slavery and plantation society softened the notions of savagery and heathenism, which indeed were increasingly attached to the planters in missionary discourse, and intensified the emphasis on pity. Slaves, Phillippo argued, were the hapless victims of a revolting system; they were

> men of the same common origin with ourselves, – of the same form and delineation of feature, though with a darker skin, – men endowed with minds equal in dignity, equal in capacity, and equal in duration of experience, – men of the same social dispositions and affections, and destined to occupy the same rank with ourselves in the great family of man.[54]

The celebration of this family of man was an important part of the new rituals introduced by the missionaries. Thus, for example, at the death of a missionary wife, Thomas Burchell instructed that the coffin should be carried by black and brown men as well as white. This was an important break with established practice, for burial grounds were strictly segregated by colour.[55] But this family of man was, like all families, internally ordered. Jostling with the language of equality in Phillippo's mind, 'neither Jew nor Greek, neither male nor female', was the language of hierarchy, undercutting that very equality he claimed to espouse. There was an evolutionary ladder, he believed, at the top of which were Europeans, and up which freed black people would climb. This assumed that black inferiority was encoded in the language of the family, naturalising relations as of parent and child. Black people were 'the sons of Africa', 'babes in Christ', children who must be led to freedom, a term which had a cluster of meanings for the missionaries, including salvation, emancipation, a free labour market and adulthood. The missionaries were the parents who would act as their teachers and guides, admonishing and improving, giving praise where praise was due.

Missionaries and planters

Amongst these fathers, teachers and guides – these patriarchal pastors – the most influential was William Knibb: 'King Knibb', as he came to be called. William Knibb was born in Kettering, the Northamptonshire boot and shoe town, in 1803. His father was a tradesman, and his mother a member of an independent church. He attended a dame school and then the town's grammar school, as well as Sunday school at the chapel. In 1816 he was apprenticed, along with his brother Thomas, to J. G. Fuller, the brother of Andrew Fuller, then the Baptist minister in Kettering and the secretary of the BMS. The BMS had a particular relation to Kettering, since it was there that the society was formed in 1792, and it was some time before it moved its administration to London. J. G. Fuller lived in Bristol, and the Knibb brothers became attached to the Baptist chapel there. In 1820 Thomas was baptised, and two years later William followed suit.[56]

In 1822 Thomas decided to become a missionary, thinking 'that it would be far more delightful, more honourable, to go to heaven from a heathen country than a Christian one'. Responding to the revival of anti-slavery sentiment in the 1820s, he chose to go as a schoolmaster to Kingston, rather than to the more familiar Baptist pastures in India.[57] Thomas's choice inspired William, and he too began to dream of a future in which he could minister to 'the swarthy sons of Africa' and become an instrument for Christ with 'the poor degraded negroes', by 'unfolding to them the wonders of redeeming love'.[58] In 1823 Thomas died, and William was accepted to replace him. After learning the recently developed Lancastrian system of teaching at the Borough Road school, he sailed for Jamaica with his new wife Mary, a fellow member of the Baptist church. A long delay off the south coast meant that he was able to preach a couple of times on the Isle of Wight, and encounter that heathenism at home which always stood as a counterpoint to the heathens abroad. Niton was 'a deplorably dark and benighted village', Knibb recorded in his journal. 'Mud was thrown at the door but I escaped unhurt. Felt thankful that I had the opportunity of unfolding to them the word of life.' His first encounter with a slave-holder was with a fellow passenger, whose very attempts to justify the system showed 'it to be complete with every enormity', from cruelty to immorality.[59]

After landing in Port Morant, the Knibbs took a boat to Kingston, where they had their first taste of Jamaica. 'I have now reached the land of sin, disease, and death,' wrote Knibb to a friend,

> where Satan reigns with awful power, and carries multitudes captive at his will. True religion is scoffed at, and those who profess it are ridiculed and insulted. . . . The poor, oppressed, benighted, and despised sons of Africa, form a pleasing contrast to the debauched white population. Though many of them seem to have lost nearly every rational idea, such is the beautiful simplicity of the gospel, that though fools, they understand it, and joyfully accept the truth as it is Jesus. . . . They are bursting through the thick

gloom which has long surrounded them, and it will be a long time ere they may be denominated by any other name than babes in Christ.[60]

Knibb's anti-slavery sentiments, bred in the nonconformist culture of provincial England, and replete with images of 'poor negroes' and benighted souls awaiting enlightenment from white missionaries, were fully confirmed by his experience of Jamaica. He was shocked by the moral degradation of slavery and the mindless existence, as he saw it, to which the enslaved were condemned. No doubt his assumptions as to the 'barren wastes' of their minds had a good deal to do with his difficulties in understanding their forms of speech and making sense of their customs and rituals. But he was convinced that his own people carried the responsibility for this appalling system, and felt ashamed 'that I belong to a race that can indulge in such atrocities'. 'The white population', he concluded, 'is worse, far worse, than the victims of their injustice.'[61]

Knibb soon started to preach, though the BMS was hesitant to give him the requisite papers, since he did not have the usual academic qualifications. In 1825 Mary Knibb had twins, and her husband was troubled at having a black wet-nurse, a sign of the difficulties associated in his mind at this time at the thought of very intimate relations between the races. To be teacher and guide of the enslaved was one thing; to have to rely on a black wet-nurse for the sustenance of his own babies was another. His attachment to whiteness was perhaps deeper than he realised. 'Dear Mary is pretty well,' he wrote to his mother in the following year, after the birth of another daughter, 'and we are truly happy in each other, which is a great mercy in this place, where all temporal pleasure is concentrated in the home. Here are no fields to walk in, and few, if any, friends to visit.'[62] By 1826, when the Jamaica Baptist Association was formed to link the churches across the island, Knibb was well established amongst the missionaries, and he served as its secretary. In 1829 he and his family left Kingston to set up a new mission on the west coast, in Savanna-la-Mar.

The Consolidated Slave Law was passed by the Jamaican House of Assembly in 1826; this confirmed new restrictions on the dissenting preachers who were proving a major irritant to the plantocracy. Tensions had increased between missionaries and planters, and the pattern of appeal to 'the government at home' and British public opinion became increasingly important. James Stephen at the Colonial Office had become convinced that complaints of cruelty and injustice should be investigated, and it was increasingly clear that the enslaved were being denied religious freedom – a right which the ameliorative legislation of 1823 had supposedly secured.[63] Despite the opposition of many planters, however, by 1833 there were sixteen Wesleyan, fourteen Baptist, eight Moravian and five Presbyterian missionaries on the island, forty-three missionaries in all, most of whom were assisted by their wives.[64]

In 1830 the Knibb family moved to Falmouth, a well-established mission station in the heartlands of plantation society. Here Knibb worked hard on the estates, on which he was allowed to preach, but many planters were still determined that the enslaved should receive no religious instruction. He was soon involved in a case that raised political temperatures considerably. Sam Swiney, an enslaved man who was a deacon in Knibb's previous congregation in Savanna-la-Mar, had been sentenced to whipping and hard labour for preaching and teaching. Knibb was outraged, since to his knowledge there was no evidence of Swiney either preaching or teaching, and he contacted the BMS as well as telling the local press. In Knibb's view, and that of the Colonial Office which investigated the case, Swiney had only prayed. The punishment was excessive, a warning to black people not to become involved with Christianity. The offending magistrate was in due course dismissed, though in the interval he had died.[65]

Not far from Falmouth, in St Ann's Bay, lived the Rev. George Bridges, the rector of that parish. Bridges was a leading advocate of slavery, an Englishman, a graduate of both Oxford and Cambridge who had gone to Jamaica as a young man. Having been educated to *critique* slavery, on arrival in Jamaica he felt that he had been misinformed. He 'found their masters a most injured and slandered race of men', and set to work to defend them. His particular enemies became the dissenting missionaries, men whom he accused of being of 'the lowest and most dangerous description', only too capable of stirring up the specious superstitions of ignorant people. It was 'the poison of sectarianism' which had disrupted the unity and purity of the church.[66] In 1829 the secretary of the Anti-Slavery Society sent an anonymous letter to the Colonial Office about Bridges' treatment of an enslaved woman, Kitty Hilton, owned by him. She had appealed for help and accused him of severely kicking and flogging her, leaving her naked. Bridges was at the centre of a complicated legal and political tangle.[67] In July 1831 he formed the Colonial Union, an organisation to protect the planting interest and the established church against the depradations of the enslaved and missionaries.

Bridges' anger towards the missionaries had its roots in a virulent defence of the established church against all others. He was passionately anti-Catholic (a sentiment which he shared with the Baptist missionaries) as well as anti-dissenter. 'The want of employment in the fields or

manufactures of England', he raged, 'sent crowds of ignorant and itinerant preachers to these shores, where they found, or expected to find,
a rich harvest, or a glorious martyrdom.' This 'cloud of itinerant preachers hastened to exchange a parish pittance in England for a lucrative profession in the West Indies'. The effect of this was that the pulpit, 'that
safe and sacred organ of sedition, resounded with the ambiguous tenets,
or at least the words, of freedom and equality; and the public discontent
might be inflamed by the promise of a glorious deliverance from a
bondage which the slave would rather apply to his temporal, than to his
spiritual condition'.[68] This was indeed the heart of the complaint against
the missionaries: the slippage that occurred between temporal and
spiritual freedom. If religious freedom were granted, what certainty
was there that the claims of the enslaved would stop there?

In 1828 Bridges published his *Annals of Jamaica*, an attempt to
reclaim the high ground from the forces of anti-slavery in Britain and to
strengthen planter resolve in Jamaica. One of the dangers of the tropical climate, he believed, reiterating familiar ideas, was that it paralysed
white men. He hoped to awaken them to the dangers they faced. 'An
Englishman', he wrote, 'born beneath a sky of varying temperature, is
continually sensible of new impressions, which keep his senses awake.
He is vigilant, active, and inconstant as the air he breathes. The West
Indian, who is constantly exposed to the same intolerant temperature,
to the same oppressed sensations, is listless, languid, and dejected.'[69]
Bridges drew on the traditions of colonial writing on the island, particularly the work of Edward Long and Bryan Edwards, who had both
articulated the colonials' desire for relative independence from the
metropolis, with a defence of slavery. He insisted that the slave trade was
of English origin, that that quintessentially English queen, Elizabeth I,
had encouraged it, and that white Jamaicans were British subjects with
a right to manage their own affairs. His hope was that the Imperial Parliament would not dare to interfere. Neither Long, Edwards or Bridges
had been born in Jamaica, but all became powerfully identified with
planter culture. Their writings were interventions in the ongoing debate
between metropolis and colony about slavery and power. As early as the
1770s, Long was utilising the stereotype of 'Quashee', which became a
stock element of pro-slavery discourse, to connote a series of what were
deemed to be specifically negro characteristics which marked off one race
from another. 'Quashee' was evasive, disguised, lazy, childlike, lying,
thieving, distrustful, capricious. But he was also kind, cheerful, a song-
ster.[70] Here was a condensation of traits and a stereotype which carried
both negative and positive poles of colonial discourse. For Long, slavery
was close to being a divine institution. His imagined Africa was a place
of barbarism and terror, and, by contrast with this, the West Indies was

a paradise, and slavery an institution which could only improve utterly uncivilised peoples. At the same time he was a convinced Whig, a defender of the House of Assembly, and a critic of the Imperial Government, with a Lockean belief in the rights of white subjects to rebel against an unruly crown.[71]

Bryan Edwards's book on the West Indies was written in 1791, and by 1806 had reached its fourth edition in London. He was well aware of his debt to Long, and drew on him for much of his detail, about obeah and African 'superstitions', for example. His book was written with the abolitionist debate constantly in mind; careful in its tone, reasoned, moderate and relatively humane, it aimed to provide an account of plantation society and the benefits that it could confer on Africans. Edwards wanted to enlist sympathy for the planters in their economic difficulties, and to convince the British public that the situation in the West Indies was more complicated than the supporters of anti-slavery allowed. The planters were not responsible for the system of slavery, he argued; slavery had always existed, and it was possible to make some improvements. His description of the different African peoples he encountered, with information collected from his own servants, recognised different ethnicities, but argued that slavery reduced these differences, that general 'negro' characteristics became more pronounced – lying, thieving, cowardice, lack of trust.[72] Negroes were brutal to animals, did not understand the meaning of love, made noise not music. Their dances were licentious, their funeral rites barbaric and riotous. Enslaved women came in for especial criticism. They were promiscuous and neglected their children. Indeed, slavery was 'unfriendly to population'.[73] On the plantations hours of work were not excessive, the cabins provided for the slaves compared very favourably with those of the Scottish or Irish peasantry, their medical care was good. 'On the whole', he concluded, in a vein that was to be repeated again and again by defenders of slavery, 'the slaves in the British West Indies ... might be deemed objects of envy to half the peasantry of Europe ... the general treatment of the Negroes in the British West Indies is mild, temperate and indulgent'.[74]

Edwards's reasoned tone was very different from the shrill polemic of Bridges. By the late 1820s the planters were infinitely more aware than heretofore of the dangers they faced from the enslaved and abolitionists alike. Bridges needed to justify racial inequalities. His case was that abolition was impractical, but he did not defend slavery in principle. Rather, he assumed, as did most protagonists of the system, that eventually it would melt away if there were no outside interference.[75] Africans needed the civilising hand of Europeans for much longer before they would be anywhere near ready for freedom. Similarly, he rejected the claims made by free coloured people for equal rights with Europeans. Slavery was for him a historic institution. He linked its formation to the subjection of women, for the 'original servitude, of the weaker sex, became the bond and seal of the social contract'. The woman became 'a constituent part' of her husband's property, 'over which he had an uncontrolled and unlimited authority'. The father then acquired the same rights over his children as over his wife, and so at the heart of the family there 'naturally sprang a mild and tender species of servitude'. Such servitude was then extended by war, and became the institution of slavery. In Bridges' account, over centuries of European history, white men, once slaves, had been able to become free men; but negroes were different. 'Kindness and indulgence have never yet been able to eradicate the generic character of deceit, ingratitude and cruelty', he maintained, amongst the *adult* objects' of negro slavery.[76]

Here we have Long's 'generic character' again. The 'vagrant tribes' of Africa, in Bridges' imagination, who refused to cultivate the soil and thus eschewed regular labour, the great civiliser, may have come from vastly different areas. The only differences across Africa, however, Bridges concluded, lay 'in the degrees of the same base qualities which mark the negro race throughout. They are a people who have never emerged from a state of primitive infancy and natural barbarity.'[77] Africa was, for Bridges as for Long, a place of horror. So, he reasoned, many of the enslaved were content to be in Jamaica, for their moral, intellectual and physical condition had improved. Amelioration had continued, and Jamaica had been 'humane in the government of a servile race which it has been her misfortune to possess'. So mild was the species of servitude which now existed, he insisted, that the enslaved had been raised 'to a level with the labouring classes in many parts of civilized Europe'.[78]

Bridges' polemic had become more shrill as the tensions had increased between planters, on the one hand, and the enslaved and missionaries, on the other. In 1826 he had instigated an attack on the Wesleyan mission in St Ann's Bay, which produced outrage in Britain and demands for a full inquiry as to the circumstances. He could not tolerate the claim which the enslaved were making: the right to worship a Christian God, for that God was a dissenting God. As Bridges was only too well aware, the demand for religious freedom always potentially opened up the demand for other kinds of freedom. Planters did not want the enslaved to learn to read any more than conservatives in England in the 1780s and 1790s had wanted working-class adults or children to learn those skills. They did not want them treated as spiritual equals, partaking of communion, addressed as 'brother' and 'sister'. They heartily disliked the idea of leaders interpreting the Bible to their classes. They knew all too well that some forms of religious belief had long been a source of radical thinking about the individual. For Bridges, enslaved African men and women were not the same as white people; they were different and inferior. Yet they were claiming the right to religious freedom.

It was well known in Jamaica that continuous efforts were being made in Britain to abolish slavery. In 1830 the House of Assembly had been forced to concede rights to free coloured and black people in an attempt to defuse some of the political tensions on the island.[79] By 1831, knowledge of the British anti-slavery campaign was widespread, and there was hope and excitement on the plantations. Then news began to circulate amongst the enslaved that the king had granted their freedom and that the planters were preventing this from being implemented, and conflict erupted. In December 1831 a major rebellion began, brutally put down by the authorities. As Mary Turner has shown for Jamaica, and Vittoria Emilia da Costa for Demerara, Christianity played a vital part in articulating new claims for freedom, just as Bridges had feared.[80] The enslaved, argues da Costa, 'appropriated symbols that originally were meant to subject them and wrought those symbols into weapons of their own emancipation'.[81] The missionary belief in the brotherhood of all men, that Africans were women and men almost like themselves, coexisted with a belief in white superiority. Turner demonstrates the contradiction at the heart of missionary teaching: while they appealed for obedience to the authorities, the missionaries insisted on the right to individual salvation, and thus opened up the question of freedom of thought. The Rev. Thomas Cooper enunciated the problem this way: if the enslaved learned Christianity, 'they would find out that they were Men, and as such would ask the Question, why are they to be treated as mere Animals – Goods and Chattels?'.[82]

New thinking was framed by new forms of organisation: the chapel community offered an alternative to the plantation. Mission churches gave opportunities for new forms of leadership and skills, and provided networks of connection which were crucial to the organisation of resistance. The political consciousness of the enslaved, suggests Turner, was 'fed and watered' by the mission churches, and came to fruition in the religious groups which they formed themselves under their 'leaders', men like Sam Sharpe, who was a deacon in Burchell's congregation in Montego Bay.[83] The rebellion was centred in the western part of the island. It was organised by Christian converts who used the mission networks, took inspiration from the Bible, and claimed the missionaries as their allies. Sharpe proclaimed the natural equality of men, and refuted the planters' claim that they could hold black people in bondage. Although a member of Burchell's church, he was heavily involved with the Native or Black Baptists. The latter had their origins in the congregations formed by black Baptists who had come to Jamaica in the late eighteenth century. White Baptist missionaries, as we have seen, were anxious from the start to dissociate themselves from the Black Baptists, since the latter's doctrines were at odds with the orthodoxies of English Baptists, their organisation was separate, and they could not be made subject to the regulation of the missions. For the Native Baptists the link between religious freedom and political freedom was explicit. The rebellion of 1831 was about creating a new society, in which black people could be free. It lasted a week, and much property was destroyed. White vengeance then began. There had been only two acts of violence against white people, but 626 of the enslaved were tried, and 312 executed. The rebellion and its aftermath played a crucial part in the recognition in Britain that slavery could not survive as a system. Sam Sharpe is now celebrated as a national hero of Jamaica.

In the wake of the rebellion, the planters wanted to expel the missionaries, whom they blamed for what had happened. As da Costa argues in the Demerara context, the planters felt that the world was against them. Their rage against East Indian traders who were challenging their dominance of the sugar market, London merchants who were ruining them with their rates of interest, colonial officials who interfered, Manchester manufacturers who believed in free trade, British consumers, abolitionists and dissenters – all became condensed into the hated figure of the missionary.[84] The missionaries had heard of the plans at the last minute, and had tried to teach obedience to civil authorities from the pulpit. But this did not save them from the wrath of the planters. Hostility was focused on the Baptists and the Wesleyans, who were most significant numerically in the rebel areas. Some missionaries were arrested, while others were threatened with lynchings and tarring and feathering.[85] Then in February 1832 a wave of violence began, orchestrated by Bridges through the Colonial Church Union which he had founded. Numerous chapels were destroyed, and leading Baptists were put on trial. Bridges identified three enemies: the missionaries, those members of the free black and coloured classes who were supporting them under the leadership of the newspaper editor Edward Jordan, and the imperial government whose 'unnatural conduct', as he deemed it, was threatening the whole system of slavery.[86] The rebellion had united the Europeans across the island, and the governor took no steps to restrain white violence. Burchell was threatened with lynching, and had to escape the island. The missionaries were forced to recognise that their work could not continue unless slavery was abolished, and that, whatever the rules of their societies, they would have to take a public stand against the system. It was at this point that the Baptists met and decided to send William Knibb to make their case in the mother country.

The war of representation

Long, Edwards and Bridges all wrote for both England and Jamaica. Their articulation of the pro-slavery case was crucial to the interests of the plantocracy, and was heavily utilised in defence of slavery as an institution. The virulence of the debate over slavery masks the links between planters and abolitionists. Both groups were united in their belief in hierarchy and order, their use of Ireland as a touchstone for colonial questions, their contempt for Africa, their assumption that Britain was the most civilised country in the world and that European empires were fundamentally a good thing. But in this period it was their differences which came dramatically to the fore. Planter interests had long been highly organised in the metropole. West Indian merchants and planters wanted their interests in the mercantile system represented in Parliament: the growth of parliamentary power made it ever more important to orchestrate that influence, particularly as anti-slavery interests became more organised themselves. As B. W. Higman shows, the 'interest' included an inner ring of those born in the West Indies, absentee planters and merchants who had never been to the colonies, colonial agents, naval and military men who had served on the islands, together with all their relatives and friends. Planters and merchants, absentees and colonists, had distinctly different concerns, and the group was never univocal. Around the 1820s there was probably a group of fifty or more in Parliament, but this steadily declined.[87] A key figure was William Burge, parliamentary agent for Jamaica, who orchestrated responses and resistance to anti-slavery initiatives.

From 1823 a propaganda war had been waged between planters and abolitionists in Britain. At stake was the question as to what was the truth about the system of slavery. Both sides were interested in mobilising public opinion, that increasingly powerful phenomenon. The abolition of the slave trade in 1807 had seemed to inaugurate a new era, but, as noted earlier, by the early 1820s it was clear that slavery was not simply going to die away as a result of the ending of the British slave trade. Pressure began to mount for other forms of change, and the Agency Committee was formed to focus public opinion more effectively on the issues. Absentee planters liked to present themselves as English property-holders rather than slave-owners, distancing themselves from what went on in the colonies. From the 1820s they were increasingly concerned with the question of compensation.[88] Slavery was defended as a well-regulated system, a necessary regime for Africans. But it became more and more difficult for the planters to conceal the brutality of slavery: the enslaved told missionaries, who reported it to their societies, the Colonial Office and MPs, and published details in the missionary press. It was the truths from the plantations which drove anti-slavery initiatives, the colony which led the metropole. Missionaries began to publish material giving their stories of slavery. A significant body of eye-witness accounts from white people thus began to challenge the planter orthodoxy that they were the ones who knew. Previously it had been medical men who supplied the most informed criticisms of the system.[89] Now missionaries, many of whom had gone to the West Indies in the 1820s with anti-slavery sympathies, were fuelling the abolitionist fans with vivid narratives of the refusal of planters to countenance Christian worship amongst the enslaved. Christianity and slavery began to seem more obviously at odds.

Crucial to this war of representation was the disputed figure of the African – what kind of a man was he, what kind of a woman was she? While the supporters of anti-slavery claimed that African men and women were brothers and sisters, the plantocracy claimed that they were fundamentally different from, and inferior to, their white superiors. While the icon of the planters was Quashee – evasive, lazy, childlike and lacking judgement – the missionaries and their allies constructed new figures, the black Christian man and woman.[90] This man and woman were childlike, and in that sense linked to established colonial discourse, but also able to accept guidance, ready to learn, ready to labour and to live in families. These men and women were human beings, with feel-ings and thoughts, and with the capacity for redemption. The attempt to construct these new Christian subjects was at the heart of the mis-sionary enterprise in Jamaica, just as it was at the heart of evangelical activity at this time in Britain.

The war over representation took place on many sites: in the press, in pamphlets, in fiction, in poetry, in paintings and engravings, in public meetings.[91] One key site in 1831 was the House of Lords, which had instituted a Select Committee on Slavery – a committee which gained urgency when the Jamaica rebellion took place at Christmas. In the Commons, a Select Committee was also established in the wake of this, taking as one of its framing propositions the view that there would be more danger if emancipation were withheld than if it were granted.[92] Both committees focused on Jamaica. The House of Lords took evidence on the condition and treatment of the enslaved, their habits and dispo-sitions, the means of improving and civilising them. Their findings, they concluded, 'were of the most contradictory Description'.[93] The House of Commons committee was formed to discuss the ending of slavery in the safest possible way, and wanted to investigate particularly whether enslaved people, once emancipated, would be industrious and maintain themselves. Their inquiry was unfinished, but they concluded that there was an urgent need for serious legislation.[94]

Both plantocracy and abolitionists had marshalled their forces and made full use of the public platforms which the select committees offered them. The same debates dominated the two sets of proceedings, and some of the same people gave evidence at both. While overseers and attornies, planters and managers, naval and military men, told one story, dissenting missionaries told another. The Duke of Manchester, governor of Jamaica from 1808 to 1827, opened the proceedings of the House of Lords with a statement which combined an insistence on the stability of the system with an assumption that the enslaved would rise and emancipate themselves whenever the opportunity arose. Asked what he thought negroes understood by emancipation, he responded that he assumed it meant, 'To have nothing to do . . . not to be obliged to work, I should say'.[95] This was one of the key issues to be fought out. Would Africans work without compulsion? The conventional wisdom of the planters was that they would not; Quashee was lazy, and slavery was a regrettable but necessary institution, part of the civilising process, along with the whip. The whip was not used to excess, but as a necessary part of the labour process. Eventually negroes might be trained to work without compulsion, but this would certainly not happen in the short term. The abolitionists, on the other hand, were convinced that negroes would work, that forced labour was a disgrace, and that Jamaica could become a free market economy. Much of the contradictory evidence in the Select Committees concerned this. Henry John Hinchcliffe, a barrister and later judge in the Vice-Admiralty court, spoke from 'my Observation of the Character of the Negro people, of which I think Indolence and Improvidence are the Two most marked Features'.[96] John Baillie Esq., a planter on the island from 1788 to 1815, insisted that the slaves were 'happy and contented' and that negroes would not work without compulsion.[97]

The plantocracy insisted that it knew the heart and mind of the negro, that the prejudicial stories spread by the anti-slavery lobby were simply not true. As Keane put it, it was impossible for any person in Britain to form a proper opinion. As for him, he was simply a military man who had arrived on the island with no prior knowledge or opinions, for he had never given Jamaica a thought. 'If a great number of the Inhabitants of this Country', he argued,

> who are very much prejudiced on this Question, which I am not, would but visit that Part of the World, and see the State of Slavery in all its Bearings, they would have a very different Feeling from what they have at this

Moment; and, speaking of the other Side of the Water, I have seen more Misery in Ireland in One Day than I have seen in the West Indies during my Service there.[98]

This comparison between Ireland, alongside Scotland, and the West Indies was a much-repeated one. William Shand, an attorney, argued that 'My sleek well-fed Negroes would form an extraordinary Contrast with the wretched half-starved Weavers in Angus and Kincardineshire'. Vice-Admiral Rowley even went so far as to say that, 'If I had been born to labour . . . I had sooner been born a black in the island of Jamaica than a white man in this country, or any other'.[99]

The planters claimed that the enslaved were both better off than some white labourers and unequal to them. 'Is there the same Variety of Character in the Negro there is in White Persons?,' Hinchcliffe was asked, and he replied 'I do not think there is,' for negroes were defined by indolence.[100] The African, argued Andrew Dignum, a solicitor who had worked in Kingston and Spanish Town, 'has no feeling'. In other words, negroes were not human beings of the same order as white people.[101] Meanwhile, William Burge, the agent for Jamaica and a key figure in orchestrating the defence of slavery, insisted that the enslaved population had as yet acquired no degree of civilisation or habits of industry, and that if emancipation were granted, the island would become 'a perfect Wilderness'. These men had 'the fire of Africa in their Blood', they were driven by 'strong Passions', they had not yet learned the restraints of civilised society.[102]

The missionaries, encouraged by the Anti-Slavery Society, were equally determined to use this platform to counter the claims of the planters and discredit that old story of the prosperity of enslaved people. There was now a sufficient body of white knowledge, from those who knew the island and had witnessed slavery at first hand, to tell a different story. Jamaica had been a 'sealed country', and the plantations a 'sealed book', for white people rarely visited them. William Taylor, who had managed property on the island, was willing to acknowledge that the missionaries knew things which others did not. 'I believe that a Missionary', he argued, 'has Opportunities of acquiring a great deal of Information from the Slaves which no other Class of Persons can; I believe that a Missionary actively employed near Estates does acquire a great deal of very intimate knowledge of the Negro Character.'[103] They did not understand, however, about sugar or labour, he continued. Those missionaries who gave evidence systematically refuted the notion that the enslaved were better off than British labourers, or that their intellect was inferior. Furthermore, it was vital for them to be able to claim that enslaved men and women were being Christianised, thus civilised, and that, once freed, they would work. The black Christian subject had feelings and thoughts, was open to redemption, accepted the guidance of Christian missionaries, wanted to buy clothes and items for their houses, and would labour. Negroes, insisted the Rev. John Barry, a Wesleyan who had been sent out by his missionary society in 1825 and had worked in Kingston and Spanish Town, 'possess as high a Degree of Intellect as the Irish Peasantry'. Or, as he put it to the House of Commons, 'They are just the same as other men.' It was their condition which was degraded, not their innate faculties.[104] The Rev. Peter Duncan, who had been in Jamaica since 1821, argued that 'the desire of liberty is so natural to man' that of course, once emancipated, those previously enslaved would work. They loved to consume, and would want to buy clothes and furniture. He did not doubt that they had equivalent energy to Englishmen in the tropics. 'I conceive that there is a sort of Lassitude,' he reflected,

> occasioned by a Residence in a tropical Climate; but if compared with Europeans, there is certainly no Inferiority whatsoever. I conceive that the emancipated Negroes manifest much greater Energy in Labour where they possess equal education – that they are superior to Europeans residing in that country. I cannot undertake to say there is a spirit of Perseverance in them equal to Englishmen residing in England.[105]

So Barry both equated negroes with the Irish peasantry while claiming that, all things considered, they were the same as other men. Duncan argued that they might not be equal to the English in England, but each was uncertain as to the question of full equality. Enslaved men and women had the right to salvation, of that there was no doubt, but once civilised by white men, the question as to whether they would really be the same remained an unresolved conundrum.

Threaded through both sets of minutes is the sound of the whip, for cruelty and its relation to labour was another key issue in this debate. Some of the supporters of the planters were determined to declare that there was no cruelty. Admiral Sir Lawrence William Halsted, who had been in Jamaica between 1823 and 1827, described the pleasant surprise he had when he arrived on the island. 'From the Papers I had read', he declared, 'and the Speeches made at different Meetings, I fully expected to find a great Degree of Cruelty exercised towards them in the Country; and I must state that, when I arrived in the Country, I was agreeably surprised to find it was quite the contrary.'[106] The Rev. Barry, however, described how, when he lived in St Thomas-in-the-Vale, he 'frequently heard, almost incessantly, the Sound of the Whip from Morning till the Time of Cessation from Work'.[107] William Taylor's observation, after thirteen years on the island, was, 'if you will have Slavery, you must have Cruelty'.[108] The two inevitably went together.

If the whip was one preoccupation, sexuality was another. The planters attacked enslaved women for their lack of feeling for their children and their vicious and difficult character. The women were 'much worse to manage than the men', they claimed.[109] The 'nearly universal' system of concubinage, with every white man in authority keeping a black or coloured mistress, was hated by the missionaries, and was at the heart of their critique of slavery.[110] They were appalled by what they saw as gross immorality and exploitation, regaling the select committees with evidence guaranteed to offend English sensibilities. When white men visited each other, said Barry, women were selected to sleep with them.[111] Duncan refused the planters' view that the women colluded with the system, as well as being uncaring of their children. He cited numerous instances he knew of black Christian women systematically refusing the advances of their overseers, despite the consequences in terms of flogging and loss of favour.[112] Indeed, the missionaries wanted to demonstrate that once black women were Christianised, they had the potential to be loving mothers and domesticated wives. It was disgusting that the master could have unlimited power over the bodies of his female slaves, and that no white man lost his respectability on these grounds. The cruelty of male relatives flogging wives, daughters and mothers was a particularly damning indictment of the way in which slavery had no respect for the family.

William Knibb gave evidence to both select committees. In January 1831 he had been harassed by the authorities and arrested in Jamaica. 'Value your privileges, ye Britons' was his message to his anti-slavery supporters in the mother country. 'Feel and pray for those poor Christian slaves who are entirely under the control of such beings. No Algerine pirate or savage Moor, would have treated me worse than I was treated by Englishmen.'[113] The order of civilisation had been turned upside down: Englishmen were savages, and the enslaved and missionaries were their victims. Knibb was threatened and pressured to leave the island, chapels were burnt, and a number of men 'came dressed in women's clothing to tar and feather me', the cross-dressing a sign of the complete breakdown of social order.[114] Thomas Burchell similarly evoked the terror of his persecution. Prior to his escape from Jamaica, he was surrounded by a mob:

> the most furious and savage spirit was manifested by some of (what were called) the most respectable white inhabitants, that ever could have been discovered amongst civilised society. They began to throng around me, hissing, groaning and gnashing at me with their teeth. Had I never been

at Montego Bay before, I must have supposed myself amongst cannibals, or in the midst of the savage hordes of Siberia, or the uncultivated and uncivilised tribes of central Africa . . . I am fully persuaded, had it not been for the protection afforded me by the coloured part of the population – natives of Jamaica – I should have been barbarously murdered – yea, torn limb from limb, by my countrymen – by so-called *enlightened*, RESPECTABLE! CHRISTIAN BRITONS![115]

Britishness, and whiteness, in the discourse of the missionaries and their allies, should mean order, civilisation, Christianity, domesticity and separate spheres, rationality and industry. When it carried another set of meanings, it was deeply disturbing: white people then became 'savages', uncultivated and uncivilised.

The Colonial Church Union of Bridges and his friends was the quintessential example of such a den of infidels, their task: to burn the houses of God and lynch his servants. It was composed, as Knibb put it, 'of nearly all the fornicators in the island'. The organisation was designed 'to stop the march of mind and religion, to protect the white rebels from deserved punishment'.[116]

It was at this point that the missionaries had decided, though not without disputes amongst themselves and with the parent society, that they must break their vows of silence on political matters and represent the case against slavery to the British public. 'My duty in the West Indies', said Knibb, 'was to instruct the Slaves in Religious Matters; when in England, I am speaking to free People.'[117] Knibb's agenda became, as he put it at a great meeting at Exeter Hall, the public meeting place of philanthropists, to 'stand forward as the advocate of the innocent and persecuted', to speak for the African in England.[118] In the process he empowered himself by representing others. 'There is nothing more delightful and interesting', he observed to a packed audience in Newcastle, 'than to plead the cause of the injured, the degraded and the oppressed.' It was particularly delightful, he continued, when his audience were fellow Christians who would rise up in indignation against oppression.[119] It was, furthermore, argued Knibb, especially pleasurable to speak on behalf of the doubly oppressed, female slaves. No Englishman, in the proper meaning of that term, could stand aside and see a woman flogged. Indeed, Englishness and slavery could not go together.

Knibb insisted that the question was one not of politics but of morality. 'All I ask', as he put it at Exeter Hall to thunderous applause,

is that my African brother may stand in the family of man; that my African sister shall, while she clasps her tender infant to her breast, be allowed to call it her own; that they both shall be allowed to bow their knees in prayer to that God who has made of one blood all nations – the same God who views all nations as one flesh.[120]

Having broken his silence, he was not to be stopped; a public lecture tour, a series of debates with an agent of the planters, evidence before the select committees, a packed agenda all concerned with the building of public support to the point at which Parliament would have to act. In one of his set-piece confrontations with Peter Borthwick, employed by the planters to make their case, Knibb called upon the love of liberty which he claimed characterised the Briton:

> I call upon you by the tender sympathies of your nature – I call upon you by that manly feeling which Britons have ever expressed – I call upon you by the love of liberty which now animates every breast, to leave no method untried till colonial slavery shall have passed away. . . . If we are united the bonds of the slave will be broken; his fetters will be snapped; the tears of the female African shall cease to flow; the trumpet of Jubilee shall sound; the banner of freedom shall be unfurled, and beneath its life-giving shade, Africa shall arise and call you blessed.[121]

Here indeed was a proud identity for Britons.

In his evidence to the select committees, Knibb had his larger audience ever in mind. But he was also concerned to persuade the lawmakers that they could delay no longer. He wanted to see the end of slavery, and he wanted the British Parliament to give emancipation as a kindness, not a right. This way the freed men and women would be bound to Britain for ever. If something was not done, the enslaved would take their own freedom by violence, he warned. Knibb demonstrated to his audience their embeddedness in the colonial system. Slavery was not something out there, it was linked to Britain in the most intimate ways. Many of the enslaved, he pointed out, were the sons and daughters of Englishmen and Scotsmen; 'they get English feelings and long for English knowledge,' they influenced other slaves, he suggested. Christian values, moreover, were spreading fast, a crucial indicator of African humanity and capacity for freedom.

Knibb was also anxious to separate the BMS from the Native Baptists, who he saw as certainly party to the rebellion. 'We have no connexion with them,' he insisted; 'they hate us with the most perfect Hatred.' They derided the Bible, they called themselves 'spirit Christians', the mind of God was revealed to them by dreams. They had their own churches, their own papers, thousands of members, and deluded black preachers who lived unholy lives and allowed sins of various kinds in their flocks.[122]

He had one further concern which shaped his evidence: his desire to speak for and represent people who could not represent themselves. No black person was invited to address the select committees, despite their being the subject matter. At one point the Rev. Duncan was asked by the Commons committee if he knew of any enslaved person who could give evidence. He replied in the affirmative, but the suggestion was not pursued.[123] Knibb went so far as to read from his examinations of black witnesses after the rebellion, thus introducing the only African testimony, though mediated through his editorial voice.[124]

The constitution of the new black subject

Emancipation was granted by the imperial parliament in 1833, and became effective from 1 August 1834. Great celebrations were held across the island, marking the death of slavery. Freed men and women joined the Baptist chapels in large numbers in the years after 1834, demonstrating by their attendance, membership and contributions their judgement of the part played by the Baptist missionaries in emancipation. Baptist membership went up by 200 per cent between 1834 and 1839, and there was a similar increase in the number of inquirers.[125] The dream of freedom was soon destroyed, however, by the realities of apprenticeship. Apprenticeship, the system masterminded by the planters at the time of the first Emancipation Act in 1834, had secured a further period of forced labour. Apprentices, the freed men and women, would learn how to become free labour. At the same time, the Colonial Office believed, the planters must learn how to work with labourers who were not enslaved.[126] Apprenticeship turned out to be slavery by another name. Joseph Sturge, Birmingham Quaker corn merchant, long-time abolitionist, celebrated in the Falmouth monument, had been concerned to monitor the system from the beginning, and this he did mainly through his contacts with the Baptist missionaries on the island.

The missionaries activated their anti-slavery friends to alert the British public. The Colonial Office had established a system of special magistrates to regulate the relations between planters and apprentices, but the magistrates were either unwilling or unable to control the planters. As early as 1835, Phillippo came to the conclusion that freedom could not mean much as long as the planters controlled both housing and labour. He started buying land in the mountains not far from his station in Spanish Town, with the idea of establishing a new settlement. The building of a chapel and a schoolroom began in October 1835, and the first lot was bought by Henry Lunan, the former head man amongst the enslaved on the neighbouring Hampstead estate.[127] Sligoville, the name given by Phillippo to the new settlement, named after the Marquis of Sligo, a governor unusually distinguished by 'his prompt and generous sympathy with the oppressed' and consequently driven out by the planters, was the first village to be established.[128] It is still there, with the Baptist chapel, Mount Zion, occupying pride of place on the hill. A notice in April 1840 in the *Baptist Herald and Friend of Africa*, the cheap weekly newspaper established by the Baptist missionaries in Jamaica, invited all 'friends of equal rights of all classes' to the dinner to be held for the opening of the new township.[129] The inaugural event was subsequently described for the British public in the *Missionary Herald*. The fifty acres, when originally bought, had been chiefly 'unreclaimed wilderness'. John Candler represented the British interest at the laying of the foundation stone for the more permanent chapel and school.[130] By 1840 one hundred families were settled, and eventually it was expected that there would be two hundred. The majority of the inhabitants were described as agricultural labourers, but there was also a schoolmaster and mistress, a shopkeeper, two butchers, four masons, one blacksmith, one straw-hat manufacturer, two gardeners, one tailor, four carpenters, one farrier and two sawyers. Most of the adults were Christians, no one sold liquor, the police unnecessary and unknown. The BMS owned the chapel and school, the mission house, the schoolmaster and mistress's house and several other cottages. Phillippo had himself, as he later explained, laid out the plan of the township and supervised its construction.[131]

The readers of the *Missionary Herald* were told how the company assembled for the opening had walked round the town naming the streets. The main road from Spanish Town was to be Victoria Road, a symbol of the hopes associated with the young queen who had ascended the throne just three years before. Prizes were given for the best cottages and grounds, and Phillippo's address focused on 'the temporal interests of the agricultural classes, both labourer and employer'. He recommended

> the several duties of honesty, industry, economy in domestic expenditure, prudent provision for the exigencies of sickness and old age, together with exhortations to a faithful and conscientious discharge of the mutual obligations of masters and servants, husbands and wives, parents and children; illustrating particularly the impolicy, as well as sin, of dishonesty in every form; the evils of idleness, and the advantages of industrious habits; the guilt of intemperance, and folly of extravagance in dress; the benefits afforded by the institution of savings banks; and the disgrace and misery almost inseparable from depending, in sickness and infirmity, on public or private charity.[132]

Industry, domestic economy, prudent provision for sickness and old age, a proper regard for the hierarchies of family and work, a refusal of the disgrace of dependence – these were to be the characteristics of the new black subject. This new subjectivity was made possible by the linked moments of conversion *and* emancipation. It was the conjunction of these two which made a particularly decisive break between *before* and *after*. While the tropes of *before* and *after* were utilised by missions across the globe, they had a particular pertinence in the colonies where slavery had been established, for only there could Christian rebirth be coterminous with the granting of political, legal and civil subjecthood.[133] In celebrating emancipation, the congregation were also dreaming of a new Jamaica. One of the hymns sung thanked God and the British nation for freedom; another dreamed of a prosperous future for the island.

> O Lord upon Jamaica shine,
> With beams of heavenly grace;
> Reveal thy power through all our coasts,
> And shew thy smiling face.
> Earth shall obey our Maker's will,
> And yield a full increase:
> Our God will crown this chosen isle
> With fruitfulness and peace.[134]

Phillippo's investment in land, allowing his church members to free themselves from dependence on the planters, was a sign of what was to come after the end of apprenticeship. When full emancipation came in 1838, Knibb orchestrated events in Falmouth and forefronted his trusted black deacons. On 1 August 1838 celebrations were held in that town, as across the whole island, to greet the end of apprenticeship, the dawning of freedom. A great procession with portraits of the emancipators – Clarkson, Wilberforce and Buxton amongst others – gathered around the coffin of slavery an hour before midnight. On one side of the coffin was painted in large letters *Cornwall Courier*, and on the other *Jamaica Standard*, two of the hated pro-slavery papers. On the plate of the coffin was inscribed 'Colonial Slavery, died July 31st, 1838, aged 276 years', and on the lower part, 'the name of Sir John Hawkins, who first brought Africans into the colonies as *slaves*'. Just before midnight, the assembled multitude sang,

> The death-blow is struck – see the monster is dying,
> He cannot survive till the dawn streaks the sky;
> *In one single hour*, he will prostrate be lying,
> Come, shout o'er the grave where so soon he will lie.

As the clock struck the final note of midnight, Knibb cried out, 'THE MONSTER IS DEAD! THE NEGRO IS FREE! THREE CHEERS FOR THE QUEEN!' There was a great burst of cheering and then the congregation sang:

> Restored the negro's long-lost rights,
> How softened is his lot!
> Now sacred, heart-born, dear delights
> Shall bless his humble cot.

The coffin was then buried, along with a symbolic chain, handcuffs and iron collar. The flag of FREEDOM together with the British Union Jack was then raised, and a tree of liberty planted. Services were then held in all the chapels in Falmouth, followed by a public meeting in the Baptist chapel, at which all the speakers, except Knibb who was in the chair, were of African descent.[135] The contrast with the Select Committee debates was striking.

These events were celebrated in the British missionary and evangelical press, demonstrating to that public the upright, responsible character of freed black men. In the Baptist chapel in Falmouth, Knibb made the opening remarks and was followed by Andrew Dickson. He thanked the people of England. 'I do truly thank God for the light of the everlasting gospel,' he said. 'I present my thanks to the people of England for the gospel.' William Kerr spoke next:

> I stand up to give hearty thanks to the people of England for send us the gospel. The gospel bring we to see this day, the gospel bring we free. No one can tell what we see one time, and what we was suffer; but the gospel bring us joy. We bless God, we bless the Queen, we bless the Governor, we bless the people of England for the joy we have. Let we remember that we been on sugar estate from sunrise a-morning till eight o'clock at night; the rain falling, the sun shining, we was in it all. Many of we own colour behind we, and many before: we get whip, our wives get beat like a dog, before we face, and if we speak we get the same; they put we in shackle; but thank our heavenly Father we not slave again. (Cheers)

Then Edward Barrett, a deacon in Knibb's church, again thanked the people of England, and recalled the terrible way in which slavery had divided families and forced men to maltreat their wives.[136]

On 2 August a huge procession of schoolchildren paraded round Falmouth. It was led by a carriage carrying six sons and daughters of ministers. The children carried banners bearing the words 'THE DAY OF JUBILEE', 'THE CHAIN IS BROKEN', 'AFRICA IS FREE, AUGUST 1838', 'LIBERTY TO THE SLAVE'. The chapel was decorated with branches, flowers, pictures of Clarkson, Wilberforce and Buxton; a banquet was held, and more trees of liberty were planted.[137]

The two days marked the beginnings of a new Jamaica, the possibilities of a new Christian patriotism, as Knibb called it in one of his sermons, one still shaped by the colonial relation, but with benevolent, emancipatory colonisers heralding a new dawn.[138] 'Come over and see the BLACK standing erect in the family of man' was the message of these events.[139] Emancipation made it possible for black men – and it was almost always men – to enter the public arena as speaking subjects. The existence of the *Baptist Herald and Friend of Africa* from 1839 meant that in the Baptist family there was a platform from which black men could speak, which allowed their words to circulate beyond the local scene to the national arena, and even to Britain, to other Caribbean islands and to the USA. They were no longer being represented, but were representing themselves.[140] That representation was still mediated by the powerful hand of the missionary, chairing the meetings, editing the journals, claiming to shape the perspectives from which their new thinking emerged, protecting them, defending them, applauding them.

At a public meeting in Falmouth in July 1839, by which time it was abundantly clear that all was not going to be plain sailing in the transition from apprenticeship to freedom, Knibb reported to his black audience that he had been in touch with Sturge and had 'felt it my duty to endeavour to cover you with the mantle of British protection'. Help was going to be needed to resist the planters' attempts to tie wages and rent. 'I pledge myself', he vowed, 'by all that is solemn and sacred never to rest satisfied until I see my black brethren in the enjoyment of the same civil and religious liberties which I myself enjoy; till I see them take a proper stand in society as men!' What he sought for them were decent wages and some independence from the estates. Deliberately addressing them as negroes, he defended the use of the word, 'because it means black, and you have no reason to be ashamed of it'. 'I hail the labouring population of Jamaica with joy,' he continued,

> and I trust that the propriety of their conduct will at all times inspire me with confidence in their behalf. Be kind to your wives; lighten their labours. I was glad, some time ago, to hear one of my people say that he wished his wife to refrain from hard labour, and turn her attention to domestic affairs, so that when he came home he might sit down and take his meals like a gentleman.[141]

Black men could be independent, not slavishly dependent, could have their own land and cottages, could marry and live with their families as patriarchal household heads. As Deacon Andrew Dickson said, 'let them act as freemen had a right to do'.[142] Let them claim their rights as voters. In the words of James Allen Senior, let them 'assert their just rights . . . and defend their characters'.[143] But those rights were still framed by missionaries, still dependent on their teaching.

Meanwhile, William Knibb asked, to the fury of the planters, 'Had the black man not the same right to every privilege of a British subject that white men had?'[144] In Lucea a celebration was held for the anniversary of emancipation in August 1838, at which the greatest cheer was for 'Britons never will be slaves'.[145] Black men and women could think of themselves and be thought of as black Britons, a term which has come in and out of the language of nation and empire.

In a symbolic moment in 1841, the foundation stone was laid for the new chapel at Mount Carey, high in the hills above Montego Bay, one of the free villages initiated by Burchell and named after the founder of the BMS. The stone was laid by Miss Burchell and a 'fine grey-headed old Christian negro', symbolising the unity of black and white, the vision of a new Jamaica.[146]

The free villages

Full emancipation, however, far from quickly opening the possibilities for a new Jerusalem, was speedily followed by a harsh struggle, as the planters tried to use their control of what had once been slave huts and provision grounds to tie rents to wages and orchestrate a new kind of forced labour. Joseph Sturge, who had visited Jamaica in 1837 to collect evidence about apprenticeship and had stayed with many of the Baptist missionaries on his tour round the island, expected that the freed apprentices would stay on the estates where they had been living, because of their attachment to the 'place of their birth, to their houses and gardens, to the graves of their parents and kindred'. For Sturge and the abolitionists the new society they dreamed of was one which celebrated free labour; their case against slavery was centrally linked to their economic argument that slavery was a less productive system than that of the free market. Drawing on the English experience, Sturge initially assumed that a new class of landless agricultural labourers would emerge, working for wages under conditions and with resources 'superior to those of a paltry agriculturalist, cultivating his little plot of land with his own hands'.[147]

The combination of planter harassment and the demand of the emancipated peasantry for their own land led to a very different outcome, as it turned out. New contracts had to be established after 1 August 1838, and estate managers attempted to coerce labour with a pincer action on rents and wages. In many instances the peasantry appealed to the Baptist missionaries to negotiate for them, and black deacons led strikes over wages in the crop season of 1838. The missionaries advised freed men and women not to sign contracts. As Swithin Wilmot has shown, during the constitutional crisis precipitated by the House of Assembly in 1838, the Baptists organised public meetings throughout the island. Members of the House of Assembly were abused as old 'slave tyrants'.[148] By June 1839 the Colonial Office was receiving resolutions from Baptist congregations refuting the allegations made against them by the planters, who were denying their rights to the houses and provision grounds they had occupied and cultivated. They insisted that they were willing to pay rents and to work for reasonable wages. As Burchell's congregations in Montego Bay, Mount Carey, Shortwood and Bethel Hill, put it:

> So far from supposing that we had any lawful claim to the houses and grounds, we have been fully and painfully taught our dependence, by notices to quit; by enormous demands of rent from husband, wife, and every child, though residing in one house; from the anomalous and unjust demand to pay additional rent for every day we, or any portion of our family, may be absent from work, whether occasioned by sickness or any other cause; from the summary ejectments which have been inflicted upon some of us, and utter destruction of provision grounds, which others of us have had to endure.

Thomas Abbott, the Baptist missionary at St Ann's Bay, who had been on the island since 1831, reported to the governor that in his experience 'the attachment of the labourers to the places of their birth, and to the burial-places of their ancestors or offspring, is so strong that they would rather make any sacrifice than leave them'.[149] But the provocations made staying almost impossible. Rents charged for every member of a family, summary eviction and the destruction of crops which had been carefully cultivated were powerful incentives to break local attachments.

'The rent question still hangs, like the sword of Damocles, suspended over the island,' commented one of the stipendiary magistrates, remarking on the bitter relations between employers and labourers. Edward Fishbourne, the magistrate in Buff Bay, reported that

> Rent continues to be the cause of most of the irritations and heartburnings which prevail throughout this parish. The objection is not to the principle of paying a fair and reasonable sum as rent, but to the amount demanded, and the modes in which it is levied. Coupling the payment of rent with the application of the tenant's labour is one cause of quarrel. Charging it for every member of a family, husbands, wives and children

above ten years of age, and deducting it from the labourer's weekly wage, without his or her consent, prevails to a great extent, which provokes the discontent and opposition of the negroes.

At Retreat Pen, on the north side of the island, Samuel Barrett, Elizabeth Barrett's brother (she was soon to be Elizabeth Barrett Browning), trying to safeguard the family fortune in the wake of emancipation, attempted to charge men, women and children rent.[150] Henry Walsh, the magistrate in Salt Gut, assured the governor that in his district the difficulties arose not from a refusal to pay rents but from the planters refusing to rent at all, 'thinking thereby, that the people will be more under their control'.[151] This desire for control, as Hugh Paget has argued, and for a landless proletariat which would give that control, was at the heart of the planters' policy over rents.[152]

Control over family labour was another vital issue for the planters. The withdrawal of the labour of women and children after emancipation was widespread, and was encouraged by the Baptist missionaries. They were firm believers in what they saw as a proper gender order, in which men worked for money and women stayed at home, caring for children and household. As Edward Barrett, now free and a deacon in Knibb's church, proudly told the Anti-Slavery Convention in London in 1840, 'while the planters during the time of slavery, compelled their children and wives to work in the fields from morning to night, they now sent their children to school, and allowed their wives to fill the station for which they were intended, that of attending to their families and homes'.[153] Such a development dismayed the planters, since women and children had been an important part of the labour force on the plantations up to 1838. This was a serious economic blow, and another reason for attempted coercion. As Fishbourne reported from Buff Bay, they again attempted to use their control over housing to control labour. 'Planters are unwilling to permit families to reside on their plantations,' he wrote, 'the females of which refuse to devote themselves to agricultural labour.'[154]

One response of the peasantry to these various attempts at coercion was resistance. Troubles over rents on the Spring Hill coffee plantation erupted in July 1839, and magistrates and constables had to be sent in. They were met with a violent reception, women being particularly conspicuous in the stone throwing that ensued.[155] The more common reaction, however, was to try and obtain land, by squatting or buying. 'I observe a great desire among the negroes to purchase land,' commented the stipendiary magistrate in the parish of Clarendon, while Fishbourne noted that the effect of planter policies was that 'many respectable people are now availing themselves of opportunities of purchasing or leasing small pieces of land where they are preparing to place their wives and children, and where they also will retire when they can quit the estates, without sacrificing the provisions now in the ground'.[156]

Buying was a real possibility for significant numbers of freed men and women. A marketing system had been established on the island for decades, and plantation owners had relied on food grown on the provision grounds of the enslaved (land which was usually not suited to sugar production), substantial quantities of which were sold in local markets. Knibb, questioned in 1842 by the Select Committee on the West India Colonies as to the 'wealth' of the negroes – which had been made much of in England – responded:

> The reason why so many of them have been enabled to purchase land has been this: during the apprenticeship, and some times during slavery, they gained money by rearing fowls, and by their own industry. During the apprenticeship they obtained a good deal of money by working over-hours, the cultivation of sugar not being able to be carried on during crop by the eight or nine hour system; so that, as a reference to the parliamentary papers will show, a number of them purchased their apprenticeship, many others saved up their money till they were free, and then purchased free-holds for themselves; so that it is not because they have had extraordinary wages since they were free, but because they were thrifty, looking forward to freedom.[157]

Some freed people were able to make independent purchases of land. Others relied on the block sales made particularly by the Baptist missionaries and then bought from them. The hunger for land was commented on everywhere.

For Lord Olivier, one-time governor of Jamaica and a passionate protagonist of the free peasantry, writing many years later, this desire for land was connected to the old-established African view that unoccupied land belonged to the king as the trustee of the people – a belief that was powerfully in play at the time of the Morant Bay rebellion, and that Philip Curtin also sees as a significant factor in the move to land settlement.[158] Sidney Mintz argues that for ex-slaves to seek the ownership of land was at one and the same time an act of Westernisation and an act of resistance to the plantation economy – an assertion of their personhood.[159] Squatting on unclaimed land was one possibility, but undeveloped land presented problems. The decline in sugar production associated with the severe labour problems in the wake of emancipation meant that estates were falling ruinate. Land was for sale. This was the opportunity which the Baptist missionaries seized.

Joseph Sturge had kept closely in touch with developments in Jamaica after 1838. He was an avid reader of Parliamentary Papers, often extracting reports for the *Anti-Slavery Reporter*, the publication of the new post-emancipation British and Foreign Anti-Slavery Society, which he had inspired. He was also in regular correspondence with several of the Baptist missionaries, including William Knibb in Falmouth and John Clark in Brown's Town, and he used this correspondence to provide reports for the English press. His early assumption that the peasantry would stay on the estates had to be abandoned in the face of the rent demands, the evictions and the struggles over wages. Freed men and women could only be made into free labourers, or peasants, if their employers would play their part too. In October 1838, only two months after emancipation, he mentioned confidentially in a letter to John Clark that 'some of us are trying to get out a little plan for the purchase of land for the establishment of independent negro villages'. 'As soon as the negroes can possibly be made independent of others in pecuniary matters,' he argued, 'I am persuaded that it will add to their happiness and moral elevation.' He added that Clark should look out for suitable spots where there would be good bargains, and that he should urge the value of independence on the negro.[160]

This notion of independence was central to the vision of Sturge, to the Baptist missionaries, and to the abolitionist public. Manhood for them was associated with independence, the capacity of a man to stand on his own feet, to look after those who were properly dependent on him, his wife and children. When Sturge urged that 'the negro' should be taught the value of independence, he meant the negro man, whilst the negro woman should learn a new form of dependence, not on her owner but on her lawful husband. Slavery had produced an unnatural phenomenon: male slaves who were entirely dependent on their masters, who could not, therefore, truly *be* men. Emancipation marked the moment at which they could cast off that dependence and learn to be men, in the image of the middle-class Englishman.[161] Being independent 'in pecuniary matters' was a central aspect of that new masculinity: becoming a householder with all the responsibilities attached to it, enjoying the freedom associated with the old maxim that 'an Englishman's home is his castle', paying for medical care and for education, celebrating the 'voluntary principle' which was at the heart of dissenting politics, the refusal of state intervention in church, in schools, in welfare. Jamaica offered an exceptional opportunity to carry this voluntary principle fully into effect. With a weak established church and a strong dissenting presence, with a state which had depended on the plantation to provide basic forms of care, the breakdown of the old system provided a moment to build a new society. The potential for that new society lay, both for Sturge and for the missionaries, in the linked moments of emancipation and conversion. Emancipation gave men and women their political, social and economic freedom. But only conversion gave them a new life in Christ, the possibility to be born anew, to be new black subjects, washed clean of old ways – new black men and women.

This was the abolitionist dream – a society in which black men would become like white men, not the whites of the plantations but the whites of the abolitionist movement, responsible, industrious, independent, Christian; and in which black women would become like white women, not the decadent ladies of plantation society, locked into their degrading acceptance of concubinage, but the white women of the English abolitionist imagination, occupying their small but satisfying separate sphere, married and living in regular households. The gender order of the abolitionists was, therefore, central to their vision of the new Jamaica. Black men would survey their families with pride, and black women would no longer be sexually subject to their masters. A new marital economy would emerge, modelled on that of the English middle classes. The mission family, both literally – the missionary, his wife and his children – and symbolically – the linked families of all those attached to the missions – provided the keystone to the new utopias. Congregations constituted families and were all part of the family of man, whether black or white. They were, furthermore, attached to the family of God in part through the familial bonds with the spirits of those departed and in heaven. Each family, as we have seen, was in theory dominated by a patriarch, connected through a chain of male power to God the Father.[162]

These free villages took some building. In November 1838 Sturge wrote to Clark, telling him again that 'We are trying to form a little land company partly for the location of negro villages'. At the same time Knibb was writing to him denouncing the planters as 'slave-tyrants' and informing him that he was on the look-out for land in his area. With his large mission based in Falmouth and surrounded by sugar estates, Knibb was at one of the centres of the struggle over rent, wages and land. He was not slow to seek help from his many supporters in England to buy that land, as we see, for example, in a letter to the Rev. James Hoby, an old friend and long-time supporter of the BMS, the minister of Birmingham's Mount Zion Baptist Church, and a close associate of Sturge's on anti-slavery issues. 'Last night I had offered me', he told Hoby,

> in a lovely spot, 500 acres of land, with a good house thereon, just where we need it, for £1,000 sterling. I shall buy it today and I earnestly beg you to procure me the loan of £500 or £600, for twelve months. Do take this to Mr. Sturge, and I am sure he will assist. I will pay interest, and I am confident that I can return the principal within the time I mention. ... The land is excellent. It is in the mountains ... My plan is to convey the house and a few acres of land to the mission, and to resell the whole

Baptist chapel and dwelling house at Sligoville, one of the first of the free villages. Visitors were impressed by the beauty of the surroundings.

From J. M. Phillippo, *Jamaica: Its Past and Present State* (John Snow, London, 1843).

of the rest to the members of the church of Christ, who may be oppressed, or who may wish to purchase. It shall be sold in lots of one, two, or three acres, so that on the erection of a house the occupier may have a vote at the elections.

The next day Knibb wrote to Sturge telling him that he had bought the land and called it Birmingham. Moreover, he intended if possible to purchase the first estate that came up for sale near him. 'The possession of 2,000 acres would teach these oppressors of men that we were beyond their power,' he argued. 'We would line our streets with gardens,' he continued, 'and the back lands would do for provisions and grass for the cattle. I do hope that my little Birmingham will never be cursed with a church establishment, or a monopoly; but that I shall live to see civil and religious liberty shedding on it all their lovely influences.'[163]

Much of Knibb's conception of the free villages and the new society is contained in these letters. Freedom had no meaning, he believed, unless the people could be rid of the oppression of the planter. The land should be bought and sold, and loans would be paid back with interest, while a portion of the land would be kept for the mission. The prime candidates for this land were church members, and the lots sold would be large enough to procure a vote, but not adequate to produce a living. Men, therefore, would continue to work on the estates and be able to return to their homes and families in the evening. It was vital to be able to demonstrate that such settlements would not undermine the employment of free labour. The new villages, named in honour of their helpers and supporters, would be havens of civil and religious liberty. They would become new communities, centred on the mission and the missionary, an alternative to the old and corrupt world of the estate. The struggle for emancipation, as Alex Tyrrell points out, was being redefined – it was becoming a movement for the civil rights of the freedmen.[164]

By January Knibb was able to tell Sturge how delighted he would be by the success of 'our little Birmingham'. It was already serving as a refuge, and about seventy families had bought land on which to build houses. 'A school-house is commenced, and the preaching of the gospel will be regularly maintained. . . . If a few sugar estates are abandoned so much the better, eventually it will be the making of Jamaica. Sugar is sweet but the liberty of man is much more sweet.' In May he was reporting to Sturge that the Baptists were particularly persecuted on the estates, and that this was producing 'a longing for a home . . . a home of their own'. He told the story of one of his church members, a poor old woman called Rasey Shaw, named after the estate on which she had been enslaved, Shawfield, where she had worked since her birth. 'Her master had that evening ordered her house to be pulled down, which was done, and she was driven into the road, without a shelter or a home.' It was this constant persecution which inspired the purchases of land. 'We have the germ of a noble free peasantry,' Knibb proudly proclaimed to Sturge, insisting that the results of freedom must be judged not in the poundage of sugar, 'but by the cottager's comfortable home, by the wife's proper release from toil, by the instructed child, and by all that joy and peace which now gladdens the hearts of the beloved people of my choice.'[165] By September, the first edition of the *Baptist Herald and Friend of Africa*, 'a cheap publication by which the labouring population might be instructed in a knowledge of the rights and privileges which belong to them as free men', blazoned on its front page an advertisement for land for sale, 'to suit buyers among the labouring peasantry' in 'Sturge's Town, New Burmingham [sic], Hoby's Town' and other free villages.[166]

Sturge, meanwhile, was pushing ahead with the Land Company. In January 1839 he told Clark that it would be small-scale and would require repayments, but that these could be over a three- to five-year period if necessary. In February ninety shares had been taken up, but by October it was still unclear whether it would succeed. Land had already been purchased for the company, however, with Clark acting as the steward. Among those properties was Sturge Town.[167] Clark bought the land for Sturge Town, about seven miles from his base in Brown's Town, and by the autumn of 1839 one hundred families had moved in and a school had been established.[168]

Knibb reported on these developments in his triumphant speech at the 1840 Anti-Slavery Convention in London on the effects of emancipation. He told his audience of the wonderful increase in 'morality, social order and domestic happiness', of the 'universal observance of marriage', of industry wherever the negroes were 'fairly treated'. He warned, however, of the attacks on wages and unjust laws, maintaining that if this persisted, 'they must and would enable the negros [sic] to obtain free settlements for themselves, where tyranny could not reach them, and the power of the oppressor could not be felt'. This was greeted with loud cheers from the audience. He was pleased to be able to tell them that there were already at least 1,000 freeholders in Jamaica, and he had just received excellent reports of a new settlement he had established. He had visited it before leaving the island, and 'he had seen the people there in their proper places and the Bible on the table'. This evoked further cheers, the 'proper places' presumably meaning women in their homes and men preparing for work. 'Already they had established in Jamaica', he continued,

> a number of free villages, one of them bearing the name of their venerable president Clarkson, another was called Birmingham, and a third they had named Victoria. (Enthusiastic cheering.) To show their respect for that esteemed man Joseph Sturge – (Loud Cheers) – they had a town which bore his honoured name, although that was not needed, for it was deeply engraven on every negro's heart. (Renewed cheers.)[169]

Sturge himself, at a meeting in Birmingham (England) in 1843 to celebrate the anniversary of 1 August, referred to the names given to the villages, 'which afford a pleasing evidence of the grateful sense entertained by the people of the exertions of those kind friends and benefactors who had exerted themselves in the cause of freedom. One village was called Wilberforce, another Buxton, and another Sturge Town.' This gratitude, of a freed people to those who had given them their freedom, was taken by the abolitionists as their right, and provided the dominant contemporary interpretation of the dynamic of emancipation. The freed men and women thanked the abolitionists and the British public, the planters

Clarkson Town. A vision of a Baptist free village, with the chapel at the centre and the small houses and gardens neatly laid out.

From Phillippo, *Jamaica*.

blamed them, and the abolitionists congratulated themselves for what they had achieved. In the abolitionist view, the emancipated peasantry owed good behaviour to the British nation for their magnanimous gift of freedom, at the cost of 20 million pounds of taxpayers' money in compensation to the planters. The naming of villages after the great figures associated with emancipation – Clarkson Town, after the indefatigable campaigner against the slave trade and slavery, Thomas Clarkson, with its main street named after Joseph John Gurney, the Quaker abolitionist; Wilberforce, renamed Refuge; Thompson Town, after George Thompson the radical anti-slavery lecturer; even Knightsville, named by John Candler after his sister-in-law, the abolitionist and feminist Anne Knight. Other villages were named after supporters and patrons, as in Hoby Town, named by Knibb for his friend. Others again were named after places in England which had significance for the anti-slavery struggle: thus Birmingham, which became New Birmingham, and Kettering, named by Knibb after his birthplace.

Kettering, Jamaica, was one of the early villages founded by Knibb, not far from his base at Falmouth and close to Wilberforce, which was up in the hills. The missionaries had to be ready to follow their congregations in the wake of emancipation, for land had to be bought where it was available. It was the willingness of the Baptists to move with the people, at a time when the Anglicans were certainly not, that was in part responsible for the scale of their influence. Knibb reported to the BMS in 1844, for example, that a third of his congregation had moved out of town, and he had to follow them.[170] The site which became Kettering was on the main route along the north coast. By August 1841 three hundred building lots had been sold, the sinking of a well was planned, a normal school (or teacher training establishment) with an English woman teacher, a Miss Anstie, who was to train 'native' young women to be teachers themselves, had been established, and Knibb's Falmouth congregation had decided to build a house for him there. This was reported in the *Baptist Herald*: 'as a testimony of the confidence they have of his integrity in the application of all monies committed to his care, they have resolved to erect for him and his family a comfortable residence, at Kettering, the corner-stone of which was laid by two of the deacons of the Church, Messrs. Barrett and Reid.'[171] Philip Cornford, newly arrived with a group of Baptist missionaries and teachers in Jamaica, described in his later reminiscences the wonderful welcome he received from Mrs Knibb at that new house and the ease with which she arranged for mattresses to be spread on the floor so that the whole party could stay.[172]

By 1842 'a beautiful village' was 'fast rising' at Kettering, and it was chosen as the place to commemorate the fifty-year jubilee of the BMS, a huge celebration attended by thousands. Knibb went the same year to England for the jubilee celebrations there, attended the services in Kettering, and was deeply moved by the graves of his son Andrew (who had died on a previous visit) and his mother, by the place of his birth and his childhood, by his meeting with his twin sister and his old Sunday school teacher. Thus the emotional links for him between the two places were bound more tightly. In December 1844 he wrote from Jamaica to J. C. Gotch, master shoe manufacturer and mainstay of the town's Baptist chapel, about the progress of little Kettering. 'The village', he reported,

is now assuming a very interesting appearance, and in a few years will be a flourishing little town. It is laid out in four hundred building lots, which, with very few exceptions, are sold. Regular streets intersect each other, and neat cottages are rising on every hand. My own dwelling-house stands in the centre, with a neat chapel and school-room adjoining, and already nearly two hundred of the members of my church have here fixed their abode. The grand road through the island, from Kingston to Montego Bay, runs close to the land, and a village named Duncan's, where there are a post-office and a market, is situated on the other side of the road. . . . Thus I dwell among my own people, though in a foreign land.

Knibb had hoped to raise the money for a new church at Kettering in memory of the jubilee, but was unsuccessful in this. The chapel eventually erected in 1862, long after his death in 1845, and repaired after the storms and hurricanes which have ravaged the modest buildings typical of country Baptist churches, still stands, just beside 'the grand road through the island', two miles from the sea and with a view of Cuba on clear days. The girls' school, run by Mary Knibb and her daughters, with regular financial help from the Ladies' Negro's Friend Society in Birmingham, survived for many years.[173]

Most of these villages were named by their missionary founders and give us little clue as to the sentiments of their inhabitants. The grateful populace of one new village, however, decided to call it Phillippo, as reported in the Jamaican *Baptist Herald*. 'In so many instances had their temporal interests been promoted by their Minister in these small settlements', they said, that they wanted to record their public obligations by 'associating his name with the place':

> To so great an extent had these been the means of promoting their domestic happiness and their agricultural usefulness, that they availed themselves of this occasion to testify their respect and gratitude to him, and unanimously named it PHILLIPPO. . . . and as the intellectual welfare of their children had been attended to by their Minister in laying the foundation of a school in the centre of the village, they named some of the streets after his children, and after the county in England with which they were connected by family ties, and with which *they themselves* were linked by friendly cherished names in the great act of Negro Emancipation.

Furthermore, they named streets after Thomas Fowell Buxton, the parliamentary leader of the anti-slavery group, Wilberforce and Joseph John Gurney, the eminent Quaker, 'whose late visit to the colony they had all recollected as one of the most interesting incidents that had occurred since their full and entire deliverance from bondage'.[174] A gravestone in the Baptist chapel at St Ann's Bay memorialising a J. Sturge Brown, schoolmaster, born in 1869, provides a more individual instance of this connection, across generations and oceans, linking the birth of a child in freedom with the work which Sturge had done, and reminding us of the importance of naming patterns in sustaining collective memories. This naming of streets, of villages and of people laid trails across centuries and oceans which still echo powerfully today as the connections of the past are reconfigured in the present. The degree of identification with powerful white men and their families indicates the extent to which, in this period of transition, the free peasantry had to rely on those with leverage in England.

For missionaries had power. The celebration of missionary names by the free peasantry was associated with the access those men had to England and the potential to challenge planter control. Missionaries, by virtue of their connections with the abolitionist press and public, with the BMS in London and with distinguished public figures, could tap into channels of influence and power. Knibb's evidence to the select committees on slavery in 1832, for example, was widely regarded as important in the struggle for emancipation. The missionaries, despite their lowly social status associated with their class backgrounds and membership of the Baptist brethren, were white Englishmen with access to the governor, and through him to the Colonial Office. They regularly pressured their English contacts to take action over issues which were blocked by the Jamaican House of Assembly. The 'mother country' was necessarily the regular site of appeal – whether for money or for assistance in challenging new laws made in the planters' interests. In the setting up of free villages, missionaries could borrow capital, negotiate with merchants and lawyers, scrutinise deeds, and act as surveyors, planners and architects. Their whiteness, their use of 'proper English', their education and their training gave them, if not the actual skills, the capacity to learn what was required for all these activities. As Phillippo summed it up in his description of the free villages in his widely read book *Jamaica: Its Past and Present State*:

> The land required for the formation of these village establishments had, in most cases, been first purchased by the missionaries, who also surveyed and laid out the allotments, superintended the construction of the roads and streets, directed the settlers in the building of their cottages, and cultivation of their grounds, supplied them with their deeds of conveyance, formed societies among them for the improvement of agricultural operations, gave them a relish for the comforts and conveniences of civilised life, and improved their domestic economy. They endeavoured at the same time, by every means in their power, to convince these simple-minded people that their *own* prosperity, as well as that of the island at large, depended on their willingness to work for moderate wages, on the different properties around them.[175]

Missionary influence over the development of the free villages depended not only on opportunities to establish settlements. The missionaries also made use of sermons, public meetings and the press publicly to argue their cause both in Jamaica and in England. By 1840 they had decided that it was essential to build an electoral base and attempt to transform the nature of the House of Assembly. As the *Baptist Herald* put it, 'If an Assembly of whites will not give relief, men of darker colour will be found to fill their places.'[176] Thomas Burchell, in his speech to a public meeting in Montego Bay in 1840, was explicit about the political intentions behind the whole drive to buy land. He argued that with their own land and their own houses built on that land freedmen could say, 'This is my own . . . this is my castle . . . We are British subjects and now none dare to molest us'. Furthermore, there was the hope, albeit a hope not to be realised, that they could in time transform the political system through an expanded franchise: if land titles were registered, black men could vote and send 'good and honest men to the House of Assembly'.[177]

The missionary vision of the new life was developed, down to the last detail, in the columns of the *Baptist Herald*. Regular leaders and features offered advice to small settlers on the proper ways of 'colonising the interior', transforming the wastelands of the hills and the untenanted areas surrounding the big estates into new and 'civilised' communities. 'It is essentially necessary', cottagers were instructed,

> that you keep your houses clean, have their walls, or plaster, washed with white-lime water twice, or at least once a year; have a good wide path to the principal door of your houses, it will not cost you much labour, as it may easily be done in your spare time. If possible have a neat painted gate at the entrance to your garden. . . . Let all the dirt or trash that may accumulate from time to time, be carefully put together into one heap in a corner of your garden, which will be of service as manure . . . have a neat white-pine or cedar table, with a good few chairs in your room, so that you and your family may be comfortably seated at meals; have a clean table-cloth, plates, knives and forks on your table, and accustom your children to come to meals with their hands and faces clean; always implore the blessing of God before you eat your food; maintain family prayer in your houses.[178]

The missionaries drew on their knowledge of England for such advice, so practical remarks for housekeepers who were in 'straitened circumstances', for example, echoed English middle-class advice to the working classes. Their awareness of the rather different Jamaican context registered periodically, with perhaps a mention of the rum-shop inserted, but this might sit next to an extract from an almanac such as *Old Humphrey's* on blackberrying in the English autumn. For the most part, however, English advice could be transposed to Jamaica – housekeepers should rise early, keep clean, have their meals at regular times, ensure that there was a place for everything and everything in its place. A poor man's home kept clean by his wife was still the best place in the world.[179] The hope was that 'the establishment of the free villages will render the Negroes more independent of the White people, and thus show the latter the necessity of treating them with justice and moderation'. The 'White people' referred to here were the planters, not the missionaries, for it was no part of the missionary dream that black people would become independent of them. An editorial in the *Baptist Herald* was gratified to note that 'the growing determination there is among the labouring population to possess a house and land is most certainly indicative of growing intelligence and industry . . . the people are becoming more and more alive to their own interests; the feelings engendered and kept alive by slavery will very soon be extinct and their place will be taken by those that freedom calls into exercise and will sustain'. 'Buy now' and 'Build now' was the advice of the missionaries, for property gave independence and encouraged industry.[180]

Threaded through missionary discourse on the free village was the vision of a new set of relations between men and women. Cottagers would be more industrious, their wives more active and managing. The 'neat white-washed cottages which are arising everywhere around us, and adorning the landscape' would become 'the abodes of happiness . . . the nurseries of piety'. Detailed instructions were offered on the necessary infrastructure for a good family life:

> You should have a middling-sized hall, sufficiently large to have a table in the centre, with chairs around, upon which the husband, wife and children can be seated, and yet have sufficient room, for a person to pass between the chairs, and walls of the house. Three bed-rooms are necessary, you cannot do well with less, if you have children of both sexes; one bed-room will be required by the parents, one for the boys, one for the girls. You should also have a small place fitted up as a pantry, where you can put up your plates, dishes, basins etc. in order. In your bed-rooms, there is no necessity to have the mat upon the floor, it is more tidy, comfortable, and convenient to have a bedstead. . . . If you have a little taste for the ornamental a picture or two, in a neat frame, would look well, but do not purchase any that are foolish, or merely daubs.[181]

The new villages were encouraged to demonstrate a proper appreciation of the division of labour between the sexes. In Hoby Town men were urged to acquire property they could call their own. Real freedom depended on the ownership of homes, 'in which they will be able to live without submitting to exorbitant rent, unfair wages, or unmanly treatment'. In Sligoville, it was triumphantly reported, every man could sit 'under his own vine and under his own fig-tree, none daring to make them afraid'. In Ewarton, children, 'no longer under the shackles of slavery, are to be seen frolicing about the road'. Marriage was increasingly celebrated, newly-weds were greeted by entire villages, 'the decencies of society are no longer outraged by insufficient and filthy apparel', and women were beginning to abandon their gaudy dress and appear modestly clad. The men worked on the estates, and after work cultivated their grounds, while the women looked after their homes and gardens, some of which even had roses at the front. The townships themselves, imagined as infants, were also constructed as large families, 'united in bonds of Christian love and fellowship . . . with one feeling to prompt and one principle to govern'.[182] That 'feeling' and 'principle' were to be orchestrated by the father of the family – the missionary.

By 1842, when Knibb gave evidence to the Select Committee on West India Colonies, he could confidently report that even the planters were now reconciled to the free villages, recognising that men who had their own property were more inclined to continuous labour. He made it clear that the Baptist missionaries had so designed the land sales that male employment was essential to family survival. He was closely questioned by George Charles Grantley Fitzharding Berkeley, a member of the committee, who 'delighted in wearing at the same time two or three different-coloured satin under-waistcoats, and round his throat three or four gaudy silk neckerchiefs, held together by passing the ends of them through a gold ring'. Such decoration was not for negroes, however. Berkeley grilled Knibb on the astonishing reports he had heard of the mahogany four-posters, sideboards and chairs owned by the Jamaican peasantry. Knibb proudly responded that 'he would be very sorry to see them as badly off as the labourers here; half of them starving', and that their desire for respectability would ensure that they would continue to work.[183] Such respectability was firmly encoded in a familial culture.

Knibb was right in seeing the villages as a fixed part of the landscape by 1842. Governor Metcalfe informed the Colonial Office as early as 1839 that he was in favour of the peasantry buying land, despite his generally conciliatory policy towards the planters. He saw it as a source of increasing stability and unlikely to have bad effects on the supply of labour. By December 1840 he had collected information on the free villages from the stipendiary magistrates at the request of the Colonial Office, and reported that the numbers of freeholders across the island had increased from just over 2,000 to nearly 8,000. In Trelawny, where Knibb had been so energetic, the number had increased from 71 to 406.[184] This increase was not, of course, only due to the Baptist missionaries. Many individuals had bought land, and some had organised themselves into collectives to facilitate purchase. In addition, other missionaries – Presbyterians, Wesleyans and Moravians – were involved in establishing new settlements, and indeed sometimes came into conflict with the Baptists, as Hope Waddell did in Mount Horeb with Thomas Burchell.[185] In *Jamaica*, published in 1843, Phillippo (over)estimated that there were already between 150 and 200 villages, that 10,000 heads of households had purchased land, and that 3,000 cottages had been built. The increase in smallholders demonstrated by the census returns of 1844 was widely commented on, and Knibb used it to argue that 'full nineteen thousand persons, formerly slaves' had purchased land.[186] George Cumper suggests that by the end of the 1840s approximately two-thirds of the former estate population had left, and perhaps half of these had gone to free settlements, particularly in the eastern part of the island.[187] Thomas Holt argues that seven years after full emancipation, more than 21 per cent of the apprentice population had become resident on peasant freeholds, and that between 1844 and 1861 there was a dramatic shift of population from the western and eastern ends of the island to the centre. The most popular land for settlement was that made available from previously developed coffee and sugar estates, which was not too distant from markets, schools and churches.[188] Overall, there is no doubt that a significant class of freeholders had emerged.

Debates over the free villages were intimately linked with controversies about the place of the free peasantry in a post-emancipation world. What kind of society was Jamaica to be? The planters were convinced that the future of Jamaica depended entirely on the estates and sugar production. Others, including many of the Baptist missionaries, believed that Jamaica could have a different kind of future with a more mixed economy and peasant production for export. But the free villages were not tied into the international market as the plantations were, and this was to have many consequences. Knibb had hoped for a significant breakthrough in black political representation through the establishment of freeholds – an aspiration that was foiled by the political chicanery of the planting interest. The free villages were iconic in these debates, for they represented those independent spaces, created despite the planters, where the emancipated could live their own way, only partially dependent on wages. For the missionaries, of course, that way was meant to be *their* way, but this was a dream that was not to be realised.

The utopian vision of the missionaries and of abolitionists such as Joseph Sturge was to build 'the good society' in Jamaica. The free villages represented the ultimate moment of this missionary fantasy. Jamaica thus became a site for acting out white visions of how black people should live. That 'good society' was informed in part by the missionaries' displacement from their own society. As dissenting ministers, their class position was uneasy, their relation to conventional forms of political power marginal. In Jamaica, because of their pivotal role in the struggle for emancipation, they glimpsed new possibilities of power, which, as they saw it, they could use on behalf of the people, to build rural idylls which could never exist in corrupted and compromised England. 'The whole island . . . had to begin the world at once,' as Knibb put it to an English audience in 1845, for in his vision there was no world as yet.[189]

For Knibb there was the possibility of a new world – neither England nor the slave plantation – where black freedmen and white missionaries could build a new society, one with which he could powerfully identify. Black people living in the image of middle-class English people were for him 'my own people', living 'in a foreign land'. At one and the same time England and Jamaica were both places in which he belonged, and likewise, freed men and women belonged to both Africa and the Caribbean. His vision – and his was the vision which most fully articulated the missionary dream to both the English and the Jamaican public – was that of a black society led, initially, by white men. He dreamed of an independent Jamaica of the future, governed by black freeholders, made in the abolitionist image. His love for Jamaica was based on a conception of black people which both gave and denied equality in the present, while promising it for the future. The missionaries fought for equality before the law and equality in political representation, yet constructed 'their' people as their pupils, learning from them the ways of the world. Such a conception was underpinned by deep-rooted assumptions about white civilisation which worked on the premiss that the corruption of some white people could be redeemed by the action of others, that a particular version of English 'freedom' must be at the heart of any civilised society. Such a conception jostled in Knibb's mind with his knowledge and experience of both white and black societies. The language of abolitionism provided the tools with which to play upon these contradictions, for a universalist rhetoric of equality was articulated with ethnocentric and patriarchal assumptions as to the inevitability of social difference. The instabilities of a missionary identity, caught between two cultures, the interpreter of the one to the other, produced the dream of a third, where Africans and Englishmen would live harmoniously, in a missionary regime, a new Jamaica.

Such a dream was built, however, on the refusal to recognise an existing black culture. For, once established, the free villages could not be maintained in the missionary image. Phillippo's fantasy of his all-seeing, all-regulating, all-supervising hand and eye – buying land, designing houses, marrying parents, educating children – reckoned without the inhabitants of 'his' villages. For they were populated by black men and women and their children who brought their own culture, shaped by slavery, the middle passage and the plantation, and honed through their encounter with Christianity and the missionaries, to build their own syncretic forms of religion, their own rituals, their own practices, their own African-Jamaican way of life.

The missionary project, to 'colonise the interior' and create a civilisation of a new kind, was to be overtaken by the emergence of that distinctive peasant culture and the decline, from the mid-1840s, of the missionary presence and influence. But that presence has left its marks – in the commanding chapels on the hills which still play such a central part in country life, in the reinforcement it gave to the family, in the tradition of 'family land'. George Cumper sees the strengthening of the family as the abiding legacy of the free villages, for these villages had little contact with estate culture, hardly used local courts and relied on the church and the family as the regulatory institutions.[190] The power of the family has, furthermore, as Jean Besson has argued, been enshrined in the tradition of 'family land': the notion that land should be handed on from generation to generation, a heritage not to be sold. The village of Martha Brae, for example, was built on land where the Baptists had strong connections, and powerful links with Knibb's church in Falmouth have survived to the present. The origin of 'family land' was intimately linked with the free villages. Rather than simply being an imposition of the missionaries, it marked a reworking of ideas of private property, 'a dynamic cultural creation by the peasantries themselves in response and resistance to the plantation system and imposed styles of life'.[191]

According to the *Baptist Herald*, it was 'the emancipated sons of Africa' who erected the memorial to emancipation in Knibb's chapel in Falmouth 'when they came into the possession of that liberty which was their right, and of which they have proved themselves to be so pre-eminently worthy'. Two Africans were represented burying the broken chain, another was 'rejoicing in the undisturbed possession of the book of God', and 'a fond mother', joyously caressed 'the infant which for the first time she can dare to regard as *her own*'. But the vision represented there was that of the missionary dream: the dream of a new Jerusalem in Jamaica, of a society of new Christian subjects, living a familial, domesticated, industrious life in villages centred around a chapel, a mission school and a mission house. While the Africans in this monument were emblematic figures, likenesses of the good man and the good woman, specific English men – Granville Sharp, Wilberforce, Sturge and Knibb – were arrayed in bas-relief on the base. They were the named architects of freedom, the agents of history. The monument, made in Birmingham in 1840, captures that post-emancipation moment when the missionaries' future seemed secure. Their contribution to the winning of full emancipation had been widely recognised both in Jamaica and in England; freed men and women had flocked to their chapels, and the creation of free villages had further reduced the power of the plantocracy. They looked ahead to universal liberty for all nations of men 'who God hath made of one blood', with themselves in the vanguard.[192] But was this future secure?

2

Fault-lines in the Family of Man 1842–1845

Native agency and the Africa mission

In their dream society, peopled with new black subjects, white missionaries needed lieutenants. They hoped to be able to train 'natives' who would eventually be able to provide their own ministry. The debate over native agency began in the 1820s, in the shadow of the Native Baptist preachers who were always present on the island. In 1830 the BMS secretary, John Dyer, was reflecting on the possibilities. There must be some amongst the thousands connected with the Jamaican churches, he thought, with gifts which could be cultivated so that they could act 'in a subordinate capacity, as instructors of their countrymen'. Eventually, they might even be capable of carrying the Gospel back to Africa. He was aware that much caution was necessary, but thought it was time that the brethren began thinking about how to effect this, 'what methods of instruction and preparation should be adopted', whenever 'suitable individuals' appeared.[1] As early as 1828, Burchell, faced with a congregation of 1,000 for a 6 a.m. prayer meeting, was wishing that he could make use of native preachers as missionaries did in India.[2] But India was an ancient civilisation: Jamaica, in the missionary imagination, had to begin at the beginning.

This was a controversial matter amongst the missionaries, not all of whom believed that black men were ready to take on such responsibilities. Given the anxiety amongst the orthodox to separate themselves from the Native Baptists – the black sheep, as it were, of the Baptist family – but hold their members, it was imperative that a policy on native agency be developed. Without shepherds, a missionary wife commented, the poor people wandered about on the Sabbath 'like sheep out of pasture and under no discipline'.[3] Lost sheep were always in danger of becoming black sheep. John Clarke, who had been in Jamaica since 1829 and was based at Jericho in St Thomas-in-the-Vale from 1834, made use of native agents from 1835. In 1839 he was very ill, and much of his work was done by Joseph Merrick and his father, 'the first native labourers in the island' to be recognised by the BMS. They were both ordained in 1839. Joseph Merrick was classified as a 'quadroon' (a person of one-quarter black ancestry), and could pass for white outside Jamaica.[4] The father and son worked together, and were encouraged to involve their close relatives: another extension of the mission family. Miss Merrick, Joseph's sister, helped John Clarke run the day-school at Jericho.[5] But Clarke was not overly optimistic about the prospects in Jamaica. 'A very common trait in the character of natives who have some knowledge', he observed, 'is that they so soon stop short and think that they know much, while they know next to nothing.' It would only be when young people came through Baptist Sunday schools, he thought, that the situation would be seriously improved.[6] Similarly, Thomas Abbott, stationed on the island from 1831, reported that he had sent 'an intelligent and pious member' of his church, Henry Beckford, to conduct public services and a day-school in Coultart Grove (named after the missionary James Coultart). He did not want in any way to underrate his services, he reported, but he was in every sense of the term 'a native assistant'. Until recently he had been enslaved, and could not be expected to have 'that learning and information, that knowledge of the scriptures', and confidence in himself, requisite to the sole and efficient management of a mission station. He had delivered an address to the Auxiliary Missionary Society 'with much propriety', and if he continued 'studious and humble', all would be well.[7]

By 1838 Knibb was arguing that they must think about 'laying the foundation of a permanent ministry in Jamaica', though he was convinced that 'for some time it will be necessary for ministers from England to have the principal stations, as fathers to the church'.[8] Thus the relations of power between 'white fathers' and 'black sons' were naturalised. Thomas Burchell, however, had serious reservations, as he explained in a letter to Dyer:

> It is not to the men, but to their present want of fitness, that I feel compelled to object. So far as the free coloured people are concerned, in consequence of their very defective and partial education, they were till lately deemed ineligible to the office of clerks or bookkeepers. With respect to the slaves, they could be instructed only by stealth, or in the Sunday school. Their acquirements, therefore, are very, very meagre indeed. Yet, this is no reflection upon them, but rather upon that accursed system under which

they have so long laboured and suffered . . . this is not the age of miracles; and it is scarcely reasonable to expect that the negro churches can grow from infancy to manhood in a day.[9]

Here was the trope of natural development again, of negro churches growing from infancy to manhood, following in the footsteps of British churches. Traces of slavery, reflected Philip Cornford, a young missionary at Rio Bueno in 1841, meant that pastors had to have special qualities, qualities which could not be 'immediately forthcoming in a native pastorate'. 'The English missionary', he continued, in a paean of praise to himself and his brethren,

> is a beloved and reverenced man. He governs readily great multitudes without an effort. He is removed from all suspicions of natural partisanship. His very look is power. 'Me lub me minister', exclaimed a poor woman at Brown's Town, 'so me could kiss him foot, but same time when me see him come *me heart tremble*'. Thus, when his character sustains a native or acquired superiority which is felt by his people, they are easily guided by his word. But the native pastor cannot yet inspire reverence.[10]

The BMS, however, anxious for the day when the mission in Jamaica would no longer require financial support, and taking into account the model of the East Indies, where converts had been employed for some time, encouraged the Jamaican missionaries to go ahead in training 'native agents'. In 1839 the missionaries decided to press for a theological institution on the island. This strategy failed to recognise, argued Burchell's contemporary biographer, 'the difference which existed in the mental development of the partially educated Hindoos and the utterly untutored children of Ham'.[11] The notion of India as an ancient civilisation, Africa as a place without culture, was deeply embedded in missionary discourse.

'Native agency' was also an issue between missionaries and their congregations, especially the leaders and deacons. In mission stations across the globe, colonisers and colonised struggled to gain mastery over the terms of the encounter, as Jean and John Comaroff have argued in relation to South Africa.[12] While missionaries claimed power over the forms of language to be used, the lessons to be taught, and who might participate in what ways, their 'flocks' had different agendas. In April 1837 John Duff of Kingston and his colleague George Lyon wrote to Secretary Dyer complaining of missionary reluctance to let black men participate in the ministry. They wrote on behalf of a group of seven who were working together and servicing seventeen stations. The suggestion had been made more than once that leaders should be sent out as helpers to pastors, but the missionaries had rejected this. 'Considering the ignorance of the country', argued Duff and Lyon, it was absurd 'that we should be folding our hands and that men should come 4,000 miles, with such heavy expense, to preach the Gospel'. The missionaries were settled only in the towns and the country places where there was easy access. Meanwhile, thousands of souls were perishing for lack of knowledge in the mountain districts, and this group was not formally allowed to attend them. 'We conceive the opposition shown to us by your missionaries', they charged, 'is from prejudice.' They had imbibed the spirit of slavery. Black men were welcomed as leaders and helpers, but any suggestion that they might do anything beyond that was greeted with disapproval. They concluded that racial prejudice was the problem, resulting in the assumption that black men could not preach. Furthermore, jealousy was at issue too, a jealousy of the influence which they, as black men, had with their classes.[13]

By 1841 Duff, Lyon and others had decided to set up their own Jamaica Native Baptist Missionary Society to further their cause. Their manifesto spoke of the lack of Christian charity amongst the white missionaries and the difficulties which they had put in the way of black pastors. The justification for this was the lack of a classical education. 'But such a sentiment we deem in direct opposition to the truths of the Gospel,' they argued. The apostles, after all, were not educated at college. Black Baptists were not opposed to learning, but did not think that classical learning was appropriate for the Jamaican pulpit, for, especially in the country parts, this would be equivalent to speaking 'in an unknown tongue'.[14]

The rules of the new society determined that they would send the Gospel into 'the most benighted parts' of the island and that, as soon as they could, they would send men to Africa. Churches 'walking orderly' would be admitted to the connection, and 'persons of known piety . . . whose testimonials as to suitable talents . . . shall be approved of' would be set apart and ordained. The Rev. John Duff, who looked after three congregations in West Kingston, St Thomas-in-the-Vale and St Andrews, was uncompromising in his critique of the late Francis Gardner, Baptist missionary and pastor of East Queen Street in Kingston from 1832 to 1838. Gardner's 'haughty, overbearing conduct' had eventually driven the native agents out of the church.[15] Similarly, G. R. Lyon, who looked after congregations in Hayse Savannah, Milk River, Chapeltown and Marley Hill, placed the responsibility for the formation of the first of these stations squarely on the shoulders of the Rev. H. C. Taylor, another of the Baptist missionaries. The latter had levied 'peculiarly oppressive' dues on his people in order to pay for the new church which had been built, and behaved 'in a manner so repugnant to every principle of brotherly love, and Christian forbearance, as to deeply wound the feelings of many of his members' and provoke a secession. Lyon had then been invited to take on the 'spiritual oversight' of the new chapel, and judging that it was quite acceptable to separate from a church 'walking disorderly', had agreed.[16] William Duggan from Spanish Town had a similar story to tell. It was Phillippo's fault that they had formed a new chapel. Phillippo, according to Duggan, had asked him to give up his business and devote himself entirely to the work of the ministry. But he would not offer him adequate travelling expenses, never mind support for his wife and three children. Duggan, therefore, refused. This was not the end of the matter, however:

> I was after this severely rebuked by him for standing up to instruct my class-people, and in various other ways, endured much misrepresentation and slander, which so wounded my spirit, that after seeking divine direction, and with the advice of many of my Christian brethren, came to the determination of separating from a Church, with whom I could not walk in peace and love.

Despite all these provocations, however, the Native Baptists declared that they would not return evil for evil and would pray for all mankind, 'even for our bitterest enemies, slanderers and persecutors'.[17]

From this report it is clear both how close and how difficult were the relations between these groups of Baptists. Some of the Native Baptists had originally been in the congregations of Liele or Baker, others were seceders from orthodox congregations. They were subject to innumerable splits amongst themselves, and no doubt sometimes returned to regular Baptist congregations. It was the intimate connections between these different Baptists that made their relations so complex. There were no simple binary divisions between them; indeed, many of them were the same people, moving from congregation to congregation as the spirit took them. But, while black Baptists could move in this way, white Baptists could not. Native Baptists, Black Baptists and orthodox Baptists were all potentially part of the same family. 'The Black Family', the family of Baptists on the island as it was called by black people, was, like all families, subject to acute tensions and contradictions.[18]

The development of 'native agency' went alongside the call for a mission to Africa. Creolised Africans, born anew as Christians, could now return to their benighted country and rescue it from 'savagery'. The Exodus motif was profoundly significant for the missionaries. They saw themselves as Moses, leading their people to the promised land, and that promised land was Africa.[19] Africa was imaged as a place of lust and evil, as the young Philip Cornford imagined it in his poem 'To Africa':

Hail! land of gloom, and woe and blood,
Where hell has rolled its mightiest flood,
And curse on curse has found a lair
On which to propagate despair.

Hail! land of victims, chains and tears,
(Unnumbered through unnumbered years)
Of captive sighs and dying groans,
Of tortured limbs and bleeding bones.[20]

Africa, said the Rev. Samuel Oughton, minister of East Queen Street
Baptist church in Kingston and one of the leading missionaries on the
island by the early 1840s, at a meeting in Falmouth on behalf of the
Africa Mission, 'was only known by her groans', 'her interior appears
like a vast desert quite unexplored'.[21] Now it could be Christianised.
Knibb was eloquent on Africa. As he told his friend Dr Hoby in 1839,
he was keen to establish a Baptist mission in West Africa. 'A beloved
brother' he told him,

> one of the despised, traduced, black Christians, an African by birth, has
> left this island . . . has worked his passage to Africa, and . . . is now on the
> spot from whence he was stolen as a boy, telling his fellow-countrymen
> the name of Jesus. . . . Think of Africa, her wrongs, her sins, her openings.
> O my Heavenly Father! work by whom thou wilt work, but save poor,
> poor, benighted, degraded, Europe-cursed Africa! My affection for Africa
> may seem extravagant. I cannot help it. I dream of it nearly every night,
> nor can I think of anything else.[22]

His affection does indeed seem extravagant, his nightly dreams of Africa
a sign of the way in which that continent had entered his unconscious,
his identification striking, his desire to assuage Europe's guilt profound.
Knibb's plan was that a small group of 'pious black men' should be
trained first in Jamaica and then in England, then one of the white missionaries should accompany them to Africa and report back in a year or
two.[23] Horace Russell has argued that African-Jamaicans probably had
less enthusiasm for an African mission than did the missionaries.[24] Certainly at the series of meetings across the island in 1841 in support of
the Africa mission, the white missionaries tended to dominate, but sometimes the deacons spoke too. Edward Barrett, one of Knibb's favourite
lieutenants, encouraged his brothers and sisters to dig deep in their
pockets for Africa, 'our' country:

> We want them to have a large chapel, like this, that a great many may
> hear. You know they call the people in Africa *savages* – *savage people*, if

Africa receiving the Gospel. A missionary vision of grateful African men and women, ready for salvation.

From the *Missionary Herald*, 1841, reproduced by permission of the British Library, BL 480.

they are *savage* to man they are not savage to God. He did not think us too savage – He sent us the Gospel – He sent us our Ministers, so that we heard the way of Salvation. We had no chapels, but God help us, and Minister help us, so that we were able to build chapels, and now we can sit in our own pews in this house, and none can make us afraid.[25]

There was considerable interest in a mission in England, probably asso-ciated with the turn to Africa after emancipation: a vision which was to come to a disastrous end in the Niger expedition, Buxton's plan to take commerce and civilisation to West Africa.[26] The BMS was hesitant at first to provide any resources, but underwent a change of heart, partly because of the strength of Knibb's persuasion at a series of public meetings in England in 1840. Joseph Sturge was doubtful, concerned that 'this great and important work' might be prejudiced by the use of agents who were not properly qualified. It was 'beautiful' to see the enthusiasm of the 'negroes to extend their blessings to the land of their forefathers', but if sufficient care were not taken, it could result in serious mischief.[27]

Knibb's plea for Africa in England was based on the claim that emancipation had been a success and that black men had proved their worth: there was, therefore, great hope for Africa. Moreover, the Jamaican congregations were on the verge of being self-supporting, so money could soon be released from England for Africa. Asked whether black men would learn Latin and Greek before sailing for Africa, he challenged his audience that they were prejudiced. 'After 1838', he told them,

> a black brother in connexion with Mr. Gardner's church . . . worked his passage out to Africa. He is on the spot from whence he was stolen, proclaiming salvation through the blood of the Lamb. You honour, and justly honour, such men as Williams and Pearce [friends of the mission and white missionaries] . . . ; and because Keith is black will you forget him?[28]

Knibb was confident that Africans had only taken up with Islam because 'Christians have not sent them a better'.[29] The field was open, the possible rewards immense.

BMS acceptance of the scheme resulted in an experienced white missionary from Jamaica, John Clarke, being sent to West Africa to investigate. When he returned to Jamaica, where an independent missionary society had been established, he was met with great enthusiasm for the cause at meetings held across the island. Money was raised in both Jamaica and England, and in 1843 the *Chilmark* was ready for departure for Fernando Po, the chosen site in West Africa, with thirty-six potential missionaries, wives and teachers, as well as a pharmacist, a doctor, a mason and some farmers.[30] The recruits were not all entirely convinced as to what they were doing. The nineteen-year-old J. T. Fuller from Spanish Town, for example, had been impelled by the entreaty of his father and the strong desire of his pastor, the Rev. James Phillippo, to send representatives of the church. But he was not yet baptised. The ship set sail from Falmouth with a big farewell led by Knibb, at which the assembled congregation sang of leaving the native land they loved, 'far in heathen lands to dwell'.[31] Thus Africa was constructed as the heathen place, ready for conversion, and Jamaica as the Christian country which could offer salvation.

Difficulties began to surface almost immediately, however. The cook on board was not prepared to cook for black people, and this was the beginning of a series of issues over race. Fuller was astonished by his first encounter 'with a savage', shocked that he wore no clothes.[32] More seriously, tensions developed between John Clarke and the other white missionaries and the black missionaries, some of whom felt themselves to be mistreated. Clarke had been judged 'peculiarly suited' for Africa, because of his 'long study of the African character, and the attention he has bestowed upon their language, customs and manners'.[33] But his judgement of the character of the native missionaries was felt to be lacking. 'I think most of our Jamaica friends will turn out well,' Clarke had written to the BMS committee, 'but they need at present constant watching, directing, instructing. In Jamaica, they have not been called out to act for themselves. They are in a new situation altogether; and if we view their former state, opportunities, habits, etc. we shall not expect too much at first.'[34] Such sentiments were not appreciated: 'They do not count us as persons at all,' argued Norman, one of the group originally from Spanish Town. 'Mr. Clarke and the rest of the Missionaries have treated us worse than they do many of the Africans,' argued Ennis, another of the group who had gone out on the *Chilmark*. They had been told that they were going as assistant missionaries, and that provision would be made for their children, but instead there were attempts to treat them like servants and to claim that they could not teach, that their children were not worth educating.[35] Many of them had received only minimal education themselves, and this was a source of resentment. Fuller had gone to Phillippo's mission school in Spanish Town, but 'the instruction given was very circumscribed as it was supposed we had not the ability for much, and so we were denied that knowledge we might have obtained'.[36] Isolated in Fernando Po, without access to friends in England that the white missionaries had, the group appealed to members of their old congregation in Spanish Town to make representations to the BMS on their behalf. They wanted above all to receive enough money to be able to pay for their passages back to Jamaica. By 1847 the Jamaicans were back on the island, the African mission having been abandoned by both the Jamaican leadership and the membership. The idea of Jamaica providing salvation for Africa was finished.

If black and coloured men were to become preachers and missionaries, they needed to be trained. In 1843 a training college was opened for native agents, set in the hills above Rio Bueno on the north coast of Jamaica, at Calabar.[37] It was to educate Baptist young hopefuls in an orthodox manner, and was initially seen as preparing them for Africa.[38] Joshua Tinson, who had been on the island since 1822, mainly at Hanover Street in Kingston, was its first principal. He had run a school in Kingston and was a deeply cautious figure. He was determined to train his young men in traditional ways, to demonstrate with his classical syllabus that black men were indeed as intellectually able as white, according to the standards of the mother country. His vision was of a Jamaican national church rooted in interdependence with Britain.[39] Recognition of the importance of a national church, with coloured and black pastors, albeit initially trained by white men, marked a crucial break with the idea of a mission staffed entirely by Europeans. The issue as to whether to train 'natives' was a difficult one for all the denominations on the island. The Methodists had always had large numbers of coloured members, and they were accepted into the ministry relatively early. But, as Robert Stewart has shown, they resented their slow promotion, and tensions around this were compounded by tensions over the marriage of white ministers to coloured creole women. There were secessions over these issues in the 1830s, one of them led by Edward Jordan and another by Thomas Pennock, who protested to the Methodist Association, 'I do in my conscience most firmly believe that many of your Missionaries are deeply prejudiced against Colour.'[40] The absence of any attempt to train black ministers would suggest that he was right. Meanwhile the Anglicans were making no attempts to train 'natives'.

The decisions over the setting up of the Africa mission and Calabar proceeded alongside the declaration of independence by the Jamaica Baptist Association. The BMS had taken the first steps on this, considering retrenchment in the early 1840s, when their financial situation was weakened by the fall-off in donations after emancipation.[41] In 1842 the missionaries themselves decided to separate financially from England and become independent. In the preceding years the large influx of church members, together with the relatively prosperous state of the freed slaves, meant that it looked possible to be self-supporting. This change marked a significant break for the missionaries, and not all of them were happy with the decision: the mission family was divided. The divide ran to some extent along the lines of the east/west division which had been established in the Jamaica Baptist Association. On the western side of the island the key figure was Knibb, full of energy, optimism and hopes for the future. On the eastern side were Burchell and Phillippo, slightly more cautious, with their doubts about 'native' agency and independence from the mother country. Until 1838 the missionaries were agents for their societies, just as sugar and coffee agents acted for their organisations, reporting back to the metropolis and being responsible on behalf of the society.[42] The assumption was that white missionaries had to interpret the Gospel to those who needed the light of European salvation. The decision to weaken the formal connection between the BMS and the Jamaican Baptists was a recognition that there were now Jamaican

Baptists, potentially a national church, which might in time be able to organise things for itself. The Jamaican move at this time to establish the mission to Africa was a statement of optimism as to the resources of the Baptist community on the island, and a statement of belief that *they* could now become the evangelisers. The Jamaican Baptists were moving from being a mission to being a church.

The Baptist family

1842 marked a high point for the mission; but this success brought its own difficulties, and the Baptist family in Jamaica, meaning all Baptists on the island, was seriously divided. The numbers of recruits bred rivalries between missionaries, and provoked envy amongst the agents of other societies on the island. In 1842 the missionaries decided to take on in public a long simmering set of disputes amongst their critics, and Knibb went to England to make their case. At the heart of these disputes, and of the difficulties of the missionaries themselves, was the relation between Native Baptists and the orthodox. The missionaries' construction of new black subjects and a new community, a new Jamaica, depended on the belief that conversion washed the sinner clean, washing away the sins of Africa and of slavery, and left new-born babes in Christ. These babes could be schooled to become new men and women, in the image of the white man and woman, potentially equal yet different. Conversion was understood as a turning-point, from which there should be no turning back; yet the widespread concern with 'backsliding' indicated how unstable that supposedly fundamental change could be.[43] The accusation made by the enemies and critics of the missionaries was that the latter deluded themselves, that their charges were not really saved: they neither understood the Gospel, nor had received Christ. Rather, these so-called Baptists were revisiting Africa, replaying African superstitions and reworking African beliefs. Far from constructing new men and women – civilised, industrious, domesticated and familial – the missionaries were providing spaces for revivals of barbaric ritual which only served to demonstrate how far freed men and women were from being truly emancipated.

The Baptist faith in Jamaica grew from the work initially done by black Baptists from North America. Black Baptist congregations were established in the Kingston, Spanish Town and Montego Bay areas. The most influential figures in those early days were George Liele and Moses Baker, and it was Baker who had invited the BMS to send missionaries to help him. One articulate critic of the Baptists was the Rev. Hope

Masterton Waddell, sent to Jamaica in 1829 by the Scottish Missionary Society and working in an area where Moses Baker had had a considerable impact. Waddell served first in Falmouth and then at Cinnamon Hill, part of the Barrett family property on the island. He settled with his wife, his 'true yoke fellow', at Cornwall, just by the sea and surrounded by numerous estates.[44] Waddell was a close associate of George Blyth, one of the most public critics of the Baptists. Waddell's autobiography, which deals with his years in Jamaica and West Africa, provides interesting insights into the vexed question of the relation between Native and orthodox Baptists. He soon encountered the effects of Moses Baker's teaching and concluded that Baker was a good man, zealous but ill informed and very superstitious. He had initiated his followers

> into a strange system of mingled truth and error, which his leaders carried to the length of a monstrous superstition. . . . The grand doctrine of these people was the Spirit's teaching. It gave life. The written word was a dead letter. If they could not read the Bible they could do without it, which was as good. The Spirit was sought in dreams and visions of the night, which thus became the source of their spiritual life. . . . Doubtless they would see and hear strange things in their excited imaginations, and the leaders could make what they liked of them. The result of such a system among such a people may be imagined.

Such a system – where leaders have too much power, there is no control from above, and no rational mind to construct boundaries – coupled with such a people, childlike, uneducated, uncivilised, easily led, prone to superstition, meant that the dangers were immense. Waddell argued that for a time the connection with the English missionaries had counteracted these influences, but that 'a permanent injury' had been inflicted.[45] This 'injury' was exposed when outbreaks of myalism occurred in 1841.

Myalism, argues Monica Schuler, stemmed from a dynamic African religious tradition.[46] Its origins were in eighteenth-century Jamaica, and Edward Long was the first European to record it. By the 1830s and 1840s myalists believed that all misfortune stemmed from malicious forces, embodied in the spirits of the dead and activated by the unfriendly. Myal men were the specialists who could identify the spirit causing the problem and exorcise it. Harm inflicted by obeah, or sorcery, which usually involved injuring others by the use of charms, poisons and shadow catching, which Patterson argues had its origins in West African 'bad medicine', could be undone by myal dance, 'good medicine'.[47] In the late eighteenth century, myalism had moved into a new phase, absorbing certain aspects of the Baptist version of Christianity. The

Baptist stress on both the inspiration of the Holy Spirit and baptism by immersion echoed traditional West African religious beliefs about the importance of water and the significance of dreams. 'Myalism', argues Stewart, 'combined the best of Christian hope with the this-world-directed power of African religion.'[48] This powerful syncretic force was mobilised to prevent misfortune. Ills, whether hunger, pain or oppression, were caused by sorcery, it was believed, and could be eradicated. The rituals of exorcism reflected forms of African identity which deeply troubled the missionaries.

John Candler, the Quaker sent by the Society of Friends to spend a year in Jamaica and report on the state of the emancipated peasantry, was astonished by his encounter with a myal man. It happened when he was travelling with Joseph John Gurney, the Quaker banker who was also visiting the island to observe the effects of emancipation. 'The doctor', described Candler,

> a black young man of about twenty, very fashionably attired, came in with the easy manners of a perfect gentleman, and taking his seat, called for a glass of water, which was brought him with haste and reverence by one of the company. At first he only professed to cure diseases by the administration of simple medicines, suited to the disease complained of; but, on being pressed further, told us that he was qualified to hold discourse with good spirits of the dead, who intimated to him all the secret and hidden evils of the human body, such as no human eye could penetrate, and that by this means he could effect cures which no white man could perform. We asked the people whether they believed this; they said with one voice, 'We do believe it', and seemed astonished at our incredulity.

Gurney then spoke to them 'on the folly of such superstition', and his own account of the meeting concluded optimistically: 'We were sorry to observe the obstinacy of their delusions, but such things will be gradually corrected by Christian instruction.'[49] The unspoken worry was that they might not be.

Waddell's definition of myalism focused on its relation to obeah. According to his observation of these African 'superstitions', any object – a nail, a fragment of cloth, a shell – might serve as the instrument or means of the malign influence associated with obeah. This object, with a spell cast upon it by the obeah man, when

> placed in a person's garden or house would find its way into his body, and afflict him with an incurable disease, or blast his property and labours, producing all kinds of misfortunes. A person under that curse felt condemned; his health and interests were ruined; everything went wrong with him; he pined away and died. The hidden 'poison' could be discovered and

counteracted only by its proper Myal antidote, which the initiated alone knew.[50]

While slavery survived, the planters worked hard to prevent any expression of these beliefs, but with emancipation and the arrival of new African labour from New Guinea, there was a revival of African rituals and beliefs. Christmas 1841 and summer 1842 brought significant expressions of such belief systems in the area of Waddell's mission; indeed, twenty-two villages were affected in the St James and Trelawny areas.[51] He was pained to observe that many of the active participants came from 'the principal missionary churches'. 'It was the strangest combination of christianity and heathenism ever seen,' he commented. Those seized with the Spirit claimed that they were sent 'to purge and purify the world'; they 'were Christians of a higher order than common'. They engaged in singing, dancing and 'various peculiar rites', rites in which Waddell tried to intervene. He went to visit a spot at which a special meeting was to be held. There he found a ring,

> around which were a multitude of onlookers. Inside the circle some females performed a mystic dance, sailing round and round, and wheeling in the centre with outspread arms, and wild looks and gestures. Others hummed, or whistled a low monotonous tune, to which the performers kept time, as did the people around also, by hands and feet and the swaying of their bodies. . . . [Waddell entered the circle and tried to address them] Some proposed that I should first sing a hymn, and I commenced one; but observing how much it affected them, ceased, and began to pray. That calmed them for a while, but soon they grew impatient, and resumed their own song, and the dancing women their performances. Turning to the manager, I said, 'If you don't keep these mad women quiet, we cannot go on with the worship of God'. Thereupon a strange hubbub arose. 'They are not mad.' 'They have the spirit.' 'You must be mad yourself, and had best go away.' 'Let the women go on; we don't want you.' 'Who brought you here?' 'What do you want with us?'[52]

In Waddell's account, a quarrel then broke out, and the myalists were defeated. These wild women, seized with the Spirit, with voices and dance, were profoundly disturbing to Waddell, given his Scottish Calvinist sense of propriety and self-control. They were mad, this was the only way to make sense of it. Their questions as to *his* sanity, *his* right to intervene, did not seriously disturb his equilibrium.

A further myal outbreak then took place on the neighbouring Palmyra estate. Waddell tried to prevent it, this time with the aid of a Baptist leader whose own 'class had joined the Myal company, and taken possession of his prayer-house for their heathenish practices'.[53] Meanwhile people on the Hampden estate were also seized with the excitement, and the teacher there, a Mr Drummond, described to Waddell the men and women 'reeling and staggering about, moaning and striking themselves', some of the men seemingly 'possessed of the devil', running up and down like mad dogs. Waddell's conclusion regarding all these manifestations was to connect them 'with a corruption of Christianity', the Native Baptist system, which, 'erring on the subject of the Holy Spirit's work in man's heart, accepted the delusions of the Myal spirit as if the operations of the Spirit of God'.[54]

The Baptist missionaries were very disturbed by these outbreaks. Philip Cornford argued that it was the scars of slavery that were to blame, and that 'the white man was king in crime', the source of the evil which left these marks. He was horrified by 'the madness' which sometimes seized the people. Families would be broken up, husbands and wives would abandon each other, mothers would leave their children, and a frenzy of screaming and howling would seize those who were taken.[55] The chapel at Salter's Hill, where Walter Dendy had been the missionary for ten years, was the site of a dramatic eruption in December 1842. 'A fearful spirit of delusions came over many persons who resided on estates near Ironside-by-the-Sea':

> Some of the members and inquirers became affected with it, and seemed fascinated as by a spell. On the 25th December they entered the chapel at Salter's Hill . . . They ran about like mad persons, jumped on the benches, began to speak wildly, and interrupted the worship. (Mr. Dendy asked the congregation to keep calm, the Myal men and women were removed and the deacons guarded the doors.) Mr. Dendy preached from Ephesians vii: 'Have no fellowship with the unfruitful works of darkness, but rather reprove them.' Towards the close a woman came in, and ran wildly about the chapel with pictures in her hands. She exhibited one, which was intended to represent the crucifixion of the Saviour, and lifting up her eyes in a peculiar manner, curtsied to it. The myalists rushed into the chapel, with frantic gesticulations. They tore away ornaments from the females, and the watch-guards of the men.

The magistrate was applied to, and the police arrived to arrest and charge the offenders, but the 'bad effects' of these practices were said to be felt by the members of the chapel for a long time to come.[56] This was home territory. Outbreaks which took place directly on missionary premises made it hard to argue convincingly that Native Baptists and myalists had nothing to do with 'proper' Baptists. Knibb's firm declarations to the select committees in 1831–2, that Native Baptists hated them and kept themselves quite separate, tell us about the missionary anxiety to draw firm boundaries where no such boundaries existed, to mark those who were within from those without, those who believed the right things from those who were deluded, those who were really Christians from those who were really heathens. The problem with these constructed binaries was that they tried to make distinct what was not, for the missionary regime of truth did not always hold.

By 1842 accusations about the relation between native and orthodox had been circulating for more than a decade. The missionaries decided to attempt to seize the initiative by going public.[57] Their main accusers were Anglican clergy, Methodist and Presbyterian missionaries, and three disaffected Baptists: Whitehorne, who had severed his connection with the BMS some ten years previously, and Kingdon and Reid, who were both still active. At the same time the BMS also went public, publishing the results of its internal investigation into the complaints.[58] The central criticisms, repeated in numerous private letters and newspapers, as well as in the pamphlet war which took place, were that the employment of leaders was degrading and demoralising, that the use of tickets of membership was deeply injurious, that baptisms had taken place too hastily and without sufficient preparation, and that superstitions were rife amongst so-called Baptist church members and inquirers. In addition, there were accusations that the missionaries had benefited financially from their large congregations, that some of them were living in ostentatious luxury quite inappropriate to their calling, and that they had relied on their wives to do work which they should have done themselves, thus offending propriety and undermining the status of the ministry as a calling.[59]

In 1838 the Rev. Richard Panton, an Anglican, had written to the BMS committee complaining that Baptist congregations were in a very corrupt state because of the presence of Native Baptists and the influence of the leaders. When the original teachers had left the island, he explained, the congregations were left under the supervision of those who could not read, had no Bibles, and fell into every excess. They were named 'Bow-Down-Baptists' because new converts had to come in on their hands and knees. They were baptised frequently, because they thought that the water washed away sin. The English Baptist missionaries, when they arrived, had had to form their congregations from these people, whose religion was mixed up with obeah and other expressions of beliefs derived from West Africa. The tickets which were given as tokens of membership, he argued, were used by the negroes as fetishes, seen as passports to heaven, buried with corpses, and understood as a reward for the contributions men and women had made to the church. The missionaries, he claimed, simply did not know what was going on in their huge congregations; they had no control, and negroes were entirely used to deception, for 'deceit and lying are the great characteristics of the negro'. Whitehorne, one of the Baptist pastors involved in making accusations, was one of the few who really knew, for he was a native and could see the truth, Panton argued.[60] Meanwhile James Reid, one of the Baptist missionaries who was himself critical of the state of the churches, took up cudgels on another much-disputed issue, complaining to the BMS that well-known fornicators were baptised and admitted by leaders, and that some of the missionaries were colluding with this shocking state of affairs.[61]

'All the Negroes in Jamaica now call themselves "Christians", generally "Baptists", though their religion differs little from their old African superstitions,' wrote one angry Congregational missionary to his committee in London. 'The bulk of them', he continued,

> are enrolled in Classes under some black Teacher as ignorant as themselves; and they are connected by the purchase of a ticket with the Baptist Congregation in the nearest Town, where they go, and receive the sacrament once a month, or once a Quarter; but they are utterly ignorant of the simplest and plainest of God's commandments. They are too ignorant to understand and profit by the Public Preaching on the sabbath; and they never see the Missionary at any other time; for they live far away from him and he has thousands attending him whom he does not know. They are perishing in their sins, and stand as much in need of instruction as the Zooloos.[62]

It was the role of the leaders in this process which particularly aroused the ire of the critics, for how could the ignorant instruct others? The Rev. George Blyth, who wrote the collective critique of the Baptists for the Presbyterians, focused particularly on the missionaries' failure to assert their authority over the leaders: rather, they left their work to them, although they were quite unfit for the task. Few of them could read, and even those who could often saw the workings of the Spirit as far more important than the dead letters of the Gospel. He quoted Waddell's claim that 'They sometimes hear and interpret dreams, and then pronounce on the spiritual state of the dreamers, and their fitness for baptism, according to their own delusions'. Pastoral inspection was also left to the leaders and deacons, men whose standards were seriously lacking, and many of whom were themselves 'proved guilty of the grossest immorality'. Furthermore, the leaders exacted money from their classes, and were responsible for shocking and disgraceful superstitious practices in their meetings. His conclusion was that there was a close connection between Native Baptists, Bow-down-Baptists and regular Baptists.[63] The Rev. Hugh Brown, another Congregationalist on the island, complained to his parent society that he had encountered Baptist leaders who taught that immersion washed away sin and gave an inner wisdom and knowledge that made it unnecessary to go and hear a white minister, 'because dem

know all him can tell them'. As Robert Stewart shows, Brown cited a
leader who claimed that his followers did not need the Bible. 'Dem no
go by the book, but by dem heart. Massa Jesus himself no go by de
book,' he taught.[64] These claims – that the inner spirit was all that was
required for salvation, that ministers provided no essential knowledge,
and that the Bible was not at the heart of the Christian message – were
profoundly disturbing to the promulgators of the version of the faith
orchestrated through the missions.

Such criticisms were not confined to rivalrous white men: an African-
American woman, Nancy Prince, an active abolitionist who had been
inspired by a visiting missionary's account of the work to be done in
Jamaica, spent several months on the island in 1840. She was hoping to
work with children and 'raise up and encourage the emancipated inhabitants'. She was not impressed by her encounter with Mr Abbott, the
Baptist missionary in St Ann's Bay, who had little sympathy for the
women's societies with which she was associated in the USA and was
determined to back his class leader, who Prince thought ignorant and
foolish, against her. To her mind the system of class leaders was deeply
unsatisfactory, and the Baptist missionaries were far too concerned with
collecting money, and not concerned enough with the state of their congregation's souls.[65]

Faced with these public denunciations, the Baptist missionaries and
their friends felt compelled to defend themselves and their methods.
Their strategies were to undermine the evidence of their critics, to
provide counter-testimony which demonstrated that they were securely
in control of their subordinates, and to draw a rigid line of demarcation
between themselves and the Native Baptists. The accusations were
spurred by envy at their success, they claimed. Those who had 'failed of
their object' found solace in attacking those who had done better.[66] More
polemically, London Missionary Society agents were 'mean, snake-like,
crawling', worse indeed than the vilest slave-owners.[67] At a speech in
Exeter Hall before a great throng who greeted him with thunderous
applause, Knibb vigorously defended his own record and that of his associates. He had felt it his duty to come, he opened, though he would have
much preferred to remain 'among the beloved people of my charge' and
'surrounded by that domestic felicity which it has been my happiness for
seventeen years to enjoy'. His wife, however, had insisted that he should
come, and that they would manage without him for the good of the
cause. This evocation of his own conjugal bliss stood him in good stead
as he launched into his salvo. There was something unmanly, he argued,
in the critics' attack on 'our poor wives' and on the female character.
But all was well, he assured his audience, in missionary homes. The wives
were making the puddings, and the husbands doing the public work. It

was entirely appropriate, he insisted, that in a society like Jamaica, women should work with other women when necessary, a claim that was contemporaneously being made in England across the class divide rather than the racial divide, and also in other parts of the globe.[68] The relation between white men and black women was historically so corrupt that much delicacy was required. Consequently, 'A great deal of the examination of females for church-fellowship devolves upon our wives,' he reported: 'It is right that this should be done by females, who, though unobtrusive, are well qualified to form a judgement, and who know what the female mind of Jamaica is; who in their humble walk never slacken, though seldom praised, but are doing a work which angels will admire, and Jesus approve.'[69] 'The infernal system of slavery', Knibb had written to a friend in England earlier, had produced 'the most fatal effects upon the female slave. As she was treated like a *brute* so all feelings of modesty and propriety were lost in her condition.' It was vital that separate work should be done with women, that separate schools should be established for girls, so that they could be trained in both knowledge of religion and domestic duties. Without this, 'the milder virtues of society' and 'the most lovely graces of Christianity' would never be able to develop in Jamaica.[70]

Knibb also defended himself against the accusation that he was living in the lap of luxury. He cited the verdict of John Candler: 'As to the dwelling houses of the missionaries, I know of no one in Jamaica, whether belonging to the Baptists or any other religious body, that is either more costly or commodious, or better furnished, than any individual with a family, who has been used to move in respectable life, is fairly entitled to.'[71] The emphasis on 'respectable life' is revealing. The house which Knibb's congregation had built for him in Kettering was a large, 'commodious' residence, a residence of the kind which merchants and professional men were used to, but a far cry from the small houses in which artisans, small tradesmen or impecunious dissenting ministers could expect to live. The leap in income and status which the most successful Baptist missionaries in Jamaica were able to make in the 1840s was undoubtedly a source of hostility and envy. Knibb described to his audience the circumstances in which he had acquired this house. He had been reporting to the members of his church about the state of the chapels under his care:

> when they found that the house in which I lived, the bed on which I reposed, and the furniture which I used was not my property, but theirs, and belonged entirely to the church, they said, 'Minister, have you took care and got a house for your wife?' I said, 'No: do you think that I would take your money without your leave, and buy a house for Mrs. Knibb?'

They replied, 'If you have not got one, it is time you had. You go to Kettering, to the land left that belongs to you, and you build a good house there, and we will pay for it.'[72]

So Knibb had taken them at their word and built 'Kettering House', costing £1,000. The name captured Knibb's and England's relation to the new village – *his* land, *his* project, *his* vision, *his* family.

Knibb's central defence was that the missionaries had done good work with the emancipated peasantry: 'there is a noble independence of mind gathering around the character of the negro,' he argued, an independence which belied the sneers of the planters that negroes could not be independent, or fully be men. Such a 'noble independence' was of course the greatest blessing of missionaries. It was upon their characters that they had to depend, it was that which gave them the strength to do the work they had to do despite the scorn of others. It was, therefore, particularly base that their characters should be under attack. He compared the work in Jamaica with that of St Paul: they might have made errors, but 'The apostle Paul could not prevent error from creeping into the church at Corinth; and do you think that William Knibb can do it at Falmouth'?[73]

Knibb's defence of the practice of using leaders depended on the figure of Edward Barrett, well known in both Jamaica and England. Barrett had been named in the 1831–2 Select Committee evidence as one of those Baptists who had tried to defend their master's property during the rebellion. At that time he had been one of the fifty leaders attached to Knibb's church.[74] He had received his freedom on Oxford estate because of his loyalty to his absentee master Edward Moulton Barrett (the father of Elizabeth Barrett Browning), whose name he had been given.[75] By 1838 he was the bookkeeper on the Oxford estate, earning £50 per annum.[76] In 1840, when Knibb attended the great Anti-Slavery Convention in London, he took with him two freedmen, Edward Barrett and Henry Beckford, who were to demonstrate by their presence and demeanour the success of emancipation. They travelled up and down the country with Knibb, appearing on platforms and speaking of their gratitude to the British public for the gift of freedom. They were painted by the artist Benjamin Haydon, with Beckford sitting at the feet of Thomas Clarkson, in his depiction of the great and good men who gathered for that historic occasion (see illustration on cover). The women, as Clare Midgley has noted, were out of the frame.[77] Edward Barrett, in Knibb's representation, was the archetypical new black subject, the responsible, industrious, Christian man. You *know* Edward Barrett, he told his audience in both England and Jamaica. He was one of those leaders who were 'so calumniated', and yet he personally had been the means of bringing 600 souls to Christ. It was he who had insisted that Knibb have his own house in Kettering, and that in the event of his death they wanted Mrs Knibb and the children to stay in Jamaica.[78] He, together with another of the Kettering deacons, had laid the corner-stone of that house.[79] 'At the first formation of our Station,' Knibb argued, 'we employed the best agency we could find.' Many superstitions had been eradicated, and only those who could read were allowed to hold office. 'So far from the Leaders and Deacons concealing sin,' he insisted, 'it is through them, nearly exclusively, that we detect it.'[80]

It was Edward Barrett's ticket which was widely reproduced in an attempt to defuse the critique of the ticket system and the ways in which it had encouraged a return to African fetishism. 'Mr. Edward Barrett', was handwritten in the centre, 'is a member of the Baptist Church in Falmouth.' The ticket was dated and signed by William Knibb, Pastor. Printed around the four borders were the exhortations 'Pray for your Children', 'Pray for Grace to live near to God', 'Pray for the Church' and 'Pray for the conversion of Africa'.[81] Surely such an item was 'not likely to mislead, demoralize, and destroy the people'.[82] The charge was that tickets were regarded with 'superstitious reverence', that they were seen as 'charms' or 'passports'. Walter Dendy, the long-established missionary at Salter's Hill, who was facing a serious outbreak of myalism in his own chapel in 1842, defended the use of them. 'I consider the advantages of tickets to be very great in such a community as this', he declared. 'They show connexion with a Christian society, and persons who are introduced to us when they have a ticket consider themselves bound to attend the means of grace and listen to instruction, who would otherwise (if not members) be tempted to regard those advantages oftentimes with indifference.'[83] Other missionaries rose to the defence of the leaders. 'Ability to read and write are, in this church, indispensable qualifications,' wrote Samuel Oughton, from East Queen Street in Kingston. And he went on to explain the strict watch which he kept over 'his' leaders:

> These leaders have to exercise a strict watch over the conduct of the people, to visit them in sickness, console them in affliction, and advise with them when in difficulty. They have also, small buildings, in various parts of the city and country, principally erected by the people, where they meet every Monday evening for reading, prayer and exhortation; and on Tuesday evening, every week, the Leaders meet on the Mission premises, to bring their reports to me, to examine cases of discipline, restoration, etc, and consult on any steps to be taken.[84]

Inevitably, however, the missionaries and their supporters were on the defensive, denying any damaging connections between traces of

Africa and the hierarchy they depended on. It was sometimes true, admitted Samuel Green, that the leaders were gang drivers from the time of slavery. But that was because 'the old drivers were usually the persons of the greatest intelligence, activity, and faithfulness'. Sometimes they were not chosen, despite their authority within the community, because they were not tender enough.[85] The missionaries had to have some way of devolving responsibilities within their congregations; it was impossible for them to do all the work themselves. Given the scale of the areas they were trying to cover and the numbers of people whose behaviour they hoped to regulate, they had to rely on others to supervise for them, and on the Word being circulated by mouth. Philip Cornford, inspired by Knibb's visit to England in 1840, was one of the band who returned with him to pursue the 'great experiment'. He was invited to work at Rio Bueno, on the north coast not far from Falmouth. When he arrived, the church had about 400 members. 'The whole of these', he explained,

> were ranked in classes according to the locality of their residence, and usually met for worship in buildings voluntarily erected for the purpose three times in the week, as well as on Sabbath evenings where their distance from the chapel rendered necessary. Each class had therefore a responsible person appointed to its management, who was called a 'Leader' ... In many cases, it must be confessed, the missionary had to make use of very defective assistants; but the alternative was, *these* with the hope of improvement, or none at all.[86]

The Baptist church in Jamaica, as Horace Russell points out, was necessarily built on African family structures and gave precedence to elders, whilst at the same time making use of existing structures from plantation communities.[87] But the missionaries also wanted to deny any pre-existing culture: they were making the world anew. They needed to convince both themselves and others that the system was at their command. As John Clarke noted, however, the leaders had their own power base, and 'they resented any interference with the size of their classes, any questioning of their reports on members' conduct, and their meetings with the missionary tended to be quarrelsome and aggressive'.[88] This Baptist family was indeed a potential hotbed of disruption and dissension.

Brother Knibb

It was Brother Knibb who was probably the key figure in holding the family roughly together. Knibb believed in a Jamaica of the future which would be governed by black men, and he encouraged black men in the present to speak, take responsibility, occupy positions of leadership within the church, and become property holders and citizens. In giving evidence to the Select Committees he had quoted testimony from black witnesses. When full emancipation came, he orchestrated events in Falmouth and forefronted his trusted black deacons.

In 1842 a debate was initiated in the *Baptist Herald* as to how the jubilee of the BMS should be celebrated. The biblical idea of jubilee carried a particular set of radical meanings, as Peter Linebaugh and Marcus Rediker have eloquently shown. Rooted in both Old and New Testament texts, a fifty-year jubilee was presaged: lands would be restored to their original owners, debts would be cancelled, slaves freed, and good tidings brought to the afflicted. Jubilee had been appropriated by the Quakers and the Diggers in seventeenth-century England, along-side Milton and Bunyan, and by radical Methodists and Baptists, African-Americans including Liele, and Paineite republicans in the transatlantic world of the 1790s. Robert Wedderburn, Jamaica-born cos-mopolitan radical, discussed it with his Maroon half-sister Elizabeth in the pages of his journal, which circulated in both London and Kingston in 1817.[89] The BMS jubilee, celebrating fifty years of the society, was the missionary version of this more radical tradition. A special medal designed for the occasion represented the triumph of the mission across East and West of the world:

It has, on the obverse, a figure of a Missionary, with the Bible lying open before him, on the one side an Asiatic kneeling; with his hand on the Bible; and his head raised as in the act of adoration for the blessings of revela-tion. On the left side of the Missionary is one of the descendants of Ham praising God for the preaching of the Gospel having a broken chain beneath his feet, over the group are two angels flying through the heavens, the one carrying an open book, designed to represent the sacred scriptures, the other with a trumpet, as emblematic of the living voice; in the back-ground is an idolatrous temple in ruins, and at a distance from it, a place erected for the worship of Jehovah, under the figure is inscribed in raised letters 'BAPTIST MISSION JUBILEE! 1842' the whole surrounded with the following inscription, 'Then shalt thou cause the trumpet of the Jubilee to sound, and ye shall hallow the fiftieth year'.

On the other side of the medal was Carey's founding motto, 'Expect great things from God. Attempt great things for God', together with historical facts about the mission. He was sure, concluded the editor, that these medals would be very popular in Jamaica.[90]

The jubilee events were held in Kettering, which had a large and con-venient 'greensward' and a beautiful setting next to Knibb's house. There

William Knibb, with the insignia of both metropole and colony. A print by George Baxter.

was a view of the sea, of Falmouth harbour and of Refuge chapel in the hills, a small country chapel where Edward Barrett was now a deacon. The celebrations were planned for months in advance. Knibb acted as secretary, and his brother Edward, who had a shop in Falmouth, laid on

Jubilee meeting at Kettering. The Knibb family house stands at the edge of the field, where thousands gathered to celebrate fifty years of the BMS.

From the *Missionary Herald*, 1843, reproduced by permission of the British Library, BL 480.

the food at moderate prices. Hymns were written, both for adults and children, a great marquee erected for four thousand people together with a special tent for the children, transport and accommodation planned. In the event 13,000 attended the three-day celebration, and the *Baptist Herald* crowed, 'We defy any country on earth to produce a peasantry more neatly attired, more consistent in their general behaviour, or more healthy in their appearance than the assembled multitude of Baptists at the Jubilee of their mission.'[91] The opening was marked with one of the specially written hymns celebrating the family of man:

> Then lift the voice, and let the song
> Winds, waves, and echoing hills prolong:
> And black and white, and bond made free,
> Swell the loud notes of Jubilee.[92]

A series of resolutions – on the achievements of the BMS, on the need for a mission to Africa, on the urgent need for further work in the country parts of Jamaica, on the importance of a theological college on the island, on the need for civil and religious liberties, on the centrality of an alliance between employers and labourers – were then proposed and seconded by the missionaries. A central theme was the distinction between Africa, an uncultivated and uncivilised place with a people sunk in 'ignorance, superstition and wretchedness', and Jamaica. 'No idol gods we own,' carolled the children, 'Nor blindly bow the knee,/ Nor pray to senseless wood and stone,/ That cannot hear or see.'[93] The creolised children of Jamaica were attached to a Christian God, not to barbaric superstitions.

But six weeks before the jubilee there had been a myal outbreak at Salter's Hill Baptist chapel. The *Baptist Herald* editorial had noted this new outbreak of 'folly and delusion' amongst these 'silly individuals', and opined hopefully that 'We cannot suppose that the error will spread very extensively and hope that all the peasantry who value the character they have so nobly earned, will discourage all such attempts at folly and wickedness'. These people were behaving as if 'they had been all their lives resident in Central Africa'. The boundaries between 'heathens', 'Bow-down-Baptists' and proper Christians were not easy to draw. White Baptists could never be mistaken for Black or Native Baptists, but Baptists who were black were always susceptible to that possibility; they could pass for either orthodox or native, their blackness providing the line of connection. Blackness, Knibb had argued, was not an identity to be ashamed of, but it had to be born anew. When blackness meant Africa, barbarism, superstition, heathenism, then it needed transformation. The Rev. Dutton spoke anxiously at the jubilee of the 'wilderness of

Clarendon', in the centre of the island, where 'the native Baptists flourish and exert an influence prejudicial, I believe, to the welfare of man and the glory of God'. 'Ignorant and superstitious notions' were being instilled, and the 'sacred rite' of Believers' Baptism was being administered in a reckless manner. He threatened the unbelievers with another baptism, 'in the lake which burneth with fire and brimstone'.[94] Hell might threaten the Native Baptists, but not, it was to be hoped, the 'neatly attired peasantry' gathered for the jubilee.

The last day focused on the condition of Jamaica, and was Knibb's opportunity to address the assembled deacons and leaders, to congratulate them on their work, to defend them from the accusations made against them, and to spur them on to greater efforts. The eyes of the world were upon them, he reminded his audience. They had made great progress, recognised even by the authorities, but the good work must be kept up. It was vital that they labour on the estates, get married (the Baptists were very proud of the number of marriages which they had performed), read the Bible in their family groups, aspire to more domestic comfort, wear clean clothes and learn to be true Christian patriots. He was seconded by Walter Dendy, who, perhaps mindful of those delinquent women who had assaulted the peace of his chapel, spoke about the importance of the education of the Christian family. He hoped to see his people

> rise in intelligence, and educate their children, and be surrounded by domestic comforts, and not only have the Bible upon their shelf, which he hoped all would possess and read, but that in every cottage there soon would be two or three small shelves, so that a small cottage library consisting not only of strictly religious works, but also of such as should be useful as it regarded this life. After the toils of day he desired to see the time as soon as the frugal meal had been partaken of, that had been prepared by the female members of the family, that the useful book should be taken from the shelf, and read by one for the benefit of all the family.[95]

A family that was educated, surrounded with domestic comforts, enjoying proper family meals together, prepared by women – this was the dream of the new Jamaican patriots.

In July 1841 a meeting had been held in Brown's Town in support of the Africa mission. Only white missionaries spoke in what was a very long meeting. Burchell opened on the special bond between Jamaica and Africa. He was followed by Knibb, who expressed his surprise that his friend, 'known to be quite a "patriarchal" man', had spoken so briefly, and chided him not to be ashamed of his standing.[96] But Burchell's and Knibb's patriarchalism had consequences. They assumed the right to dominate public proceedings, to speak at length while their black brothers spoke briefly and their white and black sisters did not speak at all. 'I have been most interested,' Knibb commented on one occasion, 'while those who have preceded me, have, in their own simple manner described the change from slavery to freedom.'[97] But who could speak better about that transition than the subjects of it? Such patronising words, combined with the skilled rhetoric of an accomplished preacher, may have silenced many others. 'I have not much to say to you,' said a Mr Wallace, at a meeting in Falmouth, 'for our dear minister . . . has taken up all my discourse so that there is nothing left for me to say.' He was 'a plain, ignorant, cane piece man', and would not have been free if it had not been for his minister. 'I was a slave once, my Christian friends', he continued,

> so that I know what it was. I was made to work when I was a very little boy, but I am thankful that our ministers came to us and preach the gospel to us, and the gospel and the people of England made us free. Well, now we must try what good we can do to other people. . . . We must try to send the gospel to Africa, we must try to get the people free, you know you have friends in Africa, and you have land there too, your father have land there or your uncles . . . you must go back.[98]

This was the testimony which the white missionaries could not give: it drew on knowledges they did not have; it connected Christianity with older African traditions in ways which were disturbing to them. As long as the missionaries occupied centre-stage, such voices were only on the margins. But such a scenario depended on the acceptance of their leadership and all that went with it. Nancy Prince attended a crowded meeting at East Queen Street in Kingston, concerned with sending a mission to Africa. She noted tartly that several ministers spoke, and there was 'one coloured minister on the platform'. 'It is generally the policy of these ministers', she continued, 'to have the sanction of coloured ministers', for it helped them to gain support.[99]

Joseph McLean, speaking at a meeting in Spanish Town, observed that

> white people often said that a black man could never make a speech, because he had got no education; but, although he could not use the same fine words, he could make the people *understand* him, and that was enough. It was not the fine words, but good sense that makes the good speech, and his hearers all understood him, his speech would be just as good as the white Gentleman's, with all his fine language.[100]

It was difficult for the missionaries to get beyond congratulating black men for their simple words, words which indicated 'powers of mind which many in the plenitude of their malice have declared that the African does not possess'.[101] They were certainly prepared to recognise that black men had minds, were capable of thinking and could be educated. But they were also convinced that they must act as the guides and educators, the patriarchs, of this new moral world. Meanwhile the white women acted as supporters and assistants, while the black women were the audience, the objects of the missionary gaze.

Joseph John Gurney and John Candler had visited Burchell at Mount Carey, where he dispensed his 'patriarchal hospitality'.[102] Candler noted that the establishment easily accommodated their party of five with three servants. They received 'handsome entertainment at a hospitable board', as well as provender for their six horses.[103] They visited 'his' free village, worshipped in 'his' chapel, stayed in 'his' home, were looked after by 'his' wife and daughter. Burchell, wrote Gurney, 'is a gentleman and a Christian'. He was a man of 'modesty, integrity and talent', once 'insulted, persecuted and imprisoned', now living 'comparatively at his ease, enjoying a delightful country residence, and exercising over many thousands of the peasantry at his various stations, an influence incomparably greater than that of any other individual in the vicinity'.[104] He had set up seven missions, and had co-operated with the establishment of six others. Thomas Burchell had come from a mercantile family, and his wife and daughter had had money of their own, most of which had been invested in chapels which were destroyed by the Colonial Church Union in the wake of the 1831 rebellion. Servants and employees had been part of the Burchell familial world in England. In appearance he was above middle height, 'manly' in looks, and altogether 'of commanding exterior'. A 'tender husband, a fond father, an affectionate brother, and a kind master' – all in all a true gentleman. His wife Hester supported him in all his activities. After emancipation, she would leave Montego Bay on a Saturday and go up into the hills to the Sunday schools attached to the free villages. In 1843 their only child was baptised in a moving ceremony. She entered the river hand in hand with the family's servant-girl, while the people assembled on the river banks sang, 'Praise ye the Lord, Hallelujah'. As Burchell described it to his brother, 'the greatest possible interest was manifested by all present . . . Esthranna is the first child of the mission family, born and brought up on the island, and publicly baptised, and that too in company with the natives. In this the people take special delight, saying, "Now we see there is no distinction".'[105] After her father's death, Esthranna and her mother continued to run the day-schools and Sunday schools attached to the mission. 'I love England,' Burchell had written not long before his death, 'but still I love home more, yea, much more.'[106] Home was Jamaica. Still, he was worried before his death by the state of the mission, by the rivalries between the missionaries, by the evident desire amongst them to be placed in the most important stations, by the divisions over the setting up of Calabar, by the seeking of financial support from the BMS despite their declaration of independence. 'We are not what we once were,' as he wrote to the committee.[107]

Knibb was different from his friend both in background and personality. Coming from an artisan family, it was a considerable leap to a town house in Falmouth and 'one of the most comfortable mansions in the parish of Trelawny' in Kettering.[108] Philip Cornford, on his arrival in 1841, was entertained by Mrs Knibb, first at Kettering House. Then he and the fourteen other new adjuncts to the mission venture all moved on to the house in Falmouth. Cornford was mindful of the criticisms which had been made of the luxurious life enjoyed by the missionaries. The house at Falmouth, as he described it,

> like the one we had left, boasted no decorations or superfluities. The walls were simply white-washed, or coloured yellow or blue. The boarded floors were bare, but bright, being polished with a brush. The chairs were of mahogany, but of common appearance and without cushions. . . . The possession of horses, etc, was indispensable in a land which did not afford a public conveyance of any kind. Servants, indeed, were numerous enough. One of these was like a footman of all-work, – butler, groom, cow-herd, coachman, valet, labourer, etc. . . . The boy 'Jerry' was required to assist at the stable, chaise-house, piggery, pasture, knife-board, fowl-house, water-cart, wood-cutting, and everywhere when required. . . . then there was a cook, but seldom seen, though often heard.

Finally there were two African girls, rescued by Knibb from a captured slave-ship and named Kate and Annie, after his two daughters.[109] Two houses, servants, horses, even African girls named after his daughters, signalling their dependence, albeit a different kind of dependence from those enslaved men and women who were named after their masters – all of this was organised by his wife, Mary, who ran the households, looked after the constant guests, cared for sick children and adults while managing her own ill health, took considerable responsibilities with the examination and training of the women in the congregation, raised money for a school in Kettering to train native female schoolmistresses which she helped to run, and looked after other aspects of the mission when William was away. As a young wife, she had witnessed a major rebellion of the enslaved and its aftermath: the threats against her husband's life, the destruction of the chapels, and the hasty leaving of Jamaica. 'I attribute most of my success in my missionary career to your excellent mother,' wrote Knibb to his daughters, while, he added, 'we are mutually impressed with the truth that we owe all to sovereign mercy, and feel that we have been unprofitable servants.'[110] Between 1825 and 1839 she had been pregnant or nursing most of the time, having given birth to four sons and five daughters. Four of these children died in infancy, and all the sons died before reaching adolescence. Two daughters survived to adulthood. The deaths of these children, and of innumerable other members of the mission family during these years, were sources of deep pain and loss. 'I preached last evening from "the whole family in heaven",' William wrote to his wife in 1843. 'In that family *there are an innumerable company of children* . . . our five sweet cherubs are there; but Oh! the loneliness they have left.'[111] The family in heaven could provide only limited consolation.

The loss of their last remaining son, William, was a particularly harsh blow. Knibb had longed for him to be a son in his own image. 'Descended as you are from a race of poor but noble-minded nonconformists,' he wrote to him, 'some of whom have suffered much for Jesus, I would have my boy catch their unquenchable spirit.'[112] He was worried by his listlessness and lack of energy, which may have been to do with his ill health but may also have been associated with the pressures of being his father's only son. The boy was mythologised after his death in a little book written by Knibb's friend Hoby at the devastated father's request. Any proceeds were to go to the Wilberforce school at Refuge, since William had intended to devote his life to the education of 'the coloured people'. Christian missionaries should not be forgotten in the history of martyrs, wrote Hoby, and 'Nor can the man of God suffer alone – his wife and children necessarily participate in, and so greatly increase every affliction'. William Junior had enjoyed an 'innate love of liberty' from his earliest years, he had stood beside his father at the memorable BMS meeting in 1832. Though only a child, he had taught many to read in Jamaica, and just before his death, he told his father that he would go as a missionary to Africa, thus realising a dream. The news that those in the congregation who had apprentices were going to free them was too much for his frail constitution. 'Though born amidst slavery', his father wrote,

> he detested it. Often did my mind exult at the deep love of liberty that he felt. It was in him, though young, a pure and lovely flame – but *it consumed* him. The thought that the members of my church would set their people free, overcame him. When he heard that all had agreed, he drew me a *ship* in full sail, with 'Liberty' on her flag, chasing two slavers; and on her pendant, 'Slavery must fall'. He bounded away with a heart too full. That night the fever took him.[113]

In the delirium of his fever, as another version of the story told it, 'his rambling words showed a mind filled with ideas of negro emancipation, and the triumphs of humanity, law and religion'.[114]

Meanwhile, the two oldest daughters, Catherine and Ann, were taken by their father to England in 1840, and settled at the school for missionary daughters which had recently been established in Walthamstow. Most of the missionaries struggled hard financially to educate their children in England. While they were travelling with him, each learned a hymn every morning, and by 1842 Knibb had baptised Catherine, a critical moment for any Baptist parent.[115] The recognition of grace was a matter for each individual, but the fear of one's children not receiving it ran very deep. On their return to Jamaica, the daughters devoted themselves to the activities of the mission, particularly the girls' schools. Annie was to marry Ellis Fray, one of the first 'native agents' trained at Calabar and a coloured man, thus demonstrating through her marriage her family's belief in the universal family.

Knibb's immediate family provided him with the emotional and practical support he needed to function effectively in the public world. In that world he faced constant attacks. In 1844 his championship of the Jamaican Anti-State Church Convention was yet another source of hostility. This was an electoral alliance, founded by the Baptists but with support from Quakers, some Congregationalists and some Presbyterians and Wesleyans. The idea was to get black and coloured representatives into the House of Assembly and challenge the control of the planters. As Swithin Wilmot comments, 'the white missionaries were the first group to politically mobilise the black peasant vote'.[116] The danger was offset by the governor calling a snap election. Since the law required the lapse of a year between the registration of a voter and his exercise of the franchise, many of the small settlers were effectively disenfranchised.[117] Nevertheless, the *Falmouth Post*, edited by Castello, maintained its assault on Knibb and the Baptists. In the early months of 1845 they were enraged by reports of local 'coffee meetings', where politics and religion made a heady and dangerous mix. These 'negro Baptists of Jamaica', they complained, were 'infinitely inferior to every other class of our native labourers'. They were possessed of 'strange ideas of liberty', were 'rude and insolent' to their employers, and were 'wedded to those superstitious practices, the love of which has been imbibed from their African forefathers'. It was all the fault of the missionaries. They had taught them to meddle with things they did not understand: myalism and 'coffee meetings' were the result.[118] An editorial in April complained of the way in which Knibb was living in splendidly furnished houses, his tables groaning with food, the best horses and gigs at the ready, and his family well provided for. Meanwhile the Baptists were egging on the peasantry, inciting them to unreasonable expectations. There were signs of rebellion, however, from amongst those same peasants, and the *Falmouth Post* was pleased to report that the missionaries were beginning to have less influence than they had had in the past.[119] There were a number of '*Native Baptist* parsons', they noted maliciously, 'who have set up for themselves . . . These . . . avail themselves of every favourable opportunity to point out to the peasantry the way they have been imposed upon.' Moreover, 'an itinerant, characterless, vagabond' was nightly inflaming audiences:

> by telling them, that Messrs. Knibb, Burchell and Co., are as prejudiced, as the planters of old, against black persons. A few weeks ago this person addressed himself in the following terms to some four or five dozen males and females . . . 'What has Mr. Knibb done for you? Has he ever invited a black man to his table? No! He looks upon and treats you as his slaves!'[120]

The paper revealed by its preoccupation with Knibb how serious a threat he posed to planter interests, inveighing against the *Baptist Herald*'s advice on wages, for example, while at the same time insisting that his influence was grossly overestimated on the island. 'He is looked upon by his followers in this colony as being of a superior order,' they sneered; 'in London, or any of the other great cities, he would sink into the insignificance from which he originally sprang.'[121] They feared his demagogy, threatening a Haitian outcome in Jamaica and warning their readers of the example of Irish leaders in Britain who had mobilised large numbers of the ignorant. A huge public meeting had taken place in Falmouth to celebrate 1 August, and a procession of 6,000 had occupied the streets, 'behaving more like savages than civilised beings'. 'Is Mr. Knibb to be the Ruler of Jamaica?,' they inquired rhetorically.[122]

In March Knibb had been despatched to England by the Jamaica Baptists to put their case for financial support to the BMS. As early as 1843 it had been clear that the missionaries faced serious financial problems. The debts associated with a large-scale building programme were extensive, and despite the severing of their dependency in 1842, they continued to seek support from the London committee. Knibb was offered a special grant of £6,000, which went some way to relieve the accumulated financial problems on the island but was meant to be the last such contribution.[123] On his return he launched back into the fray, but soon fell ill. By November, he was dead from yellow fever. His funeral service was conducted by his friend Burchell, who within a few months was dead himself. In Kingston Samuel Oughton took as his text, 'Howl, fir-tree; for the cedar is fallen'.[124] Let him be remembered, wrote one woman poet, as

> The champion of the slave
> The herald of the free,
> The day-star of the glorious morn
> Of Western liberty.[125]

In the churchyard of the present William Knibb Memorial Chapel in Falmouth, erected after the old chapel was destroyed in the hurricane of 1944 with the help of government funds, are the graves of William and Mary. Mary stayed in Kettering until her death in 1867. Both Knibb daughters died in Jamaica. A memorial stands beside the grave of husband and wife, 'erected by the Emancipated Slaves to whose enfranchisement and elevation his indefatigible exertions so largely contributed', and 'who, being dead, yet speaketh'. His voice, however, was now muted. It had been the voice of hopes and dreams, the voice of a new Jamaican patriot who wanted to see the building of a new nation, to foster a love of that nation, for 'there is not that love of country there ought to be', integrally connected to the 'old country' yet separate, peopled with new black subjects 'clothed with the comely garb of Christian civilisation'.[126]

The missionary dream depended on willing lieutenants who would extend the work of the white pastors and patriarchs. But the issue of native agency raised many difficulties and tensions between the missionaries and those they saw as their juniors and subordinates. Furthermore, the leaders to whom they gave responsibility for day-to-day supervision of the huge congregations were widely criticised by their enemies and rivals as ignorant men exercising improper power. What was more, the flocks themselves could not be relied on. Orthodox Baptist practices were always in danger of slipping into what were seen as African superstitions and rituals. Negroes were regarded as needing constant supervision if the work of educating them to be civilised subjects was to have any hope of success. While the early 1840s represented the high point of missionary hopes, spearheaded by Brother Knibb's vision of a black peasantry wielding effective political power and defeating the plantocracy, fractures were already evident within the Baptist family as well as without. The death of Knibb in 1845 marked the ending of the high watermark of post-emancipation missionary dreams.

3

'A Jamaica of the Mind' 1820–1854

⟨∽⟩

Phillippo's Jamaica

Samuel Oughton's funeral oration for Knibb, delivered at East Queen Street, the large central Baptist chapel in Kingston, represented its subject as the fallen cedar. Oughton was quite willing, however, to refer to Knibb's failings, for 'there are none, however excellent', he maintained, 'but have their faults'. Knibb's faults, to his mind, were his egotism, which 'tempted him to think more highly of himself than he ought to have done', his ambition for power combined with a dislike of rivals, and 'the conspicuous part which he took in late calamitous transactions in a neighbouring town'.[1] Knibb clearly liked to put himself centre-stage, and no one on the island could compete with him in terms of charisma. As long as he was alive, he was recognised as the leading missionary in Jamaica. The 'calamitous transactions' to which Oughton referred were the troubles in Spanish Town of the long-established missionary there, James Mursell Phillippo.

In 1843 Phillippo had published a substantial book, *Jamaica: Its Past and Present State*. It was published in Engand, but was soon after available in Jamaica. Phillippo had been based in Spanish Town for twenty years. His book aimed to unite a missionary's story with a history and a topography of Jamaica. It drew on the long tradition of Christian writing associated with conversion, together with a distinctive nineteenth-century genre, the missionary story, which told of the encounter with heathenism and its triumphant defeat.[2] This was then combined with the anti-slavery traveller's tale to produce Jamaica for England and the new Jamaica for Jamaica.[3]

English abolitionists shared an imagined place, a 'Jamaica of the mind'. This 'Jamaica of the mind' was constructed through the narratives of anti-slavery and missionary enterprise: the books, sermons, hymns, poems and engravings which poured from its presses. From the late eighteenth century, the anti-slavery lobby had been concerned to counter planter dominance in public debates. They began to publish and publicise their own reports, to utilise select committees and other public spaces, to offer eyewitness accounts (mainly from missionaries) which would challenge the planters' version of the regime of slavery.

Planters and missionaries were central to the English 'Jamaica of the mind'. It was the slave trade, slavery and emancipation which inspired Jamaica's particular genre of travellers' tales in the 1830s and 1840s. Jamaica never had its Mungo Park or its David Livingstone, for there was no 'dark continent' to explore. The Blue Mountain range never attracted the Royal Geographical Society, for the island was assumed to be 'known', mapped from the seventeenth century after its conquest by Cromwell's forces in 1655, its counties and parishes neatly demarcated with English names, its Maroon population settled as safely as it could be in defined areas. It was the plantation system, the slaves, the whip, and after 1834 the emancipated, that travellers went to see in Jamaica.

The tales written by these travellers were central to the struggle over the representation of the British West Indian islands and their peoples in the nineteenth century. But how was Jamaica produced for England, specifically in the anti-slavery narratives of the 1830s and 1840s? What was the imagined geography of the abolitionist? How was the 'travelling eye' riveted to the missionary endeavour? And what happened when the traveller's tale was mapped on to the missionary story?

The campaign against apprenticeship was spearheaded in England by the noted abolitionist Joseph Sturge, Birmingham Quaker and corn merchant. In 1837 Sturge decided to go and see for himself how the apprenticeship laws in the West Indies were working, convinced that it was vital to 'awaken the public mind'. Together with his friend and fellow Quaker, Leeds merchant Thomas Harvey, Sturge published an account of his experiences on his return, the first in a series of books written by noted anti-slavery advocates in the next twenty years. Their intention was to ascertain 'the actual condition of the negro population of those islands'. Their informants were sympathetic to anti-slavery, and their hope was that their work would stimulate a public campaign in England.[4] The book was an immediate success, provoking sharp controversy and stimulating a campaign. The Jamaican House of Assembly, fearing imperial interference, itself abolished apprenticeship from 1 August 1838.

In the years immediately following 1838, public interest in Britain in the West Indian experiment was extensive, and a series of publications sustained that interest and kept the anti-slavery viewpoint in the public eye. Sturge, Harvey and other abolitionists such as Joseph John Gurney, who visited Jamaica and published reports, were committed to the view that negroes were fellow subjects and members of the same universal human family, yet none of them believed in their equality with white people except as a future possibility. England in their view was a civilised society, Jamaica was not; but the belief was that it could become civilised with English help, that if only enough good white people, as opposed to the decadent planters of Jamaica, would go and live there, there would be more chance of them learning to be 'like us'. In writing their narratives, they constructed a sense of distance and of difference, of otherness from black people, as they observed 'the race', made comments and judgements on their manners, their 'progress' and their 'improvement', and described their dress and customs. Their writings constituted part of that English ethnographic tradition which was to become anthropology. Troubling issues – an encounter with wildly dancing women or a myal man – were marginalised, for such exhibitions disrupted the anti-slavery orthodoxy that negroes were steadily progressing towards becoming an ordered and industrious peasantry, respectful and respectable, domesticated and familial, learning the ways of civilisation and burying two histories – of Africa and of slavery.[5] By 1841 the existence of these books meant that anti-slavery supporters had a barrage of evidence at their fingertips demonstrating the first results of the 'great experiment', a counterweight to the volumes produced earlier by Edward Long and more recently by the Rev. G. W. Bridges which maintained that black people could never be like white. Phillippo's book was a contribution to this corpus.

The book was written in England. Suffering from severe ill health, Phillippo had been obliged to leave Jamaica with his wife Hannah and younger son and spend time in Hastings. Too unwell to travel, he found himself with time on his hands, unable to do the usual round of missionary events that were expected of those on leave. He decided to use the time to write a book, relying on his memory and 'his own observation and experience', together with the materials he had with him. He had been there, he knew, his eye had seen, he could authenticate. His hope was to 'give a faithful representation of Jamaica as it *was*, and as it *is*', to show the transformation which had taken place from slavery to emancipation.[6]

Phillippo had gone to Jamaica as a Baptist missionary in 1823 and had lived in Spanish Town since then. Born in Norfolk in 1798, the son of a master builder, he was brought up in the Anglican church. His mother's piety, a factor often mentioned by missionaries and ministers, made a deep impression on him, but having left home to go into farming and trade with his grandfather, he became absorbed with the worldly pleasures of country fairs and tea gardens, and together with his young male friends made fun of the worshippers at the local Independent chapel. Stirrings within his conscience, however, drove him to a Baptist chapel, despite the prejudices against dissent which he met all around him and encountered within himself. At fifteen he experienced conversion. 'I felt like Christian when he lost his burden at the sight of the Cross,' he recorded; he cast his lot 'with the despised people of God' and became a Baptist.[7]

As a child, Phillippo had loved *Robinson Crusoe* and the voyages of Captain Cook. Following his conversion, his birth as a new man in Christ, he became increasingly fascinated by missionary works of travel and adventure, and interested in 'the heathen'. 'Stirrings of desire', as his biographer Edward Bean Underhill, a later chronicler of Jamaica and secretary of the Baptist Missionary Society for many years, put it, 'for usefulness among his fellow-men began to be felt, especially among the far-off nations lying in darkness and in the shadow of death.' 'He read the missionary publications of the African traveller Campbell with avidity,' and began to train himself in useful skills – 'medicine, brick-making, house-building, cabinet work, the wheelwright's toil, agriculture, and the manufacture of articles of food and clothing, all attracted in turn his serious and ardent attention'. He started to preach, and was gradually convinced of his calling to be a missionary, to prove his Christian manhood in imperial adventure of a noble kind.[8]

Accepted as a trainee missionary by the BMS committee in 1820, Phillippo met Burchell, who became a lifelong friend, encountered a missionary wife who gave him much valuable information about the life he would lead, and talked to Dr Hoby, long-time missionary supporter. He was being inducted into the extended network of the mission family at home. He preached to small congregations in the Cotswolds, and felt 'a glowing satisfaction at the thought of spending my life in something nobler than the locality of this island will admit'. 'Heathens' and 'savage pagans of the wilderness' in far-flung corners of the empire offered a more enticing and exciting prospect than rural labourers. 'You must remember', he wrote to his parents, 'that I am to be engaged in a glorious cause.' Adopting the language of militant evangelicalism with its call to the faithful to join the army of Christ, he continued, 'Who would not lend a hand to dispel the darkness of Satan's kingdom and erect upon its ruins the kingdom of God . . . ? This world is not a place of repose for a faithful soldier of the Cross.' On moving to Bradford, he found preaching in the Yorkshire villages an excellent training for the work ahead: Yorkshire dialect presented him with almost as many difficulties as Jamaican patois, and his congregations sometimes had difficulty in understanding him. This 'soldier of the Cross' had chosen an imperial destiny, and must face its attendant problems.[9]

Trainee missionaries were well aware that they were expected to marry before leaving the country, so to secure them against the sexual licentiousness associated with slavery and Africa, and ensuring a 'help-meet' for the labours associated with a missionary station. Rumours were rife, however, as to what sort of woman the committee expected, rumours which reveal the class anxieties as to missionary work and status. Some said she should be mature in age; others focused on useful skills such as laundress or nurse, and opined that experience as a servant of all work was really the best preparation. Some claimed that a good personal appearance was quite unnecessary, as this would soon deterio-rate in tropical climes; others argued that the key qualification was an ardent spirituality. 'It was also understood', recorded Phillippo, 'that some Ministers undertook to select wives for young Missionaries who offered themselves for service,' and he told the tale of the efforts made for one young man, including the setting up of tea-parties amongst a congregation. While in the Cotswolds, Phillippo had met Hannah Selina Cecil, a young woman to whom he had become engaged, but he heard disturbing gossip as to her likely unsuitability in the eyes of the com-mittee – she was 'too delicately brought up, had too comfortable a home, had not manifested so much of a missionary spirit as to fit her for so arduous and self-denying position as that of a foreign missionary's help-meet'. Fortunately, however, the committee approved.[10]

Phillippo and his friend Thomas Burchell, who had been accepted as a trainee at the same time, were both fully expecting during their train-ing to go to 'the East', as it was called in the mission world. They were in the forefront, however, of the revived mission to 'the West'. 'I have enlisted as a soldier of the Cross,' reported Phillippo, 'and have now received the summons for active duty in a foreign land.'[11] Soldiers took orders, his order was from God. The order went to the man, as employee of the BMS, as trained missionary, as patriarch of the mission station. His new helpmeet was automatically included in that order, her free labour assumed as part of the family enterprise. In October 1823 the newly married couple embarked for Jamaica, and after an enjoyable voyage, which included evening sing-songs on deck, had arrived in Spanish Town by Christmas.

Their first encounter with black culture was dramatic, for it was Car-nival, the moment at which enslaved men and women were allowed to escape briefly from the plantation and turn the world upside down with bacchanalian festivities:

There was scarcely any passing along the streets of Spanish town from the heathenish processions encountered at every turn; while the hideous yellings of the multitudes as accompaniments to their still more revolting attitudes in their dances to the rough music of their African ancestry were more than enough to render frantic the animal that brought us thus far quietly on our way, not to anticipate the scenes of dissipation and general wickedness to which these revelries led. Some of the more respectable held their *concerts* but no one certainly unless he has resided many years in the country and discarded all European tastes and predilections could patiently endure their attempts at harmony.

Thus Phillippo encountered and codified difference, defining for himself as he wrote in his journal the moment at which the heathenism of his imagination, associated with the ancient rites of the 'dark continent', was mapped on to the sights of Spanish Town, the place which was to be his home for the next sixty years. Here was Africa in all its 'horror', with the 'revolting attitudes' of the dances the 'sign' of the lasciviousness, the licence of black sensuality rampant – this was the culture which Christianity must transform. Furthermore, the mission premises were dirty, dilapidated and inconvenient, but a good clean-up established a new beginning.[12]

The Phillippos' early years in Spanish Town were difficult – a hostile plantocracy who put every obstacle in the way of his preaching, constant difficulties with the law, and three babies lost to Hannah in less than three years. By 1825 the hostility of the authorities had somewhat abated, and the imperial government's policy of amelioration meant that dissenting missionaries could not be persecuted quite so easily. Phillippo was able to preach, and had meanwhile established Bible classes, a Sunday school, a day-school and out-stations in nearby Old Harbour and Passage Fort, all of which provided mainly for enslaved men and women. Phillippo's initial horror at the heathenism of African culture which he had encountered at Carnival was tempered by his realisation of the transformation which chapel attendance and 'proper' Christian values could bring. Baptism was the symbolic rite of passage, the public statement of transformation, the ritualised washing clean, the crossing over from one identity to another. Phillippo made use of a spectacular spot in the river above Spanish Town to fill the minds of both those baptised and the onlookers with 'a mixture of delight and awe'.[13] By 1827 he had raised enough money from England to buy the materials for a grand new chapel which could hold 1,500. Next door was a school, and the mission house, between school and chapel, was enlarged. He supervised the building work, which was done by the enslaved. The chapel still stands, looking much the same as it did in 1827, an impressive building, represented in his writing as a statement of faith and power, suitable for the capital of the country:

> There is something interesting and important in the erection of a place of worship not only as regards the special object of its erection but also in the collateral influence it is calculated to exert. It raises its sacred head with eloquence and power. It speaks of the hallowed purpose for which it is reared. . . . It shines forth as a beacon and a monument both of Philanthropy and of Prayer.[14]

He might have added that it was also a monument to Phillippo, and indeed the church is now known as Phillippo's Church.

In the late 1820s both Phillippo and his wife were involved in raising money in England to purchase the freedom of enslaved people. Hannah became embroiled in a lengthy controversy over the allegation that she had herself owned enslaved men and women, and she took the unusual step of writing personally to the BMS to vindicate her cause. In 1831 ill health brought the family to England for a while, so they were away from the island when the 1831 rebellion occurred. But Phillippo was soon drawn into the efforts spearheaded by Knibb to bring the issue of slavery to the heart of British public life. He spoke with Knibb on the celebrated occasion when Knibb first came out against slavery, did four lectures for Gurney in Norwich, addressed many public meetings for Christian organisations, and caused a sensation in Wales by travelling with Robert Smith, an escaped enslaved man from Jamaica. In Beulah, 'all soon became bustle and confusion. The shoemaker threw down his lapstone, the carpenter his axe, the blacksmith his hammer'; business stopped, the townspeople rushed to the doors and windows, 'some never having seen a black man before'.[15]

By the time he returned to Spanish Town in 1834, the Emancipation Act had been passed, and 'I was in a new world . . . surrounded by a new order of beings'.[16] The celebrations in the chapel were led by black brothers. 'Blessed Lord', said one,

> as dou so merciful pare we, to let we see dis blessed morning, we want word, we want tongue, we want heart to praise de. Debil don't do de good to us, but dou dou de good to us, for dou put it into de heart of de blessed European to grant us dis great privilege! O derefore may none of we poor sinner praise de debil by makin' all de carouze about de streets, but flock like dove to deir window to praise and glorify dy great name.[17]

Freed men and women did indeed flock to the chapels. In the years after 1834 Phillippo was engaged with the struggle over apprenticeship, organising petitions to the House of Commons, putting pressure on the

Emancipation, 1 August 1834. Emancipation was celebrated in both 1834 and 1838. On the latter occasion Phillippo shared the platform in Spanish Town Square with the governor.

From Phillippo, *Jamaica*.

Jamaican House of Assembly, which was five minutes' walk from his mission station, sending regular bulletins to the BMS secretary and the anti-slavery press, corresponding via the governor with the Colonial Office, recommending the urgent necessity of 'an immediate attempt to educate the negro in order to remove from his mind and habits of life the pernicious effects of slavery, and to fit him for a life of patient, continuous, and successful toil as a free man'.[18] This was his lifelong conviction – that a Christian education could eradicate the legacy of slavery and make men and women anew. In 1835 he began to buy land to establish free villages. 1 August 1838, the first day of full freedom, was celebrated with huge festivities in Spanish Town. Phillippo, 'the Pastor', together with the governor, greeted thousands of freed men, women and children in the main square, a striking illustration of the way in which these senior missionaries were briefly positioned, and a source of fury to the planters, who continued to treat them with 'superciliousness and contempt'.[19] Phillippo was convinced that 'the great experiment' would 'prove the most interesting that ever transpired in the annals of the world'. Hardly a modest vision. He appealed to British Christians for help: 'the fields are ripe and the harvest is great'.[20] Money was required for missionaries, chapels, schools and land; men were needed too, to be missionaries and teachers.

The years 1838–42 were immensely busy, with many new projects and thousands of members and inquirers flocking to the chapels. In 1841 Phillippo wrote to Dyer, secretary of the BMS, describing his work-load and asking for help:

> I have been alone in this district for the last seventeen years and upwards. I have eight stations, some of them full twenty miles distant from the central one, each of which requires the services of a regular minister at least once a month on the Sabbath, as well as occasional meetings on a week-day. Eight schools are under my superintendence, and are solely dependent on me for support. I have three new chapels in building, and one being enlarged, the cost of which, full £3,000 sterling, I, in some way or other, must meet. I have services to maintain three times on the Sabbath invariably in Spanish Town, and a church-meeting and Sabbath-schools to attend, besides two week-day services, all of which probably involve as much mental labour as in a respectable town in England; with marriages and funerals, visits to the sick, and a thousand other pastoral duties to discharge arising in churches of between two and three thousand members in town and country.

'I have eight stations', 'I have eight schools', 'I have three new chapels' – thus Phillippo took possession of the district, its stations, schools and chapels, occupying the landscape and filling it with *his* enterprises, claiming Jamaica as his, superintended by his imperial eye. Phillippo's vision of himself as 'alone' speaks volumes about the gap between men's reliance on their wives in mission stations (to run classes for women, to teach in schools, to visit the sick, to run the household) and the public invisibility of that work, even to those who benefited constantly from it. In addition to her work as a missionary wife, Mrs Phillippo had borne nine children by 1841, five of whom had died. Her health was bad, and she frequently had to stay at their house in the mountains at Sligoville, where the air was better than in the hot plain of Spanish Town.[21]

In 1842 both Phillippo and his wife were exhausted, and decided on a trip to England in an attempt to recover their health. It was at this point in his life, with Baptist fortunes in Jamaica flourishing in many respects (with twenty-six missionaries and their wives and eighty-two schoolmasters and mistresses), a man of forty-four with four children, two houses and eight mission stations, one of the most senior missionaries in Jamaica, based in the capital and with thousands under his wing, that Phillippo wrote *Jamaica*.[22]

Phillippo was a name well known to the anti-slavery public in England. The book was well received there, and 'had a large and remunerative circulation, three editions being rapidly exhausted'. Staunch abolitionist to the last, Thomas Clarkson, the veteran campaigner and senior surviving figure in the movement by the early 1840s, wrote to Phillippo with great enthusiasm, delighted that in his view the book vindicated yet again the great hopes attached to emancipation. Similarly, the *Anti-Slavery Reporter* encouraged its readers to purchase it without delay, and printed relentlessly optimistic extracts which focused on the progress, industriousness, politeness and improvements in dress of the emancipated classes.[23]

Abolitionist panegyrics over Phillippo's writing, and indeed the calm of his own text, masked some anxiety which had, as we have seen, been disturbing the peace of mind of the BMS and the Baptist missionaries in Jamaica. Phillippo was unhappy with the decision of the Jamaican Baptists to go independent.[24] He regretted the cutting of the umbilical cord and the loss of control over the thousands of pounds' worth of property on the island by the BMS. Jamaica was still a child as far as he was concerned, still needing succour, guidance and support from the parental committee and the imperial mother, 'the parent state'. Nor was he personally ready to stand alone, to give up the authority which his long connection with the BMS committee, with London, and with the doings of the metropolis conferred. *Jamaica* was a restatement of the ties that bound metropolis with colony. His vision was one of an infant nation. His love for Jamaica, his conviction that it was his home too, made him anxious to sustain the lines of communication with the imperial government and with the powerful abolitionist public without which, he believed, it would be exceedingly difficult to counter the political dominance of the planters. Since the island had representative government, and planters continued to dominate the House of Assembly, 'friends of the negro', as they called themselves, needed to be able to mobilise Colonial Office authority to protect the interests of the black population. Baptist missionaries might have acquired some status, but they were still regarded with contempt by much of white Jamaican society. They needed, in Phillippo's view, the protection of the anti-slavery lobby, the anti-slavery public. *Jamaica* is peppered with requests for support on particular issues from the metropolis, as well as the more general claim for an intimate and continuing connection between 'parent' and 'child'.[25]

Phillippo wanted to remind abolitionists of their continuing responsibilities, and counter the damaging accusations that had been circulat-

ing about the Baptist mission in Jamaica. He was at pains in his book
to defend the leader and the ticket system and to claim that it was properly supervised by the missionaries.[26] But the book was targeted beyond
the Baptists to a much larger public, not necessarily convinced of missionary or abolitionist truths. It aimed to tell much about Jamaica in an
entertaining way, using anecdote and dialect, making no claims to 'literary excellence' but hoping to be 'interesting and useful', and to provide
a comprehensive guide to the island and its peoples. An opening celebration of Christianity was followed by a sketch of the island's history,
its physical features, its animals and vegetables, its social and political
organisation, its government and commerce, its population – black,
white and people of colour. This framed the main part of the book
dealing with abolition, apprenticeship and total emancipation, the intellectual, social and moral condition of black people under slavery, the
bringing of Christianity, the work of the missionaries, and the transformation of religious and social life which had taken place. It ended with
a passionate plea for support for missionary work, which had taken a
people from slavery to freedom, but still had darkness to contend with
all over the world. With sufficient support Jamaica could become 'the
key-stone to the possession of the New World – a kind of rallying post
for the army of the living God', the base for the Christian conquest of
South America.[27]

Mindful of his need to convince sceptics as well as friends, Phillippo
littered his text with references to authorities, not just the expected
anti-slavery names but Long and Bridges, Select Committee reports and
the *Morning Journal*, Dr Coke (Wesley's famous associate) and Mungo
Park. Afraid of his account of slavery not being believed, for he was well
aware of how highly contested slavery was, he insisted that in case his
personal testimony was not enough, he would 'adduce representations
from historical records', including those of his political opponents, to
strengthen his case. No use of the personal pronoun was made, and
Phillippo distanced himself by appearing as 'the author', 'the writer', 'the
pastor' or 'he', his house as 'the minister's house', his wife, who scarcely
appears at all, as 'Mrs. Phillippo'. His early chapters on the physical
character of the land and its plant and vegetable life are clearly inspired
in tone by other texts he had read. In describing the landscape, he
collapses into conventional rhapsodies over the beauty of the island,
forgetting the social relations that he is at pains to describe in later chapters: the 'smiling villages' are unpeopled, the 'numerous cascades' and
rivers have nobody bathing in them, no women washing in them or men
and boys fishing. 'Jamaica', he lyrically proclaimed, 'may be reckoned
amongst the most romantic and highly-diversified countries in the world,
uniting the rich magnificent scenery which waving forests, never-failing

streams, and constant verdure can present, heightened by the pure atmosphere, and the glowing tints of a tropical sun'. His account of the vegetable and animal productions quotes Linnaeus at the beginning, to demonstrate his knowledge of systems and science, but anecdotes break up the listings of strange fruits and animals, so that we learn, for example, that 'the writer . . . once narrowly escaped having a black snake for his bedfellow'.[28]

Phillippo's glorious narrative is not of military conquest but of the conquest by Christianity and the total transformation it had brought to Jamaica. This constitutes a particular variety of 'anti-conquest', to use Mary Louise Pratt's term, since he at one and the same time secures his innocence from the history of the slave trade and slavery as perpetrated by the English, and rearticulates Jamaica to her imperial mother through her continuing need for 'civilisation' European style.[29] An anti-slavery version of English history, accepting the shame of the slave trade – 'the first Englishman who thus dishonoured himself and his country was Captain, afterwards Sir John Hawkins' – but seeing the country as redeemed by 'the eminent philanthropists Sharpe, Clarkson and Wilberforce', is combined with the notion of a 'British lion' ever ready to take up the cause of freedom. Thus one notion of Englishness is countered with another, and a claim made that the Englishness of liberty, freedom and anti-slavery is the tradition to be celebrated and remembered. The relation between England and the Caribbean carried the histories of both slavery and emancipation; Phillippo's task was to soften the memory of the first with the memory of the second, and identify England with the moment of glory, rather than the moment of shame.[30]

Distinguishing between one kind of Englishness and another, one kind of whiteness and another, is essential for Phillippo, since his worst enemies in Jamaica had always been the planters, and his hope that a particular section of the white public in England would support the missionaries against them. The distancing, objective tone that he had tried to establish in the opening chapters served him well when describing white society on the island, for planters are quite as much a species to him as are negroes. Whiteness carried no guarantees in Jamaican society – indeed, it is the disarticulation between whiteness and Englishness which had ruined white Jamaican society. 'Though the white inhabitants of Jamaica', he writes, 'retained in a considerable degree the national customs, as well as many of the domestic and social habits of their European ancestors, yet in consequence of the peculiar circumstances in which they were placed, they rapidly degenerated in their mental attainments and general accomplishments.' The females 'became addicted to pleasures' and lost their domestic skills; both sexes became proud, avaricious and prejudiced, and adultery and promiscuity were everywhere. Small improvements had taken place since 1838, he was pleased to note, but 'revolting as it may be to English feelings', adulterers were still tolerated socially. Meanwhile a darkness 'thick, gross and palpable' still reigned in religion.[31]

While white society remained a disaster, however, black society had been transformed, and it was this which Phillippo was most concerned to demonstrate. Writing as he was within an anti-slavery discourse which claimed the success of 'the great experiment' in its terms – that negroes had become industrious, domesticated and respectable – Phillippo organised his narrative through the symbolic boundaries of *before* and *after*, as many had before him. His friend David East published a book on West Africa the following year with a similar motif. As Curtin argues, missionary works often drew on older notions of the balance of vice and virtue in the 'African character'. The *before* image featured slave raiding, human sacrifice, lascivious dance and sexualised religious ceremonies, while the *after* image showed 'the mild and gentle disposition of the converted Africans, their respect for the white missionaries, their childlike innocence'.[32]

But Jamaica was not Africa. As Jean and John Comaroff have argued, missionaries in southern Africa perceived complex connections between African bodies and landscapes – here was the link between man and beast. Missionary efforts to reform African men and women ran up against an 'unresolved conflict between the incorrigibility of natural endowment and the possibility of human improvement'.[33] The removal of Africans from the 'dark continent' and their forced relocation in plantation society were seen by advocates of slavery as providing the potential for civilisation. Africans were not quite the same when they were no longer in Africa. For the abolitionists, emancipation offered the key which allowed black men and women the possibility of entry into modernity: no longer locked in another time, archaic African time or the pre-modern time of slavery, they could enter the present, as infants. In Phillippo's narrative, slavery and heathenism were of the past, and emancipation and Christianity represented the present and future. The break between slavery and emancipation was then mapped on to the Christian moment of conversion, the histories *both* of Africa and of slavery eradicated in that moment of emancipation/conversion. So Africa and slavery were connected in his discourse of *before*, and African culture rejected as a part of that savagery.

Africa for Phillippo was a place of barbarism – the darkness both of superstition (before Christianity) and of fabled tribes. The enslavement of African peoples and enforced migration to Jamaica brought new horrors: they were reduced by their oppressors to the level of 'brutes', 'the dwarfs of the rational world'. Their bodies were possessed and tortured, their minds further corrupted by white wickedness. Their lives were forcibly lived at the level of animals, their songs devoid of poetry, their thoughts 'confined within the range of their daily employments and the wants of savage life'. Slave villages were scenes of degradation: 'every negro hut was a common brothel, every female a prostitute and every man a libertine'. Marriage was not recognised, polygamy was common, and customary divorce with a plantain leaf practised. 'Like the inhabitants of all uncivilised nations', wrote Phillippo, with the superiority which came from the certainty that nineteenth-century English middle-class forms of marriage were essentially civilised, 'the men treated the women as inferior in the scale of being to themselves, exercising over those who composed their respective harems a kind of petty sovereignty'. Homes, 'if such they could be called, were embittered by all the dark passions of the fallen heart'. The people were all idle in the sense of having no inner drive to work, for the only stimulus was the whip.[34]

An underlying anxiety for Phillippo in his representation of African-isms was undoubtedly the revival of myalism on the island in 1841–2. He worked hard to provide a rational account of this, no doubt as much for himself as for his readership. The outbreak had centred on the north of the island, so had not affected him in the same way as it had those, like Dendy and Waddell, who were working in the heartlands. Phillippo admitted in *Jamaica* that myalism had revived, but hoped that 'in a very short period . . . few vestiges of the superstition will remain'. He con-nected the revival with the inadequacy of laws against it, the absence of medical care, and the claim of myal men to cure assorted ills. He was well aware of the myalist incorporation of religious phraseology and the observances which had taken place. His description of the 'pernicious follies' of the Native Baptists, whom he never names as such, is written in the past tense, as if he could will them out of the Jamaica he was rep-resenting in his writing. Their actual presence across the island, however, was all too evident. He focused on the ways in which Native Baptist leaders mysteriously blended together 'important truths and extravagant puerilities'. The preachers and teachers, he claimed, referring to 'facts which the writer has repeatedly gathered from the lips of some of the parties themselves', pretended knowledge of the Bible, but frequently could not read, tried to mimic the behaviour of John the Baptist, and set great store by dreams and visions. They were not proper Christians.[35]

Terrible superstitions had mingled with the bacchanal of carnivals. Holiday scenes, such as that he had witnessed on his arrival in Spanish Town, 'were sometimes too disgusting to be looked upon'. Funeral rites involved 'wild and frantic gesticulations', 'strange and ridiculous manoeuvres', together with the claim to speak to the dead. 'The last sad

Heathen practices at funerals. This was the missionary vision of the regrettable practices which were swept away by their teachings.

From Phillippo, *Jamaica*.

offices' after the burial were scenes of blood and violence, and 'were usually closed by sacrifices of fowls and other domestic animals, which were torn to pieces and scattered over the grave, together with copious libations of blood and other ingredients, accompanied at the same time with the most violent and extravagant external signs of sorrow; they stamped their feet, tore their hair, beat their breast, vociferated.' Nothing could be more shocking to the English middle classes than this absence of restraint, whether in sexual life or dealing with the dead.[36]

After emancipation/conversion, however, all this was changed:

The crafty Eboe; the savage, violent, and revengeful Coromantee; the debased and semi-human Moco and Angolian, with those of other tribes described by historians as 'hardened in idolatry, wallowers in human blood, cannibals, drunkards, practised in lewdness, oppression, and fraud; cursed with all the vices that can degrade humanity; possessing no one good quality; more brutal and savage than the wild beasts of the forest and utterly incapable of understanding the first rudiments of the Christian religion' – these, thousands of them, are now subdued, converted, raised to the dignity and intelligence of men, of sons and daughters of the Lord God Almighty, and are bringing forth the fruits of holiness, happiness, and Heaven.

Here was the heart of Phillippo's conversion story, that most powerful of missionary stories. Now marriage was spreading, and with it the bourgeois family with its demarcated spheres for men and women. Women had learned modesty and a sense of shame, and were looking after their homes and children. Men were working on the estates and cultivating their plots. Manners had vastly improved, families were going to church on Sundays dressed respectably rather than in gaudy attire, decent new homes and cottages were being built which facilitated a proper family life, dancing and riotous music were disappearing, funeral practices had been reformed. 'Cunning, craft and suspicion' were giving place to 'a noble, manly, and independent, yet patient and submissive spirit' – the perfect negro man, combining the independence which was so central to an English conception of manhood with patience and submission, characteristics more frequently associated with femininity in England, and marking the distinction between white and black manhood.[37]

Phillippo's conception of the family of God was central to his thinking. Such a vision resolved his dual attachment to England and Jamaica. The richness of the concept of 'family' was that it offered a way of combining inequalities of power with belonging within a family. Just as men and women, parents and children, were equal, unequal and different, so white people and black could also be contained within this embracing framework. There was no contradiction for Phillippo in maintaining that 'Children we are all/Of one great Father, in whatever clime', while believing at the same time that children and fathers had different responsibilities and different levels of authority. He challenged those theorists who argued that negroes could never reach the state of civilised man, and argued that the victims of slavery were

men of the same common origin with ourselves, – of the same form and delineation of feature, though with a darker skin, – men endowed with minds equal in dignity, equal in capacity, and equal in duration of existence, – men of the same social dispositions and affections, and destined to occupy the same rank with ourselves in the great family of man.

That destiny, however, was a long way off in most instances. He asserted his faith 'that our coloured and black fellow-creatures are equally as capable of being conducted through every stage of mental discipline and taught to arrive at as great a height of social and intellectual improvement as has ever been attained by the most privileged Europeans'. However there was no question but that the conducting and teaching was to be done by white men of the right kind. The overarching conception of the 'family of man', however, allowed for shifts in the balance between equality and difference. At moments Phillippo's lack of respect for Jamaican whites, who had abandoned their English heritage, and pride in the reformation, as he saw it, of black people led him to claim that 'the black skin and the woolly hair constitute the only difference which now exists between multitudes of the emancipated peasantry of Jamaica and the tradesmen and agriculturalists of England'. There was still, of course, a line of class division between 'peasants' and the middle classes. Phillippo's father may have been in trade, but the son was a substantial professional man.[38]

Phillippo's identification with the new black Christian subject and his desire to give his publics what he saw as an authentic account of negro reformation meant that there was a much stronger black presence in his book than in any of the previous abolitionist accounts of Jamaica. This must have been partly the effect of having lived in a predominantly black society for twenty years and having congregations made up almost entirely of, first, slaves and then freed men and women. Phillippo actually knew black people in a way that none of the visiting abolitionists could possibly do. Indeed, throughout his life he gave much longer verbatim accounts of conversations with black men and women in his reports and publications than did most other missionaries. He included many anecdotes in patois, as well as speeches and prayers. Black people had voices in his text, even if always controlled, edited and monitored by him. Almost none of them had names, and were distinguished only by gender, however; whereas his white authorities and sources are named, distinguished by occupation and public position.

Phillippo believed that a new age was dawning, and that 'The sons of Ethiopia have been too long despised by the proud descendants of a more favoured fortune'. His reading of history showed him that the equality of the African mind had been proved in the past. He was quite willing to cite Toussaint L'Ouverture as evidence of heroic African man, for Toussaint was still a hero for some abolitionists.[39] Jamaica's future rested with 'the oppressed offspring of Ham' who 'will rise at the life-giving call of Christianity, and meekly array themselves in beauty and in power'. That power rested through Christianity on white (missionary) guidance; it was missionaries who guaranteed the meekness of the race.[40]

In celebrating the missionary cause and the glorious transformation effected in Jamaica, Phillippo was in part celebrating himself. His book not only produced Jamaica for England and Jamaica for the new

Visit of a missionary and his wife to a plantation village. The missionary, in full
regalia, accompanied by his wife, is received by respectable and grateful people.

From Phillippo, *Jamaica*.

Jamaica, it also produced Phillippo as new-style imperial man, identified
with black people, leading them firmly but kindly to civilisation, a man
who had won black love and respect, who dreamed of an egalitarian
future, yet yoked the emancipated to the parent with new bonds of gratitude for the 'gift' they had received. *Jamaica* was a paean of praise to
men who had 'sacrificed' themselves altruistically to the twin ventures of
missionary and anti-slavery work. At the heart of the book is the description of the 1 August 1838 celebration, when thousands paid tribute
to the part which he had played in the winning of emancipation, and
demonstrated by their decorous conduct the truth of abolitionist pre-
dictions. A telling vignette, combined with an engraving, described the
'typical' reception of a missionary and his wife in a village – the expressions of respect, regard and delight, the efforts to entertain, the differences established through dress and seating, the occasion it all provided
for a statement about Christian benevolence. Phillippo's account of the
success of post-emancipation society is predicated on his own key role,

and that of others like him. He represents himself as the supervisory, regulatory patriarchal figure, guarding and guiding the behaviour of his flock, educating them in chapel, school, and community to be an industrious, familial, obedient people. Yet the constant assertions of success, the insistence on missionary work as the key to the future, the celebration of 'the pastor' himself, were of course underpinned by anxieties as to the political and economic instability of the island, the character of 'the negroes' as a 'race', and the role of the white man. The distinction between good and bad white people, and good and bad black people, was drawn through attachment to religion. But would it be possible to maintain these lines? Was Phillippo himself as secure as he represented himself to be to himself and his public, in his identity as beloved pastor, father of his people?

Phillippo's encounter with Jamaica was through the lens of gendered discourses of anti-slavery and missionary enterprises. His missionary story of conversion provided the structure of his narrative, the before/after of new life in Christ and new life in freedom. The imposition of this binary model allowed him to control his story, to impose a structure which explained why things were going the way he wanted them to go, and to marginalise and exclude what did not fit. His *Jamaica* of the mind was firmly in place, regulated by his pastoral/imperial eye, its symbolic boundaries in order. But could this discursive construction hold?

Phillippo returned to Jamaica in 1844, by which time his book, with his vision of the new Jamaica, had appeared there. The *Baptist Herald* quoted the *Eclectic Review*'s summation: a 'beautiful narrative', 'eloquent' as to its facts, full of generous sentiments and breathing 'universal charity'. The book was announced as on sale in Edward Knibb's shop in Falmouth, as well as through the *Herald* office. By September it was noted that nearly one hundred reviews had been published, and that almost 3,000 copies had been sold.[41]

While Phillippo had been away, his missions had been cared for by Thomas Dowson, an English missionary sent out by the BMS.[42] Dowson, who had arrived in Jamaica in 1842, sent regular reports to England which focused on how much 'the Pastor' and his family were missed and how his return was eagerly anticipated. In *Jamaica* Phillippo quoted from these letters and made friendly reference to Dowson. Not long after his return, however, tension erupted between Dowson and Phillippo, which was to transfix sectors of Jamaican society for several years and send waves of agitation to England.

While Phillippo was in England, Dowson had married into the Spanish Town congregation and established his own independent relationships with the congregations of the varied mission stations. On his return, Phillippo was happy for Dowson to continue preaching in Spanish Town while he convalesced in his beautiful and healthy mountain home in Sligoville. Dowson claimed he named him co-pastor in May 1844. But by November, relations had deteriorated, and a schism was appearing in the congregation. Dowson claimed that Phillippo, having offered him the mission house in Spanish Town, now claimed it for himself and would not allow him to preach in the chapel. He argued that Phillippo was jealous of him 'on account of the feeling evinced towards him by the people', and that the membership had become increasingly dissatisfied with Phillippo's behaviour, 'in particular . . . on account of his proud and distant demeanour, his neglect of personal attention to the sick, the poor, the ignorant, and the afflicted, and at his non-attendance at the funerals in the families of deceased members'. Furthermore, Phillippo had refused to call a church meeting where the issues could be discussed by the membership. Dowson and his supporters set up a temporary chapel, provocatively close to the main one, and consulted a lawyer in order to establish a new trust deed. New trustees appointed Dowson as pastor, and held a public meeting at which, they claimed, a majority of the members of the main Spanish Town church voted that Phillippo should no longer be their minister.[43]

Phillippo was shattered. By January he was telling Joseph Angus, the secretary of the BMS, that 'my situation and that of my family is painful in the extreme'. Phillippo's version of the story was that he had never named Dowson co-pastor. Dowson, he believed, had set his heart on the Spanish Town mission, 'these valuable premises situated in the most important city of the Island' and would leave no stone unturned to gain control of it. An attack on Phillippo's 'ownership' of the church was, in English terms, an attack on his person, since a man's masculine identity was so intimately linked to his property and profession. In March one of Dowson's sisters-in-law, a Miss MacLean, an active member of the chapel, died. Phillippo was asked for the keys to the burial ground, and refused to hand them over. This enraged Dowson and his supporters, since the family of the dead woman 'had largely contributed to the expenses of the said church, which refusal had excited much indignant feeling amongst the people, and a determination on their part to assert their right to the ground, which they believed had been purchased by their money for their use'. A crowd gathered, broke into the burial ground, and began to dig the grave before efforts at negotiation succeeded.[44]

A few days later a more serious episode occurred when the wife of one of the deacons died. Her husband was Richard Bullock, a man who was quoted approvingly by name in *Jamaica*, a rare distinction for a black man. Friends of Phillippo's in the Cotswolds had presented the

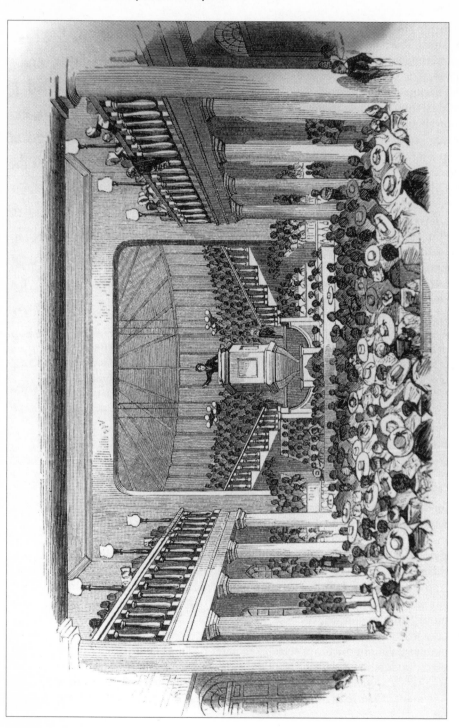

Interior of Baptist chapel, Spanish Town. This gives some indication of the scale of the chapel, and the potential power of the preacher. From Phillippo, *Jamaica*.

Spanish Town congregation with a Bible and a hymn-book for the use of the pulpit. Bullock, then enslaved and a leader in the chapel, had written to thank them, and his letter in patois was included as a demonstration of 'the simplicity and fervour of negro piety'. By 1845, however, Phillippo was not so well disposed to Bullock, since he was a supporter of Dowson. He again refused the keys to the burial ground. A crowd of several hundreds led by Dowson gathered in response, broke into the burial ground, and dug the grave. The body was then buried, according to Phillippo, 'amidst scenes not often exhibited in even a semi-barbarous community'. There was great excitement in the burial ground until well after midnight. Around three in the morning, when Phillippo and his friends thought all was quiet, they attempted to replace the fence and the gate, but 'the alarm was given and soon the whole town was aroused by the cry that I had ordered the corpse to be dug up and that I had pulled it limb from limb, and scattered it about the ground' – a fascinating rumour given Phillippo's preoccupation with 'proper' burial rites. A huge crowd assembled, and an attack was then made on the chapel, the communion vessels and Bible being seized and some damage done. The magistrates had to be called, and since they were not confident of being able to maintain the peace, the chapel was closed on their recommendation. Phillippo wrote to Angus that '[my] spirits are well-nigh broken and my health and strength prostrated', while Hannah had suffered a breakdown, having been attacked with 'hysterical fits and lost her reason for a considerable time from which she has not yet recovered'.[45]

Various attempts were made at mediation between the two parties, by other missionaries on the island and by a BMS deputation sent out in 1846. The deputation was extremely concerned about the effects of the affair. 'The mischief done by this suit cannot easily be conceived,' they concluded. 'It has divided our brethren, alienated most of the intelligent people of the town and has afforded a handle against Dissent.'[46] The brethren were certainly deeply divided, and the BMS was bombarded with angry letters from missionaries on both sides, though the majority supported Phillippo. Thomas Hands in Yallahs thought Phillippo had assumed power in ways that were 'utterly inconsistent with the principles and usages of Dissenting churches'; George Evans in Vale Lionel thought that the Baptist denomination in the island would never recover from 'the conduct of one who was looked up to as a guide'; while George Rowse from Kingston (which was a centre of support for Dowson) denounced Phillippo as 'a consummate rogue and hypocrite'.[47] Edward Hewett, on the other hand, thought that 'the conduct of Mr. Dowson has been of the basest kind'; while James Hume concluded gloomily that 'the armies of the living God have more to fear from divisions in their own camps, than from the oppositions of their enemies'.[48] Meanwhile Dowson, to the great distress of the BMS, had gone to the Jamaican Court of Chancery. The legal costs involved were enormous, and after several appeals to the BMS for help, Phillippo decided to appeal independently for support from England. A benefactor, Joseph Fletcher, took on most of the work, and an English committee functioned from London, raising money for him and providing advice. Their stated concern was that the Spanish Town mission premises had been bought initially with BMS money – that is, public funds, 'British benevolence' – and they wanted to protect those original interests and their appointee, Phillippo. They were sharply critical of the way in which Dowson and his supporters had played on what they saw as ignorance. 'The mass of the communicants are untutored and easily excited,' they argued, 'but few of them can either read or write, and many have not long enjoyed the blessings of freedom. They have been told in large and promiscuous assemblies, that their liberties and rights are invaded' – no wonder they had been led astray.[49] One of those same communicants, James A. Robertson, wrote angrily to the BMS that he knew exactly what he was doing, that he was not illiterate, and that he was fully cognisant of every decision which he and others had taken.[50] In 1850 the Court of Chancery declared in favour of Phillippo as pastor with rights to the property. This occasioned another riot, when a crowd composed mostly of women, attacked Phillippo's house, which was left 'stoned, damaged, pillaged and gutted of its furniture'. Mrs Phillippo was wounded with a stone, and the house was only saved from complete destruction by an appeal to the military. A guard had to be kept on the premises for ten days to prevent further trouble.[51]

The BMS deputation had concluded from their consultations whilst in Jamaica that 'the real and only question is, who is Pastor?' The possession of the properties, which were very extensive, given eight mission stations, including the highly desirable chapel, school and mission house in Spanish Town, went with that position. The issue as to who was the pastor was undoubtedly important, but perhaps more significant was the question of who had the right to appoint the pastor, or dismiss him? Phillippo had been appointed by the BMS and then, argued sections of the congregation, accepted by them. 'They adopted him,' they claimed; 'he was not appointed over them . . . the appointment of minister is vested in the leaders, deacons and members of the church.' This crucial distinction meant that the members could also, of course, choose to get rid of a minister they no longer accepted. Since dissenting congregations supported their own ministers financially, it was clear why they claimed rights to hire and fire. These were the moments when members could turn the patriarchal relation upside down and assert their authority over their putative 'fathers'. In Jamaica the situation was muddied by the money which had come from England through the BMS and been invested in property and men on the island. Jamaican congregations were for the most part firmly of the view, as was expressed in a series of conflicts amongst Baptist congregations across the island in the 1840s and 1850s, that mission buildings belonged to them, since they had provided the money and often built them with their own labour. In the case of Spanish Town they had certainly built it, but Phillippo had raised much of the money in England. Richard Bullock, the Spanish Town deacon, had no truck with this, however. He wrote to the BMS in 1845 complaining about Phillippo. He told them that 700 members of the congregation were opposed to him and wanted him to give up the premises, 'that we may chuse for ourselves the pastor we lik, as it is our property'.[52]

The pastor they liked on this occasion was white just like Phillippo, but questions of race were also at issue in this conflict. From the first signs of schism, Phillippo had been anxious to convince the BMS that the respectable and influential in Spanish Town were on his side. Dowson's party included 'the most uninfluential and disreputable characters', he claimed in January 1845; in March they were 'the rabble', and by April 'the very scum and refuse of the religious denominations . . . the basest rabble of the town and neighbourhood'. His black supporters were at times 'the poor deluded people' corrupted by Dowson's lust for power – unable, in other words, to think for themselves, therefore not to blame. Dowson was fanning their passions and 'exciting the worst feelings'. By July he saw them reduced to 'demi-savages', and by early 1846 he denounced them as 'infidel . . . wicked . . . profane', the struggle being a struggle between darkness and light, the forces of Satan and the army of Christ. Here were echoes of the binary division which Phillippo had made in *Jamaica* between the savage African and the emancipated/redeemed Christian – and those echoes had been picked up by the Spanish Town public.[53] 'We have already found out Mr. Phillippo to be an untrue Pastor, no protector of his people, no comforter to the sick and needy, and another thing an interferer of the dead in the grave,' said Joseph MacLean, whose relative had been refused burial.[54] Accusations of barbarism did not go only one way.

In March 1845 Phillippo noted that the whole town was in an uproar, and this had bad implications for the new edition of his book. Those people who had been prepared to have their names used for advertising purposes were no longer willing. Among the accusations of Dowson and his friends was the charge, as recounted by Phillippo, 'That I speak well of the black people before their faces, but that I have abused and vilified them on platforms in England, and especially in my Book'. He continued:

> The latter has been one of the most serious charges brought against me. It was first made by Duggan who was in the habit of reading all the portions of it which, though they might be quotations which I introduced in order to disprove what was unfavourable to the black and coloured people, he wished to be believed were my sentiments. Mr. Dowson . . . now denounces the book and has raised such prejudices against it that some of the people are ready to burn it, whilst he has quite succeeded in stopping the sale. The prejudices of the mass, indeed, are so general on this account that many of my own people have expressed their regret that I should ever have written it. . . . Thus the general opinion among the black people is, that I have abused them in a shameful manner in the book and they look upon me as a traitor to themselves and the country.

Furthermore, it was reported to Phillippo that Dowson had been rousing the people against him on various occasions by using the language of bondage and rights, telling them they would be fools to 'go back to be subjects again to his tyranny and oppression'. 'You were fools to be subjects to him so long as you had been,' he chided them, whilst excusing them from foolery because they could not help it, for 'you were under bondage'. 'Seek, then for your rights', he urged them, 'The Chapel is yours, and you *shall* have it.'[55]

Phillippo tried to convince himself that *Jamaica* had made enemies for him because of its exposure of the state of the island under slavery. This was not the case in Spanish Town. His critics there were playing on the knowledge that this patriarchal pastor had claimed too much authority, that in representing black people in his chosen image, in splitting so dramatically between good and bad, African and negro, he had betrayed black confidence. As Underhill summed it up in his biography of Phillippo many years later, the events 'greatly affected . . . (his) judgement of the negro character'. Phillippo's tale enjoyed considerable success in representing Jamaica to England, for, after all, as the Rev. Birrell remarked to a large Baptist audience in England, 'I do think that a pretty accurate idea may be formed of it without leaving our own island'.[56] Phillippo had attempted discursively to construct Jamaican society in a particular way. But Africa had survived, the paternalistic relations which his narrative had tried to set up could not hold, his possessiveness over 'his' chapel and 'his' stations was misplaced. In representing Jamaica to Jamaica, in attempting to produce Jamaica from an imperial Christian perspective, he provoked a crisis of representation, his fatherhood rejected by large numbers of his 'loving people'. The events in Spanish

Town marked the unravelling of those relations of power which his text had attempted to stabilise, the eruption of the excluded, the breakup of a particular 'Jamaica of the mind'.

The *Falmouth Post* metaphorically rubbed its hands in glee at these events. The sight of the Baptist missionaries warring amongst themselves was an unmitigated joy. It loved to tell damaging tales of how Phillippo's supporters taunted Dowson's congregation and broke up their devotions, how Miss Elizabeth Carr, the apparently respectable teacher of Phillippo's girls' school called out at the end of Dowson's ministrations one evening, 'That's a lie, Dowson, all that you have been saying this evening are lies'. Baptist influence was on the wane, and soon their friends in England would realise this.[57]

By the mid-1850s Phillippo had lost some of his faith in an earlier vision of a new Jamaica, peopled with new black subjects. In time he was able to adjust to a new understanding of his place on the island. He remained a staunch friend of the emancipated, supporting their rights time and again over the next years, defending their record, for example, on a visit to the USA in 1856–7.[58] In his evidence to the Royal Commission after Morant Bay he insisted on the peaceable atmosphere of his own district during the troubles.[59] He stayed in Jamaica until his death in 1879, and was buried beside his wife in Spanish Town. His three sons stayed on the island too – one a doctor, one a barrister, who acted for the Anti-Slavery Society in the Royal Commission hearings, and one a planter. The family regarded Jamaica as their home.

'A place of gloomy darkness'

In the period after 1845 the dramas in Spanish Town and similar events which took place in Kingston were only the most dramatic of the divisions amongst the Baptists. The Montego Bay congregation was riven with antagonisms. Thomas Williams and Isaac Beckford wrote to Dendy, who had been trying to mediate, declining the possibility of an English pastor and looking forward to the day they would be able to invite one of their own countrymen, 'who will preside over our affairs according to the rightful rules of congregationalism'. No agreement could be found, and the church split, leading to further difficulties.[60] Smaller-scale splits and secessions happened frequently, and the differences between Native Baptists and orthodox Baptists were an ever-present issue, with questions of property and authority often at the fore. One stipendiary magistrate reported a typical state of affairs in the Old Harbour area: 'The two Baptist congregations in this parish keep quite distinct from each other, though holding the same tenets,' he noted; 'those following the black native minister having quitted the white minister on account of some misunderstanding concerning the ownership of the chapel and buildings, have now built a chapel of their own, and defended two actions (for title to land) which they have gained. Both congregations continue numerous.'[61] Philip Curtin notes that all the missionary churches gained members up to 1845, but then lost between a quarter and half that membership between 1845 and 1865. In 1846 the Native Baptist congregations in Vere were stronger than all the European churches put together, and in Kingston there were sixty Native Baptist churches which encompassed half the church-going population.[62] 'The Baptists are much divided amongst themselves,' reported Governor Grey to the Colonial Office in 1849, 'and certainly have not the same power over the negro population which they possessed a few years ago.'[63] The loss of support from the emancipated was mirrored by the decline in support from the missionary public in Britain, which was distinctly less interested in the West Indies. Jamaica, it was felt, had been privileged long enough.[64]

The missionaries had held a key political position in the period of slavery, apprenticeship, and the first years of emancipation, as spokesmen for the enslaved and apprenticed, representing Jamaica to the abolitionists and the imperial government. But after 1846 they were no longer able to wield the same power and influence. Emancipation, as Douglas Hall argues, had seemed likely to threaten the political supremacy of the planters.[65] No constitutional change had taken place at the time of emancipation, but it was clear that small freehold settlements would in time mean a larger black electorate. Adult males who paid taxes on freehold lands of £6 per annum, an annual rent of £30, or direct taxes of £3 per annum had the right to vote provided they registered. It was this which had enabled Knibb and others to dream of a political future in which black freeholders would be in command. The decline of the great estates after emancipation, furthermore, meant that merchants and small farmers were better represented than they had been in the House of Assembly.

From the mid-eighteenth century the House of Assembly had been the sole originator of bills and had enjoyed considerable executive authority. Over a long period, the House had effectively taken power away from the Legislative Council and the governor and had represented itself as the local House of Commons.[66] The House of Assembly had had to suffer what it saw as a usurpation of its authority in 1833 when the imperial parliament had abolished colonial slavery. In 1838, to make sure that this did not happen again, it had felt forced to abandon apprenticeship. Both white and coloured members were determined to resist further interference from the imperial government. The coloured members were in alliance with the planters on this point, since they were particularly strong supporters of the rights of the assembly, for, as Heuman points out, island politics provided their only forum.[67] This led to a crisis and the refusal by the assembly to continue business. In January 1839 Henry Taylor, a key figure in the West India department at the Colonial Office from 1824 to 1872, submitted a paper to the Cabinet on the troublesome West Indian assemblies. He argued that there was an 'inherent and permanent incongruity of the system with the state of society', that representative institutions should be abolished, and crown colony government introduced. These societies were hopelessly divided along racial and class lines, he believed. 'Let the society of Jamaica be taken, for example', he continued:

> 320,000 black people just emancipated, still in the depths of ignorance, and by their African temperament highly excitable; about 28,000 people, partly coloured partly black, whose freedom is of an earlier date than that of the emancipated class, of whom many have property but so few were decently educated that it was thought by the Governor that their own friends would not wish to see the Assembly chiefly composed of them; and lastly, 9,000 whites possessed by all the passions and inveterate prejudices growing out of the slave system. Throw these elements into what forms or combinations we will, is it possible to bring out of them anything like a representative system properly so called?[68]

Until the mass of the population was educated and raised to new levels of civilisation, he argued, representative government could not work. The assembly would inevitably pursue only its own interests; both white men and black men were irresponsible and unrepresentative. Only the imperial government was mature enough to rule from above. The decision was taken, therefore, to suspend the Jamaican constitution for five years. This move was opposed by both Peel and the Radicals. The Prime Minister, Lord Melbourne, was forced to resign on this issue and had to abandon the scheme, and only returned after having capitulated to a policy of conciliation to the planters.[69] A new governor was appointed, Metcalfe, whose task was to find a new equilibrium. Metcalfe saw the Baptist missionaries as a serious impediment to this process, whereas the two previous governors, the Marquis of Sligo and Sir Lionel Smith had been moderately sympathetic. Jamaica was populated, Smith once commented, by 'white savages and black Christians', a view with which Knibb was very sympathetic.[70] Metcalfe's judgement both of the emancipated people and of the missionaries was much more hostile. Having served in India, he was astonished by the levels of comfort and independence enjoyed by black men and women, and thought that the Baptists had encouraged 'their negro flocks', with pernicious consequences, to think far too much of their rights and not enough of their obligations.[71] There are echoes here of the astonishment which Eyre registered over the difference between Aboriginal peoples and the freed black men and women whom he encountered in the Caribbean. Imperial travellers had racial mappings within their minds which shaped their perceptions of the new terrains they occupied.

During the 1840s an opposition party to the planters emerged in the House of Assembly, the 'Town Party', with a high proportion of coloured and Jewish merchants and professionals, but the House was still a planter stronghold. Both economically and politically, however, the planters were in a defensive position. The years 1838–46 had been a time of great initiative and enterprise for the emancipated. The Baptist missionaries' attempt to mobilise the new freeholders politically was in the context of this rebalancing of social and economic relations. It was a period of high prosperity for freed slaves, with estate wages at relatively good levels and provisions selling well. But after 1846, wages fell, the number of sugar estates was reduced, and it was more difficult to find work. Provision prices also fell because of the general depression.[72] The census of 1844 suggested that the island's population was probably about 400,000, with at least 291,000 black people, 68,000 coloured, and 15,000–16,000 Europeans plus East Indians and new African immigrants.[73]

In 1845 the Whig government had declared its intention of abandoning the sugar duties which protected the price of West Indian sugar. The primary motive was a commitment to free trade. But there was also a sense of disappointment about the pace of negro improvement. The artificially high rate of wages, which were protected by the duties, it was believed, 'and the absence of devoting more than a small portion of their time to labour, instead of proving of real advantage to them had tended to make them rather retrograde than advance in civilisation'.[74] The government's intention was to protect sugar or, rather, the sugar planters in other ways: notably by facilitating immigration. Both planters and missionaries were united against the ending of protection, anxious to defend the sugar estates which were the major employer of labour, albeit on highly contested terms, and major producers of exportable produce, seen as the key to wealth. Up to 1846 the planters had on the whole, argues Douglas Hall, been optimistic about the future of sugar, and had tried to tackle the issues regarding the need for capital investment and the supply of labour. But the crisis over duties brought a crisis of confidence. The desire of freed slaves to leave the plantations when they could, and the exodus particularly of women, who had constituted the majority of the field labour force,[75] had led to a decline in sugar production after emancipation, at a time when other countries were increasing their production. In 1820 the island was producing about 20 per cent of the world's cane sugar; by 1830, 11 per cent; by 1840, 3 per cent; and by 1851, less than 2 per cent.[76] Free trade was the final straw for many planters, and they cancelled immigration schemes, which had been designed to provide labour, and capital investment plans. In 1848 they were successful, through their pressure on the Select Committee on Sugar and Coffee in the Colonies, in delaying the date of equalisation to 1854. By then, however, they had given up hope of maintaining protection and had returned to the problem of labour as at the heart of continued sugar production. Many of the sugar estates had by this time been abandoned, hundreds failing in the late 1840s and 1850s; but neither the planters nor the imperial government were able to recognise that sugar might not be the key to the Jamaican economy.

Thomas Holt convincingly argues that from the mid-1840s the fear of a black majority stalked the debates in the Colonial Office as to the government of Jamaica. Given the relative numbers of peoples, 'democracy meant black power'. After emancipation, Colonial Office officials had tried to maintain forms of democratic practice whilst denying any substance to them. In the process, 'racism became an essential solvent for dissolving the otherwise blatant contradictions between liberal democratic ideology and colonial practice'.[77] In 1848 and 1849 there had been a series of alarms, in Westmoreland, Hanover and St James, where Governor Grey reported the view that 'the Black population entertain some evil designs'. He did not suspect any general conspiracy, but noted that the uneducated state of the labourers, recent disorders in Haiti, and rumours about the risings in Europe might have 'excited a few of the more instructed and clever of the labouring class to indulge in wild and dangerous thoughts'. He issued a proclamation assuring black people of their rights, inviting them to demonstrate that they were 'worthy to sustain the character of freemen, and to be the fathers of free families'. The Baptist missionaries, meanwhile, disavowed any responsibility for any discontent, and blamed it on the non-payment of wages.[78] In 1851 a serious riot in St David, provoked by the defeat of a candidate supported by black people, further fuelled the anxieties of the Europeans and the Colonial Office.

Holt argues that by 1850 key British policy-makers were making a distinction between the forms of government appropriate to black and white colonies. The latter needed 'benevolent guardianship'. Earl Grey thought that it was vitally important for the imperial government to maintain responsibility, for the loosening of colonial ties could unleash 'a fearful war of colour . . . and too probably all the germs of improvement which now exist there would be destroyed and civilization would be thrown back for centuries'.[79] He compared Jamaica with Canada, and argued that while it would be possible to accept self-government in the white settler colony, it was not a feasible policy for a society with a large black majority. A colony's fitness for self-government, thought the Colonial Office, would be determined by the numbers of white settlers, but in the tropics those white settlers were only 'temporary sojourners' in Stephen's term, who could not, therefore, be relied on.[80] Canada, however, was becoming an increasingly white society: more British people were emigrating there, and so reducing the French majority. In 1837 there had been a crisis over French Canadians demanding independence from Britain. This was seen as a racial struggle between the British and the French. Lord Durham, sent to sort it out, proposed in his famous report the reunification of the British and French provinces under a single governor, with ministers from the elected colonial assembly. This was the system which came to be called 'responsible government', and was to be adopted throughout the colonies of white settlement. In 1849, when the Colonial Office was seriously worried about Jamaica, it was proposed that its constitution be remodelled in the Canadian style. But Canada, the Colonial Office argued, was a totally different situation from Jamaica. In other words, it had a black majority and could not be self-governing in the forseeable future.

The year 1854 marked the final settlement of the free-trade crisis. The assembly promised to reform the constitution in return for a low-interest loan. The planters, more worried about increasing democracy than imperial authority, agreed that executive authority should rest with the governor, who was to appoint an executive committee including three members of the assembly. This would facilitate communications between the governor and the legislature.[81] Legislative powers were left with the House of Assembly, which retained the initiative on money bills and appointed a legislative council which had the rights of veto.[82] This reversed the pattern which had been to increase the powers of the legislative as against the executive. Edward Jordan, the prominent coloured member of the House of Assembly, was put on the new executive committee as a way of trying to guarantee coloured support. A new governor was appointed who was convinced that the political conflict on the island could be explained solely in terms of racial difference, a conclusion which mirrored the shifts in racial thinking which were going on in England.

On his arrival on the island, Governor Barkly requested reports from those stipendiary magistrates who remained. He was appalled by 'the description of the demoralised state of the emancipated negroes', by the indications of the 'march back to barbarism' which they provided. The labour question, he insisted, was at the root of all the problems: in

other words, the issue was that the freed slaves would not work continuously.[83] The findings were more disparate than the governor allowed.
In Portland, Charles Lake found that the small settlers were doing well.
They owned animals, traded extensively, were contributing to taxation,
and were civil and obedient and willing to work on the large estates.
They attended church properly dressed, many had got married, and
'degrading' superstitions seemed to be on the wane.[84] Similarly, Barkly
himself, on a tour of the island in June, recognised 'a decided air of progressive civilisation and comfort' in the free villages, their inhabitants
'not retrograding' either in their moral or physical condition.[85] Alexander Fyfe, in St David, saw little improvement, however. Black people's
funeral practices were lavish and inappropriate to his mind. The little
education that was available was doing no good, since it was constantly
counteracted by family life. Similarly, Henry Kent in Port Royal was
gloomy as to the morals of the people – concubinage flourished and marriage attracted few adherents. David Ewart in Kingston also saw the
black family, or rather the lack of proper family, as the root of all moral
evil. Marriages had become less frequent, and there was a 'shameful
depravity' amongst young men and women which was mainly the fault
of the parents. 'Meeting-houses with black preachers are springing up
on all sides,' recorded Kent; many of these men were totally uneducated
and it was a case of 'the blind leading the blind' which could not but
result in serious mischief.[86]

Richard Hill, the first coloured stipendiary magistrate on the island,
had been educated in England. Now serving in Spanish Town, his close
associations with the anti-slavery movement did not prevent him from
having definite opinions about innate negro characteristics. Perhaps
reflecting on the events amongst the Baptists that he had witnessed, he
felt quite confident in asserting that, 'Nothing has proved more demon-
strably a fact, than that religion, with so excitable and irrepressible a
being as the negro by temperament is, is not so much a spiritual feeling
as an animal emotion'. This would continue to be the case, he was convinced, until 'family habits' really became established. He meant, of
course, a particular set of 'family habits'. Spanish Town, he thought, was
especially subject to offences against morality and decency because of
the presence of the military. 'More indulgence', he remarked, 'is granted
to African than to European soldiers, in respect of temporary female
associates.' Licentious sexual habits were assumed to be 'natural' to
Africans, and the African regiments were 'always followed by a train of
very profligate tramps'.[87] It was a source of anxiety to many officials and
missionaries that the incidence of freedmen and women marrying had
dropped sharply in the late 1840s and 1850s: another sign of the return
to Africa.[88]

The differences between pastor and flock were discussed most fully by Thomas Witter Jackson, in St Thomas-in-the-Vale. In that area the large estates had more or less disappeared, which made clear how vital the small settlements and the peasantry were. In areas such as this the 'two Jamaicas', as Curtin named them, were all too visible. The planters' white-dominated Jamaica was that of the plains and inland valleys, the settlers' Jamaica was that of the mountain freeholds.[89] Most peasant cultivation had been established on existing estates, because of the need for local markets and transport, though some had taken place in more mountainous areas. As estates disappeared, the white population also disappeared, and the establishment of free villages meant a geographical separation between racial groups. The black population in these areas had little contact with the world of white planters, magistrates, managers or even missionaries.[90] Richard Hill's verdict in 1854 was that while one world in Jamaica was occupied with a constitutional crisis, the other was populated by 'mere creatures of sensation', who 'enquired into nothing; talked about nothing'. He meant, of course, that they did not talk about his issues, his concerns.[91]

Jackson was convinced that peasant production would spread over the land, but would it bring 'a fertilising rain or a destructive tempest'? He found the labouring classes 'patient' and 'tractable', but it was vital that their minds should be improved and their industry encouraged. 'If ever there was a time', he argued, 'that something should be done by a government for a people, this is the people and now is the time.' During the last few years, he feared, regression had been taking place. In the period before emancipation the missionary had emerged as the friend of 'the negro', his spiritual guide and temporal counsellor. But 'the negro' had not been as transformed, morally and spiritually, as all had assumed. Consequently his fall from grace, 'from the height to which he had been erroneously elevated', caused great disappointment on the one hand and glee on the other. 'Having obtained his freedom,' Jackson noted, 'the negro became less dependent on the secular aid of the missionary.' At the same time, however, the missionary had become more dependent financially on his membership, since, in the case of the Baptists particularly, financial independence from the parent society had been declared – hence the disputes between pastor and flock, which in some unfortunate instances turned into hot and fierce strife, all of which significantly reduced the influence of the missionaries. Jackson's comment on the financial problem is significant. Douglas Hall estimates that the annual average contribution of Baptist church members in 1844 was 12 shillings, by 1859 it was little over 3 shillings.[92] The free peasantry no longer had money to spare, a further consequence of which was a decline in schooling, since parents could not, or would not, make contributions for their children's education. The effects of this on the missionaries themselves were severe. In theory they no longer had the right to claim help from London and suffered from the lack of patrons in Jamaica. 'We have no wealthy persons to whom we can appeal for assistance in this community,' Walter Dendy wrote sadly to the secretary of the BMS. Indeed, there was no middle class on whom they could rely.[93] Jackson's considered judgement was that the impact of the missionaries had been most unfortunate, and that the improvement of the people could certainly not be left to them.[94]

Barkly, fresh from London, was kinder: his verdict on the Baptist missionaries in 1854 was that they were performing a vital task. The 'innate' character of the negro was the problem, and the missionaries were doing useful work in counteracting this. As an Anglican, he regretted that only the Baptists had been committed to 'following these settlers into the wilderness', and erecting chapels and schools. But that was the reality. 'Left to themselves in remote localities,' he believed, 'the people must inevitably retrograde.' 'I am bound to say', he confessed, that 'I found their congregations well dressed and orderly'; indeed, they were 'the most civilised portion of the emancipated population'.[95] Such was the official judgement in 1854. Only the Baptists had succeeded in 'civilising' Africa.

But the missionaries themselves were in deep gloom. Given the severity of the problems on the island, reported Dendy, 'I see no prospect but the abandonment of station, the breaking up of Churches, and to a great extent the overthrow of the Baptist Mission in this Island.'[96] Urgent appeals were made to England on behalf of the emancipated, particularly their educational needs:

> Through the munificence of the British nation, they are blest with the inestimable boon of perfect and entire freedom, but what will this avail if they be still left in the depths of ignorance? Left a prey to their own unrestrained passions, it is to be feared that their course will be marked by licentiousness, violence, heathenism and every species of crime and will terminate only in endless despair.[97]

The economic situation of the island was dire. Cholera in 1851, closely followed by drought and smallpox, created yet further sorrow. Missionaries themselves were cracking up, behaving badly, failing to act as models for the community. Brother Hands, for example, had 'greatly injured the cause of Christ . . . and destroyed his own usefulness' by drinking and dancing. Abandoned by the parent society and the British public, was 'endless despair' the only road for the missionaries in Jamaica?[98]

Phillippo's story was that of a man who learned the hard way. Converted as a young man, he had found meaning and inspiration in the missionary and abolitionist movements. In the post-emancipation moment he was able to exercise power and influence on a scale that could not have been imagined in the difficult years of the 1820s, when the planters had tried to block his every move. Together with the governor, he had welcomed full emancipation in the main square of Spanish Town. But his optimistic narrative of Jamaica's transformation, designed for both the British and Jamaican reading publics, which told the tale of the transformation from paganism to Christianity, from barbarism to civilisation, from Africa to the new Jamaica, overstepped the mark. 'His' church and 'his' people refused his definitions, and left him a chastened man. By the mid-1850s the prospects for the missionaries seemed gloomy: their congregations were smaller, their finances in a parlous state, and the Colonial Office had become convinced that Jamaica, with a black majority population, could not possibly be self-governing in the forseeable future.

4

Missionary Men and Morant Bay 1859–1866

Anthony Trollope and Mr Secretary Underhill

In the metropole the figure of the African remained highly contested, and part of the work of the missionaries was to counter those representations which damaged their cause. They needed to maintain the support, both financial and otherwise, of missionary and abolitionist enthusiasts. The mid-nineteenth century saw a proliferation of ways of being English in relation to Africans. In 1857 Livingstone's immensely popular *Travels* was published, bringing the explorer and the African continent into the heart of the civilising vision.[1] There were intense debates and disagreements as to what place Africans under the tutelage of Englishmen should occupy, and what role Englishmen should take. But metropolitans were united by their distance from the backward time and archaic space of both Africa and the West Indies, their shared conviction that it was they who could bring the African or the West Indian negro into modern times.[2] The appearance in 1859 of Anthony Trollope's *The West Indies and the Spanish Main* was a damaging blow to the missionary cause, and the missionaries martialled their troops, in the figure of the secretary of the BMS, Edward Bean Underhill, to reply. These two books on the West Indies, by a popular novelist and a missionary stalwart, marked a new moment of discursive instability in representations of the negro.

Trollope was a very different kind of Englishman from the missionaries. In 1858 he was asked by his employers, the Post Office, to go and 'clean up' the Post Office system in the West Indies, for the colonial postal systems were mainly managed from 'home'.[3] Before he left, he arranged a contract with Chapman and Hall for a book about his journey, which he wrote while he was away. The book was published on his return and

was an immediate success, going into a sixth edition by the following
year, as well as being published in the USA. Trollope regarded it retrospectively 'as the best book that has come from my pen. It is short, and,
I think I may venture to say, amusing, useful, and true.' This truth claim
was important to Trollope, who wrote as he travelled, never making any
notes or doing any preparation, aiming to reproduce 'that which the eye
of the writer has seen and his ear heard', 'the exact truth as I saw it'.[4]
Some readers in Britain may have believed what they read, but readers
in the West Indies were less impressed by this claim to have truthfully
represented their societies. 'Going a-Trolloping' passed into the Jamaican
vernacular as a synonym for travelling commentators who knew not
what they saw.[5]

Son of a famous author, with a brother who was also a successful
writer, Trollope had had difficulty in finding a writing voice for himself.
By 1858 he had lived in Ireland for some years, published three unsuccessful novels about that country, and started on his Barsetshire Chronicles. *The Warden* came out in 1855, and *Barsetshire Towers* in 1857,
bringing him considerable attention. *The West Indies and the Spanish
Main* was the first of what was to be a very successful series of travel
books written over the next twenty years, most of them about the
colonies of white settlement.[6]

Trollope's characteristics could be described as peculiarly English.
Indeed, his quintessential Englishness was commented on again and
again by contemporaries. 'Standing with his back to the fire, with his
hands clasped behind him and his feet planted somewhat apart,' wrote
one, 'the appearance of Anthony Trollope, as I recall him now, was that
of a thorough Englishman in a thoroughly English attitude.'[7] To another,
Trollope's views had little 'novelty in them – you were disappointed not
to find so clever a writer more original – but they were worth listening
to for their solid common sense, tending rather to commonplace sense'.[8]
This 'solid common sense' was a characteristic of both the man and his
writing. As Henry James remarked, 'with Trollope we were always safe'.
In his posthumous evaluation, he wrote of 'his great, his inestimable
merit' as 'a complete appreciation of the usual'.[9] Similarly, George Eliot,
whose husband Lewes was one of Trollope's 'dearest friends',[10] commented on the 'good bracing air' which Trollope's novels evoked for her.
His books were 'filled with belief in goodness'; they were like 'pleasant
public gardens, where people go for amusement and, whether they think
of it or not, get health as well'.[11] Thomas Carlyle was less kind. In his
caustic and cruel way, he summed Trollope up as 'irredeemably imbed-
ded [*sic*] in commonplace'.[12]

Trollope was safe and English: humorous as to the foibles of his own
people; a particular lover of the hunt; a club-man (the Athenaeum and

the Garrick); a married man who loved to flirt but was a profound believer in marriage, family and 'proper' relations between the sexes; a Church of England man who disliked enthusiasm or extremism of any kind; a supporter of deference and the English constitution; fascinated by class difference but with no sympathy for class politics; a believer in the superiority of the Anglo-Saxon race. He was kind, untroubling, riveted by the daily round of politics without being political, producing happy endings for his novels, believing in church, family and nation in ways which confirmed complacency rather than producing unsettled states of mind. These were some of the values of that 'best loved and most widely read of the Victorian novelists'.[13]

But the 'pleasant public garden' of his mind was perhaps less ordered than such a description might suggest, for the racial thinking which underpinned it raised discomforting issues for liberal opinion: issues which were most clearly articulated in his travel writing. Trollope's travels focused on the empire. He became fascinated by the colonies, particularly those which were peopled primarily by Anglo-Saxons: 'writing the empire' provided a way of affirming the connectedness and particularity of that race across the globe. He became convinced in the 1870s and 1880s that the empire did not matter enough to the English, that there was much more to be known, and it was a part of his mission to spread that knowledge in readable and accessible ways. For Trollope the empire was part of everyday Englishness, part of what was distinctive about the Anglo-Saxon race. This did not mean that he was sympathetic to imperial expansion.[14] It was important, he believed, that the 'Old World' should make informed judgements about the 'New'. His book on the West Indies inaugurated a sustained interest in non-fictional writing on colonial questions, an interest which he pursued for the rest of his life.[15] His writing on Ireland, that part of the empire which was part and parcel of 'home', remained almost exclusively fictional.[16]

Trollope's amiable Englishness was embedded in an imagined map of empire which surfaces periodically in the forty-seven novels he published.[17] His mapping of imperial places and peoples, utilising familiar language and images, brought Maori 'cannibals', Jamaican 'Quashees' and energetic white Australian settlers right into the parlour. Difference was domesticated, and binary divisions between black and white both reaffirmed and questioned in the colonising mind. The English were reassured that it was their country's right to civilise. The sites of empire were represented by the quintessential English good fellow, Anthony Trollope, in ways that English readers could take great pleasure in; for here was a favourite fictional writer transporting them to Australia, Canada and the West Indies. Here also were the serious debates of the political economists and social critics translated into the popular form of the personal travelogue, with vignettes on hotel accommodation, forms of transport and natural wonders set alongside short disquisitions on matters social and political and entertaining anecdotes of 'other' peoples.

Trollope's confidence regarding his right to provide a cartography of peoples, displaying them in his texts as they were constantly being displayed also in family magazines, newspapers, missionary sermons, novels and the plethora of other sites of cultural representation, always contained within it the anxiety as to whether those peoples were really in place. Were Jamaican planters fit to rule? Might Maori 'cannibals' eat British soldiers? Trollope's writing on the West Indies was part of contemporary debates about racial difference, quietening imperial anxieties in the wake of the 'Indian Mutiny' of 1857, yet never entirely certain that all was in place. Yet, at the same time some conventional assumptions were mocked, and some sacred cows disturbed. Trollope never fully effected closure: as Simon Gikandi argues, in his account of the West Indies he used irony 'to undermine the binaries that define the colonial relation'. The 'natural' relation between white and black was disrupted by his caustic account of the creole whites and his claim that the future lay with the coloured people of Jamaica.[18] But Trollope simultaneously reaffirmed white superiority and the inferiority of the African. In caricaturing the arguments of the anti-slavery men, he was happy to repeat the familiar claim that they did not know what they were talking about. 'Gentlemen in the West Indies', he wrote, 'see at once that the Society is discussing matters which it has not studied, and that interests of the utmost importance to them are being played with in the dark.'[19] 'Playing in the dark' provides an apt metaphor for Trollope's own colonial strategies as contradictory imperatives were played out in his writing.[20]

Trollope was an eclectic thinker, committed to an English empirical tradition which believed in the objective eye, utilising insights from various sources and with an understanding of the West Indies shaped by the long struggle over the representations of those islands and their peoples between planters and abolitionists. His oldest friend, after whom his son was named, was Henry Merivale. The Merivales were family friends of the Trollopes, and Herman Merivale, Henry's brother, was a noted colonial thinker. Merivale's formative role in colonial theory was recognised in his appointment as Assistant Under-Secretary of State for the Colonies in 1847. Between 1839 and 1841 he had given his inaugural lectures as Professor of Political Economy on 'this very popular and interesting topic', colonisation and colonies, at the University of Oxford. He argued that Europe's destiny of foreign conquest and domination was fixed and unalterable, comparing the British pattern with that of Greece and Rome.[21]

In 1861 the full text of Merivale's *Lectures* was produced in a new edition, with long additional commentaries bringing the work up to date. His project in these lectures was to convey information on an important topic, to encourage people to think about colonisation and political economy, to carefully assess the economic effects of colonisation and 'trace the progress of colonies in their second or adult stage, and up to the period when their independence, either virtual or actual, commences'. There are many signs of Merivale's influence on Trollope. Trollope was not interested in Merivale's primary concern with economic questions. But he adopted many of his other principal ideas, for Trollope was a populariser, working with elements of different intellectual and political traditions. Merivale's classical definition of 'colony' as 'a territory of which the soil is entirely or principally owned by settlers from the mother country' became Trollope's. Only the white settler colonies, therefore, were 'real' colonies. These were to be clearly distinguished from military outposts and from 'colonies of exploitation', which were primarily used as sites for the production of staples for Europe. Similarly, Merivale's trope of colonial development as an infant's growth from dependence to independence was constantly reiterated by Trollope in his later discussions of North America, Australia and New Zealand. Trollope read Merivale, and Merivale read Trollope. Merivale's comments on the West Indies are strongly evocative of Trollope, who is congratulated in Merivale's text as 'an observer of no common acuteness', though often accused of seeing 'too much with the eyes of the planter party'.[22]

Merivale saw the spirit of England as intimately linked with the colonial project, a view to which Trollope was deeply attached. 'The destiny of our name and nation is not here, in this narrow island which we occupy,' he wrote. The English spirit was progressive, capable of growth and development and emigration was, for him, a process 'dictated by nature itself'. The mother country had a special moral mission, for, having abolished slavery, she was bound 'above all communities to watch ... over the interests of the negro race'. Her responsibilities were to protect and civilise 'natives'. 'Native races must ... either perish, or be amalgamated with the general population of their country.' He was not, therefore, opposed to intermarriage. 'The feebler race must yield to the stronger; the white is destined to extirpate the savage', but there was no reason why even the lowest 'may not enter by degrees into the sphere of civilisation', though remaining always a subordinate race to the whites. All civilising attempts, Merivale believed, must commence with religious instruction, a view that Trollope did not share. Colonisation, Merivale concluded, was crucially linked to 'the sense of national honour ... the instincts of a dominant race'.[23]

The influence of a very different thinker, Thomas Carlyle, on Trollope has been much more generally recognised. At the time of the publication of *The West Indies and the Spanish Main*, and since, those who were sympathetic to the emancipated West Indian islands were sharply critical of Trollope's account, linking it with Carlyle's 'Occasional Discourse on the Negro Question'. While *The Times* welcomed the book, the anti-slavery public did not. Trollope had been raised in a family in which anti-slavery was the orthodoxy. Frances Trollope, Anthony's powerful mother, was a supporter of abolition. But her support for anti-slavery was not combined with a belief in the equality of black people. Her first sight of a slave evoked 'deep sympathy', and she found initially that 'every negro man, woman and child that passed, my fancy wove some little romance of misery'. But her encounter with the utopian community at Nashoba, established by her friend Fanny Wright to demonstrate that there was no distinction between black humanity and white, did not appeal to her. She realised that she had no desire to mix with black people, and her vision of a New Jerusalem receded. She was soon concluding that slavery was 'far less injurious to the manners and morals of the people than the fallacious idea of equality', and while she romantically characterised American Indians as 'this most unhappy and ill-used people', the fate of negroes did not figure as a tragic story.[24] Her son, brought up with anti-slavery, was part of that generation of whom John Stuart Mill remarked that they did not have the passion of their parents on these issues.[25] Trollope was not explicitly pro-slavery, but he did not believe in racial equality, and was deeply antipathetic to philanthropists.

Trollope had little taste for those whom he saw as self-righteous or self-important. Philanthropists and evangelicals came into this category; so too did Carlyle. Trollope disliked the hectoring tone of Carlyle's *Latter Day Pamphlets* which he had bought and read in 1851, and in *The Warden*, written between the publication of 'Occasional Discourse on the Negro Question' and before Trollope's own visit to the West Indies, he caricatured Carlyle as Dr Pessimist Anticant, who 'mistook the signs of the times and the minds of men, instituted himself censor of things in general, and began the great task of reprobating everything and everybody', who 'roamed at large over all matters of public interest, and found everything bad'.[26] This critique of Carlyle, and Carlyle's own damning verdict on Trollope, complicates the view of the latter as simply sub-Carlylean. Carlyle found that he agreed with *The West Indies* when he read it, and the two men apparently got on well when George Eliot took Trollope to meet the grand old man for tea two years later.[27] But the assumption made by later critics, from Lord Olivier, one-time governor of Jamaica, to Eric Williams, the Trinidadian historian and erstwhile

Prime Minister, that Trollope's book was an expurgated version of 'Occasional Discourse' does not capture the complexity of his 'common sense'.[28]

In his mapping of particular parts of the empire, Trollope was always reflecting on the differences between 'them' and 'us'. 'I wish to write of men and their manners and welfare, rather than of rivers and boundaries,' he remarked.[29] His journey was to do with the mapping of peoples, his ethnographic mission to describe difference. The observations, supposedly based on an innocent eye, provided a basis from which to later generalise about race, nation and empire.[30] While Darwin painstakingly constructed his theory of evolution from his discoveries on the voyage of the *Beagle*, Trollope engaged in a different kind of cartography, one which filled the sites of empire with men and women whom he characterised as in different stages of development: stages of development which provided the justification for different forms of colonial rule. His curiosity, and his desire to pass on the information he acquired quickly, meant that he wrote down what he saw without reflecting deeply on the judgements which he made. His writing was a craft and a livelihood to him, and he set himself a daily number of words to complete.[31] His mapping of empire was presented as descriptive, with no pretence at intellectual or philosophical depth. His contemporary, Frederick Harrison, a man with more liberal sympathies, described Trollope retrospectively as the 'photographer' of mid-Victorian England.[32] But, like all photographers and reporters, whether in London, provincial Ireland or the West Indies, he framed his pictures and constructed his narratives, working with established discourses but hoping to reinflect meanings. By visiting new sites, he aimed for fresh insights, into England and its empire. In England his ethnographic eye rested little on the poor, for whom, unlike Dickens, he had little interest or sympathy. Class and gender differences were carefully delineated inside a community which tended to exclude absolute others, the rich Jewish financier the closest thing to 'a race apart'. In the colonies he was fascinated by race, by the 'natural' differences associated with different bodies, differences which he explained, as his friend Merivale did, in terms of a hierarchical discourse. Such a discourse, with its assumptions of the backwardness of other peoples and their distance from the heartlands of civilisation, underpinned the authority of Englishness. It was the space between Ireland and England, between the West Indies and England, between the domestic and the colonial, which confirmed the right of Anglo-Saxons to rule.

Trollope's first encounter with race as difference was in Ireland, where he trained himself in careful description, learning the imaginative capacity to engage with other societies and to capture something of that otherness for consumption 'at home'. Travel writing, as Gikandi argues, is a referential gesture that brings the unknown back to the known, the strange back to the familiar.[33] Trollope's Irish novels aimed to explain Ireland to the English.[34] His particular strength in his later travel writing was his ability to provide colonial knowledge in a new register, one which entertained as well as informed. His journey to the West Indies took place in 1858, the year after the 'Indian Mutiny'. Throughout 1857 and 1858 the daily press had been centrally preoccupied with reports from India. When *The West Indies* appeared in 1858, it both reflected and was constitutive of the hardening in racial thinking which characterised the times. Trollope's ironic, gossipy, anecdotal account of the relations between races made clear to his readers that black people needed 'civilising', but reminded them that violence and force were not always the order of the day. Its style of writing belied its harsh diet of black racial inequality. India provided one model of colonial relations, the West Indies another.

The book was speedily taken up by *The Times*, a fact which Trollope himself saw as crucial to its success.[35] Always a friend to the plantocracy, and managed at this time by the son of a West Indian planter,[36] the newspaper published two long pieces based on *The West Indies*, welcoming the book with open arms. For years the paper's editorial policy had been deeply hostile to the anti-slavery lobby. Trollope's book was a valuable addition to its armoury. The real value of Trollope, the paper argued, was that he was not afraid to recognise the differences between the races and to insist, therefore, on giving the planter a chance. 'Negroes, coolies and planters; what is the position of each', it asked, 'and what are the rights of each?'

> Floods of pathetic eloquence and long years of Parliamentary struggling have taught us to imagine that the world was made for Sambo, and that the sole use of sugar is to sweeten Sambo's existence. The negro is, no doubt, a very amusing and a very amiable fellow, and we ought to wish him well; but he is also a lazy animal, without any foresight, and therefore requiring to be led and compelled. We must not judge him by ourselves.

Trollope's illustrations of negro character, the paper suggested, demonstrated that 'there is little self-sustaining power and no sense of the future in the negro – facts that are all important in determining the question of labour in the West Indies'.[37] New immigration was essential. On the same day, it published an editorial on the white colonies of settlement which argued that the public should be more aware of the potential of the new territories and the special connection between colonisation and the

Anglo-Saxon race – sentiments with which Trollope would have heartily agreed.[38]

Trollope's account of the West Indies focused on Jamaica, and his imagined interlocutor was an abolitionist. His first shock in encountering the Caribbean islands was the fact of blackness. 'The negro population', he noted, 'is of course the most striking feature of the West Indies,' and it was the inadequacies of the negro which were largely responsible for the unfortunate state of the island.[39] 'Nothing was so melancholy' as Jamaica was to him, a country 'in its decadence', a truly melancholy sight.[40] The plentiful supplies of food in that particular habitat, combined with the interference of philanthropists who had protected the negroes from low wages, had meant that labour, the great civiliser, could not get to work on its subjects. It was the absence of the need to labour as he saw it – and in this he followed Carlyle – that had provoked disaster in Jamaica. Negroes 'have no care for tomorrow, but they delight in being gaudy for today . . . they laugh and sing and sleep through life', all of which was anathema to Trollope. 'He *is* a man,' he wrote, playing directly on anti-slavery rhetoric, 'and, if you will a brother; but he is the very idlest brother.' 'God has created men of inferior and superior race', and slavery had meant a forced encounter for black people with a superior race.

This inevitably meant progress. The emancipated creole Africans were, to him, 'a servile people in a foreign land'; they had 'no idea of country and no pride of race'. Idle, unambitious and sensual, the West Indian negro 'has made no approach to the civilisation of his white fellow creature, whom he imitates as a monkey does a man'. Their religion was ritualistic, not truly reaching their minds. Their love of the Bible he compared to a Roman Catholic girl who 'loves the doll of a Madonna which she dresses with muslin and ribbons'. Their familial attachments he compared with those of a dog. If left to themselves, West Indian negroes would slip back into barbarism. Emancipation for them had meant freedom from work, rather than the desire for progress and property.[41] The English had expected too much from emancipation. The only way to remedy this was to force black people to work, a familiar refrain of the plantocracy and its supporters.[42] Yet it was their separation from barbarism, and from Africa, which made progress possible: 'There is no race which has more strongly developed its own physical aptitudes and inaptitudes, its own habits, its own tastes, and its own faults.'[43] Here creolised Africans were granted cultural patterns: 'In their liminality, these subjects are close to white civilisation, but not close enough.'[44]

If the refusal of emancipated black people to work was one major problem in Jamaica, the other was the nature of the white population. The planters had borne emancipation with 'manly courage', but the ending of protection and the difficulties over immigration had defeated them. They had become 'sore, and vituperative and unconvinced'. The planter felt that he had been ill used by the mother country; he had become 'a bore and a nuisance', and 'in his heart of hearts there dwells a feeling that after all slavery was not so vile an institution'.[45] Jamaican planters had many of the characteristics of English gentlemen, and always talked about England as 'home'. They cared about their pedigrees, their country houses, their sport, their parishes and their local politics. Staying on a sugar estate on the west of the island, Trollope found that his host's occupations 'were exactly those of a country gentleman in England'. He fished and went shooting, looked after his estate, acted as a magistrate, cared a lot about his dinner and seemed to have no interest in sugar.[46] He found such men good company, yet they were poor mimics of real English gentlemen: their towns were dirty and dismal; their roads appalling and bridges broken; their coffee plantations had gone back to bush, and their sugar estates were sold for a song; they had no time for industry, no faith in their legislature, and would have preferred Jamaica to be entirely ruled from home. Nothing could be farther from Trollope's imagined ordered, deferential and paternalistic England, that England of the Barsetshire chronicles.

Trollope did not despair, however, of the future of the West Indian islands. The best days of Jamaica were over, and white people no longer wanted to go there; but Guiana, organised as a mild despotism, was doing relatively well. Immigration to Guiana had gone ahead, and the presence of 'coolies' and 'Chinamen', both groups of whom were prepared to work, made for a more prosperous picture. Philanthropic attempts to prevent immigration should be abandoned. The hope in Jamaica, as he saw it, lay with the coloured class, whom he thought were going to be the 'ascendant race'. This he knew would deeply offend his white friends in Jamaica, for 'both the white man and the black man dislike their coloured neighbours'. Jamaican whites were fearful of the ways in which they were being displaced, but there were 15,000 of them to 70,000 coloured people. 'The coloured men of Jamaica cannot be despised much longer,' he concluded.[47] The British should let Jamaica go; they had left their sign in blood. Englishmen, he argued, had needed the wild and savage energy of their vandal forefathers; similarly, the mix in the coloured race would allow them to combine negro strength with European intellect, and this mixed with the Asian willingness to work. 'The white man has been there, and has left his mark,' he argued. There was still a little more civilising to do in terms of the spreading of commerce and education, for coloured men still could not speak with 'natural English pronunciation'; but enough white blood had entered the national bloodstream to ensure survival. Coloured women, he argued, had not yet abandoned the legacy of concubinage and illegitimate sexuality, and this was a serious sign of decadence, but the men were leading the way. 'Providence has sent white men and black men to these regions in order that from them may spring a race fitted by intellect for civilization; and fitted also by physical organization for tropical labour.'[48] Trollope believed Jamaica had a future: one that was made possible by the mixing of races. This liberal view of 'miscegenation' may have been influenced by his brother Tom's marriage to a woman whose father was the son of an Indian officer and a high-caste Brahmin. She had Scottish, Jewish and Indian blood.[49] Racial purity might be a moral imperative for the likes of Knox, but in Jamaica Trollope could see that coloured men could not simply be classified as degenerate. They were shopkeepers, parliamentarians, public servants, lawyers and doctors. Jamaican white men were unnecessarily jealous of them: the future was in their keeping.[50]

To be independent was, for Trollope, the essence of white manhood, and the best kind of independence was that which was earned. Like Carlyle, he had a high regard for labour, and a workmanlike attitude to his own writing. 'Work with fair wages has done infinitely more to civilise, and even to christianise, the so-called savage races than has the energy of missionaries,' he argued.[51] In his colonial discourse, labour was one civiliser; family was the other. Like most middle-class men of the mid-Victorian period, he believed that familial and domestic order were at the heart of social order. A good society was one in which the classes, the races and the sexes knew their place and stayed in it. As Trollope travelled the white settler colonies in the years to come, he was to argue that if these colonies were to become well established, they needed a clear gender order with bread-winning husband and father and domesticated wife and mother. The character of frontier societies meant that aspects of North America and Australia fitted very well with this notion of the idealised family, secure in its homestead. Jamaica, on the other hand, with its troubling combination of white settlement and a black majority population, demonstrated through its sexual incontinence its fundamentally decadent character. It might have a future, but it could never regenerate the race in the way that he came to believe the white settler colonies could.

As a male writer of fiction, Trollope's manhood was constantly at risk on the feminised site of the novel, particularly since so much of his writing was focused on romance and domestic life. In his travel writing that interest in manners, in dress and in emotionality could be offset with a commentary on economic and political life – of a sort which women were not supposed, in his view, to be able to make. Women who ventured out of their sphere were troubling to Trollope, perhaps partly because of his own vulnerability as a writer, and partly because of his complicated and rivalrous relation with his writing mother. The split which Victoria Glendinning points to in her biography of him, between his desire for a dutiful and ever present wife and the excitement and challenge of the independent and resourceful mother who had abandoned him, was perhaps re-enacted in his hostile response to public forms of feminism.[52] He was excited by the prospect of independent women, but castigated them for not knowing their place. But his assertion of the necessity of the 'supremacy of man over woman' was disrupted by his fascination with feminism and his preoccupation in his novels of the 1860s with the newly public presence and claims of women.[53]

His encounter with a number of white, coloured and black West Indian women on his first long journey on his own was exciting. He enjoyed flirting, though he was shocked by the extent to which white creole women in the West Indies engaged in it, and the female creole characters in his fiction are characterised as rampant flirts.[54] The period before marriage, as he saw it, was a time when women could exercise their power – a period which he explored extensively in his novels about English women. But that power must be properly contained: by marriage and men. As the Jamaican beauty who comes to live in England puts it in *Ralph the Heir*, 'I do love the idea of an English home, where things are neat and nice.'[55] Any upsetting of this gender order was deeply troubling. Black women, who do not appear in his fiction, were both exciting and disturbing to him. His first encounter with a black West Indian woman was on the island of St Thomas.

> [A]s I put my foot on the tropical soil for the first time, a lady handed me a rose, saying, 'That's for love, dear'. I took it, and said that it should be for love. She was beautifully, nay, elegantly dressed. Her broad-brimmed hat was as graceful as are those of Ryde or Brighton. The well-starched skirts of her muslin dress gave to her upright figure that look of easily compressible bulk, which, let 'Punch' do what it will, has become so sightly to our eyes. Pink gloves were on her hands. . . . What was it to me that she was as black as my boot, or that she had come to look after the ship's washing?[56]

But her blackness was enticing, 'let "Punch" do what it will', and her hands, inside those gloves, a further sign of transgression. Her beautiful elegant dress disrupted the stereotype of the African woman and reminded the reader of the illicit sexuality on which that image of the large buttocks, the sign of physicality, rested.[57]

A vignette which *The Times* chose to reproduce in full in its feature caught much of the ambivalence of Trollope's representations of 'black beauties'. 'One Sunday evening', his story began, far away in the country, as I was riding with a gentleman, the proprietor of the estate around us, I saw a young girl walking home from church. She was arrayed from head to foot in virgin white. Her gloves were on, and her parasol was up. Her hat also was white, and so was the lace, and so were the bugles which adorned it. She walked with a stately dignity that was worthy of such a costume, and worthy also of higher grandeur; for behind her walked an attendant nymph, carrying the beauty's prayer-book on her head. . . . When we came up to her, she turned towards us and curtsied. She curtsied, for she recognized her 'massa'; but she curtsied with great dignity, for she recognized also her own finery. The girl behind with the prayer-book made the ordinary obeisance. . . . 'Who on earth is that princess?' said I. 'They are two sisters who both work at my mill', said my friend. 'Next Sunday they will change places. Polly will have the parasol and the hat, and Jenny will carry the prayer-book on her head behind her.'[58]

Readers were invited to chuckle over these young black women dressed up in borrowed finery, playing at princesses. These were mill girls, not the troubling Lancashire mill girls who dominated the streets of Northern towns with their clogs and their claims for independence, but black mill girls, dressed all in white and pretending to be ladies. 'This little incident is very characteristic of the negro', pontificated *The Times*, 'who is void of self-reliance and is the creature of circumstances . . . it is evident that he [*sic*] is scarcely fitted to take care of himself.'[59]

Trollope's ambivalence regarding the mimicry which he observed both among creolised Africans and planters, both aspiring and failing in their different ways to be English, marked the distance between the domestic and the colonial, that distance which legitimated colonial rule. Yet these mimics were attractive too: the planters genial and hospitable, the black women sexually provocative and inviting. But the confident masculinity he found among these colonial gentlemen, at home with the gun, the rod, the port and the beef, assuming that negroes were born to be servants, letting nothing disturb the even tenor of their lives, was appealing rather than admirable, for it was independence which Trollope admired in men. West Indian planters were part of a dying world. And the women were to be admired and caricatured at one and the same time: confined within their eroticised black bodies.

Trollope was by no means the only author concerned with Jamaica at this time. Conflicting accounts continued to be produced by visitors to the islands and critics at home.[60] Robert Emery, for example, the man who had served as government agent for immigration in Jamaica for twelve years and who had no truck with the missionaries, published a book in 1859 arguing for the importance of new migrant labour in solving the economic problems on the island – a deliberate intervention in the struggle over immigration legislation.[61] At the same time William Sewell, a journalist for the *New York Times*, had been reporting on Jamaica and the other British West Indian islands, collecting information on the impact of emancipation in the context of the debates going on in the USA. Having gone expecting to find 'that African freedom had been a curse to every branch of agricultural and commercial industry', he had discovered the opposite: there was plenty of evidence of industry, and small proprietors and mountain settlers were doing well.[62] But the emancipated lacked ingenuity; they were imitative rather than creative, their courage and perseverance 'but hesitating, halting steps when compared with the Anglo-Saxon's rapid and determined strides'. Immigration was crucial to the future. Indians were 'docile, peaceable, intelligent, industrious, eager to learn, and apt at improvement'. Furthermore, they were British subjects and could be moved from one part of the empire to another with careful regard to their rights. The island needed European or American settlers and farmers in his view, men who would stimulate, 'by the force of example, the sluggish energy of the Creole peasantry'.[63] Once again it was those 'at home' who knew how to live and how to rule. Whiteness was no guarantee: only the distance between colony and metropolis secured proper forms of governance.

All of these writers wrote within the parameters of the debates over the character of the emancipated. Where once visitors had gone to Jamaica to see and report on slavery, now it was emancipation. Such travellers assumed the right to reflect on 'the African': for the 'nature' of the race was at the heart of the argument. Planters and abolitionists continued to represent distinctively different positions, yet they agreed that some form of colonial rule was imperative. While the supporters of the plantocracy bemoaned the laziness of the emancipated negroes, abolitionists insisted on their industriousness, obedience and gratitude to those who had freed them. Debates over immigration, which the planters saw as a solution to their economic ills, and abolitionists saw as an attack on the emancipated, provided a specific lens for the continued struggle over representation in the mid-nineteenth century. For Trollope, 'the friend of the negro' was always in sight, his narrative constructed in relation to that counter-narrative, the vision of the pious, grateful emancipated negro, celebrated by abolitionists, never far from his mind. Those visionaries, he charged, had foolishly hoped to see their 'client rise up at once with all the glories of civilization round his head'.[64] This utopian dream needed to be tempered with brutal honesty.

Trollope's depiction of the 'truth' was met with dismay by anti-slavery enthusiasts, who castigated his volume as 'sadly deficient in those elements which impart value to a traveller's observations, namely, truth, and a freedom from a tendency to caricature': it was a 'planter's book', based on 'superficial judgements'.[65] The *Morning Star* was also critical, noting that he did not say 'that he went among the blacks himself and founded his terrible condemnation of them upon personal observation and inquiry'. This book 'can possess no authority whatever', this reviewer concluded, 'in the estimation of an impartial and discriminating public'.[66] The book sold very well, however, promoted in part by *The Times*; and just as Mill and others had felt obliged to answer Carlyle, now Trollope had to be countered. As an eyewitness his evidence had a different weight from that of the armchair critics of emancipation, and he provided unwelcome ammunition to the pro-slavery forces at a time when the opposition felt itself to be weak.

The BMS had sent a deputation to Jamaica late in 1859 in response to repeated requests from their remaining missionaries on the island for help, their task to inquire into the condition of the Baptist churches. The deputation consisted of the secretary of the BMS, Edward Bean Underhill, and the Rev. J. T. Brown, minister of the Baptist church in Northampton, the Midland town where the BMS had been founded. Part of their job on their return was to spread the word as to the virtues of the emancipated peasantry. On his return to England in 1860, Brown addressed a large meeting in his home town to report on his visit. His words revealed how much had changed since those founding days, how debates over racial science had inflected missionary speech. While Carey's concerns would have been with the souls of the heathens, Brown reproduced stereotypical images of once savage, now civilised Africans, with an emphasis on physicality. He had expected to find savages, he said, 'a set of human beings with receding foreheads, repulsive countenances, flat noses and thick protruding lips'. Instead he had found a noble peasantry. 'Talk about receding foreheads,' he continued, 'in Cuba he had seen them; but in Jamaica the process of refinement had gone on to an extent beyond any thing that he could have believed.' Africans could be civilised by emancipation: in Cuba their bodies revealed their barbarism. He went on to tell a story: in conversation with an emancipated negro man, he reported what Trollope and Carlyle had said of them, and how they were up to their elbows in pumpkins.

> 'Pumpkins!', he replied, with an expression that indicated a doubt whether he should laugh or cry for they are very sensitive to these calumnies – 'Pumpkins! Never seen a pumpkin don't know how long. Pumpkins!' And he turned round and said, 'Minister, me cannot think how these people will meet Jesus, telling these lies.'[67]

This simple man met the lies of his calumniators with the faith which the missionaries had taught him: he had been Christianised and physically transformed from a savage African to a noble peasant. This was the moral of Brown's story – a story which was greeted with fury by the Jamaican press, fulminating that Brown was 'blacker than the blacks'.[68]

It was Brown's senior colleague, Edward Underhill, who took on the task of rebutting Trollope in print, publishing his book *The West Indies: Their Social and Religious Condition* in 1862.[69] The charge that Jamaica was ruined was repeated constantly on every front: in illustrations, in Parliament, in literature, in saloons, even on omnibuses, asserted one 'friend of the negro'.[70] Underhill hoped his book would help to correct the 'strange conceptions' people had. 'You know how difficult it is for people in these temperate climes to form correct views of tropical scenes,' he wrote to a friend.[71] An enthusiastic review of the book in the *Baptist Magazine* commented on its superiority to the narratives of other travellers, with Trollope no doubt in mind. 'This volume will set at rest for ever', they opined optimistically, 'all controversy' on the effects of emancipation. Unfortunately for the 'friends of the negro', Trollope's chatty diary, converted into a narrative full of lively anecdotes about his lodgings, his dinners and his encounters, appealed a great deal more to the reading public than did Underhill's careful computations and analysis. 'Only sensational books are selling,' commented Underhill sadly to his missionary friend in Jamaica, David East.[72]

Underhill was one of the second generation of the missionary venture. Born in 1813, eighteen years younger than Carlyle and seven years younger than Mill, he was an impressionable young man of twenty at the time of emancipation and the Reform Act. His father was a Baptist, and he himself was converted at sixteen. He went into business, but his real enthusiasm was the history of the Baptists. In 1849 he entered the service of the BMS, the affairs of which he was to direct for twenty-seven years.[73] In 1854 he went on a deputation to India, to report on the state of the mission there. A catalogue of misery from the missionaries in Jamaica in the late 1850s, concerning their falling numbers, financial difficulties and the continued lack of justice for black people, alongside the economic and political problems of the island, persuaded the BMS to send a deputation there. The hope was that some of the confusions between the society and those in the field would be sorted out, and that further evidence would be gleaned as to the prospects for the island into which so much BMS energy had been poured.[74] The society had not been responsible for the stations there officially since the Jamaica Baptist Union had become independent in 1842; but BMS missionaries had remained on the island, and financial and emotional links had persisted. The BMS continued to act in part as a parent figure to the 'child of their faith'.[75] A deputation had gone to Jamaica in 1846, and the Rev. Birrell's report on that occasion had greatly influenced Underhill. Birrell had drawn attention to the amount of work which needed to be done before it would be possible for black men to guide and lead in the ways that white men could, for black men to become pastors of their brethren. 'Never till I reached the spot', Birrell had declared, in a passage that imprinted itself on Underhill's mind, 'had I a just appreciation of the difficulties.' Never before had he realised the extent to which 'the education of the people in civilised countries had been carried on in the persons of their ancestors'. The creolised Africans of Jamaica had none of these hereditary advantages. 'The entire population stands intellectually at zero. Every man must rise in his own person from that point.'[76] This was a powerful formulation of the abolitionist view that emancipation meant starting the world anew: African culture was no culture. Or, as Knibb had put it, 'the whole island . . . had to begin the world at once'.[77]

Underhill became convinced that the only hope for the future of the mission in Jamaica was to train native pastors, a view that was becoming more widely shared by all denominations.[78] In 1852 he produced a document for the BMS committee making the case in favour of native agency and seeking more active support from home. 'It must be admitted', he wrote,

> that in the early stage of their Christian profession, the immaturity of the converts, the presence of evil habits acquired in a state of heathenism, idolatry and perhaps savageism, their ignorance and imperfect apprehension of the Gospel, may and do require judicious treatment from the missionary and demand from him great watchfulness, sagacity and incessant instruction.[79]

The key drawback of relying on an English pastorate, as he saw it, was that it produced dependence, that characteristic which was so unmanly. Faced with the 'superior intelligence and civilisation' of the white missionary and his family, the 'negro races' were at an 'almost immeasurable distance', confirmed by 'their rude habits', their 'confined thought' and their 'limited knowledge'.[80] In Underhill's understanding, the native candidates for the ministry had no traditions, no histories, no books on which to draw. But native pastors were essential, for Jamaica (or India, the other main site for this debate) must depend on its own sons. While Underhill worked at home to raise the profile of native agency, David East, one of his oldest friends, was appointed principal of Calabar, the training college established in Jamaica under the inspiration of Knibb. The two worked together for the next forty years. In time, wrote Underhill to East in 1853, 'as the blacks get more civilised the whole power of the island will be in their hands'. Calabar could play a crucial role in this. East's most difficult problem, Underhill suspected, would be the white pastors who would be jealous of their power.[81] While the Colonial Office had lost faith in a black future by the 1850s and was busy reining back what were now seen as unrealistic hopes, the leadership of the BMS kept theirs, despite tensions over the authority and power of the white missionaries.

Underhill's visit in 1859 was his first to the island about which he knew so much. One of his initial impressions on arrival in Kingston was that the Jamaican population was not proud of its country, and that there was a general gloom about its prospects. He travelled round the island for five months, was lyrical about its beauty (unlike Trollope, who focused on its decadence), visited all of the seventy-seven Baptist churches, talked to the thirty-eight pastors (twenty-three of whom he described as European), addressed forty-nine public meetings which nearly 20,000 people attended, preached thirty-one times to more than 14,000 people, and met 541 deacons and leaders, all men.[82] His key question related to the performance of the emancipated: had they used their twenty-three years of freedom well? This question was determined both by the exigencies of the political conjuncture in Britain and by the traditions of abolitionist thinking. Following in the line of Sturge, Harvey, Alexander, Candler and Gurney, he went to judge the African from a position of benevolent paternalism. Like his forefathers, he turned the problem of Jamaica around. Its 'ruin', whether by slavery or emancipation, was the responsibility of the planters, not the slaves or freed men and women. He was deeply critical of the planter class and its failure to move beyond its own narrow interests. Its misuse of power, its constant attempts to curtail black and coloured representation, its punitive taxation policies which weighed on the peasantry, its lax morals and refusal to effect a bastardy law (which would force fathers to take responsibility for their illegitimate children), its neglect of paternalism – all contributed to its historic failure to meet the responsibilities of a governing class. Only the British government, constantly harassed by the Baptist missionaries, had prevented a return to forms of forced labour. It was the refusal of the planters to change, he insisted, which had ruined Jamaica, not the refusal of the emancipated negroes to work.

The future of the island must belong with black and coloured people. This meant it was 'a matter of urgent interest that brown and black should be prepared by every educational, moral and religious influence, for the position they must ere long attain'.[83] Meanwhile white pastors provided a security against the antagonisms between black and coloured, and for years to come their predominance would be essential. Clearly the plantocracy could not be relied on to act justly and impartially. Rather, it was the missionaries, who should continue to occupy the most important churches, and whose 'sympathy with the wants and struggles of the people' and 'freedom from prejudices' fitted them for 'the good cause of raising the African from his degraded position'.[84] Underhill's narrative was predicated on assumptions of benevolence, paternalism and civilisation Christian style.

Underhill was delighted with the progress of the emancipated, felt that they had used their twenty-three years of freedom well, and reminded his readers that it would have been unreasonable to expect them to have reached a state of civilisation such as there was in England. He was impressed by their intelligence and fine physiques, by their manners and respectful treatment of himself and 'Mrs. Underhill', who was travelling with him, by 'the general absence of gay colours and flaunting attire', by their 'independence of opinion, manliness of manner and deep earnestness', by the way in which the 'miserable patois' of the slave had been replaced by 'euphonius [sic] and grammatical English', by their growing respect for marriage, by their neat houses and plots. Idleness, he concluded, 'was not a marked characteristic of the race'. At the same time he noted their backwardness: their serious neglect of marriage, their impure lives, their superstitious habits, their 'rude patois', their 'short and soon exhausted vocabulary', their limits intellectually. In examining students at Calabar, he found that 'the negro race' was no good at geometry and perhaps, he thought, no good at 'the higher abstractions of reasoning and calculation'. They were, after all, a people 'untrained and just emerging from barbarism'; emancipation was 'the starting point for the negro'. Without missionary training and discipline, they would be in a sorry state.[85]

The native pastors, he thought, were on the whole doing well, though sometimes they were unable 'to control the turbulent elements' of their congregations as well as might be desired. There were worrying signs of splits in some congregations, and a secession associated with obeah and superstitious practices had taken place in Sturge Town. It was essential that the churches continue to practice a severe discipline in relation to such backsliding. At the same time care and discretion were needed. Underhill believed that Christianity would take its own forms 'among the uncivilised tribes of Africa, or in the tranquil life of the polished Hindoo', and might 'display virtues which have been imperfectly developed by the cultured races of Christendom'.[86] Western Christianity might not have all the answers, and Underhill's paternalism was undercut by this recognition.

At Sligoville, one of the free villages established by Phillippo in the hills above Spanish Town, he met some of the residents and spoke with them, 'on their habits, their social condition, what England expects of them, and what is said about them'. 'What England expects of them' was a familiar theme: were they meeting the expectations of the benevolent abolitionists who had worked to free them? 'What is said about them' was presumably a check on how their habits compared with the tales of a Carlyle. As the editor of the *Missionary Herald* commented, when introducing the first reports from the deputation to the English public, the testimony of the deputation was very important, and would serve to show that 'the negro is something better than a very "funny animal" '.[87] Underhill was concerned to talk with the people he met at every opportunity, and to report their talk once transposed into 'euphonius' English. Abolitionists had long made a virtue of *knowing* what black people thought and representing those views. He noted across the island that support for white ministers had fallen off, and there had been a turn to black pastors. He was well aware that this was sometimes associated with the behaviour of the Europeans, for 'habits of command and superiority' were long established and difficult to eradicate.[88] Yet some of the Salem men he spoke to, on the north coast of the island, were glad to have continued white support. 'We must resort to white men for help and counsel,' said one; 'white people squeeze us too much if there be no white ministers to represent our case at home, as well as to meet white men here.' Another utilised the familiar parental trope: 'What the English have begun, they must carry on to the end. They were our fathers and mothers in spiritual things, and the son wants them still.' A black deacon in Montego Bay, a stronghold of the Baptists since the days of Sam Sharpe, told him, 'we are not of age yet, and we must look to England'. At a large meeting held in the Baptist church at St Ann's Bay on the north coast, where the Rev. Bridges had once terrorised the chapel and Marcus Garvey was to be born, another man spoke of their reliance on the mother country, given their lack of political representation and the power of the planters: 'We are in Jamaica; but we have no power, no hope here; all our power and hope is in England.'[89]

Underhill was well aware of the influence that could be exerted in England, but he was also concerned as to the state of public opinion there. 'I am afraid the cause of the negro is losing ground in England,' he wrote to East in 1862. Anti-slavery sentiments were still cherished, he believed, 'but now that the negro is free and the field is open for him, he is to be left to his own exertions to complete his elevation. He must now fight his own battles like other people. This I fancy is the truth of the case, notwithstanding that *The Times* continues to talk of the negro as only fitted for menial and servile labour.'[90] This was an interesting judgement – that the public was no longer prepared to see the West Indian negro as a special case, requiring particular support. By 1862 the enslaved in the southern states of America and Maori warriors were rather more present in the metropolitan imagination. Underhill himself remained convinced that civilisation depended on the missionary venture. While Trollope focused on the significance of labour and the family in civilising those whom he categorised as inferior races, Underhill saw the Baptist missionary, standing at the head of his families, as the key. In concluding his book, he cited Merivale's judgement, the very one with which Trollope would not concur, that 'the only experiments in civilising savage tribes, which offer the remotest prospects of success, are those which commence with their religious instruction'.[91]

The trials of life

While contrary representations threatened any harmonious metropolitan assumptions as to the character of the negro, social, economic and political troubles in Jamaica were seriously undermining the missionary project. John Henderson's narrative of his years in Jamaica, provided by his letters, give an eloquent account of one man's struggle to find an acceptable place for himself, once the optimistic years of the early 1840s were over. Henderson was one of those missionaries who devoted his life to the task of 'civilising subjects'. He had arrived with his wife Ann in Jamaica at the end of 1840, a time of high hopes for the Baptist missionaries. Their influence was extensive, their congregations growing apace, their aspirations for the future of their mission unlimited. Henderson had been inspired to offer his services to 'the emancipated negro' after hearing Knibb speak in England. He was to act as an assistant to Knibb, and his first task was to look after the church in Falmouth while Knibb was away.[92]

Henderson's initial impressions were positive. He found the 'attention superior to what is manifested in most of our congregations in England', and was deeply thankful that 'God had put it into my heart to leave the land of my birth and proclaim to the despised but affectionate sons of Ham the unsearchable riches of Jesus Christ'.[93] On Knibb's return to Jamaica, Henderson was invited by the new church in Waldensia to become its pastor. This was ten miles from Falmouth, where the free village of Hoby Town was being constructed. The village was named after Knibb's friend and patron Dr Hoby, who had ministered in Birmingham between 1831 and 1844, and had twice served as president of the Baptist Union in Britain. It was a beautiful, healthy spot, Henderson reported. The chapel was on the grand interior road from Falmouth: bounded on one side by the mountains, it commanded a 'delightful view

... of the vales below ... varied by hillocks and little thickets and other trees that add considerable beauty and loveliness to the whole'.[94] The couple's house was in the centre of the village, the land for which had been bought by Knibb, and about 100 cottages were being built, most of which were to be occupied by members of his church. 'Living near me,' he noted, 'I shall have many opportunities of doing them good.' Here was the patriarchal dream: the missionary with his family at the centre of the community, overseeing and correcting, training 'the despised but affectionate sons of Ham'. The recognition services for the new minister provided the occasion for the formal opening of the new township, signalling the link between pastor, chapel and community. The congregation was urged to buy land and build houses, for, 'until a man has a house he can call his own, he is in danger from the iron hand of oppression'. Those who had once been slaves, they were instructed, were now men and citizens, with rights which must be defended.[95] Henderson was soon convinced that 'the ultimate happiness of the free labourer depends on the establishment of free villages throughout the island'.[96] Every alternate week Henderson spent three days in Falmouth, the busy, prosperous town at the centre of the economic and political life of Trelawny. This freed Knibb to be in Refuge, another free village close to Kettering.[97] Between them they fostered their vision of freedom.

Henderson was thrilled by the celebrations on 1 August 1841 of the anniversary of freedom. 'When the English nation', he told his audience, 'as with one voice, united in the demand that you might enjoy those rights which belonged to you as men, I was with them and joined in that demand. When the people of England united to petition the Imperial Parliament that you might be made free, I was there, and joined in that petition.' Linking the abolitionist public at home with the freed slaves in Jamaica, he told how he had celebrated with them in spirit whilst in England on 1 August 1838, and had praised God for the gift of freedom. Then he had heard Mr Knibb speak: he had been inspired by his tales of his affectionate and kind people, how glad they were to worship together, how desirous they were to send the Gospel to Africa. 'I thought I should like to come and see you; that I should like to labour for you, and spend my days amongst you.' The welcome that they had given him, he assured them, convinced him that what Knibb had said was true, and he rejoiced that he was with them.[98] This was the picture Henderson had when he first arrived in Jamaica, a picture framed by an abolitionist regime of truth.

Between the 1840s and the 1860s Henderson wrote regularly to successive secretaries of the BMS, detailing his concerns and preoccupations, his successes and failures. These letters were an important lifeline for him, as letters were for many others, marking his connection with the parent society and the mother country, his access to the 'friends of the negro' in Britain and, if need be, the Colonial Office, reasserting his identity as Englishman, albeit far away. At the very same time, they provided a space for the missionary to articulate his relation to the colonial: a complex relationship, given the sharp hostilities with the plantocracy and the idealised stereotype of the Christian negro with which he and his generation arrived. In the process of living his adult life in Jamaica, Henderson was engaged in trying to make sense of the society and his place in it, coming to terms with the oppression and injustice which were part of everyday life for his congregations, with the vilification which he himself was subject to, with the understanding that the 'poor negro' was not quite as he had thought, and that his own fantasies of what it would be possible for him to do, who he could be, were to be disappointed. Henderson's letters give access to some aspects of one missionary's thinking about the vagaries of the particular colonial project with which he was engaged over twenty-five years, the making of Christian British negro subjects. His relation to the mother country was a vital part of who he was, and over the years the question as to where he should be resurfaced continually. When times were hard, England was always there as a possibility, with the reassuring hope that the society would find him a position 'at home'. But home became Jamaica, and the people he worked with over the decades remained 'his people'.

Despite his many dissatisfactions and miseries, he stayed on the island. He went 'home' in 1851 and 1859, and travelled round the country giving talks about the mission and raising funds for the work there. Each time he thought beforehand that he would never go back to Jamaica, but each time he returned to the home of his adult life. Henderson spoke on behalf of Jamaica, 'his' Jamaica, 'his' people, as Baptist missionaries had been doing since the 1830s. His identity was shaped in both metropole and colony, and he lived in a space that was both colonial and domestic: he mediated the one to the other, represented Jamaica to England and England to Jamaica. Metropole and colony were connected through many figures, modalities and forms of representation: one was the missionary, and Henderson enacted that role in his own particular ways. He represented the negro Christian subject to the metropolitan audience, the benevolent English teachers and guides to his black congregations in Waldensia and Falmouth. In claiming 'his' people, a construction which the *Falmouth Post*, inveterate critics of the Baptists, angrily repudiated, he produced himself as pastor and leader, father to his children, a patriarch of the mission family, albeit junior to Knibb or Phillippo. Henderson's letters can be put alongside newspaper and journal reports and Parliamentary and Colonial Office Papers in an attempt to construct an account of his life, as represented by himself and others, over this period. He was a minor figure in the missionary world, a mere irritant to the plantocracy, yet an Englishman who lived his adult life in Jamaica and continued to believe that he could contribute to making a better life for 'his' people there.

Sections from Henderson's letters were regularly excerpted, alongside those of his brethren, and published in the *Missionary Herald*, to inform the missionary public at home and encourage them in their financial support for Jamaica. In his first enthusiasm in 1841 Henderson compared the Jamaican churches most favourably with those of the early Christians at Corinth, the stewardship of St Paul with that of Mr Knibb. The island was indeed a blessed place. Only a few months later, however, Henderson's deacons were being attacked by other Baptist missionaries on the island for their supposed inadequacies.[99] The utopian moment was not to last long.

The family at Waldensia was soon extended. Henderson's brother, George, and his wife joined them in a matter of months: George to run the school which had been established there.[100] The two couples laboured together in the Falmouth area, the men preaching and teaching, the women running the households, caring for the children and the sick, establishing female schools and engaging in the thousand other tasks expected of mission wives. George Henderson's wife died after only a few months on the island. The following year he married a Miss Drayton, probably one of the five female teachers who had come with Knibb to Jamaica in 1841 as an instructor of the young, keeping romance within the extended mission family.

Henderson had been sent to Jamaica by the BMS but the declaration of independence by the Jamaica Baptist Union (JBU) in 1842 meant that missionaries from England no longer had the same claims on the society. This was to lead to many disputes as the hopes of the early 1840s dissipated and the Baptist churches and their ministers entered hard times. Since the BMS owned extensive property on the island, it retained a significant interest in the mission field. Furthermore, the missionaries themselves were loathe to give up the connection to the society, since it was their main point of access to funds and assistance, a key line of connection with the mother country. The lack of an established middle class in Jamaica and the hostility of the plantocracy to the missionaries meant that there was little chance of raising money on the island beyond the contributions made by the congregations. In the heady days after 1838 it had seemed that prosperity would continue to increase, but this had not been the case, and as church membership not only stopped increasing but began to fall, and revenues fell alongside, missionaries with BMS connections were anxious to insist on the society's obligations to them.

The great disparity in position among missionaries, some with large churches and relatively well-to-do congregations, others in villages and hamlets, meant that rivalries and jealousies were frequently in play: the mission family was rent with anger as well as bound with love. Henderson's own church at Waldensia was extended three times in two years between 1841 and 1843, when times were still good. But, like most of the missionaries, he was to suffer from serious financial problems throughout his many years on the island, and money was a constant source of anxiety. In 1845 he was engaged in dispute with the BMS committee over money which he considered was owed to him, and threatened to go public about it.[101] Between 1844 and 1845 more than £2,000 was given by the BMS to the Jamaica mission, though with considerable misgivings. In 1845 it was decided that £6,000 should be raised as a parting gift: but again this attempt at closure was unsuccessful, because the personal problems of the missionaries combined with the economic and social distress of their membership meant that help was frequently sought. Part of the task of the deputations sent to the island in 1845 and 1859 was to attempt to sort out the financial complexities of the severance between the BMS and the JBU.[102] Money to support the pastors had to come from the congregations, but there were many other issues, from those associated with property, to the costs of travel home, the debts which had been taken on in the building of chapels, and the fund which the BMS had established for widows.

The situation of widows was a difficult one, given the notion of the mission family. The pastor's stipend was understood to cover the support of his wife and family, and missionary wives worked just as hard as, if not harder than, their husbands. The widows' fund had been established to provide help for those whose husbands died in the field, leaving their widows otherwise destitute. This marked the only formal recognition by the BMS of the informal partnership, between husband, wife and children, especially daughters, on which the missionary enterprise was built. The missionaries in Jamaica were extremely anxious that this provision should extend to their wives even though they were no longer employed by the BMS. Their widows, they argued, would otherwise be left unsupported in their hour of need, at a time when they were worn down with grief and likely to be debilitated by the 'enervating climate', when they found themselves among strangers, without even the means to return home, a return which might well bring its own difficulties.[103]

Ann Henderson's only formal connections with the society, for example, were the occasions when her husband was too ill to write, and she sent reports back to the BMS.[104] Her sister in the mission family, the wife of Walter Dendy, long-time missionary on the island, whose own first name was not revealed even in the funeral service preached for her, was lauded for leading the perfect life of a missionary wife. It was a life of 'Christian activity', but she was always modest and retiring. Before coming to Jamaica, she had been a Sunday school teacher and tract distributor. Once on the island she laboured for the Sunday schools, helped in Bible classes and classes for inquirers, and ran sessions for young women. When her husband was away, she would overcome 'her natural reserve' and read the Bible, announce the hymns, and even read a sermon at the Sunday services.[105] This was in addition to caring for her children and husband and running the household. She acted as her husband's 'other half', but just as the legal definition of her marriage was that of couverture, so in her formal relations with the BMS she was covered by her husband. That husband was in the forefront of arguing with the society for widows' rights.

In 1847 Henderson was worrying again, this time about the distinctions made between junior and senior missionaries, and in 1849 he was one of a group of missionaries who wrote to the BMS committee about the terrible hardships on the island and the difficulties of surviving. They enclosed a public appeal in relation to schools for the emancipated. The late 1840s were difficult years for the missionaries as they grieved over 'a sad declension of piety in our churches' and an unwillingness to subscribe as liberally as previously. They saw that many of their members could no longer afford to contribute as they had once done, and they feared for the future of the negro.[106] Only they, the missionaries, could save them. Simple faith and piety had to be constantly struggled for: now it was 'unrestrained passions' which marked the character of the African. This was a time when several mission churches were split by disputes over ownership of property and control of the pastorate and when missionaries themselves were seriously in debt. 'I tremble for our Mission,' wrote Henderson's colleague Walter Dendy, from Salter's Hill in the mountains behind Montego Bay. Missionaries were having to survive on totally inadequate resources, and white men needed more than their coloured brethren, since they 'cannot dig the ground, or their wives stand at the wash-tub, or, cook their provisions for their respective meals'.[107] Here was an important admission: native preachers were much cheaper to support than white men, for missionaries, like other colonial officials, had to maintain their dignity and distance. Whatever their poverty, some boundaries had to be sustained, boundaries of class and colour: manual labour was out of the question for the men, and a servant to do the laundry and prepare the food was essential. George Henderson, John's nephew, born in the mission family in 1849 and later the minister at Brown's Town, recalled the significance of 'the Sunday suit' in a missionary family:

[W]hen Sunday suits became shabby, with no funds to replace them, they were carefully unpicked by our loving Mother, and her boys gathered logwood chips and boiled the dye, mixing with it copperas to turn it black, and then fixed the colour with alum. The pieces were then skilfully pressed and put together by the Mother of our love; and on Sunday we entered the chapel as proud of our renovated garments as if they had just arrived from Bond Street.

The mission children learned 'rigid economy in a practical school', but as with genteel poverty at home, appearances must be maintained.[108] Colonial rule rested on the distinction between rulers and ruled: missionaries were colonisers, though Baptist sympathy with the oppressed meant that their authority was of a different order from that of the plantocracy.

Baptist missionaries were necessarily involved in politics: their links with emancipation, their support of the freed slaves over apprenticeship, wages and housing, over the injustices of the courts and the attempts by the planters to limit the franchise, to tax the peasantry and to introduce new forms of forced cheap labour – all of these ensured a high political profile. Their celebration of the family of man and their sharp criticisms of the immorality of the island's ruling elites were equally unpalatable to the plantocracy. A Baptist version of the national anthem celebrated peace and brotherhood:

> Foe be transformed to friend,
> And Britain's power depend,
> On WAR NO MORE...
>
> Lord make the nations see
> That men should brothers be
> And form one family
> The wide world o'er.[109]

Henderson had learned from Knibb the proper connection between freedom and citizenship. Knibb's death, however, had meant that the leader was gone, and hopes of mobilising a black settler vote in close association with Baptist aspirations were dimmed. The link between British Baptists and radical black settlers was never so close again.[110] But many of the missionaries continued to defend the rights of free proprietors and labourers on the island and to act as intermediaries with the Colonial Office and the abolitionist public. In 1847, for example, Henderson wrote to the *Anti-Slavery Reporter* asking for exertions against proposed African immigration to Jamaica. It would be 'an act of great injustice on the peasantry' who were willing to work for equitable wages. 'You must, Sir', he argued, 'call upon the country to resist this scheme, or we shall be deluged with starving, superstitious strangers.' 'Coolies' would bring with them new dangers and undermine the hard work done with the emancipated: creolised Africans were one thing, Hindu or Moslem Indians, with their old-established religions, another.[111] Political tensions on the island and any claims made by the peasantry were always likely to provoke attacks on the missionaries. The planters continued to maintain the contradictory beliefs both that black people were incapable of organising themselves and that they were always conspiring against their masters, aided and abetted by wicked demagogues. The 1849 election, when the black settler vote was brought out in unprecedented numbers and African-Jamaican politicians were beginning to hope for some electoral success, saw a serious riot in Falmouth. Henderson was accused by an anonymous correspondent in the *Falmouth Post* of inciting his 'ragged regiment' against a respectable planter standing for election. Following the election, several 'followers' of the minister, together with a number of 'loose' women, had rushed to the court house with sticks and other weapons. They were stopped by the police, but 'a band of ruffians' threw rocks at 'gentlemen who were returning to their homes'.[112] In the mind of the plantocracy, Baptist missionaries were intimately associated with dangerous political claims and actions.

Henderson himself was locked in gloom, and saw few rays of sunshine on the spiritual and moral front in the late 1840s. In 1850 he was again appealing to the BMS along with three other missionaries from the Falmouth area. Their personal financial situations were dire, and the sale of books and furniture essential to their ministries looked to be the only solution to debt; they were worried about the education of their children, since Jamaica offered no adequate schooling for them, and they could not afford to send them to England. 'We desired', they wrote, 'to be instrumental in saving souls, and we expected to be able to effect a greater amount of good in this far off island, than we could have accomplished in our native country.' But their expectations had not been met. Indifference to religion was painfully on the increase, and church members were backsliding. They were losing confidence in the character of the people. 'We . . . have been deceived,' they maintained, and wanted the committee to know their feelings.[113]

'The people' were not what they had thought. Throughout that year and the next, Henderson pondered returning to England, if he could only raise the fares for himself and his four children. The serious cholera attack of 1851 had had the unexpected effect of filling the church as backsliders in large numbers returned, 'deeply anxious about their eternal interests'. But this did not shift his mood. An optimistic account of the hopes for Jamaica in the *Baptist Magazine*, the mother country's major Baptist periodical, greatly irritated him. 'There is no cause for despair', it had concluded. 'Civilisation and piety will yet spread their benign and downy wings over these once enslaved children of Ham, and Jamaica will remain a monument of England's ardent sympathy for the slave.' Such words must have reminded Henderson of his own rosy hopes of old, but they now moved him to complain of the profound ignorance of some persons as to the 'character of our peoples' and the refusal of the English public to listen to the missionaries.[114]

The Hendersons decided, however, after much debate, to visit England rather than resettle there, leave their sons at boarding-school, and return to the island. The school was to be a source of much grief, for two of the three sons died there, and the parents were convinced that the matron had not been properly attentive.[115] While many of the missionaries struggled financially to keep their sons at school in England and then to find positions for them, giving them access to the professional world, it was a terrible hardship to have them so far away and to have to rely on relatives and friends to care for them. The wider Baptist family was called upon to provide suitable schooling and apprenticeships for these mission boys. 'Separation from children is perhaps the greatest trial of a Missionary's life,' wrote Henderson's colleague, Walter Dendy; but 'to keep a child here would be to render him unfit for an honourable position in after life, and to destroy his usefulness, as there are no persons here capable to teach business habits, and in Jamaica the moral influence of society is very pernicious'.[116] Daughters were seen as less of a problem, since, if necessary, they could be educated at home on the island.

In 1854 Henderson moved to Montego Bay, to a new congregation in Union Street. Like Falmouth, the town had long been a Baptist stronghold, but since the death of Thomas Burchell, things had not gone well. The separation from the BMS meant that no more missionaries would be sent out; but 'native' pastors were only just beginning to emerge from the training at Calabar, and many of the resident white pastors were worried as to their readiness for major responsibilities. Henderson, for example, was anxious that so many churches were without guidance, and that 'unsuitable' persons were entering 'important spheres of labour'. He was encouraged by 'the manner in which those who have left the Institution are conducting themselves', but there was a danger of pushing them too far too fast.[117] The men trained on the island were only too well aware of the scrutinising eyes upon them, and the burden they carried as representatives of the potential of the negro.[118] They tended to be assigned to small congregations in the country. Town stations, Henderson argued, demanded a pastor with not only piety and prudence, but also a capacity to 'take a stand in the community . . . command respect, and exert an influence'.[119] Such men were likely to be white.

One such town station was Market Street, the Montego Bay Baptist church, left without a pastor after the return of the Rev. Cornford to England. The membership found itself split over questions of church government, and the rift continued over several years, confounding many efforts at mediation. Denied the right to the franchise for the most part, congregations utilised church government as an arena in which to learn political skills, get practice in public speaking, debate rights and forms of representation, and exercise authority in the community. Nonconformist churches also provided spaces within which the colonial relation could be tested, the power of white pastors restrained.[120] Both the BMS and the JBU got involved in the disputes in Montego Bay, and tempers ran high. In 1849 the two parties came to an agreement to invite James Reid, an Englishman not connected with the BMS who had been on the island for many years, to be their pastor. No sooner was the invitation accepted, however, than further arguments occurred relating to rights over the property, and it was determined that a second church would be formed.[121] Several of the missionaries in the area, whose sympathies lay with the seceders, were involved with the setting up of this second church, and it was to this new congregation on Union Street that Henderson went.

Henderson hoped for a reunion of the two congregations under his leadership. This depended, however, on Reid's willingness to leave, an outcome which in Henderson's mind was only proper, since he had greatly offended many of his members, 700 of whom had left. Henderson was annoyed with the way in which the BMS had conducted its part in the affair. 'The separate existence of the two churches' was a standing disgrace; his own members, having laboured to build a beautiful church, were now cut off from it and 'miserably accommodated' in expensive rented premises, and Reid had refused to call a church meeting, thus violating basic rights. 'Unless some understanding is soon come to between Mr. Reid and the people,' he warned, 'there will be an outbreak similar to that which occurred at Kingston' (where the forces of law and order had had to be called in to prevent a riot between warring factions of the congregation on East Queen's Street). People were driven to acts of desperation when pastors refused to resign despite the wishes of the majority; he feared the members would 'resort to strong measures to get rid of him'. 'Congregational principles', he asserted, 'do not appear suited to this region.'[122]

Here was a crucial point. Congregational principles might work in England, where processes of representative government were well established and church members were well trained and disciplined in the proper forms. But in Jamaica, where the House of Assembly was corrupt, voters easily bribed, and 'unrestrained passions' always in danger of taking over, more authoritative forms of rule might be more appropriate, in religious as well as political institutions.[123] Church members could not yet be relied on, he came to think, to conduct themselves properly in matters of congregational government. Meanwhile, such rows were seriously damaging the reputation of the mission. 'Our denomination here is fast becoming a by-word and a reproach,' he wrote to the BMS secretary. Henderson's conclusion was that the only hope was for new men to be sent from England.[124] Whatever his anger with the BMS, he continued to see it as providing the only solutions for the island, which was not yet ready to stand alone.

In the mid-1850s Henderson had begun to supplement his income with secular activities, since he could not maintain himself and his family on the stipend he was receiving. He constantly sought help from the BMS, but at the same time was aware that his people could support him and were failing to do so: this fuelled his sense of disappointment. He knew, however, that he was probably facing no greater financial difficulties than the brethren at home. In the early 1840s some Jamaican pastors had been far more prosperous than their counterparts in England, but that moment was long gone. In 1858 he was anxious to return to England with his wife and four children, feeling that a period in a temperate climate was essential for the health of both himself and his wife. He asked the BMS for money to help with the voyages. Hearing nothing, he became increasingly desperate, particularly for his wife, who was expecting their seventh child, and whose condition was declining. Furious and upset with the lack of response from London after his twenty years of service he packed his wife off with less than £5 in her possession to take care of herself on arrival. He himself despaired of being able to stay in Jamaica, and was dismayed at the idea of leaving his brethren, 'with whom I have been associated in the greatest harmony since the morning of my manhood', a construction perhaps more harmonious in the moment of impending departure than in the everyday.

Meanwhile serious riots in Falmouth were a painful reminder of the precarious political state of the island. 'The people', inveighed the *Falmouth Post*, 'are going wrong because they are imposed upon, and kept in a state of continual excitement by Men who call themselves the friends of freedom.'[125] John Henderson, as far as that newspaper was concerned, was one of the foremost of these agitators.[126] Land disputes were endemic across the island at this time, usually associated with settlers taking possession of abandoned estates which were subsequently claimed by purchasers or lessees. The people had developed the idea, as Holt argues, that they had rights to the land: 'such convictions were rooted deep in the moral economy of Afro-Jamaican peasants'. And they were willing to fight for them.[127]

In the summer of 1859 settlers on an estate in Westmoreland were charged with trespass, and the police arrived to evict them. When the settlers resisted, they were arrested and taken to Falmouth gaol. On 1 August, before they could be tried, a crowd of several hundred supporters took the law into their own hands and freed them. Amidst stoning from the crowd, the police fired, and two women were killed, others wounded. The crowd then set fire to the police station and marched round the building singing and making threats. The rioters, it was reported, had declared their intention of making Jamaica into another San-Domingue. They would murder the white men and make their wives into servants and concubines. They had set fire to valuable property and interfered with the due process of law. It was essential, argued the *Falmouth Post*, to have troops on the island. There were dangerous demagogues at work, and British subjects, 'who have a vast amount of capital at stake, ought not to be left to the mercy of half-civilised negroes who are misguided, and have their evil passions worked upon'.[128] Henderson himself was appalled by the violence and by the action of the police, and was anxious to distance Baptists from it all. 'The riots at Falmouth cause us to hang down our heads with shame,' he wrote; but fortunately it seemed that no Christians were involved, only 'the lowest of the low' and the 'tools of the better classes'. The 'loose women' who composed the majority of the mob were on terms of intimacy, he asserted, with many of the magistrates, and believed the police would never be allowed to fire on them. It was the immorality of the island which was erupting in this violence: there was not an official in the parish who was not living 'in open concubinage either with black or coloured females'. 'Nothing can exceed the present immoral state of the great men in this country,' he commented, and it was this corruption at the heart of the society which was to blame for present ills.[129]

While they were in England, the Hendersons addressed meetings of the faithful, and gave a fairly hopeful account of their work in Jamaica. At a meeting of the LNFS in Birmingham, for example, an organisation which had been supporting Mrs Henderson's girls' schools for some time, he spoke of the progress made there and the teachers whom they had trained.[130] Even at the Ladies' Society it was customary for the husband to be the one to speak in public. Henderson cited the neat homes and the increased taste for reading as evidence of the improvement in the peasantry, with the Bible, a hymn-book, *Pilgrim's Progress* and Dr Johnson's *Dictionary* as favourites for the bookshelves.[131] Other missionary reports received by the Ladies' Society from those whose work they supported corroborated this account of progress. Deep gloom was for the most part not in order when trying to raise funds.

On their return to Jamaica, the Hendersons found a very different atmosphere from that when they had left, for the Great Revival had spread across the island. The revival had begun in October 1860, amongst Moravian congregations in the southwest, and had then spread to Methodist and Baptist congregations.[132] The missionaries watched with amazement and somewhat mixed feelings as their congregations were seized with intense excitement and were subject to days of 'agonising convictions . . . physical prostration, piercing cries for mercy and heartrending groans'. John Clarke in Savanna-la-Mar spoke of the 'striking results' which followed from 'this amazing shaking among "the dry bones" '.[133] Phillippo described the revival as 'spreading and rolling onwards like a mighty river'. The results, he commented, as in Ireland and other places where similar revivals had taken place, 'are not altogether unmixed with evil'. But wherever the movement had been under the guidance of 'pious and devoted ministers of the Gospel', all had gone well.[134] The plus side for the missionaries was that their churches were crowded, there was a widespread conviction of sin and a huge reaction against adultery and concubinage. Innumerable couples who had been living together unmarried repented, and marriages and baptisms multiplied. The anxieties of the missionaries were associated with elements of the revival which were beyond their control, the physical convulsions which engulfed the participants, the 'degree of incoherency' about it all.[135] John Clark in Brown's Town caught the mix of reactions, scenes which were like 'heaven upon earth' alongside excitement to the point of delirium and false accusations of murder and obeah. 'But what is the chaff to the wheat?', he asked:

These are Satan's devices to hinder the work of God. That *the* work is of God no Christian can doubt . . . May God carry on the work he has begun, and permit us to realize the hopes we once so fondly cherished, but which were so utterly disappointed, of seeing the great mass of the population of this island brought up to the glorious liberty of the children of God.[136]

This was the issue for the missionaries: would God or Satan triumph? Might the revival provide the opportunity to rekindle the dream which had been disappointed in the years since the early 1840s? They were alarmed by signs of the devil's work, 'where he diffuses palpable error is in villages dark, dark as the wilds of Africa', noted one.[137] But darkness and light were in conflict; dark villages were without pastoral guidance, but where this existed, there were still great hopes of good. As always, the question was whether orthodox Baptist forms could hold their own against the syncretic forms of the Native Baptists and their associates: the physicality of the revivalists suggested the presence of violent spirits. And there were other alarming signs of Africanisms: individuals became stricken, with rigid muscles and bodies as cold as death, or myal men took advantage of the state of excitement and went amongst the crowds declaring that they were sent by God. But the missionaries held on, drawing distinctions between Satan and Christ, and hoping that, overall, the revival would increase the proper religious enthusiasm of 'their' people. By early 1862 the wild excitement had disappeared, but numbers of baptisms were high. John Clark distinguished between those who had been 'only stricken down' and those who had been 'wildly excited' with physical manifestations. It was the latter who had now returned to indifference, while the former remained steadfast: moderation turned out again to be best.[138]

The London editor of the *Missionary Herald* made sense of these reports through the notion of the superstitious and excitable negro, and emphasised the ever vital work of education. Negroes were not all right left to themselves; it was only with the care of Christian missionaries that they could become full adults. He reminded his readership of the 'excitable' and 'uninstructed' nature of the negro, and the inevitability of verbal and physical extravagance amongst such people. Whilst in Jamaica, he reported, the BMS deputation had seen in the prison of St Ann a man charged with obeah, whose 'countenance and manner were of the most sinister kind', and they were told of people who were pining away 'under the influence of the fears excited by the frauds of the obeah and myal-men'. But they did not doubt that in time education would destroy this 'vile imposture'.[139] Robert Stewart argues that the significance of revivalism was that it was open and self-confident in a way that myalism or obeah never could be: 'it broke the walls of the churches, as it were, and took to the road'. Its effect, he claims, was that Native Baptist congregations increased and Baptist Union congregations became more tightly disciplined: a widening of the gulf between Native and orthodox Baptists.[140] When Henderson returned to Jamaica early in 1862, however, he had to work extremely hard, baptising 700 and turning many away because the church was full. From his perspective the outlook seemed good, and his hold on 'his' people relatively secure.[141]

Three years later *The Voice of Jubilee* was published, a celebratory narrative of the fifty years of the Baptist Mission in Jamaica. In his introduction, East deplored the fact that in some parts of the island 'African superstition is even yet in the ascendant', as well as a 'disposition to blend with Christianity the absurdities of heathenism'. The devil was not yet dead, and in some districts had perverted the joys of religious revivalism into 'the wildest extravagances of fanaticism'. But East framed his worries about the present and the future with his satisfaction over the spread of marriage and family ties and the decline of the 'grossest abominations of African superstition'. 'We have no longer a heathen community,' he claimed. 'Brethren,' he argued, '*you are now a people*, your manhood recognised, your freedom won, your rights acknowledged.'[142] Perhaps the dream of the 1830s could still be realised.

Morant Bay and after

This optimistic account of black Jamaicans as a people, with their freedom won and rights established, represented a desire rather than something fully achieved. Nevertheless, the plans for new activities associated with the celebration of the jubilee of the BMS on the island suggested a fairly hopeful state of affairs. A great open meeting of about 10,000 was held in Montego Bay. Governor Eyre had recently been appointed, and his first efforts to improve the moral character of public servants were welcomed. Eyre himself sent a congratulatory message to the meeting on the good effects of religion, and this was well received.[143] Such friendly relations between governor and Baptists were not to last, however. Six months later the missionaries were reporting distress associated with drought, the failure of crops, a fall in wages and increase in crime.[144] Worried by the situation and the lack of initiative from the Colonial Office, Underhill, as secretary of the BMS, wrote a letter in January 1865 to the Secretary of State, Cardwell, a friend of his family, detailing the problems on the island and some possible solutions. Utilising his extensive knowledge, Underhill documented the hunger, the lack of employment and the lack of capital, and argued that the executive had failed to address the problems of the island. He called for an inquiry into legislation since emancipation, and a shift of focus away from sugar to the encouragement of small settlers producing for the export market. He insisted that with a proper system of justice and a reformed tax system capitalists would be attracted to Jamaica.[145] Underhill had become convinced that sugar did not provide the answer to the island's economic ills, and that the small settlers needed to become 'growers of produce for foreign markets'. But 'your stupid legislature', as he described it to Henderson, was incapable of thinking beyond its own interests. 'Things in Jamaica look very gloomy,' he reflected in February. 'It is another Ireland; only it seems to me the want of prosperity in Jamaica is far more owing to man's follies and fault, than to the acts of Nature.'[146] Here was Underhill accepting the arguments of political economy in relation to Ireland, a situation about which he knew little, but refusing it for Jamaica, where he had seen for himself the effects of a particular system of colonial rule.

Underhill's letter was forwarded by Cardwell to Eyre, and received an extremely hostile response. Eyre had been relying increasingly on racial explanations for the island's problems in his first year as governor. In April smallholders in St Ann sent a memorial to the Queen asking for support in buying land and setting up a company through which to sell their produce. 'This is the first fruit of Dr. Underhill's letter', inveighed Eyre: 'which represented the peasantry of Jamaica as being generally in a destitute, naked and starving condition, a representation which many of them will be quite ready to take advantage of, and try to turn to their own advantage in every way they can.' 'Nor will there be wanting persons in this colony', he continued ominously, 'to encourage and urge them on.'[147] The Baptists were clearly in Eyre's line of vision. In response to the petition, Henry Taylor at the Colonial Office, a long-time friend of Carlyle's, drafted 'a lecture in classical political economy' which instructed the labourers of Jamaica that what was needed was steady and continuous wage labour:

> the prosperity of the labouring classes as well as all other classes depends in Jamaica and in other countries upon their working for wages, not uncertainly or capriciously, but steadily and continuously, at the times when their labour is wanted, and for so long as it is wanted . . . it is from their own industry and prudence in availing themselves of the means of prosperity that are before them . . . that they must look for an improvement in their condition.[148]

While Underhill saw the executive as responsible for poverty and want, Taylor resorted to the stock response that negroes would not work. His draft became the basis for 'the Queen's Advice', a dispatch which Eyre was delighted to receive: 50,000 copies were ordered to be posted across the island and read out in churches.[149]

Meanwhile Eyre had publicised Underhill's letter and asked for responses to it. Underhill in turn encouraged the missionaries to send in as much information as possible, for Eyre would be obliged to forward it to the Colonial Office. He urged East to make sure that 'our coloured brethren' participated: 'Let them say that they are sprung from the people and that they in particular have this and that grievance to complain of.' The most should be made of the present opportunity; 'our brethren must take more interest in social and political questions than they have done,' argued Underhill.[150] At the end of April the JBU met for two days at Calabar to put together the material they had collected and produce a report. They represented seventy-three congregations with 20,000 members and 10,000 Sunday school and day scholars: their information covered almost all of the country. Their congregations were almost entirely of 'the labouring classes'. They could, therefore, with some justice claim to be amongst 'the best informed' on the social conditions of the people.[151]

This report provides a significant index of the collective views of the missionaries in the early 1860s. Poverty and malnutrition haunted the island. Underhill might have overstated the case in claiming that 'the people are starving', but large numbers were indeed 'in a starving condition'. The peasantry were much less well dressed than previously, and as a result were unable to come to church or send their children to Sunday school. The young were resistant to parental control; few marriages were taking place, and many were living openly in sin; theft had increased, and the prisons were overflowing. The causes were in part drought, the failure of the crops, the lack of employment and reductions in wages, the inadequacy of the system of justice in the petty courts and the officious actions of the police. But their returns also showed that indolence, as they described it, was much to blame. This was especially the case amongst the young who were accustomed to estate labour and unwilling to seek other employment. The 'artificial wants' of the people, they argued, 'are very few, whilst the climate is such as to induce habits of indolence'. As long as they could obtain certain comforts without much labour, they would, and they enjoyed them; but when it became more difficult, they gave up. Their standard of housing was declining, their food inferior, their clothes inadequate, self-respect had declined, and immorality had increased. 'There is no denying', pronounced the missionaries, 'that had the people more persevering energy of character they would, notwithstanding these discouragements, have accomplished more. But it must be considered that they are yet only in the incipient stages of civilisation.'[152]

The report was signed by officers within the JBU: Henderson and his brother George, East, Dendy, Millard and Claydon, all well-established BMS figures. The one coloured brother who signed was Ellis Fray, Knibb's son-in-law and one of the first men to be trained at Calabar. The language of this report reflected the disappointment of the missionaries, their tendency to fall back on a racialised understanding of African character which stressed natural indolence and absence of civilisation. While they stressed that wise legislation could help, they argued that only religion and education could transform the inner man. While Underhill asked them to engage more with social and political questions, they varied in their capacity to do this. In the detailed local reports, for example, John Clarke from Savanna-la-Mar, who was notorious for his superior attitude to Africans, castigated the laziness of many and their failure to plan. His cousin John Clark in Brown's Town, long-time friend of Joseph Sturge, had more to say about drought and crop failures.[153] All could agree, however, on the moral dimensions: without religion, civilisation could not advance. In their localities their difficulties in carrying their congregations with them had been deeply discouraging. Collectively they were depressed about the prospects for Jamaica.

The focus on the lack of desire for 'artificial wants' amongst the peasantry and the links between the character of 'the African', a tropical climate and a barbarous society were by no means new. But those associated with the abolitionists had mainly tried to counter such claims, arguing that Africans were not necessarily lazy; that, given the right conditions, they would work as industriously as any other men, would learn to want goods and commodities, and become civilised. By the 1860s, however, such arguments carried less conviction. It was Samuel Oughton who was to take up such critical ideas of African character in a public way. Missionary discourse had long contained contradictions, but this marked a new rupture. Oughton had arrived in Jamaica in 1836 and had gone to help Burchell, to whose niece he was married, with his mission stations. He had been inspired by hearing Knibb speak at Exeter Hall and, like Henderson, his first impressions were most enthusiastic. His 'very sanguine expectations' in relation to the people were more than met: they were indeed 'an interesting race'.[154]

In 1839 he went to East Queen's Street in Kingston, a large and important chapel which had gone through some difficult times but appeared to be united in wanting Oughton.[155] His first year there, however, was a difficult one, in which he was charged with defamation in connection with a magistrate whom, he claimed, had taken 'indecent liberties' with black women.[156] His anxieties, arising out of his position in 'this depraved country', were severe.[157] With his wife expecting a baby and fears that the courts would inevitably rule against him, he suffered severely, and his health declined.[158] Released on bail, he was at one stage almost overcome by the 'simple but ardent expressions of delight and affection' from 'our poor dear people'.[159] He was finally discharged as insolvent.[160]

In 1843 'an attempt was made . . . to create a division in the Church' at East Queen's Street. The 'disappointed men' were expelled, and others left after much anxiety.[161] In 1845 there was again trouble, with disputes over the control of a class house (where groups met under their leaders), between the chapel and a group of Native Baptists who attempted to seize the property: the 'poor dear people' were rather more self-willed than Oughton had imagined.[162] In 1854 a set of issues erupted violently.

The East Queen Street property, which was of significant value, had been vested in trustees when originally bought by the BMS. The trustees had gradually died, and the congregation, 'considering it to have been acquired chiefly through their contributions', decided it should be in the hands of the leaders. The last surviving Jamaican trustee was persuaded to draw up a new trust deed, and a meeting was called to elect new trustees. Oughton attempted to prevent this happening by appealing to the law, and when this failed, he applied to the governor for military protection, fearing that the property would be seized. Governor Barkly refused this, but demonstrated his support of Oughton by going personally to the chapel with the mayor and magistrates and persuading the crowd of 8,000 to 10,000 to disband peacefully. Once again the question was: who controlled the property, who had the power?[163]

An English woman member of the congregation, who had been in Jamaica for ten years, wrote to Underhill, then secretary of the BMS, with her account of these events. She was one of the few white members of East Queen's Street, and had been well aware that white society on the island would condemn her for attaching herself to a predominantly black church. Her sympathies, however, were entirely with the white pastor, and her story was one of racial hostility. 'Until I became acquainted with Mr. Oughton's family,' she told Underhill,

> I never knew how much of trial, anxiety and sacrifice of feeling was connected with a missionary's life – he has to bear with the waywardness – to battle with the obstinacy, to suffer the insolence, and misrepresentations of a set of men called Leaders, to such an extent that it would be impossible without actual observation, to credit – this however is always endured uncomplainingly.

The minister, she continued, ascended the pulpit week after week as though he were not 'pressed down by ingratitude, treachery, and malevolence'. Now, however, things had reached a new pass. Twelve of the leaders were attempting to seize the property, and the family needed help. She was convinced that there was 'a secret combination on the part of the black and coloured population against English influence . . . their object is to get rid of every white inhabitant'. Recently Mr Oughton had even been threatened with 'a large club', and the women had protected him. 'Such is the violence of the negro character when thwarted in their purpose,' she confidently stated, 'that you are never safe until their anger is over.'[164]

Oughton addressed his congregation on the occasion of the first attempted dispossession, undoubtedly stirring the very anger which he was attempting to dispel. You are doing wrong, he told them, and the authorities, both civil and military, would support him. 'I call on you', he continued, 'to return to your homes: I pity you, poor ignorant people (hisses and groans from the people).' The dispute was casting shame on the Baptists. He had never expected to be treated in this way; he had been the 'black man's friend'. He had been invited to come to Jamaica, he had been hated by every white man in Hanover, he had been begged to come to East Queen's Street, he had 'striven both in public and in private' to be the 'friend of the black man' and this was his reward. He defied them if they would not listen to him.[165]

But many of them would not. The dispute simmered on into the following year. Oughton's opponents waited until, according to the pastor, they had a chance to break in to the mission premises. 'They then proceeded to cut off all communication with that part of the Premises in which their former Pastor still resided, by erecting a strong barricade, and leaving him to continue his ministrations to the remnant of his flock, appointed one of their own number to supply his Pulpit and officiate in his stead.' The magistrates refused to eject them by force, since they tended to the view that the members probably did have the right to appoint their own minister. Like Phillippo in Spanish Town, Oughton was driven to appeal to Chancery, and once again a judgement in a missionary's favour led to a riot and an attack on his house. On the second day of rioting, marked by the intense hatred of the crowd for Oughton, the Riot Act was read. The police office report commented on the 'indescribable' nature of the 'yelling imprecations and violence' of the women, who dominated the crowd numerically. Fifty-three were arrested, and damage was done over several days.[166]

Hannah Oughton 'had removed from the beautiful vale of Gloucestershire in England', her memorial stone relates, to take on the arduous role of missionary wife.[167] She was a poet and a hymn-writer in addition to performing the usual duties associated with a mission station. She penned a poem on the death of Knibb, 'One fatal flash struck terror all around / And felled the lofty cedar to the ground', and on her husband's fortieth birthday she celebrated the gold pencil case which she presented to him. She wrote hymns for special occasions, from the opening of new churches to the anniversaries of Sunday schools. Her lines on 'Uncle Tom made free' evoked the wonderful time of emancipation and the 'sweet freedom' he enjoyed, not only of the soul but of the body too. But her faith in 'Uncle Tom's' career was sadly battered:

> But years roll'd on, – how chang'd the scene,
> Tom stands erect and free,
> His breast expanding wide is seen,
> With new-born liberty;

Prosperity sends forth her scorching rays,
And sears devotion in her upward gaze.

With wealth my Uncle's honors came,
And these gave birth to pride;
'Who dares oppose? My own I am,
And o'er the rest I'll ride'.
Thus, he who meekly wore the chain before,
Becomes a scourge to all within his power.

And step by step my Uncle trod,
The downward course of shame;
At last he seized the house of God!
And then profan'd the same,
The mourners walk and weep, and hourly moan,
Their Prophet silenc'd, and the ark undone.[168]

Prosperity had seared devotion, wealth had given birth to pride, the meek had inherited the earth and followed a path of shame, the ark of the Lord was undone. This was a bleak account of the fruits of emancipation.

Oughton had always been more interested in material questions than some of his intensely spiritual brethren. He was a town dweller rather than a countryman, even if the town in question was Kingston. Small peasants did not match his picture of civilisation. He had a strong conviction of the importance of commerce. 'This is the age of enterprise,' he had declared in one of his speeches in support of the Africa mission, 'the age of invention, the age of novelty.' In England railways were replacing horses, coals sails. Commerce and civilisation, he believed, went together, and his arguments for the mission to Africa in the early 1840s were strongly inflected with these ideas.[169] In the 1844 election he was active in promoting black candidates, but from the mid-1840s Jamaica's increasingly parlous economic state became associated in his mind with fears of a retreat into barbarism. By the early 1860s both he and John Henderson had stopped supporting a black franchise, and Oughton was in favour of authority and hierarchy on the island.[170] The death of Prince Albert in 1861 occasioned a funeral oration by him at East Queen's Street on the 'infinite diversity of conditions and powers' in the family of man. Equality of human rights and liberties was quite proper, he argued, but equality of condition was impossible, undesirable and unnatural. Inequality was indeed the 'prime spring' of human progress. Kings and labourers, princes and peasants, rich and poor, 'all these are needful and valuable each in his several place, and as each fulfils with diligence and fidelity the duties of his station'.[171]

A lecture which Oughton gave in Kingston the following year, which was repeated by popular request, focused on the terrible wages of sin. Addressing himself particularly to young men and women who had to contend with the awful examples of bastardy and concubinage which bedevilled the island, he issued a dire warning. Lawless and immoral unions could never lead to happiness, he taught, only to shame and embitterment.[172] At the same time he was intervening in a more public debate over the condition of Jamaica. God's sentence of labour pronounced on Adam, he argued, was taken to be a curse, but it was one of the greatest blessings that could have been bestowed. 'It is labour', he proclaimed, 'that has elevated our race to its present high position of individual comfort and social distinction, by stimulating thought, suggesting contrivance, and promoting invention.' It was the advancement of man from 'the wild untutored savage of the woods' to 'inhabitants of civilised states' which distinguished mankind in its most degraded and its most perfect forms. The increase of civilisation, he argued, had good effects on all, for it brought employment and a division of labour which produced new skills and knowledges and 'a higher and more dignified character'. It also meant more pay and, therefore, the possibility of increased comforts. 'Thus by the mutual action of wealth and labour on each other', he maintained, 'the interests of mankind at large are best promoted.' Inequality, the division between employer and employee, operated 'to the interest and welfare of the whole'.

The problem in Jamaica, he thought, was the lack of artificial wants, the material possessions around which a proper domestic life could be organised. In this fertile island little labour was required to survive, and the move away from the estates had meant that thousands were separated from 'civilising influences'. In the mountains the peasantry had done well to become landowners with their own homesteads, but they lacked education, medical skill and sound religious instruction. 'A horse to ride, and a showy dress' marked the limits of their ambitions. A few years ago, he reported, he had visited a squalid, dirty, comfortless cottage with little furniture: outside 'luxurious vegetation' grew in abundance. He asked why no roses were allowed to grow around the door, letting in light and air and shedding their perfume. He received the reply that roses were no good to eat. 'So long as the people of Jamaica limit their desires to the gratification of their merely animal wants,' he concluded, 'we shall never possess an active, energetic and industrious population.' England enjoyed its 'high position of wealth and importance' on account of its commerce; Jamaica was condemned to distress and poverty until 'artificial wants' were cultivated.[173] It was the people who must change. The real cause of the increase in poverty and crime was 'the inveterate habits of idleness, and the low state of moral and religious principles which prevail to so fearful a degree in our community'.[174]

Some of Oughton's concerns here overlapped with other preoccupations of the missionaries and highlight the ways in which different discourses were interwoven. Arguments about civilisation and commerce coexisted alongside notions of the family of man, as Buxton's Niger expedition and Livingstone's travels so clearly demonstrated.[175] But different elements of this discursive mix could take commanding positions at different moments. Most Baptist missionaries had been relatively untouched by notions of the significance of 'artificial wants' until their disappointments of the late 1840s and 1850s focused their minds on more negative understandings of 'the African'. At the same time, 'families of man' were always differentiated, and the decline of utopian dreams of pious and grateful freed peoples benefitting from a society dominated by Baptist missionaries produced increasing anxieties about the forms of social life which were emerging amongst the African-Jamaican peasantry. Jamaican traditions of concubinage and bastardy, always encouraged by the plantocracy, were in the forefront of missionary minds, making the struggle against immorality part of the longer struggle with a certain form of colonial rule. The figure of the black woman emerged in this context as peculiarly threatening, no longer simply a victim, rather a willing perpetrator of disorder. From the moment of emancipation and the establishment of the free villages, missionaries had been deeply anxious to encourage a particular kind of family life and to banish the immorality which, in their minds, was rife upon the island.

In 1856 the JBU had adopted a sermon of Rev. East's as a statement of its views on the relation between social habits and personal religion. East argued for the vital importance of proper relations in the household: husbands should love their wives, wives submit to their husbands, children honour and obey their parents, servants be obedient. Religion must be exemplified in daily life. Take dress, for example, which was an index of character. Women must be modest, not display a love of finery, yet take care with their attire lest they should act 'as a bait to the licentiousness of wicked men'. The humblest Christian cottage should be a model home, clean and bright, comfortable and proper, with separate sleeping quarters for parents and children, sons and daughters, and decent chairs and tables. Families should sit down to meals together rather than 'the wife standing by like a slave while the tyrant master downs his food'. It was essential that fathers should act as ministers of their own households. Sundays should be spent at church and at home, not out visiting, with the women 'flaunting' and the young men 'swaggering along with smoking cigars in their mouths'. It was habits such as these which encouraged the dreadful sin of fornication: the sin which was the bane of the island and led to such a large proportion of the cases of discipline and exclusion in and from their churches.[176]

East expanded his thoughts on suitable housing for Christian families in a paper which he wrote on the topic for his local association of Baptist churches. Family religion, he argued, was impossible without proper homes, and these must be suited to social position. Like Oughton, he drew on the analogy of nature: 'All trees are not of one uniform height ... men differ in wealth and education, in rank and office.' He laid great stress on the need for separate sleeping rooms for parents and children, boys and girls. Children have keen ears and quick eyes, he insisted. 'Scarcely any intercourse between husband and wife ... can be safely allowed in the presence even of very young children. Ideas and impressions may be conveyed to the mind, which, however little they may be thought of at the time, will, in after years, prove seeds of corruption, and supply food to a depraved imagination.' Cleanliness was vital, and the delicate matter of out-offices (toilets) needed attention: he had been reliably informed that in many country districts they were non-existent, yet building materials were abundant. The money 'frequently wasted by young people on dress and feasting at their weddings' would go a long way towards the construction of a decent modest home, and East included plans and costings to encourage action. Black female sexuality haunted his imagination, 'a land peopled with bastard children' was his nightmare. 'A woman without modesty may make a harlot: she is hardly fit to become a wife,' he concluded.[177]

While the missionaries emphasised lack of employment as a major source of woe, serious anxieties about African indolence and immorality underpinned their thinking. Their confidence in 'the African' was no longer secure, and their sense of their own role in relation to that imagined figure correspondingly troubled. When called upon for individual action, however, they took different positions. There was no one view of Underhill's letter and 'The Queen's Advice'. Henderson, alongside Hewitt, Dendy and Reid, was at one of the so-called Underhill public meetings in Montego Bay when grievances were discussed and criticisms of the government voiced. Henderson, Dendy and Reid all refused to post up copies of the Advice, arguing that the petition related to St Ann, and that in their area the peasantry were entirely loyal. Eyre was enraged by this. 'It is quite clear', he wrote to Cardwell,

> that if ministers of religion residing amongst an ignorant, debased and excitable coloured population take upon themselves to endorse and reiterate assertions such as those in Dr. Underhill's letter, to the effect that the people are starving, ragged, or naked; that their addiction to thieving is the result of extreme poverty; that all this arises from the taxation being

too heavy; that such taxation is unjust upon the coloured population; that they are refused just tribunals and denied political rights; then such ministers do their best not only to make the labourer discontented, but to stimulate resistance to the laws and constituted authorities.

By the summer of 1865, Henderson and some of his brethren were fixed in Eyre's mind as most dangerous men. Samuel Jones, however, the Baptist minister in Annotto Bay, a small town on the eastern side of the island, wrote to Eyre thanking him for the 'Queen's Advice' and saying how well it fitted with his own teaching.[178] Nor did John Clarke, 'Mr. African Clarke' as Ellis Fray called him (on account of his time in West Africa), from Savanna-la-Mar, share Henderson's criticisms of the 'Queen's Advice'; he told Eyre that he thought it would have little effect, for either good or ill.[179]

By the end of August 1865, Underhill's private opinion, expressed in a letter to East, was that the authorities themselves 'put the match to the tinder', and were raising the stakes by the publicity they had generated for his letter and the 'Queen's Advice'. He was convinced that the law was a central issue. 'These lords of sugar want to be taught that there is right and law in the land for the coloured man,' he wrote, and 'the coloured man' would have to 'boldly vindicate his right to fair dealing'. 'I know', he continued, 'that the coloured people tell lies fast enough to misrepresent often their cases; but no more than Bengalis do.'[180] Here were the 'lords of sugar', arrogant, corrupt and unjust, locked in conflict with Africans, who, like Bengalis, in the eyes of Underhill, who had visited and 'knew' both places, could not be trusted to tell the truth. Only Baptist missionaries could save the day. A month later he was writing to Henderson, sympathising with his despair over the state of the island, agreeing that the Colonial Office was dead to appeals and the Jamaican government incapable of meeting the crisis: the people 'overwhelmed with discouragement' were giving up 'their long struggle with injustice and fraud'. This letter was intercepted by the authorities, and played a part in the subsequent recriminations over the events at Morant Bay.[181] Underhill's hope remained that enough pressure could be mobilised for a Royal Commission to be set up to investigate the state of the island. England had paid a huge sum for the welfare of Jamaica, from the initial compensation to the planters to the large amounts of charitable money which had been raised. Yet the island was commercially in a very bad state and had not advanced socially in the ways that had been hoped for and expected. 'The people of England', he assured the Secretary of State, 'are deeply interested in the question, why Jamaica is in this state? Why the great and righteous act of emancipation has borne no better fruit?'[182]

On Thursday 12 October Eyre was receiving reports from St Thomas-in-the-East that 'the blacks had risen' in Morant Bay and was despatching white troops and declaring martial law. In his first report to Cardwell, he discussed the causes of 'this wicked and most wide-spread rebellion', and blamed George William Gordon, Black Baptists and political agitators who were 'exciting and stimulating ... evil passions'. Included in this attack were the Baptist ministers Henderson, Reid, Dendy, Hewitt and Maxwell, who had endorsed Underhill's letter at public meetings. Eyre added, however, that while it was his duty to point to the mischievous effects of the behaviour of these few, he was pleased to be able to say that 'the large majority of the Baptist ministers have been most anxious to support the authorities'.[183] A few days later Eyre was blaming Underhill: his letter to Henderson was a clear incitement to ministers on the island to stimulate the people 'not to give up the struggle'. If nothing could be done at home to stop such pernicious writings, and if Jamaica was to be retained at all, 'it will be necessary to pass a law in the colony authorising the deportation of all persons who leaving their proper sphere of action as ministers of religion, become political demagogues and dangerous agitators'.

The Baptist missionaries were 'really wolves in sheep's clothing, who ferment discontent and disaffection among the negro population', as one of his predecessors, Lord Metcalfe, had thought.[184] A few days later he was attacking Henderson and his friends again, charging that 'it is easy to influence the evil passions of such a population, but impossible to guide, direct, or control them when once excited'.[185] These accusations were repeated at the opening of the legislative session of the House of Assembly, in the wake of the rebellion, when Eyre proposed the abolition of the colonial constitution. A widespread rebellion had taken place, he argued, with 'savage and cruel butchery, only to be paralleled by the atrocities of the Indian mutiny'. The 'misapprehensions and misrepresentations of pseudo philanthropists in England' had played a critical part in stirring disaffection, alongside 'the inflammatory harangues or seditious writings of political demagogues' and the 'misdirected effort and misguided counsel of certain ministers of religion', all of which had their inevitable result on 'an ignorant, excitable, and uncivilised population', namely, rebellion, arson and murder.[186]

The response of the majority of the white inhabitants of the island to the events in Morant Bay was panic and fear: a conviction that all their lives were in danger. Eyre was widely celebrated as a hero who had saved them from massacre. Once Eyre realised that his actions were not straightforwardly supported in England, he was keen to collect evidence from local dignitaries confirming his account of what had happened. He issued a circular to ministers, magistrates, inspectors of police and local officials, the vast majority of whom were white, asking for information. Responses to the circular were submitted as part of his evidence to the Royal Commission, with the claim that they represented 'the feelings and convictions' of the 'large majority of the respectable inhabitants of this colony', and would go far in correcting the erroneous opinions of the British public. The documents would throw much light, he argued, 'upon the character and tone of thinking of the negro population'. Many of them were written by men 'who have spent a lifetime in the West Indies'. Their close observation of small facts and circumstances made it possible for them to know the 'tone of feeling', wishes and intentions of the peasantry.[187] Eyre's own considered judgement as to the causes and scale of the rebellion was that 'the negroes form a low level of civilization' and were 'under the influence of superstitious feelings'. He was convinced that there had been a wide-scale conspiracy, but it was not possible to get full details of negro plans or intentions, since 'as a race the negroes are most reticent, and it is very difficult to obtain from them full or specific information upon any subject'. Their object, however, had been 'to exterminate the white and coloured classes, and obtain possession of the country for themselves'.[188]

The testimony he collected revealed the fear, guilt and terror associated with colonial rule. White people in Jamaica were profoundly conscious of being a small numerical minority; many of them lived in isolated and scattered places, surrounded by those whom they exploited. The colonisers were persecuted by their relations with the colonised: they claimed to know 'the negro', yet could not know him; they claimed to rule him, yet were subject to his insolence and insubordination; they claimed to have treated him well, yet received ingratitude. The white residents of the island were enraged by what they saw as the false accounts in the British press. *'It was'* a rebellion, insisted the Rev. Hall, rector of Clarendon; 'there can be but one opinion on the subject. Those only who live at ease at a distance, safe from danger, can term it a local riot.'[189] 'People in England', argued Police Inspector Downer from St Thomas, 'are utterly ignorant of the nature of the negro, or of the requirements of the Colony.'[190] But white West Indian knowledge often owed more to fear and fantasy than to their much vamped empirical wisdom: 'I have never heard any inflammatory speeches or seen any seditious writings,' declared one gentleman, but he was convinced in his own mind that both had been made use of.[191] Similarly, several commentators noted that the evidence they had might be slight, made up of small fragments, but, put together, they 'appear to bear but one way': a point that Eyre strongly endorsed.[192]

White West Indians' claims to 'know' were undercut by their own fears as to the limits of their knowledges. Take the Hon. John Salmon,

Custos of St Elizabeth, planter, member of the House of Assembly and the Legislative Council. He had 'known' the negro for forty-five years; his family had had property on the island for nearly a century. He had been against the whip, had 'always advocated the cause of the slave', had 'strenuously' supported emancipation, and had 'continued civil and kind to the black man to the present time'. 'I think I know him, and can speak with knowledge and without prejudice and a hardened heart.' Yet one of those same black men, whom he did not know personally and had never to his knowledge addressed, had said publicly that he intended to cut his head off. This was bewildering. 'What do men with families feel', he asked, 'when they see the negro bewailed over by English papers and letters, without any correct information or knowledge? . . . Men who had only one course, to kill or be killed, to preserve their wives and daughters from pollution and death, or to protect them?'[193] Similarly, the Rev. May, rector of Buff Bay, which was not far from the site of the rebellion, told that he had been credibly informed that if the rebels had succeeded, he was high on their list for butchery. 'Does not this show', he asked, 'the fiendish spirit by which these wretches were actuated? I have lived amongst this people between 30 and 40 years, and have in every way sought their temporal and spiritual good, and this is the way they would have requited me for all my labours of love amongst them during that lengthened period.'[194]

'We know each other intimately yet not entirely,' commented an Anglican curate who had been in Jamaica since 1833.[195] A senior magistrate likewise commented that it was often 'difficult to discern the feelings and purposes of the negro'.[196] The Rev. Downie, the acting rector in Spanish Town, only three years on the island, commented how surprised he had been at the 'very insolent and defiant bearing' of many of the black population, quite the reverse of that attributed to them in England. 'I have failed to discover in them', he observed, 'that spirit of docile humility, and that ready submission to authority' which he had been led to expect.[197] An official of the Geological Survey of the West Indies remarked that the view of the negro as Christian, truthful, grateful and pious was deluded: the negroes of Jamaica were more reliant on obeah, an 'unfathomable influence', than the word of God.[198] The Rev. Panton, an Anglican curate for twenty years, put his point simply: the 'peculiar characteristics of the black man' must be taken into consideration; he was not what he was represented to be in England, 'a black Anglo-Saxon'.[199]

But if he was not a black Anglo-Saxon, what was he? He was conceited, insubordinate and insolent, and had become increasingly so in the period leading up to the rebellion. Both male and female servants had become rude, threatening and impertinent, whereas previously they had been grateful for 'the great care bestowed on them'.[200] When out on the roads they showed no respect, and the supercilious manners of those black men who proclaimed themselves to be Baptist preachers and dressed up for the part on Sundays were particularly annoying.[201] Captain Kent, a stipendiary magistrate in Port Royal, claimed that he had known trouble was coming on account of the hats:

> I was forcibly struck with many of the negroes throwing off their small scull caps and suddenly appearing in hats of at least two feet and six inches in diameter, in which no man could work, and spoke out openly that there were secret societies forming, of which these men were to be the leaders.

Since the crushing of the rebellion, he was pleased to note, the hats had disappeared.[202] A curate in Falmouth remarked that 'those who formerly used to touch their hats passed with a rude stare or turned aside', and that when he had preached on 'the wickedness and folly of rebellion', he had noted 'a marked and guilty expression . . . on the countenances of many'.[203]

At the same time 'the African' was accused of lack of moral stamina and a tendency to 'go with the stream'. This made 'Africans' subject to demagogues and easily led. Thus Underhill's letter had had a disastrous effect, along with 'the fallacious teachings and canting hypocrisy of the Baptists'.[204] 'They are an excitable race' and easily stirred to acts of violence and opposition, thought the Inspector of Revenues in Kingston.[205] Colonel Fyfe of the Maroons, who were widely blamed for some of the worst brutality in the suppression of the rebellion, blamed the Anti-Slavery Society for many of the problems of the island. 'So long as that Society exists,' he argued, 'the negro will never settle down into a sense of his real position or contentment with his lot in life.' Negroes had become convinced that they were in an inferior position and possessed less property than white people, and were dissatisfied with their lot. They built castles in the air rather than putting their shoulders to the wheel.[206] For the last three years, one magistrate opined, the black population 'had wished to place themselves on an equality with their superiors'. They had gone so far as to hold courts of their own and impose fines for offences.[207] The rector of Spanish Town, on the basis of thirty years' experience with black people, maintained that 'there is little they desire so much as the complete possession of the country and the destruction of their oppressor, the white man, who is in possession of what they imagine belongs to themselves by right'.[208]

The guilty fears of the colonisers as to the desires of those they had colonised to violently recover what they believed they had lost were linked to fantasies of rape. Given the long history of concubinage and illegitimacy, both before and after emancipation, and the connections between white male power and sexual authority, it was not surprising that white fantasies of black revenge included the rape of their wives, daughters and mothers. 'Orders were given by the leaders to kill all the males', reported the medical officer of Port Morant, 'and save all the females as they would take them for themselves.'[209] Scarcely any women submitted evidence in response to Eyre's circular, but white women expressed their gratitude to him by sending memorials thanking him for saving them from horrors worse than death.[210] The men who submitted evidence commented again and again on the immorality of the island: this was linked to the nature of black people, though at times also to the fearful immorality of some whites. Since a large number of reports came in from Anglican clergy in response to Eyre, the emphasis on the neglect of marriage and the level of prostitution was to be expected. One curate commented on the animal-like sexuality of black men and women: 'they lie together under hedges, and anywhere by stealth,' not for them the decent forms of marriage.[211] The women exposed themselves at rivers and streams, encouraging improprieties.[212] The surgeon at Morant Bay, meanwhile, focused on the savagery and violence of the women in the mob, their delight at the discovery of each new victim.[213] 'To my mind', wrote Underhill privately to East, reflecting on the white Jamaican response to the events on the island, 'there was an uneasy consciousness among the whites that they deserved some recompense from the blacks for their misgovernment and injustice. So when it came in one place they naturally expected it would extend elsewhere.'[214]

Meanwhile the missionaries themselves were divided. Samuel Oughton distanced himself from Underhill and the critics of Eyre from the beginning. Indeed, by early 1865, Underhill judged him as having 'fallen a prey to Negrophobia'. But 'he cannot harm the truth', he wrote to East.[215] At the end of 1865 Oughton was still in correspondence with Underhill as to his opinions: relations had not yet broken down. Underhill thought he might be correct in some of his judgements as to negro character, but argued that the fault lay with the government and 'the ruling class of Jamaica'.[216] By the end of January 1866 Underhill was very vexed at the support which Oughton had given to a bill regulating religious worship on the island. The purpose of this bill was to prevent the activities of native preachers, an issue on which Oughton had strong feelings. But Baptists, who had themselves had many struggles both at home and in the empire over their rights to preach and meet, had traditionally been committed to freedom of worship. Oughton's public retreat on this issue was not surprising to Underhill, but he greatly regretted it: he had had his doubts as to Oughton's relationship with black people for some time.[217]

Oughton was one of the many white residents of the island who wrote to Eyre at the beginning of 1866 thanking him for his actions in suppressing the rebellion and regretting his departure. The loyal address he signed was sent by a group of ministers in Kingston, including one other Baptist and several prominent Methodists. The evidence of their own observations together with documentary information they had available had convinced them that 'a spirit of insubordination to law has long existed among a large portion of the population of this Island'. 'The teachings of ignorant and wicked men' had fanned these flames into sedition. They were fully in support of Eyre's actions. They were shocked by the ignorant censure of the British press, which was manifestly ill informed on the real state of the colony, and which they denounced as potentially dangerous.[218] 'The course that Mr. Oughton has taken will not raise him in our estimation here,' wrote Underhill to Henderson, and indeed he would be glad when he left the island. To his friend Walter Dendy he commented caustically that Oughton would not meet a very warm welcome when he arrived in England.[219] Oughton left Jamaica later that year, regretted by few, his dreams of the 1830s long gone. His wife Hannah had died in 1862, and his youngest daughter looked after him in his retirement in Brighton. His sons all took up colonial careers across the empire: the eldest, Thomas, stayed in Kingston, where he practised as a lawyer; a second went to Antigua and was the principal of the Mico Institute there; a third was a doctor in the army; the youngest went to New Zealand. His older daughter stayed in the religious family more broadly defined, marrying the editor of the *Eclectic Review*.[220] Morant Bay was Oughton's nemesis.

The season of panic in the wake of the rebellion had its effects on other missionaries. David East, Underhill's special friend, was travelling with his daughter in Trelawny in the days after the news of the violence had broken and found no evidence of trouble. His own congregation at Rio Bueno looked and behaved as usual, and there was no sign of disloyalty. But, infected by the rumours which circulated wildly around the island, he was full of fear and was moved to preach a sermon on 29 November which enforced 'upon very high ground, loyalty to the Government, obedience to the law and the payment of taxes'. This sermon was forwarded to Eyre as a declaration of support, and published with a preface by Phillippo. East referred to the 'awful calamities' which a number of 'rebellious and seditious spirits' had brought upon the land in the eastern parishes, and argued that it was 'a rebellion against lawfully constituted authority'. Happily for everyone, however,

for our families, our homes and our churches – happily for the cause of civilisation, and for the cause of God in the land – through the vigour and promptitude of our Governor and his executive the rebellion has been crushed. Law and order have triumphed, and the infatuated rebels, with their diabolical leaders, are reaping the awful retribution with which such wickedness is sure to be overtaken.

In such times, he instructed, we must betake ourselves to our Bibles, and remind ourselves of what the Bible teaches in relation to sovereigns and their subjects.[221] This was very strong language: 'infatuated rebels', 'diabolical leaders', the triumph of law and order thanks to the vigour and promptitude of the governor. A few weeks later, East, together with Rev. Thomas Lea from Falmouth, signed an address to Eyre from the inhabitants of Trelawny, which the governor took as a mark of wholesale support. East, however, was moved to dissociate himself from this interpretation, and wrote to Sir Henry Storks, chair of the Royal Commission, clarifying his views. He deplored many of the acts of the executive, he wrote, which had taken place outside the area of martial law and the 'indiscriminate slaughter' and 'wholesale executions' which went on in the area of martial law after the rebellion had been crushed. Furthermore, he challenged the 'official representations' that a spirit of sedition and treason had been widespread.[222] Underhill watched this change of view with some wry feeling, and reflected that East had been misled by the 'strong statements' and rumours which had circulated; but he was also concerned that his signature on the address would be used in support of Eyre in Britain. Public opinion in Britain here will think 'that you all lost your heads together', he reflected.[223]

The majority of the Baptist missionaries did not wish to identify themselves with Eyre's actions, but were anxious to separate themselves from any blame for the events in Morant Bay. In the context of the summary execution of Gordon and the large-scale killings and punishments inflicted on those who were defined as rebels, they themselves had suffered little. But Eyre's accusations against them were deeply disturbing, given the Jamaican context, where feelings ran very high. His sharpest criticisms were focused on the five in the Montego Bay area whom he saw as actively encouraging rebellious sentiments. But the JBU was concerned about the ways in which his general criticisms of the nefarious influence of ministers would rebound on them. They were keen to prove their loyalty to the crown and the obedience they had taught to their congregations. Twenty-six of the missionaries, including Phillippo, Dendy, Clark, Reid and both Henderson brothers, alongside a number of their brethren trained at Calabar, prepared a memorial in Spanish Town, where the Royal Commision was meeting from January 1866. This was presented to the Secretary of State, detailing their defence. They were anxious to separate themselves from Native Baptists, with whom both Gordon and Bogle were associated. They argued that their labours were in areas remote from the disturbed parishes, and that in the political trials only one of their ministers, a black man, Rev. Edwin Palmer, and none of their church members were accused. Of the 'more respectable persons' arrested during martial law, three missionaries associated with the BMS, all men of colour, had been detained. They pointed out that amongst the memorialists more than half:

> are natives of Great Britain, and from their infancy have been educated in sentiments of warmest attachment to the British Throne and Government, that the other half, being natives of the Island, have been trained in connection with them, the most of them, having been educated in their theological institution at Calabar: that some of them have families settled in the Island, in occupation of respectable and responsible positions; and that as a Body, they are either the Trustees or holders of mission property to the value of more than £100,000, that they have therefore an interest in the country incompatible with the charges alleged.

In addition, they quoted varied commendations of their conduct from highly respectable sources, including Eyre himself. They deeply regretted that they had been refused permission to give evidence to the Royal Commission. This was because no formal charges had been made against them.[224]

In the event, several of the missionaries were able to appear before the Royal Commission. The Commission appointed by the Liberal government to investigate the causes of the events in Jamaica was chaired by Sir Henry Knight Storks, a high-ranking colonial official who had been governor of Malta. He replaced Eyre until a new permanent appointment was made. His two co-commissioners were both lawyers: Russell Gurney, a QC and Recorder of the City of London, and John Maule, barrister and Recorder of Leeds. The secretary was Charles Roundell, also a barrister. Their proceedings began in Spanish Town in January 1866, and they heard evidence from 730 witnesses between 25 January and 21 March. The report was sent to London at the beginning of April. The commissioners had intended to proceed in a systematic way, keeping each branch of the inquiry separate and distinct, taking evidence under each head consecutively. 'By this method we should have secured that order which tends so much to clearness as well as to thoroughness in the investigation.' But their systematic intentions were undermined. Witnesses were irregular in their appearance and, much more seriously, 'manifested a singular ignorance of the nature and value of evidence'. 'As regards the negroes', they concluded in their report,

It is enough to recall the fact that they were for the most part uneducated peasants, speaking in accents strange to the ear, often in a phraseology of their own, with vague conceptions of number and time, unaccustomed to definiteness or accuracy of speech, and, in many cases, still smarting under a sense of injuries sustained.

Many of them, not understanding the terms of reference of the commission, 'came to tell their tale of houses burnt or property lost, in the undisguised hope of obtaining compensation'. Even witnesses of the 'educated class' could not be restrained 'from giving opinions in general and positive terms as equivalent to facts'. The effect of this was that the commissioners had been obliged to discard a considerable amount of evidence offered to them.[225] Mr Gradgrind would have been proud of these commissioners: words which were spoken in accents other than their own, different conceptions of numbers and time, a deep sense of injustice and a desire to tell the tales of it – none of this was appropriate for English conceptions of empirically verifiable fact. Furthermore, the commissioners' questions were shaped by conventional wisdom as to 'the negro', reinforced by their own encounter with patois which was incomprehensible to them and the weight of evidence which they received on the impossibility of 'knowing' the negro.

The missionaries reported that they had encountered much distress but no evidence of hostility to the authorities. They did, however, confirm a lack of confidence in the law amongst their congregations. Several of them, encouraged by particular lines of questioning, spoke of the difficulties associated with knowing precisely what was going on in the black communities. George Henderson had seen men drilling in Trelawny; some were members of his churches. He asked them what they were doing, and they told him they were 'going to have a little amusement among themselves as Volunteers'. He told them they were acting illegally and should stop. Asked by the commissioners whether he thought the people would tell him the truth if he tried to find out about disaffection, he responded with the stereotypical view of the African propensity to lie: 'I know we have got an untruthful community.'[226] His brother John was similarly gloomy about negro character. The Great Revival, he thought, had had bad effects overall, especially when the meetings had not been under the control of ministers. Immorality and idleness had increased, and marriages were fewer; obeahism certainly existed in his district, but he had never been able to understand quite what it was. 'Then there are things about the negro which you cannot understand or fathom?', he was asked, to which he replied that he thought obeahism was 'pretty much confined to poisoning'. 'But there are secrets which the negro can carry about with him, and which you would not know?', he was further asked, and responded that he did not 'profess to understand all their secrets'.[227]

As early as December 1865 some dissenting ministers, including Walter Dendy, had sent a memorial to Eyre asking for a special commission to investigate the rebellion and regretting the 'cruel and barbarous proceedings' associated with the suppression. They were astonished at the 'astounding allegation' that the black population in general had seditious and murderous designs.[228] The arrival of Storks was the signal for numerous addresses of loyalty from Baptist congregations across the island. The congregation at Coultart Grove, for example, was typical in insisting that the events had been local and that there were no problems about loyalty. They also welcomed the change in the constitution, and were convinced that crown colony status was the best possible outcome. 'Under present circumstances', they maintained, 'this part of Your Majesty's dominions is not in a condition to be governed by representative institutions.'[229] Clark, East, the Henderson brothers, Reid and Fray all followed suit with their congregations, as did the ministers of the JBU collectively. Phillippo relied on the familiar distinction of 'before' and 'after' to explain what had happened, and remained convinced that the majority of the rebels were 'men connected with no religious society, Africans as ignorant and debased as in their native wilds'.[230]

Meanwhile Underhill believed that if he had been on the island, his fate would have been sealed. In England, however, he was safe.[231] Here was the familiar line of demarcation between colony and metropole: it was that space between England and Jamaica which made it possible for Eyre to exercise forms of repression which would have been out of the question 'at home', as Marx, an astute commentator on the imperial scene, noted.[232] But at the very same time that repression provoked a storm of protest in England as to the disjunctions in the rule of law between the two places. British subjects were British subjects – everywhere, argued Eyre's critics, and should have the same rights to the rule of law. The formal equality of British subjects across the empire, however, was belied by the informal practices of colonial rule, whether in India, Ireland, Jamaica or Australia, that distinguished between one kind of subject and another.[233]

By 1866 none of the Baptist missionaries left on the island had the same hopes or dreams as they had in the late 1830s. Of the first generation, those who had gone to Jamaica in the 1820s, Phillippo remained as a solid beacon, the venerated father figure of the mission, maintaining his faith in the capacities of the emancipated to improve. His confidence in his capacities of leadership may have been diminished, and his understanding of the wants and needs of African-Jamaican men and

women greater, but he remained convinced of the importance of the contribution which men such as he could make to the building of a new
Jamaica. Like John Clark, who had remained loyal to his chapel in
Brown's Town, he was at one and the same time a British subject and a
citizen of Jamaica. England was his place of origin and his point of
reference, but Jamaica was his home and that of his children and his
children's children. For men who had come in the white heat of the abolitionist high point and whose young manhood was formed in that
moment, it was perhaps more difficult to adapt. Their ambitions and
aspirations had been excessive; they had not shared the struggles of the
1820s and the early 1830s, or gained the political knowledge that came
with that. Some, such as John Henderson, managed, with great difficulty,
to change: not to be defeated by disillusionment with the men and
women they had hoped would be their followers, but to build new understandings of what part they might be able to play in the creation of a
more just society. Others, like Oughton, despaired and retreated into a
harsher racial vocabulary and a return to the mother country. None of
them was untouched by his experience: for to live in a colony changed
men and their ways of thinking.

Trollope's *West Indies* and Underhill's rebuttal marked the extent to
which abolitionists had lost ground by the end of the 1850s in their once-
confident depictions of the inevitable fruits of emancipation. But metropolitan commentators, whatever their particular predilections, continued
to assume the necessity and legitimacy of colonial rule. By the late 1850s
the missionaries themselves were riven with anxieties as to their congregations and their prospects. John Henderson and Samuel Oughton
provide contrasting examples of men who had once believed in and contributed to the missionary dream, but who came to very different understandings. While Henderson was convinced of the deep injustices of the
society in which he lived and felt compassion for his African-Jamaican
congregation, he abandoned the idea of black political representation
and put his hopes in reformed colonial rule. Oughton, faced with the
hostility of many of his own congregation, grew resentful and hostile
towards black aspirations. What had once been pity, with its paternalistic connotations, became antagonism and a defence of white superiority.
Morant Bay marked a watershed, as had the rebellion of 1831 in a very
different way. White missionaries, faced with black political agency, and
frightened by the white backlash against them, no longer dreamed of a
new society in which they would provide the leadership. That missionary moment was over.

PART II

METROPOLIS, COLONY AND EMPIRE

Mapping the Midland Metropolis

Living in a thriving English town shaped men's identities and imaginations as surely as living in a colony. If Jamaica was known for its plantations, sugar and slavery, Birmingham was known for its manufactories, commodities and 'sooty artisans'.[1] Whereas white travellers to Jamaica were riveted by black bodies, travellers to Birmingham were transfixed by industry. Birmingham commodities could be found across the empire, linking the town to its markets and consumers in the most material way. 'The Australian', as a *Morning Chronicle* correspondent argued in a special series on the town,

> ploughs his fields with a Birmingham ploughshare, shoes his horses with Birmingham shoes, and hangs a Birmingham bell around the necks of his cattle, that they may not stray too far from home on the hills or the rich pasture lands of that country. The savage in Africa exchanges his gold dust, his ivory, and his spices for Birmingham muskets. The boor of the Cape shoots elephants with a gun expressly made for his purpose by the Birmingham manufactures. The army, the navy, and the East India Company's service draw from Birmingham their principal supplies of the weapons of destruction – the sword, the pistol and the musket. The riflemen of the backwoods of Canada and the Hudson's Bay territories would be deprived for a while of the means of trade or sport, if Birmingham should cease its fabrication of gun barrels and locks . . . The negroes of the West Indies . . . cut down the sugar cane with Birmingham matchetts; and grass is mowed and corn is reaped, in England and the Antipodes, by scythes and sickles of its manufacture.[2]

The first ports of call for visitors to the town were its manufactories and its workshops. In the late eighteenth century travellers would go to Soho to wonder at the engines of Boulton and Watt. When the princes of Oude, the Indian principality, visited Birmingham in 1857, only months before the news of the 'Mutiny', they were conducted, as all significant visitors were, around local manufactories, the plate for the official dinner being provided by a Birmingham firm.[3] But the town was widely seen as 'uninviting and monotonous' in its outward appearance. It had no decent river, no mountains, 'nothing but a dull, and endless succession of house after house, and street after street'.[4] The improving middle-class men of Birmingham may well have been galled at these descriptions, busy as they were with the construction of public buildings from the town hall to the market hall and the free library, the endowment of new churches and chapels, the clearing of overcrowded streets, the establishment of philosophical institutions and botanical and horticultural societies, the creation of what they liked to call the 'midland metropolis'.[5] But the fact remained: Birmingham was known for its industries.

Well established as a centre for metal production from the seventeenth century, Birmingham grew rapidly from the mid-eighteenth century. The Staffordshire iron and coal industries underpinned a wide-scale development in metal manufacture. Birmingham's jewellery and plate, pistols and daggers, buttons and buckles, seals, medals and chains – known collectively as the toy trades – employed approximately 20,000 by 1759, and relied particularly on the new colonial markets. Between 1740 and 1780 the town had doubled in size, and by 1800 the population was nearly 70,000. Like several other industrial towns, its peak period of growth was between 1821 and 1831, when the population expanded by over 41 per cent, and by 1851 it had reached nearly 250,000. Birmingham specialized in finishing work and had a relatively high number of skilled workers; the initial stages in iron manufacture were usually done in the towns of the coal and iron fields. It focused on newer industries, designed for luxury markets both at home and abroad – anything that required 'the exercise of taste, skill and science' in the course of its conception and completion.[6] Birmingham trades were built on export markets: a complex network of merchants and agents operated not only in the town but also in Liverpool, London and abroad, to organise the movement of goods to European, American and African markets.[7] Developments in banking and canals and transport made this possible. The town was renowned for its inventive activities: products and raw materials were changed and adapted, tools and scientific instruments improved (though the basic tools remained the hammer, the lathe, the stamp and the press), new divisions of labour were introduced. The restructuring of the labour force, in both large and small firms, involved an expansion in female and child labour, an increasing division and specialisation by sex and age, and a drastic intensification of the pace of work. The dominance of small workshop production, which has been seen as central to the particular character of the town, associated with a tradition of co-operation between masters and men, was lessening by the 1840s, as steam power and capital investment encouraged the emergence of larger firms upon which the small masters became increasingly dependent.[8] Birmingham's economic success has been connected with the lack of institutional regulation in the town, its traditions of religious toleration, of skill and of artisanal co-operation.

The dissenting presence was well established in Birmingham by the seventeenth century, and dissenters held a significant place in town life despite the restrictions they were under. From the late eighteenth century Anglican evangelicals were also very active in the town. In the early 1830s Birmingham emerged on to the national political scene with the Birmingham Political Union, built on an alliance between classes and between Tories and Radicals, and committed to parliamentary reform. It was credited by Brummagems with having secured the Reform Act of 1832 – a story which operated as a powerful myth in the nineteenth century, for Birmingham was proud of its radical and reforming credentials.[9] In 1838 it achieved its municipal charter, though the powers of the mayor and the corporation were not confirmed until 1842. It was only in 1851 that the oligarchic system of street commissioners which had survived was abolished, and the council became *the* governing body of the town.[10]

Birmingham had all the accoutrements of a flourishing industrial town by the 1830s. It was relatively well supplied with churches and chapels, in part because of the strong evangelical presence. It boasted a general hospital and dispensary alongside specialist orthopaedic and eye hospitals, the new town hall, of which residents were inordinately proud, taverns and hotels, schools, including the well-known Free Grammar School, and a fine new market hall. Its print culture was vibrant, with booksellers, publishers, circulating and scientific libraries, local newspapers and magazines. Its main shopping areas were being improved, and trains ran to London. It had a public office, a mechanics institute, banks, a society of arts and school of design, a theatre, an institution for the deaf and dumb, a philosophical institution, penitentiaries, a school of medicine and surgery, innumerable philanthropic societies, a town mission, a fine botanical garden and a fire office. Its triennial music festival was famous throughout the region. It was lit with gas, and its water was piped in. By the 1840s it had a splendid corn exchange, an ambitious drainage scheme had begun, and there was talk not only of a library but also a lunatic asylum. The comfortable new suburb of Edgbaston was burgeoning within walking distance of the town. Birmingham's club culture was extensive, its political culture energetic: dominated by radicals and reformers of every variety, it was, particularly in the 1830s, a place of meetings, petitions and demonstrations, a place of activity.[11]

Yet it was industry which defined the town and gave it its distinctive character. In 1850 a *Morning Chronicle* series from a special correspondent described 'this remarkable town'. The first view, he noted, especially if seen from the railway station, was not prepossessing: 'from that distance it appears to be built upon a plain – and to be composed of mean, dingy, dirty brick houses – and to be enveloped in dense clouds of smoke, which are poured forth from no less than 400 tall chimneys. Neither domes, spires, nor towers are to be seen amid the mass of buildings'. Yet Birmingham remained 'the work-shop of the world', and supplied 'Europe, Asia, Africa, America, Polynesia, and Australia, not alone with trifles, but with an immense variety of necessary articles'. 'There is scarcely a house in Europe or America', he continued,

> that is not indebted for some portion of its luxury or its comfort to the enterprise and the ingenuity of the men of Birmingham. We place our feet in winter upon a Birmingham fender, and stir a Birmingham grate with a Birmingham poker. We ring for our servants with a Birmingham bell, and we write our letters of business and affection with Birmingham steel pens. Birmingham supplies our tables with spoons and forks, though not with knives, and our bed and window curtains with rods, rings and ornaments. We cannot dress or undress, whether we be men or women, without being beholden to the aid afforded us by Birmingham. It is that town which supplies half the globe with buttons for male costume, and with hooks and eyes for the costume of ladies. Pins and needles and thimbles principally come from Birmingham; and we never sit upon a chair or table, or tread upon a floor without deriving advantage from the industry of the metalworkers of that town and neighbourhood.

In death the dependence on the town continued, for coffins across the world were held together by Birmingham nails. In large and in small items, the article concluded, the town was equally industrious and successful: millions of buttons, pins, needles, screws and nails were produced each day, and even each hour, ministering 'to a greater extent than any other town in the world, to the comforts, the conveniences, the necessities and the luxuries of civilised life'.[12]

Here was the key to Birmingham's success: it produced the necessary commodities for a civilised life – the life that Baptist missionaries in Jamaica longed for their flocks to desire. Towns, as Adam Smith had argued, contributed to 'improvement and cultivation' by the market they provided for rural produce, by the spirited economic activities of their merchants, and by the forms of good government which they developed. Towns were progressive by their very nature.[13] Furthermore, Birmingham produced the commodities which encouraged people to move from a state of subsistence to one of civilisation. Civilisation for the political economists was characterised by 'artificial wants' – luxuries, which encouraged the development of an aesthetic, comforts which went beyond bare necessities. The failure to want such material goods was seen as a mark of backwardness, whether in the negroes of the West Indies or the Irish in Manchester.[14] Birmingham goods and things epitomised such 'artificial wants'; they improved those who utilised them, making them into new, civilised subjects. Take electroplated forks, invented by Birmingham's Charles Askin: their wide-scale availability meant a significant refinement in manners. As his biographer, one of the town's best-known literary men, put it:

> In every decent house in this country, and the wide world over, are seen the results of Charles Askin's labour and discoveries, and they are greatly beneficial. They create a higher degree of taste. Refined taste generates improved manners. Improved manners imply a loftier state of moral feelings, and so the tone of society is improved; the world is elevated; and its people are raised, in all that tends to create happiness, and to promote peace and goodwill.[15]

Forks transformed table manners; curtain rods and rings allowed privacy in the home; buttons and hooks and eyes meant clothes were securely fastened; steel pens made possible the easier writing of letters; saucepans meant food could be properly prepared; bells meant servants could be called; locks and keys meant property could be protected – and thereby the midland metropolis could civilise with its goods.

By the mid-1860s townsmen were proud to be able to claim that within a radius of about thirty miles, 'nearly the whole of the hardware wants of the world are practically supplied'.[16] These goods all had their origins in the workshops of Birmingham. Such items were required the world over, and colonies provided a particularly significant market for Birmingham entrepreneurs. Australia and New Zealand, for example, were the most important markets for doorknobs, while India led the sales of iron padlocks. The lock-makers were confident of their future. 'The opening-up of fresh fields of commerce in our colonies', it was argued, 'augur well for this department of local industry . . . the demand for locks and keys must necessarily extend with the growth of civilisation.'[17] Australia and India provided excellent markets for chains, cables and anchors.[18] 'There are few civilised countries which do not import English hollow-ware,' noted William Kenrick, a major manufacturer in that field and well-known Birmingham figure, 'but the best foreign markets are, as a rule, found in the British colonies.'[19] Australia was second only to Britain for the jewellery and gilt toy trades, while iron and brass bed manufacturers depended both on the colonies and dependencies of the British empire. Vast quantities of cut nails found their way to India and Australia, alongside patent wrought-iron hinges which also did well in the West Indies, Canada, New Zealand and the Cape.[20] Settlers in Australia and the Cape swore by Birmingham saddlery, and there was a flourishing market for this in India.[21]

Birmingham manufacturers were clearly proud of their sound and practical goods. They could rely on their kin across the Anglo-Saxon globe to carry their products with them, metallic symbols of the civilisation associated with commerce, private property and domesticity, signifiers of progress in the liberal mind. The empire, its colonies and dependencies were part of the everyday world of Birmingham men and women in the nineteenth century. Birmingham was not an imperial city in any obvious sense.[22] It did not depend on slavery or on raw materials from the colonies.[23] It had no black population of any size, no dockers or sailors, unlike London, Liverpool or Cardiff, no East India Docks Road or Hyderabad Barracks.[24] There were both visitors and residents of colour: Equiano visited in 1789, the Jamaican William Davidson lived there briefly in the early nineteenth century, a missionary sighted three lodging-houses for Asians in the town in 1869.[25] But these were all unusual enough to be matters of note: black missionaries or entertainers were commented on in the local press.[26] The peoples of the empire were rarely seen in the midland metropolis. Even the Irish population, from that very special 'metropolitan colony', was small in comparison with that of a place like Manchester, for it was skilled labour which was in demand in the town.[27] There were no 'hordes' of vagrants, and those 'Irish paupers that are so constant a source of expense and annoyance elsewhere, do not trouble Birmingham to any great extent'.[28] The Rev. McDonald had estimated in 1836 that the Irish population was in the region of 6,000.[29] Most of these were young men working as labourers or in the building trades, though some continued in their traditional occupation of agricultural labourer. The 1851 census indicated a virtual doubling of these figures in the aftermath of the Famine, Kaja Ziesler argues, with the Irish representing 4 per cent of the town's population.[30] 'Sturdy Catholic emigrants' found a place for themselves in Birmingham, the majority living in the overcrowded central districts of the town and maintaining their language, kinship and country connections.[31]

Yet Birmingham was *of* the empire, situated within the empire, defining itself as a town through its relation to nation and empire, imbricated with empire, long before Joseph Chamberlain articulated its political identity as imperial in the late nineteenth century. By the mid-nineteenth century its export market was closely linked to the colonies, its citizens formed a diaspora across those colonies, many of them closely maintaining their connections with their home town, families and friends. New Zealand boasted three Birminghams, Australia five, Canada ten, and even Jamaica had its New Birmingham.[32] The political, cultural and indeed domestic life of the midland metropolis was inflected with issues of race, nation and empire.

Manufacturers and merchants were ever aware of commercial imperatives. When John Bright was proposed as a parliamentary candidate by Birmingham Liberals in 1857, his candidature was unsuccessfully opposed by a Mr Dalziel on the grounds that Bright's well-known views on the desirability of peace were hardly appropriate to a town whose trading interests (in this instance their guns as well as all the other paraphernalia of military metallic supplies) depended on war.[33] But commerce with empire was only one of the multiple ways in which that empire figured in the minds and imagined landscapes of Birmingham people.

Newspaper readers, for example, could enter the imagined community of nation and empire, as well as that of the town, as they read of strange doings elsewhere and reflected on their own different and not so different daily lives. Englishmen and Brummagems did not have the same 'peculiarities of character' as 'the Hindoo', and were not locked in prejudice like 'the Sepoy'. Readers of the national periodicals which circulated amongst predominantly middle-class publics also had frequent opportunities to learn of colonial lands and peoples, as did those readers of fiction whose colonial frame of reference has been so extensively analysed.[34] John MacKenzie was the first to draw attention to the myriad ways in which empire was propagandised from the late nineteenth century through a host of popular forms from the press, postcards and cigarette cards to the exhibitions, theatre productions and music-hall performances which all played a part in the circulation of ideas about empire.[35] The work that has been carried out in this area since, from the detailed analysis of exhibitions to the deconstruction of advertisements and popular fiction, has done much to open up the imagined worlds of writers, editors, theatre managers and the makers of advertisements.[36]

We know little, however, of what people made of this plethora of representations, and, as Chartier argued, it is in the spaces between production and consumption that meanings are produced.[37] An analysis which focuses on a particular public, that of a town, can perhaps begin the task of connecting these discourses and cultural forms to their consumption. The work of historians such as Christine Bolt has told us a great deal about the particular histories of the abolitionists and the ways in which they were framed by, and constitutive of, shifts in racial thinking.[38] Meanwhile cultural critics have greatly enriched our understanding of the cultural practices of particular authors and the complex links made in their texts between race, nation and empire. But the task of connecting these two sites of analysis – the task of the cultural historian – has only just begun. The men and women of Birmingham learned about the colonial order of things through a multiplicity of forms. Here was no consolidated vision of empire, but rather a cacophony of sounds: abolitionists contending with 'scientific racists', would-be colonisers competing with the more cautious voices of those who saw empire as an unnecessary expense, exhibitors rivalling missionaries in the advertising of their wares.

But what were the many and varied sites, each with its specific audience, for the production and circulation of these representations of difference in a nineteenth-century town? And how were the identities of the men and women of Birmingham framed in this process? One site was the press. The newspaper press, argues Kathleen Wilson, was singularly important in the eighteenth century, 'structuring the national political imaginary, helping to shape the social, political and national consciousness of middling and artisanal people living in the localities and binding men and women in particular ways to the wider political processes of the state, nation and empire'. The realities of national identity, she argues, were lived through these representations. The provincial press, meanwhile, 'coaxed and shaped their readers' involvement' in war, trade and imperial expansion.[39] The same could be said of the press in Birmingham a century later. Birmingham had two weekly papers: *Aris's Birmingham Gazette*, established in 1741, and the *Birmingham Journal*. The readership of the latter has been estimated as one in four of the adult population of both sexes in the town in the heady political days of the 1830s. The town's first daily was established in 1855, soon to be followed by the very successful *Birmingham Daily Post*.[40] Local newspapers reported regularly on events in the empire, often with excerpts from national newspapers and editorial comment; they reviewed the new books of explorers and travellers, and commented in myriad ways on the differences between 'them' and 'us'. A reading of the *Birmingham Journal*, originally a Tory paper but transformed into a powerful vehicle for reform in the early 1830s, reveals a regular diet of imperial issues.[41] From November 1845 to June 1846, for example, coverage included debates on the emancipated peoples of the West Indies, with particular reference to the sugar duties and the importation of 'coolie labour'; news of the Sikh war in India and the discovery of Sikhs as brave tribal fighters, a depiction that was contrasted with that of the 'Hindoo'; comment on the beginnings of the famine in Ireland, inflected with racialised representations of the Irish as indolent and living only for the moment; advice about settling in South Australia, news of wars in New Zealand, features on exploration and the strange rituals and rites of native peoples, reports of missionary speeches.[42] Similarly, in the first three months of 1866, there was extensive coverage of the events in Jamaica following Morant Bay, continuing anxieties about India in the aftermath of 1857, much comment on Fenian activity in Ireland and the United States, reflections on the difficulties which settlers faced in New Zealand and on the troubles of the Cape, together with reviews of missionary and anthropological works.[43]

The *Birmingham Journal* saw it as part of its task to educate its readers on matters colonial, and provided special features, sometimes with maps included, for those who were not sure where such places as the principality of Oude or the region of the Punjab were. The editors confidently characterised peoples, placing them in relation to their own assumptions about nation and civilisation. 'All India', they instructed their readership during the Sikh wars of the mid-1840s,

> from the Himalayas to the southern extremity of Ceylon, and from the Gulph of Cutch, on the west, to the Mouths of the Ganges, on the east, may be said to belong to England; for the states that claim independence are so surrounded by English states, that they are comparatively powerless. The population exceeds one hundred millions; the British force is under forty thousand. But these latter are multiplied by that peculiarity of the Hindoo character which makes it easy to train him into an instrument for holding his own country in subjection. He has scarcely the idea of a country to fight for ... the Sepoys ... are found nearly as efficient as troops entirely British; and so long as nothing is done to shock their religion and prejudices, they are equally faithful.[44]

This was the character of the 'Hindoo' and the 'Sepoy': easy to train as 'an instrument for holding his own country in subjection', likely to be as solid as 'troops entirely British' as long as 'their religion and prejudices' were not disturbed.

Canada was another colony about which it was assumed that readers needed instruction. A feature on the Hudson's Bay Company appeared in the *Birmingham Journal* only weeks before Robert Knox's lectures on 'The Races of Men' (later to be published as his celebrated book) were delivered in the town.[45] Knox was fierce on the atrocious dangers of 'miscegenation', but this article carried a quite contrary view. 'The Company's servants are principally Scotch and Canadians', the writer informed his readers,

> but there is also a great number of half-breeds, children of the company's servants and Indian women. These are generally a well-featured race, ingenious, athletic and remarkably good horsemen; the men make excellent

trappers, and women, who frequently marry officers of the Company, make clever, faithful and attentive wives; they are ingenious needlewomen, and good managers.[46]

Journalistic representations of racial difference operated within a field which was continually being reworked. There were always different voices, sometimes juxtaposed. Racial representation has its own history, but it was not a closed system, rather it operated in relation with historical events, playing a part in the constitution of meaning in those events, but also being reconstituted in these moments. While stereotypical elements of these representations – as, for example, that of the negro as indolent – continually reappeared, reworked in particular forms, they never stood uncontested. Representation, in other words, was a process, a process which was central to the construction of identities, the making of self and other. At its heart was ambivalence, rooted in the twin dynamics of identification and disavowal, desire and repudiation, both key to the marking of difference. While journalists, ethnographers, missionaries and others attempted to fix 'the peculiarity of the Hindoo', for example, to know it, to name it and classify it, to write of the character of 'the race' as particular and recognisable, they were marking the continuous attempt to construct binaries, make hierarchies of difference. This was part of the effort to construct consent around particular readings of racial difference and to stabilise the field. At moments, in certain conjunctures, particular representations won wide enough consent to become hegemonic and legitimate political consequences. But these binaries were just as continuously being dissolved, the 'essential' characteristics of different peoples slipping away as times changed; the negro was no longer represented as a victim, the sepoy no longer loyal, and the imagined map of the peoples and races of the empire was reworked.

Birmingham's institutions, products of the rapid development of a new predominantly middle-class and artisan public sphere in the late eighteenth and early nineteenth centuries, were another significant source of knowledge of empire. The missionary and anti-slavery societies, for example, were devoted to the cause of disseminating information and building support. They held innumerable meetings, hosted lectures, and produced pamphlets and magazines in furtherance of their cause. Speakers from afar had an entertainment value in a Victorian town. In February 1846, for example, residents of Birmingham could hear the Rev. Peter Jones, a converted American-Indian chief, give a lecture at Ebenezer Chapel, a lecture that, as so often, was enlivened by an exhibition of idols. He had come to England to raise money for the establishment of industrial schools, aware that unless his people were 'taught to work as well as to read and write, they would remain in a half-civilised state and soon become extinct'.[47] In that same year, Frederick Douglass, travelling the country on a spectacularly successful lecture tour, spoke at the Livery Street chapel, one of the first African-Americans to be celebrated in this way in Victorian Birmingham.[48] A range of other societies and institutions debated matters imperial in a variety of ways: while 'ladies' were usually welcomed to public meetings, there were a large number of men-only venues. In 1848 the Eclectic Society discussed whether colonies were beneficial to the mother country.[49] The Mechanics Institute and the Philosophical Institution hosted lectures on colonies and on questions of race, and taught geography and history through the lens of empire. A favourite public speaker was Charles Dickens, who visited Birmingham several times and gave three Christmas readings in 1853 in support of the campaign to launch the Birmingham and Midland Institute, an ambitious educational venture, initially designed for men. 'Erect in Birmingham', he argued,

> a great educational institution – properly educational – educational of the feeling as well as of the reason – to which all orders of Birmingham men contribute; in which all orders of Birmingham men meet; wherein all orders of Birmingham men are faithfully represented; and you will erect a temple of concord here which will be a model edifice to the whole of England.[50]

Dickens's vision of concord, eloquently spoken of in *A Christmas Carol*, which he read to a packed and appreciative town hall, was a vision of domestic harmony, both at home and in the nation, which depended on keeping the boundaries of race firmly in place. The eyes of England's mothers should be on their children, not on Africa, as he had memorably laid out in *Bleak House*.[51] The establishment of the Midland Institute meant another public space for lectures, and imperial topics were favourites, with India dominating in the years after the 'Mutiny'.[52] The immensely popular minister and lecturer George Dawson ran a series of classes on English history in the late 1860s, especially for ladies, a novel idea. The first lecture was on the English [*sic*] colonies, and used as its text Caroline Bray's *The British Empire*. Participants were invited to bring a map of the British empire, coloured in red, to their first class.[53]

A national ethnological society had been founded in 1843, and by the mid-1850s lectures on ethnology in Birmingham were attracting large, respectable and 'influential' audiences. In October and November 1856, for example, Dr Latham lectured on 'The Races of Men' to a crowded auditorium, and his lectures were reproduced in the local press. Latham was concerned to defend the new discipline of ethnology as a proper science, its founders Linnaeus, Buffon, Blumenbach and Prichard

providing a worthy intellectual lineage. He had published a major ethnological survey in 1850, concerned with the narrow classification of
human species.[54] 'Linnaeus has been the first to point out in a scientific
manner the characteristics of man as a species,' he argued; Buffon had
looked at the moral peculiarities of different races, Blumenbach at the
anatomical. 'Our countryman, the late Dr. Prichard, continued these
observations with those of the philologists, and thus laid the foundation
of ethnology as it exists at the present day.' Latham was a strong supporter of Prichard, a believer in the unity of mankind and the unbridge-
able gap between apes and humans.[55] Following in his mentor's
footsteps, he insisted on the practical importance of the subject,

> especially of the question whether the differences between the races of men,
> such as the negro and European, are specific differences, like those between
> the fox and the dog, or whether they are merely the result of circumstances
> operating through great lengths of time, and producing varieties of one
> species as the shepherd's dog, and the greyhound are varieties of the species
> dog.

Latham alluded, as the report put it, to 'the bearing of this upon the
question of negro slavery, and upon our views of the future destinies of
nations', and declared that he would reserve his own opinions until he
had presented 'the facts upon which such opinions must be founded'.[56]
Latham was well aware of the challenges to a monogenist view of the
world by the mid-1850s: the discovery of new chronologies of human
existence, the increasing scientific investigation of human diversity, the
work on comparative philology – all tested the orthodoxy best expressed,
as Stocking argues, in the visual metaphor of the tree with its common
root and many branches. Knox had explicitly targeted Prichard in the
second edition of his book, and insisted that he was using the word 'race'
in a new sense, 'to designate physical entities unchanged since the beginning of recorded time'.[57] Latham adopted a Dickensian strategy for his
lectures, relying on unresolved climaxes to bring his audience back for
more. En route, he reported Lyell's conviction, for example, that 'American negroes had a better physical conformation than those of Africa,
and that the better instructed and fed negroes of Africa in many cases
approached the European type. If this were the case they would certainly
have something like evidence of inferior organisations being capable of
improvement.'[58] He himself, however, declined to give an opinion on the
subject at that stage. He built up to the declaration in his final lecture of
his commitment to the doctrine of the unity of the species. The changes
which took place over time convinced him that 'the dominant races' –
those who colonised, the European races and the more civilised races of

Asia – would slowly spread themselves over the world and would 'oblit-
erate' Aboriginals in Australia, Hottentots and Bushmen in South Africa,
and the Indians of North America. 'The minor varieties of the human
race', as he put it, 'would be gradually displaced.' 'Upon the whole', he
concluded, 'there was an approach to something like unity in the physical and moral characteristics of our race, a good deal in the way of unity
of language and creed.' Dr Latham then took leave of his subject 'by
impressing on the audience the relation which ethnology had to other
sciences, the necessity of guarding against hasty statements respecting the
principles of the science he had endeavoured to explain, and in individuals being moderate in their views upon it'.[59]

Latham spoke to the serious lecture-going public and called for moderation and reflection on matters of racial difference. Such debate, not
always in such a careful tone, was part of the agenda at the meetings of
the British Association which the town was proud to host in 1838 and
1865 and which ladies could attend as guests, and of the inaugural
meeting of the National Association for the Promotion of Social Science
(NAPSS), which took place in Birmingham in 1857.[60] Meanwhile, the
Birmingham and Edgbaston Debating Society, a group of men who from
the 1850s regularly considered matters social, political, cultural, moral
and imperial, and prepared their members for a larger political platform,
annually promoted one large-scale public debate. In 1869 the matter
under consideration was whether 'variation of species' was 'a matter of
development' or a 'special act of creation'.[61]

Exhibitions provided another form of education and entertainment
about empire. 'The most Extraordinary Exhibition of Aborigines ever
seen in Europe!' was announced in April 1847. Since it was only in Birmingham for a few days, the 'Man of Science' and the 'Student in Zoology'
were enjoined to hurry to the Athenaeum on Temple Street. Entry was
only one shilling, and private interviews could be arranged for 2s 6d.
'The Aborigines consist', the potential audience were informed, 'of two
Men, two Women and a Baby, of the Bush Tribe, from the interior of
South Africa, belonging to a race that, from their wild habits, could never
before be induced to visit a place of civilisation.' The interest excited by
their appearance had been unprecedented in Liverpool and Manchester,
and thousands had been disappointed by failing to obtain admission. The
people of Birmingham should hurry if their curiosity was to be gratified.
The newspaper advertisement for this exhibition was followed by an
extract from the celebrated South African missionary, Moffat's, commentary on the terrible fate of the Bushmen, 'hunted like partridges in
the mountains . . . deprived of what nature had made their own'. 'To the
thinking mind', concluded the editor, 'these people afford ample food
for reflection; they are the very last degree of humanity.'[62] A month later

The Times commented on this same group who were then being exhibited at the Egyptian Hall in London. The tone was significantly more hostile than that of the liberal *Birmingham Journal*:

> In appearance they are little above the monkey tribe, and scarcely better than the mere brutes of the field. They are continually crouching, warming themselves by the fire, chattering or growling, smoking, etc. They are sullen, silent, and savage – mere animals in propensity, and worse than animals in appearance. The exhibition is, however, one that will and ought to attract. The admirers of 'pure nature' can confirm their speculations on unsophisticated man, and woman also, or repudiate them, by a visit to these specimens. They are well calculated to remove prejudices, and make people think aright of the times when 'wild in his woods the noble savage ran'. In short, a more miserable set of human beings – for human they are, nevertheless – was never seen.[63]

The Times correspondent might have attended the lecture on Bushmen given by Robert Knox this same week and concluded that 'these specimens' were certainly destined to extinction. This event, which took place at Exeter Hall, usually the home of abolitionists and evangelicals, was advertised (no doubt with that in mind) as dealing with 'the great question of race, and the probable extinction of the Aboriginal races, the progress of the Anglo-African Empire, and the all important questions of Christian mission and human civilization in that quarter of the globe'.[64] Birmingham viewers of the exhibition had had the chance to listen to Knox's series of lectures three months previously.[65]

Exhibitions, as Altick has argued, provided an alternative medium to print; 'through them, the vicarious became the immediate, the theoretical and general became the concrete and specific'.[66] Their claim to educate as well as to entertain ensured a varied audience until well into the 1860s, by which time developments in engraving and photography had displaced the painted panoramas and dioramas which had enchanted their publics. The Shakespeare Rooms in Birmingham provided a regular diet of visual pleasures. In the late 1840s, for example, they offered both panoramas and dioramas on the late war in India.[67] In 1856 Professor Millar was laying on a diorama of India at the music hall. The advert promised 'a charming and colossal art production, admirably managed, and enhanced by the clever introduction of mechanical effects and coloured lights'. There were

> Ninety-five unequalled views, Displaying the magnificent Cities and Palaces, Manners and Customs, of the Inhabitants of the East, for the distance of 2,000 miles; painted on 30,000 square feet of canvas, by Phillips, Haghe, (Painters to the Queen) and Knell; being the largest diorama in the

world; universally acknowledged to be the best Exhibition ever seen in
Birmingham.

The diorama was complemented by 'a clever illustrated lecture' from a
Mr Watkins, who had been connected with the diplomatic service in
India and who spoke on Eastern life and habits.[68] By 1853 the proprietor of the Shakespeare Rooms, J. W. Reimers, had started competing
with the Athenaeum and was advertising an anatomical and ethnological museum. There were critics of this exhibit, but Reimers insisted that,
'thanks to the universal diffusion of intellectual knowledge', the inhabitants of Birmingham were far too enlightened to be prejudiced. 'We are
now in an age of progression and improvement,' he argued, 'where the
engines of terror, superstition, and bigotry are being shattered by the iron
rod of science.' Museums of anatomy and ethnology played their part in
this story of progress.[69]

Birmingham theatre-goers could encounter these issues in other
ways. Sometimes this meant seeing black actors on stage. 'The African
Roscius', for example – otherwise known as Ira Aldridge – enjoyed a
season in the town, performing Othello amongst other roles. The son of
an African-American minister, Aldridge had come to England, where
opportunities were known to be better for black actors. His marriage to
a white woman in the 1820s increased the attention of hostile pro-slavery
advocates, and he was the victim of a press campaign against him in
1833. Driven out of London, he settled in the provinces, relying on small
theatres for work.[70] Presented in Birmingham as the son of an African
prince who had become a clergyman, he was congratulated on his
'modest and unassuming manner', guaranteed to win him consideration.[71] *Uncle Tom's Cabin*, 'a Drama of powerful interest, thrilling situations, peculiar and novel characters and extraordinary scenic effects',
was playing at the Theatre Royal in May 1853, months after the spectacular success of the best-selling novel, and to coincide with the visit to
the town of Harriet Beecher Stowe. Her visit attracted much comment,
and was significant in its public celebration of a woman author, though,
as was the norm, Mrs Stowe relied on her husband to speak on her behalf
in public.[72] Meanwhile, at the concert hall, 'the Living Tableaux illus-
trative of Uncle Tom's Cabin' was showing, a much cheaper spectacle
than that at the theatre. The same week – and this was Whit week so
there were holiday novelties – there was an 'entirely new Vocal and Pic-
torial Entertainment' at the Odd Fellows' Hall, entitled 'An Emigrant's
Voyage to and Travels in Australia' which included the songs 'Onward
Oh!', 'Hurrah for a Life in the Bush', 'The Australian Settler' and 'The
Gambler's Hut'.[73] Ten years later, at a time when both town and nation
were divided over the question of the American Civil War, *Uncle Tom's*

Cabin was playing again at the Theatre Royal alongside Christy's Minstrels, demonstrating, according to one reviewer, that slave life had its bright side, exhibiting 'that practical and demonstrative humour which seems inseparable from the race, and which one can scarcely imagine to co-exist with a condition of unmitigated misery'.[74]

Birmingham, commented its well-known liberal historian J. A. Langford in his chronicle of *Modern Birmingham and its Institutions* (a volume dedicated to John Bright), had a voice on every political question. Undeviatingly Liberal, it returned only one Conservative MP between 1832 and 1871.[75] But this did not mean that the town always spoke as one. Public meetings, in the town hall, the Odd Fellows' Hall, the great churches such as Carrs Lane, gave boundless opportunities for debate, discussion and argument on the central issues of the day, from abolition to reform, from European nationalism to the Crimea, from Catholicism to the disestablishment of the state church. Sometimes those meetings were designated as 'town meetings', summoned by the mayor, usually because of pressure from particular groups or individuals, occasions for the men of the town to vote on resolutions and determine majority opinion. At other times the meetings were called by interested organisations in efforts to mobilise public opinion in particular ways. Public dinners, breakfasts and teas provided significant forms of public entertainment and debate. The huge meetings of the 1830s were preoccupied with reform and abolition. Chartism and suffrage figured largely in town life in the late 1830s, culminating in the Bull Ring riot of 1839. In the early 1840s suffrage reform and opposition to the Corn Laws were pressing issues. In 1841 a discussion took place over three nights at Ryan's Circle, with 3,000 in attendance each night, on the divisive subject of socialism, while a great Anti-Corn Law tea-party in the town hall was one of the notable events of 1843.[76]

Issues regarding empire inflected this public political life directly and indirectly. Chartism had its own implicit maps of empire, while the Colonisation Society was formed to intervene directly in matters colonial. In 1843 the emigration movement in Warwickshire called a public meeting at the town hall to hear a deputation from the Colonisation Society, protagonists of Edward Gibbon Wakefield's plan for 'a systematic method of emigration to various parts of our colonial empire'. Times were hard in Birmingham, and unemployment high. The intention was to encourage hard-working men to emigrate and thus solve the problem of poverty at home and lack of labour in Australia and New Zealand at one and the same time. The meeting was well attended, despite taking place at midday. One of the local aristocrats, Lord Lyttleton, was in the chair, and on the platform were a collection of clergymen and gentlemen, together with the two MPs for Birmingham, William Scholefield and G. F. Muntz. Francis Scott, one of the members of the deputation, insisted that they had simply come to state the facts and open the eyes of the men of Birmingham to the importance of their subject. He wanted to show them that

> the want of labour in Australia was so great that the employers had been obliged to resort to the South Sea islands, and take savages to do that which was the birthright of the labouring poor of that country. [Hear] He thought that British soil should belong to British subjects – that the soil should be tilled by British hands, and that British industry should be employed in the possessions of the British Crown. [Loud cheers]

Another member of the deputation, Walter Wrottesley, spoke from personal experience as an emigrant. He had lived and travelled in New South Wales, which, 'sixty years ago was inhabited only by the black man, and boasted not of an animal fit for human food'. Now it had become 'one of the most important colonies any country ever possessed'. Birmingham men should turn their attention to this colony. Emigration was a law of nature. America had been transformed, and now Australia was following suit. 'It was boasted', he said, that 'on Britain's dominions the sun never set, and therefore when a man left his home in this country for another on a distant shore, there met him the old English habits and customs, not amongst strangers but amongst friends, men speaking their own language and believing their own faith'.

Australia, in other words, was presented as home from home. Indeed, in some respects it was better than home. As Arthur Hodgson, a resident of South Australia for ten years and another member of the Colonisation Society put it, he regarded Australia, with its space, its 'heavenly climate' and its 'extraordinary resources' as 'a country intended by Providence to receive the surplus population of the mother land'. It was 'the Eden' 'to which they might go to have their hopes, their anticipations, their dreams realised'. William Scholefield, one of the Birmingham MPs, was not prepared to let this pass. He 'could not concur with those that thought there was any surplus population in this country [hear, hear, and loud cheering]'. However, he 'saw in emigration a most important means of benefitting the industrious classes, and in colonisation one of the very best means for extending the markets of this country'. Muntz, the other MP, went farther. He announced himself no friend to emigration or colonisation, believing them both to be expensive and injurious, 'the excrescence of an attempt to make up for a bad system of government [hear, hear]'. Despite this, he applauded the fact that the meeting had taken place and that information about the Society and its efforts had been made available.[77]

At the end of the 1840s, the European revolutions provoked much excitement in Birmingham, and European nationalisms were the galvanising topic of the 1850s, turning attention from universal brotherhood to the white brotherhood of Europe, until the 'Indian Mutiny' of 1857 transfixed both town and nation. Race returned as a central political preoccupation, played out over India, the American Civil War and Morant Bay, only displaced by the reform movement, which focused on the reconstitution of the nation in 1867.

If public life was entwined with empire, so too was private. The foods that people ate, the clothes they wore, the articles in their homes, the plants in their gardens, their psychic lives – all were marked by empire.[78] By the eighteenth century sugar, for example, had become a part of the everyday life of the English, necessary for a proper cup of tea and for the wide array of puddings for which the English were famous.[79] It was in every kitchen cupboard by the 1780s, and the abolition movement was well aware of the importance of transforming it from the simple commodity, West Indian sugar, to an item the production of which was casting a stain upon the nation. It was the women abolitionists who were in the forefront of making the consumption of sugar in the domestic environment into a moral and political question. As Clare Midgley has shown, the campaign to abstain from slave sugar was a way of bringing home to British people their personal involvement in slavery and creating an anti-slavery domestic culture. The Society for the Abolition of the Slave Trade had Cowper's poem 'Pity the Poor Africans' reprinted on fine-quality paper and distributed by the thousands with the recommendation that it made an excellent subject for conversation at the tea-table. Eighteenth-century coffee sets showing the enslaved serving white couples were displaced by anti-slavery tea sets. Sugar basins were produced bearing the motto 'East India sugar not made by slaves'. The cameo image of the kneeling slave appeared on bracelets and hairpins. The representation of the black person as commodity featured in eighteenth-century portraits as a symbol of status, comments Midgley, was replaced by the black person as victim.[80]

If the West Indies was primarily associated with sugar in the mind of the English consumer, India featured first as the land of Kashmir shawls. The Kashmir shawl was introduced from the mid-eighteenth century, and became a desirable fashion item for the wealthy woman, generating home-based production of shawls on Indian motifs and a demand for 'sale and exchange'.[81] Mrs Gaskell was well aware of the status of the Indian shawl as an item of luxury and beauty. Her heroine Margaret Hale in *North and South*, attending her cousin's wedding, helps to show off the shawls which are part of the trousseau, 'snuffing up their spicy Eastern smell' and showing off their 'gorgeous' qualities and 'brilliant colours'.[82] Indian fabrics, the lightweight muslins and silks, became fashionable, the names of the places they came from part of the conversation of middle-class women. At the same time memsahibs were publishing recipes for curry and rice in popular periodicals and modifying 'the food habits of many middle-class Britons'. Indian condiments and pickles, chutneys and spices, became a part of British cuisine, with Mrs Beeton particularly recommending the use of leftover fish and meat in curries.[83]

Family and friends were another major site of connection for Birmingham people with the empire. Take the Parkes family, living in Edgbaston from the mid-1820s. John Parkes, a Unitarian from a Warwickshire yeoman family, was running a large lace and worsted factory in Warwick in the early nineteenth century. Together with his partners he employed 500 hands, utilising a steam engine which came from Soho.[84] In 1825 the business went down in the national economic crisis, and he retired with his wife to Harborne Road, Edgbaston, the new leafy, protected suburb of Birmingham, where there were strong Unitarian connections. There it was possible to live genteelly on limited means.[85] The fourth son of the Parkes was Joseph, born in 1796, who had studied at Glasgow University and then been articled to a solicitor in London. When his father's business collapsed, he gave up his hopes of the Chancery Bar, and became a county attorney working from Birmingham. In 1824 he married Elizabeth Rayner Priestley, the granddaughter of the celebrated radical Unitarian scientist Joseph Priestley, and they lived in the town until 1833. Joseph Parkes was very actively involved in utilitarian and reforming initiatives, and played a major part in securing municipal reform both locally and nationally. In 1833 he moved to London with his wife and two young children, when he was appointed secretary to the Municipal Corporations Commission.[86]

One of Joseph's sisters, Mary, married William Swainson, who was in the army and then became a naturalist. In 1835 Mary died, leaving three boys and a girl, and William lost most of his money in speculations in Mexico. In the late 1830s he decided to emigrate and to marry his children's governess, Miss Grasby.[87] This was a time when there was great interest in New Zealand, and it was there that Swainson decided to go. Wakefield's vision of a partnership between mother country and colony, and 'a new trade – the creation of happy human beings; one country furnishing the raw material – that is, the land, the dust of which man is made; the other furnishing the machinery – that is, men and women, to convert the unpeopled soil into images of God', was one which chimed well with Unitarian and utilitarian preoccupations.[88] The Hill family in Birmingham and London were great enthusiasts for the cause. They attended the New Meeting, as did Joseph Parkes, and were in the forefront of encouraging systematic colonisation. William Swainson's decision to emigrate, therefore, was one that made sense in the context of family and friends.

The New Zealand Company was pressuring strongly for British intervention in the period leading up to the Treaty of Waitangi, sending immigrant ships and working to secure cheap land and protection for the settlers. It was not until the 1860s that Maori substantially lost control of the islands, however.[89] Control over Wellington was disputed in the 1840s between Sir George Grey, the energetic governor who arrived in 1845, and Te Rauparaha. Settlers around Wellington were encroaching on land which they believed they had bought, and there were violent confrontations. When Grey arrived, he was determined to shift the balance of power, bringing in more troops and enforcing British dominion in the areas of settlement.

The Swainsons arrived in New Zealand in 1841, and started farming in the Wellington area. Mary Swainson, (whose mother had died in 1835) born in Warwick in 1826 and age fourteen when she set out for her new life, kept closely in touch with her maternal grandparents in Edgbaston. In addition, she wrote to friends and to her childhood friend and cousin, Bessie Rayner Parkes, the daughter of Joseph Parkes. Such letters were an important source of knowledge about empire, not only to their immediate recipients but also to a circle of family and friends, and church or chapel communities, who would pass the stories of colonial life around their own overlapping networks. Women were specially important in writing them. Furthermore, such letters, particularly if they came from well-known families in the town, were sometimes excerpted in the local press. Thus the *Birmingham Journal* published extracts from the letters of the Clark family, related by marriage to the Hills and known to many in Birmingham.[90] While news of the colonies had great novelty value in Birmingham, news of the town and of events in the lives of family and friends were longed for by the emigrants. John Parkes not only wrote regularly, but also sent copies of the *Birmingham Journal* to his son-in-law, along with the *Illustrated London News* in the later 1840s. Mary confessed that she preferred the latter![91]

Mary started recording her impressions from the time of preparation for the voyage. On board she kept a diary, and once established in New Zealand, she wrote accounts of the new life, providing a picture of the world of the settlers for those at home. Not surprisingly, Maori figured significantly in the descriptions. Writing to her friend Isabel Percy, who had inquired what kind of people the natives were, Mary instructed her that 'for savages they are universally allowed to be the most intelligent', apart from the Tahitians. 'They are much better looking than any of the Australian or African tribes,' she continued confidently:

they are in colour rather darker than the Creoles, with black hair and eyes, and generally good teeth, their stature varies very much, but I should think averaged that of the English, they are mostly tatooed, some of them all over their faces, others only partly. Their expression is certainly intelligent and sometimes cunning. It is astonishing to see how quickly they learn to read and write . . . they are a very dirty people and I am afraid this generation never will become anything like clean.[92]

While the early 1840s were relatively peaceful, by 1845 there was more open military conflict and scare stories amongst the settlers. 'Most horrible it is to be obliged to say', wrote nineteen-year-old Mary to her grandparents, 'that the Natives have returned to all their old habits of cannibalism, that they mutilated the body of Capt. Grant, and scalped Mr. Philpotts besides other atrocities, it is a most dreadful thing.'

'There is a faint hope', she added, that the story about the mutilation might not be true, 'but it is very much to be feared that it is only too true.' 'The Governor', she reported, who was at this time Fitzroy, 'makes every endeavour to hide every thing that is bad on the native side.'[93] Here was a classic settler complaint: that the appointees of the Colonial Office were always more ready to 'excuse the natives' than were the settlers who really understood their ways. By 1846 local troubles with the natives meant that the Swainsons were very pleased to have a military camp established close to their house and were requesting armed men in the house for protection. The conflicts were very close to home in another sense too, for two of Mary's brothers were serving in the militia.[94] Mary was busy telling her grandparents, perhaps partly to calm her own fears, that they 'must not stop sending for fear of the Natives', as the troubles would last for a long time. Besides which, she continued, 'there really is no fear', for the new governor, Grey, was constructing military roads and establishing an armed police force, even making use of trained natives, chosen from those who had proved themselves to be peaceful and well behaved.[95] By March 1847 there was news that more troops were on their way, together with a new deputy for Grey, Mr Eyre, as skirmishes with Maori continued. The following year Mary reported that a series of earthquakes had brought more panic to the settlers than Maoris, fire, land claims and all the other innumerable difficulties they had faced, and that many were leaving, defeated by the exigencies of colonial life.[96] Mary herself chose to marry an army officer, the paymaster of the 65th Regiment, a choice which she knew would worry her grandfather, but she assured him that 'he is very different from red coats in general'.[97]

The conflicts between settlers and Maori shaped Mary's perceptions of racial difference, perceptions which she reported home. By the early

1850s, now a young married woman with children, she told her friend
Isabel of her belief in 'the extinction of races'. Despite all the improvements which natives could enjoy, 'all the care', 'the absence of native war
formerly so constant and cannibalism', yet still the race decreased. It was
'a painful thing', but must be understood as 'in the order of God's providence'. But this clarity as to the obvious differences between 'them' and
'us' could not always be maintained. The question as to whether the races
were so distinct was not easily resolved. A meeting with an old whaler
who had been married to a Maori woman left her with a mixture of feelings. Whalers had a reputation as 'the worst of our race', almost 'a race
apart'. Yet this old man tended his mixed-race children with loving care,
for their mother had died. Few could love those who were not of their
own colour as did this old man, reflected Mary. At the same time he told
his guests fearful tales of the cannibalism of his relatives, especially the
famed Te Rangiheata, who had been one of those responsible for the
Wairau massacre. Te Rangiheata had coolly shot a slave girl, 'kicked her
down the hill and made a feast of her that evening', she wrote to Isabel.
Yet this same slave-owner and cannibal had been broken-hearted at the
death of his wife. What was to be made of all this? Were the feelings of
whalers, and of natives, the same as hers? It remained a puzzle.[98]

Birmingham figured in the lives of the Swainsons through letters and
newspapers, through the boxes filled with buttons and boots, gardening
tools and watering cans, the immensely useful *Farming for Ladies*,
even 'Ladies Gauntlet Gardening Gloves', codliver oil, writing paper,
envelopes and pens, all of which were despatched to them by the family.
Mary asked for merino stockings and gloves to keep her warm in the
winter, a brown silk parasol and some cotton and muslin for the summer,
even a Ladies beaver riding hat as a real luxury, snowdrop and crocus
bulbs to remind her of home, shaded wools for knitting and ivory
needles.[99] Through the commodities they sent, the family at home added
to the picture they had of life in New Zealand. Mary's grandparents were
encouraged to read E. J. Wakefield's book, to study the map of the locality which Mary had made for them, to peruse the Wellington newspapers and Eyre's volumes of travel in South Australia, to plant the ferns
which she had sent for the garden, since, as she said, there was little
else to send. The new colony, she assured them, was a place which could,
with hard work, provide a competence, but not a fortune.[100] Indeed, the
letters make clear that money was very scarce in the Swainson family,
and that emigration brought many disappointments and no easy solutions. Mary's written accounts of the new way of life for her relatives
and friends were augmented by the visit of one of her brothers, Henry,
to Birmingham in 1847. His letters to New Zealand were much looked
forward to, for he could tell the emigrants what had changed, and

'will make us more able to fancy things as they are'.[101] So the settlers rearranged their pictures of Birmingham in their minds. Yet the family was connected across these vast spaces: the death of Mrs Parkes, Mary's grandmother, who had been especially important to her because of the death of her own mother, brought much sorrow, soothed only by the vision of a familial afterlife, in the heavenly home.[102] Though separated by thousands of miles, these families were intimately linked in their imaginations, with letters and objects providing the material connections between the midland metropolis and the colony, and with depictions of life in the two places shuttling between them, representing each to the other.

The midland metropolis was industrial in its character, yet civilising in its nature, producing commodities which improved manners and refined many. It was irredeemably provincial, dominated by middle-class men and, with no resident aristocracy, not part of the educated world in which the classics dominated, far from the court and Parliament, from society, and what was seen as the effeminacy and corruption of London. It liked to imagine itself as a moving power, leading the industrial world in things progressive. Not only was it said, for example, that one of its own shows inspired Prince Albert's vision of the Great Exhibition, but Birmingham had provided the glass and iron for the Crystal Palace and for the crystal fountain placed at the heart of the exhibition.[103] Birmingham was 'a town of the future rather than of the past'.[104] Yet Birmingham's provincialism had its metropolitan dimension: for the town was imbricated with empire. Town dwellers encountered the empire in multiple ways: in their newspapers and their novels, in their museums and their lectures, in their shows and their chapels, in their theatres and their public meetings, in their food and their clothes, in their homes and their gardens, in the worlds of their families and friends. But in those encounters and that cacophony of sounds, some voices had more weight than others. At key moments choices were made, for one view of 'the negro' rather than another, for one notion of empire rather than another. In that process identities were articulated in ways that spoke to and for significant numbers of men and women, naming the residents of Birmingham in ways that resonated with town, nation and empire.

5

The 'Friends of the Negro': Baptists and Abolitionists 1825–1842

The Baptists in Birmingham and the missionary public

Churches, chapels and denominational communities constituted one of the forms of belonging for residents of the midland metropolis. Amongst these, Birmingham Baptists were a modest but significant grouping in the town in the nineteenth century. In 1787 Birmingham had four Baptist churches with 307 members at a time when the town's population was about 35,000; by 1837 there were five churches with 1,428 members, and by 1851 ten churches with more than 4,000 members.[1] In addition to these churches with fixed buildings, ministers and memberships, there were a number of small groupings, meeting in rented accommodation, some of which became settled, others of which split or disappeared, a feature of all the groupings of New Dissent and a sign of the fissiparous nature of that movement. Birmingham Baptists included a wide range of the town's occupations: from button-burnishers to harness-makers, from schoolmasters and mistresses to lawyers, from managers to the skilled and semi-skilled artisans, both male and female. It was the latter who filled the majority of the seats on Sunday mornings.

Dissenters were marginal both socially and politically, their faith bred on deprivation and exclusion, but in rapidly growing towns such as Birmingham they were able to exert influence beyond their numbers. Each 'gathered community' of believers had autonomy: they were free to interpret Scripture in their own ways, guided by the Holy Spirit. Decisions were taken by meetings of church members, and the lives of the congregation were regulated by their pastor and community. 'Chapel', argues Clyde Binfield, acted as 'a model of self-control expressed collectively, offering a life of obedience, discipline, duty and noseyness to individuals. In a world where you had only your feet to stand on, there could be no better recipe for stepping heavenwards.'[3] The close-knit organisation and chapel and family networks of the Birmingham Baptists gave them a distinctive collective identity and presence. The ministers of the two major churches in the town, Cannon Street and Bond Street, were well-known public figures, present at significant public events and having status and power.

In 1802 Thomas Morgan, a young man of twenty-six, arrived in Birmingham to minister to the congregation of Cannon Street, situated right in the centre, next to Corporation Street as it now is, on what was to become prime land for development in Joseph Chamberlain's municipal development scheme of the 1770s.[4] Thomas Morgan was born in Pembrokeshire in 1776, the son of an Anglican farmer. He experienced conversion and was baptised in 1791, in the heady years of evangelical revival and political revolution, and decided to become a minister. He studied at Bristol College, for Baptists were encouraging their ministers to get some formal educational and theological training, to keep up with the times. There Dr Ryland, the celebrated divine, founder member of the BMS and protagonist of anti-slavery, was the principal. In Morgan's student cohort were Marshman, Chamberlain and Grant, all of whom became his friends, and all of whom were to go as missionaries to India. F. A. Cox, who was to write a two-volume official history of the BMS for its jubilee in 1842, became another intimate.[5] These were the earliest days of the BMS, when the small group of ministers who had met in Kettering and formed the society were working hard to propagate its mission, raise money for its activities, and spread its new doctrines. Thomas Morgan became a part of that group. Their history may not have been as spectacular as that of their brothers in India and the West Indies, but, as Bernard Barton wrote in his celebratory poem for the BMS jubilee, their contribution was essential. While the missionaries went forth as 'followers of the Lamb / To spread his gospel-message far and wide', the 'tarriers at home' worked hard too:

> Their aim, their object, and their hopes the same;
> Nor less to be revered their humble fame,
> Though less conspicuously such may have striven,
> Who fanned at home the missionary flame,
> Whose frequent prayers were like the missionary leaven,
> As by their household hearths they built their hopes in heaven.[6]

Evangelical Christians shared a new view of history which argued that offers of Grace were being made to Christians far beyond the traditional boundaries of Calvinist predestination. This meant a new understanding of mission, of forms of organisation, and of theology.[7] The 'gathered community' had to become a means of spreading the Word, not only at home but also abroad; they had to become mission churches. As Andrew Fuller recognised, this meant a different model of the church, since 'the first missionaries to a heathen country could not be chosen by those to whom they were sent'.[8] The task of the leaders of those who remained 'tarriers at home' was to create a missionary public: men and women who would support the missionary venture in myriad ways, ready to be called upon for action across the nation, the empire and the globe.[9]

The missionary public was one of the diverse publics which overlapped to create 'the public sphere' of the nineteenth century. In Habermas's classic model, the bourgeois public sphere was distinguished from the institutions of the state and the marketplace. 'By "the public sphere"', he argues, 'we mean first of all a realm of our social life in which something approaching public opinion can be formed.'[10] It was the sphere which mediated between society and the state, the site for the construction of a reasoned public opinion. It was identified with the demand for representative government and a liberal constitution, and with freedom of speech, of association and of the press. But Habermas, as Geoff Eley points out, was less interested in political change than in the new institutional arrangements and discourses generated by the economic, social and cultural changes which had taken place. The emergence of a public sphere was associated with the growth of urban culture, both metropolitan and provincial, the new lecture halls and assembly rooms, the development of the press and the reading public, better transport and the world of voluntary associations. Habermas sees it as vitally connected with 'rational and unrestricted discourse': 'the faculty of publicness begins with reading, thought, and discussion, with reasonable exchange among equals'.[11] Yet rationality and equality were both highly contested categories in nineteenth-century England.

As Eley has cogently demonstrated, Habermas's original proposition has been extensively utilised, revised and critiqued by both historians and social theorists. Its limitations in terms of its too narrow focus on the bourgeoisie, its neglect of other models for the creation of public spheres (as in the case of conscious nationalist projects), its lack of a conflictual basis in the competing publics and counter-publics which existed alongside each other: these are some of the issues raised. The public world as envisaged by Habermas was a world of men: feminist critics and historians have elaborated the ways in which modern political thought is gendered, as was the public sphere itself.[12] Denise Riley has drawn our attention to the distinctive world of 'the social' which emerged in the nineteenth century and which women, in their expression of gendered agency, helped to define and delineate, and to which they had access.[13] The liberal political world, as Jane Rendall argues, 'was shaped not only by rational ideas but by battles and conflicts over inclusion and exclusion'. A singular version of the public sphere, she suggests, does not encompass 'the complicated variety of ways in which women might identify with communities which stretched far beyond the borders – whatever those were – of home and family'.[14] For men too there were varieties of ways in which they might identify with the overlapping and potentially conflicting public spheres which they occupied: as civic activists, as philanthropists, as concert-goers, as Christian men. Habermas's vision of the public sphere is secular in its definition. Yet religious belonging was central to a large section of the population, and myriad practices focused around churches and chapels, structuring the daily lives of their congregations. These public places were sites for the construction of identities for men and women, for the creation of new subjects, civilised and civilising subjects. They were places of belonging, connection and identification, within which moral codes and obligations were enunciated, duties spelt out, responsibilities articulated. 'Do great things for God, expect great things from God' was Carey's injunction, which had become the call to action of the BMS.[15] He had been preaching from Isaiah 54: 2–3:

> Enlarge the place of thy tent, and let them stretch forth the curtains of thine habitations: spare not, lengthen thy cords and strengthen thy stakes; For thou shalt break forth on the right hand and on the left; and thy seed shall inherit the Gentiles, and make the desolate cities to be inhabited.

It was these words which characterised the spirit of the missionary public.

The missionary public, conceptualised as a site for the construction of the constitution of Christian subjects, both men and women, mainly from middle-class, lower middle-class and artisan backgrounds, requires an expanded notion of public and an awareness of its private and psychic dimensions. It included both men and women, though, as was so frequently the case in the early to mid-nineteenth century, men occupied the public positions. Its origins lay in a commitment to converting the heathen, whether at home or abroad, and this was the key to membership.

Access was centrally defined by faith rather than reason. Yet it relied on the press, a reading public, men and women who would attend meetings and raise money, the classic organisational structures of the voluntary association. Based in churches and chapels, it operated across town and country, had national forms of organisation, key figures who were widely known, and favourite hymns. It took specific denominational forms, which might act in co-operation or competition with each other. It provided a sphere in which public opinion on missionary questions could be articulated, where private individuals assembled to form a public body. But at the same time it operated in the private as well as the public world, defying those real and imagined boundaries, as was so often the case. Support for missionary ventures was an individual as well as a collective act; prayer was central, whether in the bedroom or the missionary meeting; belonging to the mission family across nation and empire could mean opening one's home to visitors from the field, holding small meetings in the 'privacy' of the home, hanging missionary portraits on the walls, collecting missionary books on the shelves, naming one's child after a celebrated missionary figure. Being a friend to the mission was one way of being in the world and mediating one's relation to others.

Birmingham's Baptist missionary public dated from the founding moment of the BMS, and the town played an important role in the development of the BMS. The publication of the originating document of the society, William Carey's *An Enquiry into the Obligations of Christians to Use Means for the Conversion of the Heathens*, had been paid for by Thomas Potts, a Birmingham Baptist and deacon at Cannon Street. Another deacon of the church, Thomas King, became the treasurer of the new society in 1795. Samuel Pearce, 'the Seraphic Pearce' as he was known, minister of Cannon Street from 1790, was present at the founding meeting in Kettering, and the following Sunday preached to his congregation on 'the duty of all Christians to exert themselves for the spread of the Gospel'. Amidst great enthusiasm, a large collection was taken, and an auxiliary society formed. At the same time Bond Street also formed an auxiliary.[16] Eighty years later, at a jubilee for the BMS in Birmingham, a prominent Baptist and radical, J. S. Wright, summed up the contribution which the town had made. 'No place in England', he declared,

> not excepting the metropolis, should take so great an interest as Birmingham in all that concerned the Baptist mission work. They could not claim certainly to be the birthplace of the Society, but it was the neighbouring town of Kettering, and they could say that they found the cradle, the clothes, and provided the first food for the infant.[17]

Here the local identity, that of Birmingham, was articulated in relation to the metropolis, London, to another town, Kettering, and to the nation, England. The defining of local identities in relation to a wider network – in this instance the missionary movement – helped to constitute the midland metropolis as 'a place on the landscape of the nation'.[18]

At the heart of the missionary movement was the belief that all souls had the potential for conversion. As Pearce expressed his universalistic beliefs in 1794, 'A Christian's heart ought to be as comprehensive as the universe. The Asiatic, the American, the African – all are our brethren.' Pearce desperately wanted to go to India himself, but the committee judged his work in England to be more important. Devastated, he determined that if he could not go abroad, he would do all that he could to serve the mission at home, and Carey comforted him with an insistence on the essential interconnectedness of their ventures:

> we are one, nor can rolling seas interrupt that unity of heart, which I trust we feel. We are both labouring in the same Cause, and both serving under the same Captain, only with this difference; you are employed in the centre of the army, and I am set to force an outpost of the enemy. Let us both be faithful unto death, and account it glorious even to die in such a cause.[19]

In 1798 Pearce died, a young man of thirty-three, and four years later Thomas Morgan arrived at Cannon Street, a missionary enthusiast coming to a missionary chapel. Pearce had built up the church considerably, greatly increasing its wealth and influence with new members. He had started a Sunday school, and when Morgan arrived, the chapel was being enlarged to hold 900. Pearce had married the daughter of a Baptist deacon; their son William Hopkins Pearce went out to India as a missionary; and their daughter married the youngest son of William Carey. They were indeed a part of the wider mission family of the BMS, stretching across nation and empire.[20] Within a year of arriving at Cannon Street, Thomas Morgan had also married the daughter of a deacon, Ann Harwood. Born in Birmingham, she vividly remembered the Priestley riots of 1791 when Church and King mobs attacked the houses of local radicals and Unitarians, particularly the celebrated friend of the French Revolution, Joseph Priestley. The Harwood family had at that time lived in a house belonging to a Unitarian, a house which was burnt in the riots.[21] Morgan thus linked himself in marriage to the heartland of Birmingham dissent.

In 1811 Morgan was forced to resign because of ill health, and, as their son later recorded, 'then was the character of the wife and mother tested'.[22] Family union was at the heart of nonconformist culture, and throughout their lives husband and wife gave themselves to the family and mission enterprise, seeing themselves as a partnership in the pursuit of a greater good. Faced with a husband who was unable to work for nearly ten years, Ann Morgan was compelled to support the family. She did so by establishing a boarding-school for young ladies with money borrowed from her marriage settlement. By dint of hard work and careful management, the school and land prospered, and the Morgans were able to afford to place their sons professionally, a goal which would have been out of their reach with the ministerial stipend of £100 per annum.[23] By 1815 Morgan was well enough to take on some pastoral duties again, and he became the afternoon lecturer at Bond Street chapel. In 1822 he became the minister there, a post in which he stayed until his retirement in 1846. His wife gave up the school and devoted herself to the full-time, but unpaid, role of minister's wife. 'Mr. Morgan', as his son put it,

> always inculcated family union. He thought of the earthly family as a type of the great Christian family in Heaven and on earth – all one in Christ Jesus. He desired Christian unity, not so much in cessation of denominationalism as in mutual cooperation and loving-kindness manifested by all Christians one for another, and which should be displayed in all their numerous churches and organisations, each body regardful for all other Christian peoples. What was good for churches, was also good for Christian families.[24]

Bond Street was a flourishing chapel and centre of dissenting life in the town. It had been established in 1785, its first minister Edward Edmonds, whose son George Edmonds was one of the best-known Birmingham radicals of the 1830s and 1840s. Morgan was an exceedingly successful minister and pastor. By the mid-1830s there were more than 1,000 pupils in the Sunday schools, with 170 teachers, while thirty to forty tract distributors worked from the chapel, visiting 600 houses every Sunday. Bond Street was built on the central tenets of the Baptist faith. The scriptures provided the Word of God, one God revealed as Father, Son and Holy Ghost. Adam had sinned, but there was a possibility of salvation through God's love. While Particular Baptists stressed the elect who were predestined, General Baptists had a more inclusive view of the potential for all to enjoy eternal life. It was the will of God, it was believed, 'that the Gospel of Salvation should be published to all men indiscriminately'. The sinner was justified by faith, not works, and the experience of conversion had to take place in each individual soul. Repentance must be followed by baptism – that adult baptism which marked off the sect from other New Dissenters. Christians should join together in churches where they would sing, pray, take communion, and be guided by their minister. Those churches had the right to manage their own affairs on the basis of agreed rules. Members should be disciplined if necessary and carefully watch over each other: daily behaviour, respectable dress and demeanour, proper relations between the sexes, probity in business – all of these were matters which could be spoken about and reflected upon. Parents should train their children in the nurture and admonition of the Lord.[25] It was a severe religion with its focus on faith and regulation. Good works could adorn a Christian character, but never effect salvation.

Mr Morgan was convinced that congregations should be guided by Christian patriarchs such as himself: a view which he shared with his dear friends the Rev. John Angell James, celebrated minister of Carrs Lane Congregational Church, and Joseph Sturge, Quaker corn merchant and philanthropist. The particular identity of Baptists was of deep significance, but Baptists were linked to the wider Christian family of dissenters by their shared nonconformity and the common forms of discrimination which went with that, their shared commitment to the belief in the power of religion to civilise, both at home and abroad. On many key issues these three men were agreed: their critique of the established church, the centrality of the Christian family, the vital importance of voluntary societies, temperance, anti-slavery, their revulsion at the idea of sacred music being played in the town hall. On others, such as adult baptism and the place of the Catholic establishment in England, they disagreed. Sturge was always more active than the other two on political questions, since he was a layman, and indeed his radicalism went far beyond that of James. But the friendship and mutual respect of Baptist minister Morgan born in the 1770s, Independent minister James in the 1780s, and Quaker businessman and philanthropist Sturge in the 1790s, was integral to the success of missionary and anti-slavery initiatives in Birmingham.[26]

In a widely read sermon to the London Missionary Society in 1819, John Angell James focused on the power of religion to civilise. 'Religion', he argued, 'is strictly and essentially a civilising process.' Faith raised the mind above 'sensual gratifications'; hope controlled 'pressing impulse' with 'the prospect of future benefits'; 'love establishes a law of kindness in the breast, by which the irascible passions are subdued'. 'Thus the elements of barbarism' were expelled, and industry and self-improvement followed.[27] It was religion which made England a civilised and 'a happy country', potentially the 'glory of Christendom', and it was their religious sensibilities which united these three men in their moralising ventures.[28] At the memorial after Sturge's death in 1859, James hailed him as 'a Christian, a patriot and a philanthropist', all epithets which could equally have been applied to his two friends.[29] Together the three give some access to the character of the culture of dissent, the missionary and abolitionist publics in nineteenth-century Birmingham, and their relation to the politics of race, nation and empire.

Faith was the key to their actions, but good works certainly adorned the character of the Rev. Thomas Morgan, the 'judicious Morgan' as John Angell James was to salute him in his funeral oration.[30] Morgan was active in a range of voluntary societies, most of which linked religion with radical politics, albeit indirectly, for nonconformists were wary about the political world: the missionary societies, for example, eschewed direct political involvement except in times of dire crisis. Home and foreign missions, the Peace Society, temperance and anti-slavery were his most significant spheres of action. In 1823 Morgan was a prime mover in the establishment of a Birmingham auxiliary of the BMS, an auxiliary on a town rather than a single chapel basis, which linked the Baptist churches in the area. Such unions, as has been seen in Jamaica, contributed to the development of denominational strength. The auxiliary was to aid the BMS 'in sending the gospel to the heathen'. It had the classic voluntary society structure, with subscribers, a committee, an annual general meeting, a treasurer and secretaries, a structure which, as R. J. Morris has noted, was central to the emergence of a new public sphere for middle-class men.[31] Elected officers were seen as crucial, for self-perpetuating bodies decayed, whereas voluntary bodies were vigorous and healthy.[32] Thomas Morgan was one of the secretaries, Isaiah Birt, then pastor at Cannon Street, the other.[33] The local AGM provided the opportunity for a public occasion, with a speaker, a special sermon and a collection, just as the evangelical societies all held their great May meetings in London, often at Exeter Hall. Not all Baptist congregations, by any means, supported BMS work, but Birmingham was always a centre of activity, raising money, encouraging men, and later women, to take up missionary work, holding meetings, contributing to policy. The ambitions of the Birmingham missionary public may have been small-scale in comparison with those of the men of Exeter Hall, but their efforts were designed to make the 'midland metropolis' a centre of Christian activity and the mission enterprise. In so doing, the missionary public, as Susan Thorne argues, broadened their geographical horizons from the local, to the national and the global.[34]

In October 1819 a London office of the BMS had been opened, and the new full-time, salaried secretary, the Rev. John Dyer, helped to steer the transition from a loosely structured fellowship to a formal philanthropic organisation.[35] A written constitution was adopted, with a general committee meeting annually, responsible for circulating missionary intelligence and promoting the interests of the BMS, and a central committee with monthly meetings. Annual meetings were held in London, extending over three days, with time for committee meetings, sermons, prayer meetings and an AGM. Birt and Morgan both served on the general committee of the BMS, attending the meetings which formulated policy and receiving the secretary's reports on activities in both 'the East' and 'the West' as India and Jamaica, the two main sites of the mission, were called.[36] Through these institutional structures, a national missionary public took shape, linking men of like mind across town and country, providing networks of support and people to call upon, and a sense of connection and belonging.

The organisational structures of the BMS were entirely peopled by men. Ladies did not serve on the committees, but were welcomed as members: their activities in support of missions were often a starting point for myriad other ventures. As in all these voluntary societies, their work as fund-raisers was crucial.[37] The young ladies of Birmingham, for example, sent £17 14s 6d, which they had raised for a school for girls in Calcutta, to the BMS in 1825.[38] The following year Morgan's oldest daughter was recorded as collecting the substantial sum of £424 5s 11d for female schools, the only appearance of the Morgan women in records which were permeated with the presence of their husbands, fathers and brothers.[39] A few months later the editor of the *Missionary Herald*, the domestic publication of the BMS, particularly recommended that ladies wanting to aid the Calcutta female schools might send in fancy articles for sale such as work boxes, work bags, card racks, fan mounts, netting cases, purses, portfolios, charade cases and pincushions. Fire-screens, it was noted, would not be useful articles, a comment which suggests how missionary publications circulated rudimentary geographical knowledge: India was a hot country![40]

The *Missionary Herald* began publication in 1819. Initially a four-page paper, it gradually became more substantial, particularly at times of crisis for the BMS, such as the Jamaican rebellion of 1831 and the events at Morant Bay in 1865. It appeared monthly, and carried news of the missionaries, often with carefully edited extracts from their letters alongside information about the efforts at home. The missionaries and their families became intimates of the mission public both through these regular reports and through their periodic visits and speaking tours when they returned home. Many particular connections between places and people – the Birmingham ladies and the Calcutta female schools, for example – were encouraged and sustained through these columns. News of public meetings, of special services, of AGMs, of money raised for 'the growing extension of the Redeemer's kingdom', of money sent, of special gifts, of new missionaries being sent out, of visiting missionaries speaking, of deputations, of new committee members, of the activities of the auxiliaries – these were the staple of news from home. Birmingham figured through its collections, its meetings, its sending out of books to

Jamaica especially for native preachers, a gift of steel pens from Gillott, steel pen manufacturer *extraordinaire*, to mission schools, speeches and poetic offerings from its well-known ministers, news of the selection of new pastors in the town, comment on the size of congregations.[41] Special occasions such as the designation, as it was called, of new missionaries, justified column inches. When John Griffith was designated for Jamaica at Cannon Street in 1831, the large chapel was 'excessively crowded' for the service, with the Rev. James Hoby, who had just arrived as the minister of the new church at Mount Zion, reading the scriptures, John Angell James introducing Griffith, Thomas Morgan asking the questions of the initiate, Thomas Swan, recently returned from India, addressing him on the seriousness of the task ahead.[42] Thus the Birmingham Baptists celebrated their union with each other and with the missionary enterprise. In the reporting, the mission public came to know itself as a national community, marked by locality but with the names of the same prominent men appearing time and again, speaking, attending deputations, making policy, the patriarchs of the mission family across the empire. They were the men who could lead the society's contribution to the national work of empire building, for, as the *Baptist Magazine* put it in 1826, quoting the *Monthly Review*, 'England is now the actual governor of the earth ... knowledge goes forth with it, ... tyranny sinks before it, ... in its magnificent progress it abates the calamities of nature, ... it plants the desert, ... it civilises the savage, ... it strikes off the fetters of the slave.'[43] The particular work of the society was to save heathens abroad, to civilise the savage through the influence of Christianity, and, as became clear, to 'strike the fetters off the slave'. Here the language of evangelicalism, of heathenism and salvation, was mapped on to the language of civilisation, of stages of development, of the taming of savagery and barbarism.[44]

The missionary public was both inclusive and exclusive: all were invited in, and all were sinners who could be saved, but the family of man was not undifferentiated. Once inside the mission family, the sense of belonging and community was powerful, but the price was high.[45] The culture was narrow and reproving, its rules of conduct demanding, the anxiety of evangelical Christians always present. Those who 'walked good' might rejoice in their membership of their congregation, the wider family of Baptists or the mission public. But backsliding always threatened at home, as it did abroad, and the line between sinner and saved, heathen and Christian, savage and civilised, was no more secure in Birmingham than it was in Jamaica. The men and women of Birmingham had one great advantage, however: they were white, not black, with all that meant in the missionary and wider imagination, and in a world in which slippages between barbarism in religion and in culture were so endemic, their chances of salvation seemed better.

Knowing 'the heathen'

But what did Thomas Morgan and the Birmingham mission public know of the 'heathen', and how did the mission and the missionaries represent them? Missionary sermons and publications provided one of the ways in which the empire, and indeed the globe, were mapped for their publics, and the particular peoples of different countries represented. Print culture was vital here, with its newspapers, periodicals, pamphlets and books, as were the sermons printed for special occasions, the mission-ary visits, the special prayer meetings and the hymns. Heber, bishop of Calcutta, penned one of the favourite missionary renditions, endlessly carolled by multiple generations from Birmingham to Bombay, from Kingston to Cairo. 'From Greenland's icy mountains to India's coral strand', sang the congregations,

> Where Afric's sunny fountains,
> Roll down their golden sand,
> From many an ancient river,
> From many a palmy plain,
> They call us to deliver
> Their land from error's chain.

Having helped to raise money to send missionaries overseas, the assem-bled faithful would sing of their souls 'lighted with wisdom from on high', of their duty to offer 'the lamp of life' to those more benighted than themselves, of 'heathens' in their blindness bowing down to 'wood and stone'.[46]

Birmingham's John Angell James was to become a national authority on matters spiritual.[47] In a memorable sermon of 1819 he articulated a map of the heathen world. American-Indians in his imagination were 'devoted to witchcraft, drunkenness and idolatry'; China's empire was 'groaning . . . beneath the crimes of two hundred millions of idolaters'. 'The plains of Hindostan', he averred,

> watered by the obscene and deified Ganges, would arrest your attention and produce an indescribable horror, as they disclosed the frantic orgies of Juggernaut, the flaming pile of the devoted widow, with innumerable other spectacles of idolatrous cruelty. . . . Africa would then pass by shrouded in the gloom of barbarism.[48]

These horrors would be mitigated only by the glimpses of missionaries, devotedly leading souls to Christ. But Britain, James believed, was entrusted with the task of evangelising nations. 'For this purpose', he argued, 'God has given her an empire which extends into the four quarters of the globe, and on which the sun never sets.'[49] 'The heathen nations of the present day', he instructed a congregation of young listeners,

> are a mighty wilderness of mind, a great desert in the moral world . . . an immense extent, as it were, of sand or swamp . . . Melancholy spectacle! But yours is the task, the glorious, the immortal work of enclosing, and draining, and cultivating this mental waste, of sowing it with the seeds of thought, and causing it to bring forth and blossom, and of adding it to the territory of mind, from which it now seems almost entirely cut off. Your object is compassionate. In supporting this cause, you lend your aid, to break the fetter of the captive; to raise women from their degradation, and restore them to their just rank in society; to convert the bloody tyrant into the nursing father; to give sanctity to the marriage bond . . . to terminate the reign of evil for the universal empire of mercy.[50]

This horticultural imagery, enclosing, draining and cultivating, sowing and bringing forth, stemmed from a definition of civilisation that was linked with cultivation: something that could be tended and made.[51] Here the Enlightenment scheme of the stages of development was again mapped on to Christian notions of salvation. James's emphasis on raising women from degradation, converting tyrants into fathers, giving sanctity to the marriage bond, all point to the centrality of a notion of family to this missionary project.

The first field of activity for the BMS was India, the first necessity for the missionary public to learn of the ventures there. Since the work of evangelism was dependent on financial support, the dissemination of information and the soliciting of gifts was vital. The names of Carey, Ward and Marshman were soon well known, and the Serampore Mission became the focus of Baptist efforts. Serampore concentrated on translation and education. The production of grammars and dictionaries, translations of the Bible, tracts, periodicals and vernacular newspapers – all were part of the project to evangelise.[52] Birmingham's W. H. Pearce, son of Samuel, was apprenticed to the Clarendon Press in Oxford, and set up in business in Birmingham as a printer as his long prelude to joining the missionary venture in Calcutta.[53] Serampore College was founded in 1818, to begin the task of training a native ministry: a decision which was taken much earlier in 'the East' than in 'the West' on account of British assumptions about the ancient civilisations of India and the capacity of its peoples for improvement. The success rate of European missionaries in terms of numbers of converts was very low, and the languages presented many difficulties. Pearce estimated that by 1831 there had been only forty baptisms.[54] 'Native agents', in this context, were seen as crucial.

Yet, as the Rev. John Birt put it at the AGM in 1825, 'Every instance of conversion from the heathen world is peculiarly important. The value of a soul in England is the same as in India; but the conversion of a heathen possesses far more relative importance than the conversion of an individual among us who had before been only a nominal Christian.' Souls were souls, but there were hierarchies of heathens. Here Indians were heathens, whereas English nominal Christians remained individuals. The 'absurdities and superstitions of heathenism' in India were a far cry from Birmingham. The transformations that could be hoped for in India were of a different order. Boys educated in mission schools there 'will never take their aged parents to the banks of the Ganges, there to perish in comfortless misery; they will never carry fire-brands to kindle a fire to consume a living mother, with the dead body of a father. Girls educated there, will never abandon their infants, or cast them into the Ganges.'[55] Yet the success of the missionaries could never be judged only in terms of conversions, for by their very presence and their example it was believed that they represented a promise for the future.

Such general maps of the world of heathens were made more specific in the detailed accounts of the missionaries and their allies. William Yates, soon after starting to preach amongst the natives in India, reported to the BMS that 'they are so devoted to superstition, so fettered by prejudice, and so enveloped in ignorance, that nothing but an Almighty Power can rescue them'. 'It is impossible to describe to you', he wrote to his parents, 'how low they are sunk in moral degradation.'[56] 'Suttee', in the parlance of the missionaries, became one of the symbols of this degradation, and the missionaries devoted themselves to making it a public issue in Britain, pressuring the government to take action. 'In no country', wrote the Rev. James Hoby, biographer of Yates, friend and correspondent of Knibb, and minister in Birmingham from 1831, 'has the tendency of idolatry and heathenism to dishonour the gentlest and loveliest portion of our race, been more obvious than in Hindostan. Here it is the very religion and morals of the men to offer insult and do injury to the women.'[57] It was the task of the missionaries and their supporters to raise these poor benighted women.

There was intense debate, as Lata Mani has shown, in Britain and in India in the 1820s over sati. The women who were burned, she argues, were neither the subject nor the object of the debate, but rather the ground for struggles over the nature of Indian society.[58] Once missionary activity in India had been legalised in 1813, she suggests, questions about sati became predominant in the Baptist missionaries' public representations of India. Their early attempts to describe another culture became increasingly interpretive and evaluative. Moral improvement, Christian duty and political obligation were all linked in the demand to act on sati, a demand which Wilberforce took up in the House of Commons. Sati evoked both horror and pity, sentiments which effectively raised money. Perhaps it also evoked excitement, associated with the exoticism of difference. The public campaign involved meetings, petitions, publications – all the tools of the voluntary societies and their allies.

William Yates gave the sermon at the annual meeting in London in 1826, and his words were reproduced in the missionary press. He preached on the special effects of 'Hindoo' idolatry on character, reminding his listeners how grateful they should be for the benefits of the Gospel, how tenderly they should 'pity the heathen'. 'Hindoos', he argued, 'believe tales the most monstrous and absurd.' The worst of the cruelties which followed from this was 'suttee', and he vividly evoked the scene for his audience:

> The son has his mother taken from her home, and after performing certain ablutions by the river's side, she is taken to the funeral pile, round which she is made to pass seven times. She is then conducted, in the coarsest manner, to her seat on the pile. Her cruel son makes himself ready; and when the poor widow has taken the head of the deceased on her lap, and has given the token that she is ready, he takes the torch, and kindles the fire which is at once to burn the father that begat him, and the mother that bore him. Her horrid shrieks are drowned by the shouts of the people and the noise of drums; and the multitude return home as delighted as if they had been at a feast. Behold all this in imagination, as many have done in reality, and then say if the heathen be not 'given over to a reprobate mind, to do those things which are not convenient'.[59]

Here was all the horror of a murderous son and a community which delighted in the mother's destruction. Here was the eyewitness account, the 'true picture', which the listeners and readers were invited to conjure up in their imaginations. Here were examples of the humanitarian narratives which, Laqueur argues, created pity, sympathy and the route to action.[60] The story of the widow burnt alive should remind listeners at home of the dangers of failing to keep God in their minds. 'Let us learn to be grateful for our superior station and privileges,' concluded Yates, reminding the English of their advanced 'civilisation', their respectful treatment of their womenfolk: 'Contrast your state with that of the Hindoos.'[61] Here difference was constituted in religious terms: sati was only an extreme form of the practices of 'reprobate minds'. The heathen within constantly threatened at the door, making the imagined lines between self and other psychically and culturally vital. Indians, the missionaries believed, were lying, lascivious, superstitious and idolatrous, but it was appropriate to pity them rather than be contemptuous. Their discourse intersected enough with that of colonial officials to ensure that sati was outlawed and made punishable by the criminal courts in 1829, a victory that demonstrated to evangelicals the effects they could have on public policy.

The debate about sati was part of a wider preoccupation with the position of women in indigenous Indian society. W. H. Pearce was one of the first to bring up the question of female education as central to the raising of women from the 'degradation' of indigenous culture. 'If', he argued, 'we wish to raise the females of this country to their proper level, to render their domestic life happy,' emancipate them from superstition and save their lives and souls, then we must educate them. He established a day-school, and a Mrs Wilson, 'the great instructor of native females', was sent out to him. To his mind, however, this venture was not very successful, since 'what little was learned in the school, was counteracted by the influence of evil example at home'. He therefore decided on a boarding-school which could give the children constant instruction and enable them to grow up as 'consistent characters'. The use of the boarding-school as a training ground for 'natives' was to be part of colonial policy across the empire. His sister Anne came to Calcutta to work there, a classic extension of the mission family.[62] Pearce became an authority on female education in India in England. On a visit home in 1837, he and his wife stayed with the Hobys in Birmingham for some time. Pearce lectured around the country, devoting himself to the task of raising money for new missionaries to go to India. Only ten Baptist missionaries associated with the BMS had gone to India since 1817 (there had been a serious division between the Serampore group and the BMS which had led to a split for several years), and he was convinced that India was being starved while the West Indies got the resources. When asked by young ladies to write a few words in their albums, to commemorate his visit, he liked to write something memorable. 'What will become of women and other animals in the future world?' ran one such offering. This was the inquiry of a respectable and learned Hindu. 'It correctly expresses', continued Pearce,

> the low estimate which he and his countrymen form of the female character; and which is formed and manifested in all countries where Christianity does not teach man to regard woman as his companion and friend: in circumstances so superior, and from tender concern for the welfare of your sex in circumstances so wretched, O do all you can for the present and everlasting benefit of the fifty millions of Hindoo females placed by Providence under the authority of Britain in the East.[63]

Thus were British women exhorted to recognise their superior station and do what they could for others.[64]

Since European men had no access to those women who were in purdah, and little to Hindu women, it became imperative that they had European women to work with them. The BMS was strongly opposed to unmarried men going to India, and avoided it whenever possible. Married men, they believed, would be armed against the temptations of Indian women, and the missionary wives could be drawn upon to work with their own sex. William Yates went out unmarried, to the consternation of the BMS, but soon attached himself to the daughter of a deceased missionary.[65] 'This estimable young lady', as his biographer James Hoby wrote,

> was in every respect suited to become his partner for life . . . she had, from earliest infancy, breathed a missionary atmosphere, and had been trained amidst missionary operations. With her, all which pertained to missionary life was necessarily a sober reality; she was unusually free of the romance and poetry of the undertaking, and therefore peculiarly a help-meet for such a man.[66]

Catherine Yates, as she became, was chosen as the ideal superintendent for the seminary for young ladies set up in Calcutta, an establishment which the ladies of Birmingham worked hard to support. She corresponded regularly with the wife of her husband's friend, Mrs Hoby, reporting on the progress of the girls in the schools, thanking the ladies of England for their 'deep interest in the education of the females in this benighted country', suggesting that there was cause for optimism and that the prejudice against female education was beginning to wear away.[67]

George Pearce, one of the third generation of that family to be associated with the mission, left England to work as a missionary in India in 1827. He wrote to the BMS six months after his arrival describing his reactions, a letter which was reproduced in the *Missionary Herald* and which repeated established notions of Indian depravity and wickedness. 'Of all countries', he wrote:

> none I imagine can present greater obstacles than India to the spread of divine truth. This is, indeed, the stronghold of the prince of darkness . . . I had heard and read much of the depraved character of the inhabitants of Hindosthan, but truly I may say the half had not been told me: nor can I conceive it possible for any person to form anything like an adequate idea of Indian wickedness without actual intercourse with the people. Here iniquity in all its horrid forms is practised, not by a few, but by all classes, from the highest to the lowest. Falsehood, dishonesty,

lasciviousness, superstition, and idolatry seem to be inseparable from their nature.[68]

'The stronghold of the prince of darkness', the 'depraved character' of *all* the inhabitants, the 'horrid wickedness' of Indians – these were powerful images, images which were made more specific in the accounts of particular 'depravities', as in the campaign over sati, but which were part of the repertoire of representations of India available to the British missionary public.[69]

India was exciting and exotic in the imagination of the English missionary public, but it was extremely difficult to convert 'the heathens' of those territories, and the success rate of the missionaries in India was miniscule. Jamaica offered both a similar and a different scenario. Slavery and plantation society posed a distinct set of power relations and social relations between coloniser and colonised, different from those of the ancient civilisations of India. And the 'heathens' of Jamaica heard the missionary message with enthusiasm. The pity which was called for regarding all 'heathens' was inflected in a particular way in the Caribbean, since the enslaved were subject to appalling treatment from British planters. The missionaries in Jamaica were most horrified not by what they took to be the superstitions of the negroes, though they were concerned about those, but by the practices of slavery, a British institution, and the character of the planters, British men. Slavery had acted upon the ignorance and superstition of Africans, making their character infinitely worse. Only Christianity could save them, and the saving grace was that Africans were hungry for salvation. As Lee Compère, the second Baptist missionary to go to the island from England, wrote to the BMS in 1817: 'Here are many souls continually heaving a sigh to England, and in their broken language continually crying out . . . "O Buckra come over that great big water, and instruct we poor black negro".'[70]

It was the 'simple and affecting faith' of the poor converts which received attention, rather than their 'horrid practices' of obeah, their deep attachment to the missionaries, and their enthusiasm, earnest attention and gratitude for the Gospel message which was brought to them.[71] While Indian missionaries found the India they encountered worse than that of their imaginations, the Jamaica missionaries found a readiness for the Gospel amongst these 'heathens' which contrasted most favourably with their experience in England. Thomas Knibb described a communion of 1,000 and commented: 'One of the natives said to me, "O how I should like to go to England, where the good people live who send out good men to teach us!" Poor man, thought I, you would be greatly disappointed; you would wonder to see so few remain at the table of the Lord, and so many who care for none of these things.'[72] As the missionary in Port Maria, on the north-east of the island put it, comparing the experience of ministering in Jamaica with that in England, 'With you the blessings of the Gospel descend like the dew; but with us they are heavy showers of rain.'[73]

In March 1831 the Rev. John Griffith, a young man who heard the call whilst a member at Cannon Street, and the Rev. John Shoveller provided two new Birmingham recruits for the Baptist mission in Jamaica. A poet penned questions to, and answers from, these new enthusiasts:

> Why leave your friends? Why leave your native land?
> Why your life hazard o'er the treach'rous sea?
> 'I hear my gracious Lord's divine command –
> *The love of Christ it is, constraineth me.*[74]

The vision of 'wretched men' calling for help was one widely utilised. 'The whole island redounds with the cry, "Come over and help us"', reported the *Missionary Herald* in 1831.[75] This was an inspiring vision for a mission public.

Those who were helped were reported by the missionaries to be deeply grateful. In 1829 the *Missionary Herald* published Knibb's account of the laying of the foundation-stone for a new girls' school in Kingston, the money for which had come from England. In attendance were 294 children, most of the girls dressed in white and carrying bunches of flowers. Scholars who had distinguished themselves were presented with medals, and the children sang:

> O smile on those whose liberal care
> Provides for our instruction here;
> And let our conduct ever prove
> We're grateful for their generous love.
> Through life may we perform thy will;
> Our humble stations wisely fill.[76]

'The negroes love you ardently for your kindness in sending them the Gospel,' Knibb assured the mission public. As 'a race', they were an adornment to Christianity, their simplicity heart-warming, along with their capacity to suffer for Christ's sake, to suffer for their claim to worship.[77] The lead sermon at the annual meetings of the BMS in 1830 had as its text, 'Ask, and I will give thee the heathen for thine inheritance, and the uttermost parts of the earth for thy possession', a powerful text for an expanding empire, both that of the nation and that of the society. At the AGM the chairman welcomed all to the 'one great social family' that the Baptists constituted.[78] It was Christianity which had raised England to its high place among nations, and which gave it the right and the duty to carry its mission abroad.[79] James Montgomery, the famous hymn-writer, poet and enthusiast for the missionary cause, who edited missionary journals documenting the transformation from savagery to civilisation and was convinced, though constantly troubled about it, that all peoples could improve, condensed many of these ideas of Britain as a most favoured place to which benighted Africans imploringly looked for help in his poem 'Africa'.[80] The image that he evoked was widely familiar in its visual form: the Wedgewood anti-slavery cameos of enslaved men and women beseeching their white betters, 'Am I not a man and a brother?', 'Am I not a woman and a sister?'. Montgomery's poem was published with the epigram 'Africa reaches out her fettered hand to cry to Britain'.

> To thee, our paradise of isles!
> Where mercy in full glory smiles:
> Eden of lands! o'er all the rest,
> By blessing others, doubly blest,
> To thee I lift my weeping eye,
> Send me the Gospel; or I die;
> The word of Christ's salvation give,
> That I may hear his voice and live.[81]

These were the images of Indians and Africans which had become part of the daily diet of the missionary public.

Birmingham's 'Friends of the Negro'

The earliest BMS stations had been founded in India, and resources were focused there. In 1807 Moses Baker, one of the first black Baptists active in Jamaica, wrote to Dr Ryland, principal of Bristol Academy, founding member of the BMS, and Thomas Morgan's mentor, asking for help on the island. Ryland had been keen for some time to encourage such a venture, and the first English Baptist missionary to go to Jamaica was John Rowe, one of his students.[82] The early years in Jamaica were difficult, what with the hostility of the planters and the deaths of missionaries and their wives, but by the early 1820s the revival of the anti-slavery movement brought with it a new enthusiasm for the Jamaica mission and the dispatch of Knibb, Burchell and Phillippo.

The revival of anti-slavery sentiment was felt in Birmingham too. In 1826 the Birmingham Anti-Slavery Society was formed, and Morgan was on the committee together with his friend John Angell James and

alongside such stalwarts of the Quaker community as Richard Tapper
Cadbury and Joseph Sturge. Sturge was to become another of Morgan's
special friends, and had a particular influence on his son William.
Quakers had been at the heart of the anti-slavery movement from its earliest days: the evangelical revival brought enthusiastic Anglicans and
New Dissenters into the organisations which were committed to com-
batting slavery because of the contradiction between the belief in the
right of all souls to have access to Christ and the practices of slavery.
The newly formed Birmingham society devoted itself, as did its parent
organisation, to the dissemination of information, the development of
public awareness about slavery, and the promotion of petitions for Parliament. Items were extracted from the anti-slavery press, and the editors
of local newspapers were invited to reprint them; resolutions from meetings were placed in the press; town meetings were called to debate and
publicise the issue of slavery. In addition, the society promised support,
both financial and otherwise, to London.[83] Morgan was involved in all
the activities of the early years: the publication of an address and resolutions, the establishment of connections with Liverpool and Manchester, the calling of a town meeting in 1828 to protest the slow progress
that was being made towards amelioration.[84] BMS activities and anti-
slavery activities were intimately connected. 'The friends of the negro' as
the anti-slavery supporters named themselves, in an inclusive terminology which recognised no distinctions of class or gender, were also the
friends of missions. The missionary public and the anti-slavery public
overlapped extensively, though the latter was much larger than the
former and drew on a much wider social base. Not all abolitionists were
enthusiastic Christians.

In August 1829 Joshua Tinson, one of the established BMS missionaries from Jamaica, was in Birmingham, preaching at Cannon Street and
Mount Zion, and conducting a public meeting at Carrs Lane. The following year James Coultart, one of the senior BMS missionaries from
Jamaica who had been on the island since 1817, was in Birmingham providing information to the committee of the Anti-Slavery Society.[85] The
year 1832 was immensely busy, since agitation over reform was combined with abolitionist activities amongst these liberal-minded men. The
rebellion of 1831 in Jamaica and the decision by the Jamaican missionaries to send Knibb to England to plead their cause meant a huge surge
of campaigning. Once the Reform Act had been passed, the next crucial
step was to ensure that the newly elected House of Commons would be
more sympathetic to the anti-slavery movement. 'Friends to the abolition of slavery' were requested 'not to give a promise of their votes to
any one who has not given a public pledge to support measures in Parliament for immediate emancipation.'[86] Only weeks later plans were

being made for a visit from Knibb and a public meeting at Carrs Lane. 'There was a very numerous and respectable attendance', ran the report, 'and some time before the commencement of business the seats, aisles, and avenues of the extensive building were filled to excess.' Morgan seconded the first resolution which preceded Knibb's speech, and argued that slavery was 'a great national crime', its continuation incompatible with Christianity. The resolution, which had been agreed as committee policy, argued that freedom was the birthright of every human being across the empire, and civil rights and immunities were to be enjoyed by every 'free-born subject'. Slavery was a *national* crime and a sin which could only be washed away by a popular movement which would bring about abolition. Slavery could not coexist with Christianity, and Christians must take a political stand on this. Furthermore, no man was a true Briton who did not believe that freedom was the birthright of every human being, black or white.[87]

Knibb's speech included an 'affecting statement of the condition of the slaves', a 'vindication of the missionaries' conduct in relation to the rebellion' and a declaration from Knibb that he would pursue 'an unbending and unflinching advocacy of the cause of emancipation until the system was abolished'. There were heated arguments of a political nature towards the end of the meeting, which the committee much regretted. While wanting to intervene politically themselves – by ensuring that only sympathetic MPs were elected, for example – they also wanted to keep a tight lid on what political questions were raised.[88] The respectable men of the committee were those who had been enfranchised in 1832. But they had demonstrated for reform alongside many who had not been granted the vote, and the tensions were palpable. Large meetings always carried the threat that radicals who were opposed to anti-slavery on the grounds that it was a deflection from the problems of factory slaves at home would cause 'systematic and disgraceful interruptions', undercutting the otherwise very satisfactory demonstration that 'a very large majority of the inhabitants of this Town is in favour of the immediate abolition of negro slavery'.[89]

The Act which abolished slavery, the result of much negotiation, gave substantial compensation to the planters, and imposed fixed-term apprenticeships. Nine Birmingham men, including Sturge, his brother John, Thomas Morgan and John Angell James, were signatories of the address which publicly declared against apprenticeship, to the dismay of more moderate abolitionists.[90] The key public figure amongst them was Joseph Sturge. Born near Bristol in 1793, the second son of a Quaker farming family, Sturge had little formal education and was an autodidact throughout his life.[91] Diversifying from the farming business, he set up as a corn merchant in Bewdley on the River Severn, and in 1815 his sister Sophia joined him as housekeeper and key aide. His father died when he was twenty-four, and together they took on considerable responsibilities for their widowed mother and the seven dependent children who still needed launching in the world. The idea of the Christian family was central to Sturge's thinking, and the family enterprise, designed to support the immediate family, give succour to the wider families of 'Friends' – that is, Quakers – and reach beyond through Christian philanthropy, was a key concept in the organisation of his family and household. For Sturge, as Alex Tyrrell argues, strongly influenced as he was by evangelical dissent and political economy, the inner-directed self-improving Christian was his social ideal, and the voluntary society provided the best form of collective action.[92]

The corn business was speculative and hazardous, and at twenty-two, Sturge faced bankruptcy. In 1822 he moved to Birmingham, hoping for a fresh start and realising that it would be a good base from which to develop his business, given its rapidly growing transport system and expanding markets. He began with a wharf warehouse and a one-room office and had soon established a flourishing concern. His brother Charles had gone into partnership with him in 1822, and initially stayed in Bewdley, and his sister Sophia spent one morning each week book-keeping at the office.[93] The enterprise was indeed run by and for the family. 'There are few families', wrote Sturge, 'that have been . . . more united than ours': 'what is a source of more rational satisfaction than the conviction that you have been instrumental in adding to the comfort and happiness of others, and particularly those who are dear to you?'[94] His brothers John and Edmund set up a chemical business together in Birmingham, and like Joseph, settled in Edgbaston, the new middle-class suburb of the town.[95] His statue still stands there, a commemoration of one of the great city fathers. Sturge soon diversified into canals and railways, and began to worry about his liking for business; but increasingly, Charles ran the day-to-day affairs, so that Joseph could devote his time to philanthropic works. He regarded himself, as did so many Christians of this period, as a steward, managing economic matters for the better interests of the family and the wider community.

Sturge's relationship with his sister Sophia was crucial to them both. Like many a sister in early Victorian England, Sophia devoted herself to her brother and never married.[96] She ran his household between 1815 and 1834, helping him with his work, supporting him in his philanthropic and political enterprises, discussing decisions with him: a partner, but not a wife. In 1834 he married Eliza Cropper, the daughter of his long-time associate in anti-slavery and Quaker matters, James Cropper. Faced with this marriage, Sophia decided that she could not stay in Birmingham, and she left to work as a governess.[97] Eliza, however, died in childbirth, and Sophia returned to Edgbaston. The brother and sister lived together until her death in 1845, a death which devastated him. Sophia was 'his secretary and intimate counsellor', she often wrote down his thoughts for him, she travelled with him, she watched over him, she provided Christian companionship.[98] John Angell James summed up her sisterly virtues, as he saw them, in a typically flourishing encomium:

> Never, perhaps, were the active and passive virtues of the Christian character more harmoniously and beautifully blended than in this most excellent woman. . . . She occupied and worthily tilled a most important station as the colleague, counsellor, and ever-ready helper of her distinguished brother, in all his vast designs of beneficence. She not only presided in his family and relieved him of domestic cares, but she entered with earnest and enlightened interest into all his views, and by her intelligence and method greatly aided him in keeping himself informed of the progress of events in all their details. Her sound judgement and Christian wisdom were as a staff on which he could lean with assured confidence.

Here was indeed the perfect sister, selfless and devoted. As Henry Richard, Sturge's friend and biographer, concluded, 'She absolutely identified herself with him, and lived in his life.'[99] The year following her death, Sturge married again, this time Hannah Dickinson, the daughter of a Quaker ironmaster whose sister was married to Sturge's brother Charles. The Sturge siblings had married into a series of key Quaker families in Birmingham – the Cadburys, the Southalls and the Albrights. All of them lived close by, Edmund and Joseph and their families opposite each other with a subterranean passage linking their gardens under the road.[100] Together they constituted a powerful extended family network both in the business and the philanthropic worlds.[101] Hannah had five children and, like Sophia, interested herself in the same causes as her husband, particularly anti-slavery, as well as running a large house and providing much hospitality.

Shortly after his arrival in Birmingham, Sturge became involved with anti-slavery activities. In 1826 he became secretary of the town's new Anti-Slavery Society.[102] As befitted a Quaker, he had a strong belief in rank-and-file activities, for it was vital that each individual should be moved to action. He was an energetic supporter of the view that 'the people must emancipate the slaves, for the Government never will'.[103] He was also a great protagonist of the plain men of the provinces, deeply critical of the fancy ways of the metropolis, and indeed of those whose wealth brought laxity wherever they were. By 1828 he had lost patience with the moderate character of the London leadership, and was arguing for a series of public meetings and petitions on the model of the agitation against the Test and Corporation Acts. In 1830 he came out in favour of immediate emancipation by Act of Parliament. As always, he relied on prayer and inner heart searching to bring himself to the point of political decision.[104]

The pressure from the militants led to a split in the Anti-Slavery Society and the establishment of the Agency Committee in 1831. Its self-appointed task was to rally the cause and speed on the campaign, relying on paid lecturers to carry the word across the country. Those agents – John Scoble, Captain Stuart, George Thompson – were to be Sturge's allies for years to come. Sturge himself was a key figure; so much so, argues his contemporary biographer, that 'Birmingham, next to London, was for many years the most important centre of activity for all anti-slavery operations'.[105] Sturge travelled to Ireland and Scotland to campaign, and spent significant amounts of time in London, lobbying and petitioning.

Sophia, meanwhile, was a founding member of the Ladies' Society for the Relief of Negro Slaves (a name which carried rather more exclusive connotations than did 'friend'), the organisation which became the LNFS and which effectively held together anti-slavery activities in Birmingham through not only the fat years but also the lean.[106] The minute-book presented to the Birmingham Reference Library by the Misses Sturge in 1922 demonstrates the level of organisation which was maintained and the spirit of this venture. 'Remember those in bonds, as bound with them: and them that suffer adversity as being yourselves also in the body' was their motto from Hebrews. This identification with the silent suffering of others was at the heart of their enterprise. The suffering bodies of enslaved women and their children evoked a compassion which came to be understood as a moral imperative.[107] The narratives of 'ordinary' women – Mary Prince, for example – relied on the personal body as a common bond between those who suffered and those who would help.[108] Case histories engendered a sense of association, and slavery was Britain's responsibility. As women, the Birmingham ladies believed, and especially British women with the high privileges that went with that, they had particular feelings about the degraded condition of their own sex under slavery, their children seized from them, their families broken up, their bodies flogged and prostituted. They felt it to be their duty to do something about it. Slavery was operating under British laws, and it was British hands that were dealing such bitterness.[109] Every professing Christian should ask, they insisted, 'What have *I* done for much injured Africa?'[110] Their task must be to awaken sympathy for the weakest, and to excite 'the best exertions of every Briton' on behalf of the cause. Slavery was Britain's national crime, and they must work to expiate it. Women, despite their weakness, could act:

> With humble mien, and with dejected eyes,
> Let pity follow where Injustice flies.[111]

The frontispiece of their third report showed a manacled enslaved woman sadly kneeling and others working in the background under the overseers' whip. Cowper was quoted below:

> I would not have a Slave to till my ground,
> To carry me, to fan me while I sleep,
> And tremble when I wake, for all the wealth
> That sinews bought and sold have ever earn'd.
> We have no slaves at home – why then abroad?

This was followed by a poem in the voice of an enslaved woman addressing British ladies:

> Natives of a land of glory
> Daughters of the good and brave
> Hear the injured Negro's story
> Hear, and help the *kneeling Slave*.
> Think, how nought but death can sever
> *Your* lov'd children from your hold,
> Still alive – but lost for ever –
> *Ours* are parted, bought and sold!
> Seize, then, ev'ry favouring season –
> Scorning censure or applause:
> JUSTICE, TRUTH, RELIGION, REASON,
> Are your LEADERS in our cause![112]

Such a cause required constant activity and vigilance. Meetings were held, bags and albums produced, money raised, leaflets printed, a campaign mobilised on the question of abstinence from sugar produced by the enslaved, and thousands of households visited. These were profoundly social activities: taking women out of their own homes into the homes of others, defining abolitionist ladies as those with the cultural authority to inform and improve. It was the particular job of the women, as Clare Midgley argues, to moralise the home and moralise consumption.[113] Contacts were established with female abolitionists in numerous other places and with missionary wives and their spouses in the colonies. There were letters to and from the Cape, Calcutta, Sierra Leone and Jamaica. Enslaved men and women were redeemed with their support in the period before full emancipation. Money was sent to Spanish Town to support Phillippo's schools and to Kingston to fund the training of native teachers. The Jamaica Education Society, of which Sturge was a mainstay, received regular support from the Birmingham ladies and regular reports from Mary and Annie Knibb as to the progress in the girls' schools. Sophia Sturge was a ceaselessly active secretary, utilising her brother's contacts and knowledge to further the work of the female abolitionists. When she died in 1845, her sister Lydia took over the task.[114]

From the moment of emancipation, the erstwhile members of the Agency Committee were concerned about the working of the new system of apprenticeship. Sturge had strengthened his associations with the Baptists through his support for Knibb and his cause while he was in England. In 1833 he had joined the BMS (which had always welcomed non-Baptists),[115] and in 1836 he publicly showed his support by speaking at a BMS meeting in Birmingham.[116] By the 1830s, Andrew Porter notes, 'missions both claimed and were accorded a place in a refurbished national identity'.[117] They had moved from their marginal position of the 1790s, when small groups had struggled to gain support for ventures which were often seen as dubious and dangerous, to a much closer association with the centres of national life. Missions were seen to have extended Britain's global presence and shown a serious commitment to the positive transformation of colonial societies. In West Africa, the Caribbean, India, the Cape and the South Pacific, missionary activities were seen as part of the linked processes of colonisation and civilisation. Indeed, by associating the dissenting middle classes with the nation, the missions helped the move from margin to centre which characterised the shift from dissent to nonconformity.[118]

Sturge relied on the Baptist missionaries in Jamaica to provide him with information about apprenticeship, and it soon became abundantly clear to him that apprenticeship was slavery by another name. A new organisation was formed, 'The Friends of Negro Emancipation', to deal with the new evil. This almost immediately renamed itself the Birmingham Anti-Slavery Society, since the old society was now extinct.[119] In November 1835 a great anti-slavery meeting was held at the town hall and resolved that apprenticeship be abolished. 'The most vigorous and decisive measures must be adopted', they concluded, 'for awakening the Country from its delusion on this subject.' It was Birmingham's task to do this. Some of the more moderate speakers, such as the MP Joshua Scholefield, defended compensation. The more radical, led by George Edmonds, demanded to know 'by what right was every British family taxed £5 to pay for the emancipation of the slaves? . . . was it to be endured that those villainous planters should defy the people of England, after wheedling them out of twenty millions of their money?' The Rev. Thomas Swan, once tutor at the Serampore College established by the BMS and now minister of Cannon Street, insisted that 'the country was asleep', and continued:

The people of England were slumbering, and required to be awakened
... in this highly favoured country, the Friends of the Negro were still to
be found ... he rejoiced in being able to tell the people of this country that
the people of Birmingham would not be silent; – they would cry aloud, –
their voice would be echoed throughout the kingdom, until having careered
through the remotest corners of the earth, its thunders would burst the
fetters of the slaves.

John Angell James resoundingly supported Swan. 'He congratulated his
fellow-townsmen', he concluded,

on the honours, of which they may be almost proud, of being the first
town in the Empire that had raised its public and indignant voice against
the present state of our Negro fellow-subjects; they had given the key-note
to that chorus, loud and deep, of sympathy for the Negroes and resentment against their oppressors, which was about to be raised, he hoped,
through the length and breadth of the land. . . . they had liberty, – they
enjoyed it, – and would suffer no man to take it from them.

At the conclusion of the meeting a memorial was sent to Lord Melbourne, arguing that the planters had broken their contract with the
British people and that the contract was, therefore, void. Abolition of
apprenticeship must follow.[120]
   In December the Anti-Slavery Society further resolved that 'the Anti-
Slavery public are altogether disappointed at the flagrant violation of the
apprenticeship clause and feel it necessary to reopen the question before
Parliament'. The activists, including Morgan, launched once again into
a round of deputations, publications, public meetings and petitions. A
newspaper was launched with capital raised by Sturge, for abolitionists
were well aware of the critical power of the press in struggles over public
opinion. This time the campaign was led from Birmingham, dominated
by the provinces and dissent, with no major supporting group in London.
Enough pressure was successfully exerted to ensure that the House of
Commons set up a Select Committee on Apprenticeship, but its report
was optimistic, and Sturge did not trust the evidence which had been
provided.[121] As in the previous struggles, the conflicts between planters
and abolitionists over the representation of conditions in Jamaica became
a key issue. Sturge decided to visit the West Indies himself, accompanied
by his friends and co-workers in the cause Thomas Harvey, John Scoble
and William Lloyd. He was concerned that the planters would use the
period of apprenticeship to forge a system of coercion that would defeat
the intentions of emancipation. He had been warned by Dr Philip, a representative of the London Missionary Society in the Cape and a tireless
supporter of humanitarian causes, as to the ways in which the authori-

ties had misused their power there.[122] This was the abolitionist imperial network in operation, passing critical information from the different colonies to the metropole in the hopes that pressure could be exerted on the Imperial Parliament. Sturge became determined to 'humble the Colonial Office and wake the nation from its trance'.[123]

On his visit to the West Indies, Sturge talked to officials, planters, missionaries, especially the Baptists, with whom he already had many connections, and freed men and women. The missionaries ensured that he had access to apprentices out of earshot of employers and magistrates. The deputation took down depositions from these negroes and then tested them in a variety of ways to ensure that they were hearing the truth.[124] The negro's purported capacity to dissemble was a favourite target of the pro-slavery lobby. Sturge spent short periods in Antigua, Montserrat, Dominica, St Lucia and Barbados, and a longer time in Jamaica. He visited workhouses, magistrates' courts, estates and schools. His presence on the islands was much remarked on, for his was a well-known name to planters and apprentices alike. He arrived in Jamaica with anti-slavery posters, a guarantee of hostility from his political enemies, and his clear intention was to see an end to apprenticeship. When William Lloyd arrived in Jamaica, he found some of the apprentices wearing broad-brimmed 'Sturge hats' as a gesture of defiance to their masters.[125] The report of the visit, written by Sturge together with Harvey, was designed 'to stimulate the benevolent, the Christian patriot, to lively sympathy, and to animated exertion in behalf of the oppressed'.[126] It represented the West Indies as held back only by apprenticeship, the negro and coloured populations being ready to take their places in a new society.

Sturge's and Harvey's text, written in the hopes of stirring a wave of agitation over apprenticeship in Britain, had one eye always on the planters, anxious to demonstrate both to the pro-slavery lobby and to themselves that negroes would work and that Africans could be civilised, that they were indeed of the same human family as themselves. Thus, for example, they were struck by 'the beautiful and intelligent countenances and European foreheads of many of the coloured children', so unlike the ugly caricatures of Africans. They were delighted to hear from Phillippo, when they visited his chapel and schools in Spanish Town that some of the coloured teachers were as 'useful and efficient' as any European could be. They saw 'striking proofs', from their own observation, 'of the industry of the negroes when working under a proper stimulus'.[127] Negroes were indeed equivalent to the English peasantry. They commented repeatedly on the respectable and intelligent habits of those who attended the Baptist chapels, and insisted on the vital importance of missionary teaching. It was the missionaries who were 'the best qualified to form an unprejudiced judgement of the condition of the negroes under the apprenticeship, and of their capacity for a true appreciation of the blessings of freedom'.[128] 'Tranquil and peaceable', the negroes had shown astonishing patience in the face of oppression. Yet they were 'a still injured people', and it was up to the British to put this right.[129] The planters' desperate plea for new immigrants, they argued, was a result of their failure to understand the negro character: negroes would work if fairly treated. The continued exploitation and degradation of women was a moral disgrace: women were still subjected to the treadmill, they were flogged and chained together in penal gangs. This was an insult to the British public, for if one feature had reconciled that public to the expenditure of twenty million pounds in compensation, it was the advantages which emancipation 'appeared to confer on the weaker sex, whom it professed, by exempting them from degrading punishment, to elevate at least one step towards that position which reason and humanity require that they should occupy'.[130] The imperial parliament must state 'the inherent personal and civil rights of the negroes, as fellow-subjects under the British crown, as equal members of the human family, and endowed with the same physical and moral capacities'.[131] Negroes had the right, Sturge and Harvey insisted, to the protection of the law as British subjects. Their closing peroration was full of promise for the future:

> Nothing can exceed the disposition manifested by the negro population, to acquire the comforts and even the luxuries of civilised life. The world has seen no example of so general and intense a desire for education and religious instruction, as has been shown by the apprentices on behalf of themselves and their children, within the last few years. Their conduct and their character are full of promise for the future; full of tokens of their capacity to become, when free, a well ordered, industrious, and prosperous community. . . . From the times when it was maintained that the negro was of the lower creation, to the present day, when he is recognised as of the common brotherhood of man, every pro-slavery dogma respecting his character and capabilities has been disproved by experience; every pro-slavery prophecy has been falsified by the event.

Crucial to these changes was the gradual voluntary withdrawal of women from field labour to domestic duties, 'a change not more essential to the happiness and improvement of the negroes, than to the future, permanent, advancing prosperity of the whole community'.[132]

Sturge's conclusion was that 'there had been a great violation of a solemn compact with the British people'. It was his duty to 'seek redress at the hands of Parliament and by an appeal to the British public'.[133] The framework for his thinking on race and empire was provided by the notion of the universal family of man; negroes were British subjects with

the same rights as subjects at home. At the same time he was committed to the idea of free labour as the necessary bedrock of a civilised
society, and industry as the key to prosperity and progress. The rights of
negroes were located in promise, in the hope that they would prove to
be industrious, respectable, familial, domesticated. Sturge and other abolitionists depended on an identification with black people as potentially
just like white. But that identification was always in tension with racial
difference, a marker of distinction which could be drawn upon at any
moment. Were black people really like white people? Or were they, as
the pro-slavery lobby believed, fundamentally different? Anxieties and
ambivalences clustered around this issue: sameness and difference, identification and disavowal, were constantly in play: the meanings of 'black'
unresolved. Such tensions were captured in Sturge's encounter with
James Williams which occurred at this time.

Sturge met James Williams, an apprentice who had been very badly
treated, in Jamaica. He was a powerful patron of Williams, having given
Phillippo in Spanish Town the money to free him.[134] Williams's story was
a shocking one of persistent brutality, personal vindictiveness and the
failure of the due process of law. The narrative was an anti-slavery publication, designed like *The History of Mary Prince* to provoke an outcry
and mobilise opposition, in this case to apprenticeship. The history was
written by Dr Palmer, a white Jamaican supporter of anti-slavery, who,
as a magistrate, had tried to help Williams, but was unable to in the face
of his master's hostility. Palmer was in England to seek support in relation to his own persecution by the Jamaican authorities. The text was
hurried through the press as a pamphlet, as well as being published in
the sympathetic newspaper, the *Patriot*.[135] Before any of this had happened, Sturge decided to take Williams back to England with him to meet
the anti-slavery public. It was relatively rare at this time for black people
to speak in public, and personal testimony on the horrors of plantation
life was a powerful tool. But Sturge soon found himself disturbed by the
idle life which Williams was living and the effects which all the attention paid to him was having. He had put on a large amount of weight,
and was greatly enjoying the good living to which he suddenly had
access. Sturge's response was to send him back to Jamaica. 'I think the
only means of bringing him to a proper sense of situation is for him to
be compelled to labour for his bread,' he wrote. 'I believe he is in danger
of being quite unmanageable unless he thinks he must depend upon
himself alone for support.' Writing to his friend John Clark, the Baptist
missionary in Brown's Town, Sturge confided that

> The indulgence and attention he has had has done him a great deal of harm
> but I hope will not permanently injure his character . . . if he can be kept

out of harm's way the next six or eight months even if he should turn out an indifferent character afterwards the *cause* might not suffer by it and with this view it may be well to bear with a little indiscretion or indolence in him for a time than cast him off at once.[136]

The plan was to send Williams to Kingston, where he was less likely to attract notice, not Brown's Town, where he had come from. He was to be found work and kept under a close eye. Sturge worried about Williams for some months to come, anxious that his intervention in bringing him to England might have done harm. But the episode revealed the extent to which Sturge's attitude to black people was intimately associated with what he considered their 'correct' behaviour, with a definition of them as 'good'. When their behaviour and demeanour indicated that they were not as industrious or respectable as he hoped, the paternal approval was withdrawn. Abolitionists were indeed 'friends of the negro'. But that friendship had strict limits: negroes were 'poor black clients',[137] and indications of undue independence or improper behaviour were castigated. This attempt to constitute black men, women and children in particular ways was doomed to failure; for it depended on stereotypes which could never grasp the complexity or agency of other human beings. When James Williams proved to be something other than he had been imagined to be, Sturge's disappointment was tangible. Paternalism had its other side, in forms of aggression and hostility.

The stereotype of black people which the abolitionists produced was designed to counter that of the planters, which represented 'Quashee' as lazy, mendacious, incapable of working without the whip, mentally inferior and sexually depraved. Abolitionists produced in response the stereotype of the new black Christian subject – meek victim of white oppression, grateful to his or her saviours, ready to be transformed, the kneeling figure of the enslaved man in the famous Wedgewood cameo that was so widely circulated, the engraving on the writing paper of Sophia Sturge of a vicious master brandishing a three-thonged whip over a kneeling woman chained at the neck, wrist and ankles, the pitiful loving mother, separated from her children.[138] Listen to Thomas Clarkson, the veteran abolitionist, addressing the emancipated men and women of Brown's Town and Bethany:

Ever since you have been made free I have been enquiring how you have conducted yourselves. If well, then every one of your friends in England would be pleased with what he had done for you; if badly, then you would have given an opportunity to your enemies to try to bring you back to your old Bondage; but thanks be to God, I have heard good accounts of your Conduct. I have heard that you are industrious and willing to labour, that you are obedient to your masters, that you are generally sober, that you have given up many of your old Practices and Habits, which were bad, and that you are respectable members of Society. You cannot think what pleasure these accounts have given me. I am delighted whenever I think of them, and I cannot help saying, that you have made me amends for all the Care and Anxiety I had for you ever since I took up your Cause.[139]

Clarkson's vision is of children, who are approved of when they behave and bring pleasure to the patriarch. These industrious and domesticated men and women were to embody perfection: a sure recipe for disappointment and one carrying its own potential for demonisation. Stereotypes work by reducing the complex characteristics of a person to a few essentials, fixing a type 'in nature' with a few simplified characteristics, deploying a strategy of splitting by symbolically fixing one set of characteristics, excluding what does not belong. Stereotyping tends to occur when there are gross disparities of power: it is a tool of symbolic violence.[140] Abolitionists, in their 'benevolence' to black people, in their construction of themselves as 'friends of the negro' were deeply patronising, unable to recognise the complex people whom they were encountering. When James Williams did not behave as he was supposed to, the only solution was to send him home. Distance here was crucial. For maintaining geographical distance was one way of controlling this colonial relationship. Black people belonged in the colonies. As long as they stayed there, it was easier for abolitionists to defend their rights as British subjects. As *Punch* noted caustically, 'with many of the worthy people of Exeter Hall, distance is essential to love': this was Dickens's 'telescopic philanthropy' again.[141] There was a black population in Britain, but it was very small and concentrated in a few places. Elsewhere black people were visitors, and could always be sent home. And white people could visit the colonies, even settle in them, but always have the possibility of returning home. The idea of the geographical separation between metropole and colony was critical to colonial rule: a form of rule which depended on the authority of the coloniser.

When Sturge returned home from the Caribbean, Thomas Morgan was part of the deputation which welcomed him and thanked him for all his work on behalf of the cause, for his 'unwearied attempts for the release and ultimate welfare, of the captive, the desolate and the oppressed'.[142] Again, public meetings, addresses and petitions were organised, local MPs pressured to support immediate abolition. In December 1837 the town hall was full for a meeting which declared that slavery under every form was 'repugnant to the law of God, and the spirit of the British constitution', that the British people had been pillaged of their twenty million in compensation by the planters who had not carried through emancipation, that the missionaries had been doing a grand job in the West Indies, and that parliamentary committees could not be relied on. As Sturge put it to loud cheering, 'the people must depend upon their own exertions for the emancipation of the negroes'.[143] Following this meeting, a delegation was sent to London, including Morgan, which visited virtually every MP demanding action on apprenticeship, and a town meeting was organised.[144] Sturge and Harvey published *The Narrative of James Williams* and their own book speedily, not surprisingly to be met with fierce counter-attacks and a resulting inquiry into the case of Williams.[145] Whilst huge pressure was being put on the government, which was resisting strongly, the planters in the Jamaican House of Assembly acted themselves, rather than being forced to act by the imperial parliament, and abolished apprenticeship from 1 August 1838.

Birmingham 'Friends of the Negro' were jubilant, convinced that they carried much of the credit for what had happened. Great celebrations took place on 1 and 2 August, just as they did in Jamaica. On the morning of the first, Sunday school scholars were welcomed to the town hall. They came looking 'neat and healthy', and 'the whole scene was one highly creditable to the philanthropy and liberality of the people of Birmingham'. Thomas Morgan was in the chair, and John Scoble, the national secretary of the Anti-Slavery Society, told the story of the amazing transformation whereby 'Yesterday his fellow-Christians and fellow-men, to the number of many thousands, were held the property of other men; today they were their own property – husbands could embrace their wives as their own property, and slavery, with all its gloomy and revolting features, was at an end he trusted for ever'. This was the authorised abolitionist account, with its emphasis on manhood as the possession of property in oneself, and including authority over women and children. To great cheering, Scoble told the children that he hoped they would remember this day to the end of their lives, and that 'whilst they rejoiced in their unnumbered privileges', he trusted that they would see these privileges – 'liberty of person, liberty of conscience and all the blessings and advantages which Christian instruction could afford' as the birthright of all. After several more speeches and a 'hearty meal', the children processed to the site of the new emancipation schools, the name being agreed on the spot, the money for which had mainly come from Sturge.[146]

In the evening a great meeting was held at the town hall, which was packed. A large number of ladies were present alongside the great and the good of Birmingham society. The chairman opened the proceedings by remarking that 'they had met to congratulate themselves on the final close of the apprenticeship system of slavery throughout the British dominions'. Radicals and moderate liberal opinion jostled on the platform, and reminded their audience of the ever-present tensions within such alliances. Sturge was met with great cheering, and welcomed the fact that 'Through the mighty moral influence of the people of England the sun had risen for the first time upon the freedom of a large majority of their sable brethren in the British islands of the West'. He reminded his listeners that their tasks were not finished and there was still much work to be done, but that Britons were rightly proud of their traditions of freedom and could exercise their power with mercy. He applauded the great contribution of the Baptist missionaries in Jamaica, and looked forward to the emergence of a 'sable O'Connell' who would lead his people, as O'Connell had in Ireland. Here was an interesting assertion of the rights of black people to take command of themselves, rather than being led by their white elders; but it was a vision which was not to be fully tested in Sturge's lifetime. Other speakers were more concerned with emphasising the docile, obedient, peaceful nature of the negro and celebrating achievements rather than looking to problems that remained. Edward Baines brought greetings from Leeds, and insisted that 'the people of the spirited and independent town of Birmingham' would always be in the forefront of philanthropy in the West Indies. The MP Charles Lushington was voluminous in his praise for the town. 'It had long been his wish', he told his appreciative audience,

> to visit their flourishing town, the inhabitants of which were justly distinguished for their industrial enterprise, their general intelligence, their enlightened philanthropy, and that ardent attachment to civil and religious liberty, which had evinced itself in so many acts of enlightened liberality and vigorous patriotism, for the results of which ... the empire at large had most abundant cause to be eminently grateful.

Today, he said, the negro 'had put on the decorous array of manliness and independence'. Daniel O'Connell, the Irish radical, followed with a rousing and agitational speech, arguing, as Sturge had, that they must make sure that freedom really meant freedom, while George Edmonds declared that the victory had been achieved by 'pressure from without' – Sturge's term – and that public opinion was an index or sign, while 'physical force was the thing signified'. It was this which gave power to public opinion. He reminded his audience of the 'white slaves' at home and the work to be done.[147]

The following morning a 'sumptuous breakfast' was held, with the guests of honour two white visitors from Jamaica: a solicitor, Charles Harvey, who had been prosecuted because of his support for anti-slavery activities, and a former stipendiary magistrate, Dr Palmer, the editor of James Williams's history. This was the meeting of the middle classes, and

300 ladies and gentlemen were entertained. Dr Palmer, introduced by Sturge as distinguished for his 'manly fortitude and moral courage', told how he had lived in Jamaica for twenty-three years and had initially been quite sympathetic to slavery. It was 'the discussion upon the subject in England' which had induced him to think again, another source of self-congratulation for the audience. He was returning to the island very hopeful, but asked the meeting, and England, to keep Jamaica in their sights. The MP Benjamin Hawes returned to the theme of the moral might of Birmingham. 'This town', he declared,

> was distinguished by its vast industrial resources, but it possessed higher claims to their respect . . . [in] the great moral courage it had displayed in a moment of imminent national peril. He trusted it would long continue to maintain its standing in the moral as well as the political world, and that the great influence which it justly exercised on the feeling of the country would be long found enlisted on the side of those who fought for justice, . . . liberty, and . . . the enjoyment of the principles of their common Christianity.

Charles Harvey thanked England and the missionaries who were its servants, and the Rev. MacDonnell closed the proceedings with a warning to the negroes to be sure that they guarded their newly won liberties 'against the intoxification of newly-acquired freedom'. To applause from his audience he assured the freed men and women that 'nothing would give greater pain to the men of Birmingham, than to hear that those poor creatures, rescued from thraldom, would, in the delirium of joy, arising from the acquisition of a long-lost treasure, be guilty of any excess which would induce them to weep for the exertions which they had made in their behalf'.[148] This was Birmingham's celebration for the end of apprenticeship, one in which the men of their town, particularly Joseph Sturge, and the town itself, were seen as endowed with great moral stature and power. It was a vision that had little place for black or female agency, which assumed that 'poor negroes' were grateful, and that England and Birmingham must continue to watch over them from on high.

The utopian years

Thomas Morgan had long been assisted in his public labours by his third son, William Morgan. Born in 1815, the year of Waterloo and of a major increase in imperial dominions, William was formed not by the heady days of the 1790s, as his father had been, but by the white heat of 1831–2 in Birmingham, when hundreds of thousands demonstrated for reform, and troops were at the ready in case of revolution. Educated initially at home, with his mother attending to his general needs and his father to his classical studies, he then went to school on Waterloo Street. In addition, he attended drawing classes with Samuel Lines, the Birmingham artist and abolitionist who did the designs for the LNFS leaflets 'Pity the negro'.[149] It was decided that he should train as a solicitor, and his father's friend, Joseph Sturge, suggested placing him with a Mr Weston. Thomas Morgan was nearly forty when his son William was born. His friend Sturge was seventeen years his junior and twenty-two years older than his son. He was able to be a significant friend to both father and son, occupying that intermediate position which could be so helpful to both generations. In 1830, aged fifteen, William began his training. His oldest brother Thomas had wanted to go into the ministry, but had had to give up the idea on health grounds, turning instead to business. In 1831 William became publicly involved in both the reform and the anti-slavery agitations. An enthusiastic young lad, he took charge of the anti-slavery petition which was being mounted at that time, and in 1832 he attended the great Newhall Hill reform demonstration with his father and Joseph Sturge, both of whom were sporting Union Jacks. Patriotism, in 1832, was linked to liberty and the free-born Englishman.[150]

William quickly took on significant organisational responsibilities in the Anti-Slavery Society, despite his youth. In 1833 both James Coultart and William Knibb visited the Morgan family in Regent Place, when they were in Birmingham to address meetings. These were the beginnings for William of connections with Jamaica which were to last for many years. In 1834 he was presented with a memorial at a special meeting in Cannon Street, in the form of a framed copy of the Emancipation Act in gold letters, in recognition of the work he had done for the Anti-Slavery Society. At the same time he was active in agitating for the removal of civic disabilities from dissenters and in the struggle against church rates. A year later he was in London, studying for his profession and living with his brother and sister there, taking full advantage of being in the capital to attend sessions of the House of Commons and learn more about politics. In 1836 he started work as a solicitor in Birmingham, initially in New Street, with an office right opposite Cannon Street Church. The following year he was co-founder with William Middlemore (who came from a very well-established local family) of the Birmingham Baptist Union, an organisation which linked the Baptists of the town and its close environment, aiming to strengthen connections and influence and establish new churches in the neighbourhood. In 1839, following the Chartist riot in Birmingham, he acted with Joseph Sturge and collected statements in defence of the Chartists. He was to conduct the prosecution of William May, superintendent of the Metropolitan Police, at the Warwickshire Assizes, on account of his handling of the events in Birmingham. Like his father, William Morgan was a committed radical and dissenter, linking his religious, political and professional interests closely.[151]

William was intimately involved in the struggle over apprenticeship, serving on the committee of the re-formed Anti-Slavery Society once he returned to Birmingham, acting as a delegate to London meetings and as secretary to the special assembly held in London which took as its task the visiting of every MP, helping Joseph Sturge with his visit to the West Indies, drafting annual reports, acting as secretary to the building project for the new schools which were to commemorate emancipation.[152] While his father continued to appear on public platforms and to chair and make speeches, William was the organiser, learning the job and making innumerable contacts. At the great celebrations in August 1838 his task was to announce from the platform that special medals had been struck in Birmingham which reproduced a part of the design of the candelabrum which Sturge had commissioned on behalf of the grateful apprentices of Jamaica as a gift to the marquis of Sligo, governor of Jamaica, and to read letters from those who had not been able to attend.[153] In 1839 his legal skills were in use again as he helped Joseph Sturge with the establishment of the West India Land Investment Company, a scheme to provide capital so that freed slaves could buy land for themselves. The company was not granted incorporation, but the scheme continued on a private basis.[154] Birmingham, Jamaica, or New Birmingham, as it came to be called, was one of the free villages which was established at this time, another concrete manifestation of the rich connections between the town and the Baptist missionaries and anti-slavery supporters in Jamaica.[155] Meanwhile William was responsible for the case of Charles Harvey, the Jamaican solicitor, which went to the Privy Council in 1839. It was indeed very useful to have a solicitor in the mission and abolitionist family.

Joseph Sturge had been clear in 1838 that the efforts to secure full freedom for the emancipated, and to secure abolition in other parts of the world, could not stop. The Birmingham Anti-Slavery Society continued to do this work, with Sturge, John Angell James and Thomas Morgan all centrally involved and with William Morgan as the secretary.[156] Sturge remained very closely involved with activities in Jamaica, working particularly closely with Knibb and Clark on the establishment of free villages, strongly backing the establishment of the Jamaica Education Society and raising money to set up schools, mediating with the Colonial Office in whatever ways he could to support the activities of the missionaries and protect the legal rights of the emancipated. Like

Knibb, he looked forward to Jamaica becoming a self-governing society. Jamaica, argues Alex Tyrrell, provided the testing ground for Sturge's vision of a new moral world: he was increasingly interested in applying what he had learned there to Britain and Birmingham.[157] His class politics, usually interpreted through the frame of domestic radicalism, had an imperial trajectory, with the colonial experiment informing his metropolitan vision. During the 1830s his primary commitment was to anti-slavery. By the end of that decade he became increasingly preoccupied with questions at home; the new Police Act that had been imposed on Birmingham, making the town pay for a police force which was responsible to the Home Secretary, appalled him. The Police Act, he argued, proved that 'the present administration had made up their minds both at home and in the colonies, to try to rule the mass of the people not by moral, but physical force – not as men but as brutes'.[158]

The impact on Sturge of the Chartist riots which took place in the town in 1839 and which were widely seen as provoked by the actions of the Metropolitan Police, brought the question of suffrage to the fore. He became strongly attached to the idea of manhood suffrage, a suffrage in which 'the right to have a voice in public affairs inhered in the man, and not in any accident of property or social position'.[159] By the end of 1841 Sturge was moving towards Chartism and adopted complete suffrage. In 1842 he set up the Complete Suffrage Association, of which William Morgan was the honorary secretary, which aimed to bring working-class and middle-class reformers together. Both the Morgans and Thomas Swan were closely allied with him in these efforts, but his acceptance of the six points of the Charter proved too much for many of his moderate middle-class friends, while he was too paternalistic for many Chartists. His vision continued to be that of the universal family of man, with the voluntary principle as the necessary tool with which to re-make society. He spoke of placing the rights of the enslaved and the rights of the working class 'side by side of each other on the same basis of principle'.[160] His consistent efforts to improve life for working-class people in Birmingham, from efforts to reduce the hours of work to the provision of a field in Edgbaston, from baths to walks, schools and facilities for adult education – all were part of the creation of a 'social chain', 'which in its perfect state, would unite into one harmonious whole the universal family of man'.[161] But that family would still be ruled by the patriarch, in however kindly and benevolent a manner. After Sturge's death his workmen and their families sent a letter to his widow Hannah, expressing their condolences. 'It is not an exaggeration of language to say', they wrote, 'that he loved us with a father's fondness, and had a tender concern for our happiness both temporal and spiritual. His manly gravity, his refined and exalted piety, his benevolence of heart, were alike ever conspicuous in his intercourse with us.'[162] That image of the father was crucial.

In 1840 issues of the slave trade and slavery were very present, both nationally and locally. In that year Turner exhibited *The Slave Ship*, Prince Albert addressed the inaugural meeting in Exeter Hall of Buxton's African Civilisation Society, Knibb returned to England seeking new missionaries and talking of Africa.[163] In the wake of emancipation, Buxton had turned to the non-enslaved African and the international trade in enslaved people which still flourished. Sturge had meanwhile taken the lead in the formation of a new society, the British and Foreign Anti-Slavery Society (BFASS), for his new interest in the local and the domestic scene never displaced his internationalism. It turned its sights on the persistence of the institution of slavery in other parts of the world. Its object was the universal extinction of that institution and the trade which fed it by moral, peaceful and religious means. It aimed furthermore to circulate accurate information at home and abroad, to provide a commentary on press coverage of anti-slavery and related issues, to make contacts with abolitionists in other countries, especially the USA, and to recommend free produce. Its organ was the *Anti-Slavery Reporter*, sent free to mechanics institutes and other public institutions, as well as across the empire.

The first major task of the new organisation was to host the World Anti-Slavery Convention which met in London in June 1840. Birmingham was well represented at that event. The brothers Joseph and John Sturge, the father and son Thomas and William Morgan, Richard Tapper Cadbury, John Angell James, Thomas Swan and other stalwarts represented the town. William Morgan was one of the three honorary secretaries, Joseph Sturge a vice-president. Four hundred British and Irish delegates attended, plus fifty from elsewhere, including Jamaica. William Knibb was there, together with two of the black deacons from his area, Edward Barrett and Henry Beckford, all three representing the Baptist Western Union on the island. Symbolising the connections which Sturge had made on his visit to the West Indies, he had been invited to represent Spanish Town and St Catherine's in Jamaica, while Rev. John Clarke, the Jamaican missionary, soon to set out for West Africa, was the delegate for Kingston and St Catherine's as well as for Berwick-on-Tweed, his home town. John Angell James was named delegate for Jamaica as well as for Birmingham, in recognition of his service to the cause and his associations with the island. The rich linkage between Birmingham and Jamaica was thus recognised and reinforced.[164]

Much of the first day of the convention was taken up in an unexpected manner. 'From the four quarters of the world', as the Birmingham report of the event later put it, 'men, speaking various languages, were assembled with a common object – the extirpation of slavery from the whole world . . . each gentleman had the privilege of introducing a lady to witness the proceedings'.[165] Whereas the organising committee had expected the registered delegates to be all male, the Massachusetts delegation had interpreted 'friends of the slave' as male or female, and a number of ladies had attempted to register but been refused tickets. The question of their status was raised by a US delegate, Wendell Phillips, at the beginning of the proceedings, and their presence argued for on the grounds that 'female exertion' was the 'very life' of anti-slavery. The BFASS organisers hastened to scotch such a claim, arguing that 'the custom of this country is well-known and uniform'. In matters of business ladies did not become a part of working committees. The Rev. J. Burnet underlined this view: ladies were of course crucial to the work of benevolence, but no one expected them to be delegates. There was no insult here – this was how gentlemen in England treated their wives and daughters. 'As we are in England', he concluded, 'let us act as England does.' John Angell James then spoke. A great protagonist of the separate spheres of men and women, he taught such doctrines from his pulpit and in his many public pronouncements and publications.[166] He was a great admirer of American females, he declared, but he was very sorry that this question had been raised. 'They had never before heard a single word on the question of the right of females,' he asserted. 'It was a question perfectly new in this country,' and they were not ready for it. He was delighted to have ladies present at this historic meeting; they should continue to 'be with them and around them, although they could not be amongst them'. Here was a clear statement of the proper role of women in such enterprises. His concluding sentiment, that the discord which had occurred would simply make the harmony much sweeter, was met with loud cheers. A harsher note was struck by the Baptist minister Charles Stovel, who insisted that this divisive question should stay where it belonged, in the United States, and that the serious work which they had to do – namely, the destruction of slavery – should not be disrupted by the question of the rights of women. They 'ought not to expose themselves to ridicule in this way through the whole length and breadth of the land'.[167] It was left to Joseph Sturge and William Morgan to use their procedural powers to silence the dispute.[168] Support for Knibb was widespread at the convention, and in many ways the event was a show of strength for the abolitionists, winning extensive press coverage for its speakers and debates. But the seeds of difficulties ahead were already there, with competing visions of the obligations and responsibilities of empire surfacing over free trade and indentured labour.[169]

Knibb used the opportunity afforded by his visit to England to speak and raise money in various places, with the aim of taking new missionaries back to Jamaica with him. Inevitably Birmingham was his first port of call, for it was a hotbed of Baptists and abolitionists. As Thomas Swan had put it at the AGM of the BMS the previous year, 'He came from Birmingham; and he begged to tell the meeting that he . . . had got a bad character there, and he hoped it would continue bad on that subject, and grow blacker and blacker every day. It was said that in Birmingham all the missionary meetings were anti-slavery meetings – which was not at all agreeable to some people.'[170] Knibb was in Birmingham in May, before the opening of the convention, and a great meeting was held in the town hall to welcome him, with at least 5,000 present. The chairman introduced Knibb, 'the well-known apostle of freedom', together with his two companions, 'men of colour, each of whom was a deacon of a Baptist congregation . . . they would detail to the meeting the results of that emancipation which had been achieved by the efforts of the British people'. Birmingham was checking up. This was the first time that black men, 'free British subjects', had addressed an audience in the town hall.[171] Sturge introduced Henry Beckford, a member of the Baptist missionary Abbott's congregation in St Ann's Bay, and warned his listeners that he was not used to addressing such a large number.[172] He spoke about the horrors of slavery, the mayhem and destruction which it had effected in his own family, and 'drew a very affecting picture of the state of the negroes previous to the efforts of the Christian missionaries, and contrasted it with their present happy state'. He thanked God for their deliverance. Sturge then introduced Barrett, a man whose religious beliefs had kept the negroes peaceable on Oxford estate in the rebellion of 1831 and had been offered freedom as a reward. He had asked that his son might have it in his place, a young man who could not so well endure the 'yoke of bondage'. Sturge knew that his audience would welcome the two men, 'as Christian brethren, equal in all respects to themselves in the sight of God'. Barrett defended the record of the emancipated and argued that the reason for the decline in sugar production was that while the planters had forced women and children to work on the plantations from morning till night, the freed men 'now sent their children to school, and allowed their wives to fill the station for which they were intended, that of attending to their families and homes'.

Both Barrett and Beckford focused on the family in their speeches: the ways in which it had been destroyed by the planters and the new gender order that was being created in post-emancipation society. Knibb also took up this theme in his enthusiastic account of the transformation that had taken place in Jamaica. It was right and proper, he argued,

that one of those who had witnessed the results of emancipation, should make his first report in a town, not less renowned for its manufacturing enterprise than for its determined opposition to slavery, wherever slavery was found to exist. (Cheers) When he remembered the different meetings that had been held in Birmingham in behalf of the slave – when he remembered the urgent appeals and glowing language used by many of those by whom he was surrounded he felt he was discharging some portion of that debt of gratitude which he could but feebly repay, in coming forward and laying before them some of those glorious results which had taken place in the island of Jamaica.

He would never forget, he told them, that glorious day 'when things became men', a transformation effected mainly by the missionaries. It was they who had taught the enslaved to think of their rights as men, who had struck the chains of bondage from the hands of women, put their babies in their arms, and told them that the home was their place. He was delighted to find women attending to their domestic duties and the children going to school. These were the marks of a Christian society.[173]

Knibb developed these themes in his speech, especially requesting female support. He had been anxious to speak on female education on this visit, and had suggested that breakfast and tea-parties should be arranged to ensure female participation. The female schools set up by Mary Knibb depended on ladies' support from England. Knibb was careful to thank 'those kind females who have so efficiently aided the work of education, by sending boxes of useful articles for sale'. Several young women returned with him to Jamaica as teachers.[174] Female education was seen as crucial, for slavery had brought the female character 'very low'.[175] As one of the senior missionaries in Jamaica informed the missionary public in England, they had taken the step of transforming their mixed school in Hanover to a school for girls only, a step of which Hannah More, the celebrated evangelical and protagonist of separate spheres for men and women, would have heartily approved. This was highly desirable, he thought, where it was possible. 'We have two respectable persons as teachers, a mother and daughter. The girls spend the morning in the usual school exercises, and the afternoon in needlework.'[176] Girls had to be educated to be wives and mothers in Jamaica, even more so than in England, since slavery had inculcated quite the opposite values.

Slavery was associated with the polygamous practices of Africa, on the one hand, and the horrors of concubinage and illicit sexuality, on the other. The claims for a new mission to Africa, which was a major object of the Jamaica missionaries between 1840 and 1842, also drew on representations of Africa as morally barbaric. The *Missionary Herald* educated its readers with maps of West Africa, engravings of 'Greegree men of West Africa', 'dressed out in various forms, suited to inspire terror into the minds of the poor ignorant people, and thus to perpetuate their great influence', and of Africans receiving the Gospel from the white man, being rescued from what the missionaries constructed as the terrors of superstition.[177] As always, the comparison between Britain and these other places and peoples was fully drawn out. The appeal for missionary funds for Africa was based on that contrast: English character was generous and merciful to those less privileged, pity was the key. Different constituencies could be appealed to in fund-raising projects. A female servant was reported on one occasion in the *Missionary Herald* as proposing that the society should consider a special address to servants, given their superior situation to that of negroes.[178] In 1842 the 'Women of England' were especially targeted. 'Women of England', argued Rev. Brock at an AGM of the BMS, using the same appellation as Mrs Ellis in her celebrated manual of 1839,

> I ask you to contrast the social discord there with your own peaceful habitations of joy and love. Remember those green swards of this lower world where infancy with all its innocence, and boyhood with all its roguery, and youth with all its promise, and manhood with all its vigour, and womanhood with all its gracefulness, combine to reverence your authority, and to reciprocate expressions of your tenderest love; and then remember that polygamy would be destructive of all this happiness. I am sure, therefore, that you will rejoice when you recollect that henceforth your privileges are to be enjoyed in Africa. Recollect that there woman is now the slave, that here she is the companion. . . . In England, woman is the participator of her husband's joy; in Africa, at the impulse of caprice, she is to-day his drudge, tomorrow his plaything or toy.[179]

The year 1840 was represented as the dawning of a new age. Emancipation had taken place in British colonies, and British abolitionists could turn to the wider world, focusing on the USA and Africa. But 1840 might be characterised as the swan-song for a particular phase of the movement. 'Some say all England is abolitionised,'[180] it was reported; but by 1842, attacks on Baptist missionaries for the lack of spiritual discipline and purity amongst their flock had come to a crisis, and Knibb had returned to England to defend their name. Morgans, father and son, found themselves embroiled in disturbing debates. The AGM of the BMS in London brought in Rev. Dr Campbell of the London Missionary Society to defend his co-workers. He knew, he proclaimed, that 'negro society would rise in character, and ultimately clothe itself with the comely garb of Christian civilisation . . . Emancipation is purely owing to the missionaries.'[181] This impassioned defence was followed by emotional thanks from Knibb and great enthusiasm from the floor. The Rev. A. Leslie, a missionary from India, plaintively asked the meeting not to forget 'the East' in their enthusiasm for 'the West'.

The year 1842 also saw the jubilee of the BMS, and great celebrations were associated with this. Joshua Russell, the honorary secretary, argued that for fifty years the denomination had been engaged in proclaiming liberty throughout the earth; but there was

> an obvious and special propriety in sounding this fiftieth year a louder blast, again to gladden the Hindoo and the Negro, and to kindle new and deep emotions of joy in the inhabitants of Africa . . . 'In the day of atonement shall ye make the trumpet sound throughout all your land, and ye shall hallow the fiftieth year, and proclaim liberty throughout all the land, unto all the inhabitants thereof; it shall be a jubilee unto you, and ye shall return every man unto his possession, and ye shall return every man unto his family'.[182]

Jubilee for Russell was the conversion of the heathen: not for him the wider associations with a radical political platform. The trumpet was to be sounded most loudly in Kettering, Jamaica, and Kettering, England, the metropolitan event, as it turned out, being on a considerably smaller scale than the colonial. Services and meetings were held in Kettering, England, with one of the major themes being the importance of training 'native agents'. The debate over 'native agency' and a mission to Africa had been going on in England for some time. Neither the missionaries nor the missionary public had ever been united on this subject. The ambivalence which characterised notions of racial difference within the universal Christian family found full expression in concerns as to quite what 'native agents' would be capable of. 'In the conversion of the heathen', wrote one contributor to the debate, 'we are raising up agents to carry out our designs to an unlimited extent,' supremely unaware of the potential problem as to 'our' designs not always matching 'theirs'. We hear of 'irregular teachers' in Jamaica, he continued, and from this there was much to be learned. 'If a natural outlet is not opened for the exercise of the talents and zeal of our brethren, they will break out in irregular methods.'[183] It was much better to train them and supervise them, thus minimising these dangers.

While missionary letters to the BMS carried evidence of considerable tensions over questions of power between 'native agents' and missionaries (see chapter 2), the published reports from both India and Jamaica were upbeat, stressing the transformations which occurred and the good work which could be done under European supervision. Thus an engraving of a woodcut in the *Missionary Herald* in 1839 represented a 'native' Indian missionary, Sujatali, a shining example of the work wrought by divine grace: conversion had turned him from 'a bigoted and depraved Mohammedan into a meek and lowly disciple of Christ'.[184] The editor commented in the next issue that this sketch had been very well received and that, consequently, he was now publishing an account from John Clark in Jamaica of James Finlayson, one of his deacons in Brown's Town. Once a dancing, drinking and fornicating enslaved man, he had been converted, persecuted for his faith, gained his freedom, and now gave all the proceeds of his business to the chapel and missionary work. Clark reported a recent talk he had given to local parents, encouraging them to send their children to school. 'Let "Blackee" mind his duty,' he was reported as saying:

> Let us labour honestly that we may get gold and silver, and be able to give our children education. . . . That good country that send we the Gospel, send we schools, and send we the free; and, therefore, we must carry on schools in every quarter . . . We must remember that England give more money than we can tell to make we free; and we must try to pay it all back in sending the gospel to Africa, that our brethren and sisters may see the great light we enjoy.[185]

The following month the ordination of the Merrick father and son team, which had been assisting John Clarke in Jericho, Jamaica, told another success story of native agency. Proprietors, it was reported, were seeking help from Joseph Merrick, and his literacy was contrasted with those illiterate 'self-constituted preachers' who tried to lead the people astray.[186] Such idealised accounts of new colonial subjects, full of gratitude to their Christian benefactors, were the hoped-for outcome of the missionary venture. The insistence on total conversion, total transformation, left little space for 'natives' to be anything other than perfect.

The Jamaican mission to West Africa was to be the testing ground as to whether 'natives' of one colonial site could become the missionaries of another. Knibb's enthusiasm for a Jamaican mission to West Africa had been one of the major themes of his speeches on his visit to England in 1840. One of the aims of the Jubilee Fund was to send money to assist with the establishment of Calabar, the training institution in Jamaica, so that

> liberated Africans . . . may bear the gospel to the land of their birth, and tell their benighted brethren the great things God hath done even for them . . . They will go, not, it is true, under the patronage of the mighty; not enriched with the treasures, the learning, or the wisdom which the world deems necessary; these are nature's children, trained and tutored in the school of grace.[187]

'The negroes are the men for that country', argued Russell, in relation to the proposed new mission, for Europeans could not survive in that unhealthy climate, and 'their black skins cover noble hearts'.[188]

The jubilee gave Baptists an opportunity to reflect on the great work which they saw themselves as doing for the empire: their jubilee linked conversion to civilisation, and they thanked God for fifty years of missionary activity. Ideas of the restitution of debt or the cessation of work were not for them.[189] The notion that heathens were calling out throughout that empire, 'Come over and help us', was repeated again and again in BMS literature. The hope was that negroes, Hindoos and Africans were all deeply grateful for the blessings which they received. But such assumptions were rudely questioned in 1857, when it became clear that in India there was wide-scale popular feeling against all those associated with the British. In 1842, however, 'joyful complacency' could still provide the keynote, and it could indeed seem that 'East' and 'West' were united in 'one great social family'.[190] The Rev. William Brock, a strong supporter of anti-slavery and the BMS, and a man who believed that his religion compelled him to be a citizen, waxed lyrical on the possibilities opened up by missionary work.[191] 'There is the prospect', he argued,

> of making our own country *Great* Britain. If I ever thought well of my country, I do so at this moment; and I say – 'England! with all thy faults I love thee still'. *Great* Britain, not in the acts of parliament, not in the statute book, not in queen's speeches, but great in its character, great in its resolves, great in its enterprises; great, inasmuch as it lays hold on the greatness of Omnipotence, and goes to do the work of the Lord to the very ends of the earth.

The greatness of Britain he linked to the presence of women as helpmeets, not toys or drudges but companions, a further sign of the superiority of British civilisation over all others.[192] Such hyperbole was the order of the day: from 'East' to 'West' the missionaries had heralded the breaking-up of caste, the abolition of infanticide and 'suttee', the translation of the Bible, the annihilation of slavery. Knibb spoke last at this jubilee celebration, and must have ruffled many feathers with his tactless comparison of the material comforts which he and his brethren enjoyed with the conditions in which some of the English ministers were living, 'treated more like shoe-blacks than heralds of the cross'.[193] In the following week jubilee meetings were held across the provinces, with Knibb appearing as guest of honour. In Birmingham the celebration was at the town hall, and Knibb was greeted with great enthusiasm, an old friend of the town by now. He was presented with a specially designed medal commemorating the event by Mr Davis, the medallist who was relied on for all such occasions.[194]

A few months later the Birmingham Anti-Slavery Society held its AGM at Cannon Street and demonstrated yet again the intimate connections between anti-slavery and missionary work. Sturge was in the chair, William Morgan read the annual report, and Thomas Morgan spoke. Phillippo, who was in Hastings recovering his health and writing his book, had been invited, but was not able to attend. John Clarke, missionary in Jamaica and Africa, was there, reporting on his first visit to Fernando Po, the pilot for the first missionary venture from Jamaica. He gave a 'harrowing description' of the scene in West Africa, 'arising from the combined influence of slavery and idolatry'. He called upon 'the friends of humanity not to relax in their efforts for christianising Africa', 'the most effectual way of putting an end to the twin abominations of slavery and superstition'. The Rev. Thomas Swan, loyal friend of the cause, concluded the meeting by reading out part of a letter he had received from Edward Barrett, deacon in Knibb's congregation, an indicator of a personal connection which had been established. He expressed his happiness 'that the hearts of the men of Birmingham still beat true to the anti-slavery cause, and that, while absorbed in their own cares and concerns, they could think of the interests of the slave'.[195]

Baptists, the 'friends of the negro' and of the missions, had had a good decade: one in which at many crucial points they had carried the town with them. 'Friends of the negro' were celebrated as true progenitors of the spirit of the town, demonstrating the generous and liberty-loving nature of Birmingham men. They had worked for political reform, and they had worked for emancipation. The hand of friendship had reached from the midland metropolis to Jamaica, dispensing support and wisdom to those who had been enslaved. Missionary and abolitionist knowledge of the 'heathen' and of newly converted Christian subjects was riven with paternalism and superiority, and was rooted in ideas about the proper relations of different peoples, classes and genders. It was built on an assumption that England was the most civilised nation in the world, despite its need for reform, at the heart of a mighty empire. All subjects of that empire should be able to enjoy their unique privileges, dispensed from the metropolis. But Swan's assertion that 'the hearts of the men of Birmingham still beat true to the anti-slavery cause', that this particular vision of town, nation and empire held sway, was to be severely tested in the years to come.

6

The Limits of Friendship: Abolitionism in Decline 1842–1859

'A population intellectually at zero'

If the period from the early 1830s to the early 1840s was the high moment for abolitionists in Britain, when the universal family of man looked as if it might be an achievable reality, the period from the mid-1840s to the mid-1860s saw a marked shift in the discursive terrain: a loss of confidence in the language of negro brotherhood and sisterhood, though those values were upheld by the stalwarts, and an increasing turn to the language of race to explain and justify the inequalities and persistent differences between peoples.

The failure of the Niger expedition, Buxton's attempt to send commerce and civilisation to Africa, brought considerable discredit on 'the friends of the negro' and sharp criticism in the press, notably from Charles Dickens.[1] From 1843 a serious difference of opinion emerged on the question of the tariffs that protected West Indian producers of sugar, now employing free labour, from sugar produced by the enslaved in other parts of the world. Earl Grey, Secretary of State for the Colonies in the administration of Lord John Russell, was entirely convinced of the desirability of abandoning protective legislation. He wanted to combine the abolition of the duties which protected West Indian sugar, which he saw as keeping wages unnaturally high and therefore encouraging idleness and obstructing the progress of civilisation, with encouraging European immigration. In his view, a 'rude population' needed the example of 'civilised men' to create and foster the habits of a good life.[2] Grey's support for free trade delighted Cobden and Bright, but Sturge came out in favour of the exclusion of commodities produced by enslaved labour from the British market, a position which hard-line free-traders were not prepared to support. Sturge increasingly put efforts into providing supplies of free-labour goods, a policy which was actively pursued by the LNFS. Cobden and Bright, by contrast, were wedded to the doctrine of free trade, and would not countenance exceptions.[3] Between 1846 and 1854, however, the tariffs which had protected West Indian sugar gradually disappeared, to the deep dismay of both planters and missionaries. Nothing could withstand the forward march of free trade. By 1845 the *Birmingham Journal* was quoting a hostile judgement which dismissed the BFASS as 'a clique of great unknowns, a squadron of busy-bodies who pursue great objects by small means'.[4]

Everyday abolitionist and missionary work continued, nevertheless. Miss Morgan sent a parcel of clothing to Mrs John Clarke in Fernando Po for the West Africa mission.[5] Thomas Morgan acted as one of the officiating ministers, together with Swan and Hoby, at the 'setting apart' of Jonathan Makepiece for India.[6] But the AGM of the Birmingham Anti-Slavery Society in 1844 was marked not by cheerful news of the success of the emancipated peasantry, but by gloomy reports, read by William Morgan, of conditions in Jamaica. Furthermore, there was evidence of disagreement on the subject of free trade: the mayor, in the chair, spoke strongly for it, but others were in favour of the protection of West Indian sugar.[7] While the debate over free trade raged at home, the missionaries were sending anxious reports from Jamaica of the non-payment of wages and economic depression. The planters were strongly advocating immigration as a solution to their labour problems; the missionaries were arguing equally strongly against this, insisting that no further labour was needed, only the payment of proper wages. The missionaries were hostile to both Indian and African immigration. The arrival of large numbers of 'sensualists and idolaters', or savage Africans, would do little, they felt, for the progress of the emancipated.[8] 'Discouraging accounts' were circulating as to the conduct of the emancipated peasantry, and abolitionists were increasingly thrown on the defensive, anxiously seeking reassurance that all was going well. As one of the older missionaries commented in a letter to Sturge, Jamaica was neither Paradise nor Pandemonium. 'The old state of society,' he reflected, 'if society it might be called, has been completely dissolved, and it must take time to consolidate a new and totally different kind of society.'[9] Such caution did not sit easily, however, with the utopian hopes which Knibb and others had inspired.

Knibb was in England for the AGM of the BFASS in 1845, and mounted a stirring defence of the emancipated, arguing that the problems in Jamaica were to do with the behaviour of the planters, the unreasonable taxes which had been imposed on food, and the lack of capital with which to introduce improvements on the sugar estates. The missionaries in Jamaica were facing severe problems of debt, and Knibb had come to raise money. The contributions of the freed peasantry had fallen drastically after the heady first days of gratitude. The emancipated could no longer afford to give in the way they had. The missionaries turned again to Britain. 'There is a helping hand and a helping heart still to be found in England,' Knibb proclaimed. The negroes he declared to be 'as grateful a people as any on the face of the earth'. He wanted white men to prosper too, but they must not do it on the backs of the negroes.[10] The whole island, he argued in a most memorable phrase, had 'had to begin the world at once', and it was unreasonable to expect too much. The growth of freeholding was a success story, and he told of the villages which were less well known to the abolitionist public than Sturge Town, Clarksonville and Wilberforce. Try-all, Happy-news, Standfast, Save-rents, Long-looked-for-come-at-last, August-town, Harmony, Tiswell were some of those which told a story of hope in their names.[11] They were providing havens for freed men and women, places where industry could prosper and families flourish.

In July a valedictory meeting was held for Knibb's departure, at which the address was given by Hinton, the historian of the BMS. The BMS committee had decided to give £6,000 to the Jamaica churches, which they declared to be a final gift in an effort to clear debts. Hinton argued that Jamaica could no longer be regarded as part of the missionary field, 'studded as it is with Baptist churches of great power'. The end of the mission meant that new habits were needed, particularly the habit of 'independent action', a habit which brought responsibilities as well as pleasures. This was to be a theme for the BMS. How were black men, represented as children, to become mature and take on independence, that key attribute of masculinity? When would it be possible for Europeans to stop being teachers and withdraw their paternal guidance? How was it possible to resolve the contradiction between dependence and independence, between the missionary's desire to lead and instruct and the imperative to make men? 'Make them understand', argued Hinton, referring to the emancipated,

> that they cannot combine the delights of freedom with those of subjection. . . . They may be compared to a stout little fellow that trembles at the effort of walking; but it is not an unkind thing when his mother pushes him gently off, and makes him go, teaching him to realize the strength he had, but which he did not know of. . . . It has been one of the defects of the missionary system, that it tends to produce a sense of helplessness, an attitude of weakness, in the missionary churches, by the insulated and dependent character it gives them. . . . Awake the brethren to these things, Knibb. Let them know that the eye of England is upon them; let them know that the eye, not only of the Committee and of the Society, but of the whole denomination, and of all religious communities, is upon them.[12]

Here was the image of the child being helped by the parent, of dependence, associated as it was with femininity, as being too much a part of missionary churches. Here also was the familiar message to the emancipated that 'the eye of England' was upon them, expecting them to behave in appropriate ways. In the view of the BMS, it was Knibb who was to provide the leadership and encourage new habits; the contradictions implicit in the instruction of 'manly independence' were not confronted.

Knibb himself was well known for his manly independence, and his death, only months later, was widely perceived as a serious blow to the abolitionist cause, for he had been an able and indefatigable protagonist for both enslaved and freedmen, a great believer in the 'happiness of the human family'.[13] Hinton's funeral sermon compared Knibb, the man for the West, with Yates, the man for the East: these venues required different skills if differentially racialised subjects were to be converted and civilised. Men of action were needed in the West, whereas reflective scholars, who could deal with oriental knowledge, were required for the East. While Knibb was manly and athletic, Yates, the oriental scholar, was small, pale and retiring. Yates was placed in a 'region of calms', where assiduous scholarship was possible in 'the captivating stores of oriental learning', whereas Knibb was in 'a region of storms', 'where human crime and wickedness had reached their climax, and the wild elements demanded some master spirit to confront and control their rage'.[14] The Rev. J. J. Freeman, one of the secretaries of the LMS, took up this comparison. Addressing the annual meeting of the BMS, he explained that he had never wondered at Knibb's influence over the negro population, a race whose particular features he felt entirely comfortable with delineating. 'His characteristics', he maintained,

> were just those which are fitted to secure the affection and confidence of the race. He was a man of decision, and they loved it; a man of energy, and they felt they could lean upon it; a man of blandness and candour, and those qualifications secured the affections of their hearts. A greater mistake could not be made than that of treating the negro race with harshness. . . . While Knibb was the man for the west, Yates was the man for the east. [15]

By the mid-1840s the high days of emancipation were clearly over, and the West Indies no longer so exciting for the English middle-class imagination. Abolitionist and missionary ventures both suffered from this, and the BMS had to work hard to maintain its profile. In an effort to attract younger members, they decided in 1844 on a *Juvenile Missionary Herald*, with woodcuts, sketches of the manners and scenery of foreign countries, extracts from missionary journals, and other material thought to appeal to and be suitable for children.[16] The following year a member proposed a plan for monthly missionary prayer meetings, which had been found to be very successful in Leeds. One mission station should be taken as the focus each month, 'first giving a description and an historical narrative of the place, and then an account of the origin, nature, and progress of missionary operations there'. Preparing these accounts would mean 'more correct, defined and enlarged conceptions' of missionary work: 'Ideas of places, scenes, and toils, now for the most part pictures of fancy, confused and incorrect, will become distinct and true. Imagination will be guided by that which is real.' Prayer would be more precise in its object.[17] Thus would imperial minds be educated, and imperial imaginations honed 'by that which is real': the missionary accounts.

Another new initiative was a Young Men's Christian Auxiliary. All the missionary societies were facing a fall in income in the years of economic depression, and were having to think of new ways of attracting support.[18] The Young Men's Christian Auxiliary saw as one of its tasks the guidance of those who wanted to form juvenile associations. It recommended that particular attention be given to 'the miserable state of the heathen' and 'the greatness of those privileges by which they are themselves distinguished from the children of heathen parents'. They advised the use of maps, drawings and as many objects as possible, such as idols, and argued that there was an imperative need for a missionary museum, a venture which was in fact established later in the year. There were serious worries as to the falling-off in support from young men. It was thought to be associated with the loss of novelty: 'the romance and the excitement have disappeared'; heart stirring appeals were important, and the sense of a great cause. Birmingham soon established its own Young Men's Association, which organised illustrated lectures, corresponded with missionaries, sent deputations to other places, and contributed financially to mission work. The *Missionary Herald* was pleased to be able to report a most successful meeting for the young in Kettering, when the Rev. John Clarke, missionary in Jamaica and West Africa, had spoken. He had pinned up a map of the world and a map of Africa, and the young people could ask whatever questions they wanted. In the light of this success, might it be possible for the BMS to provide 'an outline map of the world, like the one recently published by the Wesleyan Society, with the different countries marked in which our Society is labouring? And this might be followed by a short series of maps of the different countries with all the stations marked.' In this way Sunday school classes, Bible classes and families could all have access to missionary information and engage in the work of constituting properly civilised subjects at home as well as contributing to that work overseas.[19]

The Birmingham Auxiliary BMS had kept active and busy, and in 1847 organised a large event for its twenty-fourth anniversary. A 'highly respectable' gathering met in the town hall with Thomas Morgan and others on the platform. The main address came from the Rev. Birrell, who reported on the journey he had just undertaken to Jamaica. The BMS had decided to send a deputation to the island in an attempt to resolve some of the difficulties which faced the denomination there. Although the Jamaica Baptist Union had been independent since 1842, the BMS still owned considerable property on the island, and felt responsibility for the missionaries with whom they had been associated. When times became hard, those missionaries sought support from the 'parent society'. Phillippo had appealed strongly, albeit unsuccessfully, to the BMS committee for its endorsement of his case against Dowson in Spanish Town, and the BMS had also received worrying reports of divisions in other congregations and of troubles between black and white missionaries in West Africa. Very little of all this was revealed to the missionary public, but the task of the deputation was to intervene in these disputes and report on the state of the island. In June the annual meetings had been held in London, and the deputation welcomed on its return. A public meeting was held to hear an account of the moral condition of Jamaica.

The Rev. Birrell described the shock of recognition for him of the gulf between slavery and civilisation. Though convinced that 'a pretty accurate idea' of the state of Jamaica 'may be formed . . . without leaving our own island', he had found his encounter with the island disturbing and revealing. The enslaved had been 'clothed and fed, and guarded like children'. They had powerfully desired, he believed, the approval and protection of the white man. But now the situation had dramatically changed: the emancipated had to clothe and feed themselves and make their own decisions as to how to spend their money. It was his visit to Calabar, the training institution for native pastors, which clarified for him the problems to be faced. 'Never till I reached the spot', he continued,

had I a just appreciation of the difficulties in the way; never till then did I so clearly perceive the extent to which the education of the people in civilised countries has been carried on in the persons of their ancestors, – the extent to which qualities, which we deem natural and innate, are the result of subtle influences in society, the operations of which we cannot detect, and of which we cannot tell 'whence they come or whither they go'. Of all these hereditary advantages the peoples of these lands are destitute. The entire population stands intellectually at zero. Every man must rise in his own person from that point.

The notion of a population 'intellectually at zero' depended on the assumption that there were only Western forms of knowledge. Other knowledges, customs and traditions were dangerous or irrelevant, 'the hereditary advantages' of Africans non-existent. British missionaries and abolitionists believed that Africans had been literally born anew in the dual moments of emancipation and conversion. They had to begin from the beginning, learn everything.

Calabar was promising to Birrell, for it was doing this work, training young men in language, literature, mathematics, classics and biblical scholarship. He was impressed by the good manners and 'intellectual aspect' of the students, and shocked out of his erroneous assumptions, derived from nursery pictures, as to the appearance of the negroes. 'We figure them,' he commented, 'I once did and many still do – as men of no foreheads, of extravagant mouths, of preposterous nostrils', whereas 'a large majority are men of the noblest mould'.[20] Here was a man from the heartlands of the missionary and abolitionist worlds, fed and watered on tales of emancipation, who had still expected Africans to look like cartoons. His companion on the deputation, the Rev. Angus, also commented on the childlike nature of the negroes. Since the mission had begun in Jamaica, he reported, thirty missionaries had been sent out, and there were ninety-five properties still in trust to the BMS. Those missionaries had done great work, they had had to be protectors of the people in every way. 'Manly independence and self-sufficiency . . . would obviously be preferable,' but at this stage it was impossible. Like Birrell, he worked with an evolutionary view of 'the race'. The missionaries had necessarily adopted a simple evangelical style; 'the spirit of discussion, so common and perhaps so necessary in the East, they have never allowed'.[21] While ancient civilisations required such exchange, the negroes came from nowhere and carried nothing with them. Africa was vacant. While there were periodic reports in the missionary press of obeah and myalism, this was never interpreted, as in 'the East', as an alternative framework of religious belief. 'Africa' was 'lying in her darkness and in her blood', waiting for conversion and a new beginning, imagined as both empty and full of horror.[22] Africans in Jamaica, who had been locked in a second form of barbarism, that of slavery, had nevertheless had the advantage of contact with Christianity. Post-emancipation they were members of a potentially advancing civilisation, but the threat of regression to Africa always lurked in the shadows.

Birrell claimed to bring good news from Jamaica to Birmingham, but the tone of his report was significantly different from that of earlier years. They were good people, he argued. He had often heard

these poor creatures pray, and he had been delighted with them. There was a sweetness, a fervour, a simplicity in their prayers, which went to the heart. . . . The period of negro emancipation, as they all knew, was one of difficulty, in consequence of the exaggerated notions which the negroes had of liberty. . . . He hoped that the negroes would become a well-instructed and a useful people.[23]

There was considerably less enthusiasm here than in the halcyon days of the 1830s. Negroes had exaggerated ideas of liberty, expected too much without realising the hard work that was required for its achievement. The hope is more modest, that they will become 'a well-instructed and a useful people'.

On the morning after the meeting at which Birrell spoke, a '1st rate breakfast' was served in the town hall. Thomas Morgan was in the chair, and his son William and Joseph Sturge were both there. In the first hymn the mission public celebrated missionary work across the globe, and reflected on its own privileged position as givers of light to heathens in bondage to ignorance and sin, as they sang, 'From Greenland's icy mountains'. The Rev. Birrell spoke again, this time about Haiti, and was followed by the Rev. Eustace Carey, who talked about his labours in India. Both speakers paid compliments to Birmingham's proud record of missionary endeavour.

The year 1848 saw all eyes turned to Europe and to troubles at home and in Ireland. In this context anti-slavery questions were not high on the agenda, and the news from Jamaica continued to be gloomy. The late 1840s were thin years for the missionary societies, with harsh economic conditions at home reducing enthusiasm for 'heathens' abroad.[24] Colonial issues roused little interest in the House of Commons, and it was hard to rally support for immigration. 'The friends of the negro', however, remained indefatigible in their efforts. 'Immigration', argued the *Anti-Slavery Reporter*, is 'an unjust, inhuman and pernicious system.' It represented a return to the slave trade and to the oppressions associated with bonded service. Furthermore, the 'character and habits of the immigrants . . . would prove most destructive to the religion and morality of the resident labourers'.[25] The hard work which had been done to educate and civilise Africans would be undone by the arrival of 'savage' Africans and superstitious and idolatrous East Indians. There was particular concern over the sex ratio amongst immigrants, for 'the wives and families of the great bulk of the East Indian labourers have been left at home to shift as they best might', and those women who had accompanied men were mainly of 'the worst class'. This made prospects for family life very poor, and raised the spectre of new forms of sexual depravity.[26] The Jamaican Baptist Western Union organised a petition to Lord Russell, publicised in the anti-slavery press in England, protesting strongly against Kroo immigration from West Africa. The Kroomen were known to be

> idolaters of the worst class, practising the most debasing and demoralizing superstitions; fierce and ungovernable in their passions, and revengeful and cruel in their conduct. We appeal to your lordship, whether the introduction of a large body of these polygamists into the midst of our peasantry, only lately rescued from the darkness of heathenism, will not be likely to cause an awful increase of vice and crime, and ... have the worst possible effect on the advancing civilisation, morality and religion of the emancipated portion of the community.[27]

There were serious worries amongst the abolitionists that the old pro-slavery party was regaining the initiative, and that the government was far too ready to listen to the West India body. 'The fact is', argued the BFASS,

> that the West India body in this country may now be said to control the legislation in the colonies. They never possessed more power than they do at the present time; and, of course, they exult in their ascendancy. We tell them, however, that the old anti-slavery spirit, which formerly wrenched the slave from their oppression, will yet protect the freeman from their grasp.[28]

The battle ground in the late 1840s was immigration, for once the planters had failed in their attempt to retain the protective duties on sugar, when for a brief moment planters and missionaries had been at one, they returned to the question of labour. They were determined to get government support on this, and Peter Borthwick, Knibb's antagonist in the public debates over slavery in 1832, was sent by the West India interest to Jamaica to collect information to present to the British public.[29] Immigration, however, did not have the same pull, the same emotional force, as slavery. By 1849, the Rev. G. S. Bull, a popular Birmingham preacher, in the chair for a meeting of the LNFS, told his audience that from his childhood he had been identified with the interests of the African race. There was a time, he commented, 'when the question of negro slavery was fully and constantly brought before the public, but latterly it had comparatively ceased to be noticed'.[30] Despite the efforts of the faithful, and in this the ladies were exemplary, anti-slavery was in decline.

Carlyle's occasion

This was the context for Carlyle's publication of his 'Occasional Discourse on the Negro Question'.[31] Carlyle was born in 1795 in the small town of Ecclefechan, the son of a mason. Brought up as a Calvinist, he was able to benefit from the relative openness of the Scottish educational system and go to university. Intended for the ministry, he abandoned this life scheme, but an experience of spiritual rebirth, described in his book *Sartor Resartus*, after the loss of his conventional religious faith, gave him the confidence to turn increasingly to writing. At the same time he married, and became one of the growing band of professional middle-class writers, relying not only on books but on periodical writing to provide a modest income.

In recognition of the centrality of London to that market, the Carlyles moved to the metropolis, and by the 1840s, with the publication of *Past and Present*, Carlyle had become a nationally known power with the pen. He had learned from the German Romantics a grandiose conception of the man of letters. To his mind it was writers who could claim true nobility, and make a contribution which long outlived the ephemera of political life. Indeed, in 'The Hero as Man of Letters', Carlyle was to argue that this hero must be regarded as our most important modern person. 'He, such as he may be, is the soul of all. What he teaches the whole world will do and make.'[32] Carlyle had been horrified after his arrival in London, as Norma Clarke has noted, by what he saw as the unmanliness of London's writers. They were not 'red-blooded *men*', but weaklings.[33] Male writers in the 1830s and 1840s, as Mary Poovey has argued, were preoccupied with the status of their work and with the relation between their writing and other kinds of work. They conceptualised writing as a significant public activity, in part in response to the accusation that their subjection to the world of commerce and the market interfered with their role as prophet, muse or genius. Their writing gave them potential influence, but they had no institutional base or secure social position.[34] They were also fearful of the feminisation of literature, and of the place of domestic fiction.[35]

Fired with this sense of mission, to make the man of letters a figure of respect, Carlyle achieved a very considerable eminence with a literary public in the 1830s and 1840s. They welcomed his particular kind of writing, heavy with moral seriousness, redolent with spirituality, powered by its sense of its own dignity and importance, effectively distanced from the troubling world of the market. Indeed, Carlyle's critique of mechanisation was precisely the reason for his popularity in a society which had been transformed by that very process, but was simultaneously troubled by its amorality. His despair at the mechanisation of man 'in head and in heart as well as in hand' fuelled his contempt for utilitarianism, that 'dismal science', 'which reduces the duty of human governors to that of letting man alone'.[36] His bleak view of human nature drew some of its force from the Calvinist vision, and this may have contributed to his insistence on the importance of government and leadership, and of prophecy, all of which became more important to him as he grew older. Carlyle had no time for the concept of rights, countering it with his belief in the necessary dependence between master and man, a mutual dependence in which each must do his duty and his work in the world. A profound believer in the dignity of labour and the power of labour to purify fallen man, Carlyle had a deep hostility to those who would not work. 'There is a perennial nobleness, and even sacredness, in Work', he argued: 'Were he never so benighted, forgetful of his high calling, there is always hope in a man that actually and earnestly works: in Idleness alone is there perpetual despair.'[37]

For Carlyle, as Herbert Sussman argues, white masculinity was associated with an internal struggle to contain the dangers within, to master and control the potential contagion and pollution associated with male sexuality, and achieve manliness, a state which was made, not given. Maleness was untutored energy, manliness a hard-won accomplishment.[38] His hatred of philanthropy was associated with his perception that it weakened men and made them dependent on others. Such a notion of manhood was underpinned by an insistence on the essential difference between the sexes and a deep misogyny. Some men were made to rule over others, and men must be masters in their own house. Men were born to command, women to obey. 'A woman's natural object in the world is to *go out*', he argued, 'and find herself some sort of *man her superior* and obey him loyally and lovingly and make herself as much as possible into a *beautiful reflex of him*.'[39] In heroising sexual abstinence and celibacy, as in the case of his fictional Abbot Samson, Carlyle was celebrating a world of white men, uncontaminated by the dangers associated with female sexuality and the threats which women, and black men, posed to men's needful self-restraint.

In the 1830s and early 1840s Carlyle did not publish anti-abolitionist sentiments. He was, however, prepared to vent them in private. Lucretia Mott, the American abolitionist and feminist came to London in 1840 as a delegate to the Anti-Slavery Convention but was prevented from taking her official place. She visited the Carlyles at home, and noted in her diary that the conversation had not been satisfactory: 'Anti-Abolition – or rather sympathies absorbed in poor at home and own poverty and slavery . . . disappointed in him.'[40] By 1849, however, after a journey to Ireland, Carlyle's preoccupation with the troubles of the 'hungry forties' led him to an increasingly harsh, and public, position on the West Indies. He was now willing to identify himself firmly with the planters' cause. The 'Occasional Discourse on the Negro Question' was published anonymously in *Fraser's Magazine* in 1849, but republished in *The Latter Day Pamphlets* in 1853 with the significant shift of title from 'negro' to 'nigger'. In his words of introduction he commented on 'the strange doctrines and notions shadowed forth', and predicted that in 'these emancipated epochs of the human mind' he would probably find himself in a minority of one.[41] His inimitable style was immediately recognisable to the discerning reading public, and in speaking words that others would not speak, the essay provoked immediate reaction. The brief polemic argued that the effects of emancipation had been disastrous. It had led to the ruin of the colonies, the ruin of the planters, and the ruin of black people who would not work. The emancipated slaves were idle, content to live on pig's food. They had been born to be servants or slaves, and should be made to grow goods for the rest of the world, with the help of the whip if necessary. The West Indies had been purchased by British blood, and was not there for black people to grow pumpkins for themselves. Carlyle challenged the anti-slavery othodoxy of black men as brothers, arguing that black people were an inferior race.

The essay took the form of an imaginary lecture to a philanthropic organisation. Using a combination of characters with metaphorical names, proverbs, folk-tales, biblical references and social commentary, he held the polemic together with an acerbic humour strongly evocative of Dickens. Events in the sugar colonies were held up by him as a terrifying example of what would happen more generally if natural relations were unsettled. In his view black people were born to be servants to those who were wiser than them: white people were their 'born lords'.[42] The parlous state of West Indian society, with the negroes 'all very happy and doing well' but white people in a state of despair, had its origins in emancipation, which had given black people quite false expectations and dangerous opportunities.[43] While black people, best compared in Carlyle's mind with horses or dogs, were 'sitting yonder with their beautiful muzzles up to their ears in pumpkins, imbibing sweet pulps and juices; the grinder and incisor teeth ready for ever-new work', the British government and the British people were handing out millions to keep this lovely state of affairs going, while 'doleful Whites' were without potatoes to eat.[44] The only solution was to recognise the truth, so unpalatable to sentimental abolitionists, that black men had to be mastered. For Carlyle, mastership and servantship were the only conceivable deliverance from what he saw as the really dangerous forms of tyranny and slavery, when the strong, the great and the noble-minded were enslaved to the weak and the mean in the name of some foolish notion of rights. The problem of modern society was that no man reverenced another.

The place of white men as masters in the sugar islands presented no difficulties to Carlyle. In his view, proprietorship must rest with those who got the best from the land, the 'Saxon-British'. When they had first arrived, the land had been jungle and swamp, producing only 'man-eating Caribs, rattle-snakes, and reeking waste and putrefaction'. It was only when the British arrived, like the prince in 'The Sleeping Beauty', that nature was awoken and brought forth her nobler elements. The islands, wrote Carlyle, 'till the European white man first saw them . . . were as if not yet created, their nobler elements of cinammon, sugar, coffee, pepper black and gray, lying all asleep, waiting the white enchanter who should say to them, Awake!'. It was not 'Black Quashee' who made the islands what they are. Indeed,

> Before the West Indies could grow a pumpkin for any Negro, how much European heroism had to spend itself in obscure battle; to sink, in mortal agony, before the jungles, the putrescences and waste savageries could become arable, and the Devil be in some measure chained there . . . Not a square inch of soil in those fruitful Isles, purchased by British blood, shall any Black man hold to grow pumpkins for him, except on terms that are fair towards Britain.[45]

The major source of Carlyle's hostility to black people was their refusal to labour. Preoccupied with proving that writing was work of the highest order, producing food within a peasant economy did not count for him as work. Work meant sweat and toil, it meant the transformation of the sinful self, as God had decreed to Adam. 'He who shall not work shall not eat,' inveighed Carlyle;

> no Black man who will not work according to what ability the gods have given him for working, has the smallest right to eat pumpkin . . . but has an indisputed and perpetual right to be compelled, by the real proprietors of said land, to do competent work for his living. This is the everlasting duty of all men, black or white, who are born into this world.[46]

Men who would not work of their own accord must be induced by the whip if necessary, for idleness could only lead to rottenness and putrescence, to corruption and evil. Induce him if you can, argued Carlyle, with 'beneficent whip': the alternative was to 'let him look across to Haiti, and trace a far sterner prophecy! Let him by his ugliness, idleness, rebellion, banish all White men from the West Indies and make it all one Haiti, – with little or no sugar growing, black Peter exterminating black Paul . . . nothing but a tropical dog-kennel and pestiferous jungle.'[47]

Carlyle's evocation of the whip echoed the discourse of the planters and the argument which had simmered for decades as to whether black men would work without coercion. But this touched a difficult nerve for abolitionists. Missionaries and their supporters were deeply anxious as to the supposed capacities or otherwise of black people to labour. There had long been a tension between African-Jamaican desires for land and small peasant proprietorship and abolitionist convictions that working for wages was crucial. Without the cash surplus from a wage and the reconstruction of the self that went with labour discipline, men would not become the desiring subjects who wanted Birmingham forks and brass bedsteads, who would produce in order to consume. In this sense there was a thread linking Carlylean and missionary worries, and indeed, official discourse. As Thomas Holt points out, there was a 'basic complementarity' between Carlyle and Colonial Office thinking, 'though not the official rhetoric and reasoning'.[48] For official discourse on post-emancipation society had moved on, and the optimism of the 1830s had gone. Henry Taylor at the Colonial Office and Carlyle were close friends; both saw wage labour as a source of social discipline, and both distrusted democracy. Official reports and memos would not use Carlyle's language: but they reached many of the same conclusions as to the prospects for the sugar islands.

Carlyle's hostility to black men was linked to his feminisation of them: they could not exercise the self-restraint necessary for proper manliness. 'I decidedly like poor Quashee,' he wrote, 'and find him a pretty kind of man. With a pennyworth of oil, you can make a handsome glossy thing of Quashee.'[49] The black men of the Caribbean, in Carlyle's rhetoric, were pretty, supple, affectionate and amenable, none of them manly epithets. His contempt for those feminine characteristics was linked to his contempt for women. Women should know their place and not attempt to step out of it. A man must be lord in his house, just as he should be the master of his servant.

Whilst despising black people, Carlyle's worst ire was reserved for those he saw as responsible for maintaining this state of affairs. They were the philanthropists and utilitarians: the twin horrors associated with abolition which produced 'windy sentimentalists' and 'effeminate types' whose 'unhappy wedlock' could only lead to 'benevolent twaddle' and 'revolutionary grapeshot'. Together, wrote Carlyle, in lines resonant with perverted sexual imagery, they would 'give birth to progenies and prodigies, dark extensive mooncalves, unnamable abortions, wide-coiled monstrosities, such as the world has not seen hitherto'. Utilitarianism and philanthropy were reducing the duty of human governors to that of letting men alone. 'Serious men' must take a grip on this state of affairs, and realise that there was work to be done in this universe.[50]

Carlyle's blast from the fastness of his study in Cheyne Row provoked the doyen of the dismal science, John Stuart Mill, to respond. Mill, with his firm belief in the right to individual fulfilment, was a fierce antagonist of slavery. This implicit defence of that abominable system could not go unanswered. 'The author issues his opinions, or rather ordinances, under imposing auspices,' wrote Mill, 'no less than those of the "immortal gods".'[51] Carlyle spoke as one with authority, assuming that one man was born lord over another. To Mill's mind, the struggle against the law of might was the struggle for human improvement. In his brief response Mill attacked the planters for their expectation of their right to live off black people, and refuted Carlyle's gospel of work, arguing that all should take part in necessary labour, but that no one could find fulfilment in labour alone. There was no evidence, he argued, that white people were born wiser than others. He was horrified by the spectre of Carlyle, a professed moral reformer, claiming that 'one kind of human beings are born servants to another kind'. 'It is by analytical examination', he suggested, 'that we have learned whatever we know of the laws of external nature: and if he had not disdained to apply the same mode of investigation to the laws of the formation of character, he would have escaped the vulgar error of imputing every difference which he finds among human beings to an original difference of nature.'[52] Here was the nub of Mill's argument. Just as he later refuted the notion of the differences between men and women being attributable to nature, so he argued that the races were different because of their external circumstances.[53] For Mill both women and black people could potentially rise to the civilisation of British men. His concept of equality and commitment to democracy were founded on a developmental notion of human nature. His moral vision, therefore, of a free and equal society could not be achieved without a process of education.

Mill believed that Carlyle had done great mischief by throwing his weight and his persuasive powers behind the pro-slavery lobby, and indeed, from the time of its publication, 'Occasional Discourse' shifted the terms on which questions concerned with the West Indies were discussed. Mill was not alone in flying the anti-slavery banner in response to Carlyle. The *Anti-Slavery Reporter* felt bound to respond, though to reply, it argued, 'would be simply to re-open the questions which the common sense and common conscience of mankind have long ago settled'. Carlyle it decried as one 'whose Anglo-German crudities and mystified philosophies, have so tickled the fancies, or heated the imaginations of not a few amongst us, as almost to create a school'. The 'profound Carlyle', it regretted, 'raves on' with his 'oracular utterances'. In introducing the extract which he published, the editor emphasised the 'profound ignorance' of Carlyle and his ilk on social questions which fell outside their usual range, and opined that, 'whatever its momentary effect may be', the essay 'will ultimately damage the reputation of Mr. Carlyle more than any of his previous efforts had raised it in public estimation' – a judgement which was to be proved wrong. In addition to its own critique, it published one from the unitarian paper, the *Inquirer*, that argued, 'Prophecy has degenerated into raving, eloquence into mere drivelling'. The article agreed with Carlyle in his insistence on the gospel of work, but disagreed with him in his assumption that some men should compel others to do it. If black men had not acquired the taste for work, then the fault must lie in part with their white masters. God had given 'favoured nations' a mission. Had they fulfilled it?[54]

If all England had been abolitionist in 1840, it certainly was not by 1850, and the attack by Carlyle made it even more important to defend the freed men and women. But the tide was running against abolitionist truths. At the AGM of the BFASS the following year, the Rev. Brock was delighted to see Exeter Hall filled once more with an anti-slavery audience. 'I was beginning to fear', he explained, 'that the feeling in favour of the slaves was subsiding; that the sentiments of the "Latter-day Pamphlets" were doing their mischief. We have been told that we were exaggerating the evils of slavery.[55] Far from exaggerating, he insisted, the evils to be faced had not abated, as the American experience showed all too clearly.

The anti-slavery press continued to publish material on the West Indies in an attempt to keep that region in the public eye. In 1850 Candler and Alexander went on a visit to Jamaica for the Society of Friends. The publication of their report was part of the long-established Quaker tradition of investigating and reporting on conditions in the West Indies. Joseph John Gurney had been the last to go, in more propitious times, though his measured account had been less utopian in its tone than that of Sturge and Harvey. By the time of Candler's and Alexander's visit (it was Candler's second visit, he had first been there in 1840), it was widely recognised that repeal of the sugar duties had significantly altered the economic landscape: sugar production was down, there was less demand for labour, and a reduction in wages.[56] Their report stressed the variety of conditions to be found in Jamaica. They were impressed on the whole by the free villages, especially those such as Sturge Town which had a resident missionary, and saw evidence of a 'cheerful and contented peasantry'. In many areas they found the small freeholders doing well. At a meeting in St James, for example, the occasion for four Baptist churches to come together, they counted 280 horses tethered. 'Here we see the fruits of emancipation', they wrote, 'which a pro-slavery press delights to represent as a failure – a middle class of industrious people rising, in the land of their birth, to become small owners of land, on which they find it desirable to employ a horse or other beast of burden.'

But there were contrary indications too: the presence of 'coolies', with their 'refined' heathen practices, was having a prejudicial effect, as had been feared, on the morals of the emancipated, and there was an alarming revival of superstition in some places. Take Porus, for example, one of the earliest of the free villages, where a myal man, 'a sort of African rainmaker', had been. 'He pretended to be helped in his operations by angels,' they reported,

> and boasted that he could heal diseases, and make their empty wells over-flow with water. He was received as a visitor from heaven, and to do him honour they kept up revelry and dancing day and night. The police interfered to put a stop to the noise and disturbance, but the friends of superstition fought for their champion, and rescued him, till the military came and led him off to prison . . . In this large village the population is dense, and the ignorant and depraved encourage one another to evil. There is no middle class to influence them beneficially.

If conditions were mixed in the countryside, the towns were truly alarming: Kingston and Spanish Town were 'a sort of cesspool, into which much of the moral filth of the island may be said to flow'. Their overall conclusions regarding the island were extremely mixed: Jamaica was 'a suffering colony', yet the peasantry on the whole were doing well, education was vital, and the profligacy of slavery had left bitter fruits; the Sugar Act had been 'fatal' in its effects, and the planters had suffered severe losses.[57] They held to the view, however, that there was every reason to believe that the people of these colonies would occupy 'a rank in civilised society equal to that of any on the earth'.[58]

A new book on *The State and Prospects of Jamaica* also provided modest encouragement for the 'friends of the negro'. The reviewer in the *Baptist Magazine* was happy to report that an investigation of education had demonstrated that there was no disparity of intellectual power between the black child and the white. Furthermore, it was asserted that 'with slavery is departing the low forehead, the flat nose, the thick lip and the animal features which characterized the race in the days of bondage'. Yet there were problems: licentiousness, duplicity, levity, incapacity for rule, indifference to charity and greed all remained prominent negro weaknesses. Still, this was an upbeat review, minimising the author's criticisms and arguing that the field was still open, there was no cause for despair.[59] In Jamaica, on the other hand, John Henderson complained that the article 'shows how profoundly ignorant some persons are . . . of the character of our peoples'.[60]

Concerned by the shifts in opinion, Sturge was inspired to seek a review of the state of the free villages from his friend John Clark. This was published as a pamphlet as well as being covered in the *Anti-Slavery Reporter*. Clark was happy to be able to report that 'the settlement of emancipated negroes in these free villages has been productive of great good; they have become more industrious, thoughtful and frugal, and generally are desirous of occupying respectable stations in society'.[61] He was careful to provide evidence from other sources, citing new authorities on Jamaica and their conclusions as to the beneficial effects of the free villages.[62] This was a reassuring message for the 'friends of the negro'.

The publication of *Uncle Tom's Cabin* and the visit of Harriet Beecher Stowe marked something of a revival for the anti-slavery cause. The picture of a suffering Christian negro reverberated comfortably with a long tradition of anti-slavery representation in Britain. The book was a bestseller, and was speedily adapted for the theatre, as well as appearing in almanacs and song-books and being translated into wallpapers, ornaments and dolls. As Douglas Lorimer argues, Uncle Tom and Topsy came to be seen as the embodiment of 'negro character', and Harriet Beecher Stowe's response to criticisms of Uncle Tom's excessive meekness was that negroes were naturally sensitive to Christianity. 'The negro race', she suggested, 'is confessedly more simple, docile, childlike, and affectionate, than other races', and hence more attuned to the Holy Spirit.[63] The celebrated author's private visit to Birmingham in 1853, when she stayed with Joseph Sturge, provided an opportunity for the 'friends of the negro', in the guise of about 150 ladies and gentlemen from the town, to gather at Sturge's house and offer her their messages of congratulation and support. Thomas and William Morgan and John Angell James were there; an address was read by the lady secretary of the Ladies Society, since it was not a public occasion, and James 'in most eloquent terms' welcomed Mrs Stowe and her family to the 'circle of anti-slavery friends in Birmingham', a welcome to which her husband replied on account of her delicate health, and perhaps her own complex notions of a proper femininity. Beecher Stowe herself was delighted by the peace and quiet she found in the Sturge household. 'Everything seemed in order,' she remarked, with a most enjoyable extended family life, and she noted the full-length engraving of Joseph hanging in his brother's house, 'standing with his hand placed protectingly on the head of a black

Joseph Sturge. Sturge's hand rests on the shoulders of a young black child, rescued from the horrors of slavery and apprenticeship.

British School, Birmingham Museums and Art Gallery.

child', an image which accorded well with her thinking.[64] The subsequent AGM of the BFASS in London was packed, perhaps in part because of Beecher Stowe's attendance, and the audience listened to an optimistic account of developments in the West Indies, excepting Jamaica, which was described as pursuing 'her career of disaster and decay, without making any visible efforts at self-improvement'.[65]

Part of the impatience with Jamaica was associated with the political difficulties there and the determination of the planters to see no reduction in their power. The Duke of Newcastle, Colonial Secretary, warned Parliament in 1853 of the dangers of 'representative institutions without responsible government', and compared the situation in Canada and Jamaica to the great detriment of the latter. Jamaica had an anomalous constitution, with a small number of electors but a House of Assembly that had the right to veto revenue bills. Newcastle looked forward to 'the time when the black population would seek for greater power, and it was therefore the more incumbent on them to see that a sound system, such as exists in this country, should be introduced'.[66] This led to a political crisis and the replacement of the governor, Sir Charles Grey, with Sir Henry Barkly, and eventually a new constitutional settlement. But the planters continued to hold the balance of power in the House of Assembly, and it was the abolitionists' despair over this which led them to be sympathetic to the introduction of crown colony government in the wake of Morant Bay. Jamaica, they believed, could not govern itself until there was an educated black electorate.

Knibb had hoped that black self-government would happen sooner rather than later. In 1854 one of his disciples, Cornford, who had been a missionary in Rio Bueno, testified to 'the unquestioning elevation and advancing improvement of those whom slavery had so greatly degraded'. But black rule for him was a matter of the distant future. 'Black men occupy pulpits; black men fill important posts in the press, and take their places as legislators in the House of Assembly. . . . the day will come when the descendants of slaves shall possess the land tilled by their forefathers, and when no white man shall govern the islands.'[67] By the mid-1850s this looked far away. The new governor's conclusions, after a tour of the island, focused on the excessive expectations which there had been of the negroes and the need for a more realistic assessment of what was possible in the circumstances. 'That the Negroes, as a body, are not conspicuous for industry, cannot be denied by their warmest friends; but I hardly think any other race of men would have devoted themselves to unnecessary corporeal exertion, unless they had previously attained a far higher standard of civilization.' He saw 'very little ground' for the allegation that they had regressed, a common view amongst the planters.[68] Meanwhile, 'friends of the negro' in Jamaica argued that the real priority on the island was 'English energy, English habits, English enterprise, and good English morals'. The native population were 'prone to imitation' and desperately needed proper examples. They had been badly used by the planters, but would respond well to the right kind of help from England.[69] This was a familiar anti-slavery argument. There were good and bad Englishmen: the struggle over the negro was one site of the struggle between varieties of 'old Corruption' and a new moral world.

By the late 1850s even the most optimistic of anti-slavery supporters were discouraged. A plantation valued at about £80,000 during slavery sold for £500 in 1849.[70] Whatever might be said of the prosperity of the small producers and the dangers of too much attention to sugar, it was almost impossible for those honed to the discourse of free markets and large-scale industry to let go of the idea of the West Indies as a sugar bowl for Europe. Anything else was regression. Chamerovzow, the new secretary of the BFASS, compiled a report based on accounts from numerous correspondents, but heavily dependent on the views of the missionaries. There was alarming evidence, he was sorry to say, of immorality; labour was not attended to 'with that precision, regularity, vigour and despatch which distinguishes labour in England'; superstition had revived, for which African immigration was to blame; the towns were dens of iniquity, whereas the countryside was more mixed, particularly where ministers were resident; the upper classes provided no good examples. It was a common cry that expectations had been too high, and that the combined effects of sugar duties, taxes, immigration, cholera and the deaths of some key missionaries had meant less progress than had been hoped for amongst the emancipated. '[A] portion only have progressed; another portion appear to have stood still; while others have lost the ardour of their first love, and have gone back to the state in which they were before emancipation.'[71] James Mursell Phillippo, who was in England at this time, responded to the general gloom about Jamaica in the mother country by sending out a questionnaire to missionaries, proprietors, attornies and others across the island asking for their views on the state of life and labour. Again there were conflicting accounts, with hopeful reports of the condition of small freeholders from some missionaries, while planters commented on the indolence of labourers and their excessive demands for wages. They 'were little better than barbarians', said one, 'exhibiting their heathenish indulgences at their villages, especially at funerals', and knowing no churches or Sunday schools.[72]

The depressing accounts from Jamaica lent credence to the pro-slavery factions in their arguments that emancipation had been precipitate. *The Times*, a paper which had never been sympathetic to the cause, published a series of letters in its columns in late 1857, coinciding with the reaction to the 'Indian Mutiny'. 'Expertus' demanded attention to the wreck and ruin which Jamaica had become. It was a desert, with only a faint remnant of its former wealth: 'with towns at once filthy, noisome, and pathless; with mansions, once grand and stately, tottering to decay; with Jew tradesmen occupying the houses and mimicking the display of princely merchants; and with negro squatters parading their insolent idleness on lands which they have occupied without purchase, and exhausted without cultivation.' He insisted on challenging the cantings of Exeter Hall: 'the freed West-India negro slave will not till the soil for wages'. He was as obstinate as his enslaved father. The underlying message, as with Carlyle, was that only the whip would produce labour. He wished that some sensible Englishmen, 'just-minded, honest-hearted, and clear-sighted men', not parsons or dissenters or colonial officials, would go and see for themselves 'that precious *protégé* of English philanthropy, the freed negro, in his daily habits'. They would see him refusing to work except at ludicrous wages:

> they would watch him while, with a hide thicker than that of a hippopotamus, and a body to which fervid heat is a comfort rather than an annoyance, he droningly lounges over the prescribed task, on which the intrepid Englishman, unaccustomed and uninured to the burning sun, consumes his impatient energy, and too often sacrifices his life. I wish they would go out and view the negro in all the blazonry of his idleness, his pride, his ingratitude, contemptuously sneering at the industry of that race which made him free, and then come home to teach the memorable lesson of their experience to the fanatics who have perverted him into what he is.

The only negroes who were behaving acceptably, he argued, were those who had been enslaved, and slavery was the fashion of Africa. If white men left the West Indies, he believed, 'self-complacent negroes' would descend into barbarism. Cruelty to the African might be a bad thing, but 'cruelty to our own kith, kin, and countrymen' would be much worse; 'do not sacrifice English pith, toil and money to Quashee'.[73]

The Times refused to print an anti-slavery response to this letter, and published a leader commenting on the ineffectual nature of the blockade against the slave trade. This provoked a letter from Dr Livingstone arguing that the campaign against the slave trade had had real results. *The Times* followed this up with a leader on the contest that was to come over slavery and the slave trade, arguing that 'the battle over the negro' would be fought by the philanthropists with greatly diminished prestige, with their great leaders gone and their hopes blasted. Exeter Hall would have to eat humble pie, for 'politicians and the public, and even the friends of the slaves themselves, have now begun to see matters in a clearer light'. Slavery continued to be an efficient economic system, and slaves were needed to raise the cotton, sugar and tobacco which the world wanted. England could not stop it. Labour was needed in the West Indies, and 'our empire in the East may furnish the labourers', for coolies 'are ambitious and work for wages', while negroes 'go off and squat in remote districts, content to support life on a little'. If 'mutinous sepoys' had to be sent off somewhere, it might as well be to the sugar planta- tions.[74] In a further blast, a *Times* editorial argued that the emancipated had not become industrious, they did not make good labourers, the colonies were not more prosperous than slave-holding states. 'Negroes are free, but they are also brutalized,' and the West Indies were ruined. They repeated Carlyle's assertions that negroes were content to live at the level of beasts. It was clearly advantageous for Africans to be taken to countries where they could learn the dignity of labour and have access to civilisation and religion. Their capacity for elevation, however, remained in the eyes of *The Times* extremely dubious.[75]

Liberals and abolitionists were horrified by this onslaught. The *Anti-Slavery Reporter* appealed for friends to rally round, for it was clear that another anti-slavery battle would have to be fought. The *Morning Star* commented that the slave-holders in the South would be delighted. It was a 'startling revolution' in English journalism that 'an apology for slavery' should appear in such an influential newspaper.[76] A Presby- terian missionary just back from Jamaica, Rev. Robb, regretted that 'the enemy has been back at his old familiar trade of slander', and had the power to command 'the public ear' through the press, while black poeple themselves had no such access. He commented on Carlyle, *The Times* and the American press, and noted that Carlyle, 'in his own pecu- liar style . . . utters thoughts which, we fear, float through the minds of not a few genuine friends of Anglo-Ethiopia'.[77] This was an important recognition, that abolitionists were worried about the lack of industry of the emancipated, that with a part of themselves they wondered if 'the race' *was* prone to indolence, whether their expectations had been too high, their vision too utopian, whether the negro could rise to the same level of civilisation as a white person? Was 'the African' generically a 'lazy man'?[78]

The argument raged on throughout 1858. At a meeting of the NAPSS, Chamerovzow took the opportunity to read a paper on the effects of emancipation. This was a liberal gathering, yet he had to take on the case that 'the great experiment' had been a failure, and maintain a defen- sive position that there were hopeful signs of independence amongst the new wage-labourers, signs that labour was becoming the corner-stone of the economy, as it had to be in any modern society. Stephen Cave, the energetic chair of the West India Committee, wrote to *The Times* dis- puting Chamerovzow's evidence and arguing that the economic evidence of failure was clear in Jamaica, a letter which again elicited further cor- respondence.[79] Abolitionists knew that the question of racial superiority simmered in these debates. The special correspondent of *The Times* in India noted that one of the reasons for sympathy with the mutineers was 'our roughness of manner in our intercourse with the natives'. 'It is not a pleasing or popular task', he continued, 'to lay bare the defects of one's countrymen . . . I must say that I have been struck with the arrogant and repellent manner in which we often treat natives of rank, and with the unnecessary harshness of our treatment of inferiors.' 'Mean little representatives' of the white race saw themselves 'as infinitely superior to the Rajpoot with a genealogy of 1,000 years, or the Musselman whose ancestors served the early Caliphs.' 'We hate Slavery,' he concluded; 'we hate slaves too. . . . The habit of speaking of all natives as Niggers has recently become quite common.'[80]

Here was a crucial admission: the English hated slavery, a phrase much loved by abolitionists, but they also hated slaves. As a Jamaican Baptist missionary put it when reflecting on *The Times*, 'the old spirit of negro-hating seems to reign in many hearts'. 'Until men can be found that will treat the labourer as a fellow-man and a brother', he continued, it was vain to hope for better things.[81] But, furthermore, hatred and contempt were always potentially the other side of pity: even those who had pitied 'the poor negro' could not necessarily be relied on now that those 'poor negroes' were free.

'For good or evil', commented the *Baptist Magazine*, when publishing a selection from Carlyle's *Miscellaneous Essays*, 'they are perhaps the most influential of the day. . . . No-one doubts the extent and degree of their influence. Estimated, indeed, by the mere number of readers, many a foolish novelist and many a slipshod declaimer far outstrips him. But Carlyle acts upon the few who re-act upon the mass.'[82] This was indeed the crunch: the action on the few who reacted on the mass, and, it could be added, the setting of an agenda to which others had to respond. Not surprisingly, Baptists themselves were subject to this process. The editor of the *Baptist Magazine* looked forward to the day when 'we may attempt to disentangle the good and evil, the truth and falsehood, which are so strangely, almost inextricably, blended in his writings'.[83] A year later he published a piece by Carlyle on opera, with the approving note to his readers, that they would, he was sure, 'apply the pungent, biting sarcasm of this piece to many other frivolities and follies of the modern world, besides the opera'.

Carlyle's critique of opera sprang from his perception of its function in a world which lacked heroes. In this perverted society, opera was the 'appropriate heaven' of 'sweating tailors' and 'distressed needlewomen'. Those needlewomen were one of his constant preoccupations, a sign of what was wrong with the times, his preoccupation not one of sympathy but of hostility, to women in the wrong place. Carlyle's spleen and 'biting sarcasm' were focused on the 'shallow entertainment' which opera provided, when music should be 'the speech of angels'. The audience ogled each other rather than looking at the stage. The worst of these oglers was 'Prince Mahogany', tripping into the boxes of the ladies with his 'dyed mustachios and Macassar oil graciosity . . . Wretched spiritual nigger! Oh! If you had some genius, and were not a mere born nigger, with appetite for pumpkin.'[84] The 'biting sarcasm' of Carlyle's wit at the expense of the fashionable opera-going world, which was music to the ears of the Baptists, perhaps blinded them to the racism which undermined their own representations of the new Christian negro. Ideas of fellowship and brotherhood with negroes were indeed in decline; where such ideas survived, they were jostling in a discursive frame which assumed that races were different and unequal, there was no universal family.

In the spring of 1859 Charles Buxton, the official leader of the remaining abolitionists in the House of Commons, argued for a select committee on Jamaica. A new Immigration Bill had been proposed, and a new franchise introduced which raised qualifications for voters and thus further restricted the black vote.[85] He sought a full investigation. This was refused. In Birmingham a meeting was held to register a protest on the Immigration Bill, and William Morgan called for 'a determined stand by the people of England'. It was the 'duty of all Englishmen', he maintained, 'to protest'. Such calls, however, elicited little response.[86]

The arguments over immigration elicited more attacks from The Times' leader writers, complaining that the Anti-Slavery Society was interested in protecting 'the black population of the West Indies, not from oppression, but from competition'. The West Indian negro was now free, they insisted, free not to work if that was what he chose:

> Assuming the particular specimen of humanity conceived to be most unjustly dealt with, we must imagine a free and independent black squatting with his household on a bit of ground which, owing to the lack of tillage, he has come by pretty easily. His wants being remarkably few, and his indisposition to labour considerable, the balance of personal obligations leaves him at liberty to compress the whole duty of man into eating and sleeping.

Faced with the might of The Times, the incessant activity of Stephen Cave and the West India Committee, and the loss of their champion, Sturge, who died in 1859, the editor of the Anti-Slavery Reporter confessed to feeling 'like a pigmy in the hands of a Titan'.[87] But by the end of the year – the year which marked the twenty-fifth anniversary of emancipation – there was some hope that The Times was becoming more moderate in its tone. Cave, in a paper to the NAPSS, argued that emancipation had had some moral success, though economically it had been a failure. This paper was reprinted in *The Times* with a supportive leader which declared slavery to be a crime and argued that 'from England the conviction that slavery is a crime has passed to the Continent'. But the West Indies, it suggested, had become rather irrelevant, given the 'stupendous empire' which now existed, with the 'great colonies of Canada and Australia' and India 'fully conquered'.[88] Times had indeed changed.

George Dawson and the politics of race and nationalism

The midland metropolis had its own particular champion of Carlyle. George Dawson had come to Birmingham in 1844 as a young man of twenty-three, to minister to the small Baptist congregation in Mount Zion. Dr Hoby, an old friend and supporter of Knibb, an enthusiastic supporter of the missionary cause, and 'a not over-popular preacher', was ready to retire.[89] Dawson came from a Baptist family, his father kept a school, and his brothers and sisters all became teachers. After attending Glasgow University and teaching briefly, he tried the pulpit and found his metier. In Birmingham he quickly established himself as a powerful preacher, a brilliant public speaker and lecturer, 'the lion of Birmingham sermon-hunters'.[90] Dawson's theology was considerably more open than that of his Baptist congregation: his vision soon became that of a religious community that would rise above the bounds of sectarianism. From his first public appearances in Birmingham, he drew attention to the political responsibilites of Christian men, highlighting the state of the town and its poor residents, contrasting the sympathies for those far away, the 'Kaffir or Hottentot', with the neglect of those at home. His rapidly growing band of prosperous and fashionable middle-class followers built a new church for him in 1846, a church committed to a free spirit of inquiry and an open communion, and with a platform rather than a pulpit.[91]

By the late 1840s Dawson's reputation was spreading across the Midlands and the North. His extraordinarily handsome looks and 'mental magic' combined to make a considerable impact. A poet, a reader of *Punch*, a lover of 'manly exercises', a witty and sarcastic speaker, brave enough to flout convention and preach with a full moustache and beard, he was a very different kind of man from the strict dissenters of the previous generation. John Angell James was shocked by his 'lamentable departure from the straight and narrow way'.[92] In 1846 he gave a series of lectures, extensively reported in the provincial press, on the man who was to be the major influence on him throughout his life, Thomas

George Dawson. Dawson's handsome looks and charismatic style were part of his 'mental magic'.

Reproduced by permission of Birmingham Library Services.

Carlyle. Dawson claimed to act as nothing more than a 'humble sign-post' to the great Carlyle, presenting his master's thought in simple language with plenty of stories and characters. Men had lost faith 'in what a single stout heart and strong hand can accomplish', and there was a 'diseased loss of manhood, of self-reliance', he believed. One response was to live through and conquer self-doubt and difficulty, as Carlyle had done, and to celebrate heroes who provided models for life.[93] Carlyle's tortured prose and obscure ideas became in Dawson's rendition a new Anglo-Saxon common sense. In the view of many of his contemporaries, Dawson was by far the most effective single populariser of Carlyle's thinking; indeed, some of his critics saw him as entirely derivative of Carlyle, albeit spliced with a goodly dollop of Cobbett. For Charles Kingsley, Dawson was 'a kind of literary middle-man between writers like Carlyle and Ruskin and those ordinary English manufacturers, or merchants, or tradesmen, who like thought but like it well illustrated'.[94]

In 1848, Dawson, deeply affected by events in Europe, went with some of his congregation to Paris to see for himself what was going on. On his return, he determined to interpret the European revolutions to the Birmingham public. Unlike his mentor, Dawson was always a liberal, albeit of a rather Carlylean hue, since he believed that men wanted to be governed. Like his mentor, he did not believe in equality: 'Robinson Crusoe and his Man Friday were not equal,' he observed, and such differences were in the nature of things.[95] On his first coming to Birmingham, he had identified himself with the abolitionist elite in the town, and had joined the committee of the BFASS, the organisation founded by Sturge after emancipation. This membership lapsed, however, as his attention turned to race and nation as key concepts with which to rethink the crises of the late 1840s.[96] He believed in universal brotherhood, but, like Carlyle and Dickens before him, he castigated the abolitionists for focusing on abroad when there were many problems to be dealt with at home. His tone was markedly different from that of Sturge: 'the Chinese is a brother,' he maintained, 'though he does not believe the same religion, and does wear a queer tail behind him'.[97] In his 1849 lectures on Europe he argued that 'the doctrine of race meets us on every hand'. Europe was in the process of being reconstructed on racial lines, an entirely 'natural' development.[98] Some races, he argued, repeating a familiar story, were doomed to die out, but others, notably the Anglo-Saxons, were poised for further expansion.[99] 'No man with the Bible in his hand, and the history of the world to confirm it, can fail to see that it is God's will that one race shall overcome and thrust out another,' he maintained. It was hopeless to deny the findings of phrenology: 'Africa would never be a great country.' 'This principle of races is about to regulate the new division of Europe,' he asserted, and 'the square large-headed man does ever rule the world.' Drawing on the German Romantics who had so influenced Carlyle and were being interpreted to England by him, Dawson defined nation culturally, as those who speak the same language, are animated by the same literature, and ruled over by the same thinkers. His dream for the new Europe was that 'The nations and races would get themselves to themselves; that the Scandinavian people should have a clear territory and boundary; that the Slavonic race should draw themselves off; that Italy should be for the Italians, and the Teutons draw themselves into their great Teutonic clan; and then there would be peace'. Dawson's main emphasis was on race as a cultural category, but, in a society in which the language of biological difference was increasingly utilised, it was not difficult for slippage to occur both in his own thought, as in 'square large-headed men' ruling the world, and in common usage. Anglo-Saxons were culturally constituted as a special race descended from the Teutons and should occupy their empire. But negroes were all those with black skins.[100]

Like many of his generation, Dawson was a passionate supporter of European nationalisms, the romantic cause of the 1840s in the same way that anti-slavery had been the cause of the 1830s. Margot Finn argues that, from the spring of 1848, France was the centre of interest for the Chartists, but that for middle-class reformers it was the liberal and nationalist revolutions in Germany, Italy and Hungary which inspired them.[101] The French experiment was associated too much with social demands, which were more disturbing than the acceptable political demands being made in Germany, Italy, Hungary and Poland. 'We do dread', the *Birmingham Journal* remarked, 'the complete dissolution of the bonds by which society is held together; we do dread a continuous war of the classes.'[102] Dawson distinguished between the social and political causes of revolution. In a lecture on the French Revolution he reminded his audience that the work done by their Puritan forefathers meant that their basic liberties were secure. Whereas in the rest of Europe, great changes had to be brought about by force, in England the necessary measures could be carried by 'simple open speech', and 'manly fair reasoning'.[103] Middle-class reformers were keen on the moderation of Hungarian patriotism. Hungarian reformers had abolished feudalism, expanded the franchise, and established religious toleration and free speech.

It was Dawson who organised the committee to bring Kossuth, the exiled Hungarian leader of the 1848 revolution, on a triumphant visit to Birmingham in 1851. The town showed its admiration for Kossuth by mounting the largest demonstration since the days of the Birmingham Political Union, celebrating the brotherhood of lovers of freedom. 'The old heart of the men of Birmingham,' reported the *Birmingham Journal*, 'which beat warmly in the days of the Reform Bill, has been reanimated.'[104] Nearly all the factories in the town were closed, and a procession of between 60,000 and 70,000 men met Kossuth at Small Heath and escorted him to the town centre. There were six bands; flags, banners

and trade symbols were on display, and the Hungarian tricolour was flut-
tering all over the town.[105] But the brotherhood that was being celebrated
rested on an exclusive racial basis. Kossuth claimed to represent 'all who
are oppressed'. But his 'all' was strictly limited. On his grand tour of the
United States, he refused to come out against slavery, to the disgust of
the American anti-slavery groupings, and his vision of Hungarian independence was one which was exclusively Magyar – the type of pure racial
grouping that represented the new Europe to Dawson.[106]

Fuelled by the belief that 'all civilised nations which are capable
of governing themselves should be allowed to do so', Dawson established
a standing committee in Birmingham to watch and support small
nations, especially Poland, Hungary and Italy.[107] This was a brotherhood
of whiteness: there was no question of female suffrage, and the assumption was that Polish, Hungarian and Italian men were already 'civilised'
and capable of governing themselves. For Dawson, like the majority of
his compatriots, did not think that all nations were ready for self-
government. 'Nations at different times have need of different kinds of
government,' he argued; 'a childlike nation may need a strong government', and 'a nation emerging from barbarism must have a strong government'.[108] The struggles of some nations to establish themselves
became a central preoccupation for him: nations were made up of individuals, but constituted, as it were, a higher form of life, a collective
life.[109] Reform of the individual and of the nation were vitally connected.
It was perhaps Mazzini, the Italian nationalist, who benefitted most from
these efforts: with his emphasis on duties over rights and his denunciation of social conflict, he was a sympathetic figure for middle-class liberals.[110] In May 1851 the Friends of Italy was established, coinciding
with the Papal Aggression Controversy (provoked by the reinstatement
of the Catholic hierarchy in England), which raised strong feelings in
Birmingham as elsewhere, and facilitated the mobilisation of anti-
Catholic and dissenting support. Enthusiasm was widespread, with the
cause of Italian liberation becoming 'the gospel of a generation': in Birmingham there was active support, particularly from women, well into the
1860s, first for Mazzini, then for Garibaldi.[111]

But nationalism for Dawson was not just a matter of abroad. Nationalisms started at home, and the major trajectory of his speaking from
the late 1840s was a celebration of England's past and a plea for a great
national future. As early as 1845, Charles Kingsley, a passionate Anglo-
Saxonist, had proposed a vote of thanks for a lecture that Dawson gave
on the subject in Hastings, thanking him for his noble 'oration', which
had been 'expressed in the purest and simplest Saxon he had ever heard'.
In a series of lectures on English history, English literature, Anglo-Saxons
and great men – Shakespeare, Cromwell, Drake, 'Old John Bunyan',

Milton, Nelson, Wellington, Coleridge, Cobbett, Lord Palmerston, Cobden – and even one great woman, Queen Elizabeth, who, he argued, was like a man, he celebrated the race. In language that was frequently described as 'pure Saxon', for he was careful to use no words of classical or Norman derivation when a pure Saxon equivalent was to be had, with his sentences simple and uninvolved and making use of inversion, he was 'a very Cobbett in English style', and, like Cobbett, he loved all that he construed as part of the great English tradition.[112]

A belief in the unique qualities of the Anglo-Saxon race and the superiority of Anglo-Saxon institutions was widespread by the 1850s. The term was used to refer both to peoples living within the boundaries of England and to a brotherhood of English-speaking peoples throughout Britain and the world.[113] The initial response to the Crimean War was to welcome it as a struggle against despotism which was likely to have good effects for oppressed nations. Birmingham established its own Patriotic Fund in 1854, of which William Morgan was the secretary.[114] But, as the war progressed, the reports on the state of the army aroused much criticism and an attack on administrative centralisation. Such criticisms gave a great impetus to ideas of local self-government and provincial responsibilities. There was tremendous enthusiasm for these ideas in Birmingham, where men such as Joshua Toulmin Smith and J. A. Langford were eloquent on the importance of local traditions and the liberties of the free men of England.[115] David Urquhart led a national movement calling for government and ministers to return to a notion of personal responsibility to the crown and the people, arguing that local institutions were much older than Parliament. This movement, as Olive Anderson argues, did particularly well in the West Midlands, and Urquhart lived in Birmingham in 1854–5, relying on Dawson as one of his major supporters.[116]

Such ideas meshed with the widely held belief that the Anglo-Saxon folk-moot provided the origin of English political liberties. Carlyle, Reginald Horsman argues, was the first to view Saxon triumphs as the product of racial superiority: for him, Anglo-Saxonism became fused with racial thinking. The Saxons were part of the great Teutonic race, and 'He saw in the vigor of that race a transforming power in the world'.[117] The destiny of 'this great and wonderful people', Carlyle claimed, was 'first to conquer half the planet, and then show "all people" how the fruits of conquest might be effectively enjoyed'.[118] By the late 1840s, George Stocking Jr argues, the idea of an Anglo-Saxon race was an intellectual commonplace, but the focus was on hereditary and common culture, not biology.[119] Dawson enthusiastically took up these ideas, believing that 'if there was a world's work to be done, England had to do it'.[120] This provided a new twist to the established evangelical notion of the providential responsibilities of Britons. England, in Dawson's view, was 'the last of the chosen nations', and Anglo-Saxons were special partly because of the mixing which had contributed to their make-up. Emigration, he saw as a crucial response to English economic problems. 'We people the earth,' he argued; it is 'our English climate which makes hard-working men, conscious of the dignity of labour . . . We stand in order that others may learn from us.'[121] Furthermore, the particular gift of the English was their capacity to father new nations: the Greeks had created colonies, but had not had the capacity to reproduce themselves, as the English had done in the United States and Australia. 'We girdled the world round', he believed, 'by English speech, laws and institutions, by a laborious, industrious, judicious, money loving but true hearted race.'[122]

For Dawson each race had its allotted time. It was providential that neither the 'red man' nor the Aborigine could be saved. But the negroes, despite the accursed system of slavery, continued to increase and multiply, and still had their time to come. The negro of his imagination was the docile, obedient, domesticated and effeminised negro: 'their gentle, obedient, womanly natures had yet a work to do in the world God appointed, and no power could destroy that race'.[123] But his denunciation of slavery did not stop him from celebrating Hawkins as a national hero, in what he described as that most intensely national time, the time of Good Queen Bess. Unlike Phillippo, who in his book on Jamaica had distinguished between the stain of slavery and the cleansing of that stain associated with emancipation, Dawson made no attempt to separate himself from Elizabeth's grateful recognition of Hawkins's services in developing the slave trade, symbolised by her gift of a crest representing the negro, that new source of wealth and power. Yet he felt moved to remark that there was no justification for the way in which the English had suppressed the Irish rebellion. The Irish were one matter, black people another.[124] In Dawson's discourse, 'the poor negro' had been displaced by gentle, obedient and effeminate creatures; yet they were also 'ugly savages' for him, as in his chance remarks on Africans fitted with the nose-rings, ear-rings and ankle-rings from the jewellery trades of Birmingham.[125] Whereas old-time abolitionists continued to stress the chain of hierarchical connections linking them to their younger brothers and sisters, Dawson was more likely to focus on the distinctions between races.

Carlyle believed in the rule of the strong over the weak, of leaders over slaves.[126] He was horrified by the idea of manhood suffrage, and believed in separate spheres and the mastery of men over women. He was never involved in party politics, though he made celebrated public interventions, as in 1866 over Governor Eyre. Dawson, on the contrary, was actively involved in the hurly-burly of Birmingham politics. He was a great supporter of John Bright (who became Liberal MP for the town in 1857), and later of Joseph Chamberlain. From the heartlands of liberalism, therefore, Dawson articulated new discourses of race and nation, linking liberty and freedom with Anglo-Saxonism and European nationalisms. Seemingly incompatible and contradictory elements were forged by Dawson into a distinctive creed. The focus now was on the liberties of free men at home and in Europe. 'Mere parochial patriotism' was no longer enough, and Dawson encouraged the men of the midland metropolis to turn their eyes to continental Europe. In this sense he challenged a provincial mentality, and had an inclusive notion of who should enjoy the rights and duties of citizenship: but it was white men who were included in this frame.[127] He was a stalwart of the working man and parliamentary reform. He also represented himself as a supporter of women's rights, in that women should be properly educated and find appropriate work if necessary. But there was nothing more disturbing, he believed, than an effeminate man or a masculine woman. Always called 'the master' at home, Dawson's household was a classic family enterprise, with his wife and sister-in-law editing his sermons and publishing books for children. He had no time for feminists 'squeaking about their rights', any more than he believed that negroes or Indians were ready to govern themselves.[128] Dawson was indeed 'a thorough Englishman, proud of his country and its story'.[129]

Troubles for the missionary public

While Dawson and his allies were preoccupied with questions of Anglo-Saxonism and oppressed European nationalities, the Birmingham missionary public remained focused on 'the heathen'. The declaration of independence by the Jamaica Baptist Union, together with the decline of interest, and of hope, in the West Indies, meant that missionary attention turned to India in the 1850s. The BMS annual meetings in 1850 provided an opportunity for a plea for renewed interest in the mission there, after the excitements associated with emancipation. The Rev. Baptist Noel argued that:

> India was a part of the British empire. The Hindoos were our fellow-subjects. . . . The Hindoos were the slaves of the most complicated super-stition the world had ever seen, and a superstition that had degraded them. Their gods were monsters. Their books were legends of impurity. Their priests were their leaders in all iniquity. Caste was a diabolical chain, holding them in servitude, inertness of mind, and foul superstition.

But Hindoos were unable to resist 'British greatness'; they found the English superior in intellect, morals, civilisation and domestic happiness.[130] It was essential that the British send more missionaries. The following year the annual meetings again provided an opportunity to attempt to revivify work in India, as well as the idea of India at home. The Rev. Makepeace, a Birmingham man now in India, urged his audience to do by India as they had done by Jamaica: the triumphs, he promised, would be even greater. 'Remember', he argued, 'that we and its people are emphatically brethren, – that we have an identity of origin, being of the same Caucasian family, and this identity is proved by marked physical characteristics, as well as strong affinities of language'. The emphasis on the Caucasian connection was new, a mark of the interest in new forms of racial thinking. Africans could never claim this connection. Indians and British were, furthermore, fellow subjects, and 'one fraternal bond should encircle us'. The British owed a debt of gratitude for the indigos, silks, sugars and teas from India which 'we' had enjoyed, and the Hindoos were a cultivated race. 'India', he concluded, 'has been given to Britain . . . that through the power of Britain's Christianity she might be enlightened, elevated and saved. India is Britain's glory.'[131]

Makepeace was in Birmingham in July 1851, and made a big impact on his audience. He chided the churches for their 'imperturbable indifference', and invited his listeners to imagine themselves, 'the inhabitants of this noble town of Birmingham, the rising midland metropolis of our noble England', with their numbers multiplied fourfold and only one missionary to bring them the Gospel. This was a scandal and must be rectified. A fund was established to build a new mission house at Agra in the wake of this meeting.[132] In his farewell address in Birmingham in March of the following year, before he returned to India, Makepeace expressed his anxieties as to the lack of an 'earnest missionary spirit', the experience of speaking in half-empty churches, or, just as disturbing, churches which were full only because 'multitudes had come to gaze on the missionary as though he were a rare specimen from the ecclesiastical menagerie, or listen to the thrilling recital of hair-breadth escapes and strange adventures among barbarous and savage tribes'.[133] Birmingham was pleased to be able to announce, however, a very successful run of missionary meetings, with numbers and funds up. 'Missionary societies were the glory of this country,' the chair of the AGM, Henry Wright, was delighted to be able to say. It was possible to point to many islands, once peopled by savages, which were now populated by peaceful and happy races.[134] Birmingham was proud of its contribution to these transformations.

Work abroad, however, could not be prioritised at the expense of efforts at home. At the annual meetings in 1852 the Rev. Stanford declared that he had no time for the 'morbid benevolence' that 'would drop a tear for the distant heathen, and neglect the heathen in the next street'. It was important that they did not neglect 'the strange tribes of men who inhabit the unknown regions of our own metropolis'.[135] William Morgan agreed with him. In the mid-1840s he had been greatly occupied, as was Sturge, with the question of suffrage. From 1846, again with his mentor Sturge, he became interested in industrial schools and reformatories. The inhabitants of Birmingham had become alarmed by the numbers of 'juvenile outcasts' in the town, and there was considerable interest in ways of dealing with this problem. In 1851 Mary Carpenter organised a conference in Birmingham on reformatory schools, which both Sturge and Morgan attended along with Matthew Davenport Hill. 'The soul of the little ragged urchin in the streets', as the report of the conference put it,

> is as precious in the sight of God as that of a Hindoo or a Hottentot, and a saving conversion in the one case causes as great joy in heaven as in the other. Do not let us, then, leave the heathen abroad uncared for, but let us, likewise endeavour to reclaim the heathen perishing at home, and who are living in darkness as profound, and in habits as debased as in the darkest places of the heathen world.[136]

A year later Sturge opened his own school in Edgbaston, and in 1853 he greatly extended this venture in the country. It was an experiment in the provision of care for children who were seen as victims rather than in need of punishment: the regime was intended to be familial, with the superintendents acting as substitute parents.[137] Morgan lectured on these questions in Ireland in 1847, and was involved with the establishment of a similar reformatory at Saltley.[138]

Morgan was a prominent figure in the town, well known for his philanthropic and reforming ventures, his mission and chapel activities, his legal and political work. He acted on numerous voluntary bodies and was constantly on platforms for good causes. Perhaps it was his wife Henrietta, the daughter of a Nailsworth cloth manufacturer, whom he had married in 1841, though she rarely appears in public records, who made possible this ceaseless round of activity.[139] He was the joint secretary of the Birmingham Reformatory Institution, and in 1853 delivered an address to the Young Men's Christian Association which linked the themes of mission work at home and abroad and was entitled *The Arabs of the City*. Opening with an appeal for an outstretching of the hand of Christian brotherhood to 'the vicious and criminal', a plea for connection with 'the outcast', he argued that it was the absence of family ties which enabled the descent into criminality: married parents, he believed, did not bring up their children to infamy. Rescue, therefore, depended on the construction of alternative families, led by brotherhoods, which would provide safe environments for lost souls. Morgan quoted at length from his friend Matthew Davenport Hill's evidence to a select committee on the character of the criminal. Hill, himself a judge in Birmingham, had been appointed the town's first recorder in 1839. Like Morgan, he had intimate connections with colonial ventures, particularly through his family in South Australia. Hill painted a vivid portrait of the criminal, drawing on racial categories, particularly those associated with Aboriginal peoples. The criminal, in his mind, was

> indolent – averse from any settled or steady employment – averse from restraint of any kind – on the other hand, he is patient of hunger and thirst and cold – and as to dirt, he rather delights in it than otherwise . . . he would much rather be permitted to roam about at large, even suffering at times great privations, than he would be at school or at work, under the restraints which belong to civilised society.

For Morgan, who was most familiar with representations of the West Indian negro or the 'Hindoo', this image was translated to the Orient. 'This strikes me', he argued, 'as being the true picture of an Arab,' though he did not propose to follow out and illustrate the points of resemblance between 'savage life' and 'the characteristics of our criminal population'. He further quoted Macaulay's evocative description of the 'perishing and dangerous classes' as 'the human vermin which, neglected by ministers of state and ministers of religion, barbarous in the midst of civilization, heathen in the midst of Christianity, burrows amid all physical and all moral pollution, in the cellars and garrets of great cities'. For Hill, 'our criminal population' was characterised as 'a race apart', indolent, refusing restraint, unclean, yet susceptible to kindness, all evocative of other representations of 'savage' peoples. Morgan's 'Arab' was then further embroidered with Macaulay's notions of 'the human vermin' which was rotting the very fabric of the nation. Such dangers within required drastic action. Morgan went on to advocate reformatory schools which could act as industrial training asylums for 'little heathens'. Children should be given 'a bare sufficiency' of food and the 'decencies' of clothing. They should be taught religion and morality, 'the rudiments of ordinary education', habits of cleanliness, industry and order. They should learn the lessons of the home as well as those of the school, and on the importance of this he cited Mary Carpenter. He believed that the philanthropist, the political economist and the Christian missionary should join together in this project and see suffering relieved, pernicious energies turned to industry, and hearts and minds opened for the Gospel.[140] 'Little heathens' were not really different under the skin.

Given the increasing emphasis in the wider society on distinctions between races, the missionary world was at pains in the 1850s to reiterate the message of universality. Phillippo, just emerging successfully from his conflicts with his congregation in Spanish Town and once more able to speak confidently on the human family, reminded his British as well as his Jamaican audience in 1854 of the sameness of black and white. A public meeting had been held in Calabar after the annual examination of the students, and Phillippo, who had examined the young men in classics, was pleased to be able to report that they were well grounded educationally and had responded to the questions intelligently rather than mechanically. This demonstrated the fact that, 'though skins may differ, yet intellect, as well as affection, dwells in black and white the same'.[141] This was part of his appeal for more funds to sustain the college. Isaac Lord, speaking on the need for further work in India, commented on the missionary practice of seeking access to the hearts of Indian mothers through their children, and reiterated the message of universality. 'Human nature is the same all the world over,' he maintained; 'if it were not, I should really begin to think that there were some truth in those bold speculations which will have it that God has *not* made of one blood all nations for to dwell upon the face of the earth.'[142]

Visions of the sameness of human nature and of India as the most exciting field of missionary action, with its 'ancient civilisation', its venerable religion and 'powerful system of idolatry', yet its potential audience for the Christian message, were to come under serious attack during 1857.[143] Just before the news of the 'Mutiny' arrived in Britain, Underhill, the secretary of the BMS, had returned from a deputation to India to report to the committee on the mission there. The context was one of considerable concern as to the state of the mission, with the missionary societies all suffering from stationary, if not declining, incomes.[144] This was explained by the BMS committee in terms of the rapid increase in ventures at home, the multiplication of philanthropic institutions, increasing taxation and living costs, but, most alarmingly, the 'intense desire for wealth' and 'love of show' which had seized both middle and lower classes.[145] Whatever the reasons, the stationary income led them to reflect on the importance of the original spirit of their founders, who had insisted on sowing the seeds and then relying on native agency. The BMS should be teaching self-reliance, not dependence on Europeans, while at the same time Europeans should continue to be the directors of operations.

Underhill had been concerned over the issue of native agency for some time, a concern which his predecessors had shared. Clearly it provided the only way of securing a stable future, but in the eyes of Englishmen there were many difficulties attached to it. In 1852 he had written a paper for the BMS committee which explored the issue. 'It must be admitted', he wrote,

> that in the early stages of their Christian profession, the immaturity of the converts, the presence of evil habits acquired in a state of heathenism, idolatry, and perhaps savageism, their ignorance and imperfect apprehension of the Gospel, may and do require judicious treatment from the missionary, and demand from him great watchfulness, sagacity, and incessant instruction.

The assumption was that white missionaries would always be in a position to offer such guidance, an assumption rooted in the certainty of the superior qualities of English culture. It was impossible for the English missionary, Underhill argued, to enjoy 'fraternal intercourse and equality of sympathy' with his congregation, characteristics which were central to a proper pastoral relation, since in India the English were conquerers and 'lords of the soil', whereas in Jamaica, 'among the negro races their superior intelligence and civilisation place them at an almost immeasurable distance from the rude habits, the confined thoughts, and the limited knowledge of the people'. It was out of the question that native convert and English missionary could entertain each other, since both would feel out of place. This meant that the talk and exchange of opinion 'which constitutes pre-eminently the bond of brotherhood and fellowship in the Church of Christ' could never be enjoyed. This was a frank admission of the inequalities which underpinned the universalism of missionary discourse. Underhill looked forward to the development of different forms of Christianity in East and West, forms which they did not yet know, drawing on 'the uncivilised tribes of Africa' and 'the polished Hindoos', and which 'may display virtues which have been very imperfectly developed among the cultured races of Christendom'. It was clear that he did not know what these would be. Despite these problems, he was convinced that native agency must be encouraged, that it was a more financially viable long-term policy, and that the dependency of native agents on the missionaries was not desirable.[146]

These questions were in his mind as he travelled around India in 1856. His report was cautiously encouraging. 'If the lamp burn feebly,' he commented, 'it must not be forgotten how recently the people have emerged from a form of heathenism the most degrading and most demoralizing the world has ever seen'.[147] But he was seriously concerned by the dependency on the missionaries, which seemed so hard to shake off, and did not cease 'even in manhood'. The native agents were encountering many problems, and he found 'a want of moral strength . . . in the general national character', a lack which was 'fatal to the growth of . . . self-reliance'.[148]

Weeks later it began to be apparent that 'heathenism' and 'superstition' had not been thrown off, and that self-reliance was being expressed in forms fatal to the missionaries. One Baptist missionary, one missionary wife together with her daughter, and one native agent were killed in the 'Mutiny', the last reportedly 'hacked to death'.[149] Early reports from the missionaries in India focused on Satan's 'great rage' because he believed 'his time in India is short', and argued that 'the disaffection of the native troops has originated in their dread of the growing power of Christianity'. This remained the frame for missionary thinking on the 'Mutiny': it was a religious affair, 'a revolt against the changes in the national usages, institutions, and religions of Hindustan which British dominion and an evangelical Christianity have inevitably brought in their train'. For a brief time 'the ark of the Lord' had been in peril, and 'the grandest empire the world has ever known' was 'shaken to its very foundations'. Such events had 'even stirred the apathetic minds of the impassive peoples of Asia'.[150] Alongside this conviction that Christianity had threatened 'idolatry' was the view of the missionaries and their public that the 'Mutiny' was a divine punishment. The East India Company had been lukewarm in its support of the missions, and India had not had enough Christianity. The atrocities were hardly surprising, given the terrible traditions of physical abuse associated with the worship of Hindu idols which had continued to be tolerated.[151]

For months there was great reluctance to admit popular involvement; there had been 'no rising of the people'. Mohammedans had shown sympathy with the rebels and great hatred for the English, but the latter was nothing new. Hindus had been 'quiet spectators' of the rebellion, 'passive sufferers of the violence of armed men'. In September 1857 the editor of the *Missionary Herald* hoped for a good outcome: 'Confidence in idols will be shaken to the very foundation; rightly or wrongly the people of India will be inclined to attribute the success of the British arms in suppressing the revolt . . . to the superiority of Christianity.'[152] Such confidence might have been put to the test in the reports of their own agents. Shortly before he was killed, the Rev. J. Mackay, who had only recently arrived in India, wrote to the BMS describing Delhi, a city heavily influenced by Islam. The 'proud Mohammedan', he remarked, 'long accustomed to rule the country, can ill brook the British sway'. 'Our friends at home', he continued,

> can with difficulty conceive the kind of people with whom we have to deal. It is not a number of rude and savage men who are overawed with the consciousness of their own inferiority, and extend to us a deference which no one can withhold if he would from superior intelligence. But the people among whom we labour, are civilised and refined even to extravagance.

They are not only a people whose understandings have been perverted and moral perceptions blunted to such a degree that they believe themselves to be our superiors in most things, and with difficulty acknowledge their inferiority in anything but *bravery* . . . it is a startling fact, that the descendants of Europeans in this country, are unable to compete with the natives when placed side by side with them in our schools and colleges.[153]

This was indeed a startling fact for readers of the *Missionary Herald*, who were in no way prepared for the possibility that Indians might do better at school than Europeans, or for the notion that they might consider themselves and their culture superior to that of the West. These were difficult ideas to grasp, given the discourse of European superiority which was so deeply embedded in the British missionary venture. Any possibility that such thoughts might provoke serious self-doubt was crushed by the news which began to arrive of the events at Cawnpore. The talk now was only of massacre, of 'diabolical plots', of 'Mohammedan conspiracy', of 'horrid reality, so hideous, so fiendish', of 'atrocities unparalleled in the domestic annals of the English nation'. 'How little we know of the heart of the native' was the cry on every lip. The object now was clearly seen to be 'the utter extermination of the European population, and the overthrow of the British government'. There could be no reliance on the loyalty of either Moslems or Hindus; 'the only truly loyal section of the community are the Europeans, the Eurasians, and the native Christians'. Out of this crisis came the recognition that 'the Christian people of England must arise', that they, alongside the British government, had seriously neglected their duties in India, and that the East India Company policy 'of fostering caste, treating the abominations of idolatry with respect, showing favour to the bigotry of Mohammedanism, and tolerating the foul obscenities of the Hindoo temples, has been perfected, so to speak, in the organisation of the Sepoy army'.[154] East India Company rule had been a disaster. The way was open for direct rule.

The conclusion of the wider Birmingham public was much the same. John Bright, the town's new MP, was elected in the wake of the 'Mutiny'. The town chose a national rather than a local figure, a statement from the midland metropolis of their municipality's significance in the politics of the nation. Bright was a major political figure: a free-trade agitator and the architect with Cobden of the Anti-Corn Law League, a Quaker and pacifist, a middle-class reformer and a Manchester man. He had lost his seat in Manchester on account of his unpopular pacifism and anti-Crimean politics, and was invited to Birmingham, provided he would support the suppression of the 'Mutiny'. This he was prepared to do, though he had long been concerned with what he saw as the bad government of India, and had been active in the formation of the India Reform Association in 1853. In 1857 he saw the best hope for India as lying in the abolition of the East India Company.[155] The India question was 'a swamp', he wrote to Joseph Sturge; 'England cannot govern distant nations – our statesmen have no time and no principles.' He hoped that eventually India would enjoy some free institutions, for the first principle of empire to his mind, as James Sturgis argues, was that Britain should prepare the colonies for self-government.[156] Bright thought of himself as a Colonial Reformer and the colonies as sharing a common destiny, but the model here was the colonies of white settlement. Anglo-Saxons across the empire were one race, they shared common traditions and could look towards a common democratic future. Bright favoured more independence for these colonies: a shift that was steadily taking place between the 1840s and the 1860s as Canada, Australia and New Zealand all gained representative government.

A meeting of Birmingham Liberals was held to decide on Bright's candidature. J. S. Wright, a prominent supporter of the missionary cause and leading Baptist in the town, argued: 'If there was any man fully capable of contributing to the real glory of the British people, who would develop the resources and energy of the Indian Empire, and raise the sleeping capacities of the Hindoo, that man was Mr. John Bright.'[157] Here the people (interestingly British, rather than the usual English), the empire and the civilising mission to raise 'the sleeping Hindoo' were all in play, as Wright joined Sturge and Dawson, from their different positions, in support of Bright. All were united in the conviction that the rebellion must be suppressed, and that rule from London offered the best hope for the colonised. Baptists, Quakers and free-thinking nonconformist men were united in their intervention in mainstream politics, a move from the margins toward the centres of national life. And as these men moved from margins to centre, their mapping of empire shifted, and their sense of distance from those once enslaved or Indian mutineers increased. The right kind of white men, whether in Canada, Australia or Europe, could be relied on to form responsible governments: subordinate peoples, for their own good, should be ruled from London.

By the end of the 1850s Birmingham was no longer a stronghold of 'friends of the negro'. As enthusiasm for the great experiment of emancipation waned, the news from Jamaica was of decadence and distress, and events in continental Europe took centre-stage; new voices emerged – those of Carlyle and Dawson in particular – celebrating different versions of national identity. Carlyle's 'Occasional Discourse' marked a watershed: it represented a discursive break with the hegemony of universalism. Like Enoch Powell's 'Rivers of Blood' speech in Birmingham in 1968, it spoke the unspeakable, and changed the discursive terrain.[158] Dawson's articulation of Carlylean racial thinking to his version of liberalism contributed to new ideas of town, nation and empire in the 1860s and beyond. At the same time, some abolitionists had lost faith, and the optimistic visions of the late 1830s looked tarnished in the wake of the 'Mutiny'. Britons might indeed hate slavery, but their enthusiasm for racialised others was strictly limited.

7
Town, Nation and Empire 1859–1867

ᘒᘖ

New times

In May 1859 Joseph Sturge died: both Birmingham and Jamaica paid tribute. A large funeral was held in Birmingham, and Sturge's old friends John Angell James and Thomas and William Morgan were there. 'He was a Christian, a patriot and a philanthropist,' said James. He had crossed continents and oceans, sacrificed domestic comfort and ease, given his money, his time and his labour to 'the cause of our common humanity'. His home and family had provided the base for all this. A meeting was held to discuss what memorial the town might establish, and in 1862 a statue and fountain were unveiled, with John Bright, amongst others, celebrating his life and work. 'His generous nature', said the mayor, 'knew no distinctions between the different sections of God's great family.'[1] Dawson, meanwhile, noted that he was 'fond of negroes and all other sorts of low and unlovely people . . . a most impracticable man', with 'many nobly impossible and sublimely absurd ideals'.[2] Phillippo's churches in Jamaica sent an appreciative address to his family. He had been an unwavering advocate of the emancipated peasantry, defending 'their rights as men and as British subjects', and they honoured him for it. They were particularly aware of his generosity in visiting the West Indies, and they linked him with Clarkson, Wilberforce and Buxton as 'the noblest and best friends of the African race that history records'. He had devoted himself not only to the abolition of slavery but also to the raising of the African, 'by Christian education, to that rank in the scale of being, of which by his circumstances and condition he had been so unjustly deprived'.[3] As the obituary in the *Anti-Slavery Reporter* said, Sturge had fought unceasingly against pro-slavery sentiment, and in recent years had been the life and soul of the anti-slavery movement. He had recognised 'that although Great Britain had washed her hands of the slave trade and of slavery, the old pro-slavery spirit in her colonies was not extinct, and that it would constantly suggest measures of a tendency to oppress the coloured people; hence that unceasing vigilance would be necessary'.[4] Sturge had been willing personally to maintain that vigilance in the spirit of universalism, articulated through a benevolent patriarchal politics.

The LNFS in Birmingham, of which Hannah Sturge, his second wife, and other female relatives were stalwarts, decided to raise money for a memorial to the work which he had facilitated in Jamaica. 'One of the most desirable things to be impressed on the people was a sense of the value of time,' they reflected; this meant understanding how time passed. Clocks and bells would be an appropriate gift, for in some areas bells were needed to call children to school from a distance. Six bells and four clocks, all suitably inscribed, were sent off to Jamaica, a gift to encourage 'civilization'.[5] John Clark in Brown's Town was thrilled when his bell arrived. 'The bell has come', he wrote;

> It is a noble one, and will send its voice across the valleys, and to the distant hills around Sturge Town. I hope to get it mounted, and to begin its work by calling together the people for a Missionary meeting. The people who have seen it are delighted with it. The clock, I trust, will teach the people at Bethany a lesson which they greatly need – to be punctual.[6]

Sturge's great national achievement had been the abolition of apprenticeship, the campaign for which he had spearheaded from outside the political mainstream. From the late 1830s Sturge had been increasingly occupied with domestic politics, from the Corn Laws to the rights of the poor in Birmingham, Chartism and complete suffrage. He stood unsuccessfully for Parliament three times, twice in his home town, but was too radical for the voters. From the mid-1840s, Alex Tyrrell argues, he had moved away from parliamentary politics to a politics that could be implemented by individuals and voluntary societies, believing that it would be possible to lead the world into 'a new era of peace and perfectability' in this way.[7] In the 1850s he was associated with a number of unpopular causes: toleration for the re-establishment of the Catholic hierarchy in Britain, a pacifist stand on the Crimea, and a critical perspective on the British in India. He was deeply shocked by the response to the 'Mutiny' and the vengeful spirit which it produced. The *Birmingham Journal*, for example, reported seeing toy sepoys with wire collars round their necks on sale to the children of Birmingham at a fair.[8] But his unfashionable politics did not dent his reputation as a man of outstanding honour and principle in the town, and Birmingham prided itself on its loyalty to its famous sons, whether fully in agreement with their politics or not.[9] Shortly before his death, Sturge, still deeply interested in the future of the West Indies, invested in land in Montserrat, hoping to be able to demonstrate that enterprising capitalists could make money there: a policy that was to be taken up by a key Birmingham politician of the next generation, Joseph Chamberlain.[10]

The same year John Angell James, another veteran of the anti-slavery struggle, died. James had never had the scale of involvement with the West Indies that Sturge did, but he had been a stalwart supporter and a great friend to missionary work; thus his death meant that another senior figure in Birmingham associated with the cause had gone. His funeral was a major public event for the town, with tens of thousands lining the streets to show their respect. His co-pastor and successor, R. W. Dale, gave the oration, and celebrated the man who had championed the causes of evangelicalism and missionary work. The popularity of his most famous text, *The Anxious Enquirer after Salvation*, which told of the struggle for conversion, equalled, it was said, that of *Pilgrim's Progress*.[11] A great preacher with a central belief in the power of the Gospel, his church, in the widest sense, had been his family.[12] His collected sermons were published soon after his death, alongside his *Life and Letters*. These provided opportunities to celebrate his 'vigorous, clear, Saxon intellect'. Here was a man who preached with feeling and imagination, who made direct appeals to the heart. A man without genius, 'surprising originality', or 'extensive scholarship', but one who, nevertheless, in his practicality and English common sense, had achieved great things.[13] His politics were very different from those of Sturge, for he was an 'old Whig', opposed to any extension of the franchise, deeply intolerant of Catholicism, and with a profoundly conservative view of relations between the sexes.[14] He did, however, vote for Bright, on account of his views on anti-slavery and nonconformity. But missionary work had always been integral to his evangelicalism, and the idea of the Christian family of man linked these two men, both children of the late eighteenth century.

James's successor at Carrs Lane, R. W. Dale, was a man of another generation. Born in 1829, the son of a dealer in hat trimmings, he had felt James's influence on him from his adolescence, when he read his mentor's *Anxious Enquirer*, 'on my knees and in keen distress about my personal salvation'.[15] His mother had long desired that he should be a minister, and at seventeen, after experience in Sunday school work and in preaching and teaching, he was accepted at Spring Hill College, the training school for Congregational ministers inspired by James. In Birmingham he came under the influence of Dawson, a man only eight years older than himself who had already made a reputation as a leading preacher and lecturer, radical in his refusal of sectarian orthodoxies. Dawson insisted on the importance of ethical and social responsibilities, and was hostile to evangelicalism, which he saw as narrow and limiting in its effects. Part of Dale's particular contribution, complementary to that of Dawson, was to link questions of social responsibility to an evangelical faith, through the notion of Christian citizenship.[16]

James took to Dale, and in 1853 the young man became James's assistant at Carrs Lane, in 1854 his co-pastor. Dale entered adulthood at a time when the anti-slavery cause was losing its hold on the public imagination. Full emancipation had taken place when he was a child of nine, and 'the negro' occupied a different place in his imagined world than in the minds of the generation who had fought for an end to slavery. By the time of his young manhood, abolitionists were on the defensive. While Joseph Sturge and William Morgan persisted in their efforts to keep anti-slavery issues on the public agenda in the town, regular organisational efforts were confined to the women of the Ladies Negro's Friend Society, who kept the abolitionist torch burning. Dale's political initiation was through European nationalism rather than anti-slavery, and in this he followed Dawson. From the late 1840s he regularly attended public meetings in the town hall, a critical part of his training as an orator. His first public speech was in support of the Patriotic Fund in the Crimean War, when he rejoiced that 'the nation had shown itself capable of sacrifice for unselfish aims – not to extend its commerce or increase its territory, but for the sake of justice, mercy and truth'. By 1856, when Kossuth visited Birmingham, Dale had earned a place on the platform, seconding the address of welcome from the town.[17]

Events in India in 1857 turned public attention back to the empire. Racial questions took on a new urgency in the wake of the massacre at Cawnpore. While the town was riveted by tales of the 'Mutiny' in the daily press, Dale attended a lecture on India in the music hall. A resolution was unexpectedly proposed demanding full self-government for India and Dale rose to object. 'The Indian people', he urged, 'were not ready for self-government.' Even if they had been ready, this was not the time to concede it. The 'Mutiny' was still in full swing: 'England's first duty was to re-establish law and order, and to visit crime with just retribution. Till this had been done, no other policy could be considered.'[18] Europeans were ready for self-government, but subject peoples were not. While Christian nations had advanced in 'science, art, literature and manufactures', heathens were locked in 'barbarity'.[19]

As with James, Dale's faith was at the heart of his missionary enthusiasms, and Carrs Lane remained the site of missionary endeavours. Like James also, his vision of empire was one which radiated out from its Christian metropole in England: but his vision of the world as a whole

Carrs Lane chapel, site of anti-slavery meetings from the 1820s, visited by Knibb in the 1830s and 1840s, ministered to by John Angell James and R. W. Dale. Reproduced by permission of Birmingham Library Services.

was different and came to be framed by a different politics. Dale was an active supporter of the London Missionary Society: in the chair for one of its breakfast meetings in Birmingham in 1862, he reflected on the success of the work in the South Seas, India, China, Madagascar and South Africa, and hoped that the people of Birmingham would give liberally to these initiatives. Missionaries from India, Madagascar, China and Australia then spoke, the Rev. Cuthbutson from Australia reporting on the 'profound sensation' created in Australia by the news of the death of John Angell James, thus linking Birmingham to the Antipodes. The Indian missionary spoke of the 'degraded state' of India on account of the caste system and the way in which women were treated; those from Madagascar and China discussed the importance of native agency and the difficulties associated with it; the Rev. Cuthbutson remarked that the native teachers in Australia were not up to the management of churches, and were 'mere children compared with Englishmen' when it came to business. The listeners at the public breakfast could enjoy their 'very liberal repast' and reflect on the healthy state of their own society in comparison with the rest of the world.[20]

In 1864 Dale was honoured by being asked to give the annual sermon to the directors of the London Missionary Society. Reasserting his belief in Christ as the Saviour of all men, he insisted that, despite the spread of secularism in Europe, it was vital that Christians should develop and extend their missionary activities. Claiming to speak on behalf of India, China and 'the teeming races of Africa, whose existence has recently been made known to us by the courage and endurance of our own country-men', he insisted on the rights of these peoples to Christianity. The missionary public should feel cheered by the success there had been in the West Indies and elsewhere, but now was not the time to diminish European input. 'The vigour and enterprise of our English blood', he argued, 'are necessary to found new missions among vast populations as yet untouched.' And they must expect such initiatives to take time; it had taken centuries for the English to develop theological creeds and church practices. Those generations of controversy and debate ran 'in our veins', were part of a living culture and history from which others could learn. Intervening in the vexed debate over human origins, he conceded that 'the discoveries of modern science have demonstrated that all men have not a common origin'. He did not fear scientific knowledge, since, 'while the natural unity of the race is being brought into dispute, we are laying the foundations of a diviner brotherhood . . . we are gathering all into one in Christ'. That, he believed, provided the basis for 'a higher and nobler and more lasting unity than that which is imperilled by arguments founded on the structure of the skull and the texture of the hair'.[21] Nevertheless, that 'unity' was firmly rooted in the imperial responsibilities of those with English blood: his emphasis on blood and common culture marked a shift from the language of the 1830s and 1840s.

In 1864, however, it was a very domestic issue which galvanised Birmingham. A young working man, George Hall, in 'a humble condition of life', had become passionately attached to 'a very worthless woman'.[22] George and Sarah had met through membership of a choir attached to a mission chapel. They were married, but she left him the night of the wedding, preferring the company of a former lover. George attempted reconciliation several times, but was unsuccessful despite the strong support of his wife's parents. Eventually he shot and killed Sarah, and gave himself up. He was sentenced to death at Warwick Assizes in 1864. A campaign for his reprieve was led by the Baptists John Skirrow Wright and William Morgan. Wright, seven years younger than Morgan, had come to Birmingham as a child in 1834, and had started his working life as a junior clerk in a button factory. From there he moved up the ladder to become a traveller for the firm, a manager, and then a partner in 1858. He had been present as a youth when the town's charter of incorporation had been read in the town hall in 1838, and at the great celebration of emancipation: these marked the formative moments of his political life. Founder of the People's Chapel and the Birmingham Sunday School Union, a regular preacher, supporter of European nationalisms and of the early closing movement, he became an active Liberal and was to impress Gladstone by his 'simple, manly, and practical . . . English character'.[23] In 1864 Wright and Morgan were both in their forties, both family men with wives and children, both Baptists, both prominent members of the town's missionary and abolitionist publics. To them, death by hanging was too severe a sentence for a man who had been so horribly provoked by an adulterous wife.

Hall was defended at the Assizes by James Fitzjames Stephen, son of the distinguished abolitionist and Colonial Office secretary, a young barrister of thirty-four who, two years later, was to act for the Jamaica Committee against Governor Eyre. Martin Wiener shows how this case brought a series of conflicts about (what we now call) domestic violence to a head, for the judiciary was increasingly hostile to abusive husbands.[24] The Home Secretary and the Lord Chancellor believed this was a clear case of premeditated murder, leaving no grounds for reprieve. But the campaign in Hall's favour mobilised huge support. Seventy thousand people signed the petition for clemency, including the town's two MPs, the mayor, lawyers, clerics and medical men, Edgbaston ladies, working men and women, even some of Hall's female co-workers. Much was made of his good character as a steady workman, a practical Christian, a frugal and self-controlled person. 'It would be deplorable', Stephen had argued, 'if we came to look upon passion and sentiment as any excuse whatever for crime, after the fashion of Frenchmen and Mexicans.'[25] Hall was represented as an upright man, driven to destruction; an Englishman, wounded and bewildered by the behaviour of the woman he loved. Many working men were active in the campaign and, argues Wiener, by their 'disciplined and respectable behaviour', and by their insistence on his previous good character, 'they were removing the stain his action and conviction had cast over working-class masculinity'.[26] The support for Hall was a blow for manliness and domesticity: Sarah had offended against the laws of marriage by having a lover whom she preferred. Furthermore, the lover was Irish.

In 1857 Wright had presented a paper to the NAPSS conference, held in Birmingham, in which he had discussed the regrettable fact that the cheap labour of Birmingham women was essential to Birmingham's prosperity. This made for a lot of independence in young women, he argued; they were often well dressed, but knew little of household economy, of cooking or of laundry. They too frequently became wives and mothers entirely ignorant of the various important duties and responsibilities entailed, with the result that their husband's food was badly cooked, his shirt not properly washed and his home uncomfortable. With proper conditions of employment, women's work need not be morally dangerous, Wright maintained, but he was seriously concerned when it came to married women.[27] The challenge to men's power meant a more anxious focus on forms of masculinity.[28] Wright, Morgan and their supporters were defending a particular view of marriage, the same view that had been lauded at that great event in the Birmingham town hall in 1838, when freed men had been greeted as men, now able to protect their wives and children. This entailed particular notions of manliness and of femininity, and resulted in the conviction that death was an inappropriate punishment for George Hall. The maintenance of a proper gender order in Birmingham was quite as important as it was in Jamaica or the other sites of empire upon which the missionary gaze was fixed. In the context of an increasing focus on 'the woman question' at home, and increased rights for women in relation to divorce, issues of young women's independence were deeply troubling.[29] Faced with the scale of the public outcry, the Home Secretary was forced to issue a reprieve on the eve of the hanging. This was a triumph for the midland metropolis: their view had superseded that of the judiciary and the central government, a source of great local pride.

Questions of manliness were to the fore in another major preoccupation of the town in the early 1860s: the Volunteers. 'The Volunteer Force', writes Hugh Cunningham, 'was the military expression of the spirit of self-help.' Captains of industry became captains of companies, and drilled their employees: all this was seen by contemporaries as an excellent expression of improvement in class relations. Middle-class men soon lost interest, but the Volunteers remained a site in which working-class men could increase their self-esteem and begin to think of a claim to political rights.[30] A Volunteer Rifle Corps was established in 1859, with considerable enthusiasm, especially from the gun-makers. By 1860, 1,000 were enrolled in what became the Birmingham Battalion, and men of the midland metropolis were able to demonstrate their capacity to bear arms, long established as a key component of the right to full citizenship. Much debate took place over the uniforms and the band. In October 1863 a great bazaar was held at the town hall over five days to raise money for the corps, and a special song was written celebrating England as the land of the fair and the free, the home of liberty. 'Here in the heart of England born', sang the Volunteers,

> In Warwick's famous shire
> By Shakespeare's deathless name inspired,
> We glow with patriot fire.
> And thinking of our country's fame
> Our blood more warmly flows;
> For home, for Queen, for altar, we
> Would meet the fiercest foes.[31]

While the Volunteers marched out in Calthorpe Park, glowing with manly pride for their town, county and nation, a struggle over life and death was going on in the United States. Birmingham abolitionists worked hard to forefront the question of slavery in the American Civil War, and Dale, for example, refused to come out in favour of the North until Lincoln's declaration for emancipation.[32] Dawson was much more ambivalent: he supposed he was pro the North, but with little enthusiasm. He was prone to ridicule universal suffrage, and his 'wishes in favour of liberty', he argued, were as strong as ever; but immediate emancipation was a dubious strategy, and 'a general system of amelioration' in the South would be the best course.[33] Debates over the Civil War in Birmingham marked a shift in public opinion on questions of race. Whereas abolitionism had dominated public platforms in the 1830s, a much more disputed set of issues surfaced in the early 1860s, and the merits of the two sides were regularly aired. Humanitarians had rallied to the North after an initial period of uncertainty at the beginning of the war, but had been disillusioned by Lincoln's emphasis on the preservation of the Union. In 1861 the British government declared neutrality. After 1863 and Lincoln's declaration of support for emancipation, British anti-slavery loyalists were more energetic in their support of the North, alongside radicals and working-class activists. But, as Royden Harrison has shown, there were strong sympathies for the Confederacy in the working-class press, informed primarily by anti-capitalist sentiment. Many old Chartists, for example, favoured the South, and had no love for John Bright, Lincoln's most prominent supporter in Britain.[34] Probably the majority of the upper and middle classes supported the South in the war, seeing it as a fight for Southern independence, and sympathising profoundly with nationalist aspirations. Since the South was in favour of low tariffs, while the North wanted them to be high, many free-traders were also pro-Southern. 'Yankee arrogance' was heartily disliked by some, and Southern conceptions of aristocratic government were romanticised. Supporters of the South denied that slavery was the issue, and argued that the record of the North on questions of race was little better than that of the South.[35]

These issues were hotly debated in Birmingham. A great meeting was held at the town hall in December 1862, at which the town's two MPs, Scholefield and Bright, spoke on the war. Three months prior to this, Birmingham had reaffirmed its commitment to Garibaldi and Italian unification at a packed meeting in support of the Italian leader. 'No language can express', argued Dale, the degree of sympathy 'felt by the great mass of the English people for the wounded patriot' and the earnest desire for 'a free and united Italy'. In proposing a town memorial on the issue, Alderman Hawkes evoked Birmingham's tradition, in its short history as a borough, of interference on questions of liberty. They had supported Poland and Hungary in their struggles for freedom, and must now set the example to other English towns once again, in relation to Italy. The 'great men' who had made Birmingham famous were now dead: it was up to the next generation to sustain the tradition.[36]

The town had been united on Italy; but in December, when the Civil War was the topic, opinions were sharply divided, nationalist and abolitionist sentiments cutting across each other and intersecting in a range of complex positions. The mayor, Charles Sturge, one of Joseph's nephews, was on the platform together with the local elite. The town hall was 'thronged in every part', and the speeches were subject to cheering, booing, demonstrations of support and moments of disorder. Scholefield spoke first, arguing, to tremendous applause, that the first duty of a representative was to speak out frankly and plainly to those he represented. He supported the right of the South to secede, even though he regarded it as an act of folly and believed that if the secession were ever completed, it would be impossible to maintain slavery. He did not agree that the North was fighting a war for emancipation, and his own detestation of slavery was as strong as it had ever been: such a sentiment 'is almost a passion with us', he argued, a mark of Englishness. But the eight million southerners had the right to constitute themselves as a nation, and he supported their recognition.[37] Bright, for his part, deeply regretted the ravages of the war, and criticised Lincoln's failure to take up the cause of slavery; but he looked forward to the time when the continent of America would be 'the home of freedom, and a refuge for the oppressed of every race and clime'.[38]

Lincoln's declaration in favour of emancipation meant that anti-slavery enthusiasts were much more willing to take up the cause of the North. In January 1863 the *Birmingham Journal* noted a significant shift in feeling in this regard. An address had been prepared in the town to present to President Lincoln. Its intentions were twofold: to renew that 'solemn protest against slavery which was pronounced by the unanimous consent of England thirty years ago' and to show 'the Government of the Federal States that their efforts to check and finally to extinguish slavery in America are thoroughly appreciated by the people of Birmingham, who have always claimed and taken the foremost rank in the sacred cause of freedom'.[39] At the anniversary dinner of the Birmingham Chamber of Commerce, Bright celebrated the 'cause of freedom' moving onward.[40] At the same time a great meeting was held at Exeter Hall in London by the Emancipation Society, to test 'whether the feeling against slavery was really dead in the country', and the immense enthusiasm for this meeting seemed to demonstrate that it was not.[41]

If anti-slavery sentiment was alive and well, it no longer dominated the public mind. In March the productions at the Theatre Royal in Birmingham captured the ambivalent state of feeling about North and South.[42] Similarly, the records of the weekly debating society at the 'Hope and Anchor' on Navigation Street reveal the see-saw of opinion on the war and the difficulties inherent in any attempt to construct it as a battle between good and evil, as the battle over emancipation in the 1830s had been constructed. This debating society met for nearly thirty years between 1858 and 1886. Its topics in the late 1850s and early 1860s touched on every issue of the day, ranging from India to Ireland, from Napoleon to Cromwell, from church and state to education, from emigration to the monarchy, from local political issues to European nationalisms, from astronomy to phrenology, from the extension of the franchise to women's rights. Sentiments were liberal on the whole, with a unanimous vote in favour of the extension of the franchise to working-class men, strong criticism of aristocratic predominance, and support for government activity against the slave trade, for example.[43] The men who met to talk and think about these questions shared a view of themselves as active participants in the town's public life. They also shared a conception of the town as playing a part in the life of the nation, contributing to discussion of political and social questions and making public opinion. Towns such as Birmingham had a responsibility to counter the influence of landowners and aristocrats and give the voices of mechanics and tradesmen, many of whom did not have the vote, a hearing. At the 'Hope and Anchor' the view of the nation was one framed by empire. Colonies were of benefit to the metropole, and trade must be protected and prioritised; emigration provided a route for skilled labourers who could

not find work at home. At the same time, the debaters were strong supporters of European nationalisms, and ranked both Kossuth and
Garibaldi as greater men than John Bright. This sympathy for nationalism was intimately associated with a defence of English traditions of
liberty, some dating the Anglo-Saxon era as the cradle of freedom, others
convinced that Cromwell was the hero to be remembered.[44]

The American Civil War was debated repeatedly from 1861: from the
question of intervention to the trade blockade, from the seizure of pas-
sengers on board the *Trent* to the effects on the cotton industry. A discussion of Lincoln's proposal for gradual abolition split the company,
and a current of pro-Southern opinion was consistently present. 'All the
nations of Europe must acknowledge a people who are able to proclaim
and defend their own nationality,' argued Mr Moreton in January 1863,
gathering much support for this position. In February a debate over the
relative merits of North and South went on for three weeks, with thirty
eventually voting for the North, twenty for the South. A further three
weeks in June were devoted to Southern independence, Mr Monk contending that 'Justice and Humanity' demanded that a people who had
struggled so hard for freedom and self-government deserved recognition.
Mr Harris responded by arguing that 'liberty loving Englishmen', who
had gained the approbation of the civilised world with their stand on
slavery, should refuse to recognise a government, the corner-stone of
which was the destruction of human rights. The vote on this occasion
went for the South, as it did in subsequent debates on the North's
prolongation of the war and the South's right to secession. In early 1865
the 'Hope and Anchor' was ringing with denunciations of Lincoln,
and in June a debate as to whether slavery was of divine origin ran over
four nights and came to no conclusion. Yet in August there was a majority for the view that freedom would give negroes opportunities for
improvement.[45]

The men who met at the 'Hope and Anchor' probably attended the
great town meetings on the public affairs of the day, and in January 1864
Scholefield and Bright had another opportunity to speak on American
affairs in the town hall. 'The immense building was crowded in every
part,' as the *Birmingham Daily Post* described it, 'the surplus audience
swarming up the pillars, seating themselves in the windows, and running
over at every outlet into the street.' In the judgement of the editor of that
paper, it was clear that Scholefield's pro-Confederacy opinions were not
popular, but he had gained in the estimation of his constituents 'by
the frank, honest and out-spoken manner in which he avowed and justified his convictions'. Scholefield defended the right of the South to
secede, and argued that the war was not about slavery, a view which
provoked an uproar in the body of the hall. Bright, for his part,

welcomed the fact that, whatever the original intentions of the North, the war would result in the 'certain and rapid end' of 'the slavery of man', a view that was greeted with much cheering.[46] But this public enthusiasm for emancipation was not matched by activity in the town to promote such an end.

It was the ladies of the Negro's Friend Society who had worked hard in Birmingham to keep questions of emancipation on the public agenda, faithful to their own motto, 'Be not weary in well doing'. The society had met continuously throughout the 1850s and early 1860s, raising money for female educational initiatives in the West Indies, informing itself on the vexed question of immigration, keeping abreast of the struggles in the United States, working to prove the superiority of free labour to slave labour. The ladies' central aims were, as they put it, to assist in the religious education and improvement of the negroes. They met quarterly, had speakers mainly from the United States and the West Indies, published annual reports, and recommended reading to their members. Their activities were reported in the provincial and abolitionist press, keeping them, as much as possible, in the public eye. Their meetings were still addressed by men; but in the privacy of their homes they conducted their own affairs. They were in close touch with many of the Baptist missionaries in Jamaica and received regular reports as to the state of the island: John Clark, the Hendersons, Walter Dendy, David East, Mrs Knibb and Mrs Fray, all these were familiars, their letters regularly extracted in the annual reports, Birmingham a lodestar on their itineraries when they visited the mother country. The ladies saw their task as to focus on humanitarian issues rather than the nitty-gritty of politics, but their philanthropic work constantly strayed into political terrains. In the thin years of the late 1850s and early 1860s, they longed for the great days of William Wilberforce and Thomas Clarkson, and regretted the passing of their heroes.[47]

By 1864 the question of the future of freed men and women in the USA had become a pressing one, and the society, with its long experience of working with the emancipated in the West Indies, felt it had a contribution to make. Four million enslaved people were to be freed, and what was construed as their 'character' was now a key issue. 'Evidence has accumulated upon evidence', reported the Society, 'of their ability and willingness to work under the stimulus of the same motives that influence other races to labour.' The old arguments as to African idleness must once again be countered. In May 1864 the annual meeting was addressed by Mr Edward Gem from the chair. 'They must all feel deeply indebted to the women of England for the part which they took in all religious, benevolent, and philanthropic works,' he began. 'They must all feel deeply thankful to Almighty God that the hands of such men as

Wilberforce and Buxton...had been strengthened by the ladies of England.' Many of the first activists had gone to their deaths, but they had left 'a heavenly spark', a legacy of 'deep sympathy and love for the negro'. Gem went on to say that a Birmingham lady had come up with the idea of freighting a vessel for the United States, loaded with implements to assist the freedmen in their agricultural work. It would be up to the gentlemen to accomplish this object: 'if the manufacturers of the town would give some of the old stock which many of them had had in the corners of their warehouses for years', it could soon be effected. He then introduced the speaker for the evening, Mr M. D. Conway, a southerner who had left the South on account of his anti-slavery principles, who discoursed at length on the story of the negro as 'the romance of modern history'. The men and women who had escaped from slavery in myriad ways, nailed up in coffins, clinging to the wheel-houses of steamers – these were the heroes and heroines who had revealed the power and nobility of black people, he argued.

Conway's rhetoric was somewhat undercut by the vote of thanks from the Rev. Charles Vince, one of the town's Baptist ministers. He warned the 'friends of the negro' against an over-romantic view of black people. Those who were kept in bondage over generations, he argued, could not be freed without sources of weeping and mourning. 'He should not be surprised', he said, 'if many among the negroes turned out indolent and lawless.' This was one of the curses attached to slavery, and they should be prepared for it. He went on to warn against the practice of bringing freed slaves to England and 'sending them up and down the country', a practice which spoiled them and of which he heartily disapproved.[48] This warning was symptomatic of the times. The increasing presence and visibility of black abolitionists in England created its own backlash. African-Americans, including Frederick Douglass, were consistently struck by the absence of racial prejudice in England by comparison with the USA in the mid-nineteenth century. But the doubts which Sturge had found so troubling during James Williams's visit to England in the late 1830s had become more pressing by the 1860s. Too many of the black lecturers were either 'rank imposters', or men who, having 'originally a legitimate claim to sympathy, have been spoilt by over-patronage', thought his successors. Lorimer sees the class dynamic as having been critical to the treatment of black visitors, but there was also the issue of the distinction between black people 'over there' and black people in the mother country.[49] Distance did much for ideas about black people amongst anti-slavery enthusiasts. Familiarity, it seemed, bred that contempt which was the other side of pity. Black abolitionists reduced the gap between colony and metropole: their activities and claims threatened the rule of a particular kind of paternalist colonial difference. A tougher assessment of the potential of 'the negro', an insistence on a 'no-nonsense' approach which recognised their many limitations, was characteristic of many of those who continued to define themselves as sympathetic to the cause of black people in the 1860s.

The suggestion of sending a ship to the United States was taken up enthusiastically, albeit briefly, in the town, and inspired the establishment of the Freedmen's Aid Association. In June a committee was established which included William Morgan and Arthur Albright, the two who were to be the most active in the new organisation, and was unusual in including some women, though they soon disappeared from public view. A meeting was called for, the signatories for which included both Dale and Dawson.[50] An editorial in the *Birmingham Daily Post* enlisted support for the ship, arguing that almost anything made in Birmingham would be an acceptable gift. 'The chief demand is for tools,' they explained, both for husbandry and for handicrafts which could be easily taught. Nobody wanted to keep the negroes in idleness; the intention was to help them on their way, and only a start was required. 'The testimony as to their willingness to work', the paper continued, 'is literally overwhelming.' As was 'their willingness to learn. Docile, industrious, and naturally intelligent, they have been deliberately brutalised.' But now, 'these poor creatures stand up again – no longer brutes but men, full of gratitude to their deliverers, and eager to prove their manhood by honest labour'.[51]

This was the discourse of British emancipation re-utilised for the USA: negro docility, industry, gratitude and willingness to learn, strengthened by an emphasis on 'natural intelligence', to counter the claims of those who judged them mentally inferior. They were 'poor creatures' who were now freed to be men, grateful and eager to prove their manhood, only waiting for opportunity. Contributions began to come in for the ship: William Middlemore, a prominent Birmingham Baptist and proprietor of a large saddlery business, offered an assortment of his wares. Other proprietors followed suit: Albright and Wilson gave medical and sanitary chemicals; Hudson and Son, the publishers, gave fifty copies of *Course of Faith* by John Angell James; R. L. Chance, glass manufacturer, gave 100 dozen tumblers; Pumphrey Bros, engravers, 100 portraits of John Angell James.[52] Unfortunately, the reception of these articles in Carolina, Kentucky or Louisiana was not recorded in Birmingham!

Freedmen's Aid was organised across the country, and was closely associated with the BFASS: it was vital to the anti-slavery cause generally that emancipation in the USA should have a successful outcome. According to its secretary, the new organisation 'was made up mainly of earnest Anti-Slavery Men'.[53] John Bright and John Stuart Mill were its best-known figure-heads. Its priorities were to relieve physical hardship, provide educational and industrial training and Christian teaching, and improve Anglo-American relations, building on the well-established links between the British and US anti-slavery movements. As Christine Bolt argues, the associations were dominated by the middle-aged and those who had an anti-slavery history. The desire to capture 'the mind of England', and to give a 'national character' to the work, as Albright put it, was not to be fulfilled; only the faithful were mobilised.[54] In Birmingham there was an active working men's auxiliary, but this was unusual. The association was anxious not to be seen as political; rather, it stressed humanity and philanthropy. William Morgan, one of the secretaries of the Birmingham branch, was concerned that the political sensitivities associated with the issue, particularly the fear that they would be seen as meddling in American domestic affairs, should be avoided. The most effective way to do this was to focus on those familiar tropes, the suffering negro and the benevolent and responsible Anglo-Saxon. As Edmund Sturge argued, since 'the slavery and degradation of the negro in the Western World have been so largely due to the crime and cupidity of the Anglo-Saxon family, their religious, moral and social elevation will . . . be for a long time dependent on the residence among them of those of the superior race who can elevate and not degrade by their example'.[55] Pity, guilt, reparation – these were the key themes for the protagonists of the freedmen. Notions of radical reconstruction had no place on their agenda, and black male suffrage found few supporters.[56]

The freedmen caught the imagination of neither the national public nor the midland metropolis: the support was limited, and the campaign relatively short-lived, highlighting once again the shift in ethos from the 1830s. Meanwhile numerous imperial issues surfaced in the Birmingham press in the early 1860s: the rise of Fenianism in Ireland, the United States and Britain; wars in New Zealand; troubles on the Cape; debates over the unorthodox views of Bishop Colenso in Natal as to the truth of the Bible were all reported, alongside African exploration, particularly the adventures of David Livingstone.[57] The *Birmingham Journal* engaged in a typical New Year exercise in January 1863, casting its eye across the globe and including in its sweep Europe, Ireland and the United States. 'The Colonies', it concluded,

have enjoyed a course of steady if not brilliant prosperity. For once we are at peace in New Zealand and the Cape; India is setting herself in good earnest to the profitable task of extending her public works; Australia is in the happy condition of those countries which have 'no annals'; and though Canada caused the mother country some anxiety and excited more than one lively discussion at the beginning of the year, there is no reason to be dissatisfied either with her progress or her feeling towards ourselves.[58]

That same month the paper commented on the ceding of the Ionian islands, a protectorate since 1815, to Greece. This was entirely proper, it argued, since the Ionians had expressed their wish to unite their fortunes with 'the main stock of the Hellenic race' over and over again, the Greeks wanted the same thing, and 'we have come to the honest conclusion that henceforth our practice and our principles must go hand in hand'. 'It is essentially an English maxim', it concluded, 'that every nation has the right to choose its own form of Government.'[59] This was, of course, only a principle for European nations or those peopled with Europeans.

Meanwhile the distress in Lancashire caused by the cotton famine turned attention again to emigration, and the *Birmingham Journal* recommended Canada, and particularly British Columbia, as a good destination for emigrants, though those heading for the latter were warned that they must be 'men, true men, resolute, persevering, cheerful, temperate men, men of dauntless character . . . the stuff on which England's glory has been founded'.[60] Two months later it was Polish nationalists' efforts to liberate themselves from Russia which dominated Birmingham's public platforms. A town meeting was convened by the mayor, who was not himself sympathetic to the cause, but was vigorously shouted down. Dr Dale hoped that the meeting would be a demonstration of sympathetic enthusiasm for 'the heroic struggles of the Polish nation', and argued in favour of military backing for them. This sympathy with oppressed nationalities, argued manufacturer Samuel Timmins to loud cheers, was based upon 'the very truest instincts of the English heart', its love of liberty, and it was this which Count Zamoyski appealed to in his speech, which was greeted with round after round of applause from the audience.[61] Once again, it was the European nationalisms of the oppressed which inspired huge enthusiasm in the town.

Great claims were being made for the Christian missions in the early 1860s. A public lecture on 'The Results of Christian Missions' argued that the transformations wrought by missions could be tracked across the globe: Sierra Leone, which once echoed to 'the din of the war-gong and the clank of the slave-chain', was now a site of peaceful industry with the loudest sound being that of the church bell; the isles of the Pacific, 'once rank and poisonous with the worst weeds of heathenism', now 'exhale the fragrance of every Christian grace'; New Zealand, once 'cannibal and idolatrous', was now sitting at the feet of Jesus; Bengal had given her testimony that her converts had remained loyal to their God throughout the 'Mutiny'; and 'the Kraal of the Hottentot, the tent of the Kurd, and the wig-wam of the Red-man' had all born testimony to the power of the Gospel.[62] As the Baptists of Birmingham read their

Missionary Herald from the fastnesses of their homes, they could look out at this array of happenings across the world, and reflect on their privilege. As the Rev. Roberts put it:

> I look upon ourselves in this country as upon Noah in his ark of safety viewing a deluged world. Superstition and barbarism have flooded our world, but we, in our ark of Christianity, are floating on the surface. And, thank God, our ark has windows. Those windows I take to be our missionary reports; and through these we look and ascertain the state of the waters, whether they are advancing or receding.[63]

That capacity to judge 'the state of the waters' was one of the special characteristics of 'missionary nations'. By the 1860s, this could be unashamedly linked to the particular features of the Anglo-Saxon race. A new variety of racial thinking was permeating missionary discourse: negroes could be recognised by their love of excitement combined with their simplicity and empty minds, Indians by their convoluted idolatries, Anglo-Saxons by their capacities to colonise and spread the Word. 'Why may not the whole earth be ultimately brought under the influence and into the possession of the dominant race?', asked the *Missionary Herald* in 1861, a question that would have seriously troubled Joseph Sturge.[64]

Missionary meetings continued to provide a site for reflections on history and culture. The anniversary meetings of the Baptists in 1861 celebrated the 'sacred memories and associations' clustering around the names of Carey, Marshman and Ward. J. C. Woodhill, from the chair, urged his audience to read the history of their enterprise, one which had been so vital to 'the happiness and destiny of the human family', and which paralleled to his mind the acts of the apostles. 'We may view the missionary enterprise', he asserted,

> as having created a new species of literature, to which we may repair, for the most recent, and reliable, and charming delineations of the natural scenery, of the physical and mental characteristics, the manners, custom and dress, (where that luxury is indulged in) the social habits, the occupations and amusements, and religious observances of countries almost or altogether unknown before the christian missionary, with the 'lamp of life' in his hand, visited those 'distant barbrous climes' ... scattering wherever he went, the priceless double blessings of Christianity and civilisation.[65]

Those who had an inclination for the romantic or the marvellous, said Woodhill, could not do better than to read missionary literature. Those interested in maritime discovery, geographical knowledge or the boundaries of science and art could experience these wonders whilst sitting calmly at home in their armchairs.

In September 1865 the town was galvanised by the presence of the British Association for the Advancement of Science's annual conference, an event which brought a large number of prominent scientists to Birmingham and inspired the production of a series of papers on the state of Birmingham industries, which were presented to the association.[66] The British Association had an established commitment to meeting in the provinces, and it was regarded as an honour to host the annual conference. The Birmingham Central Library was opened on the first day of the 1865 meeting: a celebration of the town's commitment to knowledge. The conference provided an ideal opportunity to present the achievements of provincial scientific culture to a national audience, and Birmingham was able to act as 'a showcase for provincial talent'. The presence in the town of 'the advanced guard on the march of civilisation', as one provincial journalist described the participants, meant that the midland metropolis had yet another opportunity to place itself on the national map.[67]

The event provided an opportunity for Birmingham to engage publicly in the intense debates that were going on in the fields of comparative anatomy, ethnology and anthropology. The characteristic British tradition of race science, argues Stocking, which had been monogenist in orientation, and focused on the identification of racial stocks via linguistic as well as physical similarities between peoples, and on their migrations and interminglings over the course of centuries, had gone into decline by the 1850s. Explanations which focused on comparative anatomical and craniological approaches to race had become more prevalent. Prichard's vision, that 'just as in the beginning all men were one, so had God in the beginning revealed to all men the one true religion', no longer prevailed.[68] James Hunt, a disciple of Knox, had joined the Ethnological Society and became its joint secretary in 1863, but he was increasingly impatient with its approach. In 1863 he founded the Anthropological Society of London, arguing that while ethnology dealt with the history or science of nations, anthropology was 'the study of the whole nature of man'.[69] Ethnology, he argued, had been hamstrung by biblical dogma: anthropology, by contrast, 'would treat . . . everything pertaining to his nature'.[70] Hunt was convinced of inherent racial inequalities: negroes were incapable of mental or social advance except through intermarriage; environment was irrelevant. The influence of the Anthropological Society was limited, and its history short, but its existence signified the divisions amongst British scientists on questions of race, divisions which had intensified in the wake of the publication of Darwin's *Origin of Species* in 1859. For pre-Darwinian naturalists, living species had been created by God and were fixed in their traits. But Darwin demonstrated that species were continuously changing by a process of selection and variation, associated with struggles for survival. Adaptation was always going on, and new species forming. Species were, therefore, linked to each other in time and space by descent – a theory of evolution. As Stepan argues, despite the fact that Darwin himself was a monogenist, his evolutionary ideas were entirely compatible with the notion of a hierarchy of human races, and provided old racial ideas 'with a new scientific vocabulary of struggle and survival'.[71]

Debates over race erupted in Birmingham in 1865 at the British Association. The meeting was a major event, closely reported in the local press, a sign of Birmingham's claim to be a serious centre of intellectual and scientific inquiry. The president's address was given in the town hall, which was 'well-filled' with a 'brilliant assembly', a large proportion of whom were lady associates.[72] Sir Charles Lyell was in the chair, and the president's speech included discussion of evolution, the races of men and the specialisation of species. At the commencement of the business Dr Hunt, whose followers had come in force to support him, had requested that anthropology, 'the science of man', should be given a separate section.[73] This was refused by Sir Roderick Murchison, premier geologist and soon to be an active supporter of Governor Eyre, on the grounds that they did not want to increase the number of subsections.[74] Anthropology, therefore, stayed with geography and ethnology. A paper on 'Occidental or Western Negroes' in this section, by a Mr Crawford, opened with the observation that 'the term Negro', in so far as it was applicable to Africans, meant

> a human being with the hair of the head and other parts of the body always black, and more or less of the texture of wool, with a black skin of various shades; dark eyes, a flat face, depressed nose, jutting jaws, thick lips, and a large mouth, with oblique incisor teeth. To this is to be added a peculiar odour of the skin, offensive to and unknown in the other races of men.

Crawford went on to discuss the diversity of negroes in Africa and elsewhere, and to comment on the absence of civilisation, as he saw it, on the African continent. African negroes were obtuse, unambitious and unenterprising; their literature was 'a blank'; their architecture poor and temporary, with 'no temple, no tomb, not even a bridge'; their religion was witchcraft, their wars 'the incursions of savages', their government 'the rudest form of despotism'. Yet the negro was undoubtedly a man, he argued: 'He is equal in strength and stature to the European, but very far below him in mental endowment. He is superior in strength, but inferior in intellect, to all the races of Asia who have the same opportunities of development as himself.'[75] Furthermore, the African Negro was, 'although greatly inferior to many races, . . . far from being at the bottom of the scale', surpassing the Hottentot and the Australian, and far surpassing the races of 'oriental Negroes'. These arguments were objected to with a good deal of hilarity, a humour located in metropolitan assumptions of superiority. Hunt criticised the sources used, and Conway, that same southerner who had spoken to the Ladies Negro's Friend Society, told the audience that he had on his bookshelves 150 books written by black Africans, a point that was met with applause. Another speaker regretted that these kinds of negative statements about Africans should be made so frequently in the geography and ethnology sections of the British Association.[76]

Dr Thomas Hodgkin, the celebrated medical man and philanthropist, biographer of Prichard, firm believer in the creed that all races derived from a single origin, and enthusiastic supporter of the freedmen, had prepared a paper on 'The Transition from Slavery to Freedom' as his contribution to the debate over race at the conference. This paper had not been accepted, however, perhaps because it was seen as too overtly political in its preoccupations, and Hodgkin delivered it in London. He attributed 'the apparent inferiority of the negro race to the slow but long continued operation of causes affecting the cultivation or the neglect of the intellectual faculties'. But he also believed that emancipation should guarantee only 'the essentials of freedom', and that freedmen would need 'individual personal requisites' for admission to 'all the grades to which the free man may labour or raise himself' – a cautious judgement which perhaps prefigured the ambivalent position which Hodgkin was to take up in relation to Morant Bay and Governor Eyre.[77] The residents of Birmingham could read and listen to all this, and then attend those sessions dealing with the remarkable advances in industry and science in their own locality, as reported on by many of their local dignitaries.[78]

Birmingham men were proud of their identity as citizens of the midland metropolis. That citizenship carried with it the responsibility of civilising others. At a BMS auxiliary meeting held in the town hall in May 1863, Morton Peto was in the chair, major benefactor of the BMS, friend and patron to many of the Jamaican missionaries, MP and building constructor. Civilisation and every other blessing followed the introduction of Christianity, he argued, a line of thought which was pursued by the speaker, a former missionary from the East Indies. He appealed to the commercial interests of Birmingham men: if Christianity spread, he argued,

> there would spring up a demand for the appliances of civilised life; in fact for everything that was manufactured in Birmingham, so that it would be

one of the best investments the people of Birmingham could make if they regarded their own interests, merely, if they were to send the Gospel to India.[79]

Civilised peoples needed the locks and keys, the umbrella stands and bedsteads, the pots and pans of Birmingham manufacture. J. S. Wright was happy to make a similar point when introducing a lecture on India to the Birmingham Chamber of Commerce. He reminded his audience of the important part which Birmingham had played in sending the first Baptist missionaries to India and helping to raise that population from 'a state of degradation to one of civilisation'. Britain had great obligations to India, both spiritually and materially, he maintained. Major-General Cotton, the speaker, who had spent many years working on irrigation systems in that country, then went on to convince his listeners of the importance of this work and the benefits it could bring to all. 'These new works', he remarked,

> would not benefit one part of England, but the whole of the trades of all the towns would be improved, and Birmingham would feel the benefit amongst others. At the present time there were whole districts where there was not a pair of scissors to be found; and not one in fifty had a knife. (laughter) When the country was opened up these things would be wanted by tens of millions. (applause)[80]

Birmingham would be all the richer, once the subjects of empire were civilised.

At the beginning of 1865 the New Exchange buildings had been opened, an occasion for much celebration. Designed as a meeting place for businessmen, the Gothic structure on New Street, right in the centre of the town, was 'ornamented in the most rich and effective style'. Including different-sized assembly rooms, smoke rooms and refreshment rooms, it was a fitting place for Birmingham's merchants, manufacturers and professional men. The speeches at the luncheon which was held celebrated Birmingham, particularly its tradition of co-operation between masters and men, and the House of Commons, that 'most enlightened and most powerful assembly in the world'. In response to this toast, one of the local county MPs spoke of the spirit of commerce as *the* progressive force in English history. The English were not content to have public affairs discussed only in Parliament; rather, they formed local 'extra-mural parliaments' across the length and breadth of the land. They had social science parliaments, natural science parliaments, trade unions, church congresses and, most important of all, chambers of commerce. 'One might almost say', he remarked, 'that the Anglo-Saxon race, at that moment throughout the whole world was in Parliament of some sort.' Then John Bright spoke, telling his listeners that what happened in that building would have effects across the world. It was towns and cities which had spread the stream of commerce, civilisation and freedom, he believed: a sentiment which was met with great applause. The English people

> ought to take a special pride in the greatness of her colonies, whether on the American or the Australasian continent. (Hear, hear) They went from us, they have taken all that is best of our institutions, and of our laws and principles; our ancestors were theirs, and through their instrumentality the English language will be spoken far more universally throughout the world than any other European language.

The event concluded with a toast from Dawson to the mayor and the corporation, in which he argued that while the glory of a nation was its capacity to manage its own affairs, the especial glory of England was its capacity to manage its own local affairs. 'It was the pride of an Englishman', he concluded, 'to know that they knew how to take care of themselves.'[81]

Two weeks later Bright was in the town hall with Scholefield, reporting to their constituents at one of their annual meetings. This was the occasion when Bright took up the question of reform of the franchise to an enthusiastic audience of 5,000, arguing that the colonies already enjoyed such representation, and it was absurd that Englishmen in the mother country should be denied that right.[82] At the end of the occasion he reflected on the excellent institution of the town meeting with its MPs. The crowded platform, the full galleries, the hall so packed that it seemed impossible that men should be able to stand throughout, especially given the length of his speech – these were matters to celebrate. It was a respectable, intelligent, solid meeting, demonstrating the seriousness with which public questions were dealt with in this town. 'If all the great towns in England could take the position which you occupy', he concluded, 'and could offer such a spectacle as we see from year to year, no man might despair of his country'.[83]

The growing pride of Birmingham men was reflected in a shift in local politics in the mid-1860s, as Asa Briggs has argued. In the 1850s it was small manufacturers and traders who dominated the town council, anxious to keep down costs for ratepayers and reduce expenditure on public works.[84] From 1859, however, the economists began to lose influence, and there was increasing interest in local government reform. Large business men and leading professional men began to be recruited to the council, and a tradition of municipal service was inaugurated. George Dawson provided a significant inspiration for this, with his view of the town as the microcosm of the nation and his emphasis on moral reform. Dawson's most lasting memorial to the town was his commitment to the 'civic gospel' which he helped to articulate in the 1860s – the gospel that taught Birmingham men that to be an activist in municipal government was as beneficial to the community as to be a minister or a philanthropist. Just as the nation was the community which was to transcend difference for Dawson, so the town was to be the local manifestation of that nation. Faced with a town which was unsanitary, unhealthy and lacking in educational facilities, and which failed to answer the pressing needs of its poorer inhabitants, he sought to convince his prosperous congregation and his wider public that a new community could be built in Birmingham, a new moral world constructed on its own doorstep.

At the opening of the Free Reference Library in 1866, which he had done so much to promote (for popular education was always at the heart of his project), he argued that 'a great town exists to discharge towards the people of that town the duties that a great nation exists to discharge towards the people of that nation'. Indeed, a town like Birmingham existed 'for moral and intellectual purposes'.[85] An Improvement Act was passed for the town in 1861, and members of Dawson's church were increasingly involved in town educational and other activities.[86] The Church of the Messiah, another place of worship in the town centre, also became a locus for new thinking about the municipality, and provided Joseph Chamberlain with a launching pad for his public activities. Its minister, Rev. Crosskey, believed that of the varied methods of divine service, 'the service of a great town is one of the most honourable and in these modern days, is of increasing importance and worth'.[87]

Crosskey drew on classical references to Athens in support of his claims for the significance of the city.[88] For R. W. Dale, who also contributed to this new focus on municipal responsibility, it was the Italian city-states which provided inspiration. 'If we are true to each other and true to the town,' Dale told his congregation at Carrs Lane, 'we may do deeds as great as were done by Pisa, by Florence, by Venice in their triumphant days.'[89] This use of historic reference points, whether from the classical world or that of the Renaissance, indicates, as Clyde Binfield has argued, a less defensive posture by nonconformists in the 1860s: they were proud to contribute to urban and national life. Indeed, he sees the late 1860s as the peak point for middle-class nonconformity in the nineteenth century.[90] Nonconformists were Englishmen too, as Dale insisted, and 'decline to be excluded from the political life of the State'.[91]

For Dale the evangelical context for these arguments was critical. The year 1862 had seen a sharp conflict between established church and dissent in Birmingham, which resulted in Dale's public profile being significantly increased. He had been on the verge of leaving for Australia, which he saw as a great opportunity to engage with 'the glory and responsibility of educating a great empire and of directing the currents of its religious life and thought for a century or two to come'. The congregation at Carrs Lane, however, convinced him that he should stay, and he was to increasingly occupy himself with political questions.[92] Edward Miall, the protagonist of a class-conscious, radical nonconformity, was a significant influence here, fully conscious as he was of the power of the middle classes, yet seeking union with the working class.[93] Dale was concerned that an undue emphasis had been laid upon religious emotion, while insufficient attention was paid to the practical duties of life. Evangelicals had been too afraid of contact with worldly things, and he was anxious to redress this balance. 'The prosperous people of a free nation' must take an active part in town life; otherwise, 'the political greatness and stability of their country' would be seriously endangered.[94] He looked for an ethical revival, believing that Christians had become 'enfeebled', and that a more 'positive force' was required, involving 'strenuous virtue'.[95] What he described as 'Christian manliness', a resolute and vigorous engagement with the material world, could be expressed through Christian citizenship. Manly was indeed his favourite adjective, as Hugh McLeod argues, and it meant brisk, direct, logical, and without superfluous ornamentation. Dale's own manner was pre-eminently manly: his 'commanding presence, forceful manner, compelling earnestness and power of argument' combined with his frank, honest and vigorous style and his strong physical presence. He was indeed a 'pulpit prince' at a time when 'preaching was among the most widely popular art forms in Victorian England'.[96] But it was not necessary to attend a place of worship to hear Dawson or Dale, for both were part of municipal life at many levels.[97]

Following the death of a beloved daughter, Dale struggled to keep working. Faced with his own grief, and convinced that true Christian manliness needed to combine mind and emotions, he decided to edit a new collection of hymns. He was troubled that most recent hymns were lacking in faith, hope and joy; they were all tears and sighs and miserably sentimental. 'They are women's hymns rather than men's hymns,' he argued, and 'they are the hymns of very weak hysterical women too.' He knew that a hymn could affect a congregation far more deeply than a sermon. The new volume was *The English Hymn Book*.[98] 'I have called it THE ENGLISH HYMN BOOK,' Dale was to write in the preface,

> because I have endeavoured, as far as possible, to insert only those hymns which seem to be in harmony with the characteristic type of English piety ... in its healthier forms ... distinguished by a certain manly simplicity

... for myself, I am anxious to preserve the national type both of faith and of feeling ... I have avoided whatever seemed foreign and unfriendly to our tradition and habits.[99]

Dale became increasingly convinced of the importance of political responsibility. Speaking at a public *conversazione* with Bright in Birmingham in 1864, he stressed the duty of religious men to be responsible Christian citizens, a very different stress from that of his predecessor, John Angell James. 'I feel a grave and solemn conviction', he said, 'that in a country like this, where the public business of the state is the private duty of every citizen, those who decline to use their political power are guilty of treachery both to God and to man.'[100] He attended public meetings, and did not hide his sympathies with the Liberals, though he did not formally attach himself to a party. He abandoned the title 'Reverend' to reduce distinctions between himself and others, and became known as Dr Dale. He wanted his ministry to serve the whole population, rather than a limited number of church members. At the same time he insisted on the importance of Christian citizenship, rooted in individual experience of faith.

This was a new frame of mind, and Dale reached out to a wider audience, seeking a more inclusive fellowship through a municipal frame. He looked for 'a robust type of Christian citizen', and found that Birmingham's skilled artisans made the best listeners, ready for the 'strongest thinking'. Birmingham's business world was, 'like the scenery of Warwickshire', 'a rolling country with no projecting peaks': the apparent dominance of moderate-sized establishments and skilled workers meant fewer huge disparities of wealth.[101] He studied the conditions of business and industrial life in Birmingham, and became interested in work and wages: 'The last translation of the Bible', he once said, 'will be its translation into the vernacular of daily conduct and custom'.[102] In the early 1860s he grew a beard and a moustache, which was deeply shocking to the older members of his congregation, and began to smoke a pipe and wear grey rather than black. All of this signified his connections with the world, rather than separation from it. For James, spiritual life had to be lived through conduct and custom; for Dale, social practice was critical.

In 1865, while extensive alterations were being made at Carrs Lane, the town hall was used for services, which meant that a much more mixed congregation attended. It was at this time that Dale became involved in the struggle for reform, believing that the vote was a democratic right, rather than a privilege: the franchise should provide a peaceful and legal control for the people, all classes of the people, over the legislature and executive.[103] At the death of Palmerston in 1865, he preached a sermon which celebrated the great man's commitment to

European freedom. But at the same time Dale marked his distance from him in terms of the pursuit of national self-interest. There was another responsibility beyond that of narrow self-interest, Dale believed: 'our imperial power was not granted us by the providence of God merely that we might be able to protect our commerce in remote seas, and by the display of our vast resources extort from unwilling nations new facilities for increasing our already almost boundless wealth'. For nations, like individuals, 'the power to convert a benefit or to avert an injury is inseparably associated with the duty of using it'.[104] But the nation, the wider collective, was built on towns. Men – and Dale's focus was men – could orchestrate their individual responsibilities through their engagement with town life. In so doing they would demonstrate their capacity to act as citizens not only of the town, but of the nation and the empire. From the midland metropolis they could reach out as Englishmen, as Birmingham men, as commercial men, as makers of civilising commodities, as manly citizens, as improvers of their own town and beyond.

Morant Bay

For the protagonists of the civic gospel, the men of Birmingham had the responsibility to work for a better life for the population of the town.[105] But their responsibilities did not end there. As citizens, or citizens-to-be, of the nation, they must preoccupy themselves, as the men of Birmingham traditionally had, with the wider world. From 1865 the question of the extension of the franchise was firmly on Birmingham's political agenda: its senior MP, John Bright, was leading the countrywide demand for reform. Those skilled artisans of the midland metropolis who sought full recognition as citizens concerned themselves with all the political questions of the day, but at the end of 1865 the news arrived about the violence in Jamaica. Birmingham had strong links with the island, established over more than thirty years, but what were the reactions to the events at Morant Bay and their repercussions?

The *Birmingham Daily Post* reported from the outset that the colonists were very afraid of this 'rising or rebellion', since the white population was only about 14,000, the black 430,000: if a general insurrection were to take place, half the whites might be slaughtered before any assistance could reach them. There were only 900 troops on the island, and of these the majority were negroes who so far had remained faithful, but might defect, as the sepoys had in India. There were also references to 'the horrors of the San-Domingue insurrection': racial fear was vividly in play from the beginnings of the press coverage.[106] The

Birmingham Journal was convinced that the object of the insurrection 'embraced the systematic extermination of the white race'. But at the same time it reminded its readers that, while nothing justified violence, the negroes had 'suffered grievously at the hands of the whites'. 'Half-starved, half-naked, unable to obtain work, shut out from all participation in the government of the island, frantically apprehensive of being reduced to a condition of semi-slavery, can it be wondered at that the negroes are ready to revolt?' It noted the points of similarity between Fenian and negro disaffection, and argued that the causes of the outbreak, as well as the incidents of it, required serious attention from the government. 'The horrible thirst for blood' which appeared to have seized the white population was also deeply disturbing.[107]

The *Birmingham Daily Post* carried reports from the New York press and from the *Spectator*: the tone of the latter was not unsympathetic to the negroes, but was deeply patronising: planters, 'mulattoes [*sic*]' and negroes were all incapable of self-government, Jamaica should become a crown colony.[108]

A week later the official reports from Eyre were put in question as letters arrived from Jamaica giving different versions of the events. The political mood shifted, at least amongst those sympathetic to the emancipated. The Birmingham press relied on reports from the national press and added editorial comment. On 21 November the liberal *Birmingham Daily Post* commented that the more that became known, the worse it seemed to be; the government and the planters had given way to a 'white terror', and 'under its influence they have done things which should make every Englishman blush with shame and indignation'. It was a local riot, there was no evidence of conspiracy, and it was Eyre who had publicised Underhill's letter. Gordon's death was a 'deep stain on the nation'.[109] The *Birmingham Daily Gazette* speculated over the causes, and predicted that the evidence would show that the planters were to blame: they hoped that nothing would emerge which would reflect unfavourably on 'the negro race at this crisis of their history'. William Morgan wrote a letter in response to this editorial, thanking the editor and arguing that 'the discontent and disaffection of the black race have been fostered by influences favourable to the perpetuation of negro slavery'. Attempts were continually being made, he claimed, 'to represent the negroes as a dangerous race of mere savages'.[110] Meanwhile a meeting was organised by the Baptists in the town, to counter the accusations made against them by Eyre and first circulated by *The Times*.[111] J. T. Brown, Underhill's companion on the BMS deputation to the island, spoke about the Baptist mission on the island, and insisted that the missionaries had not been involved either in 1831 or in 1865: it was the pro-slavery lobbies which had tried to falsely incriminate them on both occasions.[112]

At the 'Hope and Anchor' Jamaica was debated in the first week of December; the motion questioned whether the policy of the governor could be justified. Those who were critical of Eyre argued that the retaliation had been excessive, that there had been a 'savage brutal bloodthirsty wholesale massacre of the innocent with the guilty', that this was 'a disgrace to the English name, to the English character, and to our English arms' – indeed a disgrace to 'the civilisation of the nineteenth century' – and that a most searching inquiry was necessary to 'redeem Old England's honour'. The supporters of Eyre argued, on the contrary, that it was absurd to govern Africans as if they were English, that 'the coloured races of Mankind' had inflicted various massacres on white people, and that severity was necessary. In the vote, fifteen supported Eyre, and twenty-nine were critical. At the end of the first week in December the *Birmingham Daily Post* noted that Brighton, Bradford, Manchester, Liverpool and Leeds had all held public meetings on events in Jamaica, and it hoped Birmingham was not going to fall behind. It was known that signatures were being collected asking the mayor to convene a town meeting, but why had nothing happened? 'Birmingham is losing, by delay, something of its ancient reputation in matters such as this,' it commented. Unless people stirred themselves, the town would no longer remain in the forefront of public opinion. Birmingham should intervene and demand a 'prompt and thorough enquiry'.[113]

Two days later, immediately after the announcement of a government inquiry, a meeting was held in the committee room of the town hall by gentlemen who were asking the mayor to call a town meeting. Alderman Sturge was in the chair, and Thomas Morgan and two of his sons and Arthur Albright and other anti-slavery activists were in attendance. William Morgan moved that a committee should be formed to present the requisition to the mayor, and Dr Dale and other faithfuls agreed to serve. William Morgan reported that they already had 300 signatures from influential residents, but that there was some anxiety as to the need for more information. Matthew Davenport Hill, for example, was reported to be advising caution before jumping to conclusions about Eyre and prejudging the issue: given the relative numbers of white people and black people on the island, the governor had faced serious problems, and it was essential to ascertain the facts.[114] Meanwhile, an Anti-Slavery Society deputation was going to see the Secretary of State, Cardwell, and it was agreed that some Birmingham gentlemen should attend that meeting, including the mayor, Edmund Sturge, Thomas and William Morgan, Arthur Albright and William Middlemore. These were the stalwarts of the anti-slavery movement in the town, the men who had been active for many years; they formed a modest grouping amongst the 250 gentlemen who attended Cardwell.[115] The mayor spoke on behalf of the town, saying that public opinion was 'much excited', feeling that 'justice to the coloured man, the honour of the English Cabinet and of the English nation', all required a thorough investigation.[116] But that excitement was limited, and Birmingham was no longer in the vanguard of anti-slavery action: all might be in favour of an inquiry, but opinions as to Eyre's actions were very varied. A correspondent for the *Birmingham Journal* noted that the 'tone of feeling' in the country at large was a re-echo of the popular views of *The Times*, a fact which did little credit to 'our humanity and national honour'. 'The unguided instincts of the mass in this country', the writer continued, 'are undeniably in favour of the white in prejudice to the black population,' and the stock notion that it was better for fifty blacks to die than one white was regrettably prevalent.[117]

The weak presence of the abolitionist interest in the town was reflected in the constitution of the Jamaica Committee, established at the end of 1865, for Birmingham was scarcely represented with five names amongst the 400 or so gentlemen.[118] On 20 December another town debating society, which had originally met in the 'Hen and Chicken' but then moved to the Midland Institute, opened its doors to the public for its session on Jamaica. The society had more than 150 menbers, and in 1862 its president had been the young manufacturer Joseph Chamberlain. The society was proud of its reputation as a training ground for the 'intellectual athlete' in 'the more vigorous . . . conflicts of public life', and of the fact that many of its members were playing 'an honourable and active part in the important public duties which are essential to the well-being of this town'.[119] The motion debated was that Eyre had been 'hasty, tyrannical and unjust': the critics of Eyre won by two votes. Meanwhile, at the 'Hope and Anchor', the first debate of the new year, on whether the Baptists and Dr Underhill had incited the negroes of Jamaica, found the majority supporting the Baptists, though a substantial minority were critical.[120]

The Ladies' Negro's Friend Society remained true to its beliefs, though deeply grieved by events in Jamaica. 'The outrages committed by the rioters at Morant Bay . . . have given occasion to the opposers of our cause to speak reproachfully,' it recorded reflectively in May 1866, in the report of the annual meeting held at the home of Mrs Joseph Sturge, as she was universally known. Doubtless, they all knew people who were ready to believe that the people of Jamaica were 'savages'. From their perspective, however, 'it would be quite as unfair to condemn the whole population of Ireland for the riots in Belfast, or the entire peasantry of England for the burning and destruction in the city of Bristol many years ago'. There was no excuse for 'negro misdeeds', but the 'terrible reprisals' were also to be greatly regretted. The violence, they argued, 'cannot fairly be attributed to any *peculiar* depravity of the negro race'. The assertion that 'the race' had no especially savage characteristics was undercut by the society's conviction that 'the race' was 'naturally impulsive and imitative in a high degree'. For the LNFS, 'the negro race' was childlike, rather than savage. The bad treatment which they experienced from white people in Jamaica must result in grievous consequences, since they were so prone to imitation. As in 1831, it was the planters, who ought to know better, who carried the burden of blame. The unspoken characteristic of the Anglo-Saxon race was that it had the capacity to lead and to rule; but this could be used or misused. There had been no justice in Jamaica: crown colony government provided the best hope of recovery from the 'abyss' of 'corrupt legislation, and still worse administration of the law'. England should have known better: 'the events of the last few months', judged the LNFS, 'solemnly instruct us, that when a nation emancipates its bondsmen, after ages of degradation and wrongs, its obligations are but half discharged; and that unless the freedmen are instructed and educated, emancipation (which is supposed to have exorcised the demon of slavery) will never produce its most beneficent results'. It hoped that this lesson would not be lost on the American people. The letters they had received from Jamaica, alongside the evidence in the Blue Books, had convinced them that there had been no conspiracy. The people had many faults, but they did not include treason or sedition. It was vital that the society continue its work: there was still much to be done, and its task was now more difficult, since the 'negro race are at this moment regarded with disfavour and distrust, while their many enemies are rejoicing in their calamities'. The degradation of the negro race, the society believed, was largely 'due to the crime and cupidity of the Anglo-Saxon family'. Hopefully, the 'more favoured race' would now shoulder its responsibilities and recognise the need for Europeans to live in the West Indies, their task being to elevate rather than degrade.[121]

The press reported fully on the hearings of the Royal Commission in Spanish Town, which began in February 1866, and evidence was accumulated of the brutality of the suppression. In March *The Times* felt obliged to recant on its initial unconditional support for Eyre and its attack on the negroes: it published a leader acknowledging that an abuse of power had taken place.[122] From February Birmingham had its own special representative in Jamaica: William Morgan. Morgan had been an anti-slavery enthusiast all his life, and in the mid-1860s was still serving as an officer of the BFASS and as one of the honorary secretaries of the Freedmen's Aid organisation in the Midlands. He was an untiring advocate of the cause of the negro, arranging meetings and petitions, following developments in different parts of the empire, giving money, time and energy. He was also still very actively involved with the Baptist church and the missionaries. The accusations against the missionaries provoked British Baptists to rally to their support; given Morgan's long association with Jamaica, it was hardly surprising that from the time the news of the events at Morant Bay arrived in England, he was busy writing letters to the press and activating the Birmingham 'friends of the negro'.

When the Royal Commission was announced, those pressure groups most heavily involved with abolitionist issues acted to secure a presence in relation to it. The Jamaica Committee, the main public organisation dealing directly with the aftermath of Morant Bay, instructed two barristers, John Gorrie and John Horne Payne, to act for it in Jamaica, following the proceedings of the commission and acting on behalf of those who had suffered under martial law. Gorrie also served as the special correspondent of the *Morning Star*, a newspaper established by Cobden and Bright in 1856, and in the forefront of criticism of Eyre from the beginning. Gorrie, trained at the Scottish Bar, had worked for the paper for some years, and had written many articles in support of the North in the American Civil War. From the moment of his arrival in Jamaica, he was besieged by victims wanting to tell him their stories, and his long vivid accounts made a significant impact in England.[123] At the same time, the BFASS resolved to send a 'Special Correspondent' to attend the hearings on the island and to assist 'the legal gentlemen representing the Jamaica Committee'. It proved difficult to raise the money for this, and it was only after a special subscription had been set up that it was possible to proceed. William Morgan was this 'Special Correspondent', his brief to investigate the legislative and administrative evils against which the society had been protesting for many years, and which had resulted in 'the present wreck of the social and industrial condition of the island'. He was to concern himself particularly with the courts. He had volunteered for this task, believing that not only the peasantry, but also the Baptist missionaries, had been falsely accused by Eyre, and that they would need all the support possible before the Royal Commission, given the hostility of the local elite.[124] While the commission had a limited brief, to concern itself primarily with the events which had taken place and only narrowly with the question of origins, the Quakers, who had sent two investigators, Thomas Harvey and William Brewin, and the BFASS were anxious to explore the deeper causes of disaffection on the island. The BFASS committee was well aware that a young criminal class had increased in Jamaica and thought that Morgan's experience in this field would be particularly relevant. They also saw his personal acquaintance with many of the oldest, most established missionaries on the island as being helpful, for it would give him access to 'the negro'. The great problem, as the committee saw it, both for Jamaica and the southern states of America, was 'how to secure good government, equal law and general education among antagonistic classes and castes, alike degraded by the habits and instincts of the old slave system'. The only solution, it believed, was to have executive government in the hands of 'men born and bred in an atmosphere of liberty'. The British government should establish a crown colony, and self-government would then become possible in time.[125]

Morgan travelled to Jamaica with Harvey and Brewin, and they arrived at the beginning of February, when the commission had just begun its public hearings. This was Morgan's first visit to Jamaica. He had been concerned with the island since the early 1830s, when in his late teens. He had corresponded with many of the missionaries, and they had visited him in Birmingham. Finally, he was to see the island for himself. Now a man of fifty-one, with a wife and seven children, he was a successful solicitor and pillar of the Birmingham liberal philanthropic community. His range of activities had broadened in the 1850s from the radical, Baptist and anti-slavery agendas to the campaign for the reprieve of George Hall and more mainstream social reform, particularly through his work with Carpenter and Hill on 'street Arabs'. Arriving on the island, he immediately got to work, and found 'a grand opportunity of exercise . . . for his practical mind'.[126] On a visit to the Kingston Penitentiary, he was shocked to see about sixty-five male prisoners exercising in the yard, dressed in sackcloth smocks with 'rebel' printed upon them in bold letters. These were men imprisoned under martial law, yet the military authorities were not permitted to use the Queen's prisons. Morgan was able to secure their release, a story that was handed down with pride in his family.[127] This outcome, he believed, 'entitles me to congratulate the *Anti-Slavery Society* that the presence of their representative in the colony brought this matter to the light, and that a large number of persons, some of whom were certainly innocent, have been restored to their families, and enabled to resume their ordinary engagements and duties in life'.[128] He was also deeply shocked, on visiting the Morant Bay area, to find that bodies were still left on the roadside, covered with lime. It would do much to heal the wounded feelings of the people, he believed, if simple graves were dug, a recognition 'that England grieves over slaughter'. He made a point of talking to 'all sorts of people' at every opportunity, and found that 'Mr. Eyre's party' firmly believed, without any evidence, that there had been 'a deep-laid scheme'.[129]

Morgan arrived in Jamaica with an analysis of the island's 'problems' already in place in his mind. The very construction of the place as a 'problem' was deeply established within English discourses on the island.

Simon Gikandi argues that 'the diverse narratives of imperial travel' share a 'theoretical unanimity: they are already animated by existing themes and delimited by discursive regulations that precede travel'. Trollope wrote a narrative that confirmed existing conventions of travel and theories about the relations between metropole and colony. Kingsley was to provide, in his *At Last*, a 'startling example . . . of the inherent circularity of imperial discourse'.[130] And Froude, who declared that he went to the West Indies to discover the real conditions of the islands, used his journey to 'affirm the essential and organic nature of Englishness'.[131] Touring, Gikandi suggests, 'becomes a form of retour: opinions formed before the commencement of the voyage are not dissipated by experience; on the contrary, they are authorized by the weight of personal observations. . . . Journeys that began with anxieties about the metropole . . . end with a sublime affirmation of the sites of Englishness.' But it was worth going, even if it was retour, because the travel itself, the observation, gave authority. The domestic audience at home could be reminded that 'in the midst of doubts about English identity and destiny . . . the alternatives to civilization and progress are barbarism abroad and decay at home'.[132] Morgan's journey certainly began with anxieties about the metropole, for it was a British governor and the British army who had acted with such brutality, and anti-negro feeling was widely circulating at home. But he was too critical of aspects of Englishness to be able sublimely to affirm its rule. The gap between metropole and colony was crucial here: the forms of Englishness which operated in the West Indies had long been anathema to anti-slavery enthusiasts. Jamaican whites did not represent the right kinds of Englishness.

Much of Morgan's commentary on his journey, both in the form of the reports he wrote and sent on the spot and the version which he submitted after his return home, contained conventional anti-slavery wisdom. Slavery had corrupted and degraded all, the extraordinary beauty of the island was juxtaposed to its 'wreck and ruin', the old problems about labour and wages persisted, and the negroes had lost heart and lost hope. But the encounters he had, and the ways in which he wrote about them, revealed the complexity of feelings and responses which his journey provoked. His pre-existing map was not quite adequate to the task. Soon after arriving, he commented on the un-English way in which people carried on. The Jamaican habit of 'exaggeration', a habit which he saw as characteristic of both white and black people, gave him pause for thought. It was a genuinely Jamaican habit, marking the colony off from the metropole and endowing it with at least the modicum of a common culture. He had soon discovered that the estimates in the press as to the numbers killed in the violence had been excessive, and he associated this 'with the wonderful tendency to exaggeration that prevails in this country'. 'Immoderate language' was constantly used in conversation, and the scale of alarm and disaffection was, in his opinion, connected to 'the careless use of the most vehement and passionate forms of speech'. This 'vicious habit' did great damage, and he looked forward to the day when more rational forms of exchange – for which, read English – would reduce the dangers which went with overheated imaginations.[133]

A meeting with a group of white women reinforced his sense of the damage done to human feelings by the cruelty of slavery, and was made sense of in terms of his existing discursive frameworks. In Bath, in the vicinity of St Thomas-in-the-East, where martial law had reigned, he spent an evening talking with 'some white ladies' who had been there throughout that time.

> Their ideas were derived from the old times of slavery, and I was much pained by their apparent insensibility to the sufferings of the 'black creatures', as they call them. While men and women alike were daily under the lash, and the flogging went on all through the day, and wire cats were being used on the bodies of women as well as men, and the outcry of agony was incessant, these ladies heard it all, yet not one expression of pity dropped from their lips when they recounted the horrors of the scene. They appeared to have taken it for granted that the punishment was necessary, and was being lawfully inflicted, and I looked in vain for some expression of womanly sympathy with persons who had evidently been exposed to an extremity of human suffering. With sorrow I found that the spirit of slavery had utterly killed that of sympathy, if it ever had any existence towards black people, in these otherwise estimable and accomplished ladies.[134]

These women were not like his friends in the LNFS, whose 'womanly sympathy' made them empathise with those in distress, or like Mary Carpenter, a profound believer in the importance of sympathy as an imaginative human quality. They were perhaps more associated in his mind with the unwomanly Sarah Hall, who had neglected the bonds of marriage and attempted to subvert the gender order by leaving her husband for her lover. In Jamaica it was the 'spirit of slavery' which had killed decent human feeling and produced a harsh insensitivity to the pain of others in women who, in other respects, were judged as 'estimable and accomplished'. The obverse of this deformation of white people was the unfortunately imitative character of the 'negro race', a stereotype which the LNFS had resorted to in its attempt to explain the violence which had taken place. Unable to treat black people as political agents responding to oppression, they projected the blame back on to the destructive character of their white rulers. Morgan was pulled between that familiar way of constructing 'the race' and a recognition that something else was going on. His passage on the white women was juxtaposed with one in which he reflected on the black women whom he saw coming down from the mountains into Bath, with their produce on their heads. This was a sight 'not to be forgotten', 'these groups of stalwart women' who were able to skilfully poise their burdens on their heads and swing along the path, 'at a pace much greater than most European labourers could manage under a similar burden'. Their clothing was 'slight, but decent', and they seemed 'cheerful, active and robust'. This was an image of an independent people, going about their business successfully, neither childlike nor depraved – a very different image from Trollope's young black mimics, pretending to be white ladies, or the pious and docile stereotypes so precious to the abolitionist imagination.[135]

Yet still he reached for European help as the route to progress. The negroes of St Thomas-in-the-East, he wrote while he was still on the island, 'are far from being the savage and brutalised people which their enemies represent them to be'. But, 'they have not yet reached that high culture and civilisation which shows itself in an extensive demand for superior articles of dress, and furniture, and food'. They were content with the food which they grew, and had little desire for articles from abroad, therefore showed little interest in the export trade. Ideas in this country, he reflected, 'are not yet fully in accordance with English notions of political economy'. Most Jamaican land was owned by small producers, and their aims were usually modest. But, 'if the remainder of the land could be brought into cultivation under European auspices, then perhaps a higher type of civilisation might be introduced, and the world would be the gainer'.[136]

But this need for European intervention was not Morgan's only response. At the end of the commission sittings, he went on a tour of the island, and was able 'to enjoy the glorious scenery of this queen of the Antilles, and to partake of the generous and graceful hospitality of its inhabitants'. He found it 'truly melancholy' to see so much land uncultivated, sugar estates abandoned, and the planters unable either to employ the same numbers or pay decent wages. But, faced with this, the labouring classes had responded with determination, slowly and painfully finding new sources of work for themselves and new ways of surviving. He was interested to discover the difficulties they faced in developing exports: inadequate shipping, for example. But he saw signs of hope. Abandoned land was coming back into cultivation, 'industrious negroes' were cutting their own cane, and small proprietors proving their skills. Like Underhill before him, he saw that large-scale sugar production could no longer be the key to the economy, and that an independent peasantry might have a future. Perhaps the ideas that prevailed in

England were not quite right for Jamaica. Yet such impulses in himself were immediately countered with a return to English values. If the people began, 'under wise and gentle government, and having the advantage of good religious teaching', to make larger profits, he argued, they might gradually come to appreciate education for their children, and 'other civilising influences and habits'. He had been delighted to discover an association at Black River, established to collect and ship produce. Such associations, 'highly esteemed in England and on the continent of Europe', had not been connected with the black and coloured populations of Jamaica. Yet here was one, its treasurer an old man who had once been enslaved, and who was spoken of highly in Joseph Sturge's book. And this association brought Morgan back to a comforting belief. 'So many intelligent Englishmen have visited the island,' he concluded, 'that I cannot but cherish the hope that a remedy will speedily be applied for some of the principal evils that afflict her.'[137] Here was the colonial dream of the 'friends of the negro' reaffirmed. Those 'intelligent Englishmen', from Sturge and Harvey, to Chandler, Gurney and Underhill, they must know best.

Once back in England, Morgan tried to make use of his new expertise. He attended a BFASS deputation to the newly appointed governor of the island, Sir John Peter Grant, who replaced Storks once he had completed his work on the commission. Harvey and Brewin were both there too. Harvey had maintained a strong interest in Jamaica ever since his visit there as a young man with Joseph Sturge. He had seen for himself the progress which had been made amongst those who had once been enslaved. There were black men in the Assembly; the headmaster of the Church of England school in Kingston was a black clergyman; the Baptists had trained and educated twenty native ministers. In his view the outbreak had had no political significance; rather, it had arisen from chronic dissatisfaction, and there was no evidence of widespread disloyalty.[138] 'Friends of the negro' must look to a better form of government as the hope for the future.

Both he and Brewin were convinced that it was the absence of religious instruction which was crucial to the disturbances. The presence of 'native Africans', freed from slave-ships, and of Native Baptists, who had been 'jealous of missionary interference' and had enjoyed little of 'effective, practical, christian teaching', were seen by them as important factors in promoting disaffection. They saw signs of improvement amongst the emancipated, particularly where missionaries had been active, noting looks of 'worth and intelligence' in Mandeville, where the LMS had a mission, and 'thoughtful and intelligent faces' in Brown's Town, where John Clark had been working for decades. But while there were hopeful indicators in some areas, 'heathen darkness' extended its shadow across large parts of the island, and it was clear to them that British intervention would be required for a long time to come. Perhaps, they argued, the 'friends of the negro' in England had underestimated the difficulties. Under slavery, the family, 'divinely instituted as the fountain of social order and of all true progress' had scarcely existed, and still there was much to be done. The greatest remedial agent must be Christianity and the work of the missionaries; but, in addition, extensive European immigration, capital, vigorous self-help, a bastardy law, improvements in the workings of the courts, in wages and in taxes were all required.[139] The deputation to Grant was hopeful that his tenure of office would see significant improvements on the island, and that his experience in India 'in dealing with the interests of all classes, especially native races' would stand him in good stead. In response, Grant enlisted their help for his work on the island, a far cry from the attitude of most governors, who had snubbed abolitionists. This more conciliatory tone ensured that the new governor soon had problems with the planters in Jamaica, who named him 'the Bengal tiger', and the 'negro Governor'.[140]

The BFASS decided to present an address to the black and coloured peoples of Jamaica as a first step in this attempt to create a new climate of hope on the island. It was important both to reassure the black population that their old friends and patrons were still in place, and to instil into them renewed commitment to the old goals. In the wake of Morant Bay there was both a great deal of fear, anxiety and depression, and a loss of confidence in some of the missionaries who had compromised their old principles and 'given way to craven fears at the time of the disturbances', pledging themselves to Eyre and alienating the affections of 'their people'.[141] Samuel Oughton's apostasy had been widely reported both in Jamaica and in Britain. The *Birmingham Journal* had made a particular point of it, noting that the support of this group of dissenting ministers was of particular importance for Eyre.[142] The 'friends of the negro' needed to reaffirm friendship. Morgan and Edmund Sturge were the two signatories from Birmingham. 'Permit us, your sincere and long-tried friends, to address a few words of hearty counsel,' the memorial began. 'The Anti-Slavery men and women of Great Britain', it continued, 'toiled hard in past years to obtain your freedom,' and they had since watched over their interests as best they could. Now they asked them to 'strengthen their hands', by showing that the black man could prove himself a good subject of the Queen. The black man needed to demonstrate that he could do more than simply support himself and his family; he must 'improve his condition by honest industry' and strive hard to educate his children. This was a turning point for Jamaica, they argued; 'Your friends hope much from you.' They were earnestly exhorted to work steadily, train their children properly, avoid violence, obey the laws, attend church and honour marriage. 'If you honour God he will bless and prosper you,' they promised, but if, once redeemed from the yoke of slavery, they remained 'the willing slaves of sin and Satan', they were warned, there was no hope for them.

The terms of this address were somewhat different from those of Thomas Clarkson thirty years earlier. 'The black man' was now a man, not a child, and if he took the wrong path, it would be his own choice. He would damn himself to perdition. But the paternalist tone, the focus on loyal subjecthood, on industry, on improvement, on family and on the man as head of the household were little changed. The 'friends of the negro' presented powerful continuities to the black subjects of Jamaica. And there were still those who were prepared to listen: Morgan received an address in response, thanking the BFASS for their 'kind words of hearty counsel' and 'long interest in us', and assuring the society that across the length and breadth of the island, 'although we are a poor and illiterate people', there were many who still thanked them for their good work.[143] At an anti-slavery meeting in Spanish Town later that year, Morgan, Underhill, Harvey and Brewin were all named as Jamaican delegates to the anti-slavery conference which was to take place in Paris, alongside Phillippo's son George, who had acted as barrister for the missionaries at the Royal Commission, and the Rev. East, thus symbolising once again the fraternal connections between England and Jamaica.[144]

Conceptualising those connections as fraternal was, however, increasingly unusual in the atmosphere of 1866 and 1867. The *Anti-Slavery Reporter*, in its review of a book on subject races by Roundell, one of the members of the Royal Commission, was dismayed that he had cut from the published version the strong condemnation of the proceedings under martial law which he had included in the spoken version of the paper presented at the Social Science Association. They disputed his implied judgement that emancipation had come too soon, and his conviction that representative institutions were unsuited to Jamaica. The remedy for Jamaica's problems, the reviewer argued, should not have been abolition of the House of Assembly, but an extension of the franchise, a view which was rarely expressed. Paternal despotism provided no answers:

> Men must feel their manhood before they can assert it, but they will not feel it any the sooner if they are always treated like children. Pride of race and pride of caste are the predominant influences in our colonies, and these – not the inferiority or unworthiness of the race governed – lie at the root of our oppressive rule.[145]

But these were unusual sentiments, and ones which were increasingly at odds with the more hostile racial discourses of the mid-1860s.

Morgan was only too well aware, in the context of the renewed sympathy for Eyre in the wake of the Jamaica Committee's attempts to prosecute him, of the 'rooted antipathy that some Englishmen cherish against all black people'. This 'spirit' was doing much mischief across the world, and Morgan would do what he could both in his home town and in the nation at large to counter it.[146] He worked hard to strengthen the connections between Birmingham and Jamaica in the period after his return, both reinforcing existing links and attempting to create new ones. He had visited particular places for the LNFS to check whether their aid was being well used. He reported that he had gone to Sturge Town with John Clark: a new school was in the process of being built there, 'on a site commanding magnificent scenery', and the large population in the surrounding area was 'looking forward with great hopefulness' to its opening.[147] In August he organised a meeting at the Birmingham Chamber of Commerce to receive a deputation from the Cornwall Agricultural and Commercial Association, one of those examples of cooperation which he had been so delighted to find. The deputation was in England to establish agency for the sale of the produce of freeholders. J. S. Wright was in the chair, and other prominent Baptists and missionary enthusiasts in attendance. Not all the audience, however, was entirely convinced of the industry of the negro. George Dixon, a prominent Birmingham figure, who was something of a sceptic on questions of racial equality, argued that the large amounts of imports and exports from Cuba, where slavery existed, pointed to the 'self-indulgence of the negro when he became free', and suggested that the absence of 'continuous labour' remained the key issue.[148]

In September Morgan was at a BMS public meeting in the town, alongside Dr Underhill. Underhill defended the attempts which had been made 'to raise the negro to a standard of a permanent and lofty character'. He argued that the people had been provoked beyond endurance, but that no excuse could be made for the behaviour of either the rioters or of Governor Eyre. The following day a large public breakfast was held in one of the town's hotels: this was a mixed event, and Morgan was accompanied by the widow of George William Gordon, who was staying with him and his family. In his address Morgan spoke about his visit to the island, and told how 'in all parts of the island he had found traces of Birmingham men and their work'. Coultart, one of the early missionaries, had a later connection with a Birmingham chapel. Griffiths, who had been sent from Birmingham in the 1830s, was buried in Spanish Town. In Four Paths, when the people discovered he had come from Birmingham, he was met with 'unbounded expressions of gratitude'. In

Falmouth, the monument to emancipation in William Knibb's church had been made by a Birmingham sculptor, and Sturge Town, a name which was met with great applause, stood as a memorial in itself to Birmingham's famous son. It was the business of England, he maintained, to help and sustain the 'black and coloured people' who were increasingly doing agricultural work. Furthermore, it was the duty of England, in his estimation, 'to elevate the coloured race', and he hoped that the representative principle would soon be re-established, since direct government from home was very expensive.[149]

The long-established 'friends of the negro' in Birmingham, the missionary and abolitionist publics, the supporters of Freedmen's Aid and initiatives to improve the lot of freed men and women in the West Indies, worked hard to make sense of what had happened in Jamaica and to sustain public interest in the cause. For a man such as Morgan the encounter with Jamaica raised new questions and possibilities and destabilised somewhat conventional anti-slavery wisdom. When Rev. Bridges had seen Jamaica for himself in the 1820s, he had decided that the metropolitan critique of slavery was misplaced. When Morgan was on the island forty years later, he saw that Jamaica was indeed a different kind of society from the metropolis and might have its own culture. Being on the island changed how men thought. But the distance from the metropolis secured the peripheral relation of the colony in metropolitan thinking. The gap between Birmingham and Jamaica was invoked as a gap in both space and time: the miles to cross the sea to the West Indies were configured as a journey back to an earlier time, and a less evolved society.[150] Jamaica was imagined as immobile without British help, its life dependent on that input. Whilst there, Morgan was able to reach for an understanding of this other place, those other peoples with their cultures located in particular histories. Once back in the metropolis, the hierarchy of relations, which had been only slightly dislodged, was reasserted. The 'elevation' of the 'coloured race' was to raise them in that evolutionary hierarchy, to improve them, to bring them into the present, but always, inevitably, behind Anglo-Saxons.

In his appeal for money which followed Morgan's address, Underhill attempted to elicit Birmingham pride, telling his audience 'that Bristol was currently contributing more than they were'.[151] Such strategies only worked, however, when there was a will to be in the forefront of a campaign, when Birmingham 'friends' wanted to demonstrate that they led the field. But the town's abolitionists were unusual in their continued preoccupation with the black population of Jamaica. In so far as events in Jamaica were discussed, it was increasingly in terms of their impact at home. At the 'Hope and Anchor' this was debated alongside questions of parliamentary reform and Fenianism (which was producing wide-scale anxiety) throughout 1866 and 1867. There was always a strong current of support for Eyre.[152] Public opinion across the country ebbed and flowed on the topic, as at the beginning of 1866 the scale of the brutality was revealed by the hearings of the Royal Commission. Once the commission had reported, radical opinion was deeply disappointed with what it saw as the weak government response, and the Jamaica Committee pursued the option of a private prosecution of Eyre. Meanwhile Eyre left Jamaica and returned to England, to be met with a welcoming banquet in Southampton which provoked a counter-demonstration. The ex-governor's defenders then mobilised to establish a defence fund, and the stakes were raised on both sides.[153]

At the end of 1866 a meeting was held in a room at the town hall by a group which then constituted itself as the Birmingham Jamaica Committee. (While large public meetings were held in Leeds, Bradford and London, Birmingham could muster only a committee.[154]) They were seeking support for the prosecution of Eyre, 'as the only course now left open to the people of Great Britain for the vindication of the rights of subject-races, and for the assertion and protection of their own freedom'. The key questions for the committee, which included Dr Dale, Arthur Albright, J. S. Wright, Rev. Vince, Charles Sturge and William Morgan, had become the status of martial law and the principles upon which England should rule her foreign dependencies. Having failed in their appeal to the government, the Jamaica Committee decided that their only recourse was to appeal to the 'British people'. The focus was on the English freedoms which had been threatened by the misuse of martial law in Jamaica: the traditional liberties of the subject must be reaffirmed.[155] It was Frederick Harrison, in a series of letters to the *Daily News* at the end of 1866, who had first brought this issue into public debate. Throughout the empire, he argued, British rule must be the rule of law, and every British citizen, whatever their colour, should be subject to definite powers. The 'terrible Indian rebellion', he believed, had sown evil seeds in the military system. It had called out 'all the tiger in our race'; 'that wild beast must be caged again'. As Bernard Semmel argues, fears of the 'wild beast' in England became increasingly strong, linked to the fears of Fenianism and of the working-class rabble.[156] At the same time, Harrison was maintaining that this was a question 'far deeper than sect or colour'. 'It does not concern Baptists, or black men, or merely the character of a public servant,' he wrote in the radical paper, the *Beehive*. He had no liking for black men, Baptists or Governor Eyre, he continued, but the question was 'whether our vast foreign dominions are to be governed by the irresponsible will of able, absolute, and iron-willed satraps'.[157] The lessons of Jamaica came back to the metropole.

Harrison's claim that all British *citizens* should be subject to the same rule of law was a confusing one, since the subjects of empire did not share the rights of citizenship.[158] In March 1866 Jamaica had been declared a crown colony, its representative institutions having been abolished in the immediate wake of Morant Bay. The *Pall Mall Gazette* wrote in February, when the bill for crown colony status was passing undisputed through both houses of Parliament, of the dangers of treating the ex-slave as though 'we believed him as fit to take care of himself, to guide himself, to judge for himself . . . as any other British subject in short'. The British should learn that 'securing civil rights to a people is one thing, and conferring on them political privileges is another'. All races and classes were entitled to justice, but all were not ready for self-government. In the context of Jamaica, it was a form of cruel and lazy neglect by the mother country to allow West Indians to rule themselves. As Christine Bolt notes, it was highly significant that Jamaica should become a crown colony and the electoral franchise be abolished at a time when black male suffrage was being hotly debated in the USA.[159] There were almost no voices raised against crown colony status in Britain: for most liberals, it was the best solution. But some anti-slavery stalwarts were unhappy about it. In a feature titled 'No Justice for the Negro' in August 1867, just after respectable working-class men had gained the vote in England and Wales, the *Anti-Slavery Reporter* lamented the fact that four West Indian colonies had lost their representative institutions. In the case of Jamaica, it admitted, this might have been necessary, though it was highly undesirable. It was not in accordance with the 'progressive tendencies, nor with the enlightened intelligence of the age'. 'In all colonies which are peopled with the African race', it noted, there was no equitable system of government; nor was there space for the 'friends of the negro' at the Colonial Office.[160]

In developing a critique of martial law, the case of Gordon, so widely publicised in Britain, was only the best known of the instances of its wrongful exercise. Morgan's activities on behalf of the imprisoned victims of courts martial provided another example: those courts should not have exercised powers over civilians. Following Harrison's intervention, John Gorrie wrote an influential pamphlet for the Jamaica Committee on this topic, in which he documented the numerous cases of improper exercise of military power 'enacted in the beautiful island of Jamaica under pretence of repressing disturbances'. 'My task has not been undertaken in vain,' he concluded,

> if it tends to deepen the resolve of my countrymen to resist at all hazards, the preposterous pretensions of Colonial Governors and military officers, to deal with human life and property as they please, without responsibil-

ity to the laws which bind society together, or to the nation which places the sword in their hands for the purpose of justice and mercy.[161]

The meeting in Birmingham was held at the end of December, in the wake of this debate over martial law. Thomas Hughes, MP and well-known author of *Tom Browne's Schooldays*, attended on behalf of the national committee. In its published report the Birmingham committee argued that it was essential

> to the maintenance of our English freedom that legal proceedings be taken to establish on their ancient foundations the great constitutional doctrines that the Crown has no power to suspend civil law; that every British subject is entitled to be tried by a jury, that Courts Martial have no authority over civilians; and that every official is responsible to the civil law for his official acts.

At the same time the events in Jamaica had raised to public prominence broader questions concerning imperial power. England had responsibility for 200 million people, 'varying in race, character, culture, religion, hopes and capabilities'. The gentlemen of Birmingham argued that 'of all tyrannies, that of a superior race over an inferior one is the most terrible'. Englishmen, who had been constant in their defence of their own liberties, and prided themselves on their sympathy with the oppressed, must not uphold government over foreign races that was not founded on principles of justice. All Englishmen should join in a practical demonstration that 'the only justification of our rule over subject races must be found in the fact that we can hold out to them the enjoyment of a higher liberty, the protection of more just and equal laws, the administration of more enlightened rulers than they could themselves secure'. The 'majesty' of the English law had been 'violated and outraged' in Jamaica: the prosecution of Eyre was necessary to demonstrate that the English held their colonial officials to account and were truly Christian rulers.[162]

Birmingham was not particularly responsive to this appeal, however, and the Birmingham Jamaica Committee was short-lived. No large 'practical demonstrations' were made; no great meetings were held in support of the prosecution of Eyre; no effigies of Eyre were burnt, as happened in Clerkenwell; no petitioners gathered with placards seeking recompense for the black victims of British injustice. Only the long-time 'friends of the negro' responded to the call. It was the reform of the franchise that dominated the political life of the town in 1867, alongside Ireland, Fenianism and anti-Catholicism.[163] The faithful continued their regular activities: the Freedman's Aid Association met, and the LNFS held a meeting in March and had a good attendance of nearly sixty. The committee assured the society's members that the gentlemen who were engaged in the prosecution of Governor Eyre and his officers were acting from the conviction, 'that the safeguards of life throughout the breadth of our vast empire are involved in this trial'.[164] In May the ladies had their annual meeting, and the Rev. East was there from Jamaica, visiting friends and hoping to raise money for Calabar.[165] In his address he spoke of the importance of the support provided by the society and kindred organisations in convincing the negro population of the island that there were people who cared for them in Britain, and who would defend their rights and liberties. In the aftermath of the recent events, he told them, 'I know of nothing which tends so much to quiet their minds, and subdue the resentment which might otherwise arise, than organisations and efforts such as yours'. He was at pains to assure his audience of the loyalty and love of order of the Jamaican peasantry and how much they had appreciated the visits of Harvey, Brewin and Morgan.[166]

But these were small meetings. In the new conjuncture of 1867, being a 'friend of the negro' was no longer a mobilising political identity, capable of drawing men and women into activity. For the thousands who attended meetings concerned with domestic political reform, questions of race and empire were relevant to their notions of citizenship, but not in ways that would have warmed the heart of Joseph Sturge. The cluster of ideas about race had shifted, and while notions of the universal family of man and the brotherhood and sisterhood of black and white lived on in the culture, they had significantly lost ground to other conceptions of racial difference. 'Friends of the negro' were now outnumbered by manly citizens.

Birmingham men

In Birmingham there were supporters of the Jamaica Committee and also of Governor Eyre. But in the new political settlement marked by the passing of the Reform Act, it was the rights of white Englishmen which were uppermost. It was Bright who raised the standard of parliamentary reform in his town meeting in January 1865, and between then and the passing of the Reform Act in July 1867, there were two years of heady political debate.[167] Bright, who represented himself as a typical English-man with Saxon qualities who believed in the common destiny of Eng-lishmen across the empire, reflected on the differentiated rights of those same Anglo-Saxons. Englishmen in the Cape, or Australia, or Canada could vote, for new constitutions had been established in the white settler colonies in the 1850s based on manhood suffrage for the colonisers.

'Only the preponderance of an Anglo-Saxon element', maintained the *Contemporary Review*, 'guarantees an inherent capacity for freedom.'[168] 'It is only in his own country', argued Bright, 'on his own soil, where he was born, the very soil which he has enriched with his labour and with the sweat of his brow, that he is denied this right which in every other community of Englishmen in the world would be accorded to him.'[169] Englishmen, Bright concluded, were 'to live like the coolies or Chinese imported into the West Indies', denied the rights that Anglo-Saxons deserved.[170] Bright's racial mapping of rights was complex, for he was in favour of the granting of suffrage to freed black men in the USA, but in favour of crown colony government in Jamaica. The right to representative government, in his mind, depended on the characteristics of the men being represented: the key characteristic was independence. 'I believe', he argued in the House of Commons in March 1867,

> that the solid and ancient basis of the suffrage is that all persons who are rated to some tax . . . should be admitted to the franchise. I am quite willing to admit there is one objection to that wide measure, which exists . . . in almost every franchise you can establish. At this moment, in all, or nearly all boroughs, as many of us know sometimes to our sorrow, there is a small class which it would be much better for themselves if they were not enfranchised, because they have no independence whatsoever, and it would be much better for the constituency also that they should be excluded, and there is no class so much interested in having that small class excluded as the intelligent and honest working man. I call this class the residuum, which there is in almost every constituency, of almost helpless poverty and dependence.[171]

Excluding the 'residuum', as Keith McClelland argues, 'was to create a boundary around a particular kind of respectable working-class man'. And, as José Harris observes, Bright's opposition to the residuum established a polarity between 'the regularly employed, rate-paying working man (possessed of a house, a wife, children, furniture, and the habit of obeying the law) [who] was the heir of the Anglo-Saxon freeman', and a residuum which was 'intemperate', 'profligate' and 'naturally incapable'.[172] Bright was not in favour of manhood suffrage, and this was a source of considerable contention in the town. But, as Patrick Joyce argues, he summoned up 'the people' in his oratory, and reconciled 'the old testament of religion with the new testament of "the people"'.[173] This was a powerful mix.

At the end of November 1865 a large meeting was held in the town hall by the National Reform League, an organisation of mainly working-class radicals, at which a resolution in favour of manhood suffrage was passed. In December Bright addressed the issue again to an audience of

6,000. 'In the galleries there was a plentiful sprinkling of the fair sex,' reported the *Birmingham Daily Post*, which relieved the 'sombre appearance produced by the mass of black hats' worn by the men.[174] In his introduction, the mayor asserted that the reason why public meetings were essential 'in this country is because Englishmen are essentially fitted by their nature to guide the government of the country'. They were peculiarly adapted, he believed, to self-government.[175] This was the essential characteristic of Englishmen, and to deprive them of the franchise was, therefore, to deprive them of their natural rights. For Bright, these were the rights of independent Englishmen: those with homes and families. The defeat of the Liberal bill in June 1866 and the condemnation of the government action in Hyde Park in July provoked huge open-air reform meetings, and in August 150,000 gathered to demonstrate in favour of change. The following March it was estimated that between 200,000 and 250,000 had congregated to express their support for residential manhood suffrage, accepting a distinction between a sober, domesticated, independent manhood and 'rough' men who were not yet ready to enjoy the vote.[176] By August the Reform Act had received royal assent, and 50,000 of Birmingham's respectable working-class men had been enfranchised.[177]

After the Reform Bill was passed, Birmingham Liberals organised a series of lectures on the social and political questions which were likely to face the new electors. Dr Dale was invited to deliver the first. Dale had been an active protagonist in the struggle for reform of the franchise, speaking at numerous demonstrations and arguing strongly for constitutional change. He had also been associated with the Birmingham Jamaica Committee, but 'the negro' was far from the centre of his political imagination in the mid-1860s. 'Manly citizenship' was the key issue for him, and what the forms of responsible action for men in the town, nation and empire should be. He greeted the half million new electors with enthusiasm: 'These 500,000 men are Englishmen like ourselves; they speak our own tongue; they have a sense of justice and honour; they are accessible to reason; they are proud of the greatness and glory of their country, and would spring to arms, every one of them, to defend its soil from invasion, or to avenge an insult to the throne.' Here were the citizen soldiers, ready to bear arms. 'Free discussion of political principles and measures is one of the highest forms of national education,' Dale argued, consciously drawing on the Birmingham tradition of open debate. These 'manly discussions' could do much to increase the general intelligence of the country and give 'robustness and vigour' to the political process and the politicians themselves. Such debate on the great issues of the day, on popular education, on the Irish Church, on foreign policy, could challenge the 'political effeminacy' and 'indolence, and

indifference' which were dangerously rife, alongside the equally dangerous 'worship of material prosperity', 'selfishness . . . cynicism and
scepticism'. For Dale the extension of the franchise meant a great
increase in the stability and security of the state, for those who should
be represented were, and felt their interests secure. The time would come,
he argued, when the franchise would need to be increased again, though
he made no mention of female suffrage. Meanwhile the new voters
had political responsibilities: they must educate their own class, through
the newspaper, the lecture and the public meeting. They must form an
intelligent body of public opinion, with views on every question of
significance. Clearly not all men could rise to be masters, and the 'great
mass of the people must always spend the greater part of their time
and strength in physical labour', but work was honourable, and the
conditions of it must be improved. Relations between masters and men
must also be attended to: co-operation, not antagonism, was the way
forward.

The town needed the energy of the new electors, and housing must
be a priority. Poverty and crime must be tackled, and assisted emigration could be an important outlet. In Australia, Canada and British
Columbia, he argued, there were vast tracts of land which could feed
millions, and which could 'augment the strength and the wealth of our
colonial possessions'. Referring to the recent events in Jamaica, Dale
reminded his audience that since they had only recently acquired political rights themselves, they would enjoy 'a quick and intense sympathy
with all who suffer injustice'. They would use their political influence to
suppress 'the atrocious spirit' which had recently appeared 'in high quarters' and licensed the 'most cruel wrongs upon races subject to our
power'. Inferior races they might be called, but in his judgement the
oppressor, whatever his culture and even his colour, was inferior to the
oppressed. In conclusion, Dale turned to the greatness of the nation and
its imperial responsibilities. This greatness was its 'magnificent inheritance'. England was the 'Queen of nations', 'rich in her material wealth
beyond the most gorgeous dreams of Asiatic kings', but richer still in the
'genius of her sons' and their tradition of freedom. They had provided
the inspiration for the 'mighty Republic of the West', for the oppressed
of every country in Europe. 'Be you worthy of your fathers,' he exhorted
the men of Birmingham, and England would continue to 'render to the
human race the most illustrious services', utilising 'our boundless wealth'
and 'our imperial power for the good of all mankind'.[178]

This vision of imperial greatness marked a different mentality from
that of the 1830s. The Baptist missionaries who had gone to Jamaica in
the 1820s had been outsiders, petitioners at the door of the Colonial
Office. The missionary and abolitionist public which had mobilised in

their support in the early 1830s did not yet control their own munici-
palities or, for the most part, vote in parliamentary elections. By the late
1860s, nonconformist men had fully entered the body politic, and were
part of the Liberal mainstream. In 1868 Gladstone fought and won the
election on the disestablishment of the Irish Church: a significant
reduction in the power of the Anglican establishment. John Bright joined
Gladstone's cabinet, the first dissenter to enjoy that position.[179] As nonconformists became more integrated, in terms of both their cultural
belonging and their status as political citizens, their relation to the
boundaries of nation and empire shifted. Once outsiders, they had
become insiders. The subject status of nonconformists was sometimes
seen as the reason for their sympathy with subject races. But this analogy
was refused: 'it is a voluntary subjection', insisted James Guiness Rogers,
and 'one from which we could be free at any moment we chose'.[180] Nonconformists exercised free will guided by their conscience; subject races
had no such choice. As those who had been marginal men moved into
the heartlands of urban and, later, national power, their mental maps
were redrawn. Birmingham men were 'citizens of no mean city': Bright
himself was convinced that a speech in the town hall was 'more read and
tells more on opinion than a speech in a debate in the Houses'.[181] The
place of their midland metropolis was now secure on the map of both
nation and empire: their independent men enjoyed the vote, their leaders
respected.

For those who were not part of the body of manly citizens, however,
other rules applied. In June 1867, just before the passage of the Reform
Act, a different issue had galvanised the town and shocked the nation.
Serious disturbances had taken place, more reminiscent, in the view of
The Times, of Belfast than of an enlightened locality such as Birmingham.[182] These were occasioned by the presence of William Murphy, a
particularly effective anti-Catholic lecturer.[183] The town's Irish population had increased considerably in the post-Famine years, though it was
probably closer to 4 per cent than the 15–30 per cent estimated for some
northern industrial towns; the predominance of skilled labour had
limited Irish immigration.[184] Despite claims to the contrary, there was
significant anti-Irish and anti-Catholic sentiment in Birmingham. The
presence of the Oratory and John Henry Newman meant that Catholicism had a relatively high profile. The restoration of the Catholic hierarchy had provoked impassioned protests, and in 1852 a series of
anti-Catholic lectures were held at the town hall.[185] In 1866 and 1867
anxieties about Fenianism, the Irish republican movement, were widespread, and Birmingham was no exception. Fenian actions in England
had brought the issues home in an alarming manner. Bright had presented a petition to the House of Commons on behalf of Fenian prison-

ers in May 1867, and was well known for his radical views on Ireland: 'there is a legitimate ground', he maintained, 'for the chronic discontent of which Fenianism is the expression'.[186] But Bright's support for the Fenian prisoners, whose stated intention was to establish an Irish republic, was extremely controversial. For the liberal *Birmingham Journal*, 'Death to the Saxon' was the Fenian watchword: when 'this treasonable conspiracy, baffled and repressed in Ireland', had assumed the form of organised conspiracy and assassination in England, it was essential that it should be firmly put down.[187] Murphy's incendiary and dramatic rhetoric had already provoked a riot in Plymouth and disturbances in Wolverhampton, and the mayor refused permission for his lectures to take place in the town hall. A special tabernacle was constructed, able to hold 3,000–4,000, in which his series on 'The Errors of Roman Catholicism' were delivered. For Murphy, 'Romanism was death, Protestantism was life'; Popish priests were murderers and cannibals, sexually perverted and destructive of the sanctity of the Protestant home and family. His audience was encouraged to stand firm to its principles and prevent any interference with the rights of Englishmen. An angry Irish crowd retaliated, with the women, it was asserted, being particularly hostile to the forces of law and order. They smashed the windows of a house associated with the Protestant Association, and fought with the police. This was behaviour entirely at variance with sober respectable manhood. Every now and again, reported the *Birmingham Daily Post*,

> the police armed with their bare swords, would make a sally to drive the crowd back, and the mob would run away from the cutlasses like so many Fenians; but no sooner had the 'cutlasses' retired than the mob, like so many more Fenians would rush back to their old quarters and again dare the police to come up to them.[188]

This slippage in the reporting between Irish and Fenians was expressive. The following day a crowd of between 50,000 and 100,000 Protestants retaliated, and there were dozens of arrests, mostly Irish, and casualties. An almost exclusively Irish street was left in ruins.[189] Murphyism, it is argued, 'reflected the reaction to Fenianism at the grass roots level'.[190] Murphy's lectures, on the dangers of popery and the threat to Protestant beliefs and institutions posed by Irish Catholics, played on popular Victorian stereotypes.[191] In their reaction to this stereotype, the defenders of Protestantism in Birmingham effected substantial damage to property and people. Throughout the rest of the year, anti-Catholic and anti-Irish demonstrations and lectures continued in the town, including, in November, a near-riot against the Fenians.[192]

The men and women involved in this violence probably belonged for the most part to Bright's residuum: clarifying in their actions the necessity for a line to be drawn between those who were ready for political citizenship and those who were not. If the Protestant crowd was as large as it was claimed, however, some of them must have been the selfsame sober men, the skilled artisans with their homes and families, who were about to receive the vote: demonstrating precisely the artificiality of the lines which were being drawn. Anti-Irish and anti-Catholic sentiments were certainly not confined to the 'rough', and Anglo-Saxonism, with its celebration of Teutonic virtues and its denigration of the Celt, was endemic. While the mayor held Murphy responsible and refused to blame the Irish, a local nonconformist minister was less tolerant. 'We allow the Irish to come amongst us', he argued, 'to absorb, to a large extent, our English labour; we tax ourselves for their support; we allow them the most perfect liberty for the exercise of their religion and we provide for them at the public expense priests of their own faith in our workhouses and gaols; and what do we get in return?'[193] His rhetorical answer was clear: Irish, Fenians and Catholics were all tarred with the same brush.

If the 'manly citizen' was an excluding identity for many of the poor, the rough and those lacking in respectability on account of their religious or ethnic characteristics, it was also an identity available only to men. The ladies of Birmingham had sat in the galleries of the town hall since its construction: watching the political gatherings of men, neither playing a full part nor totally excluded from that public space. Whereas both men and women could be a 'friend of the negro', albeit in somewhat different spheres of action and with different preoccupations, women, by definition, could not claim 'manly citizenship'. It was in the context of the demand for the extension of the franchise from 1865 that women began to make their own claims for entry into political citizenship. In June 1866 a petition was presented by Emily Davies and Elizabeth Garrett to John Stuart Mill, demanding that suffrage be extended to women householders. Three of the signatures on this petition were from Birmingham, a modest contribution from a place with such a strong reforming tradition.[194] In May 1867 Mill introduced his amendment to the Reform Bill, moving that 'person' should be substituted for 'man': an amendment which was defeated by 196 votes to 73. To the surprise of Mill, it won the support of John Bright.[195] Bright had little sympathy for feminists, who to his mind were 'miserable because they are not men'. 'My gardener', he wrote to a friend, 'says there is nothing he dislikes so much in his poultry yard as a "crowing hen" and men-women are not a pleasant addition to our social arrangements': a view which he knew was disapproved of by his sisters and daughters.[196]

The appeal of the women's suffrage movement increased after the debate generated by this amendment, as Jane Rendall has demonstrated, and societies which had been formed in London, Manchester and Edinburgh agreed to form a union known as the National Society for Women's Suffrage. A society was established in Birmingham in April 1868, with Miss Eliza Sturge, Joseph Sturge's niece, acting as secretary. She had grown up in the extended Sturge households in Edgbaston, part of the wider Quaker network to which Bright belonged. Her father Charles served as a town councillor for forty-four years, and as mayor in 1862; her aunts and cousins were active in the LNFS. As with so many of this generation of feminists, there were links with a wide variety of reforming movements. In June 1868 a public meeting was held in the Exchange Room.[197] The motion, put by the Misses Robertson and Burke, was that women should be granted the vote on the same basis as men. The exclusion of women from the exercise of the suffrage was 'unjust in principle and inexpedient in practice . . . the right of voting should be granted to them on the same conditions as those which are or may be granted to men'.[198] The meeting was judged by Lydia Becker to be a 'triumphant success', with standing room only and an audience of more than 600. The vast majority of this 'numerous and intelligent audience' then signed a petition to the House of Commons which was presented by Bright. A concerted effort was subsequently made, as in other parts of the country, to assert that women who paid taxes should be able to vote, and claims were made in the courts over this. Meanwhile, Birmingham suffragists were delighted by the efforts made, which resulted in the granting of the municipal franchise in 1869, bringing women into a closer relation to the government of their town, if not yet the nation. And on that matter they were clear that they would not allow 'the hammer and nails to lie idle'.[199]

In March 1870 Millicent Fawcett was to address a very large meeting in the town hall on 'Electoral Disabilities of Women', and two years later she spoke on 'Women's Suffrage'.[200] The focus of these women suffragists was single women and widows, lady householders, intelligent and respectable persons, who would be able, as Barbara Bodichon argued, to offer a 'healthy, lively, intelligent' patriotism and 'an unselfish devotedness to the public service'.[201] They would bring women's special moral qualities and mission into the political arena, and contribute to new forms of citizenship. These new claims, as Rendall argues, could be legitimated in part through Anglo-Saxonism. Anglo-Saxon and Germanic societies were seen as being particularly favourable to women: as Frances Power Cobbe wrote in 1868, 'Our Teuton race from the days of Tacitus, has borne women whose moral nature has been in more than equipoise with their passions; and who have both observed and obtained a freedom and a respect unknown to their sisters of the south.'[202] The movement had its Anglo-Saxon heroines, and in the debates over granting the municipal franchise to women recourse was made to notions of women's part in local government as a key component of the ancient constitution. But what united the varied strands of writing, thinking and campaigning on women's suffrage in these years was the conviction that it was part of the progressive movement of civilisation, which would bring with it more personal freedom and independence for women. 'The history of civilisation', argued Mrs Fawcett in Birmingham, 'is the history also of a steady progressive improvement in the condition of women.' Women had more freedom and independence than they had possessed in the past, and their 'elevation' continued. That freedom was constituted in relation to female others of the empire. 'Among savage races', Mrs Fawcett continued, 'women have little better lives than beasts of burden. In India a widow is sometimes compelled to sacrifice her own life at the death of her husband. In the semi-civilisations of the East we know that women are principally valued as inmates of the Seraglio.' 'We have inherited a tradition of progress and advancement,' she concluded, and this could not be halted.[203] The women of England would go forward, claiming the same rights as their husbands, fathers and brothers.

The constitution of a town and nation of manly citizens, with their dependents in place 'at home', and 'subject races' both 'at home' and in the empire in their various stages of being 'civilised', was a powerful myth for Birmingham men. In the late 1860s the emphasis of the men of the midland metropolis was on the hierarchy of races, peoples and nations and their own assumed position in that evolutionary hierarchy. This was the formative myth for Joseph Chamberlain, on which late nineteenth-century imperialism was built.

The predominant structure of feeling in Birmingham by the mid-1860s was different from that of the 1830s. The deaths of Sturge and James symbolised the passing of an older generation, formed in the crucible of the evangelical revival and the anti-slavery struggle. Their successors, men such as Dawson and Dale, had different trajectories and developed a different mental map of the world, a different politics, more concerned with the improvement of the town and its relation to the nation and empire than with Sturge's variety of universalism. Jamaica no longer had the same connotations for Birmingham people. While stalwart abolitionists continued to support ventures associated with what they saw as the improvement of the negro race, the island was no longer a compelling place in the town's collective imagination. The reaction to Morant Bay made it clear that the rights of white male citizens were very clearly delineated from those of black subjects: that Jamaica was certainly not

England. While the island became a crown colony ruled from London, the gap between metropole and colony was doubly reinforced as substantial numbers of manly citizens were granted the vote. As white women began the long struggle for full citizenship, the struggle for colonial freedom had scarcely begun.

Epilogue

When Eyre returned to England in 1866, suspended from his duties pending investigation, he was a man in his early fifties who might have hoped to have his most successful years ahead of him. But his public career was finished. In the wake of the Royal Commission's report, the government decided to take no action against him beyond confirming the ending of his term of office, and the Jamaica Committee failed in their attempts to prosecute him. Yet he was never able to re-enter public life. The attempt by the Eyre Defence Committee to reconstitute him as hero had its brief moment: but it was not a moment which lasted. Eyre was bitter as to what he saw as a gross miscarriage of justice. 'I have been persecuted and prosecuted,' he wrote to a supporter in 1869,

> for preserving the colony of Jamaica to the Crown and saving from massacre the loyal inhabitants – when an organised rebellion inaugurated by a planned and wholesale butchering of a large number of its best citizens of all ranks and colours threatened to annihilate both – and 'tho I have signally defeated and triumphed over my Persecutors in every instance I am ruined in prospects and in fortune.[1]

He finally succeeded in securing his pension, a decision which was passed in the House of Commons, but with no member of any influence speaking on his behalf and no enthusiasm from the floor.[2] He was something of an embarrassment to one and all, best forgotten in his Devonshire retreat. England was not a particularly comfortable place for this imperial man: he had lacked moderation and paid the price.

Yet his critics had signally failed in their efforts to censure him publicly. In thinking about the degree of support for the South in the Civil War, Mill had reflected on the importance of generational change: 'the generation which had extorted negro emancipation from our West India planters had passed away,' he noted; 'another had succeeded which had not learnt by many years of discussion and exposure to feel strongly the enormities of slavery'. This new generation, represented by men like Dawson in Birmingham, was liberal in some respects but not in others. Mill was struck by the lack of 'permanent improvement' in the minds of 'our influential classes', the thin veneer of liberal opinions which was all too easily exposed. This thin veneer, as Mill discovered to his cost, was swiftly unveiled when it came to 'the negro', whether in the USA or in Jamaica; to Ireland; or to women's suffrage, all issues on which Mill took a stand in his brief parliamentary career. For Mill this veneer was associated with ignorance, with 'the inattention habitual with Englishmen to whatever is going on in the world outside their own island'. The abusive letters which he received as a result of his stand against Eyre were 'evidence of the sympathy felt with the brutalities in Jamaica by the brutal part of the population at home'. In the case of Ireland, anger against Fenianism stopped people from thinking straight about 'the English mode of governing Ireland'.[3] But perhaps Mill overestimated the ignorance and unthinking reactions of those with whom he did not agree, and the extent to which improved education and increased rationality 'at home' would result in the elimination of 'brutal' or indeed racial thinking. He himself believed in a world of hierarchies: responsible government was only suitable for what he regarded as advanced societies; crown colony government was the best solution for dependencies. Similarly, his idea of citizenship was associated with self-improvement or self-cultivation. The vote was not a right as far as he was concerned: indeed, in 1865 he favoured an educational test for the franchise. Mill was no democrat, and subscribed to commonly held assumptions about civilisation and progress: in his mind, the uneducated and the lower ranks of society, whether poor white men, 'Hindoos' or women, must progress before enjoying the privileges of citizenship. What was distinctive about Mill's radicalism and that of his generation and his way of thinking was that the possibility of progression was open to all, whether inspired by a Christian universalism or a liberal humanism.[4] But in the wake of Morant Bay, Mill, like Eyre, was disappointed. Whereas Eyre felt betrayed that his saving of the colony had gone unrecognised in the metropole, Mill was dismayed that neither the English government, the judiciary or the public was sufficiently horrified by the collapse of the rule of law as it related to subject races to take action against the perpetrators. On neither side of this deeply divisive controversy did the protagonists feel they had achieved success.

Planters and abolitionists, Emilia da Costa notes, had much in common: their internecine conflicts were in part associated with what

Freud calls 'the narcissism of minor differences'.[5] It was their closeness in some respects which made it particularly urgent that they demarcate their differences. Both protagonists and antagonists of Governor Eyre in the metropole were convinced that Jamaica was not fit for representative government, and that dependencies were best ruled from London. Both sides were also convinced that black men and women were inferior or less advanced than Anglo-Saxons, though 'friends of the negro' continued to believe that 'the African' could progress. The antagonists of Eyre, as we have seen, were more preoccupied with issues about the misuse of martial law than with the systemic injustices which had produced the rebellion at Morant Bay. By the 1860s, a form of racial thinking which assumed hierarchy and inequality, and lacked the utopian vision of a Sturge or a Knibb, had become commonplace.

Take the young Charles Dilke. Dilke came from a radical background, a world of literary men, facilitators of the arts and industry. His grandfather, who was a key influence on the young Charles, was the proprietor and editor of the *Athenaeum*, and in 1846 briefly edited the *Daily News*, working closely with his friends Forster and Dickens. His father was a friend and co-worker of Prince Albert, an enthusiast for industrial exhibitions, and stood for Parliament in 1865 as a Liberal. Born in 1843, Dilke's earliest memories were of the Duke of Wellington marshalling his troops against the feared Chartist uprising in 1848, the slogan of 'No Popery' chalked on walls in 1850, and being taken to hear Kossuth speak in 1851. These were very different formative moments from those of a Joseph Sturge or a William Morgan: the demise of Chartism, the presence of anti-Catholicism and an identification with European nationalism shaped Dilke's childhood images of England. At eighteen he was a strong supporter of the North in the American Civil War, and at twenty-three he spoke at the Cambridge Union against a motion congratulating Eyre. Dilke moved away from Christianity, and became fascinated by racial difference. As a young man of twenty-one, working on a prize essay in the long vacation, he researched 'the future of the Anglo-Saxon race both in the United States and Australasia'. Having finished his degree and planning a future as a statesman, he decided to 'follow England around the world', and embarked on a journey round the English-speaking globe.[6] The letters which he wrote home whilst on his travels – lively, anecdotal and aiming to amuse as well as inform – were published as *Greater Britain*, and were an enormous success, rapidly going into three editions.[7]

Dilke regarded 'a conception of the grandeur of our race' as 'the key' with which to 'unlock the hidden things of strange new lands'.[8] He enjoyed an 'exultant patriotism of race', a conviction of a great Anglo-Saxon destiny. The 'true imperialism' for him, the doctrine 'on which our rule should be based', consisted in the linkages across countries continents between white brothers, Anglo-Saxons. Wherever he went saw 'that in essentials the race was always one'.[9] Whereas Sturge had travelled the world in the interests of abolitionism and peace, a universal family of man, Dilke travelled in the interests of a 'Greater Britain'. Dilke's confident account of the world which he saw – 'America' and Canada, Australia and New Zealand, Ceylon and India, was framed by his conception of the grandeur of the race. The binary divisions which he constructed between one race and another in his accounts of the countries he visited, were attempts to fix meanings and stop the constant slippages of difference: he mapped these peoples in ways which confirmed English notions of progress and civilisation. Wherever the English settled, they founded *new* Englands, 'new in thought as in soil'; they imposed their institutions on all others, and their pride of race stopped them intermarrying and kept them pure. He contrasted English colonisers with the French, who continually attempted to reproduce France wherever they went, and through intermarriage weakened their race.[10] For Dilke, the Anglo-Saxon race 'was the only extirpating race', possessing the particular quality that it would not amalgamate, though itself the product of fusion. The English now ploughed their own furrow, inevitably destroying other races, creating a world in an 'English mould', shaped by English language and history, offering freedom as well as moral direction to the world, free institutions, the rule of law and principles of government. The result of his survey, Dilke wrote, 'is such as to give us reason for the belief that race distinctions will long continue, that miscegenation will go but little way towards blending races; that the dearer are, on the whole, likely to destroy the cheaper peoples, and that Saxendom will rise triumphant from the doubtful struggle'.[11]

Dilke's conviction of racial superiority was combined with a sense of responsibility for those less fortunate. 'Native' races must be treated with decency. American-Indians were 'mentally, morally and physically inferior to the white man', and 'the gradual extinction of the inferior races is not only a law of nature, but a blessing to mankind'. But this inevitable outcome must not be brought about 'by cruelty or fraud'. English treatment of the 'natives' in Tasmania had been deplorable, and Queensland was in danger of becoming a 'slave republic'.[12] The white man had done enough damage already, and should learn from his mistakes. It ought to be recognised, he maintained, that the faults of the negroes were the faults of the masters. In England there was too much focus on the failure of emancipation. 'If it is still impossible openly to advocate slavery in England,' wrote Dilke, 'it has at least become a habit persistently to write down freedom.' There was constant talk of the troubles of Jamaica: little was said of the success of Barbados, where the emancipated were industrious and well conducted.[13] Yet Dilke was ambivalent as to the relation between what he understood as the essential characteristics of a race and the possibilities of reforming those characterised as inferior races. His writing on the Maori provides a case in point: Dilke was in many ways impressed by these 'robust, well-limbed and tall' men, most of them 'little darker than Spaniards', and by the seriousness with which they treated their women, a sign of a more advanced people. Yet he retreated to an essentialist definition of the race: their 'tiger-like' characteristics were 'in the blood', and would not be drawn out 'by a few years of playing at Christianity'. Missionaries had been compelled reluctantly to admit that these people whom they had seen as so open to civilising influences had turned out to be 'fickle as well as gross, not only licentious but untrustworthy'.[14]

Mill picked up this ambivalence in Dilke's thinking. He welcomed *Greater Britain* as the production of an advanced and enlightened mind, and was drawn to the young man on other grounds. Dilke was radical on 'the woman question'. After his election to the House of Commons in 1867, he supported the municipal franchise for women, and worked closely with Jacob Bright on the vote for women.[15] He saw that the Irish could be mollified by land reform 'without bringing about the disruption of the empire'.[16] Both of these were concerns close to Mill's heart. Mill was pleased with Dilke's comments about the arrogance with which the English were capable of treating 'native' populations. But he was concerned that Dilke sometimes expressed himself 'as if there were no sources of national character but race and climate'. He underestimated, Mill thought, the importance of education, legislation and social circumstances, in shaping men: he overestimated inherent racial distinctions.[17] But this was a sign of the times.

In 1869 Charles Kingsley visited the West Indies. Born in 1819, a much older and more established man than Dilke, Kingsley was of the same generation as William Morgan, and had his radical moment in the late 1840s. Anglican clergyman, anti-Catholic, Cambridge professor, one-time Christian Socialist, heavily influenced by Carlyle and yet an admirer of Mill, enthusiast for cleanliness and sanitation, a lover of England, author of those paeans of praise to English masculinity, *Westward Ho!* and *Hereward the Wake*, supporter of the South and of Eyre, antagonist of women's campaigns for the vote, Kingsley was a complex figure. His brother Henry had celebrated Eyre the adventurous explorer and friend of the Aborigine; Charles had been castigated for his support of the 'ill-used' and 'calumniated' Eyre by those who expected a rather different response from him.[18] The Kingsley brothers had West Indian connections: their grandfather on their mother's side, a judge in Barbados, came from a family which had owned property there for five generations. As a boy, Charles loved his grandfather's tales of the West Indies, of the bravery and self-possession of white folks in the face of danger, of the romance of imperial conquest.[19] Like Dilke, the letters which he wrote home were published as a volume: *At Last. A Christmas in the West Indies*. It had been his dream to go for forty years. From childhood, he had studied the natural histories, romances and tragedies of the islands. The West Indies he evoked in his writing was in part that of the childhood stories, of the past, of the age of Raleigh, of naval victories, of buccaneers and pirates, of English heroism in lands and seas peopled only by the French or the Spanish. It was an exciting place of adventure, rather than the post-emancipation site of decadence and decay – a glorious imperial history to set against the gloom of the present. On his journey Kingsley prepared himself 'to compare books with facts, and judge for myself of the reported wonders of the Earthly Paradise'.[20] An impossible task, since his vision was framed by a particular imperial gaze.[21] His discursive task was to reconcile his preconceived notions with his observations, and to confirm what he already knew: that the negro race was inferior, and that the only real hope for a West Indian future was the European.

The 'harsh school of facts' had taught Kingsley, he wrote in 1866, that the doctrine he once enthusiastically followed – that 'all men are born into the world equal, and that their inequality, in intellect or morals, is chargeable entirely to circumstances' – was wrong. This was Mill's mistake: 'to disparage, if not totally deny, the congenital differences of character in individuals, and still more in races'. 'There are congenital differences and hereditary tendencies', Kingsley was now convinced, 'which defy all education'. Irish Celts were unfit for self-government; negroes, though he was 'no slaveholder at heart', he did not like.[22] Kingsley, full of childhood stories of Admiral Rodney, his grandfather's friend and great victor over the French, was impressed by the 'gallant race of planters and merchants' that he met in the West Indian islands. And the scenery was indeed gorgeous; he wished he had Ruskin beside him to see and describe it. But the negroes defied those who tried to believe that 'all God's creatures' could be 'somewhere, somehow, reformed into His likeness'. They had the 'excitability and coarseness of half-civilised creatures'; they screamed and jabbered, used their strong incisors to tear at sugar-cane, and seemed to enjoy the 'mere act of living, like the lizard on the wall'.[23] The women were particularly disturbing to him, given his strong convictions about separate spheres for men and women. But then, he reminded himself and his readers, echoing Carlyle and Dickens, what about the tens of thousands of paupers and rogues at home who were no better? Civilisation was at risk in the metropolis: 'let us take the beam out of our own eye before we take the mote out of theirs'. It was we, he argued, who brought the negro to these islands: 'we have no right to complain of our own work. If, like Frankenstein, we have tried to make a man, and made him badly; we must, like Frankenstein, pay the penalty.'[24] Like Trollope, he had great hopes for 'the coloureds', who 'claim to be, and are, our kinsfolk', and thought that there was a future for the West Indies. Too much English blood had been lost there for those lands to be wasted. He strongly advised young white men and women to emigrate, for each such couple 'would be a little centre of civilisation for the Negro', and able to do much good.[25] It was the English who could save the colonies.

Dilke and Kingsley were very different kinds of men, though both from the upper middle class, both writers, and both public men who expected to be listened to. But they were of different generations, different convictions, different traditions and networks, and took different positions on Eyre. Each was a complex figure, whose stories merit studies in themselves. Like Eyre, the two grew and changed, their identities ruptured and differently articulated by metropolitan time, colonial time and familial time. But in the late 1860s both assumed that race was a critical mark of distinction between peoples: and in that they were creatures of their age. Racial thinking had taken a significant turn: nothing was resolved, as of course it could not be, because as a category to mark difference its discursive work could never be complete. The arguments as to the influence of climate, environment, nature and culture on the varieties of man continued to reverberate both within individuals and in the society at large, but the ground had shifted from the 1830s. A structure of feeling dominated by the familial trope and a paternalist rhetoric had been displaced by a harsher racial vocabulary of fixed differences. In the constant play between racism's two logics, the biological and the cultural, biological essentialism was, for the moment, in the ascendant, and race occupied a different place in English common sense.

And what of the missionaries and of Jamaica? A small, chastened group remained on the island, maintaining their faith in inauspicious times, but no longer believing in the dream they had once had. In Brown's Town, John Clark, great friend and correspondent of Joseph Sturge, had ministered since 1835. In 1869 he visited England for rest and recuperation. On his return to the island, he was faced with traumatic events: splits in his two main chapels and breakaway groups under a much younger, livelier minister. He called on his old friend John Henderson for help. John encouraged his nephew George, who had just finished training as a missionary, to return to the island. George had intended to go and work in Japan, 'that virile nation . . . likely to dominate the whole of the East', but allowed himself to be convinced that he should devote himself to the less exciting task in Jamaica. Jamaica had once been the place of hope and adventure: now it was recognised as more arid soil. George Henderson, himself the son of a missionary, married John Clark's daughter, and maintained the tradition of the mission family, acting as pastor until 1926.[26]

Phillippo was still in Spanish Town, still mediating between the colonial government, the planters and the peasantry. In 1872 he decided on semi-retirement, but his chosen successor did not work out. Phillippo returned to the mother country in search of a new minister for 'his' church, for he was convinced that a white pastor was necessary, both to guide 'his' flock and exercise the requisite influence on its behalf with the colonial authorities. He visited William Morgan and his family in Birmingham for four days, and they took him to parlour meetings and conferences every evening, calling on many friends.[27] But he did not want to settle in England; Jamaica was his home: there he had watched his children and his children's children grow up, there he had made friendships which nothing but death could sever. Thus he passed 'the evening of his days' in Spanish Town, and is buried next to his wife Hannah, close to what is now known as 'Phillippo's Church'. His son George was one of those white men who benefited greatly from crown colony government, for it was increasingly difficult for those of mixed race to get senior appointments. George Phillippo held important legal posts across the empire, and was eventually, in a mark of recognition which might or might not have astonished his father, rewarded with a knighthood.[28]

It was to be another fifty years before Marcus Garvey, who had grown up in St Ann's Bay, once the stamping-ground of that apologist of slavery the Rev. Bridges, was to form the United Negro Improvement Association. Garvey was a child of that dissenting tradition which Bridges had rightly feared: his father was a Methodist deacon, his mother a regular chapel-goer, and four of his teachers, he later reflected, were eminent preachers. He met his wife Amy at a debate in a Baptist church hall in Kingston on the proposition that 'morality does not improve with civilisation'. The aim of the United Negro Improvement Association was to unite all negro peoples of the world and establish their own country and government. Its motto was 'One God, One Aim, One Destiny', and its anthem, sung at the beginning and end of every meeting, that favourite missionary hymn 'From Greenland's icy mountains, to India's coral strand'.[29] What richer symbol could there be of the contradictory and ambivalent legacy of a particular colonial project?

Notes

꩜

Introduction

1 The borough arms are redolent of the complexity of the connection between England and Jamaica – the legacy of both slavery and emancipation – since the female figure who stands opposite the man is associated with the descendants of the Montague family, owners of substantial West Indian properties. See Julia Bush, 'Moving On – and Looking Back', *History Workshop Journal*, 36 (Autumn 1993), pp. 183–94.

2 Catherine Hall, 'Feminism and Feminist History', in *White, Male and Middle Class: Explorations in Feminism and History* (Polity, Cambridge, 1992), pp. 1–42.

3 Stuart Hall, 'Minimal Selves', in *Identity* (Institute of Contemporary Arts, London, 1997), vol. 6, p. 45.

4 Frantz Fanon, *Black Skins, White Masks*, 1st edn 1952 (Pluto Press, London, 1968).

5 On the remembering of empire see Bill Schwarz, *Memories of Empire* (Verso, London, 2002).

6 James Baldwin, 'Stranger in the Village', 1st edn 1953, repr in *Notes of a Native Son* (Penguin, Harmondsworth, 1995), pp. 151–65. Special thanks to Bill Schwarz for pointing me in the direction of this eloquent essay. There is now a considerable literature on whiteness. See, e.g., Vron Ware, *Beyond the Pale. White Women, Racism and History* (Verso, London, 1992); David Roediger, *The Wages of Whiteness: Race and the Making of the American Working Class* (Verso, London, 1992); Virginia R. Dominguez, *White by Definition. Social Classification in Creole Louisiana* (Rutgers University Press, New Brunswick, NJ, 1994); Bronwen Walter, *Whiteness, Place and Irish Women Inside: Outsiders* (Routledge, London, 2001).

7 Salman Rushdie, 'The New Empire within Britain', in *Imaginary Homelands. Essays and Criticism 1981–1991* (Granta, London, 1991), p. 129.

8   Simon Gikandi, *Maps of Englishness. Writing Identity in the Culture of Colonialism* (Columbia University Press, New York, 1996), pp. 129–39, p. 17.

9   See, e.g., Mike Phillips and Trevor Phillips, *Windrush. The Irresistible Rise of Multi-Racial Britain* (Harper Collins, London, 1998).

10 Gikandi, *Maps of Englishness*, p. 19.

11 Victor Kiernan used Goldsmith's evocative term 'the lords of human kind' for his innovative investigation of European attitudes to the outside world. See V. G. Kiernan, *The Lords of Human Kind. European Attitudes towards the Outside World in the Imperial Age* (Weidenfeld and Nicholson, London, 1969); Edward W. Said, *Orientalism. Western Conceptions of the Orient* (Routledge, London, 1978); *idem, Culture and Imperialism* (Chatto and Windus, London, 1993); David Scott, *Refashioning Futures: Criticism after Postcoloniality* (Princeton University Press, Princeton, 1999). See also David Scott's illuminating interview with Sylvia Wynter, 'The Re-enchantment of Humanism', *Small Axe: A Journal of Criticism*, 8 (Sept. 2001), pp. 119–207.

12 'Editorial', *Feminist Review*, 40 (Spring 1992), pp. 1–5, explores the shift which took place in the politics of the journal.

13 The term is Toni Morrison's, *Playing in the Dark. Whiteness and the Literary Imagination* (Picador, London, 1993), p. xiv.

14 '[A] form of remembrance – most often of hidden and shameful family secrets – which hover in the space between social and psychic history, forcing and making it impossible for the one who unconsciously carries them to make the link': Jacqueline Rose, *States of Fantasy* (Clarendon Press, Oxford, 1996), p. 5.

15 Leonore Davidoff and Catherine Hall, *Family Fortunes. Men and Women of the English Middle Class 1780–1850* (Hutchinson, London, 1987).

16 C. L. R. James, *The Black Jacobins: Toussaint L'Ouverture and the San Domingo Revolution*, 2nd edn (Vintage, New York, 1963); *idem*, 'Africans and Afro-Caribbeans: A Personal View', *TEN*. 8, 16 (1984), pp. 54–5.

17 Frederick Cooper and Ann Laura Stoler, 'Between Metropole and Colony: Rethinking a Research Agenda', in their edited collection *Tensions of Empire: Colonial Cultures in a Bourgeois World* (University of California Press, Berkeley, 1997), p. 4.

18 Jerry H. Bentley, Introduction to 'Perspectives on Global History: Cultural Encounters between the Continents over the Centuries', in *Proceedings of the Nineteenth Congress of Historical Sciences* (Oslo, 2000), pp. 29–45; Eric R. Wolf's book, *Europe and the People without History* (University of California Press, Berkeley, 1982), was very important in encouraging rethinking of the global nature of capitalist development.

19 Ernesto Laclau, *Emancipations* (Verso, London, 1996), cited in Stuart Hall, 'The Multi-Cultural Question', in Barnor Hesse (ed.), *Un/settled Multiculturalisms. Diasporas, Entanglements, Disruptions* (Zed, London, 2001), pp. 209–41, 234.

20 S. Hall, 'Multi-Cultural Question', p. 234.

21 Paul Gilroy, *The Black Atlantic: Modernity and Double Consciousness* (Verso, London, 1993), p. 17.
22 Partha Chatterjee, *The Nation and its Fragments. Colonial and Postcolonial Histories* (Princeton University Press, Princeton, 1993), p. 10.
23 Peter Hulme, *Colonial Encounters. Europe and the Native Caribbean 1492–1797* (Methuen, London, 1986), p. 3.
24 S. Hall, 'Multi-Cultural Question', p. 213; see also his 'When was "the Post-Colonial"? Thinking at the Limit', in Iain Chambers and Lidia Curti (eds), *The Post-Colonial Question: Common Skies, Divided Horizons* (Routledge, London, 1996), pp. 242–60.
25 As it was in the joint study with Davidoff, *Family Fortunes*.
26 P. J. Cain and A. G. Hopkins argue that 'gentlemanly capitalism' was central to an understanding of imperialist expansion. But Birmingham and Manchester, they suggest, never embraced that culture. Cain and Hopkins, *British Imperialism. Innovation and Expansion. 1688–1914* (Longman, London, 1993), p. 46.
27 In the course of researching this project, my questions have expanded and changed. In particular, I became interested in rethinking the established narratives of political history through the lens of gender and empire. See Catherine Hall, Keith McClelland and Jane Rendall, *Defining the Victorian Nation. Class, Race, Gender and the Reform Act of 1867* (Cambridge University Press, Cambridge, 2000); Catherine Hall, 'The Rule of Difference: Gender, Class and Empire in the Making of the 1832 Reform Act', in Ida Blom, Karen Hagemann and Catherine Hall (eds), *Gendered Nations. Nationalism and Gender Order in the Long Nineteenth Century* (Berg, Oxford, 2000), pp. 107–36.
28 Phillip D. Curtin, *Two Jamaicas: The Role of Ideas in a Tropical Colony 1830–1865* (Harvard University Press, Cambridge, Mass., 1955); Douglas Hall, *Free Jamaica, 1836–65: An Economic History* (Yale University Press, New Haven, 1959); Bernard Semmel, *The Governor Eyre Controversy* (MacGibbon and Kee, London, 1962); Christine Bolt, *The Anti-Slavery Movement and Reconstruction. A Study in Anglo-American Cooperation 1833–77* (Oxford University Press, Oxford, 1969); idem, *Victorian Attitudes to Race* (Routledge and Kegan Paul, London, 1971); Douglas Lorimer, *Colour, Class and the Victorians. English Attitudes to the Negro in the Mid Nineteenth Century* (Leicester University Press, Leicester, 1978); Mary Turner, *Slaves and Missionaries. The Disintegration of Jamaican Slave Society, 1787–1834* (University of Illinois Press, Urbana, 1982); Thomas C. Holt, *The Problem of Freedom: Race, Labor and Politics in Jamaica and Britain 1832–1938* (Johns Hopkins University Press, Baltimore, 1992); Robert J. Stewart, *Religion and Society in Post-Emancipation Jamaica* (University of Tennessee Press, Knoxville, 1992); Gad J. Heuman, *'The Killing Time': The Morant Bay Rebellion in Jamaica* (Macmillan, London, 1994).
29 My focus is on the social, cultural and political world of nonconformists; I do not pretend to be a theologian.

30   Stuart Hall, 'From Scarman to Stephen Lawrence', *History Workshop Journal*, 48 (1999), p. 189.

31   'What kind of racialised, gendered selves get produced at the conjuncture of the transnational and the postcolonial?': M. Jacqui Alexander and Chandra Talpede Mohanty (eds), *Feminist Genealogies, Colonial Legacies, Democratic Futures* (Routledge, New York, 1997), Introduction, p. xviii.

32   Frantz Fanon, *The Wretched of the Earth* (Penguin, Harmondsworth, 1967), introduction by Jean-Paul Sartre, pp. 21-3; 'Concerning Violence', pp. 27, 39-40, 81.

33   Said, *Orientalism*; *idem*, *Culture and Imperialism*; the definition of colonial discourse is that of Peter Hulme, *Colonial Encounters*, p. 2.

34   On the struggle over the meanings of freedom in post-emancipation Jamaica and Britain, see Holt's excellent analysis, *The Problem of Freedom*.

35   For an exemplary account of one such contestation see Semmel, *Governor Eyre Controversy*; for an essay on the gendered dimensions of this debate see Catherine Hall, 'Competing Masculinities: Thomas Carlyle, John Stuart Mill and the Case of Governor Eyre', in *White, Male and Middle Class*, pp. 255-95.

36   Kathleen Wilson, *The Sense of the People. Politics, Culture and Imperialism in England, 1715-1785* (Cambridge University Press, Cambridge, 1998), esp. pp. 24-5.

37   There is a substantial literature here, but see, e.g., K. Sangari and S. Vaid (eds), *Recasting Women: Essays in Indian Colonial History* (Rutgers University Press, New Brunswick, NJ, 1990); Nupur Chaudhuri and Margaret Stroebel (eds), *Western Women and Imperialism: Complicity and Resistance* (Indiana University Press, Bloomington, 1992); Moira Ferguson, *Subject to Others: British Women Writers and Colonial Slavery, 1670-1834* (Routledge, London, 1992); Clare Midgley, *Women against Slavery: The British Campaigns, 1780-1870* (Routledge, London, 1992); Antoinette Burton, *Burdens of History: British Feminists, Indian Women and Imperial Culture, 1865-1915* (University of North Carolina Press, Chapel Hill, 1994); *idem*, *At the Heart of the Empire: Indians and the Colonial Encounter in Late Victorian Britain* (University of California Press, Berkeley, 1998); Mrinalini Sinha, *Colonial Masculinity: The 'Manly Englishman' and the 'Effeminate Bengali' in the Late Nineteenth Century* (Manchester University Press, Manchester, 1995); Ann Laura Stoler, *Race and the Education of Desire: Foucault's 'History of Sexuality' and the Colonial Order of Things* (Duke University Press, Durham, NC, 1995); Anne McClintock, *Imperial Leather: Race, Gender and Sexuality in the Colonial Context* (Routledge, New York, 1995); Wilson, *Sense of the People*; Susan Thorne, *Congregational Missions and the Making of an Imperial Culture in Nineteenth-Century England* (Stanford University Press, Stanford, Calif., 1999); Madhavi Kale, *Fragments of Empire: Capital, Slavery and Indian Indentured Labor Migration in the British Caribbean* (University of Pennsylvania Press, Philadelphia, 1999).

38 Douglas Hall, *In Miserable Slavery. Thomas Thistlewood in Jamaica 1750–1786* (Macmillan, Basingstoke, 1989).

39 Alexander and Mohanty (eds), *Feminist Genealogies*; Avtar Brah, *Cartographies of Diaspora: Contesting Identities* (Routledge, London, 1996); Gail Lewis, *'Race', Gender, Social Welfare: Encounters in a Postcolonial Society* (Polity, Cambridge, 2000); Ann Phoenix, *(Re)Constructing Gendered and Ethnicised Identities: Are We All Marginal now?* (University for Humanist Studies, Utrecht, 1998).

40 For classic discussions of this see E. P. Thompson, *The Making of the English Working Class* (Gollancz, London, 1963); Gareth Stedman Jones, *Languages of Class: Studies in English Working-Class History, 1832–1982* (Cambridge University Press, Cambridge, 1983).

41 Davidoff and Hall, *Family Fortunes*.

42 On the development of racial thinking, see, e.g., Philip D. Curtin, *The Image of Africa: British Ideas and Action, 1780–1850*, 2 vols (University of Wisconsin Press, Madison, 1964); Nancy Stepan, *The Idea of Race in Science: Great Britain 1800–1960* (Macmillan, London, 1982); George W. Stocking Jr, *Race, Culture and Evolution: Essays in the History of Anthropology* (University of Chicago Press, Chicago, 1968); *idem, Victorian Anthropology* (Free Press, New York, 1987).

43 S. Hall, 'Multi-Cultural Question', p. 216.

44 Joanna de Groot, ' "Sex" and "Race": The Construction of Language and Image in the Nineteenth Century', in Susan Mendus and Jane Rendall (eds), *Sexuality and Subordination* (Routledge, London, 1989), pp. 89–128; repr. in Catherine Hall (ed.), *Cultures of Empire: A Reader. Colonizers in Britain and the Empire in the Nineteenth and Twentieth Centuries* (Manchester University Press, Manchester, 2000), pp. 37–60.

45 Nancy Leys Stepan, 'Race and Gender: The Role of Analogy in Science', in David Theo Goldberg (ed.), *Anatomy of Racism* (University of Minnesota Press, Minneapolis, 1990), p. 43.

46 Thorne, *Congregational Missions*, esp. ch. 5.

47 Stoler, *Race and the Education of Desire*, pp. 5, 10.

48 Cooper and Stoler (eds), *Tensions of Empire*, pp. 3–4, 7.

49 Gayatri Chakravorty Spivak, 'Three Women's Texts and a Critique of Imperialism', in *In Other Worlds. Essays in Cultural Politics* (Routledge, New York, 1985), p. 244.

50 Deborah Cherry, 'Shuttling and Soul Making: Tracing the Links between Algeria and Egalitarian Feminism in the 1850s', in Shearer West (ed.), *The Victorians and Race* (Scholar Press, Aldershot, 1994), pp. 156–70. See also *idem, Beyond the Frame. Feminism and Visual Culture, Britain 1850–1900* (Routledge, London, 2001).

51 Cited in S. Hall, 'Multi-Cultural Question', p. 216.

52 Cherry, 'Shuttling and Soul Making', p. 168. As Cherry notes, Spivak's use of the phrase 'not quite/not male' (Spivak, 'Three Women's Texts', p. 244) rewrites, as she acknowledges, Homi Bhabha's 'not quite/not white', which he elaborated in 'Of Mimicry and Man', in *The Location of Culture* (Routledge, London, 1994), pp. 85–92.

53 John Barrell, *The Infection of Thomas de Quincy. A Psychopathology of Imperialism* (Harvard University Press, London, 1991), pp. 10–11, 18–19.
54 For one excellent study of this process see Sinha, *Colonial Masculinity*.
55 Anne McClintock argues in her study *Imperial Leather* that the categories class, race and gender came into existence in relation to each other.
56 Charles Dickens, 'The Noble Savage', 1st edn 1853, in *The Works of Charles Dickens*, 34 vols (Chapman and Hall, London, 1899), vol. 34: *Reprinted Pieces*, pp. 120–7.
57 Baldwin, 'Stranger in the Village', p. 154.

Prologue: The Making of an Imperial Man

1 PP 1866 (3595) LI, part 1, Eyre to Cardwell, 20 Oct. 1865, no. 251.
2 Some of the major sources for Morant Bay and its aftermath are PP 1866 (3683) xxx, *Report of the Jamaica Royal Commission*, Part I; 1866 (3683-1) xxxi, *Report of the Jamaica Royal Commission*, Part II: Minutes of Evidence and Appendix; Hamilton Hume, *The Life of Edward John Eyre, Late Governor of Jamaica* (Richard Bentley, London, 1867); William F. Finlason, *The History of the Jamaica Case Founded upon Official or Authentic Documents, and Containing an Account of the Debates in Parliament and the Criminal Prosecutions, Arising out of the Case* (Chapman and Hall, London, 1869); Edward Bean Underhill, *The Tragedy of Morant Bay: A Narrative of the Disturbances in the Island of Jamaica in 1865* (Alexander and Shepheard, London, 1895); Sydney S. Olivier, *The Myth of Governor Eyre* (Leonard and Virginia Woolf, London, 1933); Phillip D. Curtin, *Two Jamaicas: The Role of Ideas in a Tropical Colony 1830–1865* (Harvard University Press, Cambridge, Mass., 1955); Douglas Hall, *Free Jamaica, 1836–65: An Economic History* (Yale University Press, New Haven, 1959); Bernard Semmel, *The Governor Eyre Controversy* (MacGibbon and Kee, London, 1962); Geoffrey Dutton, *The Hero as Murderer: The Life of Edward John Eyre, Australian Explorer and Governor of Jamaica 1815–1901* (William Collins, London, 1968); Christine Bolt, *The Anti-Slavery Movement and Reconstruction. A Study in Anglo-American Cooperation 1833–77* (Oxford University Press, Oxford, 1969); Douglas Lorimer, *Colour, Class and the Victorians: English Attitudes to the Negroes in the Mid-Nineteenth Century* (Leicester University Press, Leicester, 1978); Gad J. Heuman, *Between Black and White. Race Politics and the Free Coloreds in Jamaica 1792–1865* (Greenwood, Westport, Conn., 1981); *idem*, '*The Killing Time': The Morant Bay Rebellion in Jamaica* (Macmillan, London, 1994); Abigail B. Bakan, *Ideology and Class Conflict in Jamaica. The Politics of Rebellion* (McGill–Queen's University Press, London, 1990); Holt, *Problem of Freedom*.
3 Jamaica Committee, *Jamaica Papers*, nos 1–6 (Jamaica Committee, London, 1866–7).
4 PP 1866 (3683) XXX, JRC, Part I, pp. 40–1.

5   Hume, *Life of Edward John Eyre*; Finlason, *History of the Jamaica Case*.

6   Jamaica Committee, *Jamaica Papers*, esp. no. 1.

7   On the shift from British to English in this debate see Ian Baucom, *Out of Place. Englishness, Empire and the Locations of Identity* (Princeton University Press, Princeton, 1999), pp. 41–7.

8   For Carlyle's most substantial interventions on race see his 'Occasional Discourse on the Nigger Question', a revised version of his original polemic of 1849, in *English and Other Critical Essays*, vol. 2 (Dent, London, 1964); *idem*, 'Shooting Niagara: And After?', in *Critical and Miscellaneous Essays: Collected and Republished* (Chapman and Hall, London, 1899), vol. 5. For a discussion of the debate between Carlyle and Mill see Catherine Hall, 'Competing Masculinities: Thomas Carlyle, John Stuart Mill and the Case of Governor Eyre', in *White, Male and Middle Class*. On the problems associated with Carlyle's masculinity see Norma Clarke, 'Strenuous Idleness. Thomas Carlyle and the Man of Letters as Hero', in Michael Roper and John Tosh (eds), *Manful Assertions. Masculinities since 1800* (Routledge, London, 1991), pp. 25–43; Herbert Sussman, *Victorian Masculinities. Manhood and Masculine Poetics in Early Victorian Literature and Art* (Cambridge University Press, Cambridge, 1995).

9   On this new manliness see Leonore Davidoff and Catherine Hall, *Family Fortunes. Men and Women of the English Middle Class 1780–1850* (Hutchinson, London, 1987), part 1.

10 John Tosh, *A Man's Place. Masculinity and the Middle-Class Home in Victorian England* (Yale University Press, London, 1999).

11 Rev. Isaac Taylor, *Self Cultivation Recommended; or, Hints to a Youth Leaving School* (T. Cadell and Son, London, 1817), p. 17; Davidoff and Hall, *Family Fortunes*, esp. ch. 5; Leonore Davidoff, 'Regarding Some "Old Husbands' Tales": Public and Private in Feminist History', in *Worlds Between: Historical Perspectives on Gender and Class* (Polity, Cambridge, 1995), pp. 227–76.

12 For an illuminating discussion of the ideological work associated with this fiction, see Mary Poovey, *Uneven Developments. The Ideological Work of Gender in Mid-Victorian Britain* (Virago, London, 1989), esp. ch. 4.

13 P. J. Marshall, 'Britain without America – A Second Empire?', in P. J. Marshall (ed.), *The Oxford History of the British Empire*, vol. 2: *The Eighteenth Century* (Oxford University Press, Oxford, 1998), pp. 576–95.

14 Bernard Semmel, *The Liberal Ideal and the Demons of Empire. Theories of Imperialism from Adam Smith to Lenin* (Johns Hopkins University Press, Baltimore, 1993), pp. 1–3.

15 Douglas Pike, *Paradise of Dissent. South Australia 1829–1857* (Longmans Green and Co., London, 1957), esp. ch. 1.

16 R. Garnett, *Edward Gibbon Wakefield. The Colonization of Australia and New Zealand* (T. Fisher Unwin, London, 1897); C. A. Bodelsen, *Studies in Mid-Victorian Imperialism* (Scandinavian University Books, Copenhagen, 1960); Bernard Semmel, *The Rise of Free Trade Imperial-*

ism. Classical Political Economy, the Empire of Free Trade and Imperialism 1750–1850 (Cambridge University Press, Cambridge, 1970).

17 Edward Gibbon Wakefield, *A Letter from Sydney*, 1st edn 1829 (J. M. Dent, London, 1929), pp. 4, 17, 48.

18 Edward Gibbon Wakefield, *England and America*, 2 vols (Richard Bentley, London, 1833), vol. 2, p. 216.

19 Quoted in Garnett, *Edward Gibbon Wakefield*, p. 320.

20 Robert Hughes, *The Fatal Shore. A History of the Transportation of Convicts to Australia 1787–1868* (Pan Books, London, 1988), p. 323.

21 Jan Kociumbas, *The Oxford History of Australia*, vol. 2: *Possessions 1770–1869* (Oxford University Press, Oxford, 1995), pp. 123–7.

22 John Stuart Mill, *Principles of Political Economy*, 1st edn 1848, in J. M. Robson (ed.), *Collected Works of John Stuart Mill* (University of Toronto Press, Toronto, 1965), book 5, p. 963.

23 Quoted in Semmel, *Rise of Free Trade Imperialism*, p. 8.

24 Thomas Carlyle, 'Chartism', 1st edn 1839, in *Thomas Carlyle, Selected Writings* (Penguin, Harmondsworth, 1971), pp. 228–9, 214, 232.

25 Frederick Hill, *An Autobiography of Fifty Years in Times of Reform*, edited by his daughter Constance Hill (R. Bentley and Son, London, 1894); Rosamund and Florence Hill, *The Recorder of Birmingham. A Memoir of Matthew Davenport Hill* (Macmillan, London, 1878); The Martin/Clark Book Committee (eds), *The Hatbox Letters. The Story of Two Migrant Families Settling in South Australia c1850 as Recorded in their own Words* (Martin/Clark Book Committee, Adelaide, 1999); personal communication, Margaret Allen, University of Adelaide.

26 The phrase is that of George Fife Angas, a great enthusiast for South Australia, in a letter to Edward Gibbon Wakefield, quoted in Pike, *Paradise of Dissent*, p. 131.

27 J. M. Main, 'Men of Capital', in Eric Richards (ed.), *The Flinders History of South Australia. A Social History* (Wakefield Press, South Australia, 1986), p. 98.

28 Quoted in Pike, *Paradise of Dissent*, pp. 130, 131.

29 Kociumbas, *Possessions*, p. 188.

30 Semmel, *Rise of Free Trade Imperialism*, p. 195.

31 Pike, *Paradise of Dissent*, p. 169.

32 Catherine Helen Spence, *Clara Morrison. A Tale of South Australia during the Gold Fever*, 1st edn 1854 (Wakefield, South Australia, 1986).

33 Margaret Allen, 'Three South Australian Women Writers 1854–1923: Matilda Evans, Catherine Spence and Catherine Martin', Ph.D. diss., University of South Australia, Flinders, 1991.

34 Patricia Grimshaw, Marilyn Lake, Ann McGrath and Marian Quartly, *Creating a Nation* (McPhee Gribble, Victoria, 1994), p. 79.

35 Coral Lansbury, *Arcady in Australia. The Evocation of Australia in Nineteenth Century English Literature* (Melbourne University Press, Victoria, 1970).

36 Edward John Eyre, *Autobiographical Narrative 1832–39*, ed. with an introduction by Jill Waterhouse (Caliban, London, 1984), p. 1.

37   Ibid., pp. 1, 3.
38   Ibid., pp. 29, 7, 3, 31.
39   On the clash between Aboriginal and colonial understandings of land and its meanings, see Heather Goodall, *Invasion to Embassy. Land in Aboriginal Politics in New South Wales, 1770–1972* (Allen and Unwin, St Leonards, Australia, 1996).
40   Eyre, *Autobiography*, p. 46.
41   Ibid., p. 73.
42   Ibid., pp. 47–8.
43   George Grey, *Journals of Two Expeditions of Discovery in North-West and Western Australia during the Years 1837, 38 and 39*, 2 vols (T. and W. Boone, London, 1841), vol. 2, pp. 185, 190.
44   Andrew Porter, 'Trusteeship, Anti-Slavery and Humanitarianism', in Andrew Porter (ed.), *The Oxford History of the British Empire*. vol. 3: *The Nineteenth Century* (Oxford University Press, Oxford, 1999), pp. 198–221.
45   Kociumbas, *Possessions*, pp. 192–4.
46   House of Commons Committee on Aboriginals, PP 1837, VII; quoted in Kenneth N. Bell and W. P. Morrell (eds), *Select Documents on British Colonial Policy 1830–1860* (Clarendon Press, Oxford, 1928), p. 545.
47   J. Rutherford, *Sir George Grey. A Study in Colonial Government* (Cassell, London, 1961).
48   Edward John Eyre, *Journals of Expeditions of Discovery into Central Australia and Overland from Adelaide to King George's Sound in the Years 1840–1*, 2 vols (T. and W. Boone, London, 1845), vol. 1, p. 170.
49   Eyre, *Autobiography*, p. 194.
50   On the sexual and psychic meanings of the first encounters see Peter Hulme, *Colonial Encounters: Europe and the Native Caribbean 1492–1797* (Methuen, London, 1986). For one of the richest examples of the elaborations of these connections in Africa, see H. Rider Haggard, *King Solomon's Mines* (Cassell, London, 1891) and for a discussion of this, McClintock, *Imperial Leather*, pp. 1–6.
51   Eyre, *Journals*, vol. 1, p. 7.
52   Ibid., p. 20.
53   Eyre, *Autobiography*, p. 42.
54   Charles Sturt lectured at the Mechanics' Institute in Adelaide in support of Eyre's expedition: Eyre, *Journals*, vol. 1, pp. 8–9.
55   There is a very considerable debate amongst anthropologists as to the nature of Aboriginal systems of landholding; for a summary of the debate see Henry Reynolds, *The Other Side of the Frontier* (James Cook University Press, Townsville, Australia, 1981); Goodall, *Invasion to Embassy*.
56   Eyre, *Autobiography*, p. 55.
57   Julie Evans, 'Beyond the Frontier: Possibilities and Precariousness along Australia's Southern Coast', in Lynette Russell (ed.), *Colonial Frontiers. Indigenous–European Encounters in Settler Societies* (Manchester University Press, Manchester, 2001), pp. 151–72.
58   Eyre, *Journals*, vol. 1, p. 224.

59 Much more recently, that expedition has been reconstructed in a photo-graphic essay, lavishly published as part of Australia's rewriting of its own history: Edward Stokes, *The Desert Coast. Edward Eyre's Expedition 1840–1841* (Five Mile Press, Victoria, 1993); Henry Kingsley, 'Eyre, the South-Australian Explorer', *Macmillan's Magazine*, 12 (May–Oct. 1865).

60 Grey, *Journals*, vol. 2, p. 374.

61 Rutherford, *Sir George Grey*, p. 59.

62 Eyre, *Journals*, vol. 1, p. 62, cited in Kay Schaffer, 'Handkerchief Diplo-macy: E. J. Eyre and the Sexual Politics on the South Australian Frontier, in L. Russell (ed.), *Colonial Frontiers*, pp. 134–50. I am grateful to Kay Schaffer for sending me an early version of this piece.

63 See Mary Louise Pratt, *Imperial Eyes. Travel Writing and Transcultura-tion* (Routledge, London, 1992), for an analysis of the traditions of travel writing.

64 Eyre, *Journals*, vol. 1, p. x; vol. 2, p. 423; Pratt, *Imperial Eyes*, p. 7.

65 Eyre, *Journals*, vol. 1, p. xi; vol. 2, pp. 167, 172, 175.

66 Evans, 'Beyond the Frontier', p. 165.

67 Eyre, *Journals*, vol. 2, pp. 111, 156, 255; vol. 1, p. 288; idem, *Autobio-graphy*, pp. 133, 147.

68 Eyre, *Journals*, vol. 2, pp. 458–9, 489, 479.

69 Philip D. Curtin, *The Image of Africa: British Ideas and Action, 1780–1850*, 2 vols (University of Wisconsin Press, Madison, 1964), vol. 1, pp. 56, 138–9, 243.

70 One, 'proving of a vicious temper', was sent back to Australia, the other died of pneumonia at the age of seventeen: see Hume, *Life of Edward John Eyre*, p. 95.

71 Eyre, *Autobiography*, p. 213.

72 Claudia Orange, *The Treaty of Waitangi* (Allen and Unwin, Wellington, 1987); Michael Turnbull, *The New Zealand Bubble: The Wakefield Theory in Practice* (Price, Milburn and Co., Wellington, 1959).

73 Orange, *Treaty of Waitangi*; Garnett, *Edward Gibbon Wakefield*; William P. Morrell, *British Colonial Policy in the Age of Peel and Russell* (Oxford University Press, Oxford, 1930); idem, *British Colonial Policy in the Mid-Victorian Age* (Oxford University Press, Oxford, 1969).

74 Quoted in Garnett, *Edward Gibbon Wakefield*, p. 194.

75 Quoted in Semmel, *Rise of Free Trade Imperialism*, p. 126; David A. Haury, *The Origins of the Liberal Party and Liberal Imperialism: The Career of Charles Buller, 1806–1848* (Garland, New York, 1987).

76 James Belich, *Making Peoples. A History of the New Zealanders from Polynesian Settlement to the End of the Nineteenth Century* (Allen Lane /Penguin, Auckland and London, 1996), p. 182.

77 Orange, *Treaty of Waitangi*, p. 31.

78 Belich, *Making Peoples*, pp. 123–6, 179–86.

79 Despatch from Hobson to Gipps and Treaty of Waitangi, in Bell and Morrell (eds), *Select Documents*, pp. 557–63.

80 Quoted in Orange, *Treaty of Waitangi*, pp. 51, 53.

81 Belich, *Making Peoples*, pp. 192–202.

82 Grey, *Journals*, vol. 2, p. 374.

83 Dutton, *Hero as Murderer*, pp. 181, 182, 187.

84 Belich, *Making Peoples*, p. 225.

85 Quoted in Rutherford, *Sir George Grey*, pp. 221, 224, 226; Earl Henry G. Grey, *The Colonial Policy of Lord John Russell's Administration*, 2 vols (Richard Bentley, London, 1853).

86 Richard S. Hill, *Policing the Colonial Frontier. The Theory and Practice of Coercive Social and Racial Control in New Zealand 1767–1867* (Historical Publications Branch, Department of Internal Affairs, Wellington, 1986), pp. 248–9.

87 Mary Frederica Swainson, 'Letters to her grandparents in England 1840–1850', MS 198, Auckland Institute and Museum Library, 3 Aug. 1845, 4 Sept. 1847, 31 Mar. 1850, 31 May 1850; Mary Frederica Marshall, 'Letters to Mary de Lys and Isabel Percy, Warwick, from Hutt Valley and Kaiwharawhara, 1843–54', MS 198, 21 May 1843, 1 Sept. 1850, 3 Sept. 1853. Thanks to Raewyn Dalziel for pointing me in the direction of these letters.

88 New Zealand *DNB*, entry on Eyre.

89 Dutton, *Hero as Murderer*, has a brief account of Eyre's time in New Zealand. Grey also left New Zealand in 1853, in this case for South Africa.

90 Orange, *Treaty of Waitangi*; Morrell, *British Colonial Policy in the Mid-Victorian Age*; James Belich, *The New Zealand Wars and the Victorian Interpretation of Racial Conflict* (Auckland University Press, Auckland, 1986).

91 Carlyle, 'Occasional Discourse on the Negro Question', *Fraser's Magazine*, 40 (Dec. 1849); *idem*, 'Occasional Discourse on the Nigger Question'.

92 Curtin, *Image of Africa*, vol 2, p. 233.

93 Nancy Stepan, *The Idea of Race in Science: Great Britain 1800–1960* (Macmillan, London, 1982), p. xii.

94 Ibid.

95 Quoted in Curtin, *Image of Africa*, vol. 1, pp. 61–2.

96 Robert Knox, *The Races of Men: A Philosophical Inquiry into the Influence of Race over the Destiny of Nations*, 2nd edn (Henry Renshaw, London, 1862), pp. 243–4; Curtin, *Image of Africa*, vol. 2, pp. 376–80.

97 Knox, *Races of Men*, pp. v, 8, 20, 44.

98 Knox, *Races of Men*, p. 379; Eyre, *Autobiography*, p. 219. Eyre's claim to Norman lineage was primarily concerned with proving his gentility. He does not appear to be making claims for the Norman race as the progenitors of English greatness – claims which would put him seriously at odds with his later supporters, Carlyle and Kingsley, who were enthusiastic supporters of 'Saxonism'. Eyre's genealogical claim was taken up by his contemporary biographer Hume, who argued in 1867 that those who had attacked him over his conduct in Jamaica had 'also represented him as a man of no birth and without connections'. Hume also made clear, however, that he was a self-made man: *Life of Edward John Eyre*, p. 1.

99 See, e.g., the outrage occasioned by Eyre travelling on an omnibus: CO 137/376, Eyre to Newcastle, 24 Dec. 1863.

100   Eyre, *Autobiography*, pp. 218, 219.
101   Dutton, *Hero as Murderer*, p. 175.
102   Knox, *Races of Men*, p. 145.
103   Quoted in Jill Waterhouse, 'Introduction' to Eyre, *Autobiography*, p. xxviii.
104   CO 260/81, Eyre to Colonial Office, 30 Oct. 1854.
105   CO 260/82, Colebrooke to Grey, 19 Jan. 1855, no. 9, enclosure no. 1; CO 260/83, confidential letter Choppin to Eyre, 28 June 1855, enclosure no. 2.
106   CO 260/82, Colebrooke to Grey, 19 Jan. 1855, no. 9. On Taylor and the West Indies see Henry Taylor, *Autobiography of Henry Taylor 1800–1875*, 2 vols (Longmans, Green and Co., London, 1885). On the constitutional questions see C. V. Gocking, 'Early Constitutional History of Jamaica, with Special Reference to the Period 1838–66', *Caribbean Quarterly*, 6 (1960), pp. 114–33.
107   William G. Sewell, *The Ordeal of Free Labour in the British West Indies* (Harper and Bros, New York, 1861), p. 76.
108   CO 260/82, confidential letter, Eyre to Colebrooke, 2 May 1855.
109   Ibid.
110   See, e.g., John Stuart Mill, 'Civilization', *London and Westminster Review* 3 and 25 (Apr. 1836), pp. 1–28.
111   CO 260/84, confidential letter, Eyre to Colebrooke, 10 Dec. 1855.
112   On the desire for a black middle class see, e.g., Edward Bean Underhill, *The West Indies: Their Social and Religious Condition* (Jackson, Walford and Hodder, London, 1862).
113   Sewell, *Ordeal of Free Labour*, p. 80.
114   CO 260/83, Colebrooke to Russell, 7 Aug. 1855, no. 43, enclosure no. 1.
115   CO 260/84, Colebrooke to Grey, 10 Dec. 1855, no. 66, enclosure no. 1; Colebrooke to Grey, 19 Dec. 1855, no. 67, enclosure no. 1.
116   CO 260/87, Hincks to Labouchère, 1 Nov. 1856, no. 67, enclosure no. 1.
117   The quote is from the Baptist *Missionary Herald* (*MH*) (Oct. 1857), a bastion of support for emancipation and black people in the West Indies. Both Baptist missionaries in India and the abolitionist public they addressed were deeply shocked by events in India, and saw more English government, more English troops and 'more Englishmen of the right sort' as the only possible solution for India.
118   CO 260/91, Hincks to Stanley, 7 May 1858, no. 23, enclosure no. 1.
119   CO 260/91, Hincks to Stanley, 5 June 1858, no. 30, enclosure no. 3; CO 260/92, Hincks to Lytton, 20 Jan. 1859, no. 7, enclosure no. 1.
120   CO 7/113, confidential letter, Eyre to Newcastle, 20 Oct. 1859.
121   CO 7/112, Eyre to Lytton, 27 May 1859, no. 52.
122   CO 7/114, Eyre to Newcastle, 20 Mar. 1860, no. 35.
123   Rutherford, *Sir George Grey*, chs 30, 31.
124   Quoted in Belich, *New Zealand Wars*, p. 328.
125   John Eldon Gorst, *The Maori King; or The Story of our Quarrel with the Natives of New Zealand* (Macmillan, London, 1864), p. 408.
126   Holt, *Problem of Freedom*, esp. ch. 7.

127   Stanley, quoted in William A. Green, *British Slave Emancipation. The Sugar Colonies and the Great Experiment 1830–65* (Oxford University Press, Oxford, 1976), p. 119.

128   John Stuart Mill, *Autobiography*, 1st edn 1873 (Oxford University Press, Oxford, 1963), p. 288.

129   CO 137/390, Eyre to Cardwell, 19 Apr. 1865.

130   CO 137/367, Eyre to Newcastle, 7 Aug. 1862, no. 56; 8 Sept. 1862, no. 80; CO 137/368, Eyre to Newcastle, 9 Oct. 1862, no. 88.

131   On the role of coloureds in Jamaican politics see Heuman, *Between Black and White*.

132   CO 137/375, Eyre to Newcastle, 4 Nov. 1863, no. 260, enclosure no. 1.

133   CO 137/390, Eyre to Cardwell, 19 Apr. 1865, no. 90.

134   CO 137/380, Eyre to Newcastle, 18 Mar. 1864, separate communication; CO 137/381, Eyre to Newcastle, 23 Apr. 1864, no. 132.

135   Holt, *Problem of Freedom*, p. 273.

136   CO 137/384, Eyre to Cardwell, 12 Aug. 1864, no. 237; Eyre to Cardwell, 24 Aug. 1864, no. 240.

137   CO 137/384, Eyre to Cardwell, 10 Sept. 1864, no. 256; CO 137/388, Eyre to Cardwell, 2 Mar. 1865, no. 40; CO 137/390, Eyre to Cardwell, 15 Apr. 1865, no. 89, enclosure no. 1.

138   Mary Turner, *Slaves and Missionaries. The Disintegration of Jamaican Slave Society, 1787–1834* (University of Illinois Press, Urbana, 1982); Catherine Hall, 'Missionary Stories: Gender and Ethnicity in England in the 1830s and 1840s', in *White, Male and Middle Class*, pp. 205–44.

139   CO 137/388, Eyre to Cardwell, 2 Mar. 1865, no. 40; CO 137/390, Eyre to Cardwell, 19 Apr. 1865, no. 90.

140   PP 1866 (3595) LI, part 1, Eyre to Cardwell, 20 Oct. 1865, no. 251, 28 Oct. 1865, no. 257; 8 Dec. 1865, no. 321.

141   Ada Eyre to her mother, 22 Oct. 1865, 'Eyre Family Letters 1865–1903', Alexander Turnbull Library, MS 971/1195, Copies from the National Library of Australia, Canberra.

142   PP 1866 (3595) LI, part 1, Eyre to Cardwell, 7 Dec. 1865, no. 313.

143   PP 1866 (3682) XXX, pp. 116, 157–8.

144   Carlyle, 'Shooting Niagara', p. 12.

145   PP 1866 (3595) LI, part 1, Eyre to Cardwell, 8 Nov. 1865, no. 284.

146   H. Kingsley, 'Eyre, the South-Australian Explorer', part 1, p. 502; part 2, p. 57.

147   Commander Bedford Pim, *The Negro and Jamaica* (Trubner and Co., London, 1866), pp. v, 35, 50; on the Anthropological Society see J. W. Burrow, *Evolution and Society. A Study in Victorian Social Theory* (Cambridge University Press, Cambridge, 1968), p. 125; Ronald Rainger, 'Race, Politics and Science: The Anthropological Society of London in the 1860s', *Victorian Studies*, 22/1 (Autumn 1978), pp. 51–70.

148   Hume, *Life of Edward John Eyre*, pp. 201–2, 217.

149   Ibid., dedication to the Earl of Shrewsbury, p. vi.

150   Pim, *Negro and Jamaica*, p. vi; Prof. John Tyndall, quoted in Hume, *Life of Edward John Eyre*, p. 272; Thomas Carlyle, draft petition for the Eyre

Defence Committee held in the Institute of Jamaica, quoted in Olivier, *Myth of Governor Eyre*, p. 336; Carlyle, 'Shooting Niagara'. For a longer discussion of Carlyle's position see Hall, 'Competing Masculinities'.
151 For an account of the events surrounding this see Semmel, *Governor Eyre Controversy.*
152 Finlason, *History of the Jamaica Case*, p. 562.
153 Eyre to unknown recipient, 19 Nov. 1869, 'Edward J. Eyre Letters 1835–1869', Alexander Turnbull Library, MS 765/3, Copied from the Mitchell Library, Sydney, Australia.
154 *Daily News*, 10 July 1872.
155 Eyre to his daughter Mary, n.d., 'Eyre Family Letters 1865–1903', Alexander Turnbull Library, MS 971/1195, Copied from the National Library of Australia, Canberra.

Mapping Jamaica: The Pre-emancipation World in the Metropolitan Mind

1 Richard S. Dunn, *The Rise of the Planter Class in the English West Indies 1624–1713* (Cape, London, 1973).
2 Sidney W. Mintz, *Sweetness and Power. The Place of Sugar in Modern History* (Viking, New York, 1985), pp. 6, 37.
3 The first great colonial products, tobacco, sugar and tea, argues Mintz, 'were the first objects within capitalism that conveyed with their use the complex idea that one could *become* different by *consuming* differently': Mintz, *Sweetness and Power*, p. 185.
4 John Stuart Mill, *Principles of Political Economy*, 1st edn 1848, in J. M. Robson (ed.), *Collected Works of John Stuart Mill* (Toronto University Press, Toronto, 1965), vol. 3, p. 693.
5 Dunn, *Sugar and Slaves*, p. 149.
6 Richard N. Sheridan, 'The Formation of Caribbean Plantation Society 1689–1748', in P. J. Marshall (ed.), *The Oxford History of the British Empire*, vol. 2: *The Eighteenth Century* (Oxford University Press, Oxford, 1998), pp. 394–414.
7 C. L. R. James, 'From Toussaint L'Ouverture to Fidel Castro', printed as an appendix to *The Black Jacobins: Toussaint L'Ouverture and the San Domingo Revolution*, 2nd edn (Vintage, New York, 1963); Robin Blackburn, *The Making of New World Slavery. From the Baroque to the Modern* (Verso, London, 1997).
8 Mintz, *Sweetness and Power*, p. 157; see Eric Williams, *Capitalism and Slavery* (University of North Carolina Press, Chapel Hill, 1944).
9 On Barbados see Hilary McD. Beckles, *A History of Barbados: From Amerindian Settlement to Nation-State* (Cambridge University Press, Cambridge, 1990).
10 J. R. Ward, 'The British West Indies in the Age of Abolition 1748–1815', in Marshall (ed.), *Eighteenth Century*, pp. 415–39.
11 J. R. Ward, *British West Indian Slavery, 1750–1834. The Process of Amelioration* (Oxford University Press, Oxford, 1988), p. 208.

12   Ibid., p. 94.

13   Ward, 'British West Indies in the Age of Abolition', p. 433.

14   As the Rev. Bridges put it, 'their domestic institutions are unhappily founded upon a system repugnant to the spirit of the times we live in': Rev. George Bridges, *The Annals of Jamaica*, 2 vols, 1st pub. 1828 (Cass, London, 1968), vol. 1, Preface, p. vii.

15   Orlando Patterson, *The Sociology of Slavery. An Analysis of the Origins, Development and Structure of Negro Slave Society in Jamaica* (MacGibbon and Kee, London, 1967), p. 37.

16   Jane Austen, *Mansfield Park*, 1st edn 1814 (Penguin, Harmondsworth, 1966); Moira Ferguson, '*Mansfield Park*: Plantocratic Paradigms', in *Colonialism and Gender Relations from Mary Wollstonecraft to Jamaica Kincaid. East Caribbean Connections* (Columbia University Press, New York, 1993), pp. 65–89. For an analysis which focuses on Austen's interest in improving the ruling classes by transforming unscrupulous profit into scruple and value, see Kumkum Sangari, *Politics of the Possible. Essays on Gender, History, Narrative, Colonial English* (Tulika, New Delhi, 1999), pp. 164–8. For a better-known commentary see Said, *Culture and Imperialism*, p. 69–70.

17   Curtin, *Two Jamaicas*, p. 15.

18   On evangelicalism and separate spheres see Davidoff and Hall, *Family Fortunes*, esp. part 1.

19   Philip Wright (ed.), *Lady Nugent's Journal of her Residence in Jamaica from 1801–5* (Institute of Jamaica, Kingston, 1966), Introduction, p. 42.

20   Ibid., pp. 1, 2, 10.

21   King's House was built in 1773. Only the portico and frontage have survived.

22   Though Trollope was to be very dismissive of it: Anthony Trollope, *The West Indies and the Spanish Main* (Chapman and Hall, London, 1859), pp. 14–20.

23   Matthew Gregory Lewis, *Journal of a West Indian Proprietor Kept during a Residence in the Island of Jamaica*, 1st edn 1834; 2nd edn (Negro University Press, New York, 1969), p. 160.

24   Wright (ed.), *Lady Nugent's Journal*. Lady Nugent describes the court always around them at King's House, and the semi-monarchical status they occupy. See, e.g., pp. 106–23.

25   Quoted in Patterson, *Sociology of Slavery*, p. 29.

26   Eleven of the fourteen British sugar colonies had representative government prior to emancipation. Crown Colony government had been instituted in the recently acquired colonies of Trinidad, St Lucia and British Guiana.

27   Edward Brathwaite, *The Development of Creole Society in Jamaica 1770–1820* (Clarendon Press, Oxford, 1971).

28   Bryan Edwards, *The History, Civil and Commercial, of the British Colonies in the West Indies*, 1st edn 1791, 3 vols. (John Stockdale, London, 1806), vol. 2, pp. 2–5.

29 Gisela Eisner, *Jamaica, 1830–1930. A Study in Economic Growth* (Manchester University Press, Manchester, 1961), p. 127.

30 Patterson, *Sociology of Slavery*, p. 281.

31 Brathwaite, *Development of Creole Society*, p. 135.

32 Quoted in Curtin, *Two Jamaicas*, p. 56.

33 Quoted in Brathwaite, *Development of Creole Society*, p. 181.

34 Edwards, *History*, vol. 2, pp. 9–15.

35 James Stewart, *A View of the Past and Present State of the Island of Jamaica; with Remarks on the Moral and Physical Condition of the Slaves, and on the Abolition of Slavery in the Colonies*, 1st edn 1823 (Negro University Press, New York, 1969), pp. 170–1.

36 It was Lady Nugent who thought it horrid: Wright (ed.), *Lady Nugent's Journal*, p. 184.

37 Rev. David King, *The State and Prospects of Jamaica* (Johnston and Hunter, London, 1850). p. 128.

38 See Turner, *Slaves and Missionaries*.

39 Quoted in Michael Craton and James Walvin, *A Jamaican Plantation. The History of Worthy Park 1670–1970* (Allen, London, 1970), p. 125.

40 Douglas Hall, *In Miserable Slavery. Thomas Thistlewood in Jamaica, 1750–1786* (Macmillan, Basingstoke, 1989).

41 Ward, 'British West Indies', p. 435.

42 Holt, *The Problem of Freedom*, p. 88.

43 Ward, 'British West Indies', p. 435.

44 Patterson, quoting Long, *Sociology of Slavery*, p. 146.

45 See Turner, *Slaves and Missionaries*, esp. ch. 3.

46 Michael Craton, *Testing the Chains: Resistance to Slavery in the British West Indies* (Cornell University Press, Ithaca, NY, 1982); Barbara Bush, *Slave Women in Caribbean Slave Society, 1650–1838* (Indiana University Press, Bloomington, 1990).

47 Mavis C. Campbell, *The Dynamics of Change in a Slave Society: A Sociopolitical History of the Free Coloureds of Jamaica 1800–1865* (Associated University Presses, London, 1976); Heuman, *Between Black and White*.

48 Stewart, *View of the Past and Present State*, p. 335.

49 The phrase is Richard Barrett's, a leading campaigner for gradual rights to be extended to men of colour; quoted in Campbell, *Dynamics of Change*, p. 127.

50 Campbell, *Dynamics of Change*, p. 140.

51 The phrase draws on Fanon, writing about the French Caribbean: *Black Skin, White Masks*, p. 13.

52 Hilary McD. Beckles, 'White Women and Slavery in the Caribbean', *History Workshop Journal*, 36 (Autumn 1993), pp. 66–82; Brigid Brereton and Verene Shepherd, (eds), *Engendering the History of the Caribbean* (James Currey, London, 1995).

53 Trollope's judgement was that 'Kingston is a disgrace to the country that owns it': *West Indies*, p. 14.

54   Falmouth was originally to be named Barrett Town. Edward Barrett's granddaughter married Charles Moulton, and their son was Elizabeth Barrett Browning's father. He never went to Jamaica, but in 1798 inherited the Jamaican properties and, along with his brother Samuel, took the additional name of Barrett: Joseph Shore, *In Old St. James. A Book of Parish Chronicles*, ed. John Stewart (Sangsters, Kingston, 1911; new edn 1952). Trelawny Cultural Foundation, *Trelawny and its History* (no publisher, Falmouth, n.d.).

55   Philip Wright, *Knibb, 'the Notorious'. Slaves' Missionary 1803–1845* (Sidgwick and Jackson, London, 1973), p. 56.

56   N. M. Young, *The Colonial Office in the Early Nineteenth Century* (Longman, London, 1971).

57   Paul Knapland, *James Stephen and the British Colonial System 1813–1847* (University of Wisconsin Press, Madison, 1853).

58   Henry Taylor, *Autobiography of Henry Taylor 1800–1875*, 2 vols (Longmans, Green and Co., London, 1885).

59   Knapland, *James Stephen*; esp. ch. 4; D. J. Murray, *The West Indies and the Development of Colonial Government 1801–1834* (Clarendon Press, Oxford, 1965), p. 146.

60   Taylor, *Autobiography*, vol. 2, pp. 300–1.

61   Green, *British Slave Emancipation*, p. 94.

62   This paragraph is heavily dependent on Murray, *West Indies*, pp. 214–20.

Chapter 1   The Missionary Dream 1820–1842

1   *The Baptist Herald and Friend of Africa (BH)*, 17 Feb. 1841.

2   There is an enormous literature on anti-slavery. For an introduction to some of the key debates see David Brion Davis, *The Problem of Slavery in the Age of Revolution 1770–1823* (Cornell University Press, Ithaca, NY, 1975); Blackburn, *Making of New World Slavery; idem, The Overthrow of Colonial Slavery 1776–1848* (Verso, London, 1988); on slaves and missionaries in Demerara and Jamaica see Emilia Viotti da Costa, *Crowns of Glory, Tears of Blood. The Demerara Slave Rebellion of 1823* (Oxford University Press, Oxford, 1994); Turner, *Slaves and Missionaries*.

3   Peter Linebaugh and Marcus Rediker, *The Many-Headed Hydra. The Hidden History of the Revolutionary Atlantic* (Verso, London, 2000), pp. 226, 241–2, 307; Clement Gayle, *George Liele. Pioneer Missionary to Jamaica* (Jamaica Baptist Union, Kingston, 1982).

4   On the evangelical revival see Davidoff and Hall, *Family Fortunes*, esp. part 1.

5   The first Baptists were Arminian in theology, believing in general redemption and known as General Baptists. The dominant group soon became Calvinists, or Particular Baptists. By the nineteenth century the distinctions between these two were less sharp, and it was evangelical sentiments which were crucial. But the debate as to whether the privilege of communion should be extended to Christians other than those baptised as believers

continued to reverberate. Binfield argues that the Baptists were not a homogeneous group: Clyde Binfield, *So Down to Prayers. Studies in English Nonconformity* (Dent, London, 1977), p. 6.

6   A. D. Gilbert, *Religion and Society in Industrial England: Church, Chapel and Social Change 1740–1914* (Longman, London, 1976), pp. 36–9.
7   Davidoff and Hall, *Family Fortunes*, ch. 2.
8   Binfield, *So Down to Prayers*, p. 12.
9   Rev. F. A. Cox, *History of the Baptist Missionary Society from 1792–1842*, 2 vols (T. Ward and Co., London, 1842), vol. 1, p. 2.
10 William Carey quoted in E. Daniel Potts, *British Baptist Missionaries in India 1793–1837* (Cambridge University Press, Cambridge, 1967), p. 2.
11 Cox, *History*, vol. 1, p. 2.
12 On missions in the nineteenth century see Andrew Porter, 'Religion, Missionary Enthusiasm and Empire', in Andrew Porter (ed.), *The Oxford History of the British Empire*, vol. 3: *The Nineteenth Century* (Oxford University Press, Oxford, 1999), pp. 222–46.
13 Cox, *History*, vol. 2, p. 11.
14 Ernest A. Payne, *Freedom in Jamaica* (Carey Press, London, 1933), p. 21.
15 The figures are from ibid., p. 26, and Cox, *History*, vol. 2, p. 231.
16 Quoted in John Clark, Walter Dendy and James Mursell Phillippo, *The Voice of Jubilee: A Narrative of the Baptist Mission, Jamaica* (John Snow, London, 1865), p. 29.
17 William Fitz-er Burchell, *Memoir of Thomas Burchell, 22 Years a Missionary in Jamaica* (Benjamin L. Green, London, 1849), pp. 68–9.
18 Edward Bean Underhill, *Life of James Mursell Phillippo, Missionary in Jamaica* (Yates and Alexander, London, 1881), p. 181.
19 Burchell, *Memoir of Thomas Burchell*, p. 114.
20 Ibid., p. 7.
21 P. H. Cornford, *Missionary Reminiscences; or Jamaica Retraced* (Thomas Heaton and Son, Leeds, 1856), p. 45.
22 There was an extremely high level of withdrawal from the ministry in England. See Kenneth D. Brown, *A Social History of the Nonconformist Ministry in England and Wales 1800–1930* (Clarendon Press, Oxford, 1988).
23 Imperial adventure stories were, Martin Green argues, 'collectively the story England told itself as it went to sleep at night, and in the form of its dreams, they charged England's will with the energy to go out into the world and explore, conquer and rule'. Martin Green, *Dreams of Adventure, Deeds of Empire* (Routledge and Kegan Paul, London, 1980), p. 3.
24 Cox, *History*, vol. 1, p. vi.
25 Burchell, *Memoir of Thomas Burchell*, pp. 26, 27, 29, 33.
26 The phrase is Underhill's in relation to Phillippo. For many years Underhill was secretary to the BMS. *Life of . . . Phillippo*, p. 28.
27 *Baptist Magazine (BM)*, 31 (Feb. 1839).
28 Jemima Thompson, *Memoirs of British Female Missionaries with a Survey of the Condition of Women in Heathen Countries* (William Smith, London, 1841), Preface, p. xv.

29 Ibid., pp. 10, 13.
30 *BM* 36 (Dec. 1844).
31 *BH*, 12 May 1841.
32 *BM* 34 (Mar. 1842).
33 William Knibb's journal of his first voyage to Jamaica: BMS Archives, W1/3.
34 Davidoff and Hall, *Family Fortunes*, pp. 410–15.
35 Burchell, *Memoir of Thomas Burchell*, pp. 305–6.
36 The phrase is Cox's, *History*, vol. 2, p. 193.
37 James Mursell Phillippo, *Jamaica: Its Past and Present State* (John Snow, London, 1843), p. 270.
38 Clark et al., *Voice of Jubilee*, pp. 189–90.
39 On the place of the family enterprise in early nineteenth-century society see Davidoff and Hall, *Family Fortunes*, esp. Part 2.
40 Robert J. Stewart, *Religion and Society in Post-Emancipation Jamaica* (University of Tenessee Press, Knoxville, 1992), p. 72.
41 T. Middleditch, *The Youthful Female Missionary: A Memoir of Mary Ann Hutchins, Wife of the Rev. John Hutchins, Baptist Missionary Savanna-la-Mar, Jamaica and Daughter of the Rev. T. Middleditch of Ipswich; Compiled Chiefly from her own Correspondence by her Father* (G. Wightman and Hamilton Adams, London, 1840), p. 86.
42 Name cards have been compiled for the missionaries, using a wide variety of sources, and this data is derived from them.
43 John Howard Hinton, *Memoir of William Knibb, Missionary in Jamaica* (Houlston and Stoneman, London, 1847), p. 470.
44 Clark et al., *Voice of Jubilee*, p. 81.
45 *BM* 32 (Mar. 1840).
46 Payne, *Freedom in Jamaica*, p. 20.
47 *BM* 33 (Nov. 1841).
48 *BM* 38 (Sept. 1846).
49 Phillippo, *Jamaica*, p. 432.
50 Ibid., p. 437.
51 Cornford, *Missionary Reminiscences*, Appendix A, p. 108.
52 Curtin, *Image of Africa*, vol. 1, p. 223.
53 Quoted in Clark et al., *Voice of Jubilee*, p. 40.
54 Phillippo, *Jamaica*, pp. 151–2.
55 Clark et al., *Voice of Jubilee*, p. 53.
56 Hinton, *Memoir of William Knibb*, pp. 6–7.
57 Ibid., p. 9.
58 Ibid., pp. 19, 21, 29.
59 'William Knibb's Journal', BMS Archives, W1/3.
60 Hinton, *Memoir of William Knibb*, pp. 45–6.
61 Ibid., pp. 48–9.
62 Ibid., p. 75.
63 Turner, *Slaves and Missionaries*, see esp. ch. 5.
64 Ibid., p. 21.

65 CO 137/179, Belmont to Goderich, 23 Aug. 1831, enclosure 2, and Goderich to Belmont. See Wright's chapter on 'Deacon Swiney' in *Knibb, the 'Notorious'*, pp. 41–55.

66 CO 137/180, Bridges to Goderich, 5 May 1831; Bridges, *Annals*, vol. 2, p. 268.

67 Wright, *Knibb, the 'Notorious'*, pp. 51–2.

68 Bridges, *Annals*, vol. 2, pp. 294, 301.

69 Ibid., pp. 10–11.

70 On this stereotype see Patterson, *Sociology of Slavery*, pp. 174–9.

71 On Long and the other historians of the eighteenth and early nineteenth centuries see Elsa Goveia, *A Study on the Historiography of the British West Indies to the End of the Nineteenth Century* (Instituto Panamericano De Geografia e Historia, Mexico, 1956).

72 Edwards, *History*, vol. 2, p. 93.

73 Ibid., vol. 2, pp. 176, 177.

74 Ibid., p. 168.

75 Ward, *British West Indian Slavery*, p. 2.

76 Bridges, *Annals*, vol. 1, pp. 457–9.

77 Ibid., vol. 2, p. 406.

78 Ibid., vol. 1, pp. 498, 506, 509–10.

79 Heuman, *Between Black and White*, esp. ch. 2.

80 Turner, *Slaves and Missionaries*; da Costa, *Crowns of Glory*.

81 Da Costa, *Crowns of Glory*, p. xvii.

82 Cooper was a Unitarian who had worked on an estate in Jamaica and attempted to put a programme of amelioration and missionary teaching in place, to the accompaniment of great public controversy: PP 1831–2 (127) CCCVI, vol. 12, p. 794.

83 Turner, *Slaves and Missionaries*, p. 93.

84 Da Costa, *Crowns of Glory*, p. 168.

85 See, e.g., the evidence of the Rev. John Barry about his colleague Henry Bleby: PP 1831–2 (127) CCCVI, vol. 11, p. 489.

86 Turner, *Slaves and Missionaries*, p. 168.

87 B. W. Higman, 'The West Indian "Interest" in Parliament 1807–33', *Historical Studies*, 13/49 (1967), pp. 1–19.

88 Alexandra Franklin, 'Enterprise and Advantage: The West India Interest in Britain 1774–1840', University of Pennsylvania Ph.D. diss., 1992.

89 Ward, *British West Indian Slavery*, p. 185.

90 Horace O. Russell, 'The Emergence of the Christian Black. The Making of a Stereotype', *Jamaica Journal*, 16/1 (Feb. 1983), pp. 51–8.

91 David Bindman, 'The Representation of Plantation Slavery in the Eighteenth Century', unpub. paper presented at the seminar 'Reconfiguring the British', Institute of Historical Research, 1999.

92 PP 1831–2 (381) XX (Aug. 1832), p. 3.

93 PP 1831–2 (127) CCCVI, vol. 11, p. iii.

94 PP 1831–2 (381) XX, p. 4.

95 PP 1831–2 (127) CCCVI, vol. 11, p. 6.

96   Ibid., p. 14.
97   Ibid., p. 22.
98   Ibid., pp. 164, 165, 167, 183.
99   PP 1831–2 (381) XX, p. 503.
100 PP 1831–2 (127) CCCVI, vol. 11, p. 331.
101 Ibid. vol. 12, p. 821.
102 Ibid., pp. 990–2.
103 Ibid., vol. 11, pp. 566, 629.
104 Ibid., p. 430; PP 1831–2 (381) XX, p. 76.
105 PP 1831–2 (127) CCCVI, vol. 11, pp. 635, 636.
106 Ibid., p. 291.
107 Ibid., p. 472.
108 Ibid., p. 593.
109 PP 1831–2 (381) XX, p. 337.
110 Ibid., p. 101.
111 PP 1831–2 (127) CCCVI, vol. 11, p. 516.
112 Ibid., p. 698; Diana Paton, 'Decency, Dependency and the Lash: Gender and the British Debate over Slave Emancipation, 1830–34', *Slavery and Abolition*, 17/3 (Dec. 1996), pp. 163–84.
113 Hinton, *Memoir of William Knibb*, p. 121.
114 PP 1831–2 (381) XX, p. 254.
115 *MH*, May 1832.
116 PP 1831–2 (381) XX, p. 268.
117 PP 1831–2 (127) CCCVI, vol. 12, p. 776.
118 Hinton, *Memoir of William Knibb*, p. 154.
119 William Knibb, *Speech on the Immediate Abolition of British Colonial Slavery* (J. Blackwell and Co., Newcastle, 1833), p. 13.
120 Hinton, *Memoir of William Knibb*, p. 155.
121 Ibid., pp. 163–5.
122 PP 1831–2 (127) CCCVI, vol. 12, pp. 774, 757, 767, 776; PP 1831–2 (381) XX, pp. 271, 273, 278.
123 PP 1831–2 (381) XX, p. 145.
124 Ibid., pp. 271, 273. At the same time Mary Prince's *History* was reaching the British public, the first narrative of an enslaved black woman from the Caribbean. Mary Prince's story, as Moira Ferguson has shown, was mediated by the editorial intervention of Thomas Pringle, secretary of the Anti-Slavery Society, and Sarah Strickland, who wrote down her account of Mary Prince's words. The narrative immediately became a site of the war over the representation of black women. Pro-slavery critics attempted to subvert her legitimacy, while her female anti-slavery supporters were anxious to prove the validity of her claims: Mary Prince, *The History of Mary Prince, A West Indian Slave*, 1st edn 1831, ed. with an introduction by Moira Ferguson (Pandora Press, London, 1986).
125 Stewart, *Religion and Society in Post-Emancipation Jamaica*, p. xvii.
126 On Colonial Office views of apprenticeship see Holt, *Problem of Freedom*, esp. ch. 2.
127 Underhill, *Life of . . . Phillippo*, p. 184.

128 *BH*, 8 July 1840.
129 *BH*, 6 May 1840.
130 *BH*, 23 Sept. 1840.
131 *MH*, Sept. 1840; Phillippo, *Jamaica*, pp. 430–2.
132 *MH*, Sept. 1840.
133 On the use of the language of before/after see Curtin, *Image of Africa*, vol. 2, p. 327. See ch. 3 for a longer discussion of the significance of this language.
134 *BH*, 8 July 1840.
135 Cox, *History of the BMS*, vol. 2, pp. 248–52.
136 Ibid., pp. 252–4; *Falmouth Post*, 15 Aug. 1838.
137 Cox, *History of the BMS*, vol. 2, p. 258.
138 *BH*, 26 Oct. 1839.
139 *BH*, 28 Sept. 1839.
140 The activities of black men and women were also, of course, reported in other Jamaican papers, but usually from a pro-planter perspective.
141 PP 1839 (523) XXXVI, enclosure 50 in no. 29, p. 147.
142 *BH*, 13 May 1840.
143 Ibid.
144 *BH*, 4 Mar. 1840.
145 *BH*, 29 Aug. 1840.
146 *BH*, 6 Jan. 1841.
147 Quoted in Sidney Olivier, *Jamaica, The Blessed Isle* (Leonard and Virginia Woolf, London, 1936), p. 104.
148 Swithin Wilmot, 'Baptist Missionaries and Jamaican Politics 1838–54', paper presented at the 12th Conference of Caribbean Historians, Apr. 1980, pp. 1, 2; *idem*, 'The Peacemakers: Baptist Missionaries and Ex-Slaves in West Jamaica 1838–40', *Jamaica Historical Review*, 13 (1982), pp. 42–8.
149 PP 1839 (523) XXXVI, Sir Lionel Smith to Lord Normanby, 17 June 1839, enclosure 1; Smith to Normanby, 24 June 1839, enclosure 2.
150 PP 1840 (212) XXXV, Smith to Normanby, 19 July 1839, enclosure 16; *BH*, 28 Sept. 1839.
151 PP 1840 (212) XXXV, enclosure 1 in no. 9, Sir Lionel Smith to Lord Normanby, 19 July and 16 Aug. 1839, enclosure 19.
152 Hugh Paget, 'The Free Village System in Jamaica', *Caribbean Quarterly*, 10/1 (Mar. 1964), p. 42.
153 *Anti-Slavery Reporter (ASR)*, 20 May 1840.
154 PP 1840 (212) XXXV, Sir Lionel Smith to Lord Normanby, 16 Aug. 1839, enclosure 11.
155 Ibid., Sir Lionel Smith to Lord Normanby, 17 July 1839.
156 Ibid., Sir Lionel Smith to Lord Normanby, 19 July 1839, enclosure 1; 16 Aug. 1839, enclosure 11.
157 PP 1842 (479) XIII, p. 430.
158 Olivier, *Myth of Governor Eyre*, p. 171; Curtin, *Two Jamaicas*, p. 114.
159 Sidney Mintz, 'Caribbean Peasantries', in *Caribbean Transformations* (Aldine, Chicago, 1974), p. 155.

160   Joseph Sturge to John Clark, 1 Oct. 1838, in Fenn Collection, Angus Library, Regent's Park College.
161   On the construction of English middle-class manliness and femininity in this period see Davidoff and Hall, *Family Fortunes*.
162   The utopian moment in Jamaica coincided with utopian visions elsewhere. The vision of Joseph Sturge and his Baptist missionary friends was in some respects very different from that of the Owenite architects of utopias in England in this period. The longest-lived Owenite community in Britain was in existence between 1839 and 1845, precisely the period of the establishment of the free villages. Six others were established between 1821 and 1845. The inspiration to build a new society was similar to that of the Baptists, but the Owenites aimed to do it for themselves, whereas English abolitionists and even Baptist missionaries designed it for others. The communities were very different in practice. Most of the larger Owenite communities were built on the personal estates of their founders. But, as in the free villages, all aimed to build a society based on new patterns of production and distribution, new social relations. In one instance this was inspired by the critique of the destructive effects of the new capitalist world and urbanisation, in the other by the critique of slavery and the plantation system. Owenites relied on example and personal transformation, just as the missionaries stressed personal conversion as the key to the new world. Similarly, the Owenite model of communal social organisation was that of the 'enlarged family', an extended kinship network bound together by love and mutual obligation, hardly a far cry from the 'mission family' which was to be the building block of the new Jamaica. The recasting of relations between the sexes, however, was conceptualised very differently; while Owenite feminists raised questions about woman's mission, the division of labour and men's power over women, Baptist missionaries and their allies celebrated their version of the Christian marriage and family in the free village of the future. See Barbara Taylor, *Eve and the New Jerusalem. Socialism and Feminism in the Nineteenth Century* (Virago, London, 1983), esp. ch. 8.
163   Joseph Sturge to John Clark, 15 Nov. 1838, in Fenn Collection; William Knibb to James Hoby, 29 Nov. 1838, pp. 299–300, quoted in Hinton, *Memoir of William Knibb*; William Knibb to Joseph Sturge, 30 Nov. 1838, ibid., p. 300.
164   Alex Tyrrell, *Joseph Sturge and the Moral Radical Party in Early Victorian Britain* (Christopher Helm, London, 1987), p. 88.
165   William Knibb to Joseph Sturge, quoted in Hinton, *Memoir of William Knibb*, pp. 306, 307, 309.
166   *BH*, 14 Sept. 1839.
167   Joseph Sturge to John Clark, 31 Jan., 14 Feb., 1 Mar., 15 June, 1 Aug., 14 Oct., 1839, in Fenn Collection; John Clark, *A Brief Account of the Settlements of the Emancipated Peasantry in the Neighbourhood of Brown's Town, Jamaica. In a Letter to Joseph Sturge* (J. W. Showell, Birmingham, 1852).

168 *MH*, Nov. 1839.
169 *ASR*, 29 July 1840.
170 Hinton, *Memoir of William Knibb*, p. 465.
171 *BH*, 17 Feb., 2 June, 18 Aug. 1841.
172 Cornford, *Missionary Reminiscences*, p. 9.
173 Bound volume of letters from BMS missionaries 1840–46, BMS Archive on deposit in the Angus Library, William Knibb to BMS, 16 Feb. 1842; Hinton, *Memoir of William Knibb*, pp. 440, 466–7; Birmingham Ladies Negro's Friends Society (LNFS), *Annual Reports*, Birmingham Reference Library. Sister Martinelli, a sister in Immaculate Conception Convent in Kingston, born and brought up in Kettering, remembered Miss Annie Fray, Knibb's granddaughter, teaching her in the early years of this century, when interviewed in 1993. Interview with Sister Martinelli, Immaculate Conception Convent, 13 Feb. 1992.
174 *BH*, 4 Aug. 1841.
175 Phillippo, *Jamaica*, pp. 430–1.
176 *BH*, 20 Apr. 1842.
177 *BH*, 27 May 1840.
178 *BH*, 14 Dec. 1842, 15 Jan. 1840.
179 *BH*, 30 Sept. 1840.
180 *BH*, 9 Mar., 20 Apr., 1 June 1842.
181 *BH*, 11 May, 1 June, 29 June 1842.
182 *BH*, 3 Mar., 21 Apr., 19 May 1841; Phillippo, *Jamaica*, pp. 230, 231, 235, 226.
183 PP 1842 (479) XIII, pp. 422–3, 440; *DNB*, ed. Leslie Stephen, vol. 4 (Smith, Elder and Co., London, 1885), pp. 356–8.
184 Paget, 'Free Village System', pp. 47–50.
185 Rev. Hope Masterton Waddell, *Twenty-nine Years in the West Indies and Central Africa: A Review of Missionary Work and Adventures 1829–58* (T. Nelson and Sons, London, 1863), p. 155.
186 Phillippo, *Jamaica*, p. 228; Knibb, quoted in Paget, 'Free Village System', p. 51; e.g. CO 137/284, Governor Elgin to Lord Stanley, 23 Sept. 1845.
187 George E. Cumper, 'A Modern Jamaican Sugar Estate', *Social and Economic Studies*, no. 3 (1954), pp. 122, 135.
188 Holt, *Problem of Freedom*, pp. 144, 160.
189 *MH*, June 1845.
190 Cumper, 'Modern Jamaican Sugar Estate', p. 136.
191 Jean Besson, 'Family Land as a Model for Martha Brae's New History: Culture Building in an Afro-Caribbean Village', in Charles V. Carnegie (ed.), *Afro-Caribbean Villages in Historical Perspective* (Institute of Jamaica, Kingston, 1987), p. 100; *idem*, 'Reputation and Respectability Reconsidered: A New Perspective on Afro-Caribbean Peasant Women', in Janet H. Momsen (ed.), *Women and Change in the Caribbean. A Pan-Caribbean Perspective* (James Currey, London, 1993), pp. 15–37.
192 *BH*, 17 Feb. 1841.

Chapter 2   Fault-lines in the Family of Man 1842–1845

 1 BMS, Home Correspondence, H9/3, Dyer to W. Angas, Nov. 1830.
 2 *BM* 20 (Oct. 1828).
 3 *BM* 29 (Sept. 1837).
 4 *BM* 42 (Apr. 1850).
 5 *BM* 28 (Jan. 1836).
 6 *BM* 29 (Sept. 1837).
 7 *BM* 31 (Apr. 1839).
 8 Hinton, *Memoir of William Knibb*, p. 269.
 9 Burchell, *Memoir of Thomas Burchell*, p. 325.
10 Cornford, *Missionary Reminiscences*, pp. 97–8.
11 Burchell, *Memoir of Thomas Burchell*, p. 324.
12 Jean Comaroff and John Comaroff, *Of Revelation and Revolution. Christianity, Colonialism and Consciousness in South Africa* (University of Chicago Press, Chicago, 1991), vol. 1, pp. 198–9.
13 John Duff and George R. Lyon to Dyer, 1 Apr. 1837, BMS, H9/3.
14 BMS pamphlet collection 1823–51, Jamaica Native BMS, *First Annual Report 1841* (no publisher, n.d.).
15 Ibid., p. 3.
16 Ibid., pp. 7–8.
17 Ibid., pp. 21–2.
18 The term 'the Black Family' is used by Stewart, *Religion and Society*, p. 149.
19 Horace O. Russell, 'The Missionary Outreach of the West Indian Church to West Africa in the Nineteenth Century, with Particular Reference to the Baptists', Oxford D.Phil., 1973, p. 140.
20 *BH*, 8 Sept. 1841.
21 *BH*, 3 Mar. 1841.
22 Hinton, *Memoir of William Knibb*, p. 276.
23 Ibid., pp. 277–8.
24 H. O. Russell, 'Missionary Outreach', p. 140.
25 *BH*, 18 Aug. 1841.
26 On the Niger expedition see Howard Temperley, *White Dreams, Black Africa. The Antislavery Expedition to the Niger 1841–2* (Yale University Press, New Haven, 1991).
27 Joseph Sturge to John Clark, 14 Oct. 1839, in Fenn Collection.
28 Hinton, *Memoir of William Knibb*, p. 364.
29 Ibid., p. 362.
30 Horace O. Russell, 'The Church in the Past – A Study on Jamaican Baptists in the Eighteenth and Nineteenth Centuries', Jamaica Baptist Union MS (no publisher, n.d.).
31 J. J. Fuller, 'Recollections of the West African Mission of the BMS and Autobiography', BMS typescript, p. 4.
32 Fuller, 'Recollections', p. 6; 'Autobiography', p. 7.
33 *BH*, 25 Nov. 1840.

34   Quoted in Payne, *Freedom in Jamaica*, p. 80.
35   Bound volume of letters from BMS missionaries 1840–46, Shelf set V1/1, BMS MSS, letter from a group in Spanish Town to the BMS, including enclosures, 7 Aug. 1846.
36   Fuller, 'Autobiography', p. 3.
37   Hinton, *Memoir of William Knibb*, p. 458.
38   Brian Stanley, *The History of the Baptist Missionary Society 1792–1992* (T. and T. Clark, Edinburgh, 1992), p. 84.
39   Horace O. Russell, 'A Question of Indigenous Mission: The Jamaica Baptist Missionary Society', *Baptist Quarterly*, 25 (1973–4), pp. 86–93.
40   Quoted in Stewart, *Religion and Society*, p. 82.
41   Stanley, *History of the Baptist Missionary Society*, p. 77; Bolt, *Victorian Attitudes to Race*, p. 107.
42   H. O. Russell, 'Church in the Past', p. 1.
43   The same preoccupation is noted by Comaroff and Comaroff in South Africa: *Of Revelation and Revolution*, p. 199.
44   Waddell, *Twenty-nine Years in the West Indies*, p. 15.
45   Ibid., pp. 26–7.
46   This paragraph draws heavily on Monica Schuler, *Alas, Alas, Kongo. A Social History of Indentured African Immigration into Jamaica, 1841–65* (Johns Hopkins University Press, Baltimore, 1980), pp. 32–40.
47   Patterson, *Sociology of Slavery*, pp. 182–95.
48   Stewart, *Religion and Society*, p. 145.
49   John Candler, *Extracts from the Journal of John Candler whilst Travelling in Jamaica*, 2 parts (Harvey and Darton, London, 1840–1), part 1, pp. 28–9; Joseph John Gurney, *A Winter in the West Indies Described in Familiar Letters to Henry Clay of Kentucky* (John Murray, London, 1840), p. 98.
50   Waddell, *Twenty-nine Years in the West Indies*, p. 187.
51   Schuler, *Alas, Alas, Kongo*, p. 40.
52   Waddell, *Twenty-nine Years in the West Indies*, p. 187.
53   Ibid., p. 192.
54   Ibid., p. 195.
55   Cornford, *Missionary Reminiscences*, p. 24.
56   John Clarke, *Memorials of Baptist Missionaries in Jamaica, including a Sketch of Early Religious Instructors in Jamaica* (Yates and Alexander, London, 1869), pp. 162–3.
57   The imperial government had little sympathy for the Baptists in relation to the many complaints. Russell thought them dangerous and narrow-minded, and Metcalfe believed that they were preventing reconciliation between classes on the island. See W. A. Green, *British Slave Emancipation*, pp. 172–3.
58   BMS, *Circular* (J. Haddon, London, 1842).
59   Ibid.; Rev. Richard Panton, 'Memorandum of his charges against the Baptist missionaries', BMS MS H9/1, 20 Oct. 1838; James Reid, 'Letter to Angus', BMS MS W1/5; George Blyth, *Remonstrance of the Presbytery of Jamaica with the Majority of the Baptist Missionaries in that Island*

(M. Paterson, Edinburgh, 1843); Samuel Green, *Baptist Mission in Jamaica. A Review of the Rev. W. G. Barrett's Pamphlet Entitled A Reply to the Circular of the Baptist Missionary Society* (Houlston and Stoneman, London, 1842).

60 Panton, 'Memorandum'.
61 Reid, 'Letter to Angus'.
62 Quoted in Stewart, *Religion and Society*, pp. 124–5.
63 Blyth, *Remonstrance*, pp. 21, 25, 35, 37, 54, 57.
64 Stewart, *Religion and Society*, p. 134.
65 Nancy Prince, *A Black Woman's Odyssey through Russia and Jamaica. The Narrative of Nancy Prince*, introduction by R. G. Walters (Markus Wiener Publishers, Princeton, 1995), pp. 51, 75–6.
66 William Knibb, *Speech of the Rev. William Knibb before the Baptist Missionary Society* (Dyer and Dyer, London, 1842), p. iv.
67 Hinton, *Memoir of William Knibb*, p. 402.
68 On the claims made in England see Davidoff and Hall, *Family Fortunes*, part 1; for Hannah Kilham in Africa see Alison Twells, ' "So distant and wild a scene": Language, Domesticity and Difference in Hannah Kilham's Writing from West Africa, 1822–32', *Women's History Review*, 4/3 (1995), pp. 301–18.
69 Knibb, *Speech to the BMS*, pp. 8, 13, 25.
70 Knibb to C. Young, 19 Dec. 1839, BMS MS W1/3.
71 Knibb, *Speech to the BMS*, p. 13.
72 Ibid., pp. 34–5.
73 Ibid., pp. 28, 34.
74 Wright, *Knibb, the 'Notorious'*, pp. 206–7.
75 PP 1831–2 (127) CCCVI, vol. 12, p. 246.
76 PP 1842 (479) XIII, pp. 433–4.
77 Midgley, *Women against Slavery*, pp. 1–2.
78 Knibb, *Speech to the BMS*, pp. 34–5.
79 *BH*, 2 June 1841.
80 BMS, *Circular*, p. 5.
81 Edward Barrett's Ticket, BMS MS W1/3.
82 S. Green, *Baptist Mission in Jamaica*, p. 25.
83 BMS, *Circular*, p. 7.
84 Ibid., p. 4.
85 S. Green, *Baptist Mission in Jamaica*, p. 24.
86 Cornford, *Missionary Reminiscences*, p. 15.
87 H. O. Russell, 'Missionary Outreach', p. 188.
88 Clarke, *Memorials*, p. 178.
89 Linebaugh and Rediker, *Many-Headed Hydra*, pp. 289–326.
90 *BH*, 16 Feb. 1842.
91 *BH*, 12 Oct. 1842.
92 *BH*, 7 Sept. 1842.
93 Ibid.
94 *BH*, 5 Oct., 7, 14 Sept., 26 Oct., 2, 9 Nov. 1842.
95 *BH*, 2 Nov. 1842.

96   *BH*, 21 July 1841.
97   *BH*, 24 Feb. 1841.
98   *BH*, 25 Aug. 1841.
99   Prince, *Black Woman's Odyssey*, p. 53.
100 *BH*, 8 Sept. 1841.
101 Ibid.
102 Burchell, *Memoir of Thomas Burchell*, p. 411.
103 Candler, *Extracts*, pp. 36–7.
104 Gurney, *Winter*, pp. 136–40.
105 Burchell, *Memoir of Thomas Burchell*, pp. 301, 373, 404.
106 Ibid., p. 390.
107 'Bound Volume of Letters, BMS MS V1/1, 11 Aug., 29 Sept. 1840; 19 July 1844.
108 *Falmouth Post*, 8 Apr. 1845.
109 Cornford, *Missionary Reminiscences*, pp. 11–12.
110 Hinton, *Memoir of William Knibb*, p. 480.
111 Ibid., p. 458.
112 Ibid., p. 386.
113 James Hoby, *Memoir of William Knibb, Son of the Rev. William Knibb* (Thomas Ward and Co., London, n.d.), pp. 2, 43, 50.
114 Burchell, *Memoir of Thomas Burchell*, p. 332.
115 Hinton, *Memoir of William Knibb*, p. 443.
116 Wilmot, 'Baptist Missionaries', pp. 25–6; *idem*, 'The Politics of Samuel Clarke: Black Political Martyr in Jamaica, 1850–65', *Jamaica Historical Review*, 19 (1996), pp. 19–29.
117 Wright, *Knibb, 'the Notorious'*, p. 237.
118 *Falmouth Post*, 18 Feb. 1845.
119 *Falmouth Post*, 8 Apr. 1845.
120 *Falmouth Post*, 13 May 1845.
121 *Falmouth Post*, 5 Aug. 1845.
122 *Falmouth Post*, 12 Aug. 1845.
123 Edward Bean Underhill, *The Jamaica Mission in its Relation with the BMS 1838–79* (printed for the use of the committee, London, 1879), p. 5.
124 Samuel Oughton, *A Sermon Preached at East Queen St. Chapel, Kingston, on Occasion of the Death of the Rev. William Knibb* (John Snow, London, 1846).
125 BMS, MS W1/3.
126 Hinton, *Memoir of William Knibb*, pp. 471, 434.

Chapter 3   'A Jamaica of the Mind' 1820–1854

1   Oughton, *Sermon*, pp. iv, 36.
2   By the 1840s there was a significant body of 'missionary stories', from South and West Africa to India and the Pacific. The immense popularity of a poet such as Montgomery, with his enthusiasm for the missionary cause, one indication of the appetite for such publications.

3 Comaroff and Comaroff argue that what distinguished the missionary story from the traveller's tale was its 'assertively personalised, epic form': *Of Revelation and Revolution*, p. 172.

4 Joseph Sturge and Thomas Harvey, *The West Indies in 1837: Being the Journal of a Visit to Antigua, Montserrat, Dominica, St Lucia, Barbadoes and Jamaica; Undertaken for the Purpose of Ascertaining the Actual Condition of the Negro Population of those Islands*, 2nd edn (Hamilton, Adams and Co., London, 1838), p. viii.

5 Gurney, *Winter*, pp. 98, 115–16; Candler, *Extracts*, Part 1, pp. 21, 45; Part 2, p. 15.

6 Phillippo, *Jamaica*, pp. vi–vii.

7 Phillippo, 'Autobiography', BMS MS W1/1, pp. 19–20, 22.

8 Underhill, *Life of . . . Phillippo*, p. 8.

9 Phillippo, 'Autobiography', pp. 33, 40, 41, 49, 61.

10 Ibid., p. 52b.

11 Ibid., p. 64b.

12 Ibid., pp. 64b, 78–9.

13 Underhill, *Life of . . . Phillippo*, pp. 56–7.

14 Phillippo, 'Autobiography', p. 95.

15 Underhill, *Life of . . . Phillippo*, pp. 104–6.

16 Ibid., p. 121.

17 Ibid., p. 122.

18 Ibid., p. 135.

19 Ibid., p. 181.

20 Ibid., p. 162.

21 Ibid., pp. 174–5.

22 William Knibb, *Jamaica. A Speech to the Baptist Missionary Society in Exeter Hall 28 April 1842* (G. and J. Dyer, London, 1842).

23 Underhill, *Life of . . . Phillippo*, pp. 174–5; *ASR*, 4 Oct. 1843.

24 Underhill, *Life of . . . Phillippo*, p. 203.

25 Ibid., p. 100.

26 Phillippo, 'Autobiography', p. 146.

27 Phillippo, *Jamaica*, pp. v, x.

28 Ibid., pp. 35, 38, 46, 59, 122.

29 Pratt, *Imperial Eyes*, p. 7.

30 Phillippo, *Jamaica*, pp. 154–5, 174.

31 Ibid., pp. 121, 138–9.

32 Curtin, *Image of Africa*, vol. 2, p. 327.

33 Comaroff and Comaroff, *Of Revelation and Revolution*, p. 99.

34 Phillippo, *Jamaica*, pp. 189, 218–19.

35 Ibid., pp. 261–3, 270–4.

36 Ibid., pp. 242–6.

37 Ibid., pp. 386–7, 253.

38 Ibid., pp. 150, 154, 201, 208.

39 For an account of the shifting fortunes of Toussaint in the English literary imagination, see Cora Kaplan, 'Black Heroes/White Writers: Toussaint

L'Ouverture and the Literary Imagination', *History Workshop Journal*, 46 (Autumn 1998), pp. 33–62.

40 Phillippo, *Jamaica*, pp. 208–11.

41 *BH*, 17 Jan., 7 May, 24 Sept. 1844.

42 Robert Stewart has written a very full account of this episode: *Religion and Society*, pp. 83–94.

43 James Mursell Phillippo, 'Letters to Joseph Angus 1844–6', BMS MS W1/1, 20 Dec. 1844, 27 Apr. 1845; Kingston Guardian and Patriot, *Full Report of the Proceedings in Chancery of the Important Case of the Baptist Chapel, Spanish Town, October, 1845* (Kingston, 1845), W1/2, p. 21.

44 Phillippo, 'Letters', 7 Jan., 22 Mar. 1845; Kingston Guardian, *Full Report*, p. 21.

45 Phillippo, *Jamaica*, p. 325; *idem*, 'Letters', 7 Apr. 1845.

46 BMS, 'Notes of Deputation to Jamaica 1846–9', p. 57.

47 Thomas Hands, 'Letter to Angus', BMS MS W1/5, 19 Apr. 1845; George Evans, 'Letter to Angus', BMS MS W1/5, 20 Apr. 1845; George Rowse, 'Letters to the BMS', National Library of Jamaica (NLJ), MS 841, 8 Oct. 1845.

48 Edward Hewett, 'Letter to Angus', BMS MS W1/5, 6 Oct. 1845; James Hume, 'Letters', BMS MS W1/5, 28 Aug. 1851.

49 Joseph Fletcher, *Case of the Baptist Church in Spanish Town, Jamaica, and of its esteemed pastor, the Rev. J. M. Phillippo*, BMS printed circular, BMS MS HII/2.

50 James A. Robertson, 'Letter to BMS committee', BMS MS HII/3.

51 CO 137/310, Sir Charles Grey to Earl Grey, 26 July 1851.

52 BMS, 'Notes of Deputation'.

53 Phillippo, 'Letters', 23 Jan., 12 Feb., 8 Mar., 7 Apr. 1845; 6 Feb. 1846.

54 Joseph Maclean and William James, 'Letter to BMS committee', BMS MS HII/3, 17 Apr. 1845.

55 Phillippo, 'Letters', 8 Mar., 7 May, 7 June, 6 Sept. 1845.

56 Underhill, *Life of . . . Phillippo*, p. 230; *MH*, June 1847; Phillippo, 'Letters', 20 Sept. 1846.

57 *Falmouth Post*, 23 Sept., 16 Dec. 1845.

58 Underhill, *Life of . . . Phillippo*, p. 289.

59 Ibid., pp. 345–7.

60 NLJ, BMS, Correspondence 1844–54, MS 378, Dendy to Angus, 1 Aug. 1848, 9 Apr. 1849.

61 CO 137/284, Elgin to Stanley, 2 Sept. 1845, enclosure 2.

62 Curtin, *Two Jamaicas*, p. 168.

63 PP 1849 (280) XXXVII, C. E. Grey to Earl Grey, 10 Mar. 1849.

64 G. G. Findlay and W. W. Holdsworth, *The History of the Wesleyan Methodist Missionary Society*, 5 vols (Epworth Press, London, 1921), vol. 2, p. 361.

65 This paragraph and the two which follow are heavily dependent on Hall's argument. See *Free Jamaica*, esp. ch. 3.

66 Gocking, 'Early Constitutional History', p. 116.
67 Heuman, *Between Black and White*, p. 92.
68 Quoted in Gocking, 'Early Constitutional History', p. 118.
69 For accounts of the constitutional crisis of 1839 see also Holt, *Problem of Freedom*, pp. 105–12.
70 Quoted in Edward Thompson, *The Life of Charles, Lord Metcalfe* (Faber and Faber, London, 1937), p. 347.
71 John William Kaye, *The Life and Correspondence of Charles, Lord Metcalfe*, 2 vols (Smith, Elder and Co., London, 1858), vol. 2, pp. 282–3.
72 D. Hall, *Free Jamaica*, p. 169.
73 PP 1849 (280) XXXVII, Grey to Lord Grey, 10 Mar. 1849.
74 Earl H. G. Grey, *Colonial Policy*, vol. 1, p. 59.
75 Holt, *Problem of Freedom*, p. 152.
76 Ibid., p. 119.
77 This paragraph and the next draw on Holt's argument in *Problem of Freedom*, esp. pp. 214–16, 235–6, 244.
78 PP 1849 (280) XXXVII, Grey to Grey, 7 July, 22 July 1848.
79 Both quoted in Holt, *Problem of Freedom*, pp. 235–6.
80 Ibid., p. 236.
81 Gocking, 'Early Constitutional History', pp. 125–6.
82 Holt, *Problem of Freedom*, p. 249.
83 PP 1854 (1848) XLIII, Barkly to Newcastle, 21 Feb. 1854.
84 Ibid., enclosure 4.
85 Ibid., Barkly to Newcastle, 26 May 1854.
86 Ibid., Barkly to Newcastle, 21 Feb. 1854, enclosure 4.
87 Ibid.
88 W. A. Green, *British Slave Emancipation*, p. 345.
89 Curtin, *Two Jamaicas*, esp. ch. 5.
90 Green notes that the land bought for free villages was often inferior, and that African methods of cultivation were used, which meant that there was little chance of sustained prosperity. The quality of life declined, and this widened the gap between Afro-Jamaicans and Europeans: *British Slave Emancipation*, p. 304.
91 PP 1854 (1848) XLIII, Barkly to Newcastle, 21 Feb. 1854, enclosure 4.
92 D. Hall, *Free Jamaica*, p. 238.
93 BMS Correspondence 1844–54, NLJ MS 378, Dendy to Angus, 15 Apr. 1847; Dendy to Trestrail, 4 Nov. 1852.
94 PP 1854 (1848) XLIII, Barkly to Newcastle, 21 Feb. 1854, enclosure 4.
95 Ibid., Barkly to Newcastle, 26 May 1854.
96 BMS Correspondence 1844–54, MS 378, Dendy to Angus, 2 Dec. 1848.
97 *Address to the Friends of Education in Great Britain from a Meeting of Presbyterians, Independents and Baptists*, Falmouth, 15 Feb. 1849.
98 BMS Correspondence 1844–54, MS 378, Dendy to Underhill, 24 Mar. 1852.

Chapter 4   Missionary Men and Morant Bay 1859–1866

1   David Livingstone, *Missionary Travels and Researches in South Africa* (John Murray, London, 1857); see also Felix Driver, *Geography Militant. Cultures of Empire and Exploitation* (Blackwell, Oxford, 2001).
2   Johannes Fabian, *Time and the Other. How Anthropology Makes its Object* (Columbia University Press, New York, 1983).
3   Anthony Trollope, *Autobiography*, 2 vols (William Blackwood and Sons, London, 1883), vol. 1, p. 171.
4   Ibid., pp. 172–4.
5   Olivier, *Myth of Governor Eyre*, pp. 41–4.
6   For a longer discussion of Trollope's travel writing see Catherine Hall, ' "Going-a-Trolloping": Imperial Man Travels the Empire', in Clare Midgley (ed.), *Gender and Imperialism* (Manchester University Press, Manchester, 1998), pp. 180–99.
7   Mabel E. Wotton, quoted in R. C. Terry (ed.), *Trollope: Interviews and Recollections* (Macmillan, London, 1987), p. 167.
8   James Bryce, quoted in ibid., p. 168.
9   Quoted in N. John Hall (ed.), *The Trollope Critics* (Macmillan, London, 1981), pp. 3–4, 14, 20.
10 Trollope, *Autobiography*, vol. 1, p. 202.
11 Quoted in Terry (ed.), *Trollope*, p. 138.
12 Quoted in Victoria Glendinning, *Anthony Trollope* (Hutchinson, London, 1992), p. 303.
13 This description appears on the dust-jacket of Glendinning's biography, *Anthony Trollope*.
14 John Davidson, 'Anthony Trollope and the Colonies', *Victorian Studies*, 12 (Mar. 1969), pp. 305–30; Patrick Brantlinger, *Rule of Darkness. British Literature and Imperialism 1830–1914* (Cornell University Press, Ithaca, NY, 1988), pp. 4–7.
15 Trollope, *West Indies; idem, North America*, 2 vols (Chapman and Hall, London, 1862); *idem, South Africa*, 2 vols (Chapman and Hall, London, 1878).
16 His early Irish novels were *The Macdermots of Ballycloran*, 3 vols (Newby, London, 1847); *The Kellys and the O'Kellys*, 3 vols (Colburn, London, 1848). Much later he wrote *The Landleaguers*, 3 vols (Chatto and Windus, London, 1883).
17 A substantial number of these are still available in Penguin Classics.
18 Gikandi, *Maps of Englishness*, p. 95.
19 Trollope, *West Indies*, p. 221.
20 Morrison uses that metaphor in her exploration of the ways in which race haunted the literary canon of the United States, in *Playing in the Dark*.
21 Herman Merivale, *Introduction to a Course of Lectures on Colonisation and Colonies* (Longman, Orme, Brown, Green and Longmans, London, 1839), pp. xi, 39, 40.
22 Ibid., p. 340.

23 Herman Merivale, *Lectures on Colonisation and Colonies* (Longman, Green, Longman and Roberts, London, 1861), pp. vii, xii, 119, 492–3, 510–11, 520, 540, 549, 675.

24 Frances Trollope, Preface to the 5th edition of *Domestic Manners of the Americans*, 1st edn 1832 (George Routledge and Sons, London, 1927), pp. 6–7, 154, 187.

25 Mill, *Autobiography*, p. 228.

26 Glendinning, *Anthony Trollope*, p. 221; Anthony Trollope, *The Warden*, 1st edn 1855 (Robert Hayes, London, 1925), pp. 192, 195. As an older man, writing and reflecting on his life, Trollope concluded that Carlyle had exaggerated the problems of the age, for things had got better: comforts had increased, health had improved, and education had been extended: *Autobiography*, vol. 1, p. 210.

27 Hall (ed.), *Trollope Critics*, p. 274.

28 Eric Williams, *British Historians and the West Indies* (Andre Deutsch, London, 1966), p. 90.

29 Anthony Trollope, *Australia and New Zealand*, 2 vols (Chapman and Hall, London, 1873), vol. 1, p. 29.

30 I have found Gikandi's discussion of Trollope in *Maps of Englishness*, pp. 91–106 very helpful.

31 Trollope, *Autobiography*, vol. 2, pp. 103–4.

32 Frederick Harrison, *Studies in Early Victorian Literature* (Chapman and Hall, London, 1895), p. 208.

33 Gikandi, *Maps of Englishness*, esp. pp. 87–90.

34 *The Macdermots of Ballycloran*, for example, his first novel, attempted to understand the sources of violence in Irish society, particularly the Ribbonmen, and communicate that to an English audience.

35 Trollope, *Autobiography*, vol. 1, p. 175; ironically, Trollope was preoccupied in his early novels with the tyrannical power of the modern newspaper. See, e.g., Trollope, *The Warden*, 1st edn 1855 (Robert Hayes, London, 1925).

36 Richard Mullen, *Anthony Trollope. A Victorian in his World* (Duckworth, London, 1990), p. 341.

37 *The Times*, 6 Jan. 1860.

38 Ibid.

39 Trollope, *West Indies*, p. 55.

40 Anthony Trollope, 'Miss Sarah Jack, of Spanish Town, Jamaica', 1st edn 1860, repr. in Trollope, *The Complete Short Stories in Five Volumes*, vol. 3: *Tourists and Colonials* (Trollope Society, London, n.d.), p. 1.

41 Trollope, *West Indies*, pp. 56, 58, 60, 62.

42 Ibid., pp. 59–60, 62, 65.

43 Ibid., p. 55.

44 Gikandi, *Maps of Englishness*, p. 107.

45 Trollope, *West Indies*, pp. 92–3.

46 Ibid., p. 40.

47 Ibid., pp. 74, 80.

48 Ibid., pp. 64, 75, 81, 84.

49 Glendinning, *Anthony Trollope*, p. 168.

50 Trollope, *West Indies*, p. 80.

51 Trollope, *Australia and New Zealand*, vol. 1, pp. 118, 133.

52 Glendinning, *Anthony Trollope*, pp. 147–9.

53 See particularly Lady Laura in Anthony Trollope, *Phineas Finn. The Irish Member*, 1st edn 1867 (Oxford University Press, Oxford, 1992).

54 Anthony Trollope, *Ralph the Heir*, 1st edn 1871 (Penguin, Harmondsworth, 1993); *idem*, 'Miss Sarah Jack'.

55 Trollope, *Ralph the Heir*, p. 53.

56 Trollope, *West Indies*, p. 8.

57 Sander Gilman, 'Black Bodies, White Bodies. Towards an Iconography of Female Sexuality in Late Nineteenth Century Art, Medicine and Literature', in James Donald and Ali Rattansi (eds), *'Race', Culture and Difference* (Sage, London, 1992), pp. 171–97.

58 Trollope, *West Indies*, pp. 69–70.

59 *The Times*, 6 Jan. 1860.

60 See, e.g., anon., 'The West Indies, as They Were and Are', *Edinburgh Review*, 109 (Jan–Apr. 1859), pp. 421–60.

61 Robert Emery, *'About Jamaica': Its Past, its Present, and its Future* (John Evans, London, 1859), pp. 9, 26, 29.

62 William G. Sewell, *The Ordeal of Free Labor in the British West Indies* (Harper and Bros, New York, 1861), pp. 174, 177, 182, 196, 198–9.

63 Ibid., pp. 231, 252, 298, 308.

64 Trollope, *West Indies*, p. 61.

65 *ASR*, 1 Mar. 1860.

66 Quoted ibid.

67 *ASR*, 1 Oct. 1860.

68 *MH*, Nov. 1860.

69 Underhill and Brown both sent reports on every stage of their journey to the BMS. Some of this material was published in the *Missionary Herald*, see esp. Jan.–Dec. 1860.

70 *MH*, June 1862.

71 Correspondence of Dr D. J. East and Dr Underhill, 1852–95, BMS archive, Underhill to East, 31 Aug. 1861.

72 *BM* 54 (Mar. 1862); Underhill to East, 15 May 1863.

73 Ernest A. Payne, *The Great Succession. Leaders of the Baptist Missionary Society during the Nineteenth Century* (Carey Press, London, 1938).

74 Underhill, *Jamaica Mission*, pp. 5–6.

75 Edward Bean Underhill, *Christian Missions in the East and West, in Connection with the Baptist Missionary Society, 1792–1873* (Yeats and Alexander, London, 1873), p. 54.

76 Quoted in Underhill, *West Indies*, p. 295.

77 *MH*, June 1845.

78 Porter, 'Religion, Missionary Enthusiasm and Empire', p. 236.

79 E. B. Underhill, 'On the Pastorate of the Mission Churches' (1852), in *The Principles and Methods of Missionary Labour* (Alexander and Shepheard, London, 1896), p. 26.

80   Ibid., pp. 26–7.
81   Underhill to East, 16 Nov. 1853, 15 May 1852.
82   *MH*, July 1860.
83   Underhill, *West Indies*, pp. 221, 224.
84   Ibid., pp. 227, 437–8.
85   Ibid., pp. 209, 317, 296, 301, 188, 411, 423, 435.
86   Ibid., p. 302; 'On the Pastorate', p. 30.
87   *MH*, Feb. 1860.
88   Underhill was well aware of the tensions between black and white pastors which simmered and sometimes erupted on the island. The African mission had left a bad legacy (see ch. 3), and 'Mr African Clarke', as Rev. Ellis Fray, William Knibb's son-in-law and one of the first group trained at Calabar, called him, was renowned for his supercilious ways with black pastors: 'Letters from Ellis Fray to Frederick Trestrail and Edward Bean Underhill', NLJ MS 859.
89   Underhill, *West Indies*, pp. 243, 192, 315–16, 392, 327.
90   Underhill to East, 13 Aug. 1862, 'Correspondence of East and Underhill'.
91   Underhill, *West Indies*, p. 457.
92   *MH*, July, Sept., Dec. 1840.
93   *MH*, Feb. 1841.
94   *BH*, 3 Mar. 1841.
95   Ibid.
96   *BH*, 10 Mar. 1841.
97   *MH*, Aug. 1841.
98   *BH*, 25 Aug. 1841.
99   *BH*, 22 Dec. 1841.
100 *BH*, 26 Jan. 1842.
101 BMS Correspondence, Henderson to Angus, Dec. 1845.
102 Underhill, *Jamaica Mission*, p. 5.
103 BMS Correspondence, Dendy to Angus, 18 July 1848.
104 As, e.g., Ann Henderson to Underhill, 23 Jan. 1862, in Henderson, 'Letters 1841–63', NLJ MS 817.
105 D. J. East, *The Inheritance Attained: A Sermon Preached by the Rev. D. J. East for Mrs. Dendy* (Youngman and Poole, Maldon, 1866), pp. 4, 15.
106 Henderson to Angus, 2 Aug. 1847; Walter Dendy et al. to the BMS committee, 9 Feb. 1849; Address to the Friends of Education in Great Britain from a meeting of Presbyterians, Independents and Baptists in Falmouth 15 Feb. 1849, BMS Correspondence 1844–54, NLJ MS 378.
107 Dendy to Angus, 11 Jan. 1849, BMS Correspondence.
108 George E. Henderson, *Goodness and Mercy. A Tale of a Hundred Years* (The Gleaner, Kingston, 1931), p. 96.
109 *BH*, 12 Apr. 1843.
110 Many ties remained, however, between Baptists and black settlers. See, e.g., Swithin Wilmot's work on Samuel Clarke: 'Politics of Samuel Clarke'.
111 *ASR*, 1 Dec. 1847.
112 *Falmouth Post*, 4 Sept. 1849; Holt, *Problem of Freedom*, p. 231.

113   Henderson, Claydon, Gay and Hands to the BMS committee, 'Letters and Reports to the BMS about Falmouth', NLJ MS 817a, 24 Oct. 1850.

114   Henderson to Underhill, 4 Mar. 1851, 'Letters and Reports to the BMS about Falmouth', NLJ MS 814a; BM, Dec. 1850.

115   Henderson to Underhill and Trestrail, 3 May, 2 Dec. 1853; 1 Apr., 19 July 1854; in Henderson, 'Letters 1841–63'.

116   Dendy to Angus, 19 Aug. 1847, 18 Apr., 4 May 1848, in BMS Correspondence 1844–54.

117   BM, Nov. 1852.

118   Ellis Fray, a coloured man who trained at Calabar and married one of the Knibb daughters, commented on the 'heavy and peculiar responsibility' of those trained at Calabar: Fray to Trestrail, 10 Dec. 1852, in Letters to Trestrail and Underhill.

119   Dendy to Angus, 20 Dec. 1848, in BMS Correspondence 1844–54.

120   See Stewart, Religion and Society, for material on the conflicts in Methodist as well as Baptist congregations and the conflicts around 'native agency' in the Anglican church.

121   Dendy to Angus and Underhill, 19 Oct., 20 Dec. 1848; 3 Jan., 4 Jan., 11 Jan., 19 Mar., 9 Apr. 1849; in BMS Correspondence 1844–54.

122   Henderson to Trestrail, 6 May 1855; 24 July, 21 Oct. 1856; in Henderson 'Letters 1841–63'.

123   Henderson to Trestrail, 1 Apr., 9 Oct. 1854; in Henderson 'Letters 1841–63'.

124   Henderson to Trestrail, 21 Oct. 1856, in Henderson 'Letters 1841–63'; Henderson to Trestrail, 9 Dec. 1856, 19 May 1857, in 'Letters and Reports to the BMS about Falmouth'.

125   Falmouth Post, 25 Mar. 1859.

126   Falmouth Post, 8 Mar., 1 Apr. 1859.

127   Holt, Problem of Freedom, p. 266.

128   Falmouth Post, 9, 16 Aug. 1859.

129   Henderson to Trestrail, 22 Aug. 1859, in Henderson 'Letters 1841–63'.

130   Ladies' Negro's Friend Society, 36th Report (Hudson, Birmingham, 1861).

131   ASR, 1 Jan. 1861.

132   On the revival and its significance see Stewart, Religion and Society, pp. 145–8.

133   MH, Jan. 1861.

134   MH, Feb. 1861.

135   The phrase is Claydon's, the Baptist missionary in Porus where the revival had a great impact: MH, Feb. 1861.

136   Ibid.

137   MH, Mar. 1861.

138   MH, Feb. 1862.

139   MH, Feb., Mar. 1861.

140   Stewart, Religion and Society, pp. 147–8.

141   Henderson to Underhill, 4 Feb. 1862, in Henderson 'Letters 1841–63'.

142   Clark et al., *Voice of Jubilee*, pp. 7–8, 16, 24. The introduction by East was first delivered at Falmouth Baptist Church. Curtin and Stewart both argue that the revival marked the end of the alliance between black Christians and the Baptist missionaries against white hegemony. I am not convinced of this. Curtin, *Two Jamaicas*, p. 172; Stewart, *Religion and Society*, p. 173.

143   *MH*, Aug. 1864.

144   *MH*, Dec. 1864; Underhill, *Tragedy of Morant Bay*, p. xii.

145   Underhill, *Tragedy of Morant Bay*, p. xiv.

146   Underhill to East, 31 Jan. 1865; Underhill to Henderson, 28 Feb. 1865; Underhill to Millard, 28 Feb. 1865. 'Edward Bean Underhill, Extracts from Correspondence with Missionaries in Jamaica on the Disturbances, 1864–1866', BMS archive, typescript.

147   PP 1866 (3595) LI, Eyre to Cardwell, 25 Apr. 1865, no. 117, p. 645.

148   Ibid., Cardwell to Eyre, 14 June 1865, no. 222; the description of the reply as a lecture in classical political economy is Holt's, *Problem of Freedom*, pp. 277–8.

149   Ibid., li 'Papers relative to the affairs of Jamaica', Eyre to Cardwell, 22 Aug. 1865, p. 766.

150   Underhill to Hewitt, 31 Mar. 1865; Underhill to East, 15 Apr. 1865; Underhill to Phillippo, 13 Apr. 1865; Underhill, 'Extracts'.

151   'Report of the Baptist ministers to Governor Eyre', ibid., Eyre to Cardwell, 6 May 1865, no. 128, enclosure 1, p. 655.

152   Ibid., pp. 656–9.

153   Ibid., pp. 668, 669, 682.

154   *MH*, Feb. 1837.

155   *MH*, Feb. 1839.

156   Dyer to Russell, CO 137/245, 17 Sept. 1839.

157   *MH*, Feb. 1840.

158   *MH*, Aug. 1840.

159   *MH*, Oct. 1840.

160   *ASR*, 9 Sept. 1840.

161   *BH*, 25 Jan. 1843.

162   *Falmouth Post*, 29 Apr. 1845.

163   Barkly to Newcastle, 19 Jan. 1854, CO 137/322.

164   Elizabeth Holt, Letter to Edward Bean Underhill, NLJ MS 865.

165   *Falmouth Post*, 21 Feb. 1854.

166   Barkly to Herbert, 12 Mar. 1855, CO 137/326.

167   Memorial tablet in East Queen's Street.

168   Mrs Oughton, *Fugitive Pieces by a Missionary's Wife* (Muller, New York, n.d.), pp. 39–40.

169   *BH*, 3 Mar. 1841; Charles Buxton (ed.), *Memoirs of Sir Thomas Fowell Buxton* (John Murray, London, 1848).

170   Wilmot, 'Baptist Missionaries and Jamaican Politics', p. 32.

171   Samuel Oughton, *A Nation's Lamentation over Fallen Greatness. A Funeral Sermon Occasioned by the Death of His Royal Highness, Prince*

Albert at East Queen's St. 19th Jan. 1862 (Savage and Co., Jamaica, 1862), pp. 3, 4, 12, 17.

172   Samuel Oughton, *Roupell the Forger, the Lessons of his Crime and Punishment*, Lecture at East Queen St., 11th Oct. 1862, and repeated 25th Oct. 1862 by special request (M. DeCordova and Co., Kingston, 1862).

173   Samuel Oughton, 'The Influence of Artificial Wants on the Social, Moral, and Commercial Advancement of Jamaica', repr. from the *West India Quarterly*, June 1862, and bound with *Roupell the Forger*, pp. 474–83.

174   *Jamaica Guardian*, 25 Feb. 1865, cited in Heuman, '*The Killing Time*', p. 48.

175   Temperley, *White Dreams, Black Africa*; Livingstone, *Missionary Travels*.

176   D. J. East, *The Circular Letter for 1856, of the Jamaica Baptist Union* (Haddon Bros and Co., London, 1856). Included in the JBU's Memorial to the Secretary of State, 1866, NLJ MS 15, appendix 5, pp. 5, 6, 9, 10, 13, 16, 17, 18, 22.

177   D. J. East, *The Importance of Suitable Dwellings to the Cultivation of Family Religion* (J. Heaton and Son, London, 1863), pp. 4, 5, 8, 12.

178   PP 1866 (3595) LI, Part I, no. 128, Eyre to Cardwell, 6 May 1865, enclosure no. 10; Eyre to Cardwell, 22 Aug. 1865, no. 210; Eyre to Cardwell, 28 Oct. 1865, no. 257, enclosures 2, 3.

179   Eyre to Cardwell, 20 Sept. 1865, ibid., no. 237, enclosure 2.

180   Underhill to East, 31 Aug. 1865, in Underhill, 'Extracts'.

181   Underhill to Henderson, 29 Sept. 1865, in Underhill, 'Extracts'; PP 1866 (3595) LI, Part I, Eyre to Cardwell, 23 Oct. 1865, no. 253.

182   PP 1866 (3595) LI, Underhill to Cardwell, 9 Oct. 1865, no. 237, enclosure 4.

183   Ibid., Eyre to Cardwell, 20 Oct. 1865, no. 251.

184   Ibid., Eyre to Cardwell, 23 Oct. 1865, no. 253. p. 197.

185   Ibid., Eyre to Cardwell, 28 Oct. 1865, no. 257.

186   Ibid., Eyre to Cardwell, 8 Nov. 1865, no. 284, p. 313.

187   PP, 1866 (3682) XXX, pp. 3, 16, 311.

188   Ibid., pp. 1, 2, 3.

189   Ibid., p. 55.

190   Ibid., p. 64.

191   Ibid., p. 152.

192   Ibid., pp. 60, 3, 5.

193   Ibid., p. 113.

194   Ibid., p. 143.

195   Ibid., p. 158.

196   Ibid., p. 42.

197   Ibid., p. 115.

198   Ibid., p. 118.

199   Ibid., p. 157.

200   Ibid., p. 76.

201   Ibid., pp. 91, 93.

202 Ibid., p. 94.
203 Ibid., p. 60.
204 Ibid., pp. 7, 11–12, 47.
205 Ibid., p. 66.
206 Ibid., p. 193.
207 Ibid., pp. 51–2.
208 Ibid., p. 11.
209 Ibid., p. 16.
210 Ibid., pp. 478–80.
211 Ibid., p. 93.
212 Ibid., pp. 136–7.
213 Ibid., p. 34.
214 Underhill to East, 14 Apr. 1866, in 'Correspondence of East and Underhill'.
215 Underhill to East, 31 Mar. 1865, in 'Correspondence of East and Underhill'.
216 Underhill to Oughton, 16 Nov. 1865, in Underhill, 'Extracts'.
217 Underhill to Phillippo, 26 Jan. 1866, in Underhill, 'Extracts', p. 52; Underhill to East, 15 Apr. 1854, in 'Correspondence of East and Underhill'.
218 PP 1866 (3682) XXX, p. 472.
219 Underhill to Henderson, 15 Feb. 1866, p. 52; Underhill to Phillippo, 16 Feb. 1866, p. 60; Underhill to Dendy, 14 Feb. 1866, p. 58, in Underhill, 'Extracts'.
220 Oughton had given a lecture in Kingston before his departure which was published and caused great offence. He regarded the colony as 'prostrate and almost ruined', abounding in 'impiety, disorder and licentiousness'. Samuel Oughton, *Jamaica: Why it is Poor, and How it may Become Rich* (M. DeCordova, McDougall and Co., Kingston, 1866), pp. 9–20. Clarke, *Memorials*, p. 174.
221 JRC, *Report*, part II, pp. 783–4. These were not new sentiments for East. In 1863 he had written a pamphlet on *The Constitution and Government of a Church of Christ as Developed in the New Testament* (J. Heaton and Son, London, 1863), which was adopted as the circular letter of the JBU for that year. It made a clear distinction between spiritual equality and social order.
222 PP 1866 (3595) LI, part II, no. 3, Storks to Cardwell, 16 Jan. 1866, enclosure 1, p. 876.
223 Underhill to East, 16 Jan. 1866, Underhill, 'Extracts'; Underhill to East, 14 Apr. 1866, 'Correspondence of East and Underhill'.
224 JBU, 'Memorial to the Secretary of State, 1866', NLJ MS 15, pp. 4–6, appendices A–E.
225 JRC, *Report*, part I, pp. 7–8.
226 JRC, *Report*, part II, p. 885.
227 Ibid., p. 607.
228 PP 1866 (3595) LI, part II, no. 332, Eyre to Cardwell, 20 Dec. 1865, enclosure 1, pp. 425–6.
229 Ibid., no. 6, Storks to Cardwell, 20 Jan. 1866, enclosure 1.

230   Underhill, *Life of . . . Phillippo*, p. 340.

231   Underhill, *Tragedy of Morant Bay*, p. 175.

232   Marx to Engels, 27 July 1866, in Karl Marx and Frederick Engels, 'Letters on Britain', in *On Britain*, 2nd edn (Foreign Languages Publishing House, Moscow 1962), p. 541.

233   Catherine Hall, 'The Nation Within and Without', in Hall et al., *Defining the Victorian Nation*, pp. 179–233. For a fascinating account of one colonial official's struggles with these inequalities over different colonial sites see Bridget Brereton, *Law, Justice and Empire: The Colonial Career of John Gorrie 1829–1892* (University of West Indies Press, Kingston, 1997).

Mapping the 'Midland Metropolis'

1   The phrase was Carlyle's, quoted in *Showell's Dictionary of Birmingham* (Walter Showell, Birmingham, 1885), p. 31.

2   'Labour and the Poor – Birmingham', letter 1: Parochial and Moral Statistics, *Morning Chronicle*, 7 Oct. 1850.

3   *Birmingham Journal (BJ)*, 4 Apr. 1857.

4   J. G. Kohl, *Ireland, Scotland and England* (Chapman and Hall, London, 1844), pp. 8–9.

5   *BJ*, 17 June 1865. On the gender implications of this new public sphere see Davidoff and Hall, *Family Fortunes*, ch. 10.

6   William Hawkes Smith, *Birmingham and its Vicinity as a Manufacturing and Commercial District* (J. Drake, Birmingham, 1836), p. 2.

7   Pat Hudson, *The Industrial Revolution* (Edward Arnold, London, 1992), esp. pp. 121–6; Davidoff and Hall, *Family Fortunes*; Conrad Gill, *History of Birmingham*, vol. 1: *Manor and Borough to 1865* (Oxford University Press, Oxford, 1952); Victoria County History, *History of Warwick*, vol. 7: *The City of Birmingham*, ed. R. B. Pugh (Oxford University Press, Oxford, 1964).

8   Asa Briggs, *Victorian Cities* (Odhams, London, 1963); Clive Behagg, 'Masters and Manufacturers: Social Values and the Smaller Unit of Production in Birmingham, 1800–1850', in G. Crossick and H. G. Haupt (eds), *Shopkeepers and Master Artisans in Nineteenth Century Europe* (Routledge, London, 1995), pp. 137–54; idem, *Politics and Production in the Early Nineteenth Century* (Routledge, London, 1990).

9   Carlos Flick, *The Birmingham Political Union and the Movement for Reform in Britain* (Archon Books, Greenwood, Westport, Conn., 1978).

10   J. T. Bunce, *History of the Corporation of Birmingham* (Cornish Bros, Birmingham, 1878), vol. 1.

11   James Drake, *The Picture of Birmingham* (J. Drake, Birmingham, 1825); William Smith, *A New and Compendious History of the County of Warwick from the Earliest Period to the Present Time* (W. Emans, Birmingham, 1830); John Alfred Langford, *Modern Birmingham and its Insti-*

tutions: A Chronicle of Local Events, from 1841–1871, 2 vols (Osborne, Birmingham, 1873).

12 *Morning Chronicle*, 7 Oct. 1850.

13 Adam Smith, *The Wealth of Nations*, 2 vols, 1st edn 1776 (Dent, London, 1964), vol. 1, pp. 362–3.

14 On the 'barbaric' nature of the Irish in Manchester see James Phillips Kay, *The Moral and Physical Condition of the Working Classes Employed in the Cotton Manufacturies in Manchester*, 1st edn. 1832 (Cass, London, 1970).

15 E. Edwards, 'The Electro Plate Trade and Charles Askin', BRL MS 294924, pp. 32–3.

16 Samuel Timmins (ed.), *The Resources, Products and Industrial History of Birmingham and the Midland Hardware District* (Robert Hardwicke, London, 1866), preface, p. 222.

17 J. E. Tildesley, 'Locks and Lockmaking', in Timmins (ed.), *Resources*, p. 90.

18 John Jones, 'South Staffordshire Manufactures: Chains, Cables and Anchors', in Timmins (ed.), *Resources*, pp. 99–102.

19 William Kenrick, 'Cast-iron Hollow-ware, Tinned and Enamelled, and Cast-Ironmongery', in Timmins (ed.), *Resources*, p. 108.

20 J. S. Wright, 'The Jewellery and Gilt-Toy Trades'; E. Peyton, 'Manufacture of Iron and Brass Bedsteads'; R. F. Martineau, 'Cut Nails'; F. E. Martineau, 'Patent Wrought Iron Hinges'; in Timmins (ed.), *Resources*, pp. 452–62, 624–7, 613–16, 610–12.

21 Thomas Middlemore, 'The Birmingham Saddlery Trade', in Timmins (ed.), *Resources*, pp. 463–76, 472.

22 On more classic imperial cities see Felix Driver and David Gilbert (eds), *Imperial Cities. Landscape, Display and Identity* (Manchester University Press, Manchester, 1999), esp. John MacKenzie on Glasgow; Jonathan Schneer, *London 1900. The Imperial Metropolis* (Yale University Press, New Haven, 1999).

23 The importance of the gun trade affected attitudes to the slave trade. Peter Fryer notes that Birmingham gun-makers, including a well-known Quaker, complained about the abolition of the slave trade and the effects it had on their profits: Peter Fryer, *Staying Power. The History of Black People in Britain* (Pluto Press, London, 1984), p. 418. Birmingham manufacturers did not have the immediate sense of themselves as belonging to an imperial city in the way that Liverpool merchants, for example, did. See Joshua Civin, 'Slaves, Sati and Sugar: Constructing Imperial Identity through Liverpool Petition Struggles', unpub. paper presented to the Neale Colloquium on 'National Identities and Parliaments 1660–1860', University College London, 2001.

24 On the black and South Asian population in Britain in the nineteenth century see Fryer, *Staying Power*; Rozina Visram, *Ayahs, Lascars and Princes. Indians in Britain, 1700–1947* (Pluto Press, London, 1986); Folarin Shyllon, *Black People in Britain 1555–1833* (Oxford University Press, Oxford, 1977). Shyllon argues that the eighteenth-century black

population was never more than 10,000, and that the number fell in the nineteenth century as black domestics were displaced and some black people were assimilated through intermarriage: pp. 102, 159–61.

25 Fryer, *Staying Power*, pp. 110, 215, 262.

26 e.g. *BJ*, 22 Nov. 1845, 3 Jan. 1846.

27 The phrase is R. F. Foster's in *Paddy and Mr Punch: Connections in Irish and English History* (Penguin, Harmondsworth, 1993), p. 86.

28 *Morning Chronicle*, 7 Oct. 1850.

29 PP 1836 (40) XXXIV, p. 1.

30 Kaja Ziesler, 'The Irish in Birmingham 1830–1970', University of Birmingham Ph.D., 1989, p. 44.

31 Carl Chinn, ' "Sturdy Catholic Emigrants": The Irish in Early Victorian Birmingham', in R. Swift and S. Gilley (eds), *The Irish in Victorian Britain. The Local Dimension* (Four Courts, Dublin, 1999), pp. 52–74.

32 *Showell's Dictionary of Birmingham*, p. 22.

33 William Robertson, *Life and Times of the Right Honourable John Bright* (Cassell, London, 1883), p. 345.

34 See, e.g., Brantlinger, *Rule of Darkness*; Said, *Culture and Imperialism*; Cora Kaplan, ' "A heterogeneous thing": Female Childhood and the Rise of Racial Thinking in Victorian Britain', in Diana Fuss (ed.), *Human, All Too Human* (Routledge, New York, 1996), pp. 169–202.

35 John MacKenzie, *Propaganda and Empire* (Manchester University Press, Manchester, 1984).

36 Annie E. Coombes, *Reinventing Africa. Museums, Material Culture and Popular Imagination* (Yale University Press, London, 1994), and McClintock, *Imperial Leather*.

37 Cited in Lynn Hunt (ed.), *The New Cultural History* (University of California Press, Berkeley, 1989), p. 161.

38 Bolt, *Anti-Slavery Movement and Reconstruction*; idem, *Victorian Attitudes to Race*.

39 Wilson, *Sense of the People*, pp. 37–8.

40 H. E. G. Whates, *The Birmingham Post 1857–1957* (Birmingham Post and Mail, Birmingham, 1957), p. 13.

41 Asa Briggs, *Press and Public in Early Nineteenth Century Birmingham*, Dugdale Society Occasional Papers no. 8 (Dugdale Society, Oxford, 1949).

42 *BJ*, 1 Nov. 1845–13 June 1846.

43 *BJ*, 6 Jan. 3 Mar. 1866.

44 *BJ*, 28 Feb. 1846.

45 *BJ*, 16 Jan. 1847.

46 *BJ*, 14 Mar. 1846.

47 *BJ*, 2 Feb. 1846.

48 Langford, *Modern Birmingham*, vol. 1, p. 57; Fryer, *Staying Power*, p. 433.

49 George Dawson Collection, vol. 11: Lectures 1845–50, BRL 260167.

50 Langford, *Modern Birmingham*, vol. 1, p. 265.

51 Charles Dickens, *A Christmas Carol*, 1st edn 1843 (Oxford University Press, Oxford, 1988); idem, *Bleak House*, 1st edn 1853 (Penguin, Harmondsworth, 1979).

52 Langford, *Modern Birmingham*, vol. 1, pp. 293–304.
53 George Dawson Collection, vol. 12: Lectures 1851–76; Caroline Bray, *The British Empire: A Sketch of the Geography, Natural and Political Features of the United Kingdom, its Colonies and Dependencies* (Longman, Green, Roberts, Longman and Green, London, 1863).
54 Curtin, *Image of Africa*, vol. 2, p. 337.
55 Stocking Jr., *Victorian Anthropology*, p. 53.
56 *BJ*, 22 Oct. 1856.
57 Stocking Jr., *Victorian Anthropology*, pp. 49–65. The quotation from Knox is on p. 65.
58 *BJ*, 5 Nov. 1856.
59 *BJ*, 12 Nov. 1856.
60 John Alfred Langford, *A Century of Birmingham Life: or A Chronicle of Local Events from 1741–1841*, 2 vols (Osborne, Birmingham, 1868), vol. 2, p. 599; on the meeting in 1865 see ch. 8; *idem, Modern Birmingham*, vol. 1, p. 442.
61 Langford, *Modern Birmingham*, vol. 2, p. 245.
62 *BJ*, 17 Apr. 1847.
63 *The Times*, 19 May 1847, cited in Richard D. Altick, *The Shows of London* (The Belknap Press of Harvard University Press, Cambridge, Mass., 1978), p. 280.
64 Altick, *Shows of London*, p. 280.
65 *BJ*, 16 Jan. 1847.
66 Altick, *Shows of London*, p. 1; there are many other stories which could be told about the exhibiting of peoples in Birmingham. See, e.g., David Sampson, 'Strangers in a Strange Land: The 1868 Aborigines and other Indigenous Performers in Mid–Victorian Britain', Ph.D., University of Technology, Sydney, 2001.
67 *BJ*, 13 June 1846, 9 Dec. 1848.
68 *BJ*, 29 Oct. 1856.
69 *BJ*, 7 May 1853.
70 Shyllon, *Black People*, pp. 204–10; Fryer, *Staying Power*, pp. 252–6.
71 *BJ*, 22 Nov. 1845.
72 LNFS, *Twenty-eighth Report 1853* (Hudson, Birmingham, 1853), pp. 18–21.
73 *BJ*, 7 May 1853.
74 *BJ*, 28 Mar. 1863.
75 Langford, *Modern Birmingham*, vol. 1, p. 69.
76 Ibid., pp. 10, 85, 90.
77 *BJ*, 16 Dec. 1848.
78 On gardens see Rebecca Preston, ' "The scenery of the torrid zone": Imagined Travels and the Culture of the Exotic in Nineteenth Century British Gardens', in Driver and Gilbert (eds), *Imperial Cities*, pp. 191–214. On psychic lives – a much under-researched area – see Leonore Davidoff, 'Class and Gender in Victorian England', in Judith L. Newton, Mary P. Ryan and Judith R. Walkowitz (eds), *Sex and Class in Women's History* (Routledge and Kegan Paul, London, 1983), pp. 16–71, and McClintock, *Imperial Leather*.

79 Mintz, *Sweetness and Power*, p. 6.
80 This paragraph is heavily dependent on Clare Midgley, 'Slave Sugar Boycotts, Female Activism and the Domestic Base of British Anti-Slavery Culture', *Slavery and Abolition*, 17/3 (Dec. 1996), pp. 137–62; see also Lynne Walker and Vron Ware, 'Political Pincushions: Decorating the Abolitionist Interior', in Inga Bryden and Janet Floyd (eds), *Domestic Space. Reading the Nineteenth-Century Interior* (Manchester University Press, Manchester, 1999), pp. 58–93.
81 Nupur Chaudhuri, 'Shawls, Jewellery, Curry, and Rice in Victorian Britain', in Chaudhuri and Strobel (eds), *Western Women and Imperialism*, pp. 231–46.
82 Mrs Gaskell, *North and South*, 1st edn 1854–5 (Penguin, Harmondsworth, 1970), p. 39.
83 Chaudhuri, 'Shawls, Jewellery, Curry, and Rice', pp. 238, 241.
84 Jessie K. Buckley, *Joseph Parkes of Birmingham and the Part which he Played in Radical Reform Movements from 1825–1845* (Methuen, London, 1926), esp. ch. 1.
85 On Edgbaston see Davidoff and Hall, *Family Fortunes*, esp. ch. 8.
86 Buckley, *Joseph Parkes*, esp. chs 1, 2.
87 Swainson, 'Letters'.
88 Wakefield, *A Letter from Sydney*, p. 89.
89 Orange, *Treaty of Waitangi*, ch. 2.
90 e.g. *BJ*, 26 Oct. 1849.
91 Swainson, 'Letters', 4 Sept. 1847.
92 Mary to Isabel, 21 May 1843, in Marshall, 'Letters'.
93 Swainson, 'Letters', 3 Aug. 1845.
94 Ibid., 23 Aug. 1846.
95 Ibid., 19 Sept., 14 Dec. 1845; 14 Mar., 7 May 1846.
96 Ibid., 23 Mar. 1847, 24 Oct. 1848.
97 Ibid., 23 Feb. 1849; Marshall, 'Letters', Mary to Isabel, 11 Mar. 1849.
98 Mary to Isabel, 3 Sept. 1853, 24 May 1854, in Marshall, 'Letters'.
99 Swainson, 'Letters', 3 Aug., 3 Sept. 1845; 1 Nov. 1846, 18 May 1847, 29 Feb., 1 Mar., 3 Apr. 1848; 5 Sept. 1850.
100 Ibid., 11 Jan. 1846, 17 Jan. 1847, 23 Aug. 1846, 4 Sept. 1847, 25 Apr. 1848.
101 Ibid., 23 Mar. 1847, 25 Apr. 1848.
102 Ibid., 19 Sept. 1845.
103 *Showell's Dictionary*, p. 71; Langford, *A Century*, vol. 2, p. 395.
104 Rev. George Dawson, *Daily Gazette*, 5 May 1853.

Chapter 5   'The Friends of the Negro': Baptists and Abolitionists 1825–1842

1 Arthur S. Langley, *Birmingham Baptists Past and Present* (Kingsgate Press, London, 1939), p. 237; R. B. Rose, 'Protestant Nonconformity', in Victoria County History, *A History of the County of Warwick*, vol. 7: *The City of Birmingham*, ed. W. B. Stephens, p. 416. The Baptists were divided between General, Particular, and New Connexion: the dividing lines were

to do with attitudes to predestination and free will. The revised Baptist Union Constitution of 1832 opened the way for closer association between the groups. See J. H. Y. Briggs, *The English Baptists of the Nineteenth Century* (Baptist Historical Society, Didcot, 1994).

2   Birmingham File (biogaphical material has been collected since 1978 constituting a Birmingham File).

3   Binfield, *So Down to Prayers*, p. 11–12.

4   A. F. Morgan, *Kith and Kin*, privately printed (Charles Cooper and Co. Ltd, Birmingham, 1896).

5   Cox, *History of the BMS*; Morgan, *Kith and Kin*, part 1.

6   Bernard Barton in Cox, *History of the BMS*, pp. vi–vii.

7   Binfield, *So Down to Prayers*, p. 24.

8   Quoted in J. H. Y. Briggs, *English Baptists*, p. 16.

9   For two major studies of the civilising projects of missionaries at home and abroad see Thorne, *Congregational Missions*; and Alison Twells, 'The Heathen at Home and Overseas: The Middle Class and the Civilizing Mission, Sheffield 1790–1843', University of York D.Phil., 1997.

10 Jürgen Habermas, *The Structural Transformation of the Public Sphere*, quoted in Geoff Eley, 'Nations, Publics and Political Cultures: Placing Habermas in the Nineteenth Century', in Craig Calhoun (ed.), *Habermas and the Public Sphere* (MIT Press, Cambridge, Mass., 1992), pp. 289–339.

11 Eley, 'Nations, Publics and Political Cultures', p. 293.

12 Ibid.; Davidoff and Hall, *Family Fortunes*, esp. ch. 10; Davidoff, 'Regarding Some "Old Husbands' Tales"'; Nancy Fraser, 'Rethinking the Public Sphere: A Contribution to the Critique of Actually Existing Democracy', in Calhoun (ed.), *Habermas and the Public Sphere*, pp. 109–42; Joan Landes, *Women and the Public Sphere in the Age of the French Revolution* (Cornell University Press, Ithaca, NY, 1988).

13 Denise Riley, *'Am I that Name? Feminism and the Category of Women in History* (Macmillan, Basingstoke, 1989).

14 Jane Rendall, 'Women and the Public Sphere', *Gender and History*, 11/3 (Nov. 1999), pp. 475–88; C. Hall et al., *Defining the Victorian Nation*.

15 E. A. Payne argues that the original form of the motto was 'Expect great things. Attempt great things': quoted in Stanley, *History of the BMS*, p. 14.

16 William Finnemore, *The Story of a Hundred Years 1823–1923. Being the Centenary Booklet of the Birmingham Auxiliary of the Baptist Missionary Society* (Oxford University Press, Oxford, 1923), pp. 9, 15.

17 *Birmingham Daily Post (BDP)*, 23 Sept. 1893.

18 R. Q. Gray, *North and South Revisited: Locality, Nation and Identity in Victorian Britain*, Portsmouth Lecture Series (University of Portsmouth, Portsmouth, 2000).

19 Finnemore, *Story of a Hundred Years*, p. 20.

20 Langley, *Birmingham Baptists*, pp. 32–6.

21 Morgan, *Kith and Kin*, part 1.

22 Ibid., p. 9.

23 Ibid.

24 Ibid., p. 8.

25 Thomas Morgan, *A Plain Statement of the Faith and Practice of the Baptist Church Meeting in Bond Street, Birmingham* (J. Allen, Birmingham, c.1830).

26 Kenneth Brown, in his study of the nonconformist ministry, demonstrates that at least a quarter of those who began work as Congregational or Baptist ministers between 1810 and 1849 had some degree of active political life. Ministers who had personal charisma were able to exercise considerable influence. But he also cautions against forgetting the quiescent majority: Brown, *Social History*, p. 209.

27 John Angell James, 'The Attraction of the Cross', in T. S. James (ed.), *The Collected Works of John Angell James*, vol. 1 (Hamilton, Adams and Co., London, 1860), pp. 88–9.

28 Ibid., p. 82.

29 Henry Richard, *Memoirs of Joseph Sturge* (S. W. Partridge, London, 1864), p. 577.

30 Cited by Mr Woodhill in his jubilee address, 24 Sept. 1873: Birmingham Auxiliary of the BMS, 'Handbills, Newspaper Cuttings etc. 1823–80', BRL 212491.

31 R. J. Morris, 'Voluntary Societies and British Urban Elites 1780–1850: An Analysis', *Historical Journal*, 26/1 (1983), pp. 95–118; see Davidoff and Hall, *Family Fortunes*, ch. 10, on the gendered aspects of voluntary societies.

32 *MH*, July 1828.

33 Resolutions of the founding meeting: Birmingham Auxiliary of the BMS, 'Handbills'.

34 Thorne, *Congregational Missions*, p. 72. On the basis of her sampling of Congregational records across the country, Thorne argues that foreign missions were the most important of the associational activities in which middle-class evangelicals were engaged (p. 55).

35 Stanley, *History of the Baptist Missionary Society*, p. 208.

36 *MH*, July 1825, Aug. 1825.

37 Clare Midgley, 'From Supporting Missions to Petitioning Parliament: British Women and the Evangelical Campaign against *Sati* in India 1813–1830', in Kathlyn Gleadle and Sarah Richardson (eds), *Women in British Politics 1760–1860. The Power of the Petticoat* (Macmillan, Basingstoke, 2000), pp. 74–92. F. K. Prochaska, *Women and Philanthropy in Nineteenth-Century England* (Oxford University Press, Oxford, 1980), *passim*.

38 *MH*, June 1825.

39 *MH*, Oct. 1826.

40 *MH*, Nov. 1826.

41 e.g. *MH*, Mar. 1826, Apr. 1839, Oct. 1847.

42 *MH*, Apr. 1832.

43 *BM*, May 1826.

44 On the 'amalgam of enlightenment rationalism and evangelical eschatology' see Boyd Hilton, *The Influence of Evangelicalism on Social and Economic Thought, 1795–1865* (Clarendon Press, Oxford, 1988).

45 On the religious community and its advantages see Davidoff and Hall, *Family Fortunes*, ch. 1.

46 Heber was bishop of Calcutta 1822–6. Edward Said remembers singing this hymn at his colonial prep school in Cairo. Edward W. Said, *Out of Place* (Granta, London, 1999), p. 38. Thanks to Bill Schwarz for this reference.

47 On John Angell James see Davidoff and Hall, *Family Fortunes*, esp. chs 1 and 2.

48 James, 'Attraction of the Cross', pp. 112–17.

49 John Angell James, 'The Advantages and Obligations of Youth in Reference to the Cause of Christian Missions Stated and Enforced', in T. S. James (ed.) *Collected Works*, vol. 2, p. 143.

50 Ibid., p. 163.

51 Comaroff and Comaroff also found a heavy reliance on this language: *Of Revelation and Revolution*, p. 80.

52 Potts, *British Baptist Missionaries*, esp. ch. 1.

53 William Yates, 'Memoirs of the Rev. W. H. Pearce', abridged by James Hoby and published in *Memoir of William Yates D.D. of Calcutta* (Houlston and Stoneman, London, 1847).

54 Not all the missionaries were convinced of the benefits of a 'native' ministry. Eustace Carey, e.g., William's son, was dubious as to how much use they could be: *BM*, Dec. 1828; Hoby, *Memoir of William Yates*, p. 432.

55 *MH*, July 1825.

56 Hoby, *Memoir of William Yates*, pp. 80, 115.

57 Ibid., p. 158.

58 Lata Mani, *Contentious Traditions: The Debate on Sati in Colonial India* (University of California Press, Berkeley, 1998).

59 *BM*, Sept. 1828.

60 Thomas Laqueur, 'Bodies, Details and the Humanitarian Narrative', in Hunt (ed.), *New Cultural History*, pp. 176–204.

61 *BM*, Sept. 1828.

62 Hoby, *Memoir of William Yates*, pp. 402–7.

63 Ibid., pp. 451–2.

64 For an exploration of the relation between anti-slavery and imperial feminism see Clare Midgley, 'Anti-Slavery and the Roots of "Imperial Feminism"', in Midgley (ed.), *Gender and Imperialism* (Manchester University Press, Manchester, 1998), pp. 161–79. For an account of the later impact of this kind of thinking on British feminism see Burton, *Burdens of History*.

65 See, e.g., the worries about Yates going out unmarried in Hoby, *Memoir of William Yates*, pp. 35–42.

66 Ibid., p. 78.

67 Ibid., p. 161. On the development of female education in India in the 1830s and 1840s see David W. Savage, 'Missionaries and the Development of a

Colonial Ideology of Female Education in India', *Gender and History*, 9/2 (Aug. 1997), pp. 201–21.

68 *MH*, Apr. 1828.
69 For a condensed version of these associations see Cox, *History of the BMS*, vol. 1.
70 Ibid., vol. 2, p. 24.
71 Ibid., pp. 30, 32, 37.
72 Ibid., pp. 46–7.
73 *MH*, Nov. 1829.
74 *BM*, Apr. 1831.
75 *MH*, Dec. 1831.
76 *MH*, Feb. 1829.
77 *MH*, Feb. 1832.
78 *MH*, July 1830.
79 Ibid.
80 For an interesting account of Montgomery, particularly in his local context, see Twells, 'Heathen at Home and Overseas'.
81 *BM*, Sept. 1830.
82 Cox, *History of the BMS*, vol. 2, p. 18.
83 Birmingham Anti-Slavery Society, 'Minute Book 1826–37', BRL MS 152006.
84 Ibid., committee meetings, 6 Dec. 1826, 4 Apr. 1827, 28 Mar. 1828.
85 Ibid., 'Minute Book', committee meeting 16 Aug. 1831.
86 Ibid., 19 June 1832.
87 Ibid., 27 July 1832.
88 Ibid., 27 July, 4 Aug. 1832.
89 Ibid., 17 Apr. 1833. For the tensions between radicals and abolitionists see Patricia Hollis, 'Anti-Slavery and British Working-Class Radicalism in the Years of Reform', in Christine Bolt and Seymour Drescher (eds), *Anti-Slavery, Religion and Reform: Essays in Memory of Roger Anstey* (Dawson and Sons, Folkestone, 1980), pp. 294–315.
90 Birmingham Anti-Slavery Society, 'Minute Book', 16 June 1833.
91 Richard, *Memoirs of Joseph Sturge*; Tyrrell, *Joseph Sturge*.
92 Tyrrell, *Joseph Sturge*, p. 4.
93 Ibid., p. 29.
94 Richard, *Memoirs of Joseph Sturge*, p. 33.
95 On Edgbaston see Davidoff and Hall, *Family Fortunes*, ch. 8.
96 On the brother/sister tie, ibid., pp. 348–53; and Leonore Davidoff, 'Where the Stranger Begins: The Question of Siblings in Historical Analysis', in *Worlds Between*, pp. 201–26.
97 Tyrrell, *Joseph Sturge*, p. 63.
98 Richard, *Memoirs of Joseph Sturge*, p. 335.
99 Ibid., p. 367.
100 Harriet Beecher Stowe, *Sunny Memories of Foreign Lands*, 2 vols (Sampson Low Son and Co., London, 1854), vol. 1, p. 253.
101 Sylvia Lloyd Lewin, *Gaunts Earthcott to Frederick Road. An Account of the Sturges of Birmingham* (family MS, privately published, 1980).

102 Birmingham Anti-Slavery Society, 'Minute Book', 6 Dec. 1826.
103 Richard, *Memoirs of Joseph Sturge*, p. 101.
104 Tyrrell, *Joseph Sturge*, p. 51.
105 Richard, *Memoirs of Joseph Sturge*, p. 96.
106 For a much fuller discussion of this society and its context see Midgley, *Women Against Slavery*.
107 Laqueur, 'Bodies, Details'.
108 Prince, *History*.
109 Ladies' Society for the Relief of Negro Slaves, Minute Book 1825–52, BRL MS 302206.
110 *Female Society for Birmingham, West Bromwich, Wednesbury, Walsall and their Respective Neighbourhoods, for the Relief of British Negro Slaves, Second Report* (Hudson, Birmingham, 1827), p. 20.
111 *Female Society for Birmingham, West Bromwich, Wednesbury, Walsall, and their Respective Neighbourhoods, for the Relief of British Negro Slaves, First Report* (Richard Peart, Birmingham, 1826) p. 4.
112 *Female Society for the Relief of Negro Slaves, Third Report* (Hudson, Birmingham, 1828).
113 Midgley, 'Slave Sugar Boycotts'.
114 Ladies' Society for the Relief of Negro Slaves, Minute Book, *passim*.
115 Stanley, *History of the BMS*, p. 19.
116 Tyrrell, *Joseph Sturge*, p. 77; Richard, *Memoirs of Joseph Sturge*, p. 115.
117 Porter, 'Religion, Missionary Enthusiasm and Empire', p. 232.
118 Thorne, *Congregational Missions*, esp. chs 3, 4.
119 Birmingham Anti-Slavery Society, Minute Book, 16 June 1833, 8 June 1835, 23 July 1835.
120 Birmingham Anti-Slavery Society, *Report of the Proceedings of the Great Anti-Slavery Meeting Held at the Town Hall Birmingham 14 October 1835* (Hudson, Birmingham, 1835), pp. 1, 2, 5, 6, 14, 15, 16.
121 Tyrrell, *Joseph Sturge*, p. 76.
122 Richard, *Memoirs of Joseph Sturge*, p. 36.
123 Tyrrell, *Joseph Sturge*, p. 79.
124 Richard, *Memoirs of Joseph Sturge*, p. 151.
125 Tyrrell, *Joseph Sturge*, p. 81.
126 Sturge and Harvey, *West Indies in 1837*, p. viii.
127 Ibid., pp. viii, 162, 167.
128 Ibid., p. 232.
129 Ibid., pp. 229, 231.
130 Ibid., p. 336.
131 Ibid., p. 320.
132 Ibid., pp. 346–9.
133 Richard, *Memoirs of Joseph Sturge*, p. 161.
134 Joseph Sturge to John Clark, 23 Mar. 1837, in Fenn Collection, 'Letters from Joseph Sturge to John Clark', Angus Library.
135 Joseph Sturge to John Clark, 30 May, 15 June 1837, in Fenn Collection.
136 Joseph Sturge to John Clark, 15 Aug., 29 Sept. 1837, in Fenn Collection.
137 Richard, *Memoirs of Joseph Sturge*, p. 343.

138   Sophia Sturge's writing paper is found in the Fenn Collection. She occasionally wrote to John Clark for her brother when he was too busy, as on 31 Mar. 1838.

139   Thomas Clarkson's address to 'The Free Labourers of Brown's Town and Bethany', 29 Dec. 1839, in Fenn Collection.

140   Stuart Hall, 'The Spectacle of the Other', in S. Hall (ed.), *Representation: Cultural Representations and Signifying Practices* (Sage in association with the Open University, London, 1997), pp. 223–90.

141   Quoted in Driver, *Geography Militant*, p. 4; Dickens, *Bleak House*, p. 82.

142   Birmingham Anti-Slavery Society, Minute Book, 15 Dec. 1835, 9 May 1837.

143   Birmingham Anti-Slavery Society, 'Minute Book 1837–59', BRL MS 158748, 28 Dec. 1837.

144   Ibid., 19 Mar., 10, 19 Apr., 11 May 1838.

145   For the counter-attacks and the responses to them see, e.g., Joseph Sturge and Thomas Harvey, *A Reply to Letters to Joseph Sturge Esq. by William Alers Hankey Esq.* (Hamilton, Adams and Co., London, 1838).

146   *Report of the Proceedings at Birmingham on the 1st and 2nd of August in Commemoration of the Abolition of Negro Apprenticeship in the British Colonies* (Tyler, Birmingham, 1838), pp. 15–17, 19.

147   Ibid., pp. 23, 26, 30, 32, 33, 35, 36, 43, 51, 52.

148   Ibid., pp. 57, 61, 63.

149   Ladies' Society, Minute Book, 13 Apr. 1826.

150   A. F. Morgan, *Kith and Kin*, part 3, p. 3; Hugh Cunningham, 'The Language of Patriotism', in Raphael Samuel (ed.), *Patriotism: The Making and Unmaking of British National Identity*, vol. 1: *History and Politics* (Routledge, London, 1989), pp. 57–89.

151   A. F. Morgan, *Kith and Kin*, part 3, p. 3.

152   Birmingham Anti-Slavery Society, 'Minute Book 1837–59', 4 Dec. 1837, 10 Apr., 11 May, 31 July 1838.

153   *Report of the Proceedings at Birmingham*, pp. 19, 59.

154   A. F. Morgan, *Kith and Kin*, part 3, pp. 4, 5.

155   *MH*, May 1839.

156   Birmingham Anti-Slavery Society, 'Minute Book 1837–59'. The title Birmingham British and Foreign Anti-Slavery Society seems to have been used alongside the old title from 1840, when the new national organisation was formed: Birmingham British and Foreign Anti-Slavery Society (BFASS), *Report and Treasurer's Account* (Hudson, Birmingham, 1840).

157   Tyrrell, *Joseph Sturge*, pp. 89, 101. The rest of this paragraph draws heavily on Tyrrell's argument.

158   Quoted ibid., p. 98.

159   Richard, *Memoirs of Joseph Sturge*, p. 325.

160   Quoted in Tyrrell, *Joseph Sturge*, p. 120.

161   Quoted ibid., p. 155.

162   Richard, *Memoirs of Joseph Sturge*, p. 540.

163   Hugh Thomas, *The Slave Trade: The History of the Atlantic Slave Trade 1440–1870* (Picador, London, 1998), p. 789.

164   *ASR*, 15 Jan., 17 June 1840.
165   Birmingham BFASS, *Report*, p. 7.
166   For James's views on gender and separate spheres see Davidoff and Hall, *Family Fortunes*, part 1.
167   *ASR*, 17 June 1840.
168   Tyrrell, *Joseph Sturge*, pp. 108, 124.
169   On indentured labour see Madhavi Kale, ' "When the saints came marching in": The Anti-Slavery Society and Indian Indentured Migration to the British Caribbean', in Daunton and Halpern (eds), *Empire and Others*, pp. 325–44.
170   *MH*, June 1839.
171   The epithet was used by missionary Dendy's congregation to describe themselves: *ASR*, 2 Nov. 1842.
172   *ASR*, 22 Apr. 1840.
173   *ASR*, 20 May 1840.
174   *MH*, July 1840, July 1841.
175   John Clark, quoted in the *MH*, July 1840.
176   *MH*, May 1841.
177   *MH*, Oct. 1840; July, Sept. 1841.
178   *MH*, Nov. 1826.
179   *MH*, June 1841.
180   *ASR*, 12 Aug. 1840.
181   *MH*, June 1842.
182   *MH*, Mar. 1842.
183   *BH*, June 1837.
184   *MH*, July 1839.
185   *MH*, Aug. 1839.
186   *MH*, Sept. 1839.
187   *MH*, July 1842.
188   *MH*, Mar. 1842.
189   Linebaugh and Rediker, *Many-Headed Hydra*, pp. 289–92.
190   *MH*, July 1830.
191   Faith Bowers, *A Bold Experiment. The Story of Bloomsbury Chapel and Bloomsbury Central Baptist Church, 1848–1999* (Bloomsbury Central Baptist Church, London, 1999), p. 39.
192   *MH*, July 1842.
193   *MH*, June 1842.
194   *MH*, July 1842.
195   *ASR*, 30 Nov., 14 Dec. 1842.

Chapter 6   The Limits of Friendship: Abolitionism in Decline 1842–1859

1   Howard Temperley, *White Dreams, Black Africa*. Charles Dickens, Review of 'Narrative of the Expedition . . . to the River Niger in 1841', *Examiner*, 19 Aug. 1841, pp. 531–3.

2   H. G. Grey, *Colonial Policy of Lord John Russell's Administration*, vol. 1, pp. 60, 63.

3   Howard Temperley, *British Antislavery 1833–1870* (Longman, London, 1972), esp. ch. 7; Tyrrell, *Joseph Sturge*, pp. 140–2.

4   *BJ*, 31 May 1845.

5   *MH*, Feb. 1844.

6   *MH*, July 1844.

7   *MH*, 30 Oct. 1844.

8   See, e.g., *ASR*, 28 May 1845.

9   Joshua Tinson, in a letter to Joseph Sturge, *ASR*, 19 Mar. 1845.

10 *ASR*, 28 May 1845.

11 *MH*, June 1845.

12 *MH*, Aug. 1845.

13 *MH*, Jan. 1846.

14 *BM*, Jan. 1846.

15 *MH*, June 1846.

16 *MH*, Dec. 1844.

17 *MH*, Nov. 1845.

18 *MH*, Feb. 1847, Mar. 1848.

19 *MH*, Apr., Sept., Nov. 1849; Mar. 1850, Feb. 1852.

20 *MH*, June 1847.

21 *MH*, June 1847.

22 *MH*, June 1848. Thorne notes that after emancipation there was a shift in the metropole from a focus on European guilt to African guilt in the slave trade: this made the imperial civilising mission critical to Africa's future: *Congregational Mission*, p. 84.

23 Birmingham Auxiliary of the BMS, 'Handbills, etc.': Report of the 24th Anniversary of the BMS Birmingham Auxiliary, 20 July 1847.

24 Brian Stanley, *The Bible and the Flag. Protestant Missions and British Imperialism in the Nineteenth and Twentieth Centuries* (Apollos, Leicester, 1990), p. 79.

25 Birmingham BFASS committee meeting, reported in the *ASR*, 1 Dec. 1847.

26 *ASR*, 1 Mar. 1847.

27 *ASR*, 1 May 1848.

28 *ASR*, 1 June 1847.

29 *ASR*, 1 Oct. 1847.

30 *ASR*, 1 June 1849.

31 Carlyle, 'Occasional Discourse on the Negro Question'.

32 Thomas Carlyle, 'The Hero as Man of Letters', 1st edn 1841, in Thomas Carlyle, *Selected Writings* (Penguin, Harmondsworth, 1971), p. 236.

33 Quoted in Norma Clarke, 'Shock Heroic', *Times Higher Educational Supplement*, 4 May 1990.

34 Poovey, *Uneven Developments*, esp. ch. 4.

35 Sussman, *Victorian Masculinities*, pp. 16–72.

36 Carlyle, 'Occasional Discourse on the Negro Question', p. 672.

37 Thomas Carlyle, *Past and Present*, 1st edn 1843 (Dent, London, 1960), p. 189.
38 Sussman, *Victorian Masculinities*, p. 24.
39 Geraldine Jewsbury quoting Carlyle; cited in Norma Clarke, *Ambitious Heights. Writing, Friendship, Love. The Jewsbury Sisters, Felicia Hemans and Jane Carlyle* (Routledge, London, 1990), p. 99.
40 Lucretia Mott, *Lucretia Mott's Diary of her Visit to Great Britain to Attend the World's Anti-Slavery Convention of 1840*, ed. F. B. Tolles (Friends' Historical Society, London, 1952), p. 54.
41 Carlyle, 'Occasional Discourse on the Negro Question', p. 670.
42 Ibid., p. 677.
43 Ibid., p. 671.
44 Ibid.
45 Ibid., pp. 674–5; 1853 edn, p. 327.
46 Ibid., p. 673.
47 Ibid., p. 675.
48 Holt, *Problem of Freedom*, p. 284.
49 The emphasis on the feminisation of black men is sharper in the 1853 than in the 1849 edition of the essay: Carlyle, 'Occasional Discourse', 1853 edn, p. 311.
50 Carlyle, 'Occasional Discourse on the Negro Question', pp. 672–3.
51 John Stuart Mill, 'The Negro Question', *Fraser's Magazine*, 41 (Jan. 1850), p. 25.
52 Ibid., pp. 29, 31.
53 John Stuart Mill, *The Subjection of Women*, 1st edn 1869 (Virago, London, 1983).
54 *ASR*, 1 Jan. 1850.
55 *ASR*, 1 Aug. 1851.
56 D. Hall, *Free Jamaica*, ch. 3.
57 *ASR*, 1 Apr. 1851.
58 *ASR*, 2 June 1851.
59 King, *State and Prospects of Jamaica*; *BM*, Dec. 1850.
60 Henderson to Underhill, 4 Mar. 1851, in Letters and Reports to the BMS about Falmouth.
61 *ASR*, 1 Mar. 1852.
62 e.g., John Bigelow, *Jamaica in 1850: or, The Effects of 16 Years of Freedom on a Slave Colony* (Geo. Putnam, New York and London, 1851).
63 Cited in Lorimer, *Colour, Class and the Victorians*, p. 83.
64 Stowe, *Sunny Memories*, vol. 1, p. 253.
65 Ibid., p. 255; *BJ*, 7 May 1853; *ASR*, 1 June 1853.
66 'The State of Jamaica', *ASR*, 1 Sept. 1853.
67 *ASR*, 1 Nov. 1854.
68 Quoted in *ASR*, 2 Apr. 1855.
69 *ASR*, 1 Sept. 1855.
70 W. A. Green, *British Slave Emancipation*, pp. 176–7.
71 *ASR*, 1 May 1857.
72 *ASR*, 1 July 1857.

73   *The Times*, 21 Nov. 1857.
74   Ibid., 19 Dec. 1857.
75   Ibid., 29 Dec. 1857.
76   *ASR*, 1 Jan. 1858; *Morning Star*, 25 Dec. 1857.
77   *ASR*, 1 Feb. 1858.
78   Ann Whitehead, 'Continuities and Discontinuities in Political Construc-tions of the Working Man in Rural Sub-Saharan Africa', *European Journal of Development Research*, 12/2 (2000), pp. 23–52.
79   *ASR*, 1 Nov. 1858.
80   Cited in *ASR*, 1 Nov. 1858.
81   *ASR*, 1 Dec. 1858.
82   *BM*, Feb. 1858.
83   Ibid.
84   *BM*, Aug. 1859.
85   *ASR*, 1 Apr. 1859.
86   *ASR*, 2 May 1859.
87   *ASR*, 1 July, 1 Aug. 1859.
88   *ASR*, 1 Nov., 1 Dec. 1859.
89   Wright Wilson, *The Life of George Dawson* (Percival Jones, Birmingham, 1905), p. 12.
90   'George Dawson', *Christian Reformer*, new ser. 35 (Nov. 1847), p. 644.
91   Wilson, *Life of George Dawson*, pp. 15–16, 30, 57–60.
92   G. J. Holyoake, *Bygones Worth Remembering*, 2 vols (T. Fisher Unwin, London, 1905), vol. 1, p. 284; Wilson, *Life of George Dawson*, pp. 60, 170.
93   George Dawson Collection, vol. 17: Newspaper Cuttings 1845–48, *Manchester Guardian*, 31 Jan. 1846.
94   Wilson, *Life of George Dawson*, p. 212; George Dawson Collection, vol. 17: George Gilfillan, 'George Dawson', *Taits Magazine*, May 1848; Kingsley, quoted in R. W. Dale, 'George Dawson: Politician, Lecturer and Preacher', *Nineteenth Century*, 6 (1877), p. 44.
95   George Dawson Collection, vol. 11: Lectures 1845–50, 'On the Present State of Europe', lecture, p. 507.
96   Birmingham File, see p. 486, n. 2.
97   Wilson, *Life of George Dawson*, p. 22.
98   Stocking Jr remarks on the importance of the revolutions of 1848 in encouraging racial thinking: *Victorian Anthropology*, p. 66.
99   Patrick Brantlinger, ' "Dying Races": Rationalising Genocide in the Nineteenth Century', in Jan Nederveen Pieterse and Bhikhu Parekh (eds), *The Decolonization of Imagination* (Zed, London, 1995), pp. 43–56.
100 George Dawson Collection, vol. 11, 'On the Present State of Europe', lecture 1, p. 494; lecture 3, p. 510.
101 Margot Finn, *After Chartism. Class and Nation in English Radical Politics, 1848–74* (Cambridge University Press, Cambridge, 1993), pp. 74–80. Finn may somewhat overstate the case. There was a strong current of interest in Hungary, Poland and Italy amongst working-class radicals.

102 *BJ*, 15 Apr. 1848, cited in Finn, *After Chartism*, p. 80.

103 George Dawson Collection, vol. 11, 'On the Present State of Europe', lecture 1, p. 494.

104 *BJ*, 8 Nov. 1851.

105 Langford, *Modern Birmingham*, vol 1, pp. 401–4.

106 Ibid., vol. 1, p. 107; Istvan Deak, *The Lawful Revolution: Louis Kossuth and the Hungarians 1848–9* (Columbia University Press, New York, 1979), p. 345.

107 Wilson, *Life of George Dawson*, p. 113.

108 George Dawson, *The Demands of the Age upon the Church. Discourse at the Opening of the Church of the Saviour, Edward St, 8 August 1847* (E. C. Osborne, Birmingham, 1847), pp. 9–10.

109 George Dawson Collection, vol. 11, pp. 520–5.

110 Finn, *After Chartism*, esp. ch. 3.

111 John Pemble, *Mediterranean Passions. Victorians and Edwardians in the South* (Oxford University Press, Oxford, 1987), p. 10; Maura O'Connor, *The Romance of Italy and the English Political Imagination* (St Martin's Press, New York, 1998), p. 243.

112 George Dawson Collection, vol. 18: Newspaper Cuttings 1845, p. 9; vols 11–19.

113 Reginald Horsman, *Race and Manifest Destiny. The Origins of American Racial Anglo-Saxonism* (Harvard University Press, Cambridge, Mass., 1981), p. 4.

114 Birmingham File.

115 Olive Anderson, 'The Political Uses of History in Mid-Nineteenth Century England', *Past and Present*, 36 (Apr. 1967), pp. 87–105; *idem, A Liberal State at War. English Politics and Economics during the Crimean War* (Macmillan, London, 1967), ch. 4.

116 Anderson, *Liberal State at War*, p. 140.

117 Horsman, *Race and Manifest Destiny*, p. 63.

118 Carlyle, *Chartism*, p. 205.

119 Stocking Jr, *Victorian Anthropology*, p. 62.

120 George Dawson Collection, vol. 19: Newspaper Cuttings 1849–95, *Birmingham Mercury*, 15 July 1851.

121 Horsman, *Race and Manifest Destiny*; George Dawson Collection, vol. 11: 'On the Origins, Character and Doings of the Anglo-Saxons', p. 510; vol. 17, 7 May 1846; vol. 19, 15 July 1851, 10 May 1852, p. 109.

122 George Dawson Collection, vol. 19, *BJ*, 10 May 1852.

123 George Dawson Collection, vol. 19, p. 109.

124 Phillippo, *Jamaica*, p. 154; George Dawson Collection, vol. 19, p. 115.

125 George Dawson Collection, vol. 18, 29 Sept. 1873; vol. 11, 5 Oct. 1861; vol. 15: 'Speeches', 4 June 1862.

126 For Margaret Fuller's reaction to his vigorous defence of 'mere force' when she met him in 1848, see J. A. Froude, *Thomas Carlyle. A History of his Life in London 1834–81*, 2 vols (Longmans Green and Co., London, 1884), vol. 1, p. 402.

127   Peter Mandler argues that mid-Victorian intellectuals had little interest in biological racism or organic nationalism, unlike their European counterparts, and relied on the cosmopolitan science of political economy and the civilisational perspective. He does recognise the preoccupation with organic nationalism of Carlyle, Kingsley and Froude: Peter Mandler, ' "Race" and "Nation" in Mid-Victorian Thought', in S. Collini, R. Whatmore and B. Young (eds), *History, Religion, Culture. British Intellectual History 1750–1950* (Cambridge University Press, Cambridge, 2000), pp. 224–44. My argument is that the civilisational perspective amongst the men and women whom I have studied was always inflected with racial thought. See also George Dawson Collection, vol. 18, *Birmingham Morning News*, 28 July 1874.

128   George Dawson Collection, vol. 17, 'The Character and Tendencies of the Present Age', *Manchester Guardian*, 5 May 1846; vol. 11, *BDP*, 7 Feb. 1865.

129   *BDP*, 1 Dec. 1876.

130   *MH*, May 1850.

131   *MH*, June 1851.

132   *MH*, Sept., Dec. 1851.

133   *MH*, Apr. 1852.

134   *MH*, Sept. 1852.

135   *MH*, June 1852.

136   Birmingham Conference, *Report of the Proceedings of a Conference on the Subject of Preventive and Reformatory Schools, Held at Birmingham 1851*, p. 84. I owe this quote to Brenda Ann Quinn, 'India in the Making of Liberal Identities: The Case of Mary Carpenter and Harriet Martineau', University of Essex Ph.D., 2000, esp. pp. 225–37.

137   Tyrrell, *Joseph Sturge*, pp. 185–7.

138   A. F. Morgan, *Kith and Kin*, part 2, p. 7.

139   Ibid., part 3, p. 5.

140   William Morgan, *The Arabs of the City; or A Plea for Brotherhood with the Outcast: Being an Address Delivered to the Young Men's Christian Association, Birmingham 29 November 1853* (Hudson, Birmingham, 1853), pp. 6, 15–16.

141   *MH*, Mar. 1854.

142   *MH*, June 1856.

143   *MH*, July 1856.

144   Stanley, *Bible and the Flag*, p. 79.

145   *MH*, May 1857.

146   Underhill, 'On the Pastorate', pp. 26–7, 30.

147   *MH*, June 1857.

148   *MH*, Aug. 1857.

149   Ibid.

150   *MH*, May 1858.

151   Stanley, *Bible and the Flag*, pp. 101–2.

152   *MH*, Sept. 1857.

153 Ibid.
154 *MH*, Oct., Nov. 1857.
155 James L. Sturgis, *John Bright and the Empire 1811–89* (Athlone Press, London, 1969); Keith Robbins, *John Bright 1811–1889* (Routledge and Kegan Paul, London, 1979); Roland Quinault, 'John Bright and Joseph Chamberlain', *Historical Journal*, 28/3 (1985), pp. 623–46; Patrick Joyce, *Democratic Subjects. The Self and the Social in Nineteenth Century England* (Cambridge University Press, Cambridge, 1994).
156 Sturgis, *John Bright and the Empire*, pp. 45, 84–5.
157 Quoted in Robertson, *Life and Times of . . . Bright*, p. 345.
158 Bill Schwarz, ' "The only white man in there": The Re-racialization of England, 1956–1968', *Race and Class* 38/1 (1996), pp. 65–78.

Chapter 7   Town, Nation and Empire 1859–1867

1   Richard, *Memoirs of Joseph Sturge*, p. 577; John Angell James, *Christian Philanthropy: As Exemplified in the Life and Character of the Late Joseph Sturge Esq.* (Hudson and Son, Birmingham, 1859); *ASR*, 1 July 1862.
2   George Dawson Collection, vol. 15: 'Speeches', 4 June 1862.
3   Richard, *Memoirs of Joseph Sturge*, pp. 607–8. The memorial in Falmouth Baptist church in Jamaica celebrated these four men.
4   *ASR*, 1 June 1859.
5   LNFS, *41st Report* (Hudson, Birmingham, 1866), p. 21.
6   *BDP*, 29 Jan. 1867.
7   Tyrrell, *Joseph Sturge*, p. 199.
8   Ibid., p. 227.
9   A. W. W. Dale, *The Life of R. W. Dale of Birmingham* (Hodder and Stoughton, London, 1899), p. 254.
10 Tyrrell, *Joseph Sturge*, p. 232; Denis Judd, *Radical Joe. A Life of Joseph Chamberlain* (Hamish Hamilton, London, 1977).
11 Rev. A. Gordon, *The Triumphant Career and its Peaceful Close. Sermon on the Death of John Angell James, Walsall. 9 October, 1859* (Judd and Glass, London, 1859).
12 R. W. Dale, *The Funeral Sermon for John Angell James* (Hudson and Co., Birmingham, 1859).
13 R. W. Dale, *Life and Letters of John Angell James* (Nisbet and Co., London, 1861); *BM*, Mar. 1860, Oct. 1861.
14 R. W. Dale, *Life and Letters*, p. 582; Davidoff and Hall, *Family Fortunes*, esp. pp. 126–30.
15 A. W. W. Dale, *Life of R. W. Dale*, p. 16.
16 This was part of a wider movement towards Christian social action in the second half of the nineteenth century. See Boyd Hilton, *Age of Atonement: The Influence of Evangelicalism on Social and Economic Thought, 1795–1865* (Clarendon Press, Oxford, 1988).
17 A. W. W. Dale, *Life of R. W. Dale*, p. 130.

18 Ibid., p. 131.

19 *BDP*, 10 Dec. 1857.

20 *BDP*, 18 Sept. 1862.

21 R. W. Dale, *The Living God the Saviour of all Men* (Jackson, Walford and Hodder, London, 1864), p. 45.

22 A. F. Morgan, *Kith and Kin*, part 5, p. 7.

23 Eliezer Edwards, *John Skirrow Wright, M. P.* (privately published, Birmingham, 1880).

24 Martin Wiener, 'The Sad Story of George Hall: Adultery, Murder and the Politics of Mercy in Mid-Victorian England', *Social History*, 24/2 (May 1999), pp. 174–95. The rest of this paragraph is heavily dependent on Wiener's most interesting analysis.

25 Cited ibid., p. 191.

26 Ibid., p. 193.

27 James Skirrow Wright, 'On the Employment of Women in Factories in Birmingham', in *Transactions of the National Association for the Promotion of Social Science* (J. W. Parkes and Son, London, 1857), pp. 538–43.

28 Thanks to Sonya Rose for this point. Masculinity becomes a problem when men's power is challenged; otherwise it remains an unmarked category.

29 For a discussion of some of these issues see Sally Alexander, 'Why Feminism? The Women of Langham Place', in *Becoming a Woman and Other Essays in Nineteenth and Twentieth Century Feminist History* (Virago, London, 1994), pp. 135–48.

30 Hugh Cunningham, *The Volunteer Force. A Social and Political History 1859–1908* (Croom Helm, London, 1975), pp. 1, 16–18.

31 Langford, *Modern Birmingham*, vol. 2, pp. 85–100.

32 A. W. W. Dale, *Life of R. W. Dale*, p. 253.

33 Henry Parkes, *Australian Views of England. Eleven Letters Written in the Years 1861 and 1862* (Macmillan and Co., London, 1869), pp. 1–2; George Dawson Collection, vol. 11, 'An English View of the American War', *BJ*, 5 Oct. 1861.

34 Royden Harrison, *Before the Socialists. Studies in Labour and Politics 1861–1881* (Routledge and Kegan Paul, London, 1965), esp. ch. 2.

35 Semmel, *Governor Eyre Controversy*, ch. 1; Lorimer, *Colour, Class and the Victorians*, ch. 8; Bolt, *Anti-Slavery Movement and Reconstruction*, ch. 2; Harrison, *Before the Socialists*, ch. 2.

36 *BDP*, 18 Sept. 1862.

37 *BDP*, 19 Dec. 1862.

38 Ibid.

39 *BJ*, 3 Jan. 1863.

40 *BJ*, 17 Jan. 1863.

41 *BJ*, 31 Jan. 1863.

42 *BJ*, 28 Mar. 1863. An anti-slavery production was followed by one showing the 'bright side' of slave life.

43 Hope and Anchor, 'Minutes of subjects for discussion', BRL MS 103139: 11 Apr., 6 June, 18 July, 29 Aug., 19 Sept., 10 Oct., 12 Dec. 1858; 23 Jan., 10 Apr., 1 May, 3 July, 28 Aug. 1859.

44 Ibid., 25 Apr., 18 July, 24 Oct. 1858; 10 June 1860; 27 Apr. 1862.
45 Ibid., 3 Mar., 12 May, 2 June, 20 Oct., 24 Nov., 1 Dec., 25 Dec. 1861; 12 Jan., 30 Mar., 18 May, 19 Oct., 2 Nov. 1862; 4 Jan., 22 Feb., 8 June 1863; 19 June, 17 July, 6 Nov. 1864; 1 Jan., 30 Apr., 18 June, 14 Aug. 1865.
46 *BDP*, 27 Jan. 1864.
47 LNFS, *36th Report* (Hudson, Birmingham, 1861).
48 LNFS, *39th Report* (Hudson and Son, Birmingham, 1864), pp. 7–8, 25, 28–9, 32, 34–5.
49 Lorimer, *Colour, Class and the Victorians*, pp. 49, 51, 53.
50 *BJ*, 17 June 1865.
51 *BDP*, 5 Jan. 1865.
52 Birmingham and Midland Freedman's Aid Association, 'Minute Book 1864–5 including circulars, newspaper cuttings etc.', BRL MS 361222.
53 Quoted in Bolt, *Anti-Slavery Movement and Reconstruction*, p. 54.
54 Ibid., pp. 62, 70, 72.
55 Quoted ibid., p. 115.
56 Bolt, *Victorian Attitudes to Race*. On the debates *re* the black franchise see pp. 64–73.
57 On the interconnections between Fenianism, Jamaica and reform of the franchise see C. Hall, 'The Nation Within and Without', in Hall et al., *Defining the Victorian Nation*, pp. 179–233; Belich, *New Zealand Wars*; Jeff Guy, *The Heretic. A Study of the Life of John William Colenso 1814–1883* (University of Natal Press, Pietermaritzburg, 1983), esp. part 2.
58 *BJ*, 3 Jan. 1863.
59 *BJ*, 10 Jan. 1863.
60 *BJ*, 31 Jan. 1863.
61 *BJ*, 28 Mar. 1863.
62 *BM*, July 1852.
63 *MH*, June 1861.
64 'The Mission of the Anglo-Saxon Race', extract from *American Theological Review* quoted in *MH*, Nov. 1861.
65 Birmingham Auxiliary of the BMS, 'Handbills, etc.'
66 Timmins (ed.), *Resources, Products and Industrial History of Birmingham*.
67 Philip Lowe, 'The British Association and the Provincial Public', in Roy Macleod and Peter Collins (eds), *The Parliament of Science* (Science Reviews, Northwood, 1981), pp. 118–144, esp. pp. 124, 125.
68 Stocking Jr, *Victorian Anthropology*, p. 49.
69 Rainger, 'Race, Politics and Science'.
70 Stocking Jr, *Victorian Anthropology*, pp. 247–8.
71 Stepan, *Idea of Race in Science*, p. 49.
72 *BDP*, 11 Sept. 1865.
73 Stocking Jr, *Victorian Anthropology*, p. 254.
74 *BDP*, 7 Sept. 1865; on Murchison see Robert A. Stafford, *Scientist of Empire. Sir Roderick Murchison, Scientific Exploration and Victorian Imperialism* (Cambridge University Press, Cambridge, 1989).
75 *BDP*, 9 Sept. 1865.

76   *BDP*, 11 Sept. 1865.
77   Amalie M. Kass and Edward H. Kass, *Perfecting the World. The Life and Times of Dr. Thomas Hodgkin 1798–1866* (Harcourt Brace Jovanovich, Boston, 1988), pp. 504–5.
78   These sessions were published as *The Resources, Products and Industrial History of Birmingham*, ed. Timmins.
79   *BJ*, 23 May 1863.
80   *BJ*, 17 Feb. 1866.
81   *BDP*, 3 Jan. 1865.
82   See C. Hall et al., *Defining the Victorian Nation*, esp. chs. 2, 4.
83   *BDP*, 19 Jan. 1865.
84   Briggs, *Victorian Cities*, pp. 185–244; E. P. Hennock, *Fit and Proper Persons. Ideal and Reality in Nineteenth-Century Urban Government* (Edward Arnold, London, 1973), esp. ch. 3.
85   George Dawson Collection, vol. 15: Speeches, 26 Sept. 1866.
86   Wilson, *Life of George Dawson*, pp. 150–1.
87   Hennock, *Fit and Proper Persons*, p. 96.
88   Briggs, *Victorian Cities*, p. 208.
89   A. W. W. Dale, *Life of R. W. Dale*, pp. 412–13.
90   Binfield, *So Down to Prayers*, p. 106.
91   R. W. Dale, *The Politics of Nonconformity. A Lecture Delivered in the Free Trade Hall Manchester, November 1871* (Manchester Nonconformist Association, Manchester, 1871), p. 9.
92   A. W. W. Dale, *Life of R. W. Dale*, pp. 180–3.
93   Binfield, *So Down to Prayers*, pp. 110–11
94   Hennock, *Fit and Proper Persons*, pp. 155–8.
95   A. W. W. Dale, *Life of R. W. Dale*, pp. 221–2.
96   Hugh McLeod, 'The Power of the Pulpit', in Clyde Binfield (ed.), *The Cross and the City: Essays in Commemoration of Robert William Dale 1829–1895*, Supplement to the *Journal of the United Reformed Church History Society*, 6, suppl. no. 2 (Spring 1999), pp. 44–54.
97   Church- and chapel-going remained a minority activity, and the 1851 census had demonstrated that nearly half the worshippers in the town were Anglican: Davidoff and Hall, *Family Fortunes*, p. 43.
98   A. W. W. Dale, *Life of R. W. Dale*, p. 222.
99   Quoted in Clyde Binfield, 'Dale and Politics', in Binfield (ed.), *Cross and the City*, p. 117.
100   A. W. W. Dale, *Life of R. W. Dale*, p. 250.
101   Ibid., p. 137.
102   Charles Silvester Horne, 'R. W. Dale', in J. H. Muirhead (ed.), *Nine Famous Birmingham Men* (Cornish Bros, Birmingham, 1909), pp. 266, 270.
103   A. W. W. Dale, *Life of R. W. Dale*, pp. 209, 255.
104   Ibid., p. 251.
105   See Hennock, *Fit and Proper Persons*, for the details of municipal reform.
106   *BDP*, from 13 Nov. 1865.
107   *BJ*, 18 Nov. 1865.
108   *BDP*, 13 Nov. 1865.

109   *BDP*, 21 Nov. 1865.
110   *Birmingham Daily Gazette*, 17 Nov., 20 Nov. 1865.
111   *The Times*, 13 Nov. 1865.
112   *BDP*, 21 Nov. 1865.
113   *BDP*, 7 Dec. 1865.
114   *BDP*, 15 Dec. 1865.
115   *BDP*, 9 Dec. 1865.
116   *ASR*, Dec. 1865.
117   *BJ*, 6 Jan. 1866.
118   Jamaica Committee, Jamaica Papers, no. 1.
119   Langford, *Modern Birmingham*, vol. 1, pp. 241, 247.
120   BRL, 'Hope and Anchor', 10 Dec. 1865, 7 Jan. 1866.
121   LNFS, *41st Report* (Hudson, Birmingham, 1866), pp. 5–6, 9–10, 16–17,
      19, 34.
122   *The Times*, 19 Mar. 1866.
123   Brereton, *Law, Justice and Empire*, ch. 2.
124   A. F. Morgan, *Kith and Kin*, part 3, p. 10.
125   *ASR*, 15 Feb. 1866.
126   *ASR*, 16 Apr. 1866.
127   A. F. Morgan, *Kith and Kin*, part 3, p. 10.
128   *ASR*, 1 Sept. 1866.
129   *ASR*, 16 Apr. 1866.
130   Charles Kingsley, *At Last. A Christmas in the West Indies*, new edn
      (Macmillan, London, 1872). Gikandi, *Maps of Englishness*, pp. 93. 97.
131   James Anthony Froude, *The English in the West Indies: or The Bow of
      Ulysses* (Longman, London, 1888).
132   Gikandi, *Maps of Englishness*, pp. 115–17.
133   *ASR*, 1 May 1866.
134   *ASR*, 1 Oct. 1866.
135   Ibid.
136   *ASR*, 1 May 1866.
137   *ASR*, 1 June 1866.
138   *ASR*, 1 Mar. 1867.
139   Thomas Harvey and William Brewin, *Jamaica in 1866. A Narrative of a
      Tour through the Island with Remarks on its Social, Educational and
      Industrial Condition* (A. W. Bennett, London, 1867), pp. v, 11, 17, 20, 28,
      32–3, 56, 67, 71–2.
140   *ASR*, 1 Aug. 1866, 1 Jan. 1867.
141   *ASR*, 1 Oct. 1866.
142   *BJ*, 16 Feb. 1866.
143   *ASR*, 1 Apr. 1867.
144   *ASR*, 15 July 1867.
145   *ASR*, 15 Feb. 1867.
146   *ASR*, 1 Sept. 1866.
147   LNFS, *41st Report*, p. 25.
148   *ASR*, 1 Oct. 1866.

149 *BDP*, 27 Sept. 1866, Birmingham Auxiliary of the BMS, 'Handbills, etc.'.

150 Doreen Massey, 'Travelling Thoughts', in Paul Gilroy, Lawrence Grossberg and Angela McRobbie (eds), *Without Guarantees. In Honour of Stuart Hall* (Verso, London, 2000), pp. 225–32.

151 *BDP*, 27 Sept. 1866.

152 Hope and Anchor, 'Minutes', 7 Jan., 16 Sept. 1866; 7 Apr. 1867.

153 Semmel, *Governor Eyre Controversy*, ch. 3; C. Hall, 'Competing Masculinities', in *White, Male and Middle Class*.

154 *ASR*, 15 Feb. 1867.

155 Birmingham Jamaica Committee, *The Jamaica Question. A Statement of the Grounds on which the Birmingham and District Jamaica Committee Appeal to the Public for Assistance in Aid of their Funds* (Hudson and Son, Birmingham, 1867).

156 Semmel, *Governor Eyre Controversy*, pp. 131–40. Harrison is quoted on p. 131.

157 Quoted in Bolt, *Victorian Attitudes to Race*, p. 84.

158 See C. Hall, 'Nation Within and Without', in Hall et al., *Defining the Victorian Nation*, pp. 179–233.

159 Quoted in Bolt, *Victorian Attitudes to Race*, p. 89.

160 *ASR*, 15 Aug. 1867.

161 Jamaica Committee, *Jamaica Papers*, no. 6: *Illustrations of Martial Law in Jamaica. Compiled from the Royal Commission and Blue Books by John Gorrie, Barrister at Law of Jamaica and Counsel of the Jamaica Committee before the Royal Commission* (Jamaica Committee, London, 1867), p. 102.

162 Birmingham Jamaica Committee, *Jamaica Question*, pp. 1, 6–7.

163 C. Hall, 'Nation Within and Without'.

164 *ASR*, 1 May 1867.

165 *MH*, June 1867.

166 *ASR*, 15 Aug. 1867.

167 This section draws heavily on the work of Keith McClelland, Jane Rendall and myself: C. Hall et al., *Defining the Victorian Nation*.

168 Quoted in Eric Foner, *Nothing but Freedom. Emancipation and its Legacy* (Louisiana State University Press, Baton Rouge, 1983), p. 30; on the new constitutions of the white settler colonies in the 1850s see Miles Taylor, 'The 1848 Revolutions and the British Empire', *Past and Present*, 166 (Feb. 2000), pp. 146–80.

169 *BDP*, 19 Jan. 1865.

170 Quoted in John Breuilly, Gottfried Niedhart and Anthony Taylor (eds), *The Era of the Reform League: English Labour and Radical Politics 1857–1872. Documents Selected by Gustav Mayer* (Palatium Verlag in J. and J. Verlag, Mannheim, 1995), p. 194.

171 *Hansard's Parliamentary Debates*, 3rd ser., vol. 186, cols 626–42.

172 Keith McClelland, 'England's Greatness, the Working Man', in C. Hall et al., *Defining the Victorian Nation*, pp. 71–118, esp. pp. 97–8; José Harris, 'Between Civic Virtue and Social Darwinism: The Concept of the

Residuum', in David Englander and Rosemary O'Day (eds), *Retrieved Riches: Social Investigation in England 1840–1914* (Scholar Press, Aldershot, 1995), p. 74.

173   Joyce, *Democratic Subjects*, p. 94.

174   *BDP*, 13 Dec. 1865.

175   Ibid.

176   Langford, *Modern Birmingham*, vol. 2, pp. 350–7.

177   Quinault, 'John Bright and Joseph Chamberlain', p. 626.

178   R. W. Dale, *The Politics of the Future. A Lecture to New Electors* (Hudson and Son, Birmingham, 1867), pp. 1–2, 5, 7, 9, 11, 14, 17, 20.

179   Interestingly, it was more than Bright could cope with, and he resigned in 1870 having suffered the second breakdown of his adult life: Robbins, *John Bright*, p. 205.

180   I owe this point and this quotation to Robbie Gray, *North and South Revisited*, p. 11.

181   The phrase was Dr Dale's and was used in his obituary: *Daily Post*, 14 Mar. 1895; Robbins, *John Bright*, p. 201.

182   *The Times*, 20 June 1867.

183   For a longer account of this episode, see C. Hall, 'Nation Within and Without', pp. 215–20.

184   Ziesler, 'Irish in Birmingham', p. 44; Alan O'Day, 'The Political Organization of the Irish in Britain 1867–1890', in Roger Swift and Sheridan Gilley (eds), *The Irish in Britain 1815–1939* (Pinter, London, 1989), pp. 183–211.

185   Langford, *Modern Birmingham*, vol. 1, p. 411.

186   *Hansard*, 3rd ser., vol. 186, cols 1939–31.

187   *BJ*, 16 Sept., 23 Nov. 1865.

188   *BDP*, 17 June 1867.

189   *BDP*, 18 June 1867.

190   Patrick Quinlivan and Paul Rose, *The Fenians in England 1865–1872: A Sense of Insecurity* (John Calder, London, 1982), p. 33.

191   D. M. MacRaild, 'William Murphy, the Orange Order and Communal Violence: The Irish in West Cumberland 1871–1874', in Panikos Panayi (ed.), *Racial Violence in Britain, 1840–1950*, rev. edn (Leicester University Press, Leicester, 1996), pp. 44–64; see also Walter L. Arnstein, 'The Murphy Riots: A Victorian Dilemma', *Victorian Studies*, 19 (1975–6), pp. 51–72.

192   Langford, *Modern Birmingham*, vol. 2. pp. 300–2.

193   Quoted in Ziesler, 'Irish in Birmingham', p. 74.

194   Ann Dingsdale, 'Generous and Lofty Sympathies: The Kensington Society, the 1866 Women's Suffrage Petition and the Development of Mid-Victorian Feminism', University of Greenwich Ph. D. 1995, p. 103.

195   Mill, *Autobiography*, pp. 257–8.

196   Robbins, *John Bright*, pp. 194, 214.

197   On women's suffrage in 1867 see Jane Rendall, 'The Citizenship of Women and the Reform Act of 1867', in C. Hall et al., *Defining the Victorian Nation*, pp. 119–78. I have been much influenced by her analysis. On the

relation between anti-slavery and feminism see Midgley, 'Anti-slavery and Feminism in Nineteenth Century Britain'.

198   Langford, *Modern Birmingham*, vol. 2, p. 367.
199   National Society for Women's Suffrage, Birmingham Branch, *First Annual Report* (W. E. Harris, Birmingham, 1869).
200   Rendall, 'Citizenship of Women', pp. 144, 155.
201   Bodichon cited ibid., p. 163.
202   Cited ibid., p. 170.
203   Mrs Fawcett, *Women's Suffrage. Speech Delivered in the Town Hall, Birmingham, December 6 1872*, repr. for *Birmingham Morning News*, p. 5; Burton, *Burdens of History*; Midgley, 'Anti-Slavery and the Roots of Imperial Feminism'.

Epilogue

1   Edward J. Eyre, Letter to unknown recipient, 19 Nov. 1869: 'Eyre Letters 1835–1869', Alexander Turnbull Library, MS 765/3, Copied from the Mitchell Library, Sydney, Australia.
2   *Daily News*, 10 July 1872.
3   Mill, *Autobiography*, pp. 228, 244, 254.
4   I am drawing here on the discussion of Mill in C. Hall et al., *Defining the Victorian Nation*, pp. 62–70.
5   Da Costa, *Crowns of Glory*, p. 34; Sigmund Freud, *Civilisation and its Discontents*, in *Penguin Freud*, vol. 12: *Civilisation, Society, Religion* (Penguin, Harmondsworth, 1991), p. 305.
6   Stephen Gwynne and Gertrude M. Tuckwell, *The Life of the Rt. Hon. Sir Charles Dilke*, 2 vols (John Murray, London, 1917), vol. 1, pp. 11, 14, 52, 56.
7   Sir Charles Wentworth Dilke, *Greater Britain: A Record of Travel in English Speaking Countries during 1866 and 1867*, 1st edn 1867, 3rd. edn (Macmillan, London, 1869), p. vii.
8   Ibid.
9   Gwynne and Tuckwell, *Life of . . . Sir Charles Dilke*, pp. 65, 68; Dilke, *Greater Britain*, p. vii. Dilke was influenced by Renan, a theorist of race and nation who believed that the regeneration of inferior or degenerate races by superior races was part of the providential order of things: Ernest Renan, 'What is a Nation', 1st edn 1882, repr. in Homi Bhabha (ed.), *Nation and Narration* (Routledge, London, 1990), pp. 8–22; on Renan see Robert Young, *Colonial Desire. Hybridity in Theory, Culture and Race* (Routledge, London and New York, 1995), pp. 68–72.
10   Dilke, *Greater Britain*, pp. 47, 85.
11   Ibid., pp. 223, 225, 572.
12   Ibid., pp. 88, 389.
13   Ibid., pp. 17–18.
14   Ibid., pp. 257, 263, 274.
15   Gwynne and Tuckwell, *Life of . . . Sir Charles Dilke*, vol. 1, p.72.

16 Dilke, *Greater Britain*, p. 215.

17 Gwynne and Tuckwell, *Life of... Sir Charles Dilke*, vol. 1, p. 70.

18 Kingsley claimed he had been 'cursed for it, as if I had been a dog': Charles Kingsley, *His Letters, and Memories of His Life, Edited by his Wife*, 4 vols (Macmillan, London, 1901), vol. 3, pp. 241–2; H. Kingsley, 'Eyre, the South Australian Explorer'.

19 C. Kingsley, *His Letters*, vol. 1, pp. 5–6; Susan Chitty, *The Beast and the Monk. A Life of Charles Kingsley* (Hodder and Stoughton, London, 1974).

20 C. Kingsley, *At Last*, p. 1.

21 Gikandi, *Maps of Englishness*, pp. 97–102.

22 C. Kingsley, *His Letters*, vol. 3, pp. 248–9, 265; vol. 4, p. 50. The Kingsley family had been paid compensation in 1834 for the enslaved men and women on their properties. 'Emancipation ruined me,' Kingsley wrote in 1867.

23 C. Kingsley, *At Last*, pp. 7, 16, 20–1, 32–3.

24 Ibid., p. 297.

25 Ibid., pp. 130, 298.

26 Henderson, *Goodness and Mercy*, pp. 121–6.

27 Underhill, *Life of... Phillippo*, p. 412.

28 H. P. Jacobs, *Sixty Years of Change 1806–1866* (Institute of Jamaica, Kingston, 1973), p. 107.

29 Rupert Lewis, *Marcus Garvey. Anti-Colonial Champion* (Karia Press, London, 1987); John Henry Clarke (ed.), *Marcus Garvey and the Vision of Africa* (Vintage, New York, 1974); Judith Stein, *The World of Marcus Garvey. Race and Class in Modern Society* (Louisiana State University Press, Baton Rouge, 1986). Garvey built on the tradition of Alexander Bedward, Native Baptist. See Roscoe M. Pierson, 'Alexander Bedward and the Jamaican Native Baptist Free Church', repr. from *Lexington Theological Quarterly*, 4/3 (July 1969).

Bibliography

Manuscript sources

Alexander Turnbull Library

Edward J. Eyre Letters 1835–1869, MS 765/3, Copied from the Mitchell Library, Sydney, Australia.
Eyre Family Letters 1865–1903, MS 971/1195, Copied from the National Library of Australia, Canberra.

Angus Library, Regent's Park College

Fenn Collection

Auckland Institute and Museum Library

Swainson, Mary Frederica, 'Letters to her grandparents in England 1840–1850', MS 198.
Marshall, Mary Frederica, 'Letters to Mary de Lys and Isabel Percy, Warwick, from Hutt Valley and Kaiwharawhara, 1843–54', MS 198.

Baptist Missionary Society (archive on deposit in the Angus Library)

General Missionary Correspondence WI/1, WI/2, WI/3, WI/5.
Home Correspondence HII/2, HII/3, H9/1, H9/3.
Bound volume of letters from BMS missionaries 1840–1846 (shelf set V1/1).
BMS Pamphlet Collection 1823–51.
BMS, 'Notes of Deputation to Jamaica 1846–9'.
Correspondence of Dr D. J. East and Dr Underhill, 1852–95.
Fuller, J. J., 'Recollections of the West African Mission of the BMS and Autobiography', BMS typescript.
Underhill, Edward Bean, Extracts from Correspondence with Missionaries in Jamaica on the Disturbances, 1864–1866.

Birmingham Reference Library

Birmingham Anti-Slavery Society, 'Minute Book 1826–37', BRL 152006.
Birmingham Anti-Slavery Society, 'Minute Book 1837–59', BRL 158748.
Brimingham Auxiliary of the BMS, 'Handbills, Newspaper Cuttings etc. 1823–80', BRL 212491.
Birmingham and Midland Freedman's Aid Association, 'Minute Book 1864–5 including circulars, newspaper cuttings etc.', BRL 361222.
Bond Street Baptist Church, BRL 212477.
Edwards, E., 'The Electro Plate Trade and Charles Askin', BRL 294924.
Female Society for Birmingham for the Relief of British Negro Slaves, Album, BRL 361221.
George Dawson Collection, 21 vols, BRL 260167.
Hope and Anchor, 'Minutes of subjects for discussion', BRL 103139.
Ladies' Society for the Relief of Negro Slaves, Minute Book 1825–52, BRL 302206.
Cash Book belonging to the Female Society for the Relief of British Negro Slaves for Birmingham, West Bromwich, BRL 302205.
Memorial of the First of August 1838, BRL 217752.

National Library of Jamaica

BMS Correspondence 1844–54, MS 378.
Duckett, Rev. Angus, Letters to Revs Trestrail and Underhill, MS 868.
Fray, Rev. Ellis, Letters to Revs Trestrail and Underhill, MS 859.
Henderson, 'Letters 1841–63', MS 817.
Holt, Elizabeth, 'Letter to Edward Bean Underhill', MS 865.
Jamaica Baptist Union, Memorial to the Secretary of State, 1866, MS 15.
Letters and Reports to the BMS about Falmouth, MS 817a.
Millard, Rev. B., Letter to Revs Trestrail and Underhill, MS 857.
Milliner, Rev. G., Letters to Rev. Underhill, MS 886.
O'Meally, Patric, Letters to Revs Trestrail and Underhill, 1858–63, MS 873.
Rowse, George, Letters to the BMS, MS 841.
Sibley, Elizabeth and Sibley, Charles, Letters to the BMS, MS 880.

Public Records Office

CO 137/178 Jamaica January–July 1831.
CO 137/179 Jamaica July–December 1831.
CO 137/180 Jamaica Offices/Individuals 1831.
CO 137/181 Jamaica January–March 1832.
CO 137/245 Jamaica May–September 1839.
CO 137/284 Jamaica May–September 1845.
CO 137/285 Jamaica October–December 1845.
CO 137/309 Jamaica January–June 1851.
CO 137/310 Jamaica July–August 1851.
CO 137/322 Jamaica January–March 1854.

CO 137/326 Jamaica January–June 1855.
CO 137/366 Jamaica June–September 1862.
CO 137/367 Jamaica October–December 1862.
CO 137/368 Jamaica January–March 1862.
CO 137/370 Jamaica January–February 1863.
CO 137/371 Jamaica March–April 1863.
CO 137/372 Jamaica May–June 1863.
CO 137/373 Jamaica July 1863.
CO 137/374 Jamaica August–September 1863.
CO 137/375 Jamaica October–November 1863.
CO 137/376 Jamaica December 1863.
CO 137/378 Jamaica January 1864.
CO 137/379 Jamaica February 1864.
CO 137/380 Jamaica March 1864.
CO 137/381 Jamaica April 1864.
CO 137/382 Jamaica May 1864.
CO 137/383 Jamaica June 1864.
CO 137/384 Jamaica July–September 1864.
CO 137/388 Jamaica February–March 1865.
CO 137/390 Jamaica April 1865.
CO 137/395 Jamaica November 9–30, 1865.

CO 260/81 St Vincent September–December 1854.
CO 260/82 St Vincent January–June 1855.
CO 260/83 St Vincent July–October 1855.
CO 260/84 St Vincent November–December 1855.
CO 260/85 St Vincent January–May 1856.
CO 260/87 St Vincent October–November 1856.
CO 260/89 St Vincent January–August 1857.
CO 260/91 St Vincent January–December 1858.
CO 260/92 St Vincent January–July 1859.

CO 7/112 Antigua July–September 1859.
CO 7/113 Antigua October–December 1859.
CO 7/114 Antigua January–May 1860.

Parliamentary papers

PP 1831–2 (127) CCCVI, vols 11 and 12, Select Committee of the House of Lords on the State of the West India Colonies.
PP 1831–2 (381) XX, Select Committee of the House of Commons on the Extinction of Slavery throughout the British Dominions.
PP 1836 (560) XV, Select Committee of the House of Commons on the Working of the Apprenticeship system in the Colonies.
PP 1836 (40) XXXIV, 'Report on the State of the Irish Poor in Great Britain', being Appendix G, Commission for Inquiry into the Condition of the Poorer Classes in Ireland.
PP 1839 (523) XXXVI, Papers Relative to the West Indies.

PP 1840 (212) XXXV, Papers Relative to the West Indies.
PP 1842 (479) XIII, Select Committee of the House of Lords on the West India Colonies.
PP 1847/8 (685) XLIV, Papers Relative to Jamaica.
PP 1849 (280) XXXVII, Papers Relative to the Affairs of the Island of Jamaica.
PP 1854 (1848) XLIII, Papers Relative to the Affairs of the Island of Jamaica.
PP 1866 (3595) LI, Papers Relative to the Disturbances in Jamaica, Parts I, II, III.
PP 1866 (3682) XXX, Papers Laid before the Royal Commission of Inquiry by Governor Eyre.
PP 1866 (3683) XXX, Report of the Jamaica Royal Commission, Part I: Report.
PP 1866 (3683-1) XXXI, Report of the Jamaica Royal Commission, Part II: Minutes of Evidence and Appendix.
Hansard's Parliamentary Debates.

Newspapers and periodicals

Anti-Slavery Reporter
Baptist Herald and Friend of Africa
Baptist Magazine
Birmingham Daily Post
Birmingham Mercury
Birmingham Morning News
Daily News
Edinburgh Review
Falmouth Post
Fortnightly Review
Fraser's Magazine
Macmillan's Magazine
Manchester Guardian
Missionary Herald
Morning Chronicle
Morning Star
The Times
Westminster Review

Unpublished Doctoral theses

Allen, Margaret, 'Three South Australian Women Writers, 1854–1923: Matilda Evans, Catherine Spence and Catherine Martin', Ph.D., University of South Australia, Flinders, 1991.
Dingsdale, Ann, 'Generous and Lofty Sympathies: The Kensington Society, the 1866 Women's Suffrage Petition and the Development of Mid-Victorian Feminism', Ph.D., University of Greenwich, 1995.

Evans, Julie, ' "To keep within proper bounds . . .': Edward Eyre and the Colonised Peoples of Australia, New Zealand and the Caribbean', Ph.D., University of Melbourne, 1998.

Franklin, Alexandra, 'Enterprise and Advantage: The West India Interest in Britain 1774–1840', Ph.D., University of Pennsylvania, 1992.

Quinn, Brenda Ann, 'India in the Making of Liberal Identities: The Case of Mary Carpenter and Harriet Martineau', Ph.D., University of Essex, 2000.

Russell, Horace O., 'The Missionary Outreach of the West Indian Church to West Africa in the Nineteenth Century, with Particular Reference to the Baptists', Oxford D.Phil., 1973.

Ryall, Dorothy Ann, 'The Organization of the Missionary Societies, the Recruitment of the Missionaries in Britain and the Role of the Missionaries in the Diffusion of British Culture in Jamaica during the Period 1834–1865', Ph.D., University of London, 1959.

Sampson, David, 'Strangers in a Strange Land: The 1868 Aborigines and Other Indigenous Performers in Mid-Victorian Britain', Ph.D., University of Technology, Sydney. 2001.

Twells, Alison, 'The Heathen at Home and Overseas: the Middle Class and the Civilizing Mission, Sheffield 1790–1843', D.Phil., University of York, 1997.

Ziesler, Kaja, 'The Irish in Birmingham 1830–1970', Ph.D., University of Birmingham, 1989.

Books, articles, pamphlets and speeches published before 1914

Address to the Friends of Education in Great Britain from a Meeting of Presbyterians, Independents and Baptists, Falmouth, 15 Feb. 1849.

Anon., 'George Dawson', *Christian Reformer*, Nov. 1847, new series, 35.

Anon., 'The West Indies, as They Were and Are', *Edinburgh Review*, 109 (Jan.–Apr. 1859).

Austen, Jane, *Mansfield Park*, 1st pub. 1814 (Penguin, Harmondsworth, 1966).

Baptist Missionary Society, *Circular* (Haddon, London, 1842).

Bigelow, John, *Jamaica in 1850: or, The Effects of 16 Years of Freedom on a Slave Colony* (George Putnam, New York and London, 1851).

Birmingham Anti-Slavery Society, *Report of the Proceedings of the Great Anti-Slavery Meeting Held at the Town Hall Birmingham 14 October 1835* (Hudson, Birmingham, 1835).

Birmingham British and Foreign Anti-Slavery Society, *Report and Treasurer's Account* (Hudson, Birmingham, 1840).

Birmingham Conference, *Report of the Proceedings of a Conference on the Subject of Preventive and Reformatory Schools, Held at Birmingham*, 1851.

The Birmingham Ladies' Negro's Friend Society, *Reports* (Hudson, Birmingham, 1828–1870).

Birmingham Jamaica Committee, *The Jamaica Question. A Statement of the Grounds on which the Birmingham and District Jamaica Committee Appeal to the Public for Assistance in Aid of their Funds* (Hudson and Son, Birmingham, 1867).

Blyth, George, *Remonstrance of the Presbytery of Jamaica with the Majority of the Baptist Missionaries in that Island* (M. Paterson, Edinburgh, 1843).

Bray, Caroline, *The British Empire: A Sketch of the Geography, Natural and Political Features of the United Kingdom, its Colonies and Dependencies* (Longman, Green, Roberts, Longman and Green, London, 1863).

Bridges, George Wilson, *The Annals of Jamaica*, 2 vols, 1st edn 1828, 2nd edn (Cass, London, 1968).

Bunce, J. T., *History of the Corporation of Birmingham* (Cornish Bros, Birmingham, 1878), vol. 1.

Burchell, William Fitz-er, *Memoir of Thomas Burchell, 22 Years a Missionary in Jamaica* (Benjamin L. Green, London, 1849).

Buxton, Charles (ed.), *Memoirs of Sir Thomas Fowell Buxton* (John Murray, London, 1848).

Candler, John, *Extracts from the Journal of John Candler whilst Travelling in Jamaica*, 2 parts (Harvey and Darton, London, 1840–1).

Carlyle, Thomas, *Chartism*, 1st edn 1839, in Thomas Carlyle, *Selected Writings* (Penguin, Harmondsworth, 1971).

Carlyle, Thomas, 'The Hero as Man of Letters', 1st edn 1841, in Thomas Carlyle, *Selected Writings* (Penguin, Harmondsworth, 1971).

Carlyle, Thomas, *Past and Present*, 1st edn 1843 (Dent, London, 1960).

Carlyle, Thomas, 'Occasional Discourse on the Negro Question', *Fraser's Magazine*, 40 (Dec. 1849).

Carlyle, Thomas, 'Occasional Discourse on the Nigger Question', a revised version of his original polemic of 1849, in *English and Other Critical Essays*, vol. 2 (Dent, London, 1964).

Carlyle, Thomas, 'Shooting Niagara: And After?', in *Critical and Miscellaneous Essays: Collected and Republished*, 7 vols (Chapman and Hall, London, 1899), vol. 5.

Clark, John, *A Brief Account of the Settlements of the Emancipated Peasantry in the Neighbourhood of Brown's Town, Jamaica. In a Letter to Joseph Sturge* (J. W. Showell, Birmingham, 1852).

Clark, John, Dendy, Walter and Phillippo, James Mursell, *The Voice of Jubilee: A Narrative of the Baptist Mission, Jamaica* (John Snow, London, 1865).

Clark, John, *Memorials of Baptist Missionaries in Jamaica, including a Sketch of Early Religious Instructors in Jamaica* (Yates and Alexander, London, 1869).

Cornford, P. H., *Missionary Reminiscences; or Jamaica Retraced* (Thomas Heaton and Son, Leeds, 1856).

Cox, Rev. F. A., *History of the Baptist Missionary Society from 1792–1842*, 2 vols (T. Ward and Co., London, 1842).

Dale, A. W. W., *The Life of R. W. Dale of Birmingham* (Hodder and Stoughton, London, 1899).

Dale, R. W., *The Funeral Sermon for John Angell James* (Hudson and Co., Birmingham, 1859).

Dale, R. W., *Life and Letters of John Angell James* (Nisbet and Co., London, 1861).

Dale, R. W., *The Living God the Saviour of all Men* (Jackson, Walford and Hodder, London, 1864).

Dale, R. W., *The Politics of the Future. A Lecture to New Electors* (Hudson and Son, Birmingham, 1867).

Dale, R. W., *The Politics of Nonconformity. A Lecture Delivered in the Free Trade Hall Manchester, November 1871* (Manchester Nonconformist Association, Manchester, 1871).

Dale, R. W., 'George Dawson: Politician, Lecturer and Preacher', *Nineteenth Century*, 6 (1877).

Dawson, George, *The Demands of the Age upon the Church. Discourse at the Opening of the Church of the Saviour Edward St, 8 August 1847* (E. C. Osborne, Birmingham, 1847).

Dickens, Charles, *A Christmas Carol*, 1st edn 1843 (Oxford University Press, Oxford, 1988).

Dickens, Charles, *Bleak House*, 1st edn 1853 (Penguin, Harmonsworth, 1979).

Dickens, Charles, 'The Noble Savage', 1st edn 1853, in *The Works of Charles Dickens*, 34 vols (Chapman and Hall, London, 1899), vol. 34: *Reprinted Pieces*, pp. 120–7.

Dickens, Charles, Review of 'Narrative of the Expedition to the River Niger in 1841', *Examiner*, 19 Aug. 1841, pp. 531–3.

Dilke, Sir Charles Wentworth, *Greater Britain: A Record of Travel in English Speaking Countries during 1866 and 1867*, 1st edn 1867, 3rd edn (Macmillan, London, 1869).

Drake, James, *The Picture of Birmingham* (J. Drake, Birmingham, 1825).

East, D. J., *The Circular Letter for 1856, of the Jamaica Baptist Union* (Haddon Bros and Co., London, 1856).

East, D. J., *The Constitution and Government of a Church of Christ as Developed in the New Testament* (J. Heaton and Son, London, 1863).

East, D. J., *The Importance of Suitable Dwellings to the Cultivation of Family Religion* (J. Heaton and Son, London, 1863).

East, D. J., *The Inheritance Attained: A Sermon Preached by the Rev. D. J. East for Mrs. Dendy* (Youngman and Poole, Maldon, 1866).

Edwards, Bryan, *The History, Civil and Commericial, of the British Colonies in the West Indies*, 2 vols, 1st edn 1791, 4th edn (John Stockdale, London, 1806).

Edwards, Eliezer, *John Skirrow Wright, M. P.* (privately published, Birmingham, 1880).

Emery, Robert, *'About Jamaica': Its Past, its Present, and its Future* (John Evans, London, 1859).

Eyre, Edward John, *Autobiographical Narrative 1832–39*, ed. with an introduction by Jill Waterhouse (Caliban, London, 1984).

Eyre, Edward John, *Journals of Expeditions of Discovery into Central Australia and Overland from Adelaide to King George's Sound in the Years 1840–1*, 2 vols (T. and W. Boone, London, 1845).

Fawcett, Mrs, *Women's Suffrage. Speech Delivered in the Town Hall, Birmingham, December 6 1872*, repr. for *Birmingham Morning News*.

Female Society for Birmingham, West Bromwich, Wednesbury, Walsall, and their Respective Neighbourhoods, for the Relief of British Negro Slaves, First Report (Richard Peart, Birmingham, 1826).

Female Society for Birmingham, West Bromwich, Wednesbury, Walsall, and their Respective Neighbourhoods, for the Relief of British Negro Slaves, Second Report (Hudson, Birmingham, 1827).

Female Society for the Relief of Negro Slaves, Third Report (Hudson, Birmingham, 1828).

Finlason, William F., *The History of the Jamaica Case Founded upon Official or Authentic Documents, and Containing an Account of the Debates in Parliament and the Criminal Prosecutions, Arising out of the Case* (Chapman and Hall, London, 1869).

Froude, J. A., *Thomas Carlyle. A History of his Life in London 1834–81*, 2 vols (Longmans Green and Co., London, 1884).

Garnett, R., *Edward Gibbon Wakefield. The Colonization of Australia and New Zealand* (T. Fisher Unwin, London, 1897).

Gaskell, Mrs, *North and South*, 1st edn 1854–5 (Penguin, Harmondsworth, 1970).

Gilfillan, George, 'George Dawson', *Taits Magazine*, May 1848.

Gordon, Rev. A., *The Triumphant Career and its Peaceful Close. Sermon on the Death of John Angell James, Walsall. 9 October, 1859* (Judd and Glass, London, 1859).

Gorst, John Eldon, *The Maori King; or The Story of our Quarrel with the Natives of New Zealand* (Macmillan, London, 1864).

Green, Samuel, *Baptist Mission in Jamaica. A Review of the Rev. W. G. Barrett's Pamphlet Entitled A Reply to the Circular of the Baptist Missionary Society* (Houlston and Stoneman, London, 1842).

Grey, Earl Henry G., *The Colonial Policy of Lord John Russell's Administration*, 2 vols (Richard Bentley, London, 1853).

Grey, George, *Journals of Two Expeditions of Discovery in North-West and Western Australia during the Years 1837, 38 and 39*, 2 vols (T. and W. Boone, London, 1841).

Gurney, Joseph John, *A Winter in the West Indies Described in Familiar Letters to Henry Clay of Kentucky* (John Murray, London, 1840).

Haggard, H. Rider, *King Solomon's Mines* (Cassell, London, 1891).

Harrison, Frederick, *Studies in Early Victorian Literature* (Chapman and Hall, London, 1895).

Harvey, Thomas and Brewin, William, *Jamaica in 1866. A Narrative of a Tour through the Island with Remarks on its Social, Educational and Industrial Condition* (A. W. Bennett, London, 1867).

Hill, Frederick, *An Autobiography of Fifty Years in Times of Reform*, edited by his daughter Constance Hill (R. Bentley and Son, London, 1894).

Hill, Rosamund and Hill, Florence, *The Recorder of Birmingham. A Memoir of Matthew Davenport Hill* (Macmillan, London, 1878).

Hinton, John Howard, *Memoir of William Knibb, Missionary in Jamaica* (Houlston and Stoneman, London, 1847).

Hoby, James, *Memoir of William Knibb, Son of the Rev. William Knibb* (Thomas Ward and Co., London, n.d.).

Hoby, James, *Memoir of William Yates D. D. of Calcutta* (Houlston and Stoneman, London, 1847).

Holyoake, G. J., *Bygones Worth Remembering*, 2 vols (T. Fisher Unwin, London, 1905).

Horne, Charles Silvester, 'R. W. Dale', in J. H. Muirhead (ed.), *Nine Famous Birmingham Men* (Cornish Bros, Birmingham, 1909).

Hume, Hamilton, *The Life of Edward John Eyre, Late Governor of Jamaica* (Richard Bentley, London, 1867).

Jamaica Committee, *Jamaica Papers*, nos 1–6 (Jamaica Committee, London, 1866–7).

James, John Angell, *Christian Philanthropy: As Exemplified in the Life and Character of the Late Joseph Sturge Esq.* (Hudson and Son, Birmingham, 1859).

James, T. S. (ed.), *The Collected Works of John Angell James*, 17 vols (Hudson and Co., Birmingham, 1860–4).

Kay, James Phillips, *The Moral and Physical Condition of the Working Classes Employed in the Cotton Manufactures in Manchester*, 1st edn 1832 (Cass, London, 1970).

Kaye, John William, *The Life and Correspondence of Charles, Lord Metcalfe*, 2 vols (Smith, Elder and Co., London, 1858).

King, Rev. David, *The State and Prospects of Jamaica* (Johnston and Hunter, London, 1850).

Kingsley, Charles, *At Last. A Christmas in the West Indies*, new edn (Macmillan, London, 1872).

Kingsley, Charles, *His Letters and Memories of His Life. Edited by his Wife*, 4 vols (Macmillan, London, 1901).

Kingsley, Henry, 'Eyre, the South-Australian Explorer', *Macmillan's Magazine*, 12 (May–Oct. 1865). Parts 1 and 2.

Kingston Guardian and Patriot, *Full Report of the Proceedings in Chancery of the Important Case of the Baptist Chapel, Spanish Town, October, 1845* (n.p., Kingston, 1845).

Knibb, William, *Speech on the Immediate Abolition of British Colonial Slavery* (J. Blackwell and Co., Newcastle, 1833).

Knibb, William, *Jamaica. A Speech to the Baptist Missionary Society in Exeter Hall 28 April 1842* (G. and J. Dyer, London, 1842).

Knibb, William, *Speech of the Rev. William Knibb before the Baptist Missionary Society* (Dyer and Dyer, London, 1842).

Knox, Robert, *The Races of Men: A Philosophical Inquiry into the Influence of Race over the Destiny of Nations*, 2nd edn (Henry Renshaw, London, 1862).

Kohl, J. G., *Ireland, Scotland and England* (Chapman and Hall, London, 1844).

Ladies' Negro's Friend Society, *Retrospect of the Work of Half a Century of the Ladies' Negro's Friend Society* (Newman, London, 1875).

Langford, John Alfred, *A Century of Birmingham Life: or A Chronicle of Local Events from 1741–1841*, 2 vols (Osborne, Birmingham, 1868).

Langford, John Alfred, *Modern Birmingham and its Institutions: A Chronicle of Local Events, from 1841–1871*, 2 vols (Osborne, Birmingham, 1873).

Lewis, Matthew Gregory, *Journal of a West Indian Proprietor Kept during a Residence in the Island of Jamaica*, 1st edn 1834; 2nd edn (Negro University Press, New York, 1969).

Livingstone, David, *Missionary Travels and Researches in South Africa* (John Murray, London, 1857).

Merivale, Herman, *Introduction to a Course of Lectures on Colonisation and Colonies* (Longman, Orme, Brown, Green and Longmans, London, 1839).

Merivale, Herman, *Lectures on Colonisation and Colonies* (Longman, Green, Longman and Roberts, London, 1861).

Middleditch, T., *The Youthful Female Missionary: A Memoir of Mary Ann Hutchins, Wife of the Rev. John Hutchins, Baptist Missionary Savanna-la-mar, Jamaica and Daughter of the Rev. T. Middleditch of Ipswich; Compiled Chiefly from her own Correspondence by her Father* (G. Wightman and Hamilton Adams, London, 1840).

Mill, John Stuart, 'Civilization', *London and Westminster Review*, 3 and 25 (Apr. 1836); repr. in *Collected Works of John Stuart Mill*, vol. 18: *Essays on Politics and Society*, ed. J. M. Robson (University of Toronto Press, Toronto, 1977), pp. 117–48.

Mill, John Stuart, *Principles of Political Economy*, 1st edn 1848, in J. M. Robson (ed.) *Collected Works of John Stuart Mill*, vols 2 and 3 (Toronto University Press, Toronto, 1965).

Mill, John Stuart, 'The Negro Question', *Fraser's Magazine*, 41 (Jan. 1850).

Mill, John Stuart, *Considerations on Representative Government*, 1st edn 1861, in J. M. Robson (ed.), *Collected Works of John Stuart Mill*, vol. 19 (Toronto University Press, Toronto, 1977).

Mill, John Stuart, *The Subjection of Women*, 1st edn 1869 (Virago, London, 1983).

Mill, John Stuart, *Autobiography*, 1st edn 1873 (Oxford University Press, Oxford, 1963).

Morgan, A. F., *Kith and Kin*, privately printed (Charles Cooper and Co. Ltd, Birmingham, 1896).

Morgan, Thomas, *A Plain Statement of the Faith and Practice of the Baptist Church Meeting in Bond Street, Birmingham* (J. Allen, Birmingham, c.1830).

Morgan, William, *The Arabs of the City; or A Plea for Brotherhood with the Outcast: Being an Address Delivered to the Young Men's Christian Association, Birmingham 29 November 1853* (Hudson, Birmingham, 1853).

Mott, Lucretia, *Lucretia Mott's Diary of her Visit to Great Britain to Attend the World's Anti-Slavery Convention of 1840*, ed. F. B. Tolles (Friends' Historical Society, London, 1952).

National Society for Women's Suffrage, Birmingham Branch, *First Annual Report* (W. E. Harris, Birmingham, 1869).

Oughton, Mrs, *Fugitive Pieces by a Missionary's Wife* (Muller, New York, n.d.).

Oughton, Samuel, *A Nation's Lamentation over Fallen Greatness. A Funeral Sermon Occasioned by the Death of His Royal Highness, Prince Albert at East Queen's St. 19th Jan. 1862* (Savage and Co., Jamaica, 1862).

Oughton, Samuel, *Jamaica: Why it is Poor, and How it may Become Rich* (M. DeCordova, McDougall and Co., Kingston, 1866).

Oughton, Samuel, *A Sermon Preached at East Queen St. Chapel, Kingston, on the Occasion of the Death of the Rev. William Knibb* (John Snow, London, 1846).

Oughton, Samuel, *Roupell the Forger, the Lessons of his Crime and Punishment*, Lecture at East Queen St., 11th Oct. 1862, and repeated 25th Oct. 1862 by special request (M. DeCordova and Co., Kingston, 1862).

Oughton, Samuel, 'The Influence of Artificial wants on the Social, Moral, and Commercial Advancement of Jamaica', repr. from *West India Quarterly*, June 1862, and bound with *Roupell the Forger*, pp. 474–83.

Parkes, Henry, *Australian Views of England. Eleven Letters Written in the Years 1861 and 1862* (Macmillan and Co., London, 1869).

Phillippo, James Mursell, *Jamaica: Its Past and Present State* (John Snow, London, 1843).

Pim, Commander Bedford, *The Negro and Jamaica* (Trubner and Co., London, 1866).

Prince, Mary, *The History of Mary Prince, a West Indian Slave*, 1st edn 1831, ed. with an introduction by Moira Ferguson (Pandora Press, London, 1986).

Report of the Proceedings at Birmingham on the 1st and 2nd of August in Commemoration of the Abolition of Negro Apprenticeship in the British Colonies (Tyler, Birmingham, 1838).

Richard, Henry, *Memoirs of Joseph Sturge* (S. W. Partridge, London, 1864).

Robertson, William, *Life and Times of the Right Honourable John Bright* (Cassell, London, 1883).

Sewell, William G., *The Ordeal of Free Labor in the British West Indies* (Harper and Bros, New York, 1861).

Shore, Joseph, *In Old St. James. A Book of Parish Chronicles*, ed. John Stewart (Sangsters, Kingston, 1911; new edn 1952).

Showell's Dictionary of Birmingham (Walter Showell, Birmingham, 1885).

Smith, Adam, *The Wealth of Nations*, 2 vols, 1st edn 1776 (Dent, London, 1964).

Smith, William, *A New and Compendious History of the County of Warwick from the Earliest Period to the Present Time* (W. Emans, Birmingham, 1830).

Smith, William Hawkes, *Birmingham and its Vicinity as a Manufacturing and Commercial District* (J. Drake, Birmingham, 1836).

Spence, Catherine Helen, *Clara Morrison. A Tale of South Australia during the Gold Fever*, 1st edn 1854 (Wakefield, South Australia, 1986).

Stewart, James, *A View of the Past and Present State of the Island of Jamaica; with Remarks on the Moral and Physical Condition of the Slaves, and on the Abolition of Slavery in the Colonies*, 1st edn 1823 (Negro University Press, New York, 1969).

Stowe, Harriet Beecher, *Sunny Memories of Foreign Lands*, 2 vols (Sampson Low Son and Co., London, 1854).

Sturge, Joseph and Harvey, Thomas, *A Reply to Letters to Joseph Sturge Esq. by William Alers Hankey Esq.* (Hamilton, Adams and Co., London, 1838).

Sturge, Joseph and Harvey, Thomas, *The West Indies in 1837: Being the Journal of a Visit to Antigua, Montserrat, Dominica, St. Lucia, Barbadoes and*

Jamaica; Undertaken for the Purpose of Ascertaining the Actual Condition of the Negro Population of those Islands, 2nd edn (Hamilton, Adams and Co., London, 1838).

Taylor, Henry, *Autobiography of Henry Taylor 1800–1875*, 2 vols (Longmans, Green and Co., London, 1885).

Taylor, Rev. Isaac, *Self Cultivation Recommended; or, Hints to a Youth Leaving School* (T. Cadell and Son, London, 1817).

Thompson, Jemima, *Memoirs of British Female Missionaries with a Survey of the Condition of Women in Heathen Countries* (William Smith, London, 1841).

Timmins, Samuel (ed.), *The Resources, Products and Industrial History of Birmingham and the Midland Hardware District* (Robert Hardwicke, London, 1866).

Trelawny Cultural Foundation, *Trelawny and its History* (no publisher, Falmouth, n.d.).

Trollope, Anthony, *The Macdermots of Ballycloran*, 3 vols (Newby, London, 1847).

Trollope, Anthony, *The Kellys and the O'Kellys*, 3 vols (Colburn, London, 1848).

Trollope, Anthony, *The Warden*, 1st edn 1855 (Robert Hayes, London, 1925).

Trollope, Anthony, *Barchester Towers* (Longman, London, 1857).

Trollope, Anthony, *The West Indies and the Spanish Main* (Chapman and Hall, London, 1859).

Trollope, Anthony, 'Miss Sarah Jack, of Spanish Town, Jamaica', 1st edn 1860, repr. in Trollope, *The Complete Short Stories in Five Volumes*, vol. 3: *Tourists and Colonials*. (Trollope Society, London, n.d.).

Trollope, Anthony, *North America*, 2 vols (Chapman and Hall, London, 1862).

Trollope, Anthony, *Phineas Finn. The Irish Member*, 1st edn 1867 (Oxford University Press, Oxford, 1992).

Trollope, Anthony, *Ralph the Heir*, 1st edn 1871 (Penguin, Harmondsworth, 1993).

Trollope, Anthony, *Australia and New Zealand*, 2 vols (Chapman and Hall., London, 1873).

Trollope, Anthony, *South Africa*, 2 vols (Chapman and Hall, London, 1878).

Trollope, Anthony, *Autobiography*, 2 vols (William Blackwood and Sons, London, 1883).

Trollope, Anthony, *The Landleaguers*, 3 vols (Chatto and Windus, London, 1883).

Trollope, Frances, Preface to the 5th edition of *Domestic Manners of the Americans*, 1st edn 1832 (George Routledge and Sons, London, 1927).

Underhill, Edward Bean, 'On the Pastorate of the Mission Churches' (1852), in *The Principles and Methods of Missionary Labour* (Alexander and Shepheard, London, 1896).

Underhill, Edward Bean, *The West Indies: Their Social and Religious Condition* (Jackson, Walford and Hodder, London, 1862).

Underhill, Edward Bean, *Christian Missions in the East and West, in Connection with the Baptist Missionary Society, 1792–1873* (Yeats and Alexander, London, 1873).

Underhill, Edward Bean, *The Jamaica Mission in its Relation with the BMS 1838–79* (printed for the use of the committee, London, 1879).

Underhill, Edward Bean, *Life of James Mursell Phillippo, Missionary in Jamaica* (Yates and Alexander, London, 1881).

Underhill, Edward Bean, *The Tragedy of Morant Bay: A Narrative of the Disturbances in the Island of Jamaica in 1865* (Alexander and Shepheard, London, 1895).

Underhill, Edward Bean, 'On the Pastorate of the Mission Churches', prepared for private circulation in 1852, published in *The Principles and Methods of Missionary Labour* (Alexander and Shepheard, London, 1896).

Waddell, Rev. Hope Masterton, *Twenty-nine Years in the West Indies and Central Africa: A Review of Missionary Work and Adventures 1829–58* (T. Nelson and Sons, London, 1863).

Wakefield, Edward Gibbon, *A Letter from Sydney* (J. M. Dent, London, 1929).

Wakefield, Edward Gibbon, *England and America*, 2 vols (Richard Bentley, London, 1833).

Wilson, Wright, *The Life of George Dawson* (Percival Jones, Birmingham, 1905).

Wright, James Skirrow, 'On the Employment of Women in Factories in Birmingham', in *Transactions of the National Association for the Promotion of Social Science* (J. W. Parkes and Son, London, 1857).

Wright, Philip (ed.), *Lady Nugent's Journal of her Residence in Jamaica from 1801–5* (Institute of Jamaica, Kingston, 1966).

Yates, William, 'Memoirs of the Rev. W. H. Pearce', abridged by James Hoby and published in *Memoir of William Yates D.D. of Calcutta* (Houlston and Stoneman, London, 1847).

Books and articles published after 1914

Alexander, M. Jacqui and Mohanty, Chandra Talpade (eds), *Feminist Genealogies, Colonial Legacies, Democratic Futures* (Routledge, New York, 1997).

Alexander, Sally, *Becoming a Woman and Other Essays in Nineteenth and Twentieth Century Feminist History* (Virago, London, 1994).

Altick, Richard D., *The Shows of London* (The Belknap Press of Harvard University Press, Cambridge, Mass., 1978).

Anderson, Benedict, *Imagined Communities: Reflections on the Origin and Spread of Nationalism* (Verso, London, 1983).

Anderson, Olive, *A Liberal State at War. English Politics and Economics during the Crimean War* (Macmillan, London, 1967).

Anderson, Olive, 'The Political Uses of History in Mid-Nineteenth Century England', *Past and Present*, 36 (Apr. 1967), pp. 87–105.

Arnstein, Walter L., 'The Murphy Riots: A Victorian Dilemma', *Victorian Studies*, 19 (1975–6), pp. 51–72.

Bakan, Abigail B., *Ideology and Class Conflict in Jamaica. The Politics of Rebellion* (McGill–Queen's University Press, London, 1990).

Baldwin, James, 'Stranger in the Village', 1st edn 1953, repr. in *Notes of a Native Son* (Penguin, Harmondsworth, 1995), pp. 151–65.

Barrell, John, *The Infection of Thomas de Quincy. A Psychopathology of Imperialism* (Harvard University Press, London, 1991).

Baucom, Ian, *Out of Place. Englishness, Empire and the Locations of Identity* (Princeton University Press, Princeton, 1999).

Behagg, Clive, 'Masters and Manufacturers: Social Values and the Smaller Unit of Production in Birmingham, 1800–1850', in G. Crossick and H. G. Haupt (eds), *Shopkeepers and Master Artisans in Nineteenth Century Europe* (Routledge, London, 1984), pp. 137–54.

Behagg, Clive, *Politics and Production in the Early Nineteenth Century* (Routledge, London, 1990).

Belich, James, *The New Zealand Wars and the Victorian Interpretation of Racial Conflict* (Auckland University Press, Auckland, 1986).

Belich, James, *Making Peoples. A History of the New Zealanders from Polynesian Settlement to the End of the Nineteenth Century* (Allen Lane/Penguin, Auckland and London, 1996).

Bell, Kenneth N. and Morrell, W. P. (eds), *Select Documents on British Colonial Policy 1830–1860* (Clarendon Press, Oxford, 1928).

Bentley, Jerry H., Introduction to 'Perspectives on Global History: Cultural Encounters between the Continents over the Centuries', in *Proceedings of the Nineteenth Congress of Historical Sciences* (Oslo, 2000), pp. 29–45.

Besson, Jean, 'Family Land as a Model for Martha Brae's New History: Culture Building in an Afro-Caribbean Village', in Charles V. Carnegie (ed.), *Afro-Caribbean Villages in Historical Perspective* (Institute of Jamaica, Kingston, 1987).

Besson, Jean, 'Reputation and Respectability Reconsidered: A New Perspective on Afro-Caribbean Peasant Women', in Janet H. Momsen (ed.), *Women and Change in the Caribbean. A Pan-Caribbean Perspective* (James Currey, London, 1993), pp. 15–37.

Bhabha, Homi, 'Of Mimicry and Man', in *The Location of Culture* (Routledge, London, 1994), pp. 85–92.

Bindman, David, 'The Representation of Plantation Slavery in the Eighteenth Century', unpub. paper presented at the seminar 'Reconfiguring the British', Institute of Historical Research, 1999.

Binfield, Clyde, *So Down to Prayers. Studies in English Nonconformity* (Dent, London, 1977).

Binfield, Clyde (ed.), *The Cross and the City. Essays in Commemoration of Robert William Dale 1829–1895*, supplement to the Journal of the United Reform Church History Society, vol. 6 (supplement no. 2), Supplement to the Congregational History Circle Magazine, vol. 4 (Supplement no. 1) (Spring 1999) (URC History Society, Cambridge, 1999).

Blackburn, Robin, *The Overthrow of Colonial Slavery 1776–1848* (Verso, London, 1988).

Blackburn, Robin, *The Making of New World Slavery. From the Baroque to the Modern* (Verso, London, 1997).

Bodelsen, C. A., *Studies in Mid-Victorian Imperialism* (Scandinavian University Books, Copenhagen, 1960).

Bolt, Christine, *The Anti-Slavery Movement and Reconstruction. A Study in Anglo-American Cooperation 1833–77* (Oxford University Press, Oxford, 1969).

Bolt, Christine, *Victorian Attitudes to Race* (Routledge and Kegan Paul, London, 1971).

Bowers, Faith, *A Bold Experiment. The Story of Bloomsbury Chapel and Bloomsbury Central Baptist Church, 1848–1999* (Bloomsbury Central Baptist Church, London, 1999).

Brah, Avtar, *Cartographies of Diaspora: Contesting Identities* (Routledge, London, 1996).

Brantlinger, Patrick, ' "Dying Races": Rationalising Genocide in the Nineteenth Century', in Jan Nederveen Pieterse and Bhikhu Parekh (eds), *The Decolonization of Imagination* (Zed, London, 1995), pp. 43–56.

Brantlinger, Patrick, *Rule of Darkness. British Literature and Imperialism 1830–1914* (Cornell University Press, Ithaca, NY, 1988).

Brathwaite, Edward, *The Development of Creole Society in Jamaica 1770–1820* (Clarendon Press, Oxford, 1971).

Brereton, Brigid *Law, Justice and Empire. The Colonial Career of John Gorrie 1829–1892* (University of the West Indies Press, Kingston, 1997).

Brereton, Brigid and Shepherd, Verene (eds), *Engendering the History of the Caribbean* (James Currey, London, 1995).

Breuilly, John, Niedhart, Gottfried and Taylor, Anthony (eds), *The Era of the Reform League: English Labour and Radical Politics 1857–1872. Documents Selected by Gustav Mayer* (Palatium Verlag in J. and J. Verlag, Mannheim, 1995).

Briggs, Asa, *Press and Public in Early Nineteenth Century Birmingham*, Dugdale Society Occasional Papers no. 8 (Dugdale Society, Oxford, 1949).

Briggs, Asa, *Victorian Cities* (Odhams, London, 1963).

Briggs, J. H. Y., *The English Baptists of the Nineteenth Century* (Baptist Historical Society, Didcot, 1994).

Brown, Kenneth D., *A Social History of the Nonconformist Ministry in England and Wales 1800–1930* (Clarendon Press, Oxford, 1988).

Buckley, Jessie K., *Joseph Parkes of Birmingham and the Part which he Played in Radical Reform Movements from 1825–1845* (Methuen, London, 1926).

Burrow, J. W., *Evolution and Society. A Study in Victorian Social Theory* (Cambridge University Press, Cambridge, 1968).

Burton, Antoinette, *Burdens of History: British Feminists, Indian Women and Imperial Culture, 1865–1915* (University of North Carolina Press, Chapel Hill, 1994).

Burton, Antoinette, *At the Heart of the Empire: Indians and the Colonial Encounter in Late Victorian Britain* (University of California Press, Berkeley, 1998).

Bush, Barbara, *Slave Women in Caribbean Slave Society, 1650–1838* (Indiana University Press, Bloomington, 1990).

Bush, Julia, 'Moving On – and Looking Back', *History Workshop Journal*, 36 (Autumn 1993), pp. 183–94.

Cain, P. J. and Hopkins, A. G., *British Imperialism. Innovation and Expansion. 1688–1914* (Longman, London, 1993).

Campbell, Mavis C., *The Dynamics of Change in a Slave Society: A Sociopolitical History of the Free Coloureds of Jamaica 1800–1865* (Associated University Presses, London, 1976).

Chatterjee, Partha, *The Nation and its Fragments. Colonial and Postcolonial Histories* (Princeton University Press, Princeton, 1993).

Chaudhuri, Nupur and Stroebel, Margaret (eds), *Western Women and Imperialism: Complicity and Resistance* (Indiana University Press, Bloomington, 1992).

Cherry, Deborah, 'Shuttling and Soul Making: Tracing the Links between Algeria and Egalitarian Feminism in the 1850s', in Shearer West (ed.), *The Victorians and Race* (Scholar Press, Aldershot, 1994), pp. 156–70.

Cherry, Deborah, *Beyond the Frame. Feminism and Visual Culture, Britain 1850–1900* (Routledge, London, 2001).

Chinn, Carl, ' "Sturdy Catholic Emigrants": The Irish in Early Victorian Birmingham', in R. Swift and S. Gilley (eds), *The Irish in Victorian Britain. The Local Dimension* (Four Courts, Dublin, 1999), pp. 52–74.

Chitty, Susan, *The Beast and the Monk. A Life of Charles Kingsley* (Hodder and Stoughton, London, 1974).

Civin, Joshua, 'Slaves, Sati and Sugar: Constructing Imperial Identity through Liverpool Petition Struggles', unpub. paper presented to the Neale Colloquium on 'National Identities and Parliaments 1660–1860', University College London, 2001.

Clarke, John Henry (ed.), *Marcus Garvey and the Vision of Africa* (Vintage, New York, 1974).

Clarke, Norma, *Ambitious Heights. Writing, Friendship, Love. The Jewsbury Sisters, Felicia Hemans and Jane Carlyle* (Routledge, London, 1990).

Clarke, Norma, 'Shock Heroic', *Times Higher Educational Supplement*, 4 May 1990.

Clarke, Norma, 'Strenuous Idleness. Thomas Carlyle and the Man of Letters as Hero', in Michael Roper and John Tosh (eds), *Manful Assertions. Masculinities since 1800* (Routledge, London, 1991), pp. 25–43.

Comaroff, Jean and Comaroff, John, *Of Revelation and Revolution. Christianity, Colonialism and Consciousness in South Africa* (University of Chicago Press, Chicago, 1991).

Coombes, Annie E., *Reinventing Africa. Museums, Material Culture and Popular Imagination* (Yale University Press, London, 1994).

Cooper, Frederick and Stoler, Ann Laura (eds), *Tensions of Empire: Colonial Cultures in a Bourgeois World* (University of California Press, Berkeley, 1997).

Craton, Michael, *Testing the Chains: Resistance to Slavery in the British West Indies* (Cornell University Press, Ithaca, NY, 1982).

Craton, Michael and Walvin, James, *A Jamaican Plantation. The History of Worthy Park 1670–1970* (Allen, London, 1970).

Cumper, George E., 'A Modern Jamaican Sugar Estate', *Social and Economic Studies*, no. 3 (1954), pp. 119–60.

Cunningham, Hugh, *The Volunteer Force. A Social and Political History 1859–1908* (Croom Helm, London, 1975).

Cunningham, Hugh, 'The Language of Patriotism', in Raphael Samuel (ed.), *Patriotism: The Making and Unmaking of British National Identity*, vol. 1.: *History and Politics* (Routledge, London, 1989), pp. 57–89.

Curtin, Philip D., *Two Jamaicas: The Role of Ideas in a Tropical Colony 1830–1865* (Harvard University Press, Cambridge, Mass., 1955).

Curtin, Philip D., *The Image of Africa: British Ideas and Action, 1780–1850*, 2 vols (University of Wisconsin Press, Madison, 1964).

Da Costa, Emilia Viotti, *Crowns of Glory, Tears of Blood. The Demerara Slave Rebellion of 1823* (Oxford University Press, Oxford, 1994).

Daunton, Martin and Halpern, Rick (eds), *Empire and Others: British Encounters with Indigenous Peoples 1600–1850* (UCL Press, London, 1999).

Davidoff, Leonore, 'Class and Gender in Victorian England', in Judith L. Newton, Mary P. Ryan and Judith R. Walkowitz (eds), *Sex and Class in Women's History* (Routledge and Kegan Paul, London, 1983), pp. 191–214.

Davidoff, Leonore, 'Regarding Some "Old Husbands' Tales": Public and Private in Feminist History', in *Worlds Between: Historical Perspectives on Gender and Class* (Polity, Cambridge, 1995), pp. 227–76.

Davidoff, Leonore, 'Where the Stranger Begins: The Question of Siblings in Historical Analysis', in *Worlds Between*, pp. 201–26.

Davidoff, Leonore and Hall, Catherine, *Family Fortunes. Men and Women of the English Middle Class 1780–1850* (Hutchinson, London, 1987).

Davidson, John, 'Anthony Trollope and the Colonies', *Victorian Studies*, 12 (Mar. 1969), pp. 305–30.

Davis, David Brion, *The Problem of Slavery in the Age of Revolution 1770–1823* (Cornell University Press, Ithaca, NY, 1975).

Deak, Istvan, *The Lawful Revolution: Louis Kossuth and the Hungarians 1848–9* (Columbia University Press, New York, 1979).

de Groot, Joanna, ' "Sex" and "Race": The Construction of Language and Image in the Nineteenth Century', in Susan Mendus and Jane Rendall (eds), *Sexuality and Subordination* (Routledge, London, 1989), pp. 89–128; repr. in Catherine Hall (ed.), *Cultures of Empire: A Reader. Colonizers in Britain and the Empire in the Nineteenth and Twentieth Centuries* (Manchester University Press, Manchester, 2000), pp. 37–60.

Dominguez, Virginia R., *White by Definition. Social Classification in Creole Louisiana* (Rutgers University Press, New Brunswick, NJ, 1994).

Driver, Felix, *Geography Militant. Cultures of Empire and Exploitation* (Blackwell, Oxford, 2001).

Driver, Felix and Gilbert, David (eds), *Imperial Cities. Landscape, Display and Identity* (Manchester University Press, Manchester, 1999).

Dunn, Richard S., *The Rise of the Planter Class in the English West Indies 1624–1713* (Cape, London, 1973).

Dutton, Geoffrey, *The Hero as Murderer: The Life of Edward John Eyre, Australian Explorer and Governor of Jamaica 1815–1901* (William Collins, London, 1968).

Eisner, Gisela, *Jamaica, 1830–1930. A Study in Economic Growth* (Manchester University Press, Manchester, 1961).

Eley, Geoff, 'Nations, Publics and Political Cultures: Placing Habermas in the Nineteenth Century', in Craig Calhoun (ed.), *Habermas and the Public Sphere* (MIT Press, Cambridge, Mass., 1992), pp. 289–339.

Evans, Julie, 'Beyond the Frontier: Possibilities and Precariousness along Australia's Southern Coast', in L. Russell (ed.), *Colonial Frontiers* (Manchester University Press, Manchester, 2001), pp. 151–72.

Fabian, Johannes, *Time and the Other. How Anthropology makes its Object* (Columbia University Press, New York, 1983).

Fanon, Frantz, *Black Skin, White Masks*, 1st edn 1952 (Pluto Press, London, 1986).

Fanon, Frantz, *The Wretched of the Earth* (Penguin, Harmondsworth, 1967), introduction by Jean-Paul Sartre.

Feminist Review, 'Editorial', *Feminist Review*, 40 (Spring 1992), pp. 1–5.

Ferguson, Moira, '*Mansfield Park*: Plantocratic Paradigms', in *Colonialism and Gender Relations from Mary Woollstonecraft to Jamaica Kincaid. East Caribbean Connections* (Columbia University Press, New York, 1993), pp. 65–89.

Ferguson, Moira, *Subject to Others: British Women Writers and Colonial Slavery, 1670–1834* (Routledge, London, 1992).

Findlay, G. G. and Holdsworth, W. W., *The History of the Wesleyan Methodist Missionary Society*, 5 vols. (Epworth Press, London, 1921).

Finn, Margot, *After Chartism. Class and Nation in English Radical Politics, 1848–74* (Cambridge University Press, Cambridge, 1993).

Finnemore, William, *The Story of a Hundred Years 1823–1923. Being the Centenary Booklet of the Birmingham Auxiliary of the Baptist Missionary Society* (Oxford University Press, Oxford, 1923).

Flick, Carlos, *The Birmingham Political Union and the Movement for Reform in Britain* (Archon Books, Greenwood, Westport, Conn., 1978).

Foner, Eric, *Nothing but Freedom. Emancipation and its Legacy* (Louisiana State University Press, Baton Rouge, 1983).

Foster, R. F., *Paddy and Mr. Punch. Connections in Irish and English History* (Penguin, Harmondsworth, 1993).

Fraser, Nancy, 'Rethinking the Public Sphere: A Contribution to the Critique of Actually Existing Democracy', in Craig Calhoun (ed.), *Habermas and the Public Sphere* (MIT Press, Cambridge, Mass., 1992), pp. 109–42.

Freud, Sigmund, *Civilisation and its Discontents*, in *Penguin Freud*, vol. 12: *Civilisation, Society, Religion* (Penguin, Harmondsworth, 1991).

Fryer, Peter, *Staying Power. The History of Black People in Britain* (Pluto Press, London, 1984).

Gayle, Clement, *George Liele. Pioneer Missionary to Jamaica* (Jamaica Baptist Union, Kingston, 1982).

Gikandi, Simon, *Maps of Englishness. Writing Identity in the Culture of Colonialism* (Columbia University Press, New York, 1996).

Gilbert, A. D., *Religion and Society in Industrial England: Church, Chapel and Social Change 1740–1914* (Longman, London, 1976).

Gill, Conrad, *History of Birmingham*, vol. 1: *Manor and Borough to 1865* (Oxford University Press, Oxford, 1952).

Gilman, Sander, 'Black Bodies, White Bodies, Towards an Iconography of Female Sexuality in Late Nineteenth Century Art, Medicine and Literature', in James Donald and Ali Rattansi (eds), *'Race', Culture and Difference* (Sage, London, 1992), pp. 171–99.

Gilroy, Paul, *The Black Atlantic: Modernity and Double Consciousness* (Verso, London, 1993).

Glendinning, Victoria, *Anthony Trollope* (Hutchinson, London, 1992).

Gocking, C. V., 'Early Constitutional History of Jamaica, with Special Reference to the Period 1838–66', *Caribbean Quarterly*, 6 (1960), pp. 114–33.

Goodall, Heather, *Invasion to Embassy. Land in Aboriginal Politics in New South Wales, 1770–1972* (Allen and Unwin, St Leonards, Australia, 1996).

Goveia, Elsa, *A Study on the Historiography of the British West Indies to the End of the Nineteenth Century* (Instituto Panamericano De Geografia e Historia, Mexico, 1956).

Gray, R. Q., *North and South Revisited: Locality, Nation and Identity in Victorian Britain*, Portsmouth Lecture Series (University of Portsmouth, Portsmouth, 2000).

Green, Martin, *Dreams of Adventure, Deeds of Empire* (Routledge and Kegan Paul, London, 1980).

Green, William A., *British Slave Emancipation. The Sugar Colonies and the Great Experiment 1830–65* (Oxford University Press, Oxford, 1976).

Grimshaw, Patricia, Lake, Marilyn, McGrath, Ann and Quartly, Marian, *Creating a Nation* (McPhee Gribble, Victoria, 1994).

Guy, Jeff, *The Heretic. A Study of the Life of John William Colenso 1814–1883* (University of Natal Press, Pietermaritzburg, 1983).

Gwynne, Stephen and Tuckwell, Gertrude M., *The Life of the Rt. Hon. Sir Charles Dilke*, 2 vols (John Murray, London, 1917).

Hall, Catherine, *White, Male and Middle Class: Explorations in Feminism and History* (Polity, Cambridge, 1992).

Hall, Catherine, ' "Going-a-Trolloping": Imperial Man Travels the Empire', in Clare Midgley (ed.), *Gender and Imperialism* (Manchester University Press, Manchester, 1998), pp. 180–99.

Hall, Catherine, 'The Nation Within and Without', in Hall et al., *Defining the Victorian Nation*, pp. 179–233.

Hall, Catherine, McClelland, Keith and Rendall, Jane, *Defining the Victorian Nation: Class, Race, Gender and the British Reform Act of 1867* (Cambridge University Press, Cambridge, 2000).

Hall, Catherine, 'The Rule of Difference: Gender, Class and Empire in the Making of the 1832 Reform Act', in Ida Blom, Karen Hagemann, and Catherine Hall (eds), *Gendered Nations. Nationalism and Gender Order in the Long Nineteenth Century* (Berg, Oxford, 2000), pp. 107–36.

Hall, Catherine (ed.), *Cultures of Empire: A Reader. Colonizers in Britain and the Empire in the Nineteenth and Twentieth Centuries* (Manchester University Press, Manchester, 2000).

Hall, Douglas, *Free Jamaica, 1836–65: An Economic History* (Yale University Press, New Haven, 1959).

Hall, Douglas, *In Miserable Slavery. Thomas Thistlewood in Jamaica 1750–1786* (Macmillan, Basingstoke, 1989).

Hall, N. John (ed.), *The Trollope Critics* (Macmillan, London, 1981).

Hall, Stuart, 'When was "the Post-Colonial"? Thinking at the Limit', in Iain Chambers and Lidia Curti (eds), *The Post-Colonial Question: Common Skies, Divided Horizons* (Routledge, London, 1996), pp. 242–60.

Hall, Stuart, 'Minimal Selves', in *Identity* (Institute of Contemporary Arts, London, 1997), vol. 6; repr. in H. A. Baker Jr., M. Diawara and R. H. Lindeborg (eds), *Black British Cultural Studies: A Reader* (University of Chicago Press, Chicago and London, 1996), pp. 114–19.

Hall, Stuart, 'The Spectacle of the Other', in S. Hall (ed.), *Representation*, pp. 223–90.

Hall, Stuart, 'From Scarman to Stephen Lawrence', *History Workshop Journal*, 48 (1999), pp. 187–97.

Hall, Stuart, 'The Multi-Cultural Question', in Barnor Hesse (ed.), *Un/settled Multiculturalisms. Diasporas, Entanglements, Disruptions* (Zed, London, 2001), pp. 209–41.

Hall, Stuart (ed.), *Representation: Cultural Representations and Signifying Practices* (Sage in association with the Open University, London, 1997).

Harris, Jose, 'Between Civic Virtue and Social Darwinism: The Concept of the Residuum', in David Englander and Rosemary O'Day (eds), *Retrieved Riches: Social Investigation in England 1840–1914* (Scholar Press, Aldershot, 1995), pp. 67–87.

Harrison, Royden, *Before the Socialists. Studies in Labour and Politics 1861–1881* (Routledge and Kegan Paul, London, 1965).

Haury, David A., *The Origins of the Liberal Party and Liberal Imperialism: The Career of Charles Buller, 1806–1848* (Garland, New York, 1987).

Henderson, George E., *Goodness and Mercy. A Tale of a Hundred Years* (The Gleaner, Kingston, 1931).

Hennock, E. P., *Fit and Proper Persons. Ideal and Reality in Nineteenth-Century Urban Government* (Edward Arnold, London, 1973).

Heuman, Gad J., *Between Black and White. Race, Politics and the Free Coloreds in Jamaica 1792–1865* (Greenwood, Westport, Conn., 1981).

Heuman, Gad J., *'The Killing Time': The Morant Bay Rebellion in Jamaica* (Macmillan, London, 1994).

Higman, B. W., 'The West Indian "Interest" in Parliament 1807–33', *Historical Studies*, 13/49 (1967), pp. 1–19.

Hill, Richard S., *Policing the Colonial Frontier. The Theory and Practice of Coercive Social and Racial Control in New Zealand 1767–1867* (Historical Publications Branch, Department of Internal Affairs, Wellington, NZ, 1986).

Hilton, Boyd, *The Age of Atonement: The Influence of Evangelicalism on Social and Economic Thought, 1795–1865* (Clarendon Press, Oxford, 1988).

Hollis, Patricia, 'Anti-Slavery and British Working-Class Radicalism in the Years of Reform', in Christine Bolt and Seymour Drescher (eds), *Anti-Slavery,*

Religion and Reform: Essays in Memory of Roger Anstey (Dawson and Sons, Folkestone, 1980), pp. 294–315.

Holt, Thomas C., *The Problem of Freedom: Race, Labor and Politics in Jamaica and Britain 1832–1938* (Johns Hopkins University Press, Baltimore, 1992).

Horsman, Reginald, *Race and Manifest Destiny. The Origins of American Racial Anglo-Saxonism* (Harvard University Press, Cambridge, Mass., 1981).

Hudson, Pat, *The Industrial Revolution* (Edward Arnold, London, 1992).

Hughes, Robert, *The Fatal Shore. A History of the Transportation of Convicts to Australia 1787–1868* (Pan Books, London, 1988).

Hulme, Peter, *Colonial Encounters: Europe and the Native Caribbean 1492–1797* (Methuen, London, 1986).

Hunt, Lynn (ed.), *The New Cultural History* (University of California Press, Berkeley, 1989).

Jacobs, H. P., *Sixty Years of Change 1806–1866* (Institute of Jamaica, Kingston, 1973).

James, C. L. R., *The Black Jacobins: Toussaint L'Ouverture and the San Domingo Revolution*, 2nd edn (Vintage, New York, 1963).

James, C. L. R., 'Africans and Afro-Caribbeans: A Personal View', *TEN*.8, 16 (1984), pp. 54–5.

Joyce, Patrick, *Democratic Subjects. The Self and the Social in Nineteenth Century England* (Cambridge University Press, Cambridge, 1994).

Judd, Denis, *Radical Joe. A Life of Joseph Chamberlain* (Hamish Hamilton, London, 1977).

Kale, Madhavi, ' "When the saints came marching in": The Anti-Slavery Society and Indian Indentured Migration to the British Caribbean', in Daunton and Halpern (eds), *Empire and Others*, pp. 325–44.

Kale, Madhavi, *Fragments of Empire: Capital, Slavery and Indian Indentured Labor Migration in the British Caribbean* (University of Pennsylvania Press, Philadelphia, 1999).

Kaplan, Cora, ' "A heterogeneous thing": Female Childhood and the Rise of Racial Thinking in Victorian Britain', in Diana Fuss (ed.), *Human, All Too Human* (Routledge, New York, 1996), pp. 169–202.

Kaplan, Cora, 'Black Heroes/White Writers: Toussaint L'Ouverture and the Literary Imagination', *History Workshop Journal*, 46 (Autumn 1998), pp. 33–62.

Kass, Amalie M. and Kass, Edward H., *Perfecting the World. The Life and Times of Dr. Thomas Hodgkin 1798–1866* (Harcourt Brace Jovanovich, Boston, 1988).

Kiernan, V. G., *The Lords of Human Kind. European Attitudes towards the Outside World in the Imperial Age* (Weidenfeld and Nicholson, London, 1969).

Knapland, Paul, *James Stephen and the British Colonial System 1813–1847* (University of Wisconsin Press, Madison, 1953).

Kociumbas, Jan, *The Oxford History of Australia*, vol. 2: *Possessions 1770–1869* (Oxford University Press, Oxford, 1995).

Laclau, Ernesto, *Emancipations* (Verso, London, 1996).

Landes, Joan, *Women and the Public Sphere in the Age of the French Revolution* (Cornell University Press, Ithaca, NY, 1988).

Langley, Arthur S., *Birmingham Baptists Past and Present* (Kingsgate Press, London, 1939).

Lansbury, Coral, *Arcady in Australia. The Evocation of Australia in Nineteenth Century English Literature* (Melbourne University Press, Victoria, 1970).

Laqueur, Thomas, 'Bodies, Details and the Humanitarian Narrative', in Hunt (ed.), *New Cultural History*, pp. 176–204.

Lewin, Sylvia Lloyd, *Gaunts Earthcott to Frederick Road. An Account of the Sturges of Birmingham* (family MS, privately published, 1980).

Lewis, Gail, *'Race', Gender, Social Welfare: Encounters in a Postcolonial Society* (Polity, Cambridge, 2000).

Lewis, Rupert, *Marcus Garvey. Anti-Colonial Champion* (Karia Press, London, 1987).

Linebaugh, Peter and Rediker, Marcus, *The Many-Headed Hydra. The Hidden History of the Revolutionary Atlantic* (Verso, London, 2000).

Lorimer, Douglas, *Colour, Class and the Victorians: English Attitudes to the Negro in the Mid-Nineteenth Century* (Leicester University Press, Leicester, 1978).

Lowe, Philip, 'The British Association and the Provincial Public', in Roy Macleod and Peter Collins (eds), *The Parliament of Science* (Science Reviews, Northwood, 1981), pp. 118–44.

MacKenzie, John, *Propaganda and Empire* (Manchester University Press, Manchester, 1984).

MacKenzie, John, ' "The Second City of the Empire": Glasgow – Imperial Municipality', in Felix Driver and David Gilbert (eds), *Imperial Cities, Landscape, Display and Identity* (Manchester University Press, Manchester, 1999), pp. 215–37.

MacRaild, D. M., 'William Murphy, the Orange Order and Communal Violence: The Irish in West Cumberland 1871–1874', in Panikos Panayi (ed.), *Racial Violence in Britain, 1840–1950*, rev. edn (Leicester University Press, Leicester, 1996), pp. 44–64.

Main, J. M., 'Men of Capital', in Eric Richards (ed.), *The Flinders History of South Australia. A Social History* (Wakefield Press, South Australia, 1986).

Mandler, Peter, ' "Race" and "Nation" in Mid-Victorian Thought', in S. Collini, R. Whatmore and B. Young (eds), *History, Religion, Culture. British Intellectual History 1750–1950* (Cambridge University Press, Cambridge, 2000), pp. 224–44.

Mani, Lata, *Contentious Traditions: The Debate on Sati in Colonial India* (University of California Press, Berkeley, 1998).

Marshall, P. J., 'Britain without America – A Second Empire?', in P. J. Marshall (ed.), *The Oxford History of the British Empire*, vol. 2: *The Eighteenth Century* (Oxford University Press, Oxford, 1998), pp. 576–95.

Martin/Clark Book Committee (eds), *The Hatbox Letters. The Story of Two Migrant Families Settling in South Australia c1850 as Recorded in their own Words* (Martin/Clark Book Committee, Adelaide, 1999).

Marx, Karl, and Engels, Frederick, *On Britain*, 2nd edn (Foreign Languages Publishing House, Moscow, 1962).

Massey, Doreen, 'Travelling Thoughts', in Paul Gilroy, Lawrence Grossberg and Angela McRobbie (eds), *Without Guarantees. In Honour of Stuart Hall* (Verso, London, 2000), pp. 225–32.

McClelland, Keith, 'England's Greatness, the Working Man', in Catherine Hall, Keith McClelland and Jane Rendall, *Defining the Victorian Nation: Class, Race, Gender and the British Reform Act of 1867* (Cambridge University Press, Cambridge, 2000), pp. 71–118.

McClintock, Anne, *Imperial Leather: Race, Gender and Sexuality in the Colonial Context* (Routledge, New York, 1995).

McD. Beckles, Hilary, *A History of Barbados: From Amerindian Settlement to Nation-State* (Cambridge University Press, Cambridge, 1990).

McD. Beckles, Hilary, 'White Women and Slavery in the Caribbean', *History Workshop Journal*, 36 (Autumn 1993), pp. 66–82.

McLeod, Hugh, 'The Power of the Pulpit', in Clyde Binfield (ed.), *The Cross and the City: Essays in Commemoration of Robert William Dale 1829–1895* (Spring 1999), pp. 44–54.

Midgley, Clare, *Women against Slavery: The British Campaigns, 1780–1870* (Routledge, London, 1992).

Midgley, Clare, 'Anti-Slavery and Feminism in Nineteenth-Century Britain', *Gender and History*, 5/3 (Autumn 1993), pp. 343–62.

Midgley, Clare, 'Anti-Slavery and the Roots of Imperial Feminism', in Clare Midgley (ed.), *Gender and Imperialism* (Manchester University Press, Manchester, 1998), pp. 161–79.

Midgley, Clare, 'Slave Sugar Boycotts, Female Activism and the Domestic Base of British Anti-Slavery Culture', *Slavery and Abolition*, 17/3 (1996), pp. 137–62.

Midgley, Clare, 'From Supporting Missions to Petitioning Parliament: British Women and the Evangelical Campaign against *sati* in India 1813–1830', in Kathryn Gleadle and Sarah Richardson (eds), *Women in British Politics 1760–1860. The Power of the Petticoat* (Macmillan, Basingstoke, 2000), pp. 74–92.

Mintz, Sidney, 'Caribbean Peasantries', in *Caribbean Transformations* (Aldine, Chicago, 1974), pp. 146–57.

Mintz, Sidney W., *Sweetness and Power. The Place of Sugar in Modern History* (Viking, New York, 1985).

Morrell, William P., *British Colonial Policy in the Age of Peel and Russell* (Oxford University Press, Oxford, 1930).

Morrell, William P., *British Colonial Policy in the Mid-Victorian Age* (Oxford University Press, Oxford, 1969).

Morris, R. J., 'Voluntary Societies and British Urban Elites 1780–1850: An Analysis', *Historical Journal*, 26/1 (1983), pp. 95–118.

Morrison, Toni, *Playing in the Dark. Whiteness and the Literary Imagination* (Picador, London, 1993).

Mullen, Richard, *Anthony Trollope. A Victorian in His World* (Duckworth, London, 1990).

Murray, D. J., *The West Indies and the Development of Colonial Government 1801–1834* (Clarendon Press, Oxford, 1965).

O'Connor, Maura, *The Romance of Italy and the English Political Imagination* (St Martin's Press, New York, 1998).

O'Day, Alan, 'The Political Organization of the Irish in Britain 1867–1890', in Roger Swift and Sheridan Gilley (eds), *The Irish in Britain 1815–1939* (Pinter, London, 1989), pp. 183–211.

Olivier, Sidney, *Jamaica. The Blessed Isle* (Leonard and Virginia Woolf, London, 1936).

Olivier, Sydney S., *The Myth of Governor Eyre* (Leonard and Virginia Woolf, London, 1933).

Orange, Claudia, *The Treaty of Waitangi* (Allen and Unwin, Wellington, 1987).

Paget, Hugh, 'The Free Village System in Jamaica', *Caribbean Quarterly*, 10/1 (Mar. 1964), pp. 40–55.

Paton, Diana, 'Decency, Dependency and the Lash: Gender and the British Debate over Slave Emancipation 1830–34', *Slavery and Abolition*, 17/3 (Dec. 1996), pp. 163–84.

Patterson, Orlando, *The Sociology of Slavery. An Analysis of the Origins, Development and Structure of Negro Slave Society in Jamaica* (MacGibbon and Kee, London, 1967).

Payne, Ernest A., *Freedom in Jamaica* (Carey Press, London, 1933).

Payne, Ernest A., *The Great Succession. Leaders of the Baptist Missionary Society during the Nineteenth Century* (Carey Press, London, 1938).

Pemble, John, *Mediterranean Passions. Victorians and Edwardians in the South* (Oxford University Press, Oxford, 1987).

Phillips, Mike and Phillips, Trevor, *Windrush. The Irresistible Rise of Multi-Racial Britain* (Harper Collins, London, 1998).

Phoenix, Ann, *(Re)Constructing Gendered and Ethnicised Identities: Are We All Marginal Now?* (University for Humanist Studies, Utrecht, 1998).

Pierson, Roscoe M., 'Alexander Bedward and the Jamaican Native Baptist Free Church', repr. from *Lexington Theological Quarterly*, 4/3 (July 1969) (Institute of Jamaica, Kingston).

Pike, Douglas, *Paradise of Dissent. South Australia 1829–1857* (Longmans Green and Co., London, 1957).

Poovey, Mary, *Uneven Developments. The Ideological Work of Gender in Mid-Victorian England* (Virago, London, 1989).

Porter, Andrew, 'Religion, Missionary Enthusiasm and Empire', in Andrew Porter (ed.), *The Oxford History of the British Empire*, vol. 3: *The Nineteenth Century* (Oxford University Press, Oxford, 1999), pp. 222–46.

Porter, Andrew, 'Trusteeship, Anti-Slavery and Humanitarianism', in Porter (ed.), *The Oxford History of the British Empire*, vol, 3: *The Nineteenth Century* (Oxford University Press, Oxford, 1999), pp. 198–221.

Potts, E. Daniel, *British Baptist Missionaries in India 1793–1837* (Cambridge University Press, Cambridge, 1967).

Pratt, Mary Louise, *Imperial Eyes. Travel Writing and Transculturation* (Routledge, London, 1992).

Preston, Rebecca, ' "The scenery of the torrid zone": Imagined Travels and the Culture of Exotics in Nineteenth-Century British Gardens', in Felix Driver and David Gilbert (eds), *Imperial Cities, Landscape, Display and Identity* (Manchester University Press, Manchester, 1999), pp. 194–211.

Prince, Nancy, *A Black Woman's Odyssey through Russia and Jamaica. The Narrative of Nancy Prince*, introduction by R. G. Walters (Markus Wiener Publishers, Princeton, 1995).

Prochaska, F. K., *Women and Philanthropy in Nineteenth-Century England* (Oxford University Press, Oxford, 1980).

Quinault, Roland, 'John Bright and Joseph Chamberlain', *Historical Journal*, 28/3 (1985), pp. 623–46.

Quinlivan, Patrick and Rose, Paul, *The Fenians in England 1865–1872: A Sense of Insecurity* (John Calder, London, 1982).

Rainger, Ronald, 'Race, Politics and Science: The Anthropological Society of London in the 1860s', *Victorian Studies*, 22/1 (Autumn 1978), pp. 51–70.

Renan, Ernest, 'What is a Nation?', lst pub. 1882; repr. in H. Bhabha (ed.), *Nation and Narration* (Routledge, London, 1990), pp. 8–22.

Rendall, Jane, 'The Citizenship of Women and the Reform Act of 1867', in Catherine Hall, Keith McClelland and Jane Rendall, *Defining the Victorian Nation: Class, Race, Gender and the British Reform Act of 1867* (Cambridge University Press, Cambridge, 2000), pp. 119–78.

Rendall, Jane, 'Women and the Public Sphere', *Gender and History*, 11/3 (Nov. 1999), pp. 475–88.

Reynolds, Henry, *The Other Side of the Frontier* (James Cook University Press, Townsville, Australia, 1981).

Riley, Denise, *'Am I that Name? Feminism and the Category of Women in History* (Macmillan, Basingstoke, 1989).

Robbins, Keith, *John Bright 1811–1889* (Routledge and Kegan Paul, London, 1979).

Roediger, David, *The Wages of Whiteness: Race and the Making of the American Working Class* (Verso, London, 1992).

Rose, Jacqueline, *States of Fantasy* (Clarendon Press, Oxford, 1996).

Rose, R. B., 'Protestant Nonconformity', in Victoria County History. *A History of the County of Warwick*, vol. 7, ed. W. B. Stephens: *The City of Birmingham*, pp. 411–82.

Rushdie, Salman, 'The New Empire within Britain', in *Imaginary Homelands. Essays and Criticism 1981–1991* (Granta, London, 1991), pp. 129–39.

Russell, Horace O., 'A Question of Indigenous Mission: The Jamaica Baptist Missionary Society', *Baptist Quarterly*, 25 (1973–4), pp. 86–93.

Russell, Horace O., 'The Emergence of the Christian Black. The Making of a Stereotype', *Jamaica Journal*, 16/1 (Feb. 1983), pp. 51–8.

Russell, Horace O., 'The Church in the Past – A Study on Jamaican Baptists in the Eighteenth and Nineteenth Centuries', Jamaica Baptist Union MS (n.p., n.d.).

Russell, Lynette (ed.), *Colonial Frontiers. Indigenous–European Encounters in Settler Societies* (Manchester University Press, Manchester, 2001).

Rutherford, J., *Sir George Grey. A Study in Colonial Government* (Cassell, London, 1961).

Said, Edward W., *Out of Place* (Granta, London, 1999).

Said, Edward W., *Orientalism. Western Conceptions of the Orient* (Routledge, London, 1978).

Said, Edward W., *Culture and Imperialism* (Chatto and Windus, London, 1993).

Sangari, Kumkum, *Politics of the Possible. Essays on Gender, History, Narrative, Colonial English* (Tulika, New Delhi, 1999).

Sangari, K. and Vaid, S. (eds), *Recasting Women: Essays in Indian Colonial History* (Rutgers University Press, New Brunswick, NJ, 1990).

Savage, David W., 'Missionaries and the Development of a Colonial Ideology of Female Education in India', *Gender and History*, 9/2 (August 1997), pp. 201–21.

Schaffer, Kay, 'Handkerchief Diplomacy: E. J. Eyre and the Sexual Politics of the South Australian Frontier, in L. Russell (ed.), *Colonial Frontiers* (Manchester University Press, Manchester, 2001), pp. 134–50.

Schneer, Jonathan, *London 1900. The Imperial Metropolis* (Yale University Press, New Haven, 1999).

Schuler, Monica, *Alas, Alas, Kongo. A Social History of Indentured African Immigration into Jamaica, 1841–65* (Johns Hopkins University Press, Baltimore, 1980).

Schwarz, Bill, *Memories of Empire* (Verso, London, 2002).

Schwarz, Bill, ' "The only white man in there": The Re-racialization of England, 1956–1968', *Race and Class*, 38/1 (1996), pp. 65–78.

Scott, David, *Refashioning Futures: Criticism after Postcoloniality* (Princeton University Press, Princeton, 1999).

Scott, David [interview with Sylvia Wynter], 'The Re-enchantment of Humanism', *Small Axe: A Journal of Criticism*, 8 (Sept. 2001), pp. 119–207.

Semmel, Bernard, *The Governor Eyre Controversy* (MacGibbon and Kee, London, 1962).

Semmel, Bernard, *The Rise of Free Trade Imperialism. Classical Political Economy, the Empire of Free Trade and Imperialism 1750–1850* (Cambridge University Press, Cambridge, 1970).

Semmel, Bernard, *The Liberal Ideal and the Demons of Empire. Theories of Imperialism from Adam Smith to Lenin* (Johns Hopkins University Press, Baltimore, 1993).

Sheridan, Richard N., 'The Formation of Caribbean Plantation Society 1689–1784', in P. J. Marshall (ed.), *The Oxford History of the British Empire*, vol. 2: *The Eighteenth Century* (Oxford University Press, Oxford, 1998), pp. 394–414.

Shyllon, Folarin, *Black People in Britain 1555–1833* (Oxford University Press, Oxford, 1977).

Sinha, Mrinalini, *Colonial Masculinity: The 'Manly Englishman' and the 'Effeminate Bengali' in the Late Nineteenth Century* (Manchester University Press, Manchester, 1995).

Spivak, Gayatri Chakravorty, *In Other Worlds. Essays in Cultural Politics* (Routledge, New York, 1985).

Stafford, Robert A., *Scientist of Empire. Sir Roderick Murchison, Scientific Exploration and Victorian Imperialism* (Cambridge University Press, Cambridge, 1989).

Stanley, Brian, *The Bible and the Flag. Protestant Missions and British Imperialism in the Nineteenth and Twentieth Centuries* (Apollos, Leicester, 1990).

Stanley, Brian, *The History of the Baptist Missionary Society 1792–1992* (T. and T. Clark, Edinburgh, 1992).

Stedman Jones, Gareth, *Languages of Class: Studies in English Working-Class History, 1832–1982* (Cambridge University Press, Cambridge, 1983).

Stein, Judith, *The World of Marcus Garvey. Race and Class in Modern Society* (Louisiana State University Press, Baton Rouge, 1986).

Stepan, Nancy Leys, *The Idea of Race in Science: Great Britain 1800–1960* (Macmillan, London, 1982).

Stepan, Nancy Leys, 'Race and Gender: The Role of Analogy in Science', in David Theo Goldberg (ed.), *Anatomy of Racism* (University of Minnesota Press, Minneapolis, 1990), pp. 38–57.

Stewart, Robert J., *Religion and Society in Post-Emancipation Jamaica* (University of Tennessee Press, Knoxville, 1992).

Stocking, George W. Jr, *Race, Culture and Evolution: Essays in the History of Anthropology* (University of Chicago Press, Chicago, 1968).

Stocking, George W. Jr, *Victorian Anthropology* (Free Press, New York, 1987).

Stokes, Edward, *The Desert Coast. Edward Eyre's Expedition 1840–1841* (Five Mile Press, Victoria, 1993).

Stoler, Ann Laura, *Race and the Education of Desire: Foucault's 'History of Sexuality' and the Colonial Order of Things* (Duke University Press, Durham, NC, 1995).

Sturgis, James L., *John Bright and the Empire 1811–89* (Athlone Press and University of London, London, 1969).

Sussman, Herbert, *Victorian Masculinities. Manhood and Masculine Poetics in Early Victorian Literature and Art* (Cambridge University Press, Cambridge, 1995).

Taylor, Barbara, *Eve and the New Jerusalem. Socialism and Feminism in the Nineteenth Century* (Virago, London, 1983).

Taylor, Miles, 'The 1848 Revolutions and the British Empire', *Past and Present,* 166 (Feb. 2000), pp. 146–80.

Temperley, Howard, *White Dreams, Black Africa. The Antislavery Expedition to the Niger 1841–2* (Yale University Press, New Haven, 1991).

Terry, R. C. (ed.), *Trollope: Interviews and Recollections* (Macmillan, London, 1987).

Thomas, Hugh, *The Slave Trade: The History of the Atlantic Slave Trade 1440–1870* (Picador, London, 1998).

Thompson, Edward, *The Life of Charles, Lord Metcalfe* (Faber and Faber, London, 1937).

Thompson, E. P., *The Making of the English Working Class* (Gollancz, London, 1963).

Thorne, Susan, *Congregational Missions and the Making of an Imperial Culture in Nineteenth-Century England* (Stanford University Press, Stanford, Calif., 1999).

Tosh, John, *A Man's Place. Masculinity and the Middle-Class Home in Victorian England* (Yale University Press, London, 1999).

Turnbull, Michael, *The New Zealand Bubble: The Wakefield Theory in Practice* (Price, Milburn and Co., Wellington, 1959).

Turner, Mary, *Slaves and Missionaries. The Disintegration of Jamaican Slave Society, 1787–1834* (University of Illinois Press, Urbana, 1982).

Twells, Alison, ' "So distant and wild a scene": Language, Domesticity and Difference in Hannah Kilham's Writing from West Africa, 1822–32', *Women's History Review*, 4/3 (1995), pp. 301–18.

Tyrrell, Alex, *Joseph Sturge and the Moral Radical Party in Early Victorian Britain* (Christopher Helm, London, 1987).

Victoria County History, *History of Warwick*, vol. 7: *The City of Birmingham*, ed. R. B. Pugh (Oxford University Press, Oxford, 1964).

Visram, Rozina, *Ayahs, Lascars and Princes. Indians in Britain, 1700–1947* (Pluto Press, London, 1986).

Walter, Lynne, and Ware, Vron, 'Political Pincushions: Decorating the Abolitionist Interior', in Inga Bryden and Janet Floyd (eds), *Domestic Space. Reading the Nineteenth Century Interior* (Manchester University Press, Manchester, 1999), pp. 58–93.

Walter, Bronwen, *Outsiders Inside: Whiteness, Place and Irish Women* (Routledge, London, 2001).

Ward, J. R., *British West Indian Slavery, 1750–1834. The Process of Amelioration* (Oxford University Press, Oxford, 1988).

Ward, J. R., 'The British West Indies in the Age of Abolition 1748–1815', in P. J. Marshall (ed.), *The Oxford History of the British Empire*, vol. 2: *The Eighteenth Century* (Oxford University Press, Oxford, 1998), pp. 415–39.

Ware, Vron, *Beyond the Pale. White Women, Racism and History* (Verso, London, 1992).

Whates, H. E. G., *The Birmingham Post 1857–1957* (Birmingham Post and Mail, Birmingham, 1957).

Whitehead, Ann, 'Continuities and Discontinuities in Political Constructions of the Working Man in Rural Sub-Saharan Africa', *European Journal of Development Research*, 12/2 (2000), pp. 23–52.

Wiener, Martin, 'The Sad Story of George Hall: Adultery, Murder and the Politics of Mercy in Mid-Victorian England', *Social History*, 24/2 (May 1999), pp. 174–95.

Williams, Eric, *Capitalism and Slavery* (University of North Carolina Press, Chapel Hill, 1944).

Williams, Eric, *British Historians and the West Indies* (Andre Deutsch, London, 1966).

Wilmot, Swithin, 'Baptist Missionaries and Jamaican Politics 1838–54', paper presented at the 12th Conference of Caribbean Historians, Apr. 1980.

Wilmot, Swithin, 'The Peacemakers: Baptist Missionaries and Ex-Slaves in West Jamaica 1838–40', *Jamaica Historical Review*, 13 (1982), pp. 42–8.

Wilmot, Swithin, 'The Politics of Samuel Clarke: Black Political Martyr in Jamaica, 1851–65', *Jamaica Historical Review*, 19 (1996), pp. 19–29.

Wilson, Kathleen, *The Sense of the People. Politics, Culture and Imperialism in England, 1715–1785* (Cambridge University Press, Cambridge, 1998).

Wolf, Eric R., *Europe and the People without History* (University of California Press, Berkeley, 1982).

Wright, Philip, *Knibb, 'the Notorious'. Slaves' Missionary 1803–1845* (Sidgwick and Jackson, London, 1973).

Young, N. M., *The Colonial Office in the Early Nineteenth Century* (Longman, London, 1971).

Young, Robert, *Colonial Desire. Hybridity in Theory, Culture and Race* (Routledge, London and New York, 1995).

Index

Page numbers in italics refer to illustrations